THE ALABAMA GUIDE

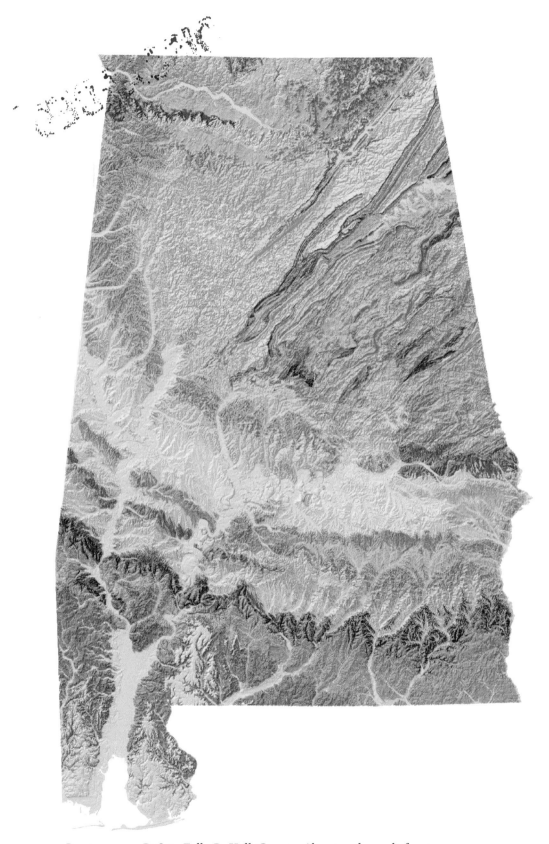

Previous page: DeSoto Falls, DeKalb County. Above: geology relief map.

THE ALABAMA GUIDE

Our People, Resources, and Government

2009

FOREWORD BY GOVERNOR BOB RILEY

PRODUCED FOR THE GOVERNOR'S OFFICE BY THE STAFF OF THE
ALABAMA DEPARTMENT OF ARCHIVES AND HISTORY
Montgomery

HORACE RANDALL WILLIAMS, EDITOR
CHRISTINE GARRETT, ASSOCIATE EDITOR

Alabama Department of Archives and History
P.O. Box 300100
Montgomery, AL 36130
www.archives.alabama.gov

This work is being distributed to the book trade by the University of Alabama
Press. For information on this book, including for the order of copies, please visit
the Press website at www.uapress.ua.edu.

Library of Congress Cataloging-in-Publication Data

The Alabama guide : our people, resources, and government 2009 / foreword
by Governor Bob Riley ; produced for the Governor's Office by the staff of the
Alabama Department of Archives and History ; Horace Randall Williams, editor ;
Christine Garrett, associate editor.
    p. cm.
Includes index.
ISBN-13: 978-0-8173-1656-3 (cloth : alk. paper)
ISBN-10: 0-8173-5537-5 (cloth : alk. paper)
ISBN-13: 978-0-8173-5537-1 (pbk. : alk. paper)
ISBN-10: 0-8173-1656-6 (pbk. : alk. paper)
1. Alabama—Handbooks, manuals, etc. 2. Alabama—Politics and government—
Handbooks, manuals, etc. 3. Alabama—History. I. Williams, Randall, 1951. II.
Garrett, Christine, 1979. III. Alabama. Dept. of Archives and History.
    F324.A43 2009
    976.1'064—dc22
    2009020602

Design by Randall Williams
Printed in the United States by RR Donnelley

On the Locust Fork of the Black Warrior River, Blount County.

FOR THE PEOPLE OF ALABAMA

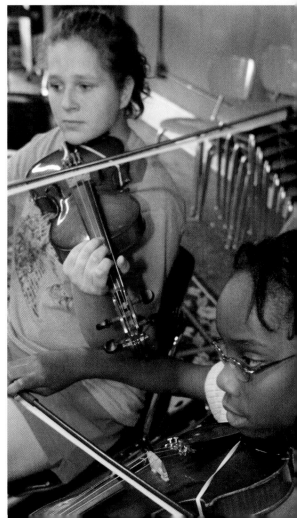

Contents

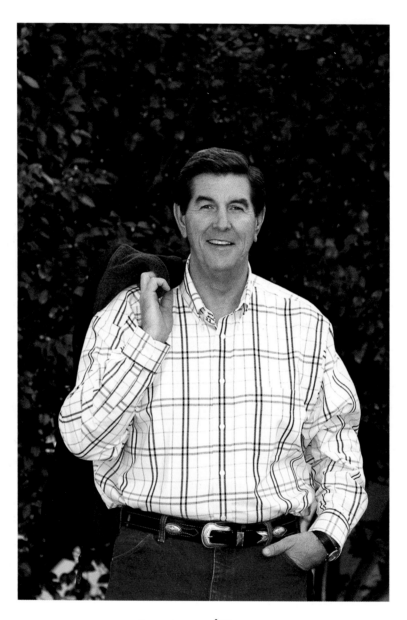

Bob Riley

FOREWORD

GOVERNOR BOB RILEY

On behalf of the people of Alabama, I take great pleasure in presenting to you this first edition of *The Alabama Guide*. For residents, the guide serves as a reference and a source of fascinating information about our history, culture, and natural wealth. For those unfamiliar with our state, we hope these pages illustrate why Alabama is an outstanding place to live, work, and raise a family. Alabama is blessed with abundant natural resources and dedicated people whose character and hard work have built a state that I am proud to call home.

The Alabama Guide begins with "The Land," a detailed overview of the state's geology and natural environment that draws upon the research of expert geologists and cartographers. Alabama's beautiful landscape was formed over millions of years during which continents shifted, oceans advanced and receded, and mountains arose. This chapter explains why fossils of great sea creatures are found in Alabama hundreds of miles from the present-day ocean, and how our abundant mineral riches came to be in specific locations.

When you are ready to take a break from geology, skip ahead to the exciting stories that compose "Historical Alabama." Learn about the people of Alabama from the earliest Indians to today's increasingly diverse population, told in words, pictures, and maps. Based on the research of esteemed Alabama historians and supplemented with the extensive holdings of our Department of Archives—the nation's oldest state historical department—the result is an excellent general history of Alabama. Pictures of artifacts, early maps and drawings, and many wonderful historical photographs make this an accessible resource for students and a useful tool for anyone who wants to get acquainted with our state.

For a more contemporary overview, take a look at the next section, "Alabama Today." Colorful photographs and accompanying descriptions give a snapshot of modern Alabamians making a living, enjoying leisure, and furthering their education.

Part Two of *The Alabama Guide* is a reference work containing valuable information for citizens and anyone who needs to understand and interact with state government. All three branches—executive, judicial, and legislative—are covered, with profiles of the departments, contact information, and brief biographies of every constitutional officer, legislator, state judge, and cabinet member.

Part Three of the book contains a chapter on demographics and statistics that uses charts and tables to reveal trends about population, economics, education, race and ethnicity, and more. The other chapter in this section describes the numerous official symbols and emblems of Alabama. Part Four contains appendices, a bibliography, acknowledgments, and the index.

Thus you have *The Alabama Guide*. I hope this new resource will help you better understand our state, appreciate its enormous potential, and work effectively with its departments of government.

The Alabama Guide provides a glimpse of our past and present. I am proud of our accomplishments; but I know the future will be even brighter because I believe in Alabama—in her goodness, her character, and, most of all, I believe in her people.

The Tennessee River Valley, north Alabama.

THE ALABAMA GUIDE

1

THE LAND

Entering the state along any major highway, travelers are greeted with the familiar big green signs that proclaim, "Alabama The Beautiful." The signs do not lie. There are many spectacular vistas in America, and Alabama has been blessed with more than its share, spread across a varied topography that includes seashore, mountains, plains, river deltas, and piedmont.

Eighty million years ago, about two-thirds of the state's 52,423 square miles were under water. What we now call the Gulf of Mexico extended as far north as present-day Jemison and Alexander City in the center of the state, and perhaps as far north as the Tennessee line in the northwestern corner. Even earlier, before shifting tectonic plates caused land masses to slam into one another, forming mountains and oceans, "the land that was to become Alabama lay beneath a warm, shallow ocean somewhat south of the earth's equator. As this was long before the Appalachian or Rocky mountains were formed . . . only a small portion of North America rose above the ocean's surface. A narrow upland extended from present-day New Mexico through the northern reaches of the North American continent—a region known to geologists as the Canadian Shield. Alabama's rocks dating to this time show that it lay beneath the warm seas to the south of this land area in the form of a shallow, marine shelf onto which near-shore muds and limy sediments were accumulating. The continental interior must have been the source for the sand and mud in Alabama's Cambrian sediments," writes geologist James Lacefield in *Lost Worlds in Alabama Rocks*.

Over the few hundred million years after the Cambrian Period, Alabama's land mass began to emerge. First, the vast ocean alternately rose and fell, depositing sea rocks along the shorelines. Then mountain building began to shape eastern North America as continents collided and the resulting friction forced melted rocks to erupt from the

View from Pulpit Rock in Cheaha State Park, Alabama's highest elevation.

ALABAMA MARBLE QUARRY, SYLACAUGA, ALABAMA—3

A 1950s picture postcard of the Alabama marble quarry at Sylacauga.

earth's surface. These igneous rocks can be seen today in the Appalachian Mountains as far south as eastern Alabama, notes Lacefield. Also during this period when seawater ebbed and flowed, limestone deposits such as those in present-day Shelby and Chilton counties were formed. The ingredients for Portland cement and for agricultural and chemical lime are mined from quarries cut deep into these ancient formations. And along I-59 near Fort Payne, volcanic ash deposits can be seen within the limestone. These are just a few of the geological clues that testify to the forces which gradually created Alabama's stunning natural beauty.

PHYSIOGRAPHIC SECTIONS OF ALABAMA

Occurring over eons of time, the geologic processes left modern Alabama with widely varied physical landscapes. According to the *Encyclopedia of Alabama*,

> The characteristics of the Earth's surface are the result of the interactions of those geologic processes that wear it away and those that rebuild it. Destructive processes include weathering, which is the disintegration or decomposition of stationary solid material by agents such as gravity and water, and erosion, which is the breaking down, loosening, and movement of solid material. Water, wind, and ice are the main agents of erosion. Much of our landscape is the result of differential erosion, the varying resistance of individual rocks to wearing down.
>
> Geologic processes that build the landscape include deposition, magmatism, and deformation. Deposition is the addition of material, called sediment, that was eroded in one area to another part of the Earth's surface. Magmatism is the generation, rise, and solidification of molten rock (magma) formed by partial melting of the Earth's interior. Deformation is the change in size, shape, and location, as a result of heat and stress.

By studying the land's features and understanding the geologic processes, scientists classify landscapes into physiographic regions, each based on the area's most significant features. The characteristics include "rock type and age, geologic structure, and history." Geologists divide North America into eight physiographic regions. Each region is subdivided into provinces, then into sections, and then into districts. Follow this geologic chain far enough, and one might expect to find a zip code. Working from small to large, Huntsville, for example, is in the Tennessee Valley District, in the Highland Rim Section, within the Interior Low Plateaus Province, within the Appalachian Highlands Region.

According to the 1975 *Geological Survey of Alabama Map* by C. D. Sapp and J. L. Emplaincourt, Alabama has five physiographic sections, three in the Appalachian Highlands Region, one in the Interior Plains, and one in the Atlantic Plain regions:

A 1906 geological and artesian water map by State Geologist Eugene A. Smith.

An Alabama geologist points to fossils in an exposed rock face.

- In the APPALACHIAN HIGHLANDS REGION, for example, the (1) *Piedmont Upland section* is a plateau that slopes from one thousand and more feet above sea level in the north to about five hundred feet in the south, where it meets the East Gulf Coastal Plain section; the (2) *Tennessee Valley and Ridge section* has zigzagging ridges and deep valleys in the west and the broad valley of the Coosa River; and the (3) *Cumberland Plateau section* consists of mostly flat uplands formed on Pennsylvanian sandstone and cut by three major valleys falling from northeast to southwest.
- In the INTERIOR PLAINS REGION, the (4) *Highland Rim section* consists of two east-west valleys which developed as soft limestone eroded, separated by a low ridge of harder, less erosive sandstone.
- In the ATLANTIC PLAIN REGION, the (5) *East Gulf Coastal Plain section* is flat in places but also has rounded and eroded hills, some steep slopes, flatwoods, and the floodplains of the Alabama and Black Warrior rivers.

The section descriptions that follow (arranged from north to south across Alabama) are adapted from UAB professor Mike Neilson's articles in the *Encyclopedia of Alabama*.

HIGHLAND RIM PHYSIOGRAPHIC SECTION

The Highland Rim is the southernmost section of the Interior Low Plateaus province in the Appalachian Highlands Region and is the smallest and northernmost physiographic section in Alabama, occupying about seven percent of the state. It occurs as a roughly rectangular area in northwest and north central Alabama, including Lauderdale, Limestone, Madison, Colbert, Lawrence, and Morgan counties, and continues northward into central Tennessee and Kentucky. It is bordered by the Cumberland Plateau to the southeast and the East Gulf Coastal Plain to the southwest. The landscape consists of a prominent east-west ridge separating two valleys. Elevations reach about 900 feet along the Alabama-Tennessee border and drop to about 420 feet where the Tennessee River flows back into Tennessee.

The landforms in the Highland Rim are the result of differential erosion of the underlying rocks. These rocks consist of middle- to upper-Paleozoic sedimentary rocks (490 to 323 million years before the present), most of which formed during the Mississippian period (353 to 323 million years before the present). The main ridge-forming rock is known as the Hartselle Sandstone, and the valleys cut through the Bangor Limestone and Tuscumbia Limestone Formations.

DISTRICTS: The Highland Rim is comprised of three districts: the Little Mountain, the Moulton Valley, and the Tennessee Valley.

NATURAL RESOURCES: Numerous quarries extract limestone from both the Tuscumbia and Bangor Formations. With the exception of one quarry, which produces dimension stone used for architectural and decorative purposes, the limestone is used as construction aggregate.

HIGHLAND RIM

TV	Tennessee Valley
LIM	Little Mountain
MOV	Moulton Valley

CUMBERLAND PLATEAU

WB	Warrior Basin
JCM	Jackson County Mountains
SM	Sand Mountain
SQV	Sequatchie Valley
BM	Blount Mountain
MV	Murphrees Valley
WV	Wills Valley
LOM	Lookout Mountain

ALABAMA VALLEY AND RIDGE

COV	Coosa Valley
COR	Coosa Ridges
WR	Weisner Ridges
CAV	Cahaba Valley
CAR	Cahaba Ridges
BBC	Birmingham-Big Canoe Valley
AR	Armuchee Ridges

PIEDMONT UPLAND

NP	Northern Piedmont Upland
SP	Southern Piedmont Upland

EAST GULF COASTAL PLAIN

FLH	Fall Line Hills
BP	Black Prairie
CH	Chunnenuggee Hills
SRH	Southern Red Hills
F	Flatwoods Subdistrict
BH	Buhrstone Hills Subdistrict
LH	Lime Hills
HD	Hatchetigbee Dome Subdistrict
SPH	Southern Pine Hills
DP	Dougherty Plain
CL	Coastal Lowlands
A, Ad	Alluvial-deltaic Plain

———	District boundary
▬▬▬	Region boundary

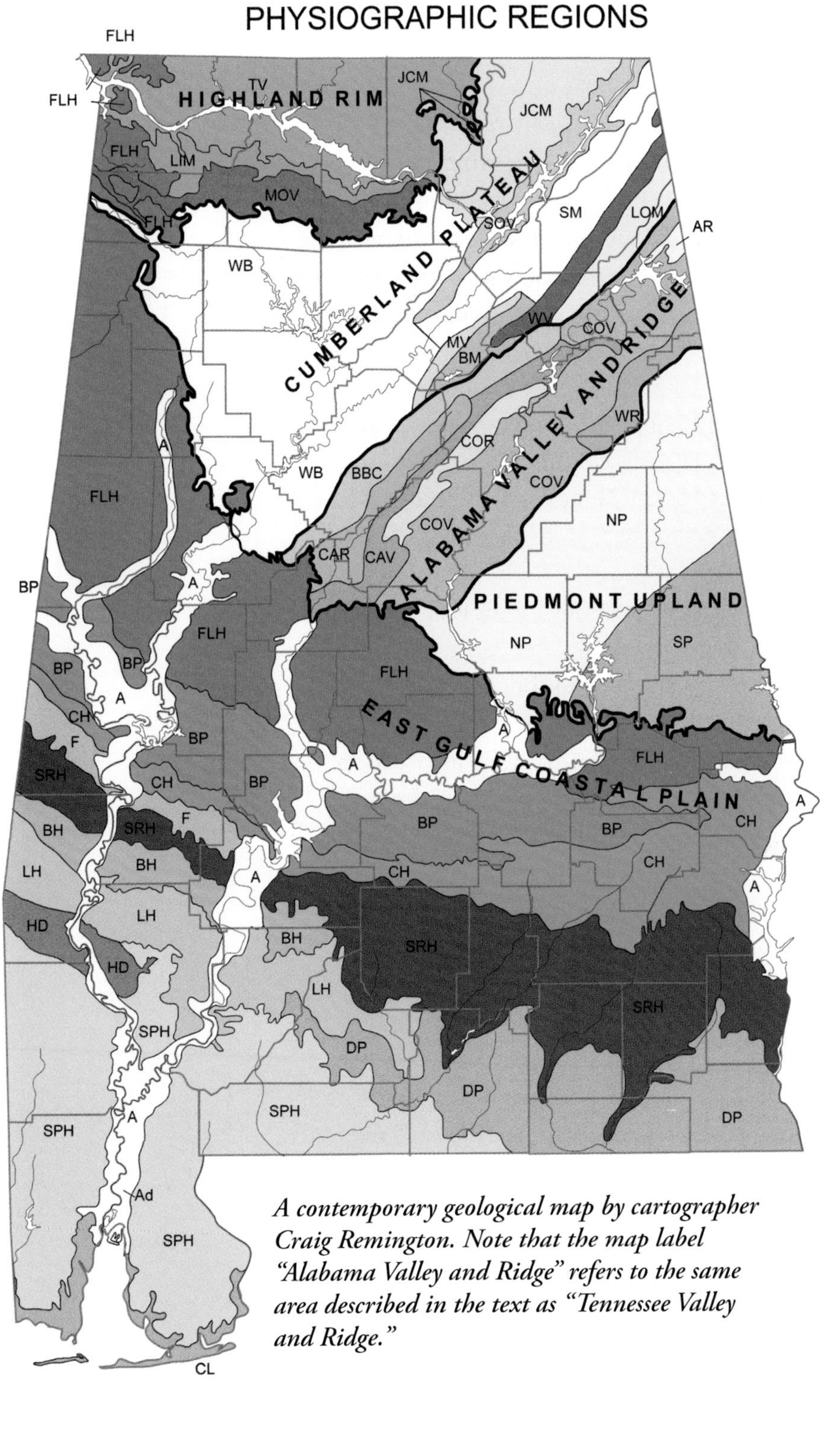

PHYSIOGRAPHIC REGIONS

FLH

HIGHLAND RIM
TV
JCM
JCM
FLH
FLH
LIM
MOV
SOV
SM
LOM
AR
WB
WV
COV
MV
BM
CUMBERLAND PLATEAU
COR
WR
WB
BBC
COV
ALABAMA VALLEY AND RIDGE
FLH
NP
CAR
CAV
COV
BP
A
PIEDMONT UPLAND
FLH
NP
SP
BP
FLH
BP
CH
F
A
SRH
BP
EAST GULF COASTAL PLAIN
A
BH
SRH
F
FLH
A
LH
CH
BP
BP
A
HD
BH
CH
CH
BP
A
LH
BH
HD
CH
SRH
LH
SPH
DP
SRH
DP
A
DP
SPH
SPH
SPH
Ad
SPH
CL

A contemporary geological map by cartographer Craig Remington. Note that the map label "Alabama Valley and Ridge" refers to the same area described in the text as "Tennessee Valley and Ridge."

CUMBERLAND PLATEAU PHYSIOGRAPHIC SECTION

The Cumberland Plateau is the southernmost section of the Appalachian Plateaus province of the Appalachian Highlands Region. Its relief features and landforms differ significantly from those of adjacent sections. It occupies about 15 percent of the state in central and northeastern Alabama, encompassing mainly Jackson, DeKalb, Marshall, Blount, Cullman, Winston, and Walker counties, continuing into Georgia and Tennessee. The landscape consists of flat-topped high-elevation plateaus separated by deep, steep-sided valleys. The plateaus slope gently from the northeast to the southwest. The highest elevations are above fifteen hundred feet in DeKalb and eastern Madison counties, and the lowest elevations are about two hundred feet, near Holt Lock and Dam in Tuscaloosa County.

The landforms are the result of erosion of the underlying Paleozoic rocks, which range from 550 million to 290 million years old. The most resistant rocks are sandstones of various ages, and these form the ridges. Pennsylvanian sandstones underlie the major plateaus. The valleys cut through softer shale, limestone, and dolomite. Of these three, limestone is most easily weathered and eroded, and thus the deepest valleys are floored in this rock type. The Wills, Murphrees, and Sequatchie valleys developed where the presence of anticlines—arched folds in rock layers—exposed the more easily eroded rocks. The plateaus of Lookout and Sand mountains developed on down arches in rock layers known as synclines.

Silt deposits have formed a small sandy creek delta along this stretch of the Sipsey River in Tuscaloosa County.

Active surface mine near Horse Creek in Walker County.

DISTRICTS: The Cumberland Plateau is divided into eight districts: Warrior Basin, Jackson County Mountains, Sand Mountain, Sequatchie Valley, Blount Mountain, Murphrees Valley, Wills Valley, and Lookout Mountain.

NATURAL RESOURCES: The Cumberland Plateau contains economic deposits of Pennsylvanian-aged bituminous coal. The deposits are divided geographically into four regions, or fields: the Warrior Basin, Plateau, Cahaba, and Coosa. During the nineteenth century, the Coosa and Cahaba fields were the source of coal for Alabama's fledgling iron industry and for the Confederacy. Much of the coal mining in the twentieth century was surface mining, and the scars can be seen throughout the area. Recent reclamation efforts have begun to restore the landscape. Coalbed methane is also an important economic resource in the Cumberland Plateau. A by-product of coal formation, the gas is extracted from several areas in the Warrior Basin, mainly in Tuscaloosa, Walker, and Jefferson counties.

TENNESSEE VALLEY AND RIDGE PHYSIOGRAPHIC SECTION
The Tennessee Valley and Ridge section in Alabama is the southernmost section of the Valley and Ridge province of the Appalachian Highlands Region. The Valley and Ridge section occupies about 9 percent of the state. It occurs as a roughly northeast-trending rectangular area in central and east-central Alabama, mainly encompassing Shelby, St. Clair, Calhoun, Cherokee and parts of Jefferson, Bibb, Talladega, and Etowah counties and continues northeast into Georgia and Tennessee.

The Red Mountain Cut, on Highways 31 and 280 leading into downtown Birmingham, provides a spectacular view of the layers of iron ore which were extensively mined until the early 1970s.

The Valley and Ridge borders the Cumberland Plateau section to the north and west, the Piedmont Upland section to the southeast, and the East Gulf Coastal Plain section to the southwest. The landscape developed on tightly folded and thrust-faulted rock layers and thus consists of numerous uniquely zigzagging ridges separated by deep steep-sided valleys. The landscape formed on Paleozoic sedimentary rocks that range in age from Cambrian to Pennsylvanian, around 540 to 290 million years before the present age. The ridges are composed of Pennsylvanian sandstone belonging to the Pottsville Formation, whereas the valleys cut through shale, limestone, and dolomite.

DISTRICTS: The Valley and Ridge is comprised of seven districts: Coosa Valley, Coosa Ridges, Weisner Ridges, Cahaba Valley, Cahaba Ridges, Birmingham-Big Canoe Valley, and Armuchee Ridges.

NATURAL RESOURCES: The Red Mountain Formation crops out on the slopes of Red Mountain in the Valley and Ridge and along the slopes of the Big Wills, Murphrees, and Sequatchie valleys of the Cumberland Plateau. The iron-ore deposits within the formation attracted both Native American artisans and European settlers, and Jones Valley became the center of Alabama's iron and steel industry during the late-nineteenth and early-twentieth centuries. The red color is the result of hematite, a red iron-oxide mineral that was the main reason for Birmingham's establishment and growth and a major part of the economy of the Birmingham area. Although hematite was mined sporadically along Red Mountain's length, extensive and long-term mining took place only in the Birmingham area in the three seams: the Big Seam, the Irondale Seam, and the Ida Hickory Nut Seam.

Red Mountain iron ore was used sporadically during the Civil War, notably in the Oxmoor and Irondale furnaces, but its use did not take off until the late nineteenth century, when coke replaced charcoal as the main source of energy. In 1876, Levin Goodrich succeeded in producing pig iron using the Red Mountain ore and coke made from local coal. Numerous coal seams, most notably the Pratt seam in the nearby Warrior basin, guaranteed a constant source of coke. Limestone and dolomite, used in iron manufacturing, were also extremely abundant in the Birmingham-Big Canoe Valley. Mining of the Red Mountain ore continued until the early 1970s, and a total of about 375 million tons of ore was removed in all.

PIEDMONT UPLAND PHYSIOGRAPHIC SECTION

The Piedmont Upland section is part of the Piedmont province of the Appalachian Highlands Region. It occupies about 9 percent of the state in a triangular area in east-central Alabama that includes Verbena in Chilton County, Piedmont in Cleburne County, and Phenix City in Russell County. It is bordered by the Tennessee Valley and Ridge section of the Valley and Ridge province to the northwest and the East Gulf Coastal Plain to the south. The Piedmont consists of a plateau that slopes from the north, with elevations commonly above one thousand feet, to the south, where it contacts the Coastal Plain at about five hundred feet.

The Piedmont developed on northeast-southwest trending belts of Precambrian to Paleozoic (around one billion years to about three hundred million years in age) metamorphic rocks that are highly deformed and bordered by faults. The most common rock types are slate, phyllite, marble, quartzite, greenstone, schist, amphibolite, and gneiss, some of which are among the oldest rocks in Alabama. Chewacla State Park, located just south of Auburn, in Lee County, is in the Southern Piedmont Upland and contains the oldest known rock in Alabama, a gneiss dating from 1.05 billion years ago. A characteristic small-scale feature of the Piedmont is saprolite, or "rotten rock," which forms where decomposition of the original rocks to depths up to twenty to forty feet changes the minerals present in rocks but retains their texture and structure.

Although described as a plateau, the relatively flat nature of the Piedmont is only obvious in its southern region. The northern part contains many of the highest peaks in the state, including Mt. Cheaha, the state's highest point at 2,407 feet, and numerous northeast-trending steep-sided ridges. The point at which the Piedmont's relatively rugged landscape becomes flat serves as a dividing line between the Northern Piedmont Upland district and the Southern Piedmont Upland district. The boundary

Moores Mill Creek at Chewacla State Park, near Auburn.

is the Brevard Fault Zone, which roughly follows the course of the Tallapoosa River in the vicinity of Lake Martin, in Tallapoosa County. In Randolph County the boundary swings toward the northeast and follows the valley of High Pine Creek, passing just north of Roanoke.

DISTRICTS: The Piedmont is comprised of the Northern Piedmont Upland and the Southern Piedmont Upland districts. The Northern Piedmont Upland is underlain by slate, quartzite, phyllite, marble, gneiss, and schist, and the rugged nature and high elevations of the northwestern part of the upland are caused by varying rates of erosion of these rock types. The highest elevations and greatest relief (changes in elevation) occur near the northwestern edge of the Northern Piedmont. Erosion-resistant quartzite comprises the high ridges, whereas the flat areas at lower elevations, mainly in the vicinity of Sylacauga in Talladega County, are underlain by marble, which is extremely susceptible to chemical weathering. The Southern Piedmont Upland is underlain by schist, gneiss, and amphibolite. These rocks resist erosion equally, accounting for the flatness of the area. Rivers have cut valleys up to two hundred feet deep in the plateau.

NATURAL RESOURCES: Historically, the Piedmont Upland was valued for its mineral resources. Between 1840 and 1934, about 33,000 ounces of gold were extracted from many small workings in the Northern Piedmont and in the Brevard Fault Zone. About one-third of all gold mined in Alabama came from a series of quartz-gold veins found at Hog Mountain, thirteen miles north of Alexander City, in Tallapoosa County. Today, no extensive gold-mining operations exist in the state, and no extensive prospecting is presently taking place.

There are several marble quarries near Sylacauga in Talladega County and at Auburn in Lee County. Most of the quarried material is used for crushed stone, but the white Sylacauga marble from the Alabama Marble Company's quarry is mined in larger blocks, known as dimension stone, and is used for architectural purposes.

EAST GULF COASTAL PLAIN PHYSIOGRAPHIC SECTION

The East Gulf Coastal Plain section is the southernmost part of the Coastal Plain province of the Atlantic Plain Region and is Alabama's largest physiographic section, occupying about 60 percent of the state. The section encompasses parts of forty of Alabama's sixty-seven counties. Its northern boundary, often known as the Fall Line, forms a large sweeping curve from Phenix City in Russell County, to the Alabama-Mississippi border west of Florence in Lauderdale County. The Coastal Plain continues northwest into Mississippi and northeast into Georgia. Although called a plain, the Coastal Plain includes a wide variety of landscapes. It is flat and relatively featureless in some areas, but elsewhere it consists of rounded and eroded hills, topographic features known as cuestas (ridges with a gentle slope on one side and a steep slope on the other)

Cotton field in the rolling hills of the Alabama Black Belt.

and flatwoods (slightly higher and drier areas within generally low-lying terrain), and the floodplains of the Alabama, Tombigbee, and Black Warrior rivers.

The Coastal Plain developed on geologically young sedimentary rocks (from about 140 million years ago to the present) and sediment (gravels, sands, silts, and clays). The rocks are mainly chalk, sandstone, limestone, and claystone. The beds slope gently southward at about forty feet per mile and are progressively younger from the Fall Line to the coast. Locally, higher elevations are underlain by more resistant material (in some areas it is sediment, in others sedimentary rock) and the lowlands are underlain by softer material. The type of resistant material varies from one physiographic district to another.

Numerous cuestas and intervening flatwoods form a distinctive landscape. The cuestas are roughly northwesterly to southeasterly, and each north-facing slope is steeper than the south-facing slope, which indicate the dip of the underlying beds. The flatwoods valleys tend to appear as distorted V shapes in profile, with a gentler northern slope and a steeper southern slope. The elevation difference between the top of cuesta and the floor of the flatwoods, known as relief, can reach three hundred feet. Major cuestas occur in the Black Prairie, Chunnenuggee Hills, and Southern Red Hills districts.

DISTRICTS: Eight districts occur in this section: Fall Line Hills, Black Prairie, Chunnenuggee Hills, Southern Red Hills, Lime Hills, Southern Pine Hills, Dougherty Plain, and Coastal Lowlands.

NATURAL RESOURCES: Oil and gas are significant economic resources in the Coastal Plain. Alabama's output in 2003 placed the state sixteenth in the nation in petroleum production and tenth in the nation in natural gas production. Alabama's oil and gas fields occur in two areas in the Coastal Plain. Oil is extracted from Jurassic strata at depths of more than ten thousand feet beneath the southwestern counties, and gas is extracted at depths of greater than two thousand feet in the southern Mobile Bay field.

ALABAMA'S RIVER SYSTEMS

IN THE CUMBERLAND PLATEAU: The Warrior and Tennessee River systems drain most of the Cumberland Plateau. Each has a distinctive drainage pattern.

The Tennessee River flows southwest in the Sequatchie Valley from the Alabama-Tennessee border to Guntersville in Marshall County, where it abruptly changes direction and flows northwest through the Jackson County Mountains and into the Highland Rim physiographic section. The change in direction has been attributed to a large northwest-southeast-trending structure called the Anniston Cross-Strike Structural Discontinuity, a northwest-trending zone of highly crushed rocks. This geologic feature caused a zone of weakness which the river cut into by erosion.

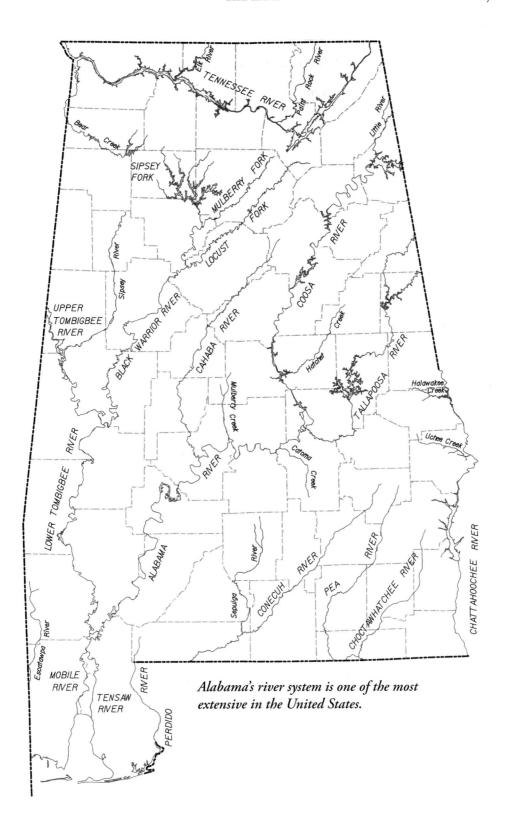

Alabama's river system is one of the most extensive in the United States.

Little River Canyon, near Fort Payne.

The Black Warrior system has two different flow patterns. Its eastern tributaries, the Mulberry and Locust forks, rise between Cullman, Gadsden, and Guntersville and flow southwest in a trellis pattern, consisting of long, relatively straight stream segments with smaller short tributaries joining at right angles. The northern tributary, the Sipsey Fork, flows in a distinctive rectangular pattern. Several individual straight stream segments flow either southwesterly or southeasterly and make approximately right-angle bends at various points.

One particularly scenic area in the Cumberland Plateau occurs where the Little

River has cut into the plateau, forming the Little River Canyon. Below the falls at DeSoto State Park, the river has cut about 90 feet into the plateau and flows at an elevation of 1,143 feet. Where the river enters the Coosa River valley west of Hurley in Cherokee County, its bed has descended about 500 feet and flows at an elevation of 650 feet. The valley profile is V-shaped, with the river occupying all of the lowlands. The canyon is about 1,200 feet wide at DeSoto Falls and widens to about 2,600 feet at its mouth, near Hurley. The river flows to the southwest throughout most of its course in the canyon, cutting through the sandstones of the Pottsville Formation. Numerous waterfalls occur along its course where tributaries flow off the plateau to join the main part of the river. About one mile before it exits the canyon, the river changes course to the southeast, where it has begun to erode the softer Mississippian shale underlying the Pottsville sandstone.

IN THE COASTAL PLAIN: Five main rivers drain the Coastal Plain: the Chattahoochee, Choctawhatchee, Conecuh, Alabama, and Tombigbee-Black Warrior. With the exception of the Tombigbee River, the rivers generally flow south to southwest across the physiographic districts and all cut though the prominent cuestas and hills. In many places the tributaries flow at right angles to the main streams in the valleys and flatwoods. This pattern can be explained by the variable erosive force of the rivers. The streams with higher discharge had sufficient erosive power to cut through both resistant and soft materials and formed major southwesterly trending rivers. Smaller tributaries tend to erode only the softer materials, thus forming the cuesta-flatwoods landscape.

The Alabama River, the largest in the state, forms at Wetumpka in Elmore County, at the joining of the Coosa and the Tallapoosa rivers. From there it flows southwest and is joined by the Cahaba below Selma in Dallas County, and the Tombigbee near Mount Vernon in Mobile County, where it becomes the Mobile River before emptying into Mobile Bay. The Alabama has a well-defined alluvial plain composed of material deposited by the river itself. The plain reaches up to six miles wide in Clarke County, and the river meanders over it for its entire course. Smaller alluvial plains occur along the Cahaba, Black Warrior, Tombigbee, and Chattahoochee rivers.

To aid river navigation, the Tennessee Valley Authority (TVA) constructed three locks on the Alabama south of Montgomery from 1969 to 1972. In addition, TVA built the Millers Ferry Dam and Robert F. Henry Dam and related hydroelectric plants. The Alabama, which is the fourth-largest river system in the United States based on discharge, brings five million tons per year of suspended sediment and 62,500 cubic feet-per-second of water into Mobile Bay. The Mobile-Tensaw Delta (see page 22) formed where the Alabama flows into Mobile Bay. It is shaped like a distorted triangle and begins just south of I-65 near Creola in Mobile County, widening to about seven miles in the south at the I-10 Bridge. The location of the southern terminus of the

Delta depends on the balance between sediment being transported by the river and deposited in the Delta and erosion of that sediment by wave and tidal action and human activity.

The Tombigbee and Black Warrior rivers join at Demopolis in Marengo County, and are part of the $2 billion Tennessee-Tombigbee Waterway. Approved by Congress in 1946, the aim of the waterway was to shorten the distance that freight had to be carried to the Gulf Coast. The TVA excavated a twenty-seven-mile-long, twelve-foot-deep navigation canal to join the headwaters of the Tombigbee at Pickwick Lake on the Tennessee River and constructed 205 miles of canals, five dams, and ten locks on the Tombigbee River. The Heflin and Bevill lock-and-dam systems are located in Alabama, and the rest are in Mississippi.

IN THE HIGHLAND RIM: The Tennessee River flows through the valley in a north-westerly direction, and its small tributaries flow from Little Mountain and the northern uplands into the main river. Throughout most of its course, the Tennessee flows wide and deep in its own alluvium, which is the loose material deposited by the river when it floods. Prior to construction of Wilson and Wheeler Dams, the river consisted of rapids, shoals, and shallow water between present-day Florence and Decatur, where it cut through the Tuscumbia Limestone and struck the more resistant Fort Payne Chert. In 1924 Wilson Dam and its locks were completed at Florence, and in 1936 Wheeler Dam and its locks were completed upstream, thus making the Tennessee River navigable. The Tennessee Valley Authority operates three hydroelectric plants on the river, and the two largest plants in the state, the Wheeler and the Wilson plants, lie within the Highland Rim section.

IN THE PIEDMONT: More than half of the Piedmont is drained by the Tallapoosa River and its tributaries. The main trunk of the system is about two hundred miles long, entering the state near Muscadine in Cleburne County, and leaving the Piedmont at Tallassee in Tallapoosa County. The system drains about 3,300 square miles. On a regional scale, the Tallapoosa and Little Tallapoosa rivers are a series of relatively straight segments broken up by abrupt changes in direction. The dominant flow directions are to the southwest, south, and west. The

Diagram illustrates drainage area of the Tallapoosa River in east Alabama.

Sunset over Neely Henry Lake on the Coosa River in Calhoun County.

most abrupt change occurs near Belltown in Cleburne County, where the Tallapoosa turns from the southwest to the south. Floodplains vary from less than fifty feet to more than one mile wide.

At the Fall Line, the boundary between the Piedmont Upland and the Coastal Plain, the Tallapoosa's gradient (drop in elevation per mile) increases, and the river flows through rougher terrain. Alabama Power constructed four dams along this stretch of the river: Martin Dam (1926), Yates Dam (1928), Thurlow Dam (1930), and Harris Dam (1983), the last being built over rapids seventy-seven miles upstream from Martin Dam.

IN THE VALLEY AND RIDGE: The Coosa River System drains some 5,350 square miles in Alabama, most of it in the Valley and Ridge. The river enters Alabama in Cherokee County and flows southwesterly until it passes into the Piedmont section, north of Lay Lake Dam. Several main tributaries flowing from the Cumberland Plateau join the Coosa near Gadsden, including the Little River, Big Canoe Creek, Little Canoe Creek, and Big Wills Creek. The main channel ranges from three hundred to five hundred feet wide and is flanked in places by banks up to twenty-five feet in height near Gadsden. North and east of Hokes Bluff, in Etowah County, the river meanders across its own floodplain, which is about fifteen miles wide. To the southwest, the valley narrows and deepens along the boundary between St. Clair and Calhoun counties, where the river cuts through the more resistant shale and sandstone of the northern edge of the Coosa Ridges district. Neely Henry Dam is located on the Coosa at the southern edge of the ridges. To the south, the valley widens to about 20 miles across near Pell City, in St. Clair County, and the river begins to meander again. The meanders are less pronounced here because the dolomites of the Knox Group contain varying amounts of chert, and the river's meanderings are restricted by ledges of more resistant rocks along its course. Logan Martin Dam, located south of Pell City on the Coosa, was built on one of these ledges. The seven dams on the Coosa River together produce 58 percent of Alabama Power's hydroelectric power.

SPECIAL GEOLOGICAL FEATURES

THE MOBILE-TENSAW DELTA

Directly north of Alabama's Mobile Bay, within a broad river valley that leads northward to the confluence of the Tombigbee and Alabama Rivers, lies a vast region of wetlands known by various names, including the Mobile-Tensaw Delta, the Mobile Delta, or simply the Delta. This region is home to some of the most diverse wildlife in Alabama, and indeed in the entire United States. The Delta played a major role in the exploration and settlement of Alabama and is currently at the center of a clash between conservationists on the one side and developers and business interests on the other. The Delta is Alabama's principal remaining natural terrain and has been designated a national landmark.

The Mobile-Tensaw Delta includes sections of Baldwin, Clarke, Mobile, Monroe, and Washington counties in southwestern Alabama. The region features numerous interconnected stream systems, floodplains, swamps, bayous, lakes, and forests, and it is home to an abundance of species of flora and fauna, including 500 plants, 300 birds, 126 fishes, 46 mammals, 69 reptiles, and 30 amphibians. The Delta is about 45 miles long, ranges up to 16 miles wide, and encompasses about 300 square miles. Ecosystems vary among 20,000 acres of open water; 10,000 acres of marsh; more than 70,000 acres

Cypress swamp in the Tensaw Delta.

Cottonmouth water moccasin.

of swamp; and more than 85,000 acres of bottomland forest. As a result of restoration and conservation efforts by a combination of federal and state agencies and private citizens, 185,500 contiguous acres of federal and state property are now preserved in the Delta.

The valley in which the Delta now lies began forming several million years ago when separate inland streams joined together in their southward flow across land formerly covered by the Gulf of Mexico. About 18,000 years ago, during the last major ice age, the water line in the Gulf of Mexico probably was about 400 feet lower than it is at present, and Alabama's coastline was about 60 miles south of its present location. Thus

Grasshopper on palmetto leaf.

at that time streams of the Delta valley extended far beyond their present southern termination at the head of Mobile Bay.

As global temperatures began to rise, the glacial age slowly came to an end, and the melting of glaciers caused worldwide sea levels to rise. Gulf waters now cover the lower courses of ancient streams as well as their valleys, floodplains, and associated ecosystems (including many areas inhabited by prehistoric peoples). Present-day Mobile Bay is a drowned section of an ancient river valley. Inundation of the area probably began about 5,000 years ago and reached present-day levels (although with some fluctuation) slightly more than 2,000 years ago. The water level in the Gulf of

View from the deck of Alabama's new 5 Rivers Delta Resource Center near Mobile.

Mexico continues to rise at a rate of about two millimeters per year, continuing to drown the southernmost areas of the Delta.

Rivers in the Delta region include the Tombigbee, Alabama, Mobile, Middle, Tensaw, Apalachee, Raft, Spanish, and Blakeley. Of these, the Tombigbee, Alabama, and Mobile are important transportation routes. The Mobile River is the southernmost river channel of the Tennessee-Tombigbee Waterway. Numerous small streams intercon-

nect with Delta rivers, and their courses divide, converge, and constantly change, resulting in continual erosion and redistribution of sediment deposited by former streams. The Delta also receives drainage from adjacent uplands.

Many Delta streams develop meander channels (channels that wander in sweeping curves), resulting in erosional widening of the Delta valley. These streams constantly shift positions, and numerous sections of abandoned channels have filled with sediment or become isolated lakes. Those that formed in the extreme bends of former stream channels are called oxbow lakes. A network of abandoned river channels provides alternative drainage routes during flood stages of primary streams. Most stream channels in the Delta have developed "levees" (narrow ridges of sediment along their banks), which tend to prevent water from overflowing stream banks during moderate increases in stream flow. During these periodic increases in flow (usually after heavy spring rains), streams overtop these natural levees and cover large areas of the Delta called floodbasins. As water levels subside, flood-basin waters return to the adjacent flowing streams.

Evidence of human habitation in the Delta dates back thousands of years. [See "The First Alabamians" in the History chapter.] The area supplied these early inhabitants with abundant fish, shellfish, game animals, plant material, and clay and mineral resources. Indians of the Mississippian period built earthen mounds adjacent to Bottle Creek and the Tensaw River. As the Mississippian tradition declined, other peoples moved into the area, including the Alabamas, the Mobilians, the Taensas, the Creeks, and the Choctaws. The Tensaw River is named for the Taensa, and the Alabama and Mobile rivers are named for those groups.

Spanish forces passed through the area in the mid-1500s, and the French arrived in 1702, leading to the establishment of a fort and town upstream from present-day Mobile in an area of the wetlands that often flooded; in 1711 Jean-Baptiste Le Moyne de Bienville oversaw the relocation of the town downriver to its present site. In 1813 the Delta settlement of Fort Mims, located in present-day Baldwin County, was the site of an attack by Creek Indians in which more than 250 settlers, militiamen, and slaves were massacred. In April 1865, the last major battle of the Civil War took place

The Tensaw Delta, opening into Mobile Bay.

Large alligator in the Tensaw Delta.

at the fortified town of Blakely (often known as Fort Blakely) on the Delta's southeastern rim. In the mid-1920s, a public roadway, now called the Causeway, was extended east-west across the lower part of the Delta to link the western and eastern shores of Mobile Bay. U.S. Interstate Highway 65 and a railway line now cross the Delta, and U.S. Interstate Highway 10 now crosses the northern part of Mobile Bay.

The Delta long has been a prime agricultural location as well as a source of fish, game, timber, lumber, pulpwood, sand, clay, gravel, oil, and gas. Primary uses of the Delta today are recreation and education, including boating, fishing, hunting, wildlife observation, and study of wetland ecology. The Delta is home to many of the stops on the Alabama Coastal Birding Trail.

Conservationists presently are concerned about the effects of upstream dams on stream flow and sediment loads, stream pollution, decline in fish populations, effects of invasive alien plant and animal species, and stream-channel dredging. Some restoration advocates propose restoring ecological conditions in the lower Delta to their former status (pre-Causeway conditions) by improving tidal flow between the lower Delta and Mobile Bay. There are also concerns that continued commercial development of the U.S. 90 Causeway will result in diminished scenic and ecological qualities in the lower Delta. — EVERETT SMITH, Fairhope, in the *Encyclopedia of Alabama*

THE WETUMPKA CRATER

About 83 million years ago, a cosmic object (an asteroid or comet estimated to have been about 1,250 feet in diameter) struck what is now Elmore County on the eastern side of the city of Wetumpka. All that remains of the meteoritic impact crater formed by the collision is a crescent-shaped ridge of hills rising up to 300 feet above the surrounding river plains. Bald Knob, the highest point on the rim, and other parts of the crater remnant are clearly visible to travelers entering Wetumpka on U.S. Highway 231 and Alabama Highway 14.

The crater structure was first noted in 1969 by a group of geologists from the Geological Survey of Alabama, including team leader Thornton L. Neathery. In 1976 Neathery and his co-workers published a paper proposing that a meteor had created the feature, which they called the Wetumpka astrobleme. Its origin was not proven conclusively until 1999 when scientists completed a 630-foot-deep drilling operation at the crater's center. The scientists found that the minerals contained in the subsurface samples revealed evidence of deformation characteristics resulting from high pressure and massive sudden impact. Such minerals are found only in structures formed by cosmic impacts and at nuclear-test sites. In addition to the physical analysis,

Eroded section of the Wetumpka impact crater.

Satellite image of the Wetumpka crater. The arching road from the bottom left to the top center traces the remaining portion of the crater rim.

the material was subjected to geochemical testing at a laboratory in Vienna, Austria, which revealed meteoritic elements such as iridium, cobalt, nickel, and chromium and confirmed their meteoric origin. In 2002 the research team published its results in *Earth and Planetary Science Letters* and officially established Wetumpka as the 157th known impact crater on Earth.

The Wetumpka impact crater, which is approximately 4.7 miles wide, formed during a time in geological history when the sea level was much higher than it is today. Much of southern and central Alabama was under the shallow waters of the northern Gulf of Mexico, and the shoreline ran roughly from Tuscaloosa County to northern Elmore County and eastward to northern Russell County. The Wetumpka impact thus occurred about 15 miles offshore in water about 100 feet deep. The rim is made of hard, crystalline rocks, and the interior area is composed of softer, sedimentary materials. There is also an area of highly disturbed sediments outside the crater's rim on the southern side of the crater that were washed into place by the catastrophic resurgence of sea water forced away from the area by the impact.

The Wetumpka impact event was the greatest natural disaster in Alabama history. Energy released by the impact was roughly 175,000 times greater than the nuclear explosion in Hiroshima in 1945. The collision produced a huge earthquake, a tsunami, an atmospheric blast wave (hurricane-force, straight-line winds), and a cascade of falling rocks, which would have been ejected from the developing crater bowl. Many thousands of living things, including dinosaurs, other reptiles, and aquatic life, along the Gulf shoreline of Elmore County were decimated by this event. The Wetumpka impact did not have global consequences, however, and is not linked to any global extinction of animals or plants in the geological record.

Wetumpka, which means "rumbling waters" in the Creek Indian language, is an appropriate name for an impact crater formed in sea water. The crater is celebrated annually by the city of Wetumpka, which sponsors lectures and public tours. In 2002, the Alabama Historical Association erected a roadside historical marker describing the crater on U.S. Highway 231 in front of the Elmore County Health Department.

—DAVID T. KING JR., Auburn University, in the *Encyclopedia of Alabama*

STEPHEN C. MINKIN PALEOZOIC FOOTPRINT SITE

The Steven C. Minkin Paleozoic Footprint Site in Walker County is the most prolific source of vertebrate trackways of its age in the world. It is an important resource for scientists for a number of reasons: the fossils found within it are well-preserved, abundant, and diverse, and thus scientists can study multiple examples of a given species or behavior; the deposit records the footprints of some of the earliest reptiles; and it contains the oldest known examples of schooling and herding behavior. The site is named for the man who led the effort to preserve the site.

The fossil trackways are preserved in dark gray shale that formed as mud on a freshwater tidal flat about 315 million years ago. Scientists know that this was the likely environment from a combination of clues. For example, the trackway layer lies on top of a coal deposit that formed on land, and associated rocks contain known marine (sea-dwelling) fossils, indicating that the trackways formed near  the shoreline. The shale contains traces of land-dwelling organisms (amphibians and reptiles) and aquatic organisms (fish), but no exclusively marine organisms. Marine deposits nearby contain brachiopod shells and the traces of resting trilobites, both absent from the trackway deposits, but no remains of land dwellers.

The coal deposit, once a swamp forest, is one of the reasons that the trackways were discovered. The Minkin Site is located at the former Union Chapel coal mine. In 1999, a high school teacher learned that the grandmother of one of his students owned the coal mine. The teacher visited the mine and soon found something he knew was important: tracks of an ancient amphibian. He reported the find to what was then the

Fossils from the Minkin Site. Above: Crossing horseshoe crab trackways. Left: Millipede trackways. Opposite page: Amphibian trackway and fly larva burrow.

Birmingham Paleontological Society (now the Alabama Paleontological Society), and some of its members visited the site. They informed professional paleontologists, and the two groups together began a race to collect the specimens and struggled to preserve the site. By law, surface mines in Alabama must be reclaimed shortly after mining operations end, and the Minkin Site was scheduled for reclamation. The preservation effort was spearheaded by geologist and amateur paleontologist Steve Minkin, and was named for him following his untimely death. It represented a true collaboration between dozens of amateurs and professionals. Their efforts were successful, and the Minkin Site is now preserved in perpetuity thanks to the New Acton Coal Mining Company, the Alabama Department of Conservation and Natural Resources, and dedi-

cated paleontologists. In 2005, this same group published the first major scholarly work about the trace fossils and the site: *Pennsylvanian Footprints in the Black Warrior Basin of Alabama.* The contents range from historical essays to technical discussions of the trackways.

The Minkin Site features a cliff, the high wall of the former mine, partially surrounded by a large mass of broken rock that was moved during the coal-mining process. This rock consists primarily of slabs of shale that range from a fraction of an inch to several feet in thickness. The fossils are found on or in some of these slabs. Nearly 3,000 specimens have been collected so far and many more await discovery. In addition to the hundreds of footprints and trackways left by reptiles and amphibians, the Minkin Site also features undulating traces made by fish swimming in very shallow water; horizontal and vertical burrows of fly larvae; walking, resting, and jumping traces made by horseshoe crabs and other arthropods; and worm burrows. The trace fossils occur with the carbonized remains of ferns, treelike cycads, giant horsetails, and other plants. These plants lived in swamps adjacent to tidal flats on deltas and rimming bays and lagoons. These tidal flats were home to fish, insects, worms, amphibians, horseshoe crabs, and other creatures that left traces of their activities in soft mud (now shale). Fragments of plant material were periodically washed out onto the tidal flats or into the adjacent shallow bays.

The Minkin Site is not generally open to the public, but visits are easily arranged. The Alabama Paleontological Society conducts monthly collecting expeditions, and interested persons can go along. Specimens of scientific value must be donated to a museum so that they are available for future study. —DAVID C. KOPASKA-MERKEL, Geological Survey of Alabama, in the *Encyclopedia of Alabama*

The State House at Cahawba

ALABAMA'S STATE CAPITOLS

STATE HOUSE. TUSCALOOSA, AL.

As a separate territory and state since 1817, Alabama has had five capitals. Saint Stephens, in southwest Alabama, was the territorial seat of government. The first Constitutional Convention assembled in Huntsville in 1819, and the first state legislature met there. But Governor William Wyatt Bibb had chosen Cahaba (or Cahawba), at the confluence of the Cahaba and Alabama rivers, as the site for the new capital. In 1826, after six years, the legislature moved the capital to Tuscaloosa. With the occupation of more Indian land in the 1830s, Tuscaloosa was too far from the population center of the state, and in 1846, Montgomery was selected as the new capital. Montgomery has served as Alabama's capital since 1847. Top, a drawing of the Capitol in Cahaba. Center, the Capitol in Tuscaloosa. Bottom, an 1880s view of the present Capitol on "Goat Hill" in Montgomery.

2

HISTORICAL ALABAMA

EDWIN C. BRIDGES

Alabama's history is rich and fascinating. Virtually every major issue in American history has played out in Alabama, often in dramatic ways. From Stone Age mammoth hunting to Space Age rocket building, it is difficult to find a topic in American history not vividly illustrated in Alabama.

Yet, Alabama history is not just the story of America writ small. Alabama has its own unique character and flavor. While America's story is generally one of repeated successes, Alabama's story mixes success with generous doses of struggle and failure. Like the rest of the South, Alabama embraced slavery and suffered defeat in the war that ended slavery. The state struggled again after the Civil War, emerging with a segregated social and political system. Through the civil rights movement, African Americans overturned that system.

Hardship and struggle are not unique to Alabama, of course, but Alabama's blend of these elements is. Cycles of success and hardship have tempered the character of Alabama as its people have acted and reacted to the challenges of their times. The result is a history that is complex, varied, and full of life.

This section of *The Alabama Guide* offers an overview of Alabama's history from prehistory to efforts by Alabamians today to prepare for the future. In recent years, Alabama has experienced considerable success in economic development efforts. New building and rebuilding are opening doors of opportunity across the state. And Alabamians are working together with a new sense of community to address common problems. For people all too conscious of the handicaps of the past, the sense of a budding resurgence makes this an exciting and hopeful time. The remainder of this book will draw a more complete portrait of Alabama today.

This essay is a synthesis of a large and growing body of scholarship, both past and present. It is not intended as an official history of the state; like all works of historical analysis, it reflects the judgment and perspective of the writer. The author has been the director of the Alabama Department of Archives and History since 1982.

THE FIRST ALABAMIANS (12,000 BC–1702 AD)

The first humans in North America eventually became known as Indians. What we know of them is based on archaeology, the study of past life through the excavation of sites and analysis of artifacts. Archaeologists have organized the story of Indian life into broad periods based on such indicators as tools, ways of securing food, and social organization. The first Alabamians arrived as hunters toward the end of the last Ice Age. Over thousands of years, they developed new tools and new methods of sustaining themselves. Gradually, their numbers increased, and their society became more complex. By the time of the Middle Ages in Europe, they had built a sophisticated culture with walled towns and a well-developed system of agriculture—a culture that collapsed under the massive losses caused by European diseases.

The Paleo Indians (12,000–8500 BC)

Beginning around fourteen thousand years ago, the Paleo-Indian Period was the time of the Ice Age hunters. Large glaciers extended far south into what is now the United States. Because so much of the earth's water was locked in ice, the level of the oceans was substantially lower than now. Exposed land connected Asia and North America. Asian hunters pursuing game were able to cross into North America, and some migrated southward into what is now Alabama. The climate and the vegetation they found resembled that of today's Minnesota.

Archaeological evidence indicates that the first Alabamians moved into the southeastern part of North America pursuing large animals such as mammoths and giant bison. Archaeologists differ over how much the Paleo Indians relied on this megafauna. They also hunted smaller animals and gathered foods such as nuts and berries. But large animals were an important part of their diet. Living together in small bands, these early Indians moved frequently to follow their food sources. Because these sources were not reliable and because of the dangers intrinsic to a hunting and nomadic existence, the lives of the Paleo Indians were difficult, precarious, and usually brief.

Our scant information about the Paleo Indians comes from the study of their stone tools, such as spear points and scrapers, as well as bone fragments, seeds, and other

A fossil mammoth molar. The ridges were for grinding grasses. (Actual size, about eight inches across.)

A Paleo-Indian point.
(Actual size, 2.5 inches long.)

remains found in caves. Visitors today can see an example of early Indian habitation at Russell Cave in Jackson County. Over the course of thousands of years, the residue of one generation after another piled up on its floor—to a depth of more than thirty feet. Archaeological research has been a process of carefully scraping off and analyzing layer after layer of this accumulated debris.

The Archaic Indians (8500–1000 BC)

The occupation of Russell Cave may date from the end of the Paleo Period or, more likely, the start of the next period, called Archaic, which began around 8500 BC. Looking back from the perspective of thousands of years, archaeologists see significant differences between Paleo and Archaic life. Yet most researchers agree that no specific time marks the transition from one lifestyle to another. The process of adaptation and development was long and slow.

The Archaic Period lifestyle emerged as the last Ice Age ended. Warmer temperatures brought a new environment to Alabama and new challenges to the Indian inhabitants. A major change was the disappearance of large animals, such as the mastodons, on which the Paleo Indians had relied for food. Scientists are not certain whether these extinctions were caused by climate change or over-hunting. Regardless of the cause, the Indians had to find other food sources and to adapt to new environmental conditions.

Fortunately, the warming climate brought increases in the numbers of smaller animals such as rabbits, deer, and turkeys. There were also more edible plants—nuts, berries, roots, and greens. The Archaic Indians were skillful gatherers and hunters. As they took advantage of these new sources, their diet gradually shifted to one with more vegetable content. They had dogs, but none of the other domesticated animals such as cattle, pigs, and horses that became an important part of life in Africa, Asia, and Europe.

The Archaic Indians became more skilled in tool making. They learned to shape stones by grinding, not just by chipping, and they fashioned projectile points tailored for specific animals. They also created crude pots by scraping out soft stones with harder ones. Pots were an important advancement because they retained more of the nutritional value of cooked food. Instead of dripping uselessly into the fire, the juices

In continued use from the Archaic into the Mississippian periods, Russell Cave provides clues to the development of prehistoric society over the course of 10,000 years.

of food cooked in pots became part of a stew. The Archaic Indians also developed trade networks to acquire materials not available locally. Although their overall numbers increased, they still lived in small, extended-family bands, skirmishing occasionally with other bands over territory and resources.

Toward the end of the period, the Archaic Indians acquired two new skills that greatly improved their lives. They learned to heat clay to produce ceramic pots, and they began rudimentary agriculture. Cultivated plants such as squash and sunflowers helped ensure a more reliable food supply. Ceramic pots made cooking and food storage much easier.

This grinding stone and the steatite bowl on the opposite page reflect the shift from nomadic life to a more settled society.

With these innovations, the Archaic Indians were able to stay longer in one place, and they began settling into year-round communities. This sedentism in turn allowed them to accumulate more material to make their lives secure and comfortable. Their population gradually increased, and, as a result, their social organization became more complex. Archaeologists today see this increasing complexity in the ornaments and special treatment of privileged individuals found in Archaic burial remains.

Steatite bowl, used before ceramic pottery was developed.

The Woodland Indians (1000 BC–900 AD)

The Woodland Period is distinguished by a higher level of technological and social complexity. Woodland Indians became skilled potters, producing pots to fit a wide variety of functions and frequently demonstrating beautiful artistry. They learned to use the bow and arrow, improving their ability to secure game. They also became more skilled at cultivating plants, relying even more heavily than their ancestors on food they grew for themselves.

With a more reliable food supply and a greater accumulation of material objects, the Woodland Indians remained longer in settled communities. And with an increased attachment to one place, they began building earthen mounds for important ceremonies and for the burial of their dead. Studies of these burials show a continued increase in social differentiation as well as an increasingly rich aesthetic and spiritual life.

Archaic projectile point.

The Mississippian Culture (900–1550)

The Mississippian Period continued the Woodland pattern of growth and increased complexity, raised to a still higher level—all made possible by the cultivation of corn. Planted with squash and beans, corn proved to be a versatile and efficient nutritional source. It could be grown in quantity in the rich alluvial soil of Alabama river valleys. And it could be dried and stored in pots to provide sustenance throughout the year.

Decorated pot, reflecting Mississippian artistry.

Clay plate with incised rattlesnakes, a common Mississippian motif.

Sustained by this plentiful new food supply, the Mississippian population increased substantially. Towns became larger, and some were even protected by fortified walls. Many towns were knit together in organized systems, with larger chiefdoms governing smaller ones.

The Mississippians expanded the Woodland practice of building mounds. The largest Mississippian site in Alabama—and one of the largest in North America—was located in Hale County. Twenty-six mounds, arranged around a large open plaza, remain today at Moundville. Some of these mounds appear to have been places of residence, while others were ceremonial sites. A large part of the town was enclosed inside a protective wall. Archeological evidence shows an extensive network of smaller Mississippian towns all along the river valleys of Alabama. The total Mississippian population may have exceeded one hundred thousand when the first Europeans arrived.

Cultural Collapse

Indian history in Alabama shows a complex interplay between people and their environment. Through each epoch of environmental change, humans eventually found new ways of supporting themselves. They suffered frequent disasters, and by modern standards their lives were hard even in the best of times. But they gradually adapted and moved forward to a greater level of cultural complexity.

The Mississippian culture was the culmination of thousands of years of this development, but it too suffered disaster. Archaeologists do not know why, but Mississippian society appears to have been in distress even before the arrival of the first Europeans. Moundville was probably abandoned by the mid-1400s. Yet thousands of Indians were still living in substantial towns when the Spanish conquistador Hernando de Soto arrived in Alabama in 1540.

The four narratives that came from the de Soto expedition are the first written accounts of life in Alabama. They describe numerous towns along the major rivers and the corn-based system of agriculture of Mississippian culture. The narratives also describe the Indians' resistance to the more than seven hundred Spanish invaders, many of whom were on horseback, protected by armor and wielding metal implements of war.

Led by Chief Tuscaloosa, the Indians mounted a fierce nine-hour attack at a walled town named Mauvilla. The Spanish reported that thousands of warriors joined the assault and that thousands were killed. The reports probably exaggerated the numbers but, even so, Mauvilla was probably the largest battle waged by Indians against European invaders in what would become the United States. Today, finding the location of that fabled site is one of the great quests of Alabama archaeology.

Although de Soto defeated Tuscaloosa at Mauvilla, his victory was costly. The accounts report forty Spanish killed and many more wounded. De Soto also lost valuable horses and supplies. Unwilling to turn back empty-handed toward the Gulf, he continued westward. His own death in 1542 near the Mississippi River marked the collapse of his expedition.

Coalescent Societies (1550–1702)

While Tuscaloosa's warriors suffered heavy casualties at Mauvilla, the war losses were trivial compared to those from European diseases. For thousands of years, Europeans had tended livestock that did not exist in North America. They had developed some degree of resistance to the respiratory viruses and other diseases such as smallpox that occasionally mutate from domesticated animals to humans.

For the native population of North America, the communicable diseases brought by Europeans were a catastrophe. Some archaeologists estimate that as much as 90 percent of the native population may have died in the years following the first contact with Europeans. The entire Mississippian culture was virtually destroyed. The population loss was so great that large tracts of land were left uninhabited. Buffalo from the western plains began migrating into Alabama to graze in relative tranquility on native river cane.

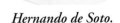

Hernando de Soto.

In the decades after de Soto, the Mississippian survivors in Alabama struggled to recover and rebuild. They regrouped in small towns, usually along rivers or creeks. Their political and social structures had suffered terrible blows, but the survivors became the nuclei of the new tribes that would emerge—the Creek, Choctaw, Alabama, Chickasaw, and Cherokee. The basic technical skills, social tradi-

Mississippian mounds and plaza at Moundville, in Hale County.

tions, and values of these modern tribes were largely carried over from their Mississippian ancestors.

After the first destructive wave of Spanish explorers passed through Alabama in the mid-1500s, there was little contact between Indians and Europeans for more than a century. When Europeans returned in the late 1600s, they found Indians living in scattered clusters of small towns. Still emerging from a long rebuilding process, the Indians were much weaker than they had been two centuries earlier. Lacking political unity, numerical strength, or comparable technological resources, they were at a huge disadvantage in resisting the onslaught of new people who began settling around them.

A Struggle for the Land (1702–1814)

In January 1702, a party of French-Canadian colonists sailed into Mobile Bay. On a bluff upriver from the bay, they built the first European settlement on the land that would become Alabama. The largest native group, the Creek Indians, initially prospered in their dealings with the French colonists and with traders from the Spanish and English colonies. They played the Europeans against each other and traded deerskins for products they wanted.

The aftermath of the American Revolution brought a formidable new challenge to the Creeks from people who were more interested in land than in deerskins. The relentlessly expanding settlements of the new United States threatened the Creek way of life. Differences over how to respond to these intrusions triggered bitter internal struggles within the Creek Nation, leading to civil war and attacks by U.S. forces.

Alabama Indians in the Early 1700s

By the early 1700s, three European nations had established colonies that almost encircled what is today the state of Alabama. The Spanish held the Florida Gulf Coast. The British were moving down the Atlantic Coast, settling their new colony of Carolina. The French were developing Louisiana, including the lower Mississippi Valley and the western Gulf Coast.

A century-and-half after the arrival of Europeans and their diseases, the total number of Indians living in Alabama had declined to probably less than twenty thousand. Of these, the Creeks were by far the largest tribal group. The name "Creek" was used for a loose-knit confederation of smaller tribes and villages extending across present-day Alabama and Georgia. In Alabama, they lived along the Coosa and Tallapoosa rivers and in the Chattahoochee River Valley. A closely related tribe, the Alabamas, lived along the river that today bears their name. Choctaws and Chickasaws claimed large tracts of hunting land in the western part of Alabama, but their primary homes were outside the present state boundary. The Cherokees would not move into the territory until the late 1700s.

The Creeks sustained themselves by growing crops, hunting, fishing, and trading. Early European traders described Creek life in pleasant

This portion of a 1721 map by John Senex shows what is now Alabama and surrounding states, with the major Indian communities and European settlements.

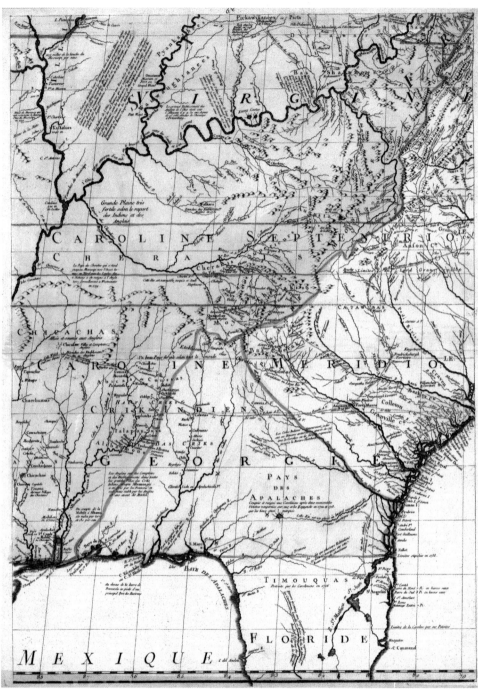

Above: The 1756 French map by John Mitchell shows overlapping French and English claims to territory still occupied by Indians. Opposite page: Top, a drawing by Philip Georg Friedrich von Reck, a young German colonist, shows an Indian village from the early 1700s. Bottom, a replica of a "wattle and daub" house at the Fort Toulouse-Fort Jackson historic site near Wetumpka.

terms. Women tended house and garden, cooked, and raised the children. Men hunted, cleared land, provided protection, traded, and made canoes, tools, and other implements. Elaborate ceremonies punctuated the changing of the seasons.

Though they were connected in a loose political union, most Creeks thought of themselves primarily as members of their town and clan. Creek

towns, called *talwa*, were small communities, usually of just a few hundred people. Their houses were "wattle and daub"—branches or canes interwoven around support posts, then plastered with clay. Houses were arranged in orderly fashion around a central public square, which also contained a winter council house. There was usually an open field for games. All of the land was for the common use of the entire *talwa*; there was no concept of exclusive, individual property ownership.

The Development of Indian Trade

European traders began visiting the Creeks in the late 1600s. They offered a variety of appealing objects, from cloth to metal implements and jewelry. Initially, the British wanted slaves in exchange—captured Indians from other tribes whom the British took to work on their plantations.

Trade beads, right, and brass gorget, below, are examples of objects that were common in early European-Indian trade.

After several decades of experimentation, the British gradually replaced Indian slaves with people taken from Africa or the West Indies. The Creeks continued their commerce with the Europeans by selling deerskins. As deerskin products became popular in Europe, traders from South Carolina and Georgia led pack trains into Alabama loaded with goods the Indians wanted. They returned to the coast loaded with deerskins.

Trade led to political and military alliances between Indian towns and European traders. Indians used European help in battles against their old enemies. Europeans sought to use the Indians against their colonial rivals and other tribes allied to those rivals. The Creeks were especially successful among southeastern Indians in exploiting trade and diplomacy to strengthen their power.

The Establishment of Mobile

The first European settlement in Alabama was Mobile. In 1702, Pierre Le Moyne d'Iberville and his brother, Jean Baptiste Le Moyne de Bienville, led a group of mostly French Canadians into Mobile Bay. After an initial encampment on Dauphin Island, these settlers built a fort and small town on a bluff upriver from the Bay. In 1711, they relocated back down the river to Mobile's present site. Mobile served as the capital of

Bienville and Iberville, founders of Mobile.

French Louisiana until 1718, when colonial offices were transferred to Biloxi (Mississippi). Two years later, French officials moved the capital farther west, to the newly established town of New Orleans.

In trade, the Creeks favored British goods, but they sought to keep a balance between the European powers. To offset the aggressively expanding British, the Creeks allowed the French to establish an inland outpost near the center of the Upper Creek settlements. Built in 1717, Fort Toulouse was located where the Coosa and Tallapoosa rivers converge to form the Alabama River. This fort was the easternmost point of French settlement in southern North America.

In 1721, the French sought to strengthen their base at Mobile by importing enslaved workers. They had already established African slavery in their West

French soldiers brought this cannon upriver from Mobile to Fort Toulouse in the early 1700s and left it behind when they abandoned the fort in 1763. The carriage was built much later for display purposes.

Indies colonies, so the expansion to Mobile was an easy step for them. French laws governing slavery were not as severe or rigid as later slave codes of the antebellum South. French slaves had rights which, though limited, were protected by law. For example, slaves could buy their freedom and even own other slaves.

Racial and national lines were relatively fluid in colonial Alabama. Living together in close proximity for many decades, European, Indian, and African cultures interacted in a rich frontier blend. This cultural openness extended as well to Indian-controlled parts of Alabama. Creeks were usually welcoming to outsiders. When children were born to Creek women, they were treated as Creeks regardless of the father's origin.

American Revolution Upsets the Creek Power Balance

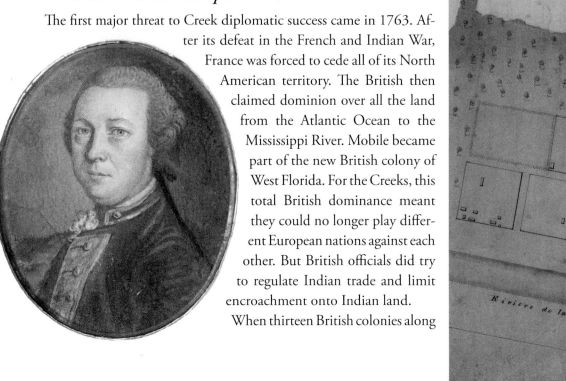

The first major threat to Creek diplomatic success came in 1763. After its defeat in the French and Indian War, France was forced to cede all of its North American territory. The British then claimed dominion over all the land from the Atlantic Ocean to the Mississippi River. Mobile became part of the new British colony of West Florida. For the Creeks, this total British dominance meant they could no longer play different European nations against each other. But British officials did try to regulate Indian trade and limit encroachment onto Indian land.

When thirteen British colonies along

the Atlantic Coast rose up in revolution against the British in 1776, their sister colony of West Florida remained loyal to the crown. Mobile and the Creek lands became a sanctuary for fleeing loyalists and escaped slaves. Then in 1780, the Spanish took advantage of Britain's vulnerability to reclaim their old colony of Florida, attacking and seizing Mobile in their campaign. The thirty-year Spanish occupation that followed added still more national and ethnic variety to the cultural mix of the Mobile Bay area.

The United States' victory in the American Revolution was a disaster for Alabama Indians. After the war, the Americans claimed all former British territory below Canada, except for Florida, which remained under Spanish control. The question of how the U.S. government would treat Indians inside this territory remained open, but the danger was readily apparent to Creek leaders. Americans wanted land, not trade. As soon as the Revolutionary War was over, American settlers began looking westward, eager to take possession of this vast, fertile territory.

Opposite page, top: At Fort Toulouse today, historically accurate replicas of buildings, furnishings, tools, and weaponry allow visitors a glimpse into French colonial life. Opposite, bottom: Major Robert Farmar was the officer in charge of Mobile after the British took control. Below: A 1780 map of Mobile following the city's fall to Spain.

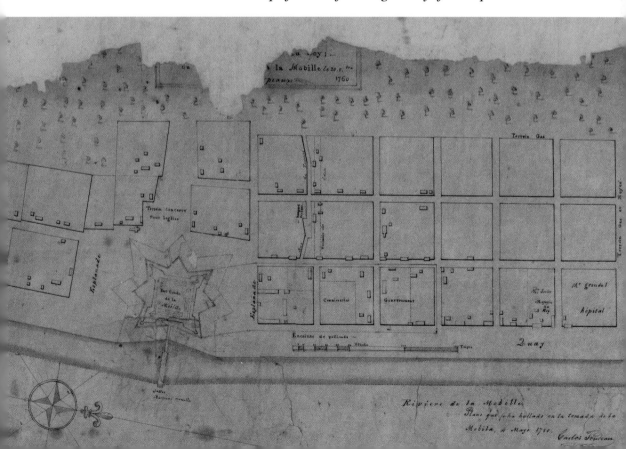

Creek Efforts To Protect Their Land

After the Revolution, Georgia argued that its boundaries extended all the way to the Mississippi River. As restless Georgia settlers began intruding more frequently onto Creek lands, violent skirmishes erupted between Indians and settlers all along the frontier. In 1789, after the new U.S. government was formed under the Constitution, President George Washington quickly initiated steps to restore peace to the southern frontier. He invited a Creek delegation, led by Alexander McGillivray, to visit him in New York and discuss terms for a treaty.

McGillivray had emerged after the American Revolution as the Creeks' most influential and able leader. He was the son of a long-time Scottish trader and an Indian woman from one of the most prominent clans. Though he received a European-style education in Charleston, South Carolina, McGillivray returned during the Revolution to live with his Creek family near present-day Wetumpka. His ability to work easily in both Indian and American cultures strengthened his effectiveness as a Creek leader.

This medal was given as a token of honor to Creek leaders at the 1790 treaty conference in New York. Below, John Trumbull's drawings of two Creek chiefs who attended the conference.

In the summer of 1790, the Creek delegation traveled from Alabama to New York City. There, at the nation's temporary capital, they signed the Treaty of New York, the first treaty entered into by the United States under its new Constitution. It was a landmark in American–Indian relations.

In the treaty, the Creeks ceded an additional tract of

The 1797 Bradley map shows Alabama as part of Georgia's western territory, with the locations of some major Indian towns and lines showing Spain's boundary claims.

land to the Americans. But the United States, in turn, committed itself to "solemnly guarantee to the Creek Nation, all their [remaining] lands within the limits of the United States." This guarantee outraged most white inhabitants along the southern frontier. They regarded Indian land as a great treasure to which they were entitled. The idea that the federal government would deny them access to this bounty ignited a fierce backlash. Georgians denounced the treaty provisions as a federal infringement on "states' rights"—the first of many times southerners would invoke this doctrine.

Despite President Washington's hopes, relations between the Creeks and their Georgia neighbors continued to deteriorate. The deerskin trade was in disarray as the deer population fell, yet the Indians still wanted European goods to which they had become accustomed. Unscrupulous American traders encouraged Indians to run up debts, which the traders expected to convert into cessions of land. Meanwhile, settlers continued to encroach onto Creek territory in violation of the terms of the Treaty of New York. As the struggle intensified, the untimely death of Alexander McGillivray in 1793 left the Creeks without an effective leader.

The Mississippi Territory

The Creeks were not the only opponents to Georgia's western land claims. Other states also challenged the claims. During the American Revolution, all states except Georgia had agreed that unsettled western lands would be shared as common property, won in the collective struggle for independence. Congress established the Mississippi Territory in 1798 to provide governance for disputed land that Spain had ceded in a 1795 treaty. Finally, in 1802, Georgia formally surrendered its claims to land west of the Chattahoochee River. This land was added to the Mississippi Territory, which then included most of today's states of Alabama and Mississippi. Natchez became the territorial capital.

In the treaty with Spain, all land below the 31st parallel, which included the Mobile Bay area, remained in Spanish hands. The only Alabama portion of the Mississippi Territory with any American settlers was a small tract upriver from Mobile and above the 31st parallel. This area, known as the Tensaw, was organized by the territorial government as part of Washington County. Its chief town was St. Stephens, located at the site of the old Spanish fort and mission San Esteban.

Settlement Pressure Builds

As the deerskin trade declined, many Creeks adopted American practices of farming, husbandry, and trade. Others were unable or unwilling to change their lifestyles. Raising garden crops had always been women's work for the Creeks. To give up traditional male duties and become tied to a plow was an insult to the dignity of Creek warriors. It meant abandoning a cherished way of life.

As envisioned in the Treaty of New York, President Washington appointed a federal representative, former Revolutionary War colonel Benjamin Hawkins, to work with the Indians. Part of Hawkins's mission was to encourage the Creeks to adopt American-style farming. Those who were most successful in taking up these new skills tended to be mixed-blood descendants of traders, such as Alexander McGillivray. But many Creeks grew increasingly resentful at pressure by the U.S. government to give up the way of life of their forefathers.

In 1805, the Cherokees ceded their hunting lands in Alabama north of the Tennessee River. Thousands of farmers from Georgia and Tennessee crossed over to settle in this rich agricultural area. At the same time, an additional cession of land by the Choctaws allowed the Tensaw settlement to expand northward.

Meanwhile, in 1803 the United States secured a far larger acquisition by purchasing Louisiana from France. After the Louisiana Purchase, President Thomas Jefferson wanted to establish an efficient land route connecting Washington

Benjamin Hawkins, appointed by President Washington as Superintendent of Indian Affairs in the South.

and New Orleans. The most direct path ran down the eastern piedmont through Georgia and then across Creek territory. Building this new road through Indian land would require the permission of the Creeks.

In 1805, President Jefferson invited a group of Creek headmen to another treaty conference—this one in Washington. Although they did not fully represent all parts of the Creek Nation, the delegates authorized the building of what would become the "Federal Road." Crossing the Chattahoochee River below present-day Phenix City, the Federal Road roughly paralleled today's I-85 and I-65 southwest to Mobile. It ended at Ft. Stoddard, an American fortification in the Tensaw settlement just north of the Spanish line.

The Red Sticks Rise in Resistance

As settlers continued encroaching on Indian land, new voices rose to fan the flames of Indian resentment. Two Shawnee war leaders, Tecumseh and his younger brother who was called The Prophet, preached united Indian resistance to the Americans. They urged a return to tradi-tional ways of life and the expulsion of white settlers from Indian land.

William McIntosh led the delegation that met with Thomas Jefferson.

From Alabama up to the Ohio River Valley, the brothers traveled through Indian territory, denouncing the expansionist Americans and urging spiritual renewal among the Indians. In an 1811 Creek Council meeting at Tuckabatchee, a Creek town along the Tallapoosa River, Tecumseh was re-ported to have proclaimed: "Back whence they came, upon a trail of blood, they must be driven. . . . Burn their dwellings! Destroy their stock! . . . War now! War forever!"

As tensions grew between the Americans and Creeks, hostile Creeks who were called Red Sticks became more aggressive. By contrast, leaders of the Creek National Council feared American power and struggled anxiously to preserve peace. In 1812, in response to American threats, Council members executed four Creek warriors who had killed several American settlers. Disagreements among the Creeks over these executions widened the division between the two sides. This internal tension became as great as that between the Creeks and the Americans and led to armed clashes.

That same year, war erupted again between the United States and Great Britain. Many Red Stick leaders saw the War of 1812 as a time of opportunity. They reasoned that American troops would be tied up fighting the British and that the British might even provide help for the Red Sticks. American settlers all along the frontier realized the danger of Indian attack and began preparing for conflict.

In the summer of 1813, a group of Red Sticks traveled to Pensacola to secure weapons from the Spanish, who were then British allies. On their return, near Burnt Corn Creek, the Red Sticks were assaulted by a band of territorial militiamen accompanied by friendly Indians. Red Stick success in repelling this attack increased their confidence and prompted near panic among the Tensaw settlers.

The Creek War

Following the Burnt Corn skirmish, some four hundred American settlers, U.S.-allied Creeks, and enslaved African Americans gathered for protection at a makeshift fort on the farm of settler Samuel Mims. On August 30, more than seven hundred Red Sticks led by William Weatherford attacked and destroyed the fort. Although some occupants escaped, the Red Sticks brutally killed two hundred fifty men, women, and children. It was the largest and most successful assault by Indians on an American fortification in U.S. history.

News of the "Fort Mims Massacre" and graphic descriptions of mutilated victims prompted rage across the United States. Militia units from the Mississippi Territory, Georgia, and Tennessee quickly mobilized to suppress the Creek uprising. Assisted by Indian allies, they attacked Red Stick villages from the north, east, and west—burning Creek homes and destroying their crops.

A blood-letting instrument that belonged to William Weatherford.

After a series of crushing defeats through the fall and winter of 1813–14, many remaining Red Sticks retreated for a last stand to Horseshoe Bend—a peninsula formed by a loop of the Tallapoosa River. General Andrew Jackson's mixed army of Tennessee militia, regular U.S. troops, and friendly Indians attacked and destroyed

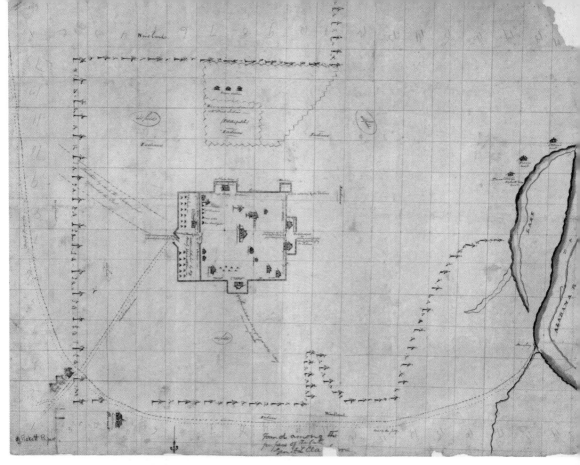

QUE-NA-WA.

Above: A map of the scene at Fort Mims, drawn by the burial party. Left: The Red Stick leader Menawa, who was second-in-command of Creek forces at the Battle of Horseshoe Bend.

the Red Stick camp. They killed hundreds of warriors, as well as many family members who were with them.

A few months later, in August 1814, Jackson summoned Creek leaders to a treaty conference. They met at Fort Jackson, built on the site of old Fort Toulouse. There, Jackson required Creek leaders, all of

Above: Horseshoe Bend National Military Park, in Tallapoosa County, near Dadeville.
Below: A map of the "Battle of the Horse Shoe," drawn by a member of General
Jackson's staff.

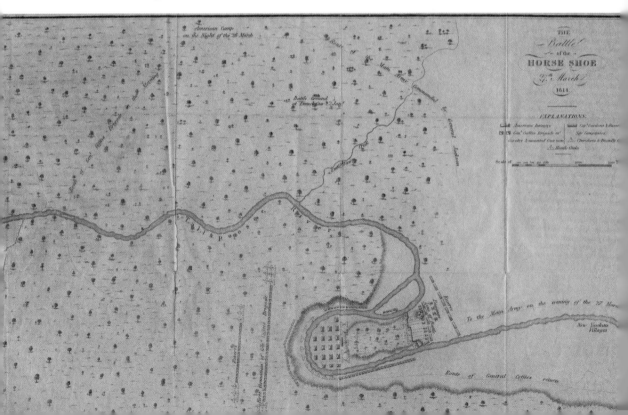

whom represented towns that had helped the Americans, to sign a new treaty. The Creeks ceded to the United States approximately twenty-two million acres of land—much of what would become the state of Alabama.

Consequences of the War

The war and the Treaty of Fort Jackson were a death blow to Creek power. The Creeks retained a reserve east of the Coosa River and extending into Georgia, but many of their towns and fields had been destroyed. A great part of their hunting land was lost. While some Creeks inside the reserve area recovered and continued to pros-per, many entered a period of degradation, poverty, and even starvation.

For Andrew Jackson, the Creek War was a triumph. Horseshoe Bend was his first great national success. After the treaty was signed, Jackson sent his forces to the Gulf Coast, where they repulsed a British attack on Fort Bowyer, south of Mobile. When the British regrouped for another attack farther to the west, Jackson met them at the Battle of New Orleans. His astound-ingly one-sided victory colored the lackluster War of 1812 with an afterglow of glory and confirmed Jackson as a national hero.

In the years after the Treaty of Fort Jackson, new settlers swarmed into the lands taken

General Andrew Jackson,
painted by his friend, Ralph Earl.

from the Creeks. With appetites whetted by years of delay, these settlers were eager to seize the opportunities before them. Their arrival and their energy would lead to the creation of the state of Alabama.

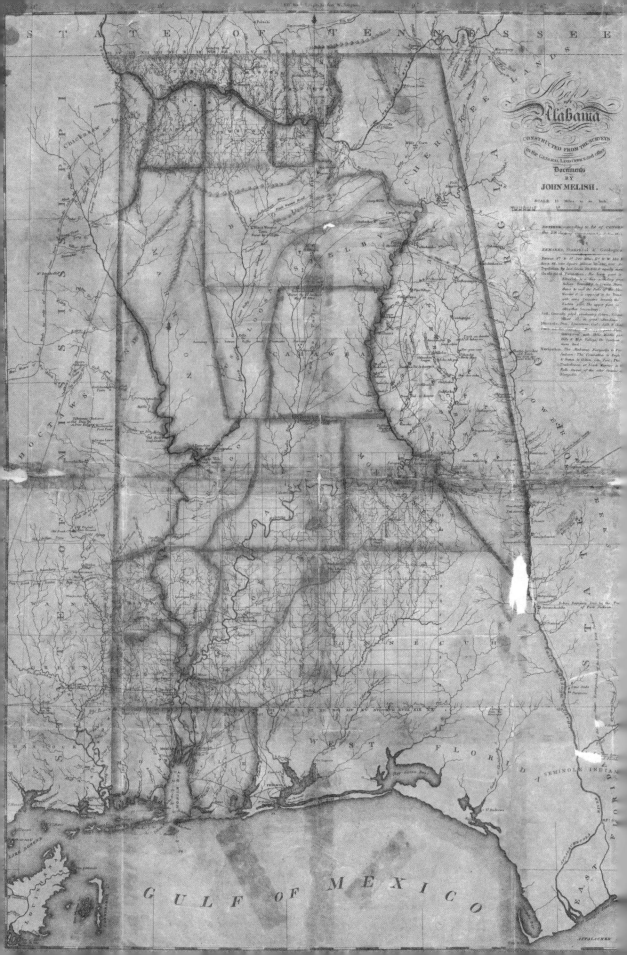

COTTON STATE (1814–1861)

Fired by the promise of new land, hundreds of thousands of settlers flooded into Alabama. Planters brought slaves to produce cotton for the world market. Yeoman farmers sought places where their families could make a better life. In less than forty years, these new arrivals transformed Alabama from frontier wilderness into the "Cotton State." Alabama became a prosperous cornerstone of the Old South, but the cost of this prosperity was high because it depended in large measure on slavery. While a growing abolitionist movement denounced slavery as evil, Alabama's economy grew to depend on it.

Alabama Fever

Reports of fertile land available in Alabama created a near mania in older states, where years of continuous farming had depleted the soil. Alabama offered new farm land, and plenty of it. A period of high cotton prices sweetened the attraction. The Industrial Revolution was accelerating in Europe and New England, and textile manufacturing was the leading industry. As increasing demand drove up cotton prices, planters were beguiled by visions of the fortunes to be made in Alabama.

A North Carolinian wrote of this new land mania: "The Alabama Feaver [sic] rages here with great violence and has carried off vast numbers of our citizens." From Georgia, the Carolinas, and Virginia, planters scurried to cash in. They sold their old homes and set out with their families and slaves for Alabama.

Above: British traveler Basil Hall made this sketch of a settler's cabin. Opposite: The 1818 Melish map of the new Alabama Territory. The Creek reserve is the arc of land on the east, along the Georgia line. Grid marks reflect the new land survey.

Small farmers not motivated by high cotton prices also caught Alabama Fever. From the mountains of Tennessee and the backcountry of the Carolinas and Georgia, tens of thousands of yeoman farmer families were drawn to Alabama. Few of these families owned slaves. They had to rely on the work of their own hands. They grew, raised, hunted, made, or bartered for almost everything they had. But for these yeoman farmers as well as planters, Alabama land offered a chance to improve their lives.

Sketches by Basil Hall depict the pine forests that covered much of the land and a typical early settlement (this one was Columbus, Georgia).

Federal Land Sales Shape the Pattern of Settlement and Politics

Land sales in the Mississippi Territory were governed by federal laws. After the land was surveyed and divided into tracts, it was first offered at auction. Speculators, developers, and planters competed in these auctions for fertile river-valley land and for potential town and mill sites. After the auctions, the remaining land was available for purchase at $1.25 an acre in 160-acre parcels.

Initial auctions were held in 1809 in Nashville, Tennessee, for tracts in the Tennessee Valley region, and in 1817 in Milledgeville, Georgia, for central Alabama land. For many yeoman farmers, even the base price of $1.25 an acre ($200 for a 160-acre parcel) was an impossibly large amount. Some tried borrowing the money. Others squatted on unclaimed land, hoping they might eventually raise the money to buy it but knowing they might have to move if someone bought the land from underneath them. Many squatters expected to keep moving.

In an interesting way, federal land policy shaped future Alabama politics. Wealthy planters purchased large prime tracts in river valleys and across the fertile Black Belt. These areas would remain under planter domination for generations. So many prominent Georgia planters bought land in Alabama that they immediately formed a political network, transposed from Georgia to the new territory. Yeoman farmers were left with more remote and less productive tracts. They settled the hill country and the Wiregrass, where society and culture today still bear their imprint.

Statehood

In 1817, Mississippi was admitted to the Union as a separate state. The rest of the old Mississippi Territory became the new Alabama Territory, with St. Stephens as its capital. William Wyatt Bibb, a former U.S. senator from Georgia, was territorial governor.

As new settlers poured in, the population of the Alabama Territory grew quickly. In early 1819, Congress authorized Alabamians to begin the process of admission to the Union. That summer, delegates to a territorial convention met in Huntsville and drafted Alabama's first constitution. At the time, it was the most democratic of any in the Union. All white men were eligible to vote even if they did not own property, and frequent elections ensured governmental accountability to the public will.

On December 14, 1819, President James Monroe signed the resolution of Congress admit-

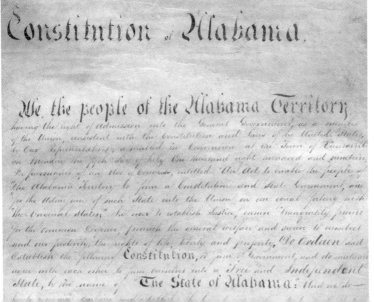

Above: William Wyatt Bibb became territorial governor in 1817 and Alabama's first governor two years later.

Left: Alabama's first Constitution, adopted in 1819.

ting Alabama as the twenty-second state in the Union. Cahaba, a site selected by Governor Bibb, became the state capital, although after just a few years the capital would be transferred to Tuscaloosa.

Early Alabama Politics

Most of Alabama's first state officials were, like Governor Bibb, members of the Georgia planter network. They had connections in Washington and were leaders by habit and tradition. But just as Alabama became a state, the economy collapsed under the weight of a worldwide depression. Cotton prices fell and banks retrenched. The Planters and Merchants Bank of Huntsville, the first and largest bank in the state, squeezed its debtors to repay their loans. Then, the bank refused to pay off its own paper notes in gold or silver of equal value.

Seal of Alabama's first bank.

The bank's policies infuriated Alabama voters. It had been chartered by the state, and its owners included leading members of the "Georgia aristocracy." Political opponents of the Georgians denounced the bank, the state officials who had chartered it, and the planters who owned it. They urged Alabama voters to reject "royal party" leaders, whom they accused of misusing their offices for personal enrichment. Voters responded, and the Georgia aristocracy was soundly defeated in the 1821 elections.

The 1821 elections reflected a deep cultural division between planters and yeoman farmers. Planters tended to view government as an instrument for promoting the economic development of the state. They favored banks, improved transportation, and education. Yeoman farmers, by contrast, were descendants of people who had lived under some type of aristocracy for as far back in time as their collective memory could recall. Having just thrown off the yoke of British monarchy in their fathers' time, they feared anything that might lead to a new aristocracy in America. They were intensely suspicious of governments, banks, great wealth, or anything new that smacked of "special privilege."

A Huntsville story illustrates this class tension. Leroy Pope was a wealthy Georgia planter who bought land around Big Spring, now the heart of downtown

The development of the mechanical cotton gin led to increased prosperity and the expansion of slavery.

A drawing by Stephen Button of the first Capitol at Montgomery, which burned on December 14, 1849, the thirtieth anniversary of Alabama's statehood. The present Capitol was built on its foundations.

Huntsville. John Hunt, a yeoman farmer who had squatted at the site, had to give up his place and move on. Pope then laid out a new town and proudly named it "Twickenham," after a then-fashionable suburb of London. Madison County delegates to the territorial assembly appealed to yeoman farmers back home by voting to rename the town Huntsville in honor of the unfortunate squatter Pope had supplanted.

A major theme of Alabama politics for the rest of the antebellum period was some version of this struggle between planters and yeoman farmers. American historians point to the election of President Andrew Jackson in 1828 as the beginning of the bumptious politics of the common man—of "Jacksonian Democracy." Those politics had already begun in Alabama, and Jackson, looking across the state line from nearby Nashville, was watching closely.

Cotton State

Alabama grew rapidly after statehood. In 1819, the population totaled approximately seventy thousand. By 1840, it had grown to six hundred thousand. Part of this growth was onto the land that had been reserved for the Indians. After years of disgraceful mistreatment by traders, land grabbers, and public officials, most Indians were forced out of Alabama in the mid-1830s. As settlers moved onto this newly

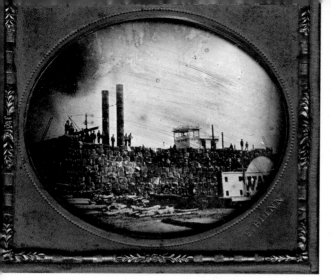

Bales of cotton piled high on the decks in this ambrotype image, left, of the steamboat Wave *were symbolic of Alabama's cotton prosperity, which made possible grand antebellum homes like the one on the right on a Greene County plantation.*

seized land, the state's population center shifted, prompting calls to relocate the capital from Tuscaloosa to a more central location. In 1846, the legislature voted to move to Montgomery. A majestic new Capitol was built overlooking the town on a high point known locally as Goat Hill.

Cotton prices fluctuated erratically after the Panic of 1819, but the early 1830s brought "flush times" to Alabama. Prices remained relatively high and production increased dramatically. Successful planters reaped enormous profits. Steamboats, which had first appeared in Alabama in the early 1820s, helped planters get more cotton to market. Starting in the 1840s, an expanding network of railroads supplemented the steamboats. Alabama's cotton production continued to grow through the 1840s and 1850s, increasing by more than three hundred percent over the two decades.

As Alabama became the "Cotton State," Mobile, its principal port, became the "Cotton City." A British visitor to Mobile in 1858 caricatured the

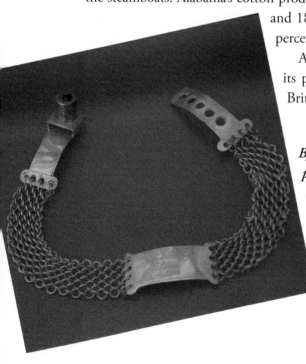

By law, slaves could not leave their owner's property without a pass or token. This brass collar and others like it were the tokens worn by William T. King's slaves when they were sent on business beyond the plantation. The collars discouraged the slaves from running away and also protected them from being mistaken for runaways.

place of cotton in the lives of Alabamians: "They buy cotton, sell cotton, think cotton, eat cotton, drink cotton, and dream cotton. They marry cotton wives, and unto them are born cotton children. It is the great staple, the sum and substance of Alabama."

Cotton production dwarfed every other economic enterprise in Alabama. Much of the state settled into a routine that followed its annual cycle. Beginning with preparation of the land and planting in the spring, work continued through a hot summer of hoeing and tending. Picking began in August, followed by ginning, and then the excitement of selling. Winter was a time for repairs and for getting ready to begin the cycle again the next spring.

Yeoman farmers participated only marginally in the cotton economy during Alabama's early years. They pursued a "safety-first" agriculture, focusing on what they needed for survival. But as time passed and prices stayed high, more yeoman farmers were enticed into trying their hands at raising cotton. A significant part of the production increase through the 1850s appears to have come from yeoman farmers. By 1860, Alabama produced more cotton than any other state except Mississippi. The combination of increased production and high prices brought wealth that was almost dizzying.

Cudjo Lewis was the last survivor of a slave ship brought illegally to Mobile in 1860.

Slavery

The great flaw in this prosperity was that so many of the workers who made it possible were enslaved. Most early Alabama slaves had been brought from older plantations along the Atlantic Coast, where they may have grown tobacco, rice, indigo, or cotton. Many were descendants of slave ancestors who had been in the United States since the 1600s. Others were more recent arrivals from the West Indies or Africa. Though Congress formally closed the Atlantic slave trade in 1808, smugglers brought in new shipments of Africans as late as the onset of the Civil War. Africatown, north of Mobile, was settled by Africans from a slave ship that arrived in 1860.

Life for slaves in Alabama varied widely. Some were skilled craftsmen, enjoying recognition and respect for their abilities. House servants on the large plantations also

Above: Bill of sale for Jim, a slave boy sold for $800. Right: James Williams, an escaped Alabama slave whose oral history, written by J. G. Whittier, was the first slave narrative published by the American Anti-Slavery Society.

held a more privileged status. Slaves belonging to small farmers usually worked closely with their owners and shared many of the same living conditions. Regardless of their positions, all slaves were deprived of the most fundamental freedoms. They were subject to arbitrary, capricious, and cruel acts by their owners. Families were often split apart when members were sold, never to be seen again.

Generally, life was hardest for field hands on large plantations. They usually worked in gangs directed by an overseer whose objective was to maximize production. Treatment was often impersonal and brutal. A compensation for this harsher life was their community. In the "quarters," slaves had their own society. There, despite whatever constraints the owner may have imposed, they could nurture their own culture and traditions. Over the course of years, accommodations and understandings tended to develop between slaves and owners. These traditions set a kind of informal framework in which daily plantation life was played out.

As the number of slaves increased in Alabama, the institution of slavery grew more rigid and restrictive. Before Alabama became a state, a number of African Americans had lived in freedom among the Indians and in areas of European control. Some had intermarried with Indians and with whites. But as new planters and slaves poured into the state through the 1830s, slaves came to outnumber whites in some areas, often by large margins. Many whites in those areas feared possible slave uprisings. Each report of an incident elsewhere increased anxiety in the slaveholding regions of Alabama.

Starting in the 1830s, the state legislature began enacting laws to tighten controls over the slaves. One act made it illegal to teach slaves to read and write. Others made it more difficult for owners to free their slaves or for slaves to purchase their own freedom. After 1835, any slave who was freed had to leave the state within a year. Militia units that had once provided defense against Indians now prepared to suppress slave uprisings.

Social Change

Early Alabama was a raucous frontier culture. There were few churches and schools. Alcohol consumption was high and gambling was widespread. The institutions of law were still in their infancy. A visitor to St. Stephens in 1820 described the former territorial capital as "a rough frontier town with streets full of hogs wallowing in mud-holes, barrooms, drunkards lying in and out of doors, scarlet women, bloody fights, shootings and killings, gambling games going on day and night." In many parts of the state, frontier-like conditions continued through the start of the Civil War.

The institutions of social order tended to emerge first in planter-dominated areas and towns, and to spread gradually outward. A series of religious revivals through the 1830s led to massive increases in the number of churches and active church members. Social improvement organizations such as temperance societies sought to cleanse communities of their defects. Amid the increasing zeal, alcohol consumption fell dramatically.

Communities established primary schools, and the first colleges began appearing—LaGrange Col-

English-born naturalist Philip Gosse made this 1838 sketch of Pleasant Hill in Dallas County, where he tutored plantation owners' children.

Above: Greek Revival style brick church, built in 1839 in Mooresville, Limestone County. Left: Wooden statue of Minerva, the goddess of wisdom, from the Eufaula Female Academy.

lege (1829), Spring Hill College (1830), the University of Alabama (1831), and Judson Female Institute (1839). Fraternal groups such as the Masons built lodges across Alabama. Traveling companies of actors brought theatrical productions. The primary form of graphic art was portraiture, but artists also painted murals in fine new homes that were built with the increasing profits from cotton. Almost every town had at least one newspaper. Alabama writers of frontier humor attracted national attention.

Just two generations after Alabama was opened to settlement, the frontier was in retreat. Although more than half the land still remained in the public domain in 1850, large portions of Alabama had taken on the appearance of a stable, ordered society.

Economic Diversification

Some Alabamians were concerned about the state's dependence on cotton. They called for economic diversification and urged planters to invest part of their profits in new industries. Daniel Pratt, who founded Prattville, was one of Alabama's leading exponents of industrial development. Originally from Vermont, Pratt moved to Alabama from Georgia in 1833 and set up a plant to manufacture cotton gins. Building on his success making gins, he also established an iron foundry, a textile mill, and a large shop producing doors and sashes.

Pratt had trouble finding workers, however. Yeoman farmers were loath to surrender their considerable independence for the demeaning status of hired worker. Pratt had to supplement his workforce with slave labor. Despite this obstacle, other Alabamians followed Pratt's lead. By 1860, fourteen textile mills were operating in Alabama.

The most important industrial effort of the time was railroad construction. Because railroads were expensive to build, many states provided subsidies to promote expanded railroad service. In Alabama, the long-standing hostility of yeoman farmers toward "special interests" made railroad subsidies a contentious political issue. In the mid-1850s, Governor John Winston endeared himself to the yeoman farmers of north Alabama by repeated vetoes of railroad subsidy legislation.

During the Civil War, this mill in Prattville made Confederate military uniforms.

Defending the "Southern Way of Life"

Governor Winston's chief political opponent, William Lowndes Yancey, focused on a different issue, defense of the South's "way of life." Since the 1830s, northern anti-slavery spokesmen had grown more assertive in their denunciations of slavery. Many white Alabamians recoiled at the outside criticisms. They became defensive about their institutions, some even arguing that slavery was beneficial. They could truthfully

William Lowndes Yancey, leader of the secession effort in Alabama.

argue that slavery had been generally accepted for all of recorded history. They were, however, unable or unwilling to see that the world was changing or to acknowledge that plantation slavery as practiced in the South was different in many respects from the slavery that was accepted in the Bible.

William Lowndes Yancey was a fiery and forceful speaker who had won fame by attacking threats to southern interests. As the national dispute over slavery grew more bitter, Yancey's following in the South grew larger. He denounced abolitionists and argued that any federal restriction on slave ownership was a violation of the U.S. Constitution. He urged the southern states to secede unless the federal government guaranteed what he maintained were their fundamental rights.

In the mid-1850s, the Republican Party emerged in the North, pledged to prevent the expansion of slavery into the western territories. For Yancey, this policy was a direct challenge to the South's interests. When the Republican nominee, Abraham Lincoln, was elected president in 1860, Yancey and his supporters were ready to act. Governor A. B. Moore immediately called for the election of delegates to a special state convention. Most Alabama voters, all of whom were white men, realized that this election was a crossroads in the state's history.

In the election, Yancey's allies won a majority of seats, although the balance was relatively close, 54-46. Meeting in the House chamber of the State Capitol, the delegates adopted Alabama's Ordinance of Secession on January 11, 1861.

Some white Alabamians feared disaster, and a substantial percentage had opposed the decision to secede. But most joined after the vote in support of their new government. African Americans, of course, were not asked their opinions. Less than forty-two years after Alabama's admission to the Union, the Secession Convention declared her to be a sovereign and independent state.

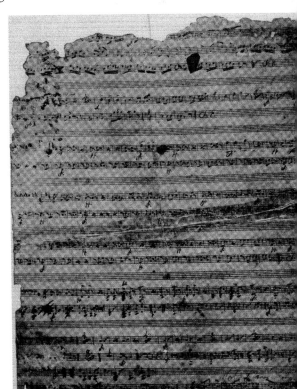

An Ordinance

To dissolve the Union between the State of Alabama and other states united under the compact styled "The constitution of the United States of America"

WAR AND RECONSTRUCTION (1861–1875)

The Civil War was a defining historical event for Alabama. In later years, white Alabamians would study the deeds and honor the memories of their fallen ancestors. Black Alabamians would celebrate Emancipation Day each year, recalling the jubilation of freedom.

But these memories masked a much harsher reality. The war years were hard and destructive for most white Alabamians. For African Americans, the initial freedom brought by the war was followed by another ten years of intense and ultimately unsuccessful struggle known as Reconstruction. The legacy of war and reconstruction would weigh on Alabama with leaden hands for generations afterward.

Creation of the Confederacy

Alabama's Ordinance of Secession served a double purpose. It declared Alabama's independence. It also invited other seceding states to send delegates to Montgomery—to consult "with each other as to . . . our common peace and security." In February 1861, a month after Alabama's secession, delegates from six states met in the Senate chamber of the Alabama State Capitol (the Texas delegates arrived later). They drafted a provisional constitution organizing the new Confederate States of America, and they elected a provisional president, Jefferson Davis of Mississippi, and vice-president, Alexander Stephens of Georgia.

When Davis arrived in Montgomery on February 17, William Lowndes Yancey famously proclaimed, "The man and the hour have met." The next day, the band played "Dixie's Land" as Davis's procession climbed Market Street to the Capitol. Lacking a national anthem, the band chose "The Marseillaise," the

The original band score of "Dixie."

This lithograph of a painting by James Massalon depicts the inauguration of Jefferson Davis on the steps of the Capitol, February 18, 1861.

anthem of the French Revolution, as Davis stepped from his carriage. He took the oath of office at the top of the front steps of the Capitol. Two days later, Davis wrote to his wife: "Upon my weary head was showered smiles, plaudits, and flowers; but beyond them I saw troubles and thorns innumerable."

The creation of the Confederacy fired most white Alabamians with a new patriotic fervor. In the northern Alabama hill country, many continued to oppose secession. Some openly supported the Union. But after the formation of the new government, even most who had questioned the decision to secede joined their neighbors in hoping for Confederate success.

The Outbreak of War

Abraham Lincoln was sworn in as president of the United States on March 4, 1861, a few weeks after Davis's inauguration. The Confederate government chose that day to unveil its new flag, accentuating its status as an independent nation. By then, Confederate agents had taken over most Federal property in their territory. Only two important installations remained under Federal control—Fort Pickens in Pensacola and Fort Sumter in Charleston. The newly inaugurated President Lincoln served notice that he would not give up either of these fortifications.

To the Confederate government, the continuation of Federal troops on their soil was a violation of national sovereignty. On April 11, the Confederate secretary of war authorized General P. G. T. Beauregard "to reduce" Fort Sumter if the Federal forces refused to evacuate. A bombardment began the next day, and the fort surrendered on April 14. The day after the surrender, President Lincoln called for seventy-five thousand volunteers to help suppress "the insurrection."

President Lincoln's call implied military action against the seceding states. Refusing to support this action, Virginia, North Carolina, Tennessee, and Arkansas followed the original seven states in seceding. In grateful recognition of Virginia's importance, the

The mortar in this photograph is believed to have fired the first shot of the Civil War. Immediately after the surrender of Ft. Sumter, it was transferred by railroad to Pensacola, where this photo was taken, for use against Ft. Pickens. A substantial portion of the soldiers at Pensacola were Alabamians. En route from Charleston to Pensacola, the train passed through Montgomery, where the mortar was displayed to the public.

Charles W. Faust and David Clinton Faust, Company B, 10th Alabama Infantry.

Confederate Congress voted to transfer the capital from Montgomery to Richmond. After four months at the center of the world's stage, the spotlight shifted away from Alabama in May 1861, as her citizens prepared for war.

For many young men going off to service, and for the young women who cheered them, the call to arms stirred a sense of adventure and excitement. Most expected a short, glorious, and relatively painless war. The First Battle of Manassas (Bull Run) in July 1861 shocked both North and South with its horrific bloodshed. Both sides realized they had to prepare for warfare on a scale far beyond their initial expectations. But not even the most pessimistic could have envisioned the extent of the suffering, or the changes, that would follow.

An Economy Struggling to Support the War

The war effort demanded a full mobilization of Alabama's economy. Planters and farmers tried to grow more food crops. Textile mills ramped up production. Confederate officials established new iron furnaces, ordnance plants, salt works, and arsenals. And railroads strained to deliver all these supplies to the fronts. By 1864, approximately

Opposite page: Tannehill Ironworks produced ordnance, skillets, pots, and ovens for the Southern army. On March 31, 1865, the works were destroyed during U.S. General James Wilson's raid on Alabama's war industry. This photo was taken in the 1920s. Above, Tannehill Ironworks today is a state historic site at McCalla, Jefferson County.

ten thousand white workers and black slaves labored in war production at the river town of Selma, a number exceeding the town's total pre-war population.

One of President Lincoln's first actions after Fort Sumter was to order a naval blockade of southern ports. Although blockade runners conducted their daring business throughout the war, the net around the South tightened a little more each month. Alabamians quickly felt the impact. They could no longer earn money by selling their cotton, but the cost of goods coming through the blockade continued to climb. Savings and resources accumulated through the years of prosperity began to leach away.

Women in Mobile rioted in 1863 over food shortages and high prices.

With many farmers now in uniform and without any food imports, the residents of an agricultural state faced the bitter irony of food shortages. As early as the spring of 1862, protests over the shortages required the imposition of martial law in Tuscaloosa. In September 1863, Mobile women rioted because of the lack of bread. By the end of the war, many items that had been commonplace were virtually unattainable, and some areas in Alabama faced starvation conditions.

Early Fighting in North Alabama

The first Federal attack struck Alabama less than a year after the bombardment of Fort Sumter. In February 1862, a flotilla of gunboats steamed up the Tennessee River, landing unchallenged at Florence. They seized Huntsville in April and soon controlled much of the Tennessee River Valley. In the ebb and flow of combat over the next three years, Confederate forces were sometimes able to reassert power in parts of the region. Guerilla units, which sprang up to help them, drew civilians into this deepening struggle.

The resulting conflict was brutal and destructive. One historian called this fighting in northern Alabama "a bitter Alabama civil war within the Civil War." When one side seized power, its supporters often punished those who had been in control before. When that side was overthrown, the former victims took their revenge. In some areas such as Lawrence County, this cycle was repeated more than fifteen times, becoming harsher with each repetition. Neighbors and even family members were pitted against each other. The loss of life, buildings, crops, and livestock wasted large portions of northern Alabama.

One of Alabama's most famous battles was a series of skirmishes in late April and early May of 1863. Confederate troops under General Nathan Bedford Forrest chased a raiding party of Federal troops eastward across northern Alabama. After the Federals surrendered, the Alabama Legislature and state newspapers showered special praise

Emma Sansom's portrait was painted by Samuel Hoffman of Montgomery, based on a photograph of her when she was nineteen. Nathan Bedford Forrest's was by the famous artist Nicola Marschall.

upon a young woman, Emma Sansom, who had helped guide Forrest across Black Creek in Etowah County.

Effects on the Lives of Women

Sansom was recognized as a heroine, yet many Alabama women performed heroic work during these years. Some, like Mobile's Kate Cumming, broke tradition and became nurses. They attended their patients amid gore and hardship that are almost unimaginable today. Thousands more women labored in war industries. Wives of planters frequently assumed the duties of plantation management, in times that were far more difficult than their husbands had known.

Wives of yeoman farmers faced the most crushing burdens. Unless they had family to fall back on, they had to plow, plant, harvest, cut wood, make repairs, and tend animals for their survival. This work was in addition to their already substantial burdens of keeping

Despite her parents' belief that respectable women should not serve as nurses to soldiers, Kate Cumming served in Mississippi, Tennessee, and Georgia. Her journal of her experiences was later published and gives a unique view of the war.

house, cooking, and raising children. Alabama state and county governments established relief programs to assist needy families. With the scarcity of supplies and lack of funds, however, this assistance was usually inadequate.

African Americans in the War

Even more disruptive to Alabama's traditional social order were the changes in the lives of African Americans. Many slaves remained at work, helping their owners survive. Some even accompanied officers to war as menservants. Thousands of others were forced to maintain railroads and build fortifications, or to work at munitions plants, iron furnaces, or salt works.

When Union troops first swept into northern Alabama, Federal officials did not free slaves as a matter of policy. Escapees were given protection and often employment, but they were regarded as "contraband," a legal term for material that could be seized from an enemy because it helped them make war.

This legal hairsplitting became unnecessary after January 1, 1863. On that day President Lincoln's Emancipation Proclamation freed all slaves in the rebellious states. Escape to Union-held territory now clearly meant freedom, and a Union that was com-

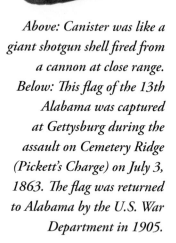

mitted to end slavery was a cause African Americans could happily fight for. Escaped slaves joined the Union army in large numbers. By the war's end, as many as nine thousand former Alabama slaves were fighting as U.S. soldiers.

African Americans were not the only Alabamians who fought with the Federal forces. Many Unionists, especially from northern Alabama, also joined the U.S. Army. The First Alabama Cavalry U.S.A. was composed entirely of Alabama Unionists.

The Hardships of Combat

Above: Canister was like a giant shotgun shell fired from a cannon at close range.
Below: This flag of the 13th Alabama was captured at Gettysburg during the assault on Cemetery Ridge (Pickett's Charge) on July 3, 1863. The flag was returned to Alabama by the U.S. War Department in 1905.

For four long years, tens of thousands of Alabama soldiers—Confederate and Union, white and black—fought on, despite unrelenting hardships. For the poorly supplied Confederate troops, conditions were particularly harsh, but soldiers on both sides endured similar misery. They often slept on the hard ground with no shelter. They suffered forced marches of dozens of miles while carrying weapons and full packs—with shoes falling apart, little food, and in snow, mud, or heat—all for the opportunity to charge into murderous artillery and rifle fire.

As the war progressed, clever engineers devised ever more lethal ways to kill. Finely made rifles could strike down approaching soldiers at a thousand yards. Exploding artillery shells ripped through whole ranks of charging troops. As a charging force drew closer, the artillery changed from shells to canister—cans of iron balls that would splatter out of the barrel, tearing bodies apart.

If they survived, the soldiers had to pick themselves up, haul off their wounded friends, bury their dead ones, and be prepared to do it all

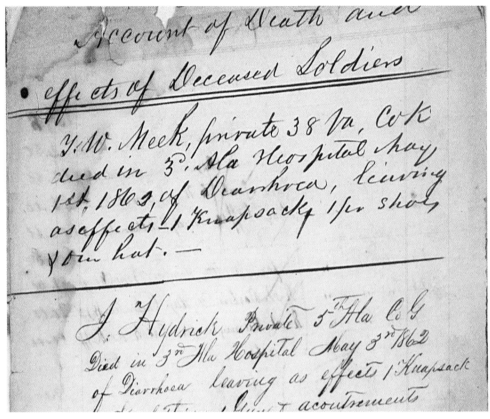

A register records deaths and personal effects from one of three Richmond, Virginia, hospitals run by Juliet Opie Hopkins for Alabama soldiers.

again—and again. It is no wonder that accounts of hardship and heroism lived on with such potency afterward. The Civil War was a story of suffering, courage, and sacrifice on an epic scale.

Growing Resistance to the War

As the central government in Richmond grew desperate for men and supplies, it established a compulsory draft, raised taxes, impressed slaves, and restricted economic activity. The Confederacy had been created in part to safeguard states' rights. Alabamians now found themselves under a central government far more intrusive than anything they had experienced in the Union. After losses at Vicksburg and Gettysburg dimmed Confederate prospects, the demands from Richmond seemed even more onerous.

In August 1863, Alabama held new state elections. Most politicians who had been elected in 1861 because of their support for secession were soundly defeated. New officials concentrated less on supporting the Confederacy than on defending the state. They stressed their concerns about Alabama's rights and occasionally clashed

Major John Pelham served in Major General J. E. B. Stuart's Horse Artillery. He was mortally wounded at Kelly's Ford in Virginia. Prior to his enlistment in the CSA military, Pelham had been a cadet at West Point. He resigned shortly before graduation. Following his death, Stuart wrote Pelham's parents telling of his grief over the loss of their son, who was like a brother to him.

Hd Qrs Cav.y Division A. of N. Va.
March 29th 1863.

My Dear Sir —

With the deepest grief, I approach a subject which has doubtless brought to your household sorrowful wailing. I refer to the death of your son — my comrade — friend, all but brother, John Pelham who was to me as a younger brother — whose place on my staff — at my fireside — in my Division, — but most of all at the head of the corps to which his genius has imparted so much efficiency and fame — the Horse Artillery — is vacant, — and that vacancy sends a pang to my heart that knew him, and in the space elapsed, a nation's wail is heard from out your capitol, mourning her lost hero — so noble — so chivalrous — so pure — so beloved.

I know that man's sympathy is emptiness, to one who has lost as you have, the promise and hope of a noble son — but when I tell you, I loved him as a brother, you will permit me to share with you a grief so sacred, so consoling.

He has won a name, immortal on earth, and in heaven he will reap the reward of a pure heart and guileless heart. I attended church with him the Sabbath

with Confederate officials when state interests differed from those of Richmond.

The Costs of War Mount

Unlike the Tennessee Valley, central and southern Alabama remained free from Union raids for much of the war. Then, in July 1864, General Lovell Rousseau drove southward, destroying thirty miles of railroad tracks between Montgomery and Opelika. The raid cut off supplies needed by Confederate troops defending Atlanta against General William T. Sherman. The next month, Admiral David Farragut led a Union naval force into Mobile Bay. He achieved victory and a kind of immortal-

Top: In February 1864, Mobile was warned to expect attack. Bottom: By August, Union forces had bombarded Fort Morgan, above, and controlled Mobile Bay.

ity with the order later attributed to him: "Damn the torpedoes! Full speed ahead!" (Torpedo was the name then used for floating mines, which Confederates had placed at the entrance to Mobile Bay.)

Following these two Confederate defeats, the peace movement grew stronger in Alabama. In September 1864, the state legislature began debating a resolution urging the Confederate government to explore negotiations with the Union. Jefferson Davis traveled to Montgomery in person to speak before the legislature and urge persever-ance: "There is but one duty for every Southern man. It is to go to the front."

Above: The naval foundry in Selma was burned by Union troops, April 5, 1865.

Determination was not enough, however. By late 1864, conditions were desperate in much of Alabama. Fearing for the very survival of their wives and children, many soldiers began to desert. Since deserters faced capture and punishment, they often banded together for self-protection, sometimes joined by men who had fled from the Confederate draft.

Law and order deteriorated. In parts of northern Alabama and along the Florida border, armed bands roamed the countryside, foraging, plundering, and terrorizing helpless civilians. Some bands were large enough to skirmish successfully with Confederate troops sent to subdue them. Ever-increasing numbers of escaped slaves contributed to the chaos.

Major Thomas Goode Jones, later governor of Alabama, was an adjutant to General John Gordon. Jones tied a napkin onto his sword (below) as he rode toward Union lines at Appomattox to secure a meeting between Grant and Lee.

The End of Combat

In the spring of 1865, Union forces launched a coordinated offensive aimed at central Alabama and Mobile. Federal cavalry units destroyed iron furnaces in Shelby, Jefferson, Tuscaloosa, and Bibb counties. They burned the

University of Alabama and the huge Confederate manufacturing complex in Selma. They met only token opposition because there were simply no Confederate troops available. After seizing Selma, Union forces turned toward Montgomery, entering the capital on April 12, three days after Lee's surrender at Appomattox. It was four years to the day after the bombardment began at Fort Sumter.

Alabama's last pocket of Confederate resistance was in the southwestern part of the state. An overwhelming Union force captured Fort Blakeley on April 9, but Confederate troops continued futile maneuvering until May 4. That day, General Richard Taylor surrendered the Department of Alabama, Mississippi, and East Louisiana at Citronelle, Mobile County. Taylor's was the last major Confederate command east of the Mississippi River to surrender.

The Challenges of Reconstruction

With the great engines of war finally stilled, it was time to repair the damage and to reestablish social order. But the years of Reconstruction were almost as bitterly contested as the war itself.

In his last speech, President Lincoln described the enormous challenges of "the

Harper's Weekly *depiction of the depot of the Army of the Cumberland (Union) at Stevenson, Jackson County, December 1863.*

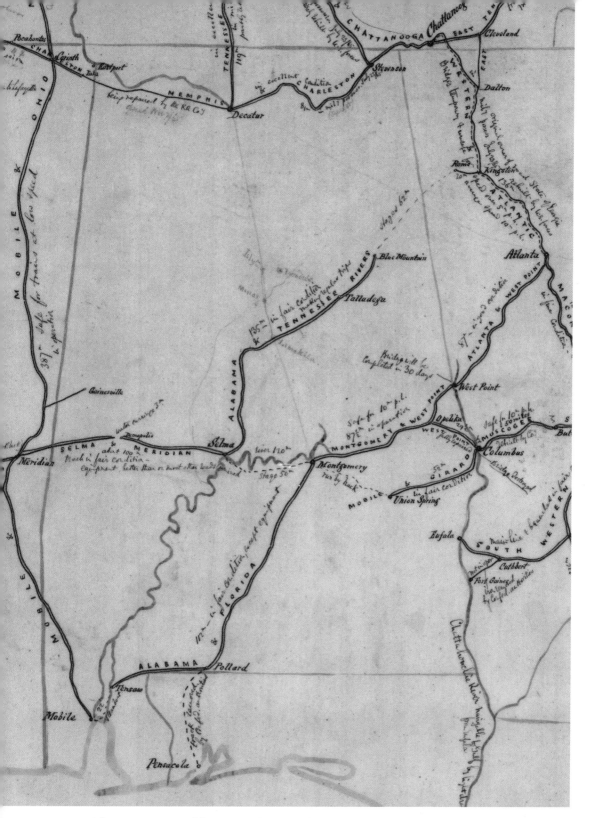

This map, prepared between July 23 and September 6, 1865, describes the conditions of Alabama railroad lines at the end of the Civil War.

re-inauguration of national authority." He wanted a speedy return of rebellious states to "their proper relation with the Union." He also urged that qualified blacks be granted the right to vote. John Wilkes Booth was in the audience in front of the White House and heard Lincoln's speech. Reportedly, it was Lincoln's views on African American voting that fixed Booth's resolve to assassinate the President.

A reconstruction program that achieved both of Lincoln's goals would have been difficult even for a president of his extraordinary skill. Unfortunately for the South and the nation, the burden fell to far less skillful hands after Lincoln's murder. The next ten years degenerated into a power struggle among multiple groups with competing and often changing interests. The outcome of this struggle in Alabama was a new political framework that would hold sway for most of the next century.

Economic and Racial Challenges

As the war was ending, Congress set up the Freedmen's Bureau (officially, the Bureau of Refugees, Freedmen, and Abandoned Lands) to deal with postwar problems in the South. One immediate task was feeding the many people, black and white, who faced starvation. Restoring the economy was an even more difficult task.

The collapse of Confederate power left hundreds of thousands of ex-slaves suddenly free simply to walk away. Many went to find family members from whom they had been separated. Others followed Federal troops. Still others moved to towns. Many more stayed in what had been their homes, or

NOTICE.

—o—

Head Quarters Cavalry Force,
Military Div. West Mississippi,
Eufaula, Ala,, May 1, 1865.

GENERAL ORDERS,
No. 6.

For the maintainance of order in Eufaula, during its occupation by the Federal forces, the following rules will be observed :

1st. The soldiers of this command are forbidden to interfere with the persons or property of Citizens.

2nd. During the existing armistice, Confederate Officers and Soldiers will be permitted to pass to their homes unmolested.

3d. Citizens will continue their legitimate business, but will not be allowed to congregate upon the streets.

4th. The patrol heretofore organized by the Civil Authorities, will confine themselves to the government of Citizens and Confederate Soldiers, and will not interfere with the United States Forces.

5th. Capt. E. E. Thornton is announced as Provost Marshal, and a sufficient Provost Guard has been organized to insure quiet and order.

By order of
Brevet Major General
B. H. GRIERSON,

S. L. Woodward,
Assistant Adjutant Gen'l.

May 1, 1865, order establishing martial law in Eufaula.

| MONTH. | WHITE. | | | | | COLORED. | | | | | Total No. of Men. | Total No. of Women. | Total No. of Children. | Aggregate. | Bushels Corn. | Pounds Bacon. | Pounds Pork. |
	Men.	Women.	Male.	Female.	Total.	Men.	Women.	Male.	Female.	Total.							
December 1866	1,648	4,289	4,930	5,229	16,096	760	1,272	1,657	1,584	5,273	2,408	5,561	13,400	21,369	17,458	52,920	......
January 1867	644	2,307	3,217	3,558	9,726	250	476	570	858	2,154	894	2,783	8,203	11,880	9,957	21,702	......
February 1867	255	1,151	1,546	1,787	4,739	96	314	181	261	852	351	1,465	3,775	5,591	1,559	3,685	8,600
March 1867	1,736	5,365	6,715	8,193	22,009	1,080	2,267	1,995	2,398	7,740	2,816	7,632	19,301	29,749	19,977	42,742	4,200
April 1867	2,024	5,782	7,419	10,177	25,402	601	2,502	2,452	2,782	8,337	2,625	8,284	22,830	33,739	16,720	33,088	3,200
May 1867	1,255	4,457	5,721	7,205	18,638	901	1,876	1,963	2,395	7,185	2,156	6,333	17,284	25,773	12,910	26,350	......
June.......... 1867	298	2,781	3,222	4,632	10,883	398	1,210	1,367	1,890	4,865	696	3,941	11,111	15,748	13,367	12,786	3,500
July 1867	1,040	3,539	4,701	4,336	13,616	425	1,048	731	819	3,018	1,465	4,582	10,587	16,634	7,935	13,919	......
August 1867	539	1,281	1,974	2,344	6,138	292	694	692	539	2,217	831	1,975	5,549	8,355	......	8,970	......
Total........	9,439	30,902	39,445	47,461	127,247	4,803	11,654	11,608	13,526	41,591	14,242	42,556	112,040	168,838	99,883	216,162	19,500

Above: 1867 chart from the report of General Wager Swayne, assistant Freedmen's Bureau commissioner for Alabama, showing numbers of people fed. Below: Part of a freedmen's contract between Willis Bocock of Waldwick Plantation, Marengo County, and some of his former slaves.

returned to them after satisfying themselves that they really could leave.

Congress had debated proposals to provide land and supplies for the freedmen, but the measures had not passed. There was no clear policy about how the ex-slaves were to support themselves and become members of society. Another major complication was the wretched condition of Alabama's farms, factories, transportation systems, and banking and credit mechanisms.

Alabama planters generally hoped to resume growing cotton during the summer following the war's end. Most acknowledged that slavery was dead, but they needed their former slaves to work the crops. With few other viable options, the Freedmen's

Contract made the 3d day of January in the year 18[70] between us the free people who have signed this paper of one part, and our employer, Willis. P. Bocock, of the other p[art]. We agree to take charge of and cultivate for the year 1870, [a] portion of land, say   acres or thereabouts, to be laid o[ff] to us by our employer on his plantation, and to tend the sam[e] well in the usual crops, in such proportions as we and he m[ay] agree upon. We are to furnish the necessary labor, say an average hand to every 15 acres in the crops, making in all   average hands; and are to have all proper work done, ditc[hing] fencing, reparing &c, as well as cultivating and saving the crops of all kinds, so as to put and keep the lan[d]

Bureau acceded to this planter vision. Bureau officials encouraged former slaves to return to work, but with a system of written contracts to protect the freedmen's rights. The contracts were to be enforced by the Bureau.

This new arrangement proved unsatisfactory to almost everyone. Planters pushing for maximum production often treated their new contract workers as they had their slaves. Workers, fully conscious of their freedom, were repelled by conditions that resembled slavery. They especially abhorred the gang labor system.

Within a few years, the labor contracts had evolved into a new system. Workers would cultivate assigned tracts of land on a "shares" arrangement. The landowner provided land and supplies. The farm worker planted, tended, and harvested the cotton crop. At the end of the season when the cotton was sold, there was a settling up, with each receiving a share of the proceeds. Sharecropping spread across much of Alabama agriculture, for both black and white farmers.

Lewis Parsons, appointed by President Andrew Johnson, served as Alabama's provisional governor from June 21 to December 13, 1865. He reinstated all state laws—except those pertaining to slavery— in force prior to secession.

Presidential Reconstruction

Alabama politics in the postwar years was as chaotic as the economy. Like Lincoln, President Andrew Johnson advocated a speedy return of states to the Union, offering relatively easy terms to his old enemies. But unlike Lincoln, Johnson showed little interest in protecting the rights of freedmen.

African Americans were not allowed to vote in the first Alabama elections after the war. The federal government did not require black voting, and, in fact, blacks could not vote in many northern states. But the exclusion of African Americans in the August 1865 election signaled the posture of white Alabama leaders toward the freedmen. When the legislature met that fall, it not only ignored the rights of African Americans, it enacted laws clearly designed to abridge those rights.

This loyalty oath is unusual in that it was signed by a woman, Mrs. Sallie K. Huey of Perry County. According to her pardon application, Huey was guilty of "giving aid to the rebellion by contributing to soldiers in the army and their families, and by the sympathies of a Southern woman." While she was not under arrest for her activities, the Confiscation Act threatened to take away her property, valued at more than $20,000.

White Unionists were another source of political contention in Alabama. They had suffered intensely during the previous four years and bitterly resented the plantation-region politicians whom they blamed for starting the war. Expecting to have a major role governing the postwar state, they were furious at the number of former Confederates in the new government.

To these loyal Unionists, to African Americans, and to many Republicans in the North, Alabama's postwar government was an outrage. The old planter aristocracy appeared to be back in the saddle. Across the North, angry politicians asked their constituents if they had fought such a costly and bloody war for such an outcome. The constituents' responses translated into a sweeping 1866 national election victory by "radical Republicans."

Congressional Reconstruction and White Reaction

Radical Republicans in Congress wanted to protect the rights of southern blacks. They also wanted to punish the secessionist whites whom they saw as having caused the war. The 1867 Congress moved quickly, enacting a series of Reconstruction laws. These laws abolished the state governments that had been set up under President Johnson and established a system of military rule across the former Confederacy. They required the election of new state and local governments with black men having the right to vote and to hold office. Whites who had violated their oaths to the United States by engaging in rebellion were to be disfranchised.

The Alabama Legislature elected under these Reconstruction laws convened in July 1868. Its twenty-seven black members comprised almost 25 percent of the total body. Although the number did not fully reflect the percentage of African Americans in the population (then around 45 percent), it signaled a different world from that just a few years earlier.

The new Reconstruction government faced a staggering list of problems. It had to rebuild the state and reestablish government services despite a faltering economy and inadequate resources. Desperate for money, the Alabama Legislature turned to virtually the only revenue source available—property taxes. But the tripling of property taxes in a time of economic hardship and declining cotton prices was a political disaster, fueling bitter resentment from both large and small landowners.

After African Americans registered to vote on a large scale in 1867, hostile whites in Alabama began forming secret terrorist organizations such as the Ku Klux Klan. Their goal was to intimidate blacks and white Republicans and prevent them from controlling the government. Despite the presence of federal troops, these paramilitary bands grew more brazen and more violent. In

James Rapier was a delegate from Florence to Alabama's 1867 Constitutional Convention and served in the U.S. House of Representatives in 1873–75. Born a free black, he was educated in Canada and returned to Alabama at the end of the war.

Alabama's 1867 voter registration records (the example here is from Shelby County) were created as a direct result of a Reconstruction act passed by the U.S. Congress on March 23, 1867. The act required the commanding officer in each military district to register all male citizens, black and white, twenty-one years or older, in each county who were qualified to vote and had taken the loyalty oath to the United States.

An 1868 $1,000 bond for the Eufaula, Opelika, Oxford, and Guntersville Railroad, with attached redemption coupons.

some parts of the state, the violence escalated into guerilla warfare.

Through the early 1870s, the state's finances continued to deteriorate, with a worldwide depression compounding the misery. A major thrust of state recovery efforts had been to promote railroad construction by guaranteeing millions of dollars of railroad bonds. Through a combination of bribery, fraud, bad management, and bad luck, some of the railroads failed. When the burden of paying the interest on these bonds fell to the state, the government itself faced bankruptcy.

The End of Reconstruction

In the 1874 election, the Democrats—then called the Democratic and Conservative Party—put together a coalition that would secure their control of Alabama politics for decades to come. Denouncing the corruption and spending excesses of the Reconstruction government, the Democrats forged a new alliance between planter and yeoman farmer interests. Their platform called for clean government, reduced taxes, and the restoration of white control. The Democratic victory in 1874 would effectively

George Houston served as governor from 1874 to 1878. His election marked the end of Reconstruction in Alabama and the establishment of what would be called "Bourbon" rule.

eliminate the Republican Party from Alabama politics for more than a century, creating a one-party system which lasted until the 1960s.

Following the 1874 election, Governor George Houston summoned a convention to fix his campaign platform into constitutional law. The Constitution of 1875 established strict limits on the ability of state and local governments to raise taxes. It centralized authority in Montgomery and banned any government support for private enterprises such as railroads.

Recognizing that federal intervention remained a possibility, the authors of the new constitution avoided provisions that were overtly discriminatory against blacks. But by the mid-1870s, the national Republican Party was growing weary of the effort to remake the South. It had its own problems with the depression and turmoil in President Ulysses Grant's administration. Without continued federal oversight, white leaders in Alabama and across the South gradually implemented a new system of legally enforced racial separation, which became known as "segregation."

Union victory in the Civil War had ended Alabama's old social and political order based on slavery. But the new order that emerged after Reconstruction was hobbled by continued racial discrimination, economic distress, corrupt electoral practices, and a government that tended to avoid positive leadership. As Alabamians struggled to rebuild their state in the generations after the war, their greatest obstacles were burdens from the past—the legacies of slavery, class conflict, war, and Reconstruction.

Mines, Mills, and Mules (1875–1929)

Alabama leaders recognized the urgent need to rebuild the state's economy in the years after the Civil War and Reconstruction. They welcomed new railroads, coal mines, iron furnaces, textile mills, and lumber mills, which brought a surge of economic activity to the state. By the early 1900s, Alabama had become the most heavily industrialized state in the South.

Most Alabamians, however, still lived on farms. They were locked into the annual cycle of cotton production—and to the poverty that resulted from exhausted soil and decades of depressed cotton prices. Alabama government continued generally in the pattern set in 1875, focusing on low taxes, minimal services, and racial segregation. By the early 1900s, economic growth and reform initiatives brought improved conditions to towns and cities. But with the exception of a few occasional years of higher prices, such as during World War I, rural Alabamians continued to endure year after year of economic hardship.

Industrialization

In 1871, builders of the major north-south railroad line through Alabama connected with a new east-west line. The junction was in the middle of the state's mineral belt. A company of local citizens and outside financiers established a new town there and named it

Top: Oxen haul pine logs through town for the Eufaula Lumber Company. Right: Engineer and industrial developer John T. Milner built the North and South Railroad that connected the Alabama and Tennessee rivers and helped Birmingham become an industrial center.

"Map of the City of Birmingham, Alabama and Suburbs" by H. Schoel, published by Rand McNally & Co. of Chicago in 1888 for the Elyton Land Co.

Birmingham, after the coal and iron center in England. They expected their city to become a new industrial center for America.

The Civil War had shown the industrial potential in Alabama's mineral belt. Alabama mines and furnaces had produced a substantial portion of the Confederacy's iron. After the war, political and business leaders saw the development of these mineral resources as one way to rebuild their state's economy.

Alabama entrepreneurs pursued other forms of industry as well. Pre-war lumber mills had been mostly small, local operations. Now, expanding railroads required wood for crossties, bridges, stations, and shops. Railroads also made it easier to ship lumber outside Alabama. With huge tracts of uncut forest, especially the stately longleaf pine of the coastal plain, lumbering grew rapidly through the late 1800s and into the early 1900s. Its sawmills eventually consumed most of Alabama's longleaf pine forests.

Above: A train preparing to unload logs into a log pond at the Kaul Lumber Company in 1915 in Kaulton, Tuscaloosa County. Below: A group of men surrounded by carts piled with wood on a street in Huntsville in the late nineteenth century.

Decade after decade, Alabama industry expanded dramatically. By the 1880s, new textile mills began moving to Alabama from the northeastern states. Other mills were established by Alabama entrepreneurs such as B. B. Comer and Benjamin Russell. Almost ten thousand Alabamians worked in textile mills in 1900. That number doubled by 1920 and continued to rise. Pig iron production grew from virtually nothing in 1860 to more than a million tons per year by 1900. By then, three-quarters of America's pig iron exports came from Alabama. Birmingham grew so fast it became known as the "Magic City."

Working conditions in these mines and mills were hard and often dangerous, especially by today's standards. To thousands of tenant farmers and sharecroppers, however, these jobs seemed better than life on the farm. The readiness of many workers to accept any available job allowed factory owners to keep industrial wages low. Yet, even low wages were higher than what most farm work provided. The wages were also

Above: A textile mill at Tallassee Manufacturing Company, c. 1870. Incorporated in 1852, the company was home to one of the earliest cotton manufacturing plants in the state of Alabama. Right: In 1897, B. B. Comer established Avondale Mills, a cotton manufacturing firm, in Birmingham. In the following years, he and his sons expanded the company by acquiring mills in other towns, including Sycamore, Sylacauga, Pell City, and Alexander City.

Sloss Furnace, Birmingham, Ala.

This 1907 postcard depicts the Sloss Furnaces, which produced pig iron from 1882 to 1971 and was a world leader in production of the smelted metal during World War I. Today the remains of the Sloss works are a major historic site in Birmingham.

high enough to attract immigrants from eastern and southern Europe, introducing a new element of cultural diversity to Alabama.

Rural Alabama

Despite Alabama's industrial growth, the 1920 census listed more than 78 percent of the state's population as rural. The chief cash product continued to be cotton. Before the Civil War, cotton prices had fluctuated but remained relatively high for long periods of time, producing great wealth. For almost four generations after the war, however, the pattern was reversed. Farmers endured long periods of depressed prices, punctuated only occasionally by a "good year."

Many farmers, white and black, remained trapped in the sharecropping system that had evolved during Reconstruction. Through the course of planting and tending a year's crop, they borrowed money to pay for their supplies. When they harvested their crops and settled up, they were frequently unable to clear their debts, which then carried over to the next year. This pattern continued year after year, often generation after generation.

The debt system lent itself to abuse and exploitation. Landowners, storekeepers,

Top: Farmers crowding Court Square in downtown Montgomery to sell their cotton, c. 1880. Bottom: Strawberry picking in Elmore County, c. 1910.

and gin operators kept the books. Many sharecroppers, white and black, were illiterate, or at least not in a position to challenge those on whom they were economically dependent. If they were cheated, they knew that the legal system usually favored the owners. And creditors demanded that indebted farmers grow cotton, the most reliable cash crop, curbing the diversification that might have helped the farmers economically and could have improved the fertility of the soil.

Above: Gin day at Mount Hope, Lawrence County, c. 1927. Below: African American woman with oxen and plow, c. 1900; specific location unknown.

Above: An Alabama home "cotton factory," exact location unknown, c. 1900. This photograph illustrates steps in the production of cotton cloth. Right: A rural family on their porch near West Blocton, in Bibb County, c. 1900. Opposite page: Congregation on the front steps of the Autaugaville Methodist Church in the early 1900s.

For much of rural Alabama, conditions resembled those we think of today in third-world countries. The first yeoman farmers had moved into Alabama in the early 1800s searching for a better life. Now their grandchildren sank into cycles of seemingly perpetual impoverishment. For the descendants of former slaves, conditions resembled a new kind of bondage—not as complete as slavery, but clearly not the kind of freedom they had anticipated in the days of Jubilee.

Rural life was not all hardship and poverty. Family, church, music, crafts, sports, and community gatherings all provided leavening for the spirit. And rural Alabamians pursued these activities with all the more zeal because their work life was so hard.

The continuing struggle for economic survival could toughen people and make them stronger. It could also grind down both body and spirit. In both its strengthening and its scarring, the long years of rural poverty left a deep imprint on Alabama society.

Town Life

Alabama towns fared better than rural areas in the years after the Civil War. All across the state—along the new railroad lines and especially at road intersections and railroad junctions—new towns appeared and old ones grew. These towns were the homes of merchants, bankers, lawyers, doctors, gin operators, craftsmen, mechanics, teachers, ministers, barbers, public officials, and a varied array of laborers. They served the agricultural regions around them, and some were home to the new mills.

Each town had its own unique flavor, depending on its history, geography, and the functions it served. But all towns had many elements in common—churches,

Steam-powered traction engine on Randolph Street on the north side of the square in Huntsville, c. 1900.

schools, social organizations, and interlinked businesses. The town was a focal point for the geographic area around it, especially on Saturdays, when farm families came to shop and socialize.

Over the decades, town life developed its own rhythm and character. People lived in neighborhoods. In warm weather, their windows stayed open, and they gathered in the evening on porches while their houses cooled. Generations of children grew up together, often related to each other and attending the same schools and churches. Exposure to the outside world was limited. Most people's lives centered on their family, their church, and their town.

Today's recollections of small-town life tend to be colored by nostalgia. The towns provided warmth, nurture, and a comfortable stability for many residents. But town society could also be rigid and oppressive. Most towns were divided clearly by both race and class, of which all inhabitants were keenly conscious.

An apparent irony of town life was the emergence, despite such closeness and conformist pressures, of a strain of vigorous individualism. The towns were full of "characters." Idiosyncratic habits and foibles were known and generally accepted as part of the social mix. Harper Lee's iconic town of Maycomb in *To Kill a Mockingbird* is one of the best-known literary depictions of this remarkable culture, a way of life that appeared in different versions in hundreds of places across Alabama.

African American Life

African Americans were part of all these developments, though encumbered with special limits and hardships caused by racial discrimination. In rural Alabama, a small percentage of African Americans acquired land and some degree of independence. Most, however, remained farm workers or sharecroppers, economically dependent on white landowners.

Sawmills, coal mines, and iron furnaces provided a degree of economic opportunity for some African Americans, but the jobs were usually segregated. Blacks were limited to the lowest levels of work, often the most difficult and dangerous. Despite these limits, black workers often became mainstays for many Alabama businesses, large and small.

Towns and cities offered a wider range of opportunities than rural Alabama. In towns, African Americans created their own institutions, often paralleling those of their white neighbors. After the Civil War, one of the first actions blacks had taken was to establish their own churches. Black craftsmen, businessmen, and professionals

Hand-tinted photo of a cotton farmer and children, c. 1900.

emerged to serve their own communities, and sometimes the white community as well. Benevolent and fraternal organizations enriched the social life of the community and helped people work together to overcome common obstacles and threats. One of the compensating benefits of segregation was that African American schools and churches nurtured community life and provided space for personal development.

Though town life was more free, the limits to that freedom for African Americans were often strict, and brutally enforced. In the decades after Reconstruction, whites gradually implemented laws requiring racial separation in public facilities. The laws and practices became almost universal by about 1900. And the legal restrictions were supplemented by social expectations of public deference by blacks to whites. For the police and courts, the maintenance of order included the maintenance of segregation. Defiance by blacks brought the danger of jail, and perhaps a term as a convict laborer leased out to a coal mine or lumber mill. Vigilante actions, such as lynching, were a constant threat to any black person who transgressed, or even was thought to have transgressed, one of segregation's rules.

African American students and their teacher standing outside a one-room schoolhouse in Lowndes County, c. 1910. This photograph was part of a survey documenting rural school conditions.

Political Agitation and Reaction

In the years after Reconstruction, government expenditures were kept low to reduce the tax burden. Business leaders maintained that these low taxes also contributed to economic growth by helping to attract new industries. The anemic tax collections, however, limited the ability of the state and local governments to provide services. Education in Alabama was funded at only a fraction of the national average. Public health issues were delegated to the Alabama Medical Association. Welfare consisted of little more than county poorhouses. And prisoners were leased to private employers to avoid the costs of housing them. In fact, their lease fees became an important source of government revenue.

As the rural economy continued to languish through the 1880s, farmers grew more resentful. They felt exploited and thought the government should do more to improve conditions. In the industrialized parts of Alabama, workers began reacting against their treatment by corporate managers, who were then consolidating and tightening controls to increase profits. By the early 1890s, these grievances melded into one of the major political uprisings in Alabama history, the Populist Movement.

Growing out of a series of self-help organizations for farmers, the Populist Movement urged a broad slate of initiatives to improve the lives of working people. Proposals ranged from the regulation of railroad rates to a looser monetary and credit policy, from better schools to the establishment of farmers' cooperatives. Excitement about the Populist cause spread rapidly, and thousands of Alabama farmers and industrial workers joined the bandwagon. In one of its most radical turns, Populist leaders reached out to black Alabamians who suffered many of the same hardships.

Political advertisement from Reuben Kolb's gubernatorial campaign in 1894. The rooster was then the symbol of the Alabama Democratic Party.

Reuben Kolb, Populist candidate for governor in 1892 and 1894. Prior to running for governor, he had served as Alabama's Commissioner of Agriculture, 1886–90.

Historians generally believe that Reuben Kolb, the Populist leader in Alabama, would have been elected governor in 1892 or 1894 if fraudulent votes from Black Belt counties had not been used to defeat him. Some of the same practices that had been used to regain control during Reconstruction were now used to beat back the Populist challenge. Both landowners and industrialists wanted to keep their political power to protect their economic interests. The threat of the Populist insurgency united them in resistance.

Although the defeated Populists faded as a statewide force by the late 1890s, conservative Democrats feared the possibility of another eruption. At the same time, the clearly corrupt methods they had used to win exposed a glaring flaw in their system. Solutions to both concerns converged in the call for a new constitution. More restrictive voting requirements could remove African Americans as a political threat and thus eliminate any further need for corrupt voting practices. These same voting requirements might also reduce the number of poor white voters, who had supported the Populists.

The 1901 Constitution was written in large part to restrict voting by blacks and poor whites. Literacy requirements and cumulative poll taxes (that grew larger each year they were not paid) became major barriers to popular suffrage. Also, local registrars were given, as a practical matter, almost unchecked power to make a final determination of who could register. When the 1901 Constitution was approved in a statewide referendum, the margin of victory came from the Black Belt counties. Thousands of African Americans saw their votes manipulated one more time—to ensure their future disfranchisement.

Reform Movements

A major irony in the adoption of the 1901 Constitution was that it opened the door to more reform initiatives. Before 1901, dissent by whites could be stifled by claims that it threatened the Democratic Party unity that was necessary to preserve

Delegates to the 1901 Alabama Constitutional Convention. The larger photo in the center is that of John Knox, who served as president of the convention.

Constitution of the State of Alabama.

1901.

We, the people of the State of Alabama, in order to establish justice, insure domestic tranquillity and secure the blessings of liberty to ourselves and our posterity, invoking the favor and guidance of Almighty God, do ordain and establish the following constitution and form of government for the State of Alabama:

Article 1.

Declaration of Rights.

That the great, general and essential principles of liberty and free government may be recognized and established, we declare:

1. That all men are equally free and independent; that they are endowed by their Creator with certain inalienable rights; that among these are life, liberty and the pursuit of happiness.

2. That all political power is inherent in the people, and all free governments are founded on their authority and instituted for their benefit; and that, therefore, they have at all times an inalienable and indefeasible right to change their form of government in such manner as they may deem expedient.

3. That no religion shall be established by law; that no preference shall be given by law to any religious sect, society, denomination or mode of worship; that no one shall be compelled by law to attend any place of worship; nor to pay any tithes, taxes or other rates for building or repairing any place of worship, or for maintaining any minister or ministry; that no religious test shall be required as a qualification to any office or public trust under this State; and that the civil rights, privileges and capacities of any citizen shall not be, in any manner, affected by his religious principles.

4. That no law shall ever be passed to curtail or restrain the liberty of speech or of the press; and any person may speak, write and publish his sentiments on all subjects, being responsible for the abuse of that liberty.

5. That the people shall be secure in their persons, houses, papers and possessions from unreasonable seizures or searches; and that no

The first page of the 1901 Constitution, the sixth and current state constitution.

Three young laborers photographed by pioneering documentarian Lewis Hine at Avondale Mills, Birmingham, 1910. Hine's photos in mines, mills, and factories helped arouse the American public to demand new child labor laws.

white rule. With African Americans effectively removed from voter rolls, white control was assured. Now, white politicians were more free to attack each other and to call for reform. The establishment of the Democratic direct primary in 1902 restored the power of white voters to choose their leaders, a role that Democratic state conventions had played since the end of Reconstruction.

The early 1900s were the years of America's Progressive Movement. In Alabama, reformers proposed limits on the sale of alcohol, regulation of railroad rates, restrictions on child labor, abolition of the convict lease system, improvements in public health, better schools, and women's suffrage. Alabama was hard ground for reformers to plow, but leaders such as Julia Tutwiler, Margaret Murray Washington, Edgar Gardner Murphy, and Pattie Ruffner Jacobs were moral forces who were hard to ignore.

Reformer Julia Tutwiler devoted her life to improvements in education, prison conditions, opportunities for women, and other causes.

The Alabama
Anti-Saloon League

Rev. W. B. CRUMPTON, President, Montgomery, Ala.
Rev. I. D. STEELE, Secretary and Treas., Birmingham, Ala.

What It Proposes

FIRST—To federate the Churches, Sunday Schools, Temperance Societies and other moral forces of the State in a conservative, persistent, and determined movement against the saloon.

SECOND—To create a healthy, sane, and powerful public opinion in favor of Local Option.

THIRD—To secure the nomination and election of such persons to the next General Assembly of Alabama as will pledge their support to a General Local Option Bill, permitting counties, cities, or subdivisions of the same, to settle the saloon question within their bounds by popular vote, without other recourse than formal petition presented to the proper authority.

FOURTH—To organize the temperance sentiment of Alabama into a permanent and perpetual Anti-Saloon force. And to press the fight for civic righteousness, asking for that fundamental principle of Democratic government—the right of the majority to rule.

For information address

S. E. WASSON,
Acting Supt. Alabama Anti-Saloon League,
DECATUR, ALA.

And occasionally, they were successful. Their collective impact helped set a new standard of social consciousness in Alabama that would live on after them.

One major impetus for reform grew out of women's involvement in the temperance movement. Campaigns for temperance had existed before the Civil War and continued afterward in many Alabama churches. As a socially acceptable avenue for women to enter the public sphere, the temperance movement also gave women a chance to speak out on other policy issues. Julia Tutwiler, for example, served as a link between the Women's Christian Temperance Union (WCTU) and prison reform. She also advocated educational improvement and women's rights, in addition to being the author of "Alabama," the state's official song.

In 1904, the temperance movement in Alabama received an infusion of new energy with the establishment of the Anti-Saloon League. Temperance advocates helped elect Governor B. B. Comer, who persuaded the legislature to pass an act prohibiting the manufacture or sale of alcohol in the state after December 31, 1908. Alabama became a "dry" state a decade before prohibition was enacted nationally.

Alabama women's clubs were another center of reform energy. The Alabama Federation of Women's Clubs was established in 1895 and the Colored Women's Clubs in 1898. By the early 1900s, both groups were heavily involved in a variety of causes—educational improvement, youth services, child labor reform, and the creation of libraries.

Reform efforts brought many women into sustained engagement in public policy issues, yet they were still unable to vote. The Alabama Equal Suffrage Association, founded in 1912, launched a campaign to amend the state constitution and allow women to vote. Though the effort was gaining ground, it did not succeed before the Nineteenth Amendment to the U.S. Constitution was enacted in 1920. With women's

Opposite: Anti-Saloon League handbill. Above: Women's suffrage booth at a state fair in Birmingham, 1914.

suffrage finally achieved, the Alabama Equal Suffrage Association disbanded—to reemerge as the League of Women Voters.

Education

Education was a central interest of most progressive leaders. In the impoverished decades after the Civil War, illiteracy actually increased in Alabama, peaking—or rather hitting bottom—around 1900. With only meager state financial support and few standards, education was left largely to local communities. As a result, some affluent communities had good schools, but these places were the exception.

More common in Alabama were oversized classes in rundown buildings with underpaid teachers working a truncated school year. Students bought their own books or did without. In the postwar years, former slaves and their children were particularly hungry for the education that earlier had been denied them by law. Small allocations of state funds, local initiatives, and outside support allowed blacks in many communities to establish schools, but maintaining these schools was a continuing struggle.

Higher education was also underfunded and equally chaotic in organization. By the turn of the century, Alabama had scores of institutes and colleges. Many were church-supported. Others were created by local community leaders. Some were "normal schools," established to train teachers. Some were created especially for women, others for African Americans. Talladega College, for example, began as a grade school founded by two former slaves and became a college in 1867 with the support of the American Missionary Association, an arm of the Congregationalist Church.

Alabama's best known institution of higher education for blacks was Tuskegee In-

Top: 1871 view of Woods Hall, one of the University of Alabama's earliest buildings. Bottom: Old Main, 1883, was the first building on what later became Auburn's campus. It burned in 1887 and was replaced by Samford Hall.

Above: Booker T. Washington speaking to a crowd of African Americans in the early 1900s. Below left: Washington at the height of his career as president of Tuskegee Institute, when he was the best-known African American leader in the U.S. Below right: Tuskegee professor George Washington Carver was a research scientist, a devoted teacher, and a promoter of improved agricultural practices.

stitute. In 1881, organizers of a new school for African American students in Macon County brought in a twenty-five-year-old principal named Booker T. Washington. Under his leadership, Tuskegee became a national center of African American education and culture.

Washington labored in some of the hardest years of racial discrimination, under the gaze of a watchful white society. He established a curriculum that he believed fit the times, stressing vocational skills that would help his students become financially independent. He thought that when African Americans earned financial success and respect within their communities, the doors of full citizenship would gradually open for them.

Doors certainly opened for Washington. He dined at the White House and consulted regularly with leading national businessmen. Their support helped Tuskegee Institute grow and prosper. Washington hired the famous scientist George Washington Carver and sponsored an extension program in which advances in agriculture and home life were shared with black farmers, craftsmen, and their wives across Alabama.

Though Washington talked publicly about cooperation with the white leadership, he also worked vigorously to defend black rights, usually behind the scenes. Some African American leaders then, and many later, questioned Washington's strategy. There is no question, however, that his impact on the lives of thousands of Alabamians was substantial and positive.

By the 1920s, the general Progressive drumbeat for education had achieved a variety of successes—increased pay for teachers, better overall funding, special vocational schools, strengthened requirements for local schools, and better financial support for state normal schools and universities. Alabama's illiteracy rate was finally declining, and educational institutions were established on a stronger footing.

Third-grade students working with crafts at Minor School, Birmingham, c. 1910.

Left: Like numerous World War I American soldiers, William Dumas died of disease before reaching Europe. He died at Camp McClellan in March 1918. His family received a Gold Star medal in recognition of their loss. Right: Leon McGavock, a sergeant from Birmingham, died of disease in France just a month before the armistice. His family also received a Gold Star.

World War I

The United States was engaged in World War I for only eighteen months, but the war triggered an important surge of economic and social activity in Alabama. Approximately seventy-five thousand Alabama men, black and white, served in the military, and Alabama units fought in some of the most important engagements of the late part of the war. Alabama's 167th Infantry served with distinction at Chateau-Thierry, Saint Mihiel, Croix Rouge Farm, and the Argonne.

The war claimed more than six thousand of Alabama's sons, but it brought a new stirring of national patriotism that had been mostly dormant in Alabama since the Civil War. It also stimulated the economy, as industries increased production to meet the demands of warfare. Cotton prices shot up, bringing farmers a few good years. Military bases in Alabama provided jobs and an infusion of money for their host communities.

For many African Americans, reports of high-paying war jobs in northern facto-

Top: The 67th U.S. Infantry garrisoned at Camp Sheridan, near Montgomery, September 1918. Bottom: A train carrying recruits on their way to join the army stopped in Conecuh County. Phrases such as "To Hell Mit The Keiser" and "Mobile to Berlin" were written on the side of the train.

ries proved irresistible. Black migration from Alabama to the North set a pattern that would continue for decades afterward. The war also brought new people to Alabama. While in Alabama for military training, Minnesota soldier F. Scott Fitzgerald met Montgomery socialite Zelda Sayre. Military service, economic opportunity, and new experiences growing out of World War I permanently altered the lives of tens of thousands of Alabamians.

The Twenties

In the 1920s, the division between urban and rural Alabama became sharper than ever. Urban Alabama enjoyed growing prosperity. People had jobs, and wages were rising. Radios and movies opened up the outside world. Telephones linked people to distant friends and relatives, or to neighbors down the street. The number of automobiles increased by almost 400 percent between 1920 and 1930. Birmingham built the South's

tallest skyscrapers. Alabama Power Company completed a series of hydro-electric dams and power lines that supplied electricity to Alabama towns and cities. New appliances powered by electricity made urban life easier and more comfortable.

Conditions in rural Alabama were the complete opposite. Agricultural prices fell again after World War I. The same old problem of depressed cotton prices was compounded by the spread of the boll weevil and continued depletion of the soil. A decade later, Alabama farmers would joke bitterly that they never noticed when the Great Depression hit; for them, the misery of the twenties just continued.

Politically, Alabama enjoyed the leadership of two strong, reform-oriented governors during the twenties. Thomas Kilby (1919–23) was a successful businessman-

Dauphin Street in downtown Mobile, c. 1920.

Right: Construction of the Alabama Power Company's Mitchell Dam, c. 1922. This photograph shows workers guiding the sluice gate for Unit Number 2 into place. Below: Lay Dam on the Coosa River near Clanton. Construction began in 1910 and was finished in 1914. With an installed capacity of 110,000 horsepower, this was Alabama's first hydroelectric plant combining power generation and river improvement.

M·D·456

Placing Gate in #2 Unit.

Top: A farmer near Camp Hill, Tallapoosa County, plowed along the contours of the land to help reduce erosion. Bottom: Unchecked erosion is documented in a Farm Security Administration photo. Inset, the boll weevil forced Alabama farmers to diversify their crops, and sometimes to abandon farming entirely.

turned-politician from Anniston. He used his considerable skill to update the tax system, strengthen education, build roads, and improve public health services. He also led in creating the State Docks in Mobile and the Child Welfare Department, the beginning of professional social work in Alabama.

Bibb Graves (1927–31) continued many of Kilby's initiatives. Graves ended, finally, the convict lease system (Alabama was the last state to stop this practice). In addition to strengthening educational programs and human services, Graves used gas taxes and vehicle registration revenue to expand highway construction. Unfortunately for Graves and for Alabama, the Great Depression hit during the last year and a half of his administration. The earlier contrast between prosperous cities and impoverished rural Alabama was now unhappily resolved: urban Alabamians joined their rural cousins in economic depression.

Above: Governor Thomas Kilby (1919–23) brought a variety of important reforms and new initiatives to Alabama government. Right: Lorraine Tunstall was appointed by Governor Kilby as the first director of the Alabama Department of Child Welfare, the predecessor to today's Department of Human Resources.

DEPRESSION AND WORLD WAR (1929–1950)

The Great Depression, the New Deal, and World War II brought an avalanche of change that touched the lives of every Alabamian. Hundreds of thousands of people moved—from farms to cities, to new jobs, and to new lives. These dramatic changes in the economy brought new experiences, new opportunities, and new wealth. The impact of all these changes would shake the foundations of the political and social system that had prevailed since the end of Reconstruction.

The Great Depression

Despite World War I and the Roaring Twenties, most Alabamians in 1929 still lived on farms and in poverty. Society remained segregated, and African Americans were still denied basic citizenship rights. Entrenched interest groups kept taxes low and defended the existing social order. In most standard measures of social welfare, Alabama hovered near the bottom of national charts.

Above: In Alabama as in the nation, the priority of President Franklin D. Roosevelt's New Deal was to get people back to work. This photo is of a Civil Works Administration road construction project in Burnt Corn, Monroe County.

Benjamin Meek Miller served as governor of Alabama from 1931 to 1935. A staunch conservative, he led the effort to enact Alabama's first income tax to keep schools open.

The stock market crash in October 1929 triggered a series of nationwide financial disasters. Businesses closed. Workers were laid off. Banks collapsed. Property values plunged. With the Great Depression, Alabama lost the benefits of what had been its economic strength—industrial production. Coal mines, iron furnaces, textile mills, and lumber mills all suffered massive layoffs and some total shutdowns. President Franklin D. Roosevelt declared Birmingham "the worst-hit city in the country." County relief agencies provided some assistance to thousands of the desperate jobless, but thousands more fell through the safety net. Men and women walked the streets looking for work. Whole families jumped freight trains, searching for a place to catch hold; many lived in hobo camps.

Governor Benjamin Meek Miller's correspondence files (1931–35) are filled with pleas from destitute citizens:

From Tuscaloosa:

I have a wife and five children & have nothing to eat & we are in need of clothes. I am a farming man but the man I am farming with is not able to help me.

From Frisco City:

As I am a widow woman and have 4 children to take care of and haven't any way in this world to make a living for them, I am writing to you for advice and help. . . . I haven't an ear of corn or nothing else to my name, and so I don't know what in the world I am going to do for a living.

The New Deal

Following his inauguration in March 1933, President Franklin D. Roosevelt initiated program after program to restore the economy—his New Deal. Economists differ on the long-term economic wisdom of many New Deal programs. There is little doubt, however, that these programs brought practical relief to struggling Alabamians. Direct assistance provided small monthly payments to many who were destitute. Public works programs provided jobs for hundreds of thousands of Alabama workers, which also meant assistance for their families. Alabamians today still benefit from many of these New Deal projects, from state parks to roads, schools, and public buildings.

To restore crop prices, new agricultural laws paid landowners to take land out of production. A variety of follow-up programs then gave assistance to the tenant farmers and sharecroppers displaced by the crop reduction program. Wage and hour laws brought increased pay to Alabama factory workers. New rural electric cooperatives began providing power to areas where service was not economically viable for private companies. Electrification brought an array of conveniences that made rural life much easier. Washing machines replaced washboards and boiling pots. Refrigeration allowed people to store perishable food, improving the quality of their diets. Water pumps brought running water and indoor toilets.

Stone tower on Mt. Cheaha in Talladega National Forest. It was built by the Civilian Conservation Corps (CCC), a New Deal program that put young men to work improving parks and forests.

Above: Wilson Dam in Colbert County on the Tennessee River. Construction lasted from 1918 to 1924. The dam not only generated power, but also allowed navigation around Muscle Shoals. Right: President Roosevelt signed the act creating the Tennessee Valley Authority on May 18, 1933. Alabama Representative Lister Hill, a sponsor of the bill, is second from right.

President Roosevelt inherited a long-standing controversy over the huge Wilson Dam on the Tennessee River. Construction of the dam began during World War I to provide electricity needed for making ammunition. The dam was not completed until after the war was over, and a major political dispute then developed over who would control it. The Tennessee Valley Authority (TVA) emerged in 1933 as the New Deal's resolution of this dispute, though controversy continued.

TVA was a program for economic development, flood control, social welfare, and river navigation grafted onto a construction and electrification project. It targeted one of the nation's most depressed regions. TVA not only provided construction jobs for workers, it also gave them housing and training. Its dams and locks opened up the

Tennessee River for navigation and promoted the growth of new industry. When U.S. industrialization began to pick up in anticipation of World War II, ready access to cheap electricity and cheap labor made Alabama's Tennessee Valley region an attractive location for war-production plants.

The New Deal had many critics. Opponents pointed out numerous examples of waste and mismanagement. Others complained about favoritism in the dispensing of benefits. Even beneficiaries complained about other beneficiaries who they thought were abusing the system. One frequent complaint was that some New Deal managers insisted on treating African Americans by the same standards as whites. Some business owners protested government competition with private industry. Other businessmen objected to relief payments for workers who were on strike.

The New Deal's position toward labor was indeed something new to Alabama. In addition to allowing relief checks for striking workers, Roosevelt secured congressional passage of legislation that protected unions and prescribed standards for their treatment by management. Using these tools, the United Mine Workers, after years of unsuccessful strikes, finally secured contracts for most of Alabama's miners.

Juanita Coleman, teacher and National Youth Administration leader, listening to one of her pupils read in a 1939 adult literacy class in Gee's Bend, Wilcox County.

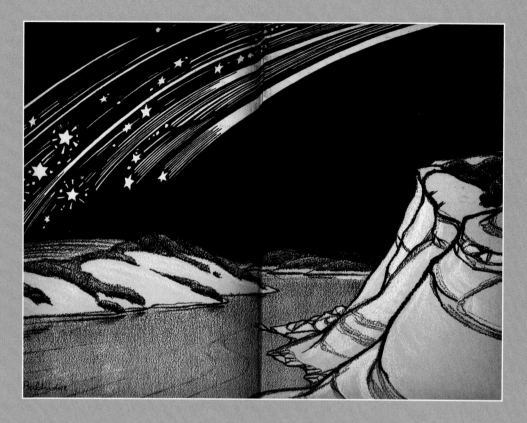

REMEMBERING WHEN STARS FELL ON ALABAMA

In the midst of the Great Depression, Alabamians and the nation were transported through words and music a century back in time. Through the night of November 12–13, 1833, Americans were stunned by the most amazing meteor shower in the country's history. Tens of thousands lit up the sky in a show that grew increasingly intense until they were obscured by the light of the dawning sun. People across the United States were terrified. Many thought the great shower marked the end of the world.

The *Huntsville Democrat* described "this most awful and sublime appearance . . . . For several hours, thousands, and even millions of these meteors appeared in every direction to be in constant motion." The spectacle was no more intense in Alabama than in other states, but it was seared into Alabamians' memories.

Then in the 1920s, New Yorker Carl Carmer came to teach at the University of Alabama. In 1934, he published a book of essays, entitled *Stars Fell on Alabama*, based on his experiences and travels in the state. The book's name came from interviews with "black conjure women" whose fathers had recalled the "awful event." And almost a century later, Carmer found that people still reckoned dates in relation to "the year the stars fell." For Carmer, falling stars was as good a way as any other for explaining the special character of this "strange country in which I once lived and from which I am now returned."

That same year, 1934, Mitchell Parish provided words and Frank Perkins the music to a song using Carmer's title. In August, the Guy Lombardo Orchestra recorded the tune for Decca Records, and it became a hit. It has since been recorded by more than a hundred other singers, from Frank Sinatra to Jimmy Buffett.

The lyrics include:

> I can't forget the glamour,
> Your eyes held a tender light,
> And, stars fell on Alabama last night.
> . . . My heart beat like a hammer,
> My arms wound around you tight,
> And, stars fell on Alabama last night.

The illustration at the top of the facing page was used on the end sheets of the 1934 first edition of Carmer's book; the smaller image below is the title page from the book. Above: The cover and a portion of the sheet music from the song.

Three New Deal Projects in Alabama: Top: Completed in 1940, the Alabama Department of Archives and History building was one of the last Works Progress Administration projects in the nation. Left: Trapping rats in Geneva was part of a project of the Civil Works Administration, 1934. Below: Elyton Village apartments were built by the Housing Authority of the Birmingham District, with U.S. Housing Authority aid. They were opened for occupancy in June 1940.

Left: William Bankhead was Speaker of the U.S. House of Representatives from 1936 to 1940. His father and brother both represented Alabama in the U.S. Senate. Below: His actress daughter, Tallulah, was honored at a dinner given by Rep. Frank Boykin (standing), with Sen. John Sparkman (left), and Sen. Lister Hill (right).

Despite all criticisms, the New Deal was enormously popular in Alabama. Members of the Alabama congressional delegation were ardent New Dealers. In fact, they became some of its leading advocates in Congress. Senators John Bankhead Jr., Hugo Black, and Lister Hill (Black's successor) were influential in much of the New Deal legislation. Senator Bankhead's brother, Will Bankhead, became Speaker of the U.S. House of Representatives for the last half of the 1930s. Congressman Henry Steagall of Ozark chaired the important House Banking Committee and was co-author of the landmark Glass-Steagall Act of 1933, which established a new legal framework for American banking and created the Federal Deposit Insurance Corporation (FDIC).

World War II

While the economic effectiveness of the New Deal may be debated, there is little argument about the impact of World War II. It transformed Alabama's economy—from struggling and sluggish to fully mobilized and throbbing with vitality. The renewed activity began in the late 1930s, as military regimes in Germany and Japan began attacking their weaker neighbors. Programs to assist America's allies and to rebuild the U.S. military generated large orders for Alabama mills and furnaces.

As the build-up continued, existing factories in Alabama expanded and new ones were constructed. Ordnance plants and arsenals were in themselves huge construc-

Above: In this 1944 photograph, workers at Redstone Arsenal tape together cardboard containers that could have been used to ship grenades, smoke bombs, or a variety of other munitions manufactured at the arsenal during World War II. Below: A ship being built in Mobile.

tion projects. Fourteen thousand workers descended on the small town of Childersburg to build a plant on a scale never seen before in Alabama, and rarely in the world. Huntsville was transformed by the Huntsville and Redstone arsenals. In addition to producing iron and steel, Birmingham supported massive munitions production, parts manufacturing, and airplane repair operations.

Shipbuilding in Mobile drew so many workers to the port city that there were not enough beds to accommodate them all. Residence facilities scheduled bed usage so that people who were off duty could sleep in the beds of those who were working. Mobile natives were dazzled by the transformation

of their city. The city's shipyards became principal producers of "liberty ships," tankers, destroyers, mine sweepers, and cargo vessels. At their peak of activity, Mobile shipbuilders launched a ship every week.

Across Alabama, industries strained to produce at the highest possible capacity. Textile factories ran at full speed, twenty-four hours a day. Lumber mills could not produce enough wood to satisfy the demand. Workers who had been laid off during the Depression returned, worked overtime, and were asked if they had friends or relatives willing to work. Thousands of Alabamians left farms to take advantage of these jobs and of wages that exceeded anything they had known before. For those who continued to farm, rising demand drove up prices for their crops. Many farmers enjoyed real profits for the first time in their lives.

Cadet Richard M. Wright of Richmond, Indiana, during training at Maxwell Field during World War II.

As the U.S. government evaluated site options for new military bases, large tracts of cheap land and mild weather that allowed year-round training made Alabama an attractive choice. Alabama air bases included Brookley Field at Mobile, Courtland Air Base in Lawrence County, Craig Field at Selma, Maxwell Field and Gunter Field at Montgomery, Napier Field at Dothan, and Tuskegee Army Air Field, where the famous Tuskegee Airmen trained. More than 100,000 air cadets trained at Maxwell alone, joined by thousands more French and British pilot trainees. Former cotton fields became touch-and-go runways.

In addition, the army built major infantry bases at Anniston (Fort McClellan) and Ozark (Fort Rucker). Camp Sibert at Gadsden was a training center for chemical warfare, and the Anniston Ordnance Depot was an important storage facility. Later in the war, camps for German prisoners were opened at Aliceville, Camp Rucker, Fort McClellan, and Opelika. Smaller camps were set up across the state where prisoners worked on farms, at sawmills, or on special construction projects.

German prisoners working in the greenhouse at the Aliceville Internment Camp, which held 6,000 from 1942 to 1945. The majority were captured in 1943 from the German Afrika Korps.

African Americans also benefited from this economic revitalization, though most businesses still practiced segregation. In the spring of 1943, President Roosevelt's Committee on Fair Employment Practices ordered Alabama Dry Dock to allow some of its seven thousand African American workers into skilled labor positions. When twelve blacks were upgraded to welders, white workers rioted, requiring army troops from Brookley Field to restore order. Changes in race relations were limited and slow. Even the military remained segregated. Thousands of African Americans continued to leave Alabama for work in northern plants.

Women in Alabama had worked in war industries during the Civil War, but the percentage of women working during World War II was much higher. At some large facilities they made up nearly half of the total labor force. They worked in crafts and

African American servicemen testing the frequency of a radio after installing it in a basic trainer plane at the Tuskegee Army Airfield.

Woman working in the shipyards in Mobile during World War II.

in duty areas that previously had not been open to women. Women also joined the Women's Army Auxiliary Corps, serving in a variety of support and administrative functions. Still others became nurses, helped the Red Cross, or staffed USO facilities.

Alabamians not in military service or working in war production were involved in the war effort in other ways. They drilled in civil defense to prepare for German attacks. They grew victory gardens, recycled everything that might have military value, and bought war bonds. And they endured the rationing of key commodities needed by soldiers, from sugar and meat to tires and gasoline.

War mobilization was a great engine that drew the entire state into its workings. In World War I, the Selective Service drafted approximately 74,000 men from Alabama. In World War II, 321,000 men served, approximately a third of the state's male population. Virtually every family had at least one member in uniform, and every day they followed newspaper and radio reports on military action overseas.

As deeply as the war touched the lives of ordinary Alabamians, nothing could compare to its impact on Alabama soldiers. Many Alabamians distinguished themselves in military service. Approximately six thousand Alabamians lost their lives in combat or captivity, and many more suffered serious wounds.

Eugene B. Sledge of Mobile kept a small notebook of his experiences as a marine serving in the Pacific. He later compiled his notes into a book, *With the Old Breed.* Many historians regard Sledge's memoir as the best account of the war by an American

Left: Harriett Engelhardt of Macon County (left) with co-worker in front of their American Red Cross Clubmobile. These portable kitchens traveled with the U.S. Army Corps in Europe. Each was run by three American women who prepared coffee and doughnuts for servicemen. Engelhardt was killed in October 1945 in a jeep accident. Below: Members of the Sheffield Citizen Defense Corps and enlisted men from the Courtland Army Air Base during a scrap drive in March 1945.

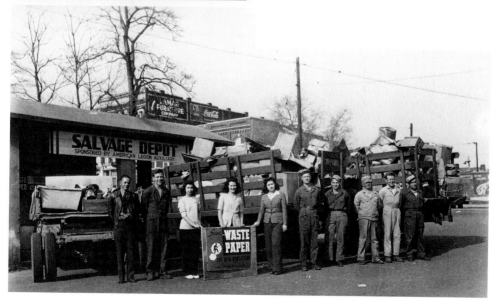

Above: Alabama soldiers in New Guinea, May 1944. Left: Mobile native Eugene B. Sledge enlisted and served in the Pacific Theater. His memoir is a compelling account of the war. Below: Sledge and other members of Company K-3-5, 1st Marine Division, with a captured Japanese flag and weapons following a battle in 1944 or 1945.

serviceman. The hardships and horrors he describes seem almost beyond endurance. His work has a clarity and humanity that offers readers at least some sense of the combat experience:

> On a battlefield rain made the living more miserable and forlorn and the dead more pathetic. To my left lay a couple of bloated Japanese corpses. . . .

Each dead man still wore two leather cartridge boxes. . . . Beside each corpse lay a shattered and rusting Arisaka rifle, smashed against a rock by some Marine to be certain it wasn't used again.

War is brutish, inglorious, and a terrible waste. Combat leaves an indelible mark on those who are forced to endure it. The only redeeming factors were my comrades' incredible bravery and their devotion to each other.

The Aftermath

The decades of the Great Depression and World War II left an indelible mark on Alabama. Manufacturing had crashed and then been revitalized. New wealth had surged through the state's economy. In rural Alabama, the old sharecropping system was in collapse. Hundreds of thousands of Alabamians had moved from farms to towns and cities. Landowners used their federal subsidies to buy tractors and mechanize production. Many converted to raising livestock or poultry. Some planted their land in pine trees to supply the growing paper industry. Within the space of a generation, Alabama tilted from a primarily rural to a primarily urban state.

During the war, many Alabamians had left their homes and experienced life in other cultures. Some married people from those other cultures. A wider range of experiences, greater mobility, and money to do things they could not do before—all changed people's lives, often in profound ways. Veterans' benefits after the war may have been as transformative as the war itself. Returning soldiers were able to attend college, and many were the first members of their families ever to do so. They could also buy homes with low-interest loans.

Because of their training and experiences, Alabamians after the war were more skilled, knowledgeable, and confident. A new generation of leaders and producers was ready to step forward. They started businesses, expanded old ones, and enticed outside industries to move to Alabama. Alabama's attractions still included lower wages, but the wage gap between Alabama and the nation was closing.

For African Americans, the New Deal and the war brought a peculiar blend of opportunity and insult. War jobs and service had opened many areas previously limited to whites. But these opportunities were usually hedged by racial restrictions. So many blacks left Alabama that the state recorded a major decrease in its percentage of African American residents. The veterans who did return home, however, faced the same system of segregation they had left. They had loyally served their country as men and returned to be called "boy."

As he was leaving office, conservative governor Frank Dixon (1939–43) warned his fellow Democrats that their own party was "dynamiting their social structure." Dixon was right. Many of the New Deal programs made an effort to treat African Americans equitably. Although the military remained segregated through World War

II, the Roosevelt administration had made concerted efforts to provide opportunities for black advancement. For thousands of African Americans, opportunities for work, military service, and travel outside Alabama had provided exposure to life where segregation was not the rule.

As New Deal programs and the impact of the war challenged the practices of segregation, the legal foundation for these practices was also weakening. America's enemies in World War II had used claims of racial superiority to justify their barbarous

Workers with a mechanical cotton picker on Price McLemore's Oaks Plantation in Montgomery County, c. 1950.

World War II veterans taking advantage of the GI Bill enroll at Alabama Polytechnic Institute (now Auburn University). P. M. Norton (back to camera), college coordinator of veterans affairs, registers some of the more than 4,300 GIs entering API in 1946.

brutality. Americans had to look again at their sanctioning of racial discrimination in the United States. Gradually, the U.S. Supreme Court began chipping away at the system of segregation it had enabled in its 1896 *Plessy v. Ferguson* decision.

In 1944, the Court ruled that Alabama's system of white-only primaries was illegal. The Democratic Party could no longer deny registered black voters, however few they were, the right to vote in its primaries. In 1946, the Court rejected the Boswell Amendment to the Alabama Constitution. That amendment had allowed registrars to decide if they thought an applicant understood the U.S. Constitution well enough to be allowed to vote. Adding to the weight of these court decisions was President Harry Truman's 1948 executive order desegregating the U.S. military. With so many bases in Alabama and so many Alabamians in the service, this order was a major new threat to segregation.

As Alabama entered the 1950s, the underpinnings of its old social and political system were collapsing. The economy had changed, and people had changed. The system of segregation remained, but it was in jeopardy. Its challengers were gathering force.

Times of Change and Civil Rights (1950–1980)

Alabama emerged from World War II with a reenergized economy. Economic activity in turn triggered widespread social changes, the most dramatic of which was the civil rights movement. African Americans' assertions of their civil rights returned Alabama to the center stage of American history. But the transformation in Alabama in the decades after World War II extended beyond the civil rights movement. It touched almost every aspect of life, from access to education to the use of air conditioning. In Huntsville, even as their fellow Alabamians struggled over civil rights, scientists and engineers orchestrated the landing of a man on the moon.

Alabama at Mid-Century

Midway through the twentieth century, economic issues still dominated Alabama politics. Governor James E. "Big Jim" Folsom—a truly larger-than-life figure—pushed for programs to help working people. Alabama's congressmen continued to support the economic agenda of the New Deal. Alabama Senator John Sparkman's place as the vice presidential running mate to Adlai Stevenson on the 1952 Democratic Party ticket reflected those continued links. Across the state, chambers of commerce redoubled their efforts to attract new industries with more jobs. A progressive young representative named George Wallace made a name for himself sponsoring legislation to promote industrial recruitment. And in Huntsville, a team of former German scientists began setting up facilities to build rockets for the U.S. Army.

The same year that the rocket team arrived in Huntsville (1950), a Mont-

During the 1946 gubernatorial campaign, "Big Jim" Folsom carried a mop and a "suds bucket" to dramatize his plans to clean up state government. The suds bucket also collected contributions.

Left: John Sparkman represented Alabama in the U.S. Senate from 1946 to 1979 and was the Democratic nominee for vice president in 1952. He played key roles in the army's establishment of a military chemical plant at Huntsville and in encouraging the army to make Redstone Arsenal its center for missile and rocket research. Right: Dr. Wernher von Braun was director of the Marshall Space Flight Center from 1960 to 1970. Under his leadership, the center developed and produced the Saturn V rocket used in the Apollo moon missions.

gomery police officer shot and killed Hilliard Brooks Jr., an African American army veteran wearing his uniform. His offense was that he had boarded a city bus through the whites-only front door.

The Montgomery Bus Boycott (1955–56)

The issue of segregated buses was an old one for African Americans in Montgomery. They had boycotted city streetcars half a century earlier when the original segregation ordinance was enacted in 1900. The issue grated even more harshly after Brooks's death. At a forum for city commission candidates in February 1955, the first item on a list of concerns presented by African American leaders was "the present bus situation."

The specific practices of bus segregation varied among southern cities. In Montgomery, there were three sections: the front one reserved for whites; the back section for blacks; and a middle section to be adjusted by drivers based on the ratio of black and white riders. In practice, the "adjustment" worked only one way, with African Americans being di-

A 1964 photo of Rosa Parks.

rected to surrender seats to whites. Rudeness by white drivers frequently added to the insult blacks felt in having to give up their seats. On December 1, 1955, Rosa Parks was told to "adjust," but she remained seated and was arrested.

Though she worked as a seamstress, Parks was also a long-time secretary for the Montgomery Chapter of the National Association for the Advancement of Colored People. Resentment in Montgomery's African American community over her arrest turned quickly into plans for a boycott. To manage the boycott, a group of black leaders organized the Montgomery Improvement Association (MIA). For their president, they chose a twenty-six-year-old minister who had recently moved to Montgomery. He was highly educated, extraordinarily articulate, and unencumbered by traditional community factionalism. His name, of course, was Martin Luther King Jr.

In retrospect, it seems almost miraculous that the MIA could have found and chosen

These photographs of Martin Luther King Jr. were taken February 21, 1956, after his arrest with other boycotters. The mug shot became part of his police file and includes the handwritten date of his death, later noted by a police official. The second photo shows King as the mug shot was being taken, with the Reverend Ralph Abernathy in the right background. This picture, by Montgomery photographer Paul Robertson, was published in Life *magazine.*

such a man for that moment. King's Christian beliefs and training enabled him to develop the strategy of nonviolent resistance, setting a tone for the protests that attracted widespread admiration and respect. His ability to express his beliefs made him one of the greatest orators in American history. Under King's leadership, the Montgomery Bus Boycott continued for 382 days, until federal courts ordered that the buses be desegregated. This victory helped launch the national civil rights movement.

The ending of legalized segregation was a long, complex process, fought out in thousands of court suits and encounters, large and small, across the United States. But Alabama remained a focal point, as one clash followed another. Many of these clashes—such as the Freedom Rides (1961), the Birmingham Campaign (1963), and the Selma-to-Montgomery March (1965)—were major national news stories. They are remembered today as landmark events in the story of the civil rights movement.

The Freedom Rides (1961)

After the Montgomery Bus Boycott, most white Alabamians embraced the idea of massive resistance as their best strategy for preserving segregation. They hoped that if all whites stood together in a determined refusal to integrate, they might maintain their "way of life." They were fully conscious that their forebears had succeeded in resisting federal pressure during Reconstruction. Through the late 1950s, as hopes hardened into strategy, the pressure inside the white community to hold the line became intense. Whites who suggested compliance with the law or negotiations with black leaders were often abused and harassed.

For a few years after the boycott ended in 1956, it seemed that this strategy might succeed. No schools were integrated, and Alabama's social and political structure remained essentially unchanged. So, the

Violent attacks on the Freedom Riders in Alabama dominated headlines in state newspapers, and also around the world.

arrival in Alabama of a group of black and white riders traveling together on interstate buses presented a jarring challenge. The Freedom Riders were testing a recent U.S. Supreme Court decision—written, incidentally, by Alabamian Hugo Black—that rejected segregation in interstate bus terminals.

When the first integrated bus arrived in Anniston on Mother's Day, May 14, 1961, a hostile crowd attacked it and slashed its tires. A few miles outside Anniston, flat tires forced the bus to stop, and members of the mob who had followed attacked again. They set the bus on fire and tried to block the exit doors. Only the presence on board of an armed undercover officer prevented a far greater disaster. Later, another group of Freedom Riders was attacked by a Ku Klux Klan-led mob in the Birmingham bus terminal. Some of these riders were seriously injured.

Though some riders were lost through injury and some gave up heart, national news stories inspired many others to join and continue the rides. When another bus left Birmingham for Montgomery on May 20, it was escorted by state troopers who were to be replaced by local police once the bus reached Montgomery. Inside Montgomery, however, local police were conspicuously absent. When riders emerged from the bus, they were attacked by a waiting mob armed with baseball bats and pipes. Some riders, including Troy native and future Georgia congressman John Lewis, were seriously injured. John Seigenthaler, a special representative of U.S. Attorney General Robert Kennedy, was knocked unconscious.

The next night, Martin Luther King Jr. spoke to a rally at the black First Baptist Church. A large mob of angry whites began attacking the federal marshals who tried to protect the church; the mob even threatened to burn the church down. Nearly a thousand people were trapped inside overnight, as King talked by phone with Attorney General Kennedy. Governor John Patterson had to summon the Alabama National Guard to restore order.

The Freedom Riders broke the stalemate that had followed the end of the Montgomery Bus Boycott. President John Kennedy, who initially had sought to placate southern whites, now committed more openly to the protection of civil rights. Inside Alabama, some business leaders, such as Winton Blount, publicly denounced mob violence and soon began new efforts to open lines of dialogue with the African American community.

White Resistance

Most white Alabamians, however, favored continued resistance, a sentiment that no politician could ignore and that many sought to exploit. The most successful of the exploiters was George Wallace. He had lost the 1958 race for governor, in part because he was seen as the more moderate candidate on racial issues. By the early 1960s, Wallace had become segregation's passionate defender.

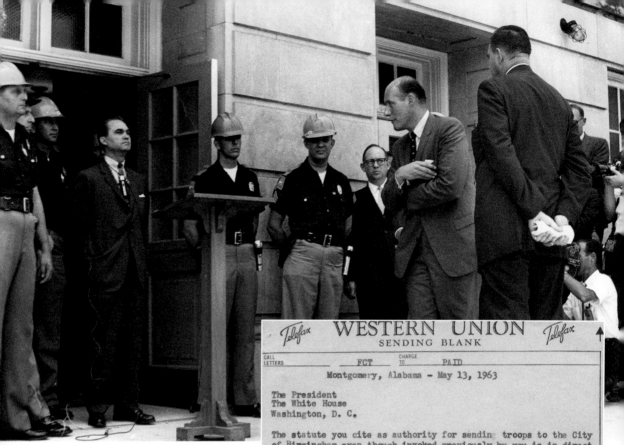

The statute you cite as authority for sending troops to the City of Birmingham even though invoked previously by you is in direct conflict with Art. 4, Section 4 of the Constitution of the United States which states that the U.S. shall guarantee to every state of the Union a republican form of government and which also provides that the U.S. can use its National Military forces to quell

Governor George C. Wallace facing U.S. Assistant Attorney General Nicholas Katzenbach outside Foster Auditorium, University of Alabama, June 11, 1963, during the "Stand in the Schoolhouse Door." Inset: May 13, 1963, telegram from Wallace challenging President John F. Kennedy over the presence of federal troops in Alabama.

Governor Wallace gave voice to white fears that reached back to the earliest days of slavery. One key to his success was that he framed his arguments in terms of traditional political doctrines, appealing to "states' rights" and "law and order." These arguments were not unreasonable in themselves, but they were a veil of superficial respectability that covered, without concealing, underlying white resentment over challenges to the traditional order.

The social and economic disruptions in the mid-twentieth century had left many white Americans with a sense of loss and fear. Tradition did seem to be under attack on a broad front, and the vigorous assertions by African Americans of their rights was the most threatening point of assault. Governor Wallace's resistance to these protests appealed to white voters from both inside and outside of Alabama. His presidential campaigns of 1964, 1968, and 1972 drew support from across the nation. Despite his considerable political success, however, Wallace was still most conspicuous as a counterpoint to Martin Luther King. His high-profile defiance helped make King's attacks more dramatic and kept Alabama a national battleground in the war to end segregation.

The Birmingham Campaign (1963)

While Wallace was taking his first oath of office as governor in January 1963, Reverend Fred Shuttlesworth and Dr. King were planning new protests in Birmingham. Their goal was to desegregate lunch counters in downtown stores. At first, however, their protests failed to gain much attention.

Then in May, campaign leaders revised their tactics, encouraging school children to join the marches. These students were instructed to invite arrest by defying Public Safety Commissioner Eugene "Bull" Connor. As he tried to enforce a state-court injunction against the demonstrations, Connor filled the jails and temporary holding cells with demonstrators. But new marchers stepped in to replace the arrested ones. Exasperated, Connor also adopted new tactics—fire hoses and police dogs.

On the evening of May 3, 1963, national newscasts showed demonstrators being slammed into walls by water hoses and attacked by dogs. These images, and more violence afterward, triggered renewed efforts by embarrassed white business leaders to reach a settlement. In the resulting agreement, King and Shuttlesworth substantially achieved their goals of desegregating downtown businesses. In June, the national news featured Wallace "standing in the schoolhouse door" as he sought to prevent the inte-

Name: SHUTTLESWORTH, FRED LEE, N/M
DOB 3/18/22, 5'9", 152 lbs., brown eyes, black hair.
Address: Birmingham, Alabama and Cincinnati, Ohio.
Occ.: Baptist Minister
Arrest: DC and Unlawful Assembly.
Lengthy arrest record Felony Convictions.
Organization: President S C E F, Secretary S C L C and is a member of Alabama Christian Movement for Christian Rights, and C O R E.
Associates: Numerous.

Reverend Fred Shuttlesworth's record from the Alabama Department of Public Safety's "Individuals Active in Civil Disturbances." Distributed to law enforcement officials, the two-volume set included the names, descriptions, and photographs of individuals involved in the civil rights movement as well as others with the American Nazi Party.

Aftermath of the bombing of the 16th Street Baptist Church, September 15, 1963.

gration of the University of Alabama. His "stand" amounted to a staged capitulation, and the university was peacefully integrated that same day.

The lowest point in the Birmingham story came that September. As public schools prepared to integrate, black and white community leaders worked together to ensure a peaceful process. But on Sunday morning, September 15, members of the Ku Klux Klan exploded dynamite by a side wall of the Sixteenth Street Baptist Church. The blast killed four young girls—Addie Mae Collins, Denise McNair, Carole Robertson, and Cynthia Wesley. The moral bankruptcy of segregation was painfully seared into the nation's consciousness.

Selma-to-Montgomery March (1965)

If the Montgomery Bus Boycott opened the modern civil rights movement, the Selma-to-Montgomery March sealed its success. Since the days of Reconstruction, white political power had been based on controlling the ballot box. The success of the voting-rights march dealt a smashing blow to that system of control and opened Alabama politics to meaningful African American participation.

For more than two years before the Selma-to-Montgomery March, members of the Dallas County Voters' League and the Student Nonviolent Coordinating Committee had worked to promote voter registration. In late 1964, Dr. King's Southern Christian

Leadership Conference joined them in the campaign. They found a useful foil in Dallas County sheriff Jim Clark, as they had with Bull Connor and with Governor Wallace. Clark came across on television as an almost perfect caricature of a bully.

After a state trooper killed a young black man in nearby Marion, civil rights leaders called for a protest march to Montgomery. On Sunday, March 7, John Lewis and Hosea Williams led demonstrators across Selma's Edmund Pettus Bridge. Although they were on the highway to Montgomery, most marchers were still wearing their church clothes. They were hardly prepared to walk fifty miles. Yet, as they descended the east side of the bridge, a phalanx of state troopers and sheriff's officers lined up across the highway in front of them.

Governor Wallace had specifically instructed the head of the Department of Public Safety to avoid violence. After a brief warning to march leaders, however—and without giving them time to respond—the officers waded into the crowd, firing tear gas canisters and flailing marchers with their billy clubs. Television and news photographers captured the images. "Bloody Sunday" became another national outrage.

Marchers crossing the Edmund Pettus Bridge at the start of the Selma-to-Montgomery March, March 21, 1965. Right: Singer/songwriter Joan Baez and actress Susan Sarandon chat near the end of the march.

Dr. King came immediately to Selma and began organizing plans for another march. During this interval, President Lyndon Johnson, anguished by images of the violence, delivered a televised address to the nation. He announced his intention to send Congress a bill that would provide federal protection for black voting rights across the South. He ended his address with the words, "And, we shall overcome."

After several weeks of demonstrations, meetings, legal maneuvers, and preparations, the march actually began on March 21. This time it included people from across the United States who came to Selma because they were upset by what they had seen in the news. When the marchers reached Montgomery on March 25, masses of supporters greeted them and joined the protest, swelling their numbers to approximately twenty-five thousand. They paraded up the same street Jefferson Davis had traveled a century earlier to take his oath of office as president of the Confederacy.

When he addressed the crowd, Dr. King stood in front of the Alabama Capitol, just yards below the spot where, two years earlier, Governor Wallace had proclaimed "Segregation Forever." King's speech was one of the great moments of his career:

> How long will it take? . . . Not long, because no lie can live forever.
> How long? Not long, because you shall reap what you sow. . . .
> How long? Not long, because the moral arc of the universe is long, but it bends toward justice.

The effects of Bloody Sunday, the Selma-to-Montgomery March, and the subsequent Voting Rights Act are still felt across the South and the nation. Under federal protection, African American voters began registering in huge numbers, won election to public office, and quickly became active participants in Alabama politics.

A Time of Change in Alabama

The civil rights movement was the dominant story in Alabama during the mid-twentieth century. But it played out against a background of still broader social change that included such diverse elements as urbanization, economic growth, automobiles, air conditioning, television, health-care improvements, feminism, improved educational opportunities, and even new eating habits. These changes touched almost every aspect of life in Alabama. The civil rights movement grew out of this larger pattern of change while at the same time contributing to it.

In such a massive social upheaval, it is difficult to separate cause from effect. Yet clearly, federal money was a driving force in transforming Alabama's economy and in triggering many of the social changes that followed. From the New Deal onward, federal money flowed into Alabama through a variety of channels: programs for social welfare, military bases, aid for education, highway construction, the TVA, agricultural

Left: Aerial view of the Republic Steel Corporation's plant in Gadsden, April 1967, reflects continued industrial production in Alabama. Below: This 1960s scene inside the plant shows hot-rolled strip steel entering the tower at the new pickling line which began operations in mid-1964. In the tower the strip was sprayed with hydrochloric acid, leaving it with a clean, scale-free surface.

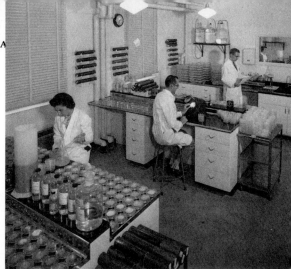

Top left: Women operating pressing machines at a textile mill in the 1940s or 1950s. Top right: Laboratory work at the Southern Research Institute in Birmingham, c. 1950s. The institute was the first independent research center in the South when it opened in 1944. Its scientists conducted research across a wide range of disciplines including medicine, space technology, energy, and engineering. Above: Mid-20th century aerial view of the Mobile Paperboard Corporation. The company was established in 1923.

subsidies, rocket research and development, and health-services assistance. Decade after decade, Alabama received far more money from Washington each year than it sent in taxes, by some estimates as much as 50 percent more.

The impact of this change on rural Alabama was dramatic. The farm population continued to decrease, and the small towns that had serviced the rural economy lost their sustenance. Hundreds of small communities that had been such an important part of Alabama life began to wither as Alabama became a predominantly urban state.

At the same time, city people began moving to the suburbs, partly in an effort to recapture the feel of small-town life. But work and residence were no longer connected, and the sheer size of cities brought anonymity. Alabamians were increasingly drawn into the churn of a new, more impersonal economic and social environment.

While many Alabamians regretted what was lost, most voted with their feet for opportunities to improve their lives. People were willing to leave their homes to take advantage of better jobs. They even moved to other states if they could not find what they wanted nearby. An expanding system of higher education and new technical and community colleges opened still more doors of opportunity.

Many of the changes in Alabama reflected those taking place all across America, which also makes them significant. Alabama, like the broader South, had been separated from the rest of the nation for generations, first by slavery and then after the Civil War by poverty, segregation, and one-party politics. Now, Alabama was becoming more like the rest of the United States.

Paul "Bear" Bryant being carried off the field by his players after winning a game during the 1973 season. Sylvester Croom (59) later became the Southeastern Conference's first African American head football coach.

A Man on the Moon

No place in Alabama exemplified the currents of modernization more than Huntsville. The approximately 120 German scientists and engineers who arrived there in 1950 were accompanied by other talented American colleagues, and they were soon joined by many more. Redstone Arsenal became the center for army missile development. When the Soviet Union launched Sputnik in October 1957, the United States initially tried to counter with a satellite launched by the navy's Vanguard rocket. After the Vanguard's embarrassing failure, the government turned to the army's Jupiter rocket, which had been developed at Redstone.

The success of Wernher von Braun's Army Ballistic Missile Agency led to a massive expansion of the rocket program and of Huntsville. The National Aeronautics and Space Administration (NASA) opened the Marshall Space Flight Center in 1960. The Army Missile Agency was transferred to NASA, and von Braun became the Marshall Center's director.

Two years later, in September 1962, President Kennedy committed the United States to landing a man on the moon before the end of the decade. The work of planning, organizing, and executing this program fell to the Marshall Center. And the new Saturn rocket that von Braun's team developed would be the launch vehicle.

By the mid-1960s, thousands of scientists and

Redstone research and development missile number CC-56 launches at Atlantic Missile Range, Cape Canaveral, Florida, September 17, 1958. This missile, a major step forward in U.S. rocketry, was named for the arsenal at Huntsville where it was designed and produced.

engineers worked in Huntsville for NASA. Thousands more were employed by project contractors. On July 20, 1969, when Neil Armstrong stepped onto the surface of the moon, the Marshall staff and all Alabama celebrated one of the great achievements in human history, and their own part in having made this achievement possible.

The space program in Huntsville suffered major reductions following its great success. Yet Redstone survived, the Marshall Center continued, and many of the contractors remained. Huntsville staggered for a while, but new enterprises emerged out of the remarkable assembly of talent and energy that had gathered there. Huntsville became one of the South's major centers of research, engineering, and high-technology industry.

During these same years, Birmingham experienced a transformation of its own. Through the 1950s and '60s, the coal, iron, and

The Marshall Space Flight Center provided the rockets that powered Americans to the moon, developed the space shuttle propulsion system, and managed the development of Skylab, Spacelab, space station nodes, the Hubble Space Telescope, the Chandra X-ray Observatory, and many scientific instruments. Marshall continues to be at the forefront of space exploration as its scientists are designing the Ares I and Ares V rockets that will return America to the moon.

steel industries suffered dramatic reductions. While some parts of those industries, such as the manufacturing of cast iron pipe, continued to grow, many others closed or drastically downsized. Like Huntsville, Birmingham found new areas of opportunity. Medical services and research provided a platform for future growth as the University of Alabama at Birmingham became a medical center of national stature.

By the early1980s, the legal underpinnings of the post-Civil War political and social structures had finally given way. Alabamians would still feel the impact of the previous years of segregation, one-party political rule, and debilitating rural poverty. But improved economic conditions, new civil rights laws, two-party politics, urbanization, and a host of related changes unleashed new energy and created new opportunity.

Above: Aerial view of the University of Alabama at Birmingham campus in 1955, at the beginning of its long period of extraordinary growth. Below: The School of Public Health is one of many buildings in the UAB/Birmingham Medical Center Complex that now dominates Birmingham's Southside.

Alabama Since 1980

The years since 1980 have been a time of continued change and growth. Alabamians have had to restructure their social and political institutions while addressing the expanding challenges of a global economy. Although the state has enjoyed substantial success, it is too soon to judge the lasting impact of these efforts. Both the rebuilding and the global challenges continue today. This section is an overview of changes that have taken place in Alabama over the last three decades. It is also a preface to the contemporary picture of the state that the remainder of this book will provide.

Politics

George Wallace won his second election as governor in 1970 after a bitter, racially tainted campaign. Several years later, he sought reconciliation with African Americans in

Alabama, visiting the congregation of Martin Luther King's former church in his wheelchair to apologize. When Governor Wallace ran for the Democratic gubernatorial nomination for the fourth time in 1982, African American voters provided his victory margin. Of course, racial conflict did not disappear in Alabama after the 1970s, but Governor Wallace's career reflects the structural change taking place in state politics.

African Americans entered political life with enthusiasm and determination after their successes of the 1960s. In 1979, an African American college professor, Richard Arrington Jr., became mayor of Birmingham, the state's largest city. Joe Reed, chairman of the Alabama Democratic Conference, led a sustained push to increase the number of elected African American officials. His efforts were supported by federal court orders that reapportioned the legislature and restricted at-large representation in local

Oscar Adams Jr., appointed to fill a vacancy by Governor Fob James in October 1980, became the first African American to serve as a justice on the Alabama Supreme Court. Two years later, he won a full term, becoming the first African American elected to a statewide constitutional office.

government. These court rulings removed or minimized barriers that had effectively barred blacks from elective office in majority-white communities.

By the 1980s, the representation of African Americans in the Alabama Legislature fully reflected their state population percentage. Black senators and representatives, as well as hundreds of elected local officials, were able to use their political power not only to address racial issues, but also to participate in all areas of public policy development.

At the same time that African American political participation grew, a resurgent Republican Party began challenging the old one-party political system. Efforts to build a new Republican Party in Alabama began during the Eisenhower administration, but Barry Goldwater's sweep of the state in the 1964 presidential election secured the Republican foothold. Alabama has usually voted Republican in national elections since that year.

Guy Hunt from Cullman County was the first Republican governor elected since Reconstruction and served 1987–1993.

Despite these Republican successes, Democrats have continued to dominate legislative and local elections. The first Republican governor since Reconstruction, Guy Hunt, was not elected until 1986, and then only after a bitter internal dispute among Democrats. The continued strength of the Democrats and the persistence of Republican challenges have brought new partisan divisions to Alabama politics. But they have restored a two-party political system for the first time since Reconstruction.

Other political changes in Alabama have mirrored those occurring in the rest of the nation. More women have been elected to political office. After the Alabama Legislature switched from biennial to annual sessions in 1976, senators and representatives who were understood to be serving on a part-time basis faced almost full-time demands. Service became almost impossible for people with full-time jobs or other responsibilities at home. The growing reliance on broadcast media in elections has required more money for campaigns and has driven many politicians into a constant fund-raising mode. More associations and interest groups have become politically active, and the number of lobbyists has skyrocketed.

This photograph from the Gulf of Mexico includes both a well and a production platform, where natural gas from multiple wells is collected and piped to onshore facilities. Oil and gas production in Alabama's offshore waters became a major new economic factor in state life starting in the 1980s.

Economic Development

The discovery of substantial fields of oil and natural gas beneath the Gulf of Mexico has been a stroke of great fortune for Alabama. In anticipation of this windfall, Governor Fob James proposed that revenue from the lease sales, taxes, and fees be placed in a trust fund. The fund would continue to grow over time, but only the interest could be spent. Governor James's proposal was approved as a constitutional amendment in the 1982 election. A second trust fund proposed by Governor Wallace was added in 1985.

Another stroke of good fortune was a September 1993 announcement by Mercedes-Benz that the company would build its first North American automobile assembly plant in Alabama. Governor Jim Folsom Jr. had led an aggressive effort to recruit Mercedes. The direct benefits of new jobs would be considerable, but the recruitment team also believed that Alabama's selection by such a highly respected firm would cause other companies to give the state a second look.

Persuading Mercedes-Benz to build their first North American auto assembly plant in Alabama was a major success for Alabama political and economic development leaders. Today the plant produces second-generation M-Class, R-Class, and GL-Class vehicles and has had a positive impact on the region's economy of over $1.5 billion.

Above: The Alabama Manufacturing Facility of Hyundai Motor America, located near Montgomery. Right: The plant began operations in 2005 and was the company's first manufacturing facility in the United States. It currently produces Sonatas and Santa Fe SUVs.

Following upon this success, Governor Don Siegelman led efforts to attract two more auto assembly plants—Honda and Hyundai—to Alabama. Governor Bob Riley continued Alabama's aggressive recruitment efforts, winning the largest private economic development project in American history with a new ThyssenKrupp steel plant now under construction north of Mobile. Revenue from the oil and gas trust fund helped support these and other projects.

The growing number of automobile assembly plants has had the secondary benefit of attracting a variety of parts suppliers and fabricators. Meanwhile, continued expansion of high-technology and defense-related work in the Huntsville area, the growth of medical services and research in Birmingham, and the expanded activity of the State Docks in Mobile have all contributed to further economic diversification. Many domestic Alabama industries have also expanded—especially banking, construction, engineering, insurance, real estate development, and forest products.

Following the Mercury, Gemini, and Apollo programs, the Marshall Space Flight Center has continued to play a leading role in the United States' space effort. For nearly thirty years, the center has been responsible for many aspects of the space shuttle's propulsion system, including solid rocket boosters, main engines, and external tanks.

On a different front, the Retirement Systems of Alabama, led by its CEO, David Bronner, began construction in the late 1980s of a network of challenging and elegantly designed golf courses across the state. The beauty of the courses—and their heavy promotion through media channels also owned by RSA—have raised Alabama's profile as a tourist destination. In 1992, Alabama voters applied 10 percent of the Alabama Trust Fund earnings to a program called Forever Wild. This money is being used to purchase and preserve large tracts of land that have special value as scenic locations or natural habitats, adding important new attractions to Alabama's inventory of beautiful places.

The golf courses, natural areas, and continued efforts of the Department of Con-

Above: Golfers at Hoover's Ross Bridge course, part of the Robert Trent Jones Golf Trail, a network of beautiful courses across the state. Below: Alabama's Gulf Coast contains thirty-two miles of beautiful beaches with sugar-white sand. Miles of additional shoreline—with a different terrain and type of natural beauty—surround the Mobile, Perdido, Bon Secour, Grand, Portersville, Heron, Weeks, Oyster, Amica, and Wolf bays, which open into the Gulf of Mexico.

servation and Natural Resources have helped make the beauty of Alabama's land more easily accessible to tourists. Combined with cultural and historical attractions, these improved natural and recreational offerings have contributed to a dramatic expansion of tourism in Alabama. At the same time, the white-sand beaches along Alabama's Gulf Coast and the mild year-round climate have generated an extraordinary surge of recreational and residential growth in Baldwin County.

Alabama has also suffered economic setbacks during the last three decades. The global economy and importation of cheaper foreign-made clothing have devastated the state's textile industry. Other traditional Alabama industries, such as steel and lumber, have also been stressed by competition from imports. The closure of Fort McClellan in Anniston was a major blow to east-central Alabama. These losses and a number of areas that remain in poverty from the past, especially the western Black Belt, continue to pose challenges. Yet the overall story of Alabama's economy over the last decade has been one of growth and new opportunity that has benefited tens of thousands of Alabama workers.

Society, Education, and Culture

The end of official segregation broke down legal barriers that divided Alabamians. It did not, however, immediately change all the social institutions, traditions, and habits that had developed through the entire course of earlier history. In almost every sphere of public life—from housing to medical care, from churches to cultural organizations—Alabamians began the process of rebuilding their society on a new, inclusive basis. The changes have been wrenching for many, and the process is far from over. Yet, it is important to note that change has proceeded steadily now for more than thirty years.

One of the most traumatic areas of change has been in education. Schools have always been more than just places for learning skills. They are social and cultural

ACCESS (Alabama Connecting Classrooms, Educators, and Students Statewide) uses online and interactive video conferencing technology to link classrooms and offer coursework, including Advanced Placement and languages, to students in schools where those courses may not be available.

institutions that reflect the interests and values of their constituent communities. The separate worlds of black and white schools in Alabama before the 1960s contained many elements that were unfair, especially in the inadequate resources provided for black students. Yet, for both blacks and whites across the state, their schools were cherished institutions that served a community-building function for many decades.

While the desegregation of Alabama schools was necessary, it was also painful. Through the years of segregation, the schools had come to reflect separate cultural traditions. The merging of white and black schools brought these cultural differences clashing together. Both communities regretted aspects of what they had lost, and each often had trouble understanding or sympathizing with the problems of the other. African Americans may have lost more than whites because their schools were more frequently closed or converted to some alternative use. One specific result in many parts of the state was an increase in the number of private schools, which had the effect of reenforcing racial and economic divisions.

Because of its central importance, education reform has been the dominant political issue in Alabama over the last thirty years. Though it has also been a major concern nationally, educational improvement has had a special urgency in Alabama because the schools have been rebuilding from the days of segregation. Alabama politicians of all persuasions agree on the importance of improving education, though they often disagree on how reform is to be accomplished.

One recent set of reform initiatives has drawn bipartisan support. During the 1990s, the Alabama State Department of Education began experimenting with an intensive concentration called the Alabama Reading Initiative. Improved test scores from pilot schools have led to a major investment in the program statewide. The techniques used

The Mobile Museum of Art, founded in 1963, has a new 95,000-square-foot structure with more than 6,000 objects in its permanent collection, including pieces from the American South, North and South America, Europe, Africa, and Asia.

The Alabama Shakespeare Festival in Montgomery is one of the largest such festivals in the world. ASF offers twelve to fourteen plays in rotation throughout the year, including at least three works by Shakespeare. The performances attract hundreds of thousands of visitors annually.

in the Alabama Reading Initiative are also now being applied to a parallel initiative for mathematics and science.

The last thirty years have been a time of change in many other areas of Alabama life as well. Until the 1990s, the overwhelming majority of Alabama citizens were born in the state. This pattern meant that Alabama citizens were deeply rooted and felt a strong sense of attachment to the state. It also meant that Alabamians did not have as much exposure to outside views as people in other states. Over the last three decades, this pattern has changed dramatically as Alabama's reviving economy has brought new people into the state.

New Alabamians have come from other parts of the United States and also from other countries. The impact of immigrants from Latin America has been particularly strong. In some schools, Hispanic children now make up a substantial percentage of the student population. Immigrants from Asia, a rarity thirty years ago, are present in almost every town, often in substantial numbers. From Mexican construction workers to Chinese restaurant owners, from Japanese and Korean automobile engineers to Indian computer specialists, new residents have enriched the state with a substantial infusion of talent and energy.

Another area of significant development has been the arts. In the last twenty years, Mobile and Montgomery have built major new art museums, while Huntsville's continues to grow and Birmingham's has undergone a major expansion. All four cities have either formed or substantially expanded symphonic orchestras. The growth of classical music has been more than matched by that of popular music. Muscle Shoals became a national recording and production center, and many state musicians have gained national followings.

The Alabama State Council on the Arts has nurtured the development of community arts programs across the state. One of the Council's most significant achievements has been in promoting renewed interest in traditional arts. From pottery and quilting to shape-note singing and bluegrass music, the traditional arts have enjoyed a lively resurgence. One group of these traditional artists has attracted international attention and admiration: growing out of years of poverty and hardship in their Black Belt community, quilters in Gee's Bend produced work of extraordinary originality and beauty. Their quilts are now shown to large, appreciative audiences in major art museums across the United States.

In theater, the late Montgomery businessman Winton Blount built a major new facility to serve as home for the Alabama Shakespeare Festival, which moved to Montgomery from Anniston in 1984. Every year, the Shakespeare Festival offers productions that attract audiences from across the nation and enrich the lives of fans in Alabama. Alabama writers have also experienced a renaissance. While none has risen to challenge the eminence of Harper Lee, the community of writers in Alabama is large and diverse.

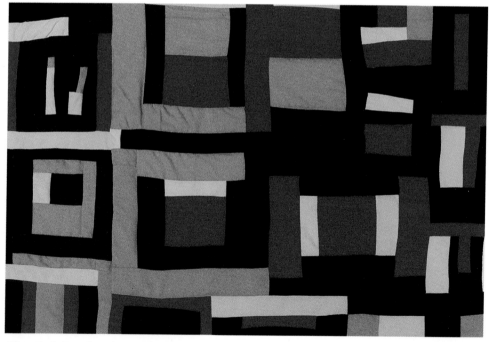

This Gee's Bend quilt was designed by Mary Lee Bendolph in 1998 as an example of the "Housetop" variation. Bendolph's daughter, Essie B. Pettway, stitched the quilt in 2001 using cotton corduroy, twill, and assorted polyester. It is part of the "Quilts of Gee's Bend," an exhibition that has traveled to major museums across the United States.

Over the last forty years, fishing has grown from a casual recreation to become a popular sport and also a major tourist attraction for Alabama. This photograph is from beautiful Lake Guntersville in Marshall County.

In sports, the dominance of football in Alabama may be challenged only by outdoor recreations such as hunting and fishing. Both Bassmasters and Buckmasters began in Alabama and have become national organizations. The race track at Talladega is a major stop on the NASCAR circuit and home of the International Motor Sports Hall of Fame and Museum. As other sports such as basketball and soccer have also grown in popularity, baseball and especially softball have expanded to community and church leagues, with lights glowing in ball fields across Alabama on warm summer nights.

Conclusion

Looking back at Alabama history as a whole, we see a remarkable story. For decades, historians, anthropologists, political scientists, and other scholars have produced a body of literature that makes the story accessible. Another way to learn history is to visit Alabama's numerous historic sites, museums, and archives where objects from the past can be viewed personally. These relics link us directly to the lives of those who went before us.

Learning more about our history is important in many ways. Our understanding of history helps us judge how things came to be as they are. And because this understanding helps frame the way we respond to issues today, it should be as accurate and complete as possible.

For Alabama, there is a special need for better historical understanding. Many of

Symbolic of the change that the state has witnessed over the past several decades, Alabama native and civil rights leader Reverend Joseph Lowery, with his wife Evelyn, joins then-senator Barack Obama and a multiracial crowd of many thousands in March 2008 at the annual commemoration of the Selma Bridge Crossing.

the great challenges we face are the clear products of our history. A broadly shared understanding of our common past can help us identify and overcome these long-standing barriers. Indeed, much of what is sketched in the following section of this book reflects what Alabamians have achieved working together over the last thirty years. We invite readers to consider the descriptions of "Alabama Today" in light of the long path we have traveled in reaching this point.

As Alabama ends its first decade of the twenty-first century, most Alabamians feel positive about the direction of our state. Yet at the same time, international financial upheavals are a jarring reminder of the need to strengthen the state's economic infrastructure. We must continue working for success in a fiercely competitive global economy while rebuilding our social institutions on a more inclusive basis. The achievements of the recent past have shown what is possible. Sustaining and expanding these achievements in the years to come is the great challenge of our time.

3

ALABAMA TODAY

On Saturday evenings on WUAL-FM, Lance Kinney, the host of a bluegrass radio show, makes listeners smile each week when he closes by saying, "There are only two kinds of people . . . those who are from Alabama, and those who wish they were."

But what of those lucky folks who presently call Alabama home? Increasingly, there are far more than two kinds of them. For a century and a half after the removal of the native Indian tribes, we had a historical image of being a state of whites from western Europe and blacks from Africa. Now, however, Alabama's 2006 population of about 4.6 million also includes measurable populations of residents whose family origins are in Korea, Mexico, China, Cuba, Vietnam, and many other countries. These new Alabamians add their own traditions to the workplace, the schoolhouse, and the marketplace while they absorb the rich mix of Native American, European American, and African American culture which has defined "the heart of Dixie" in literature, art, and the popular imagination. The effects are obvious in language, food, dress, religion, music, and even roadside folk art.

Demographers predict that these trends will continue. Thus, Alabama in the twenty-first century will be more crowded and more diverse than it was in the twentieth century. Yet all these Alabamians will share the fundamental goals of making a living, establishing homes, educating themselves and their children, worshipping as they choose, enjoying their leisure, and participating in civic and social life.

In the pages to follow, we look at an overview of how today's Alabamians work, go to school, and play.

The assembly line at Montgomery's Hyundai plant.

ALABAMIANS AT WORK

In 1900, Alabama was a distinctly rural society, with more than half its population making a living, such as it was, from a cotton-dominated agricultural economy. By 2000, only 44 percent of Alabamians lived in rural settings, and only a small percentage of those rural residents actually worked in agriculture. Like the nation's, Alabama's economy has become diverse, global, and more oriented toward manufacturing, banking, service, and technology sectors. Alabamians today have a wide variety of occupational choices.

As this book was being prepared, Alabama's workers were suffering along with everyone else in the global economic downturn that became a crisis in 2008. Alabama, however, was faring better than many other states, and the officials in charge of the state's economic development attributed this relative good news to the aforementioned diversification and to a steadily growing workforce. Employment in wholesale trade in Alabama, to cite just one example, is expected to increase from 77,910 in 2004 to 87,720 in 2014.

Job growth can be partially credited to the increased emphasis in recent years on training workers for higher-paying, more technical careers. Leading this effort has been the Alabama Industrial Development Training (AIDT) agency, which was established to help new and expanding Alabama companies recruit and train an outstanding workforce. AIDT is consistently recognized for its excellence. Most recently, the program was ranked second in the nation in the 2007 *Expansion Management* site consultant survey of how states prepare for and recruit new industries.

Other characteristics cited as making Alabama attractive, in addition to an able workforce, are low operating costs, no inventory tax, sales and use tax abatements for qualifying companies, the lowest property taxes in the U.S., property tax abatements for qualifying companies, and one of the lowest overall corporate income tax burdens in the U.S.

The following pages offer overviews of some of the dominant industrial categories in which Alabamians earn their livings in the twenty-first century. (The information in this section was largely adapted from the Economic Development Partnership of Alabama, www.edpa.org.) Some industries—such as agriculture, mining, and banking—would have sounded familiar to Alabamians in 1909, though on closer inspection the practices of the occupations are vastly different today. Others—such as automotive manufacturing and aerospace—have emerged only in the past few decades.

Automotive Industry

Before 1997, the number of passenger vehicles produced in Alabama equaled exactly zero. That year the first M-Class SUV rolled off Mercedes' production line, and less than a decade later Alabama had built its 2,000,000th automobile. In 2007, Mercedes-Benz, Honda, and Hyundai made 739,019 cars and light trucks in Alabama, with the help of more than 90 automotive suppliers of parts ranging from brakes to headlamps. Alabama ranks 5th in U.S. car and light truck (minivans-pickups-SUVs) production. Car and truck engine manufacturing, from the likes of Toyota and International Diesel, began in Alabama in 2001. By 2007, combined capacity had risen to 1.2 million engines annually.

In fact, over the last decade, the automotive industry has invested more than $7 billion and created more than 135,000 new jobs in Alabama. Motor vehicles were Alabama's top export in 2007 at over $5.4 billion—equivalent to 38 percent of the state's total exports. The automotive industry now represents approximately 11 percent of the state's manufacturing gross domestic product.

The impact on the state's labor force has been profound.

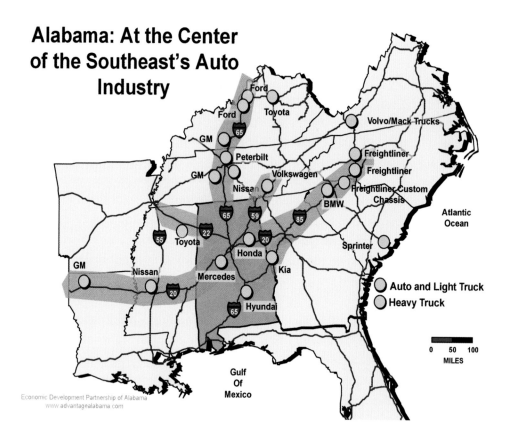

Alabama: At the Center of the Southeast's Auto Industry

The auto industry in Alabama accounted for 48,457 direct jobs and 85,769 indirect jobs in 2007 with a total payroll of $5.2 billion. Weekly wages in motor vehicle manufacturing averaged $1,302 in 2006, significantly higher than the $696 per week average for all Alabama industrial wages, and even higher than the $813 average weekly wage across all Alabama manufacturing industries.

A snapshot of Alabama's vehicle and engine assembly plants reveals:

Wheel assembly at Honda's plant in Lincoln, Talladega County.

- Mercedes-Benz U.S. International, Tuscaloosa County: capital investment over $1 billion; 4,000 workers; capacity of 174,000 vehicles annually from a plant of more than 3 million square-feet; serviced by 35 auto-related suppliers in Alabama; producing the M-Class SUV, R-Class Grand Sports Tourer, and GL-Class luxury SUV.
- Honda Manufacturing of Alabama, Talladega County: capital investment of $1.4 billion; 4,500 workers; capacity of 300,000 vehicles and engines annually from a plant of 3.15 million square feet; serviced by 25 auto-related suppliers in Alabama; producing the Odyssey minivan, Pilot SUV and V6 engines, and the Ridgeline pickup.
- Hyundai Motor Manufacturing, Montgomery County: capital investment of $1.4 billion; 3,000 workers; capacity of 300,000 engines and vehicles annually from a plant of 2 million square feet; serviced by 34 suppliers in Alabama; producing the Sonata sedan and Santa Fe SUV and V6 engines.
- International Diesel of Alabama, Madison County: capital investment of $350 million; 400 workers; capacity of 250,000 engines annually from a plant of 700,000 square feet; producing International's line of vee engines, the MaxxForce 5, MaxxForce 7, MaxxForce 11, and MaxxForce 13, and the 6.4-liter Power Stroke Diesel engine for Ford Motor Company.
- Toyota Motor Manufacturing Alabama, Madison County: capital investment of $490 million; 950 workers; capacity of 390,000 engines annually from a

plant of 440,000 square feet; producing V8 engines for the Tundra and Sequoia and V6 engines for the Tundra and Tacoma.

In addition to the workers at the major plants, thousands of Alabamians also work in the smaller suppliers that have sprung up in the state to make and sell vehicle components. These plants are located in counties including Chambers, Lee, Talladega, Tallapoosa, Montgomery, Cullman, Autauga, Jackson, St. Clair, Etowah, Dallas, Escambia, Jefferson, Colbert, and Barbour. Some recent suppliers have located in Alabama to service the new Kia plant which is being built in West Point, Georgia, just across the Alabama line.

Aerospace/Defense

Alabama is home to more than three hundred aerospace companies in the fields of space and defense, aviation, and maintenance, repair, and overhaul (MRO). The space and defense cluster of the industry is centered in north Alabama around Redstone Arsenal and the Marshall Space Flight Center with significant activity around U.S. Army Fort Rucker near Ozark and Maxwell Air Force Base in Montgomery. Aviation companies in both the commercial and defense sectors are located throughout the state, with concentrations in central and southeast Alabama. The MRO industry is spread across the state.

Though it remains to be seen what will actually happen after congressional wrangling, Alabama made big aerospace news in 2007 with the announcement that Northrop Grumman and the maker of Airbus planes had won a multibillion-dollar Air Force contract to build tankers used to refuel military aircraft mid-flight. The manufacturing facilities would be built in Mobile. The contract was estimated to be worth between $30 billion and $40 billion over ten to fifteen years. It is the first of three awards worth up to $100 billion over thirty years to replace the entire Air Force fleet of nearly six hundred tankers.

Aerospace equipment and parts are among Alabama's largest exports, valued at more than $293 million in 2007. Some 140,000 Alabamians work directly or indirectly in aerospace in these sectors: engineering and research and development services (36 percent); aircraft maintenance, repair, and overhaul (19 percent); information technology services (16 percent); guided missile and space vehicle and parts manufacturing (20 percent); and aircraft parts manufacturing and MRO (6 percent).

North Alabama is a world leader in the research and design of missile systems, aviation technology and rocket design, and propulsion. More than two hundred aerospace and defense companies are located in North Alabama, employing more than 40,000 people (one out of twelve residents in the Huntsville area is a scientist, engineer, or technologist). Nearly every major aerospace company is represented in

Technology workers at the Marshall Space Flight Center in Huntsville, Madison County.

the region, including Lockheed Martin, Raytheon, Northrop Grumman, and Boeing. The University of Alabama in Huntsville and Alabama A&M University have strong research partnerships with NASA and the Army as well as private industry. K–12 schools emphasize science and technology and expose students to the aerospace industry.

REDSTONE ARSENAL: This massive military complex near Huntsville, dating to World War II, is home to the Marshall Space Flight Center and is the center of testing, development, and doctrine for the U.S. Army's missile programs. Redstone's 40,000-plus acres house the Aviation and Missile Command; Tactical UAV (Unmanned Aerial Vehicles) Project Office; Ordnance Munitions and Electronic Maintenance School; Redstone Technical Test Center (RTTC); and other operations. The RTTC, for example, provides flight testing of small rockets and guided missiles and life cycle testing for weapon system components and/or subsystems. These services are supplied to the Department of Defense (DoD), its contractors, and friendly governments. More than 14,000 military and civilian personnel work at Redstone. With the scientists and engineers at the Marshall Center, they have significantly increased per capita income and education levels in the north Alabama area.

MARSHALL SPACE FLIGHT CENTER: The Marshall Space Flight Center in Huntsville opened in 1960 and is named in honor of General George C. Marshall, the Army chief of staff during World War II, secretary of state, and Nobel Prize winner for his

Testing a reaction control engine at Marshall Space Flight Center. The test was part of a series of engine tests under the Space Launch Initiative, which seeks to improve the safety and efficiency of reusable launch vehicles.

world-renowned "Marshall Plan." The Saturn V moon rocket was developed here by Wernher von Braun's team of rocket engineers. The center remains one of NASA's largest and most diversified installations, where engineers and scientists use state-of-the-art equipment and facilities to manage the key propulsion hardware and technologies of the space shuttle, develop the next generation of space transportation and propulsion systems, oversee science and hardware development for the International Space Station, manage projects and direct studies that will help pave the way back to the moon, and handle a variety of associated scientific endeavors to benefit space exploration and improve life here on Earth.

UNITED LAUNCH ALLIANCE FACILITY: This complex in Decatur produces the Boeing Delta IV rockets and may be the world's only assembly-line manufacturing plant for satellite rockets. Originally designed for the U.S. Air Force Evolved Expendable Launch Vehicle (EELV) program and commercial satellite business, the Delta IV rockets are intended to reduce the cost and effort needed to launch payloads into orbit. Delta IV models are available in medium to heavy capacities tailored to suit specific payload size and weight ranges. The facility completed its first rocket in 2000, and in 2008 the government increased the Delta IV contract with Boeing by $1.7 billion to extend its work through the end of the 2009 fiscal year.

THE ALABAMA SPACE GRANT CONSORTIUM (ASGC) includes seven PhD-granting universities (Auburn University, Tuskegee University, University of Alabama at Birmingham, University of South Alabama, University of Alabama in Huntsville, Alabama A&M University, and University of Alabama), all with space-related research activities; seven affiliates; and the U.S. Space and Rocket Center. Several other small colleges and schools in Alabama are affiliated with Space Grant Activities through NASA's Experimental Program to Stimulate Competitive Research (EPSCoR). NASA's Marshall Space Flight Center is an ex-officio member of the consortium. As a participant in the National Space Grant College and Fellowship Program, the ASGC promotes America's continued preeminence in aerospace. The consortium is housed in Huntsville, home to NASA's Marshall Space Flight Center, making NASA's technology available to all Alabama institutions of higher education. The consortium, established in 1989, leverages its NASA funds by more than two-to-one.

The ALABAMA AEROSPACE INDUSTRY ASSOCIATION links aerospace companies together across the state to collaborate and solve common problems. The Tennessee Valley Corridor connects the science and technology assets of the region with the nearby Oak Ridge National Laboratory, U.S. Air Force Arnold Engineering Development Center, and other research facilities. And the Alabama Space Exploration Initiative is an alliance of the state government, NASA, universities, and industry to support the space program.

U.S. SPACE AND ROCKET CENTER: This tourism and education complex is adjacent to the Marshall Center in Huntsville. Its Space Camp, Aviation Challenge, Mach II, and Mach III programs use space to excite and educate children ages nine to eighteen in math, science, and technology. Teamwork, self-confidence, and communication are taught through state-of-the-art simulations, missions, rocket building, and robotics. Additional programs are offered for parents with their children, for adults, and for the visual- or hearing-impaired. The center's archives contain the papers of Dr. Wernher von Braun and other rocket scientists, a collection of thousands of books, technical documents pertaining to the early space program, all of NASA's special publications from the early years, congressional records from the early space program, science fiction data from the 1920s forward, the papers of World War II ordnance officers, and the space collection of Frederick Ordway III, who was the technical advisor for the movie *2001: A Space Odyssey*.

Military Bases

Almost seventy thousand Alabamians are active- or reserve-duty personnel on the state's military bases, which include Maxwell Air Force Base and its Gunter Annex

A CH-47 Chinook helicopter picks up a "sling load" during a joint training exercise of the Army helicopter and crew from Fort Rucker along with firefighters and active-duty and reserve personnel at Maxwell Air Force Base.

in Montgomery; the Anniston Army Depot; Fort Rucker in Dale County (with additional property in Coffee, Geneva, and Houston counties); Redstone Arsenal (see "Aerospace/Defense" above); U.S. Coast Guard facilities; and a number of National Guard posts around the state:

- Maxwell AFB is home to Air University, part of Air Education and Training Command; is the U.S. Air Force's center for Joint Professional Military Education; and is the base for the 42nd Air Base Wing, the 908th Airlift Wing, and the 754th Electronic Systems Group.
- Gunter Annex provides logistics and computer systems analysis and training; serves as headquarters for the Standard Systems Group, which provides U.S. bases around the world with data-processing and communications computer systems to aid with the gathering and analysis of intelligence information; and hosts some of Air University's classes and facilities.
- Anniston Army Depot serves as the designated Center of Industrial and Technical Excellence for combat vehicles, artillery, bridging systems, and small caliber weapons. Depot personnel conduct maintenance, repairs, and overhauls on a variety of military vehicles, including those damaged in combat.
- Fort Rucker serves as the Army's primary flight training base. The U.S. Army Aviation Center of Excellence and the U.S. Army Aviation Museum are located at the base.
- The Coast Guard Aviation Training Center, located in Mobile, is the Coast

Guard's aviation and capabilities development center; serves as an operational air station; trains pilots in operating the HU-25 Guardian, the HH-60 Jayhawk, the HH-65 Dolphin, and the HC-144 Ocean Sentry; conducts search and rescue, homeland security, and environmental protection missions; and oversees an area from the Louisiana/Texas border to the eastern edge of the Florida panhandle. Group Mobile coordinates search-and-rescue missions; enforces laws regarding fisheries, boating safety, and law enforcement; and is currently replacing and updating all buoys in its area of responsibility. Mobile is also home to a Coast Guard Marine Safety Office.

- Alabama Army National Guard is headquartered in Montgomery. Its major commands are the 167th Theater Support Command, Birmingham; HHC 115th ITSB, Decatur; the 20th Special Forces, Birmingham; the 31st Chemical Brigade, Northport; and the 62nd Troop Command, Montgomery.

- The Alabama Air National Guard's headquarters are also located in Montgomery. Its major commands are the 187th Fighter Wing, Montgomery; the 117th Air Refueling Wing, Birmingham; and the 226th Combat Communications Group, Montgomery.

Agribusiness and Forestry

From statehood until the mid-twentieth century, Alabama was largely rural, and a significant portion of the state's economy was based on agriculture. Today, farming and animal husbandry remain important, and farmland still covers about 26 percent of the state. But in recent decades both forestry and large-scale agriculture have displaced most of the state's family farms. As agriculture became increasingly capital-intensive, small farmers had to expand or find other occupations. In 2006, Alabama was one of the country's leading cotton producers, but the crop accounted for only 3.5 percent of the state's total farm and forestry income.

Some farmers shifted from crops to the rapidly growing production of poultry, livestock, and fish. These animal products accounted for 82 percent of the agricultural cash receipts in Alabama in 2005–06, while crops accounted for the other 18 percent. Broilers are the most valuable farm product in the state, with Alabama ranking third in the nation in broiler production at more than one billion birds. Poultry made up 66 percent of the total cash receipts for all agricultural commodities (excluding forestry) in 2006. Alabama also ranked second in the nation behind Mississippi in catfish sales with total sales amounting to $97.6 million. Alabama ranked third in the nation for peanut production, with 613,250,000 pounds produced in 2005, and fifth in the nation in sweet potato production.

Greenhouses, nurseries, and sod are also an important source of farm income, with receipts for 2005 totaling $276.1 million—ranking Alabama 17th in the nation.

Making candy from Alabama-grown pecans at Priester's in Ft. Deposit.

Alabama has the second-largest timberland base in the United States with nearly 23 million acres. Total farm and forestry receipts were more than $5.15 billion for 2005–06.

Forest Products

The forest products industry—which began in the 1800s with lumbering and turpentining and expanded in the 1900s into paper and other products—is today among the state's largest manufacturing sectors, producing an estimated $15.6 billion worth of products in 2005 and directly employing approximately 59,000 Alabamians with an annual payroll in 2005 estimated at $2.3 billion. In fact, there are approximately 850 forest-products manufacturing operations in the state, ranging from family-owned operations like Nixon Cabinet Company in Limestone County to international corporations like Kronospan GmbH in Calhoun County. The latter is a manufacturer of wood-based panels and particle board, and, over the past few years, it has created 700 new jobs and invested $500 million in a plant expansion.

Alabama's forest products industry has been the state's largest consistent source of new investment. During the ten-year period ending in 2005, the industry invested $5.9 billion in capital for new plants, expansions, and modernizations.

In 2005, the various segments of Alabama's forest products industry produced goods estimated at: lumber and woods products, $5.2 billion; pulp and paper products, $2.5 billion; and furniture and other secondary wood products, $2.5 billion. The wood products manufacturing industry output decreased by 12 percent in 2007 to $1.1 billion, but the output of the paper and allied products industries rose by 1.5 percent to $3.1 billion.

INDUSTRY-UNIVERSITY COLLABORATION: The Forest Products Development Center at Auburn University's School of Forestry provides a technical information and analytical support base to facilitate and encourage forest-based economic development in Alabama. The center serves as a contact point for companies exploring new investment or market opportunities within Alabama. The center can either directly provide or assist in providing numerous technical studies, marketing studies, and evaluations.

Specialized equipment makes quick work of felling trees in Alabama's managed pine forests.

Coal, Iron, and Steel

Though Alabama is no longer among the largest iron and steel producing states, the coal, iron, and steel industry was the driving force of Alabama's economic growth from the mid-1800s until its decline in the mid-20th century. The sector remains a significant part of the state's economy. Total coal production in the state in 2008 was 20.5 million tons. Almost 12 million tons came from underground mining, employing 2,522 workers; and 8.55 million tons came from surface mining, employing 1,331.

Employment and business sales in the iron and steel industry in 2006 included: 47 iron and steel mill operations with 4,760 workers and $1.39 billion in sales; four ferroalloy manufacturers with 285 workers and $77 million in sales; and 37 iron and steel foundries with 5,460 workers and $2.1 billion in sales.

A market for some of the iron and steel is provided by about 18 plants in the state that purchase iron and steel to manufacture pipes and tubes, rolled steel shapes, and steel wire. Among the largest of these companies are Hanna Steel, Southland Tube, and Tubular Products.

The National Alabama Corporation railcar manufacturing plant to be built in the Florence-Muscle Shoals area will also be a heavy consumer of steel and will boost Alabama's industrial consumer base for steel.

Nucor's $167 million sheet steel galvanizing facility in Decatur, with capacity for about 500,000 tons annually, will employ about 100 workers.

U.S. Pipe announced in May 2007 that it would be investing $45 million in a new state-of-the-art ductile iron pipe plant adjacent to its existing facility in Bessemer;

Longwall machine at No. 4 Mine, Jim Walter Resources in Brookwood.

Above: Construction of the Thyssenkrupp plant in Calvert. Inset: Dr. Ekkehard D. Schulz, executive board chairman of ThyssenKrupp AG, on the left, with Governor Bob Riley at the plant's ground-breaking ceremony.

operations were to begin in 2009, creating some 100 jobs. This will be the first new ductile iron pipe plant built in the United States in more than fifty-five years.

The iron and steel industry will see significant expansion with the state's most recent economic development recruitment success—the massive $3.7 billion plant being built by German steelmaker ThyssenKrupp AG in northern Mobile County, slated for completion in 2010. An estimated 2,700 workers at the plant will manufacture and process carbon and stainless steel for high-end manufacturers, including the automotive, construction, utility, appliance, and machinery manufacturing industries.

The University of Alabama at Birmingham's Bevill Biomedical Building contains over 220,000 square feet of space for research, mainly in immunity and virology.

Medicine, Healthcare, and Biotechnology

Alabama is home to seven research universities, a highly accomplished contract research organization, a brand new biotechnology research institute, and more than 90 life sciences companies with a total of 2,400 employees, $622 million in sales, and $104 million in capital. The state has produced six FDA-approved cancer drugs and is on the forefront with major initiatives for flu vaccines, cancer treatment, the National Institutes of Health (NIH) Roadmap of biomedical research needs, and more. Alabama's research institutions received almost $234 million in NIH funding in 2007.

New additions to Alabama's growing biotechnology infrastructure include the Shelby Interdisciplinary Biomedical Research Building, a $100-million, 340,000 square-foot, interdisciplinary biomedical research facility that opened in March 2006 at the sprawling University of Alabama at Birmingham Medical Center complex. The twelve-story facility increased the amount of research space for the university by 25 percent, adding new research laboratories and research support areas including a state-of-the-art microscopy area, offices, administrative space for graduate programs, and conference rooms.

Another major new facility, the $130-million Hudson Alpha Institute for Biotechnology, opened in November 2007. The institute conducts research in biotechnology and partners with for-profit companies to develop new biotech products. Dr. Richard Myers, former professor and chair of genetics at the Stanford University School of Medicine and director of the Stanford Human Genome Center, is the scientific director of Hudson-Alpha. The facility includes a 260,000 square-foot main building that houses biotech companies and facilities for eight teams of scientists hired by the institute. The institute has recruited fifteen companies to the campus. The announced initial employment was 500-600; it is expected to employ 1,600 within ten years.

The 156-acre Auburn University Research Park is located just south of the Auburn campus along the I-85 corridor between Atlanta and Montgomery. Auburn University has major technical competencies in the fields of biotechnology, pharmacology, agriculture, composite materials, and biological and chemical detection systems. In August 2007, Northrop Grumman Corporation announced that it will locate one of its new national workforce centers in Auburn.

Recent Alabama company achievements include:

- Gambro Renal Products, part of Gambro Groups, a Sweden-based global leader in kidney and cell-based therapies, is building a 100,000 square-foot manufacturing plant in Opelika.
- BioCryst Pharmaceuticals, based in Birmingham, produces the intravenous Peramivir flu treatment; the BCX-4208 compound, a PHP inhibitor; and Fodosine, an oncology drug used in Europe, Asia, Australia, and other countries.

- Brookwood Pharmaceuticals' scientific team has industry-leading experience in a wide-range of drug delivery systems—with particular depth in long-acting parenterals. Based in Birmingham, Brookwood was founded in 2005 as a spinoff from Southern Research Institute and in 2007 was acquired by Minnesota-based SurModics, Inc., but it remains in Birmingham and operates as a separate business unit.
- Southern Research Institute is an independent, not-for-profit center for scientific research, based in Birmingham. For sixty-five years, Southern Research has provided pharmaceutical, biotechnology, government, and academic partners with high-quality essential services in support of numerous drug and vaccine discovery and development programs. Six FDA-approved anti-cancer therapies have been discovered at Southern Research.
- Vaxin, Inc., is a Birmingham-based biotechnology company developing vaccines and other biological products for public health needs. The company uses proprietary technology for non-invasive delivery to the nasal passages or to the skin. Vaxin's lead programs include vaccines for influenza, anthrax, avian influenza, tetanus, and Alzheimer's.
- The Montgomery-based ProEthic Pharmaceuticals, Inc., is a specialty pharmaceutical company enhancing treatment strategies through pharmaceutical products directed at the primary-care physician. Products in the ProEthic pipeline include medicines for acute migraine and acute pain.

Banking

As late as the 1970s, Alabama's banking industry was led by independent local banks and a few statewide holding companies. Beginning in the 1980s, the nationwide trend toward banking consolidation led to the emergence of strong regional banks. Birmingham emerged as the one of the top ten banking centers in the U.S. Today, Alabama includes some 148 different banks with more than 1,300 branches located throughout the state. Banks play an important role in economic development by taking deposits through checking accounts and savings accounts and then lending these funds to consumers to purchase goods or to small businesses to help fund their operations.

Fortunately for Alabama, even during the global economic crisis of 2008–09, its banking industry has continued to perform relatively well as compared to many other areas of the U.S. According to the FDIC, as of December 2008, 148 commercial banks operated in Alabama with total assets of $266 billion and more than 52,808 employees. In addition, 9 savings institutions operated in Alabama with $5.9 billion in assets and 1,654 employees. The Alabama State Banking Department is the primary regulator for approximately 90 percent of the assets in Alabama's 127 state-chartered banks.

Nationwide, Alabama ranks 12th in terms of total assets under control, higher than all southeastern states except for North Carolina, which ranks first with $2.3 trillion in total assets, and Georgia, which ranks eleventh with $293 billion in total assets. Alabama's relatively high ranking is the direct result of the strategy of many Alabama banks to expand into other states through mergers and acquisitions, allowing them to increase their total assets.

As of December 31, 2008, the largest bank in Alabama was Regions Bank. It was established in 1871 and accounts for nearly 60 percent of total banking assets in this state. Its size was largely the result of the merger with AmSouth Bank in 2006. In 2004, another large consolidation of banking in Alabama occurred with the acquisition of SouthTrust Bank by Wachovia, a North Carolina bank. The most recent data indicate that as of the 1st quarter of 2009, the FDIC-insured banks in Alabama had a return on assets (ROA) of 0.05 percent and a return on equity (ROE) of 0.38 percent (compared to ROA of 0.25 percent and ROE of 2.58 percent, respectively, for all FDIC-insured institutions).

Two major organizations represent the banking industry in Alabama. The Alabama Bankers Association was organized in 1890. The association provides assistance to banks through educational programs, governmental affairs initiatives, and dissemination of information. The Community Bankers Association of Alabama, established in 1980, also promotes sound banking practices through education, representation, and other services to its member banks, which are typically community banks.

Service, Travel, and Tourism

As in many states, service industries contribute significantly to Alabama's economy. At the top of the list are community, business, and personal services (private health care, law firms, software developers, engineering companies) along with wholesale (groceries, machinery, mined products) and retail

Hospitality and service industry employment has grown in Alabama.

trades (auto dealerships, discount and food stores). Other significant employment is found in government services (public schools, public hospitals, military); finance, insurance, and real estate; and transportation, communication, and utilities.

Increasingly in recent years, tourism has played a substantial role. The Alabama Tourism Department indicated in 2008 that the state's tourism and travel industry had increased by 10 percent over the previous year. In 2008, an estimated 22.4 million visitors to Alabama spent more than $9.3 billion and paid more than $685 million in state and local lodging and sales taxes. Baldwin County led the state with almost $2.3 billion in travel-related spending, Jefferson County was second with $1.5 billion, Madison County was third at $900 million, and Mobile County ranked fourth with $890 million. Montgomery County was fifth with $542 million. The number of jobs in Alabama's hospitality industry grew 4 percent, an increase of more than 7,000 jobs. The industry was responsible for approximately 115,000 direct jobs and 55,000 indirect jobs for a total of 170,000—this represents more than 8.5 percent of all non-agricultural jobs in Alabama.

An analysis conducted by Auburn University Montgomery indicated that every $80,872 in travel industry spending creates one direct job in Alabama; for every two direct jobs created, the state's economy indirectly creates one additional job.

Textiles

The development of the cotton gin, Alabama's dominant role as a producer of raw cotton, and an abundant supply of non-union labor led to a thriving textile industry in the state in the nineteenth and twentieth centuries. By the late 1900s, however, increased competition from overseas manufacturing had severely diminished the textile industry in Alabama as well as other southern states.

Nevertheless, textile and/or apparel plants are still operating in 55 of Alabama's 67 counties, and the industry employs more than 22,500 Alabamians in approximately 260 companies with more than 315 plant sites, according to the Alabama Textile Manufacturers Association (ATMA).

Using the most recent data available, ATMA estimates that one of thirteen manufacturing jobs in Alabama is in the textile/apparel industry, with an annual payroll exceeding $638.5 million and generating more than $160 million in state taxes each year. Textile/apparel shipments by Alabama corporations were valued at $9.8 billion (including fiber) annually.

Chemicals, Plastics, and Rubber Products

Chemical manufacturing contributed $2.28 billion to Alabama's $133.9 billion gross domestic product in 2005. Plastics and rubber product manufacturing contributed an additional $1.02 billion. In 2006, Alabama had 176 manufacturers of plastics

Ciba chemical manufacturing plant at McIntosh, on the Tombigbee River.

products and 62 of rubber products. The highest concentration of manufacturing and employment was in plastic plumbing fixtures, resilient flooring, and miscellaneous plastic products.

Plastics and rubber product manufacturing employment was 14,830 in 2006: 8,435 in plastic products and 6,396 in rubber products. Under the current economic conditions, growth in Alabama's automotive manufacturing sector is uncertain but should enable plastics/rubber product employment to increase. Long-term projections indicate employment in the sector is expected to reach 15,750 in 2014, up from 13,640 in 2004.

Transportation and International Trade

Alabama is home to major distribution operations of numerous nationally known companies, including Home Depot, Wal-Mart, McLane Company, ACE, Target, C&S Wholesale Grocers, and SYSCO. In addition, Alabama was ranked 25th in the U.S. for exports in 2006, and Alabama companies shipped products to 180 countries. These activities, and the jobs of the thousands who move these goods and services, are dependent on the state's extensive transportation and trade network.

Alabama water corridors connect to more than 15,000 miles of inland waterways

Wood products packaged for shipment from the state docks at the Port of Mobile.

in 23 states. The Alabama channel at the Port of Mobile bisects the 1,300-mile Intra-coastal Waterway, giving access to markets from Texas to Florida. The Alabama State Port Authority projects that its ongoing $300 million expansion of the Port of Mobile will result in it becoming the sixth-busiest deepwater port in the United States, with connecting service to railroads and immediate access to freight forwarding through the Brookley Airport Complex, located adjacent to the port. The port is adjacent to I-10 and I-65 and has four million square feet of cargo handling capacity. The port's core business includes coal, forest products, frozen poultry, iron and steel products, aluminum, and containers. The port and intermodal facilities have been instrumental to increasing Alabama's trade.

Alabama offers 2,000-plus miles of railroad track service by five Class I railroads. Five interstate highways converge in Alabama, allowing goods to be shipped to major markets. The completion of the new Interstate 22 linking Birmingham to Memphis will make Birmingham the hub of four interstate highways and will rank Birmingham with Atlanta and Nashville as the Southeast's top three interstate hubs.

Alabama is served by seven major commercial airlines and seven commuter airlines operating through six commercial airports. International flights are easily accessible via direct flights to major connecting cities. In addition, Alabama is located between two of the country's largest air freight centers—Memphis and Atlanta. Alabama has 92 public-use airports. Through the Alabama Airport Improvement Program and the Federal Aviation Authority Airport Improvement Program, cities can develop airports for industrial and other civil use. Most public-use airports have lighted runways and can accommodate corporate aircraft. The Huntsville Intermodal Center is an inland port located at Huntsville International Airport, offering domestic and international services including on-site inspectors of U.S. Customs and the U.S. Department of Agriculture. Panalpina provides 12-14 weekly international cargo flights to Europe, Asia, and Mexico.

ALABAMIANS AT SCHOOL

Today's Alabamians have much to be proud of in their educational system. From preschool through graduate school, in both public and private settings, there are many examples of award-winning programs, innovative approaches, and nationally recognized teachers. Though serious challenges remain, energized citizens and organizations are working hard to strengthen the state's educational institutions. In the following pages, we will learn about Alabama's recent efforts in K–12, postsecondary, and higher education.

K–12

The state's 1,538 public schools, with approximately 750,000 students, are under the combined administration of the Alabama State Department of Education and 131 local systems across the state. Alabama now spends about $6.3 billion a year on public K–12 education, employing about 100,000 school personnel, serving one billion school meals annually, and operating 7,000 school buses traveling almost 500,000 miles each school day.

One feature of education funding in Alabama is the relatively high percentage of state support. Through constitutional and statutory restrictions, Alabamians have dedicated most of the proceeds of the state's sales and income taxes to education. Because of the growth of these revenue sources over the years, Alabama teachers—once woefully underpaid compared to their counterparts in other states—have enjoyed substantial recent salary increases. In the decade from 1997 to 2008, funding for instruction and school operations grew 57 percent after inflation. Although still not at the national average, salaries for Alabama teachers now compare favorably to those in the southeastern region.

One of the state's great challenges has been rebuilding a unified public educational system from the legacy of a segregated and impoverished past. Both the general public and state political leaders have recognized the seriousness of this challenge. They are also conscious of the central importance of education in preparing the state's children for the future. In virtually every election, improving education is a top candidate priority.

One major effort toward improvement has been through modifications to the "Foundation Program," which establishes the formula for distributing state funds

to local schools. Major adjustments in the late 1990s have significantly increased funding for school systems in the poorer parts of the state.

Another set of efforts has also shown signs of real success over the past decade—initiatives that focus intensely on nurturing fundamental skills. A cornerstone has been the Alabama Reading Initiative (ARI), developed by the State Department of Education. The goal of ARI is to enable every child to become a successful reader by improving the quality of reading instruction. The initiative provides extensive training to teachers to help them teach in proven and effective ways. This training integrates the best practices of phonics and the

Above: Students at Foley Middle School, Baldwin County. Below: A class at William L. Radney Elementary School in Alexander City.

Students use a clinometer and GPS during an activity in a program within the Alabama Math, Science, and Technology Initiative.

whole-language approach. With its effectiveness established through a series of tests and its procedures standardized over a decade, the Alabama Reading Initiative is now being extended to school systems across Alabama.

So far, the results have been impressive. From the fall of 2003 though the spring of 2008, for example, third graders improved from 44 percent to 69 percent proficiency on the DIBELS test in oral reading fluency. As State Superintendent of Education Dr. Joe Morton reported recently, "The United States Department of Education (USDE) published an entire publication simply called 'Alabama' that praised the accomplishments ARI has made in our state. Not in recent memory has Alabama served as a model for other states to emulate in educational programs. Now we are leading the nation in fourth-grade reading gains. We are seeing improvement never experienced by any other state according to the National Assessment of Educational Progress (NAEP)."

Similarly, the Alabama Math, Science, and Technology Initiative (AMSTI) seeks to improve teaching and learning in math and science. AMSTI was designed by a committee of K–12 educators, higher education representatives, and business leaders. Like the ARI, AMSTI provides teachers with extensive professional development and with equipment and materials needed to improve math and science instruction. The methods focus on hands-on, activity-based instruction.

External evaluations indicate that AMSTI is highly successful. Students in AMSTI schools scored dramatically higher on the Stanford Achievement Test in math, science, and reading and on the Alabama High School Graduation Exam compared to similar schools that had not participated in AMSTI. As of 2008, AMSTI had trained approximately 16,000 teachers and administrators and provided services to more than 300,000 students. By the 2009–10 school year, approximately half of all Alabama schools will be served by AMSTI.

This focus on the quality of instruction is just part of a larger drive to improve Alabama's public school systems. Alabama educators have worked to increase graduation rates, and the state ranked sixth in the nation in graduation improvement rates between 2002 and 2006. Another positive indicator is the number of students taking Advanced Placement (AP) tests. In 2008, the number of students taking the tests increased by 24.3 percent, compared with the national average of 8.6 percent. Scores improved as well. The number of students achieving scores of 3.5 or higher grew by 7.8 percent, compared with the national average increase of 5.7 percent. From 2002

Students in a computer lab at Sumter County High School in York.

The 2009 first- and second-place state champions, with their creative writing teacher at Loveless Academic Magnet Program (Montgomery), in the Alabama State Council on the Arts' Poetry Out Loud program.

to 2008, the increase in Alabama was 69 percent.

Several school districts around the state have had notable success with magnet schools in attracting students to accelerated programs in academics, arts, and technology. The Loveless Academic Magnet Program (LAMP) High School in Montgomery, for example, was honored by Governor Riley and the State Board of Education in 2008 for being the top academic high school in the state, the 25th best in the nation, and the fifth best magnet school in the nation, in various national educational rankings. Out of a 2009 graduating class of about eighty students, fourteen were National Merit Scholarship Program semifinalists.

In addition, two specialized public high schools consistently win national honors. The Birmingham-based Alabama School of Fine Arts is a state-operated residential and day school for especially talented students in arts fields such as music, dance, writing, and sculpture. The Mobile-based Alabama School of Mathematics and Science is a state-operated residential school for students pursuing advanced studies in math, science, and the humanities. Alabama is also home to a number of college-preparatory independent schools and church-related schools. Many of these private schools offer excellent training, and, collectively, they contribute to the range of options available for parents and students.

Postsecondary Education

Another important educational advance for Alabama over the last half century has been the development of a statewide system of two-year community and technical colleges. The purpose of the system has been to make higher education accessible and affordable to every citizen. An open enrollment policy, low tuition costs, and a variety of services to remove entrance barriers help make this next step in educational advancement an easy one. And the number of college sites across the state makes physical access convenient for virtually every Alabamian.

Like K–12 education, the Alabama Community College System is administered

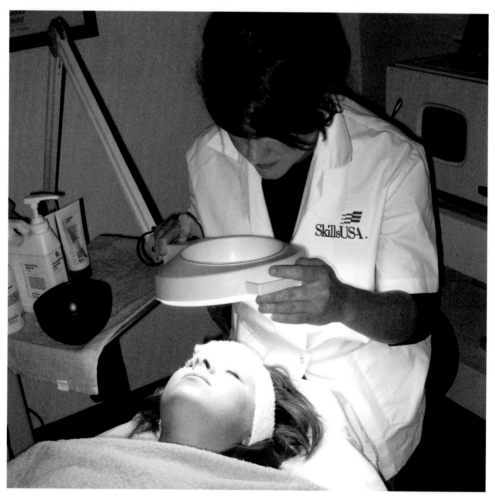

Cosmetology training at Northeast Alabama Community College's (Rainsville) Salon Institute.

Alabama Technology Network training course on milling machinery.

by the State Board of Education. The system consists of twenty-two comprehensive community colleges, four technical colleges, and Athens State University. Many of these schools (see listing, page 332) have branch facilities which allow them to extend their reach. The system also includes an array of adult education services and workforce development programs, including the Alabama Industrial Development Training Institute and the Alabama Technology Network. Altogether, the Alabama Community College System serves approximately 300,000 people each year.

One major traditional form of service for the Community College System has been as a bridge to four-year colleges and universities. The community colleges have made it possible for thousands of students who might not otherwise have been able to continue their education to become college graduates. For thousands of other students, the Community College System has provided the means for acquiring advanced technical skills and improving their ability to earn a living. The System also offers GED preparation and assistance to students who have experienced a break in their education and wish to return.

For the State of Alabama itself, the Community College System has been an extremely important economic development tool. Alabama officials have been able to use the training services of the technical colleges and other System programs as an inducement to attract new industries and better-paying jobs to the state. The System's Office of Workforce Development supports this goal by providing a wide range of services to help both job seekers and employers. The Alabama Career Center System provides job placement and training assistance to prospective workers. Alabama Industrial Development Training (AIDT) provides skills assessment and training programs for existing, expanding, and new businesses. The Alabama Technology Network (ATN) links two-year colleges, the University of Alabama System, Auburn University, and the Economic Development Partnership of Alabama to solve the needs of the state's existing manufacturing industry. The Community College System's Workforce Development director also serves as the director of the Governor's Office of Workforce Development, strengthening coordination between the System and the economic development efforts of the state.

An example of the System's efforts is AIDT's Ready to Work (RTW) program. It provides a hands-on career path for adults with limited education and employment experience. RTW's workplace environment provides trainees the entry-level skills for employment with most businesses and industries in Alabama. Successful completion of the training requires regular attendance and punctuality; instructor-certified "satisfactory" achievement of work ethic, organizational skills, attitude, and motivation; instructor-certified "satisfactory" achievement of problem-solving skills, workplace behaviors, computer skills, job acquisition skills, and manufacturing skills; attainment of acceptable assessment levels on applied mathematics, reading for information, and locating information; and a passing score on the written Alabama Certified Worker Examination.

As society has become more complex, lifelong learning has become an essential tool for individual success and for the economic health of the state itself. The Alabama Community College System performs a vital service to Alabama citizens, providing tools they need to improve their work skills and the quality of their lives. And the system serves as a foundation stone for the state's economic development efforts by helping provide existing and prospective employers with workers who are ready and able to contribute to the success of their businesses.

Higher Education

Alabama's four-year colleges and universities provide the state's citizens a wide array of educational options. They range from the University of Alabama System, with more than 50,000 students and three campuses, to Talladega College, with 350 students. The two largest and best-known universities are the University of Alabama and Auburn University, but Alabama also has a number of institutions that began as regional schools or branches and have become substantial centers of learning in their own right. The state is also home to a number of private colleges and universities. The most historically famous of these, Tuskegee University, became a national center of African American education under the leadership of Booker T. Washington. [See page 330 for a listing of and contact information for all Alabama colleges and universities.]

The following overview will begin with the state's three best-known schools and then briefly describe other state-funded universities in Alabama.

The historic University of Alabama campus in Tuscaloosa, with the Denny Chimes tower on the Quad in the foreground.

THE UNIVERSITY OF ALABAMA SYSTEM. The University of Alabama was officially established by the state in 1820, the year after Alabama became a state, though it did not formally open its doors to students until 1831. Its mission is "to advance the intellectual and social condition of the people of the State through quality programs of teaching, research, and service." The university began an engineering program (one of five in the nation at the time) in 1837; a medical college (in Mobile) in 1859; and a law school in 1872. The University of Alabama became a military school during the Civil War, and all but seven buildings were burned to the ground by Union troops in 1865. The first football team formed in 1892, the first women enrolled in 1893, and the first band organized in 1914–15. Today, the University of Alabama offers 80 undergraduate programs, 69 masters programs, 6 education specialist programs, 56 doctoral programs, and 1 law program to more than 25,000 students.

The medical college moved to Birmingham in 1945, paving the way for today's University of Alabama at Birmingham (UAB). Its academic buildings and medical complex now extend across much of Birmingham's Southside. The growth of UAB has been driven both by the research and health-services functions of the medical school and by the school's role as an urban university in Alabama's largest urban center. UAB and the medical school have made Birmingham a health-care center of national stature and have substantially strengthened Birmingham's economy.

In 1950, the University of Alabama opened an extension campus at Huntsville, in part due to the demand for education from the U.S. military personnel and scientists at Redstone Arsenal. In 1961, Wernher von Braun addressed the Alabama Legislature and asked for funds to build a research institute on the university campus. He observed that "opportunity goes where the best people go, and the best people go where good education goes." The legislature responded with $3 million for a new facility, further accentuating the research and technology capacities of what in 1966 became the University of Alabama in Huntsville (UAH).

Each of the three campuses of the University of Alabama System—Tuscaloosa, Birmingham, and Huntsville—has its own president, its own curriculum, and its own program priorities. The three institutions are governed collectively by the Board of Trustees of the University of Alabama System, whose work is supported by the office of the system chancellor.

Left: Auburn University students working in a lab. Below: The school's Department of Fisheries and Allied Aquacultures' off-shore research vessel "Mary Lou." Auburn is among the few American universities designated as a land-grant, sea-grant, and space-grant research center.

AUBURN UNIVERSITY. Established in 1856 as the East Alabama Male College, Auburn became the first land-grant college in the South in 1872, and its name changed to the Agricultural and Mechanical College of Alabama. Fraternities were formed in 1878 and became officially recognized by the school in 1883. In 1892, Auburn admitted its first women and organized its first football team. In 1899, the name was changed again, to the Alabama Polytechnic Institute, to reflect the school's scientific emphasis within its traditional liberal arts curriculum. As a land-grant university, Auburn also has the responsibility to support agriculture, forestry, and animal husbandry in Alabama. These services expanded with the 1887 Hatch Experiment Station Act, the Second Morrill Act of 1890, and the 1914 Smith-Lever Act into a substantial, federally supported extension service.

As the university grew and other programs expanded as well, the name of the school changed again in 1960 to Auburn University. The main campus had an enrollment during fall of 2008 of 24,137, and it currently offers degrees in thirteen schools and colleges at the undergraduate, graduate, and professional levels. Auburn University at Montgomery was established as a separately administered branch campus in 1967. AUM has developed rapidly as well, especially after moving to a 500-acre campus east of Montgomery in 1971. Current enrollment at AUM is about 5,000.

TUSKEGEE UNIVERSITY is a private school, but it receives state assistance. Founded in 1881, the school was led by Booker T. Washington until his death in 1915. In the

Tuskegee University student conducting a science experiment.

The Alabama A&M Maroon & White Marching Band performs during a Veterans Day Parade in Huntsville.

segregated South of the day, Washington was an advocate of self-reliance and vocational education. He promoted African American businesses and was instrumental in the building of black schools throughout the South. He also recruited George Washington Carver and other scholars to the school, formed alliances with white politicians and philanthropists, initiated a major extension service program, and maintained a lifelong devotion to his institution and to the South. Under later presidents, the U.S. Veterans Administration Hospital was created on land donated by the Institute, and a School of Veterinary Medicine was established. (Nearly 75 percent of black veterinarians in America today are Tuskegee graduates.) During World War II, the Tuskegee Airmen flight training program came to the Institute; the all-black squadrons were forerunners of the civil rights movement.

Tuskegee attained university status in 1985. It now has almost 3,000 students enrolled in five colleges: Agricultural, Environmental, and Natural Sciences; Business and Information Science; Engineering, Architecture, and Physical Sciences; Liberal Arts and Education; and Veterinary Medicine, Nursing, and Allied Health.

Other state universities in Alabama include:

ALABAMA **A&M UNIVERSITY** opened in 1875 as the Huntsville Normal School with William Hooper Councill, a former slave, serving as principal and president. In 1878, industrial education was added to the curriculum, and the legislature subsequently changed the school's name to State Normal and Industrial School at Huntsville. In 1891, the school became a land-grant university and added agricultural and mechanical studies. The school relocated to allow room for growth and changed its name to the State Agricultural and Mechanical College for Negroes. In 1919, it became a junior college and in 1939 began offering senior level coursework. The school became fully accredited in 1963. Today, the university serves more than 5,000 students and offers a variety of degrees, including doctorates.

ALABAMA **STATE UNIVERSITY** grew out of what was originally known as the Lincoln School, a private school established in 1867 for blacks in Marion. Seven years later, the state acquired the school, and it became the first state-supported school for blacks in

Dr. Karyn Scissum Gunn, director of biomedical research and training programs at Alabama State University.

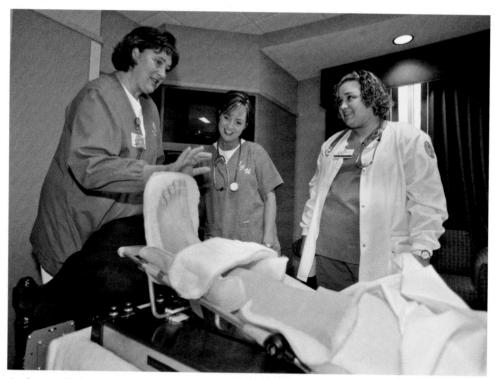

Jacksonville State University nursing students.

the United States. In 1887, the school relocated to Montgomery as the Normal School for Colored Students. By 1929, the school had expanded into a four-year institution, called the State Teachers College. As the school and its programs continued to grow, it became Alabama State College (1954) and Alabama State University (1969). ASU continues to evolve and now offers undergraduate, graduate, and specialist degrees in more than forty academic programs to more than 5,000 students.

JACKSONVILLE STATE UNIVERSITY was founded in 1883 as a state teacher's college, Jacksonville State Normal School. The school used the site and equipment of an earlier school, Calhoun College, that had closed. In 1930, the school became Jacksonville State Teachers College, and its role broadened. Twenty-seven years later, the school was renamed Jacksonville State College and began offering graduate degrees. It has been known by its present name since 1966 and has had its own board of trustees since 1967. The school now serves almost 10,000 students and offers nationally accredited programs in 38 specialized fields.

TROY UNIVERSITY was founded in 1887 as Troy State Normal School. The school's focus was entirely on teacher education until after World War II, when its student body doubled due to the G.I. Bill. New degrees were added to serve the larger student population, and in 1957 the school's name was changed from Troy State Teacher's College to Troy State College. In the 1950s, Troy began an extension program with courses at nearby military bases. Extension courses at Fort Rucker and Maxwell Air Force Base eventually grew into full academic campuses in Dothan and Montgomery, respectively. Troy has expanded its partnership with the military so that it now operates educational programs around the world. In 1967, Troy began operating under its own board of trustees, independent of the State Board of Education. To emphasize the change, the school became Troy State University; in 2004 it dropped "State" from its name. Nearly 30,000 students are now enrolled at Troy University facilities in 17 states and 11 countries.

Troy University's "Sound of the South" marching band at the New Orleans Bowl in 2006.

University of Montevallo theater students performing in the Palmer Theatre.

THE UNIVERSITY OF MONTEVALLO began as the Alabama Girls' Industrial School in 1896, with 150 students. It aimed to provide skills that would prepare women for futures not dependent on farm or mill work or reliance on male family members. In 1911, the name changed to Alabama Girls' Technical Institute. In 1923, a name change to Alabama College, State College for Women reflected the end of high school courses. The school was the first in the state to offer home economics degrees, and it also pioneered social work education, becoming only the second school in the nation to offer the program in 1925. It admitted its first men in 1956, and in 1969 it was renamed the University of Montevallo. Other changes included new programs such as pre-med, pre-law, and business administration as the school has sought to fulfill its mission today as "Alabama's public liberal arts university." Its average annual enrollment is around 3,000.

THE UNIVERSITY OF NORTH ALABAMA dates back to 1830 with the opening of LaGrange College in Franklin County, the first college chartered by the Alabama Legislature. In 1854, the majority of the faculty and all the students moved the school to Florence, and the name was changed to Wesleyan University. The Methodist school closed in 1871, and the state established the State Normal School at Florence on the same property. The school became a state teachers college in 1929, and graduate programs were added in 1957, when the name changed again—to Florence State College. In 1967, the state placed the school under a board of trustees independent of the State Board of Education, and in 1974, it became the University of North Alabama, underscoring its role as a comprehensive, regional university. More than 7,000 students attend UNA.

THE UNIVERSITY OF SOUTH ALABAMA began as an extension of the University of Alabama in 1944, offering associate degrees only. In 1960, the extension director and a group of Mobile businessmen petitioned the legislature to establish a state university in south Alabama. USA was formally established in 1963 and accredited in 1968. The following year, Brookley Field, a former air force base, was added to its campus. In 1969, the legislature approved the establishment of a medical school, and USA began acquiring medical facilities. The medical school opened in 1973. Today, USA has more

Intercollegiate athletes at the University of South Alabama, here taking on the University of West Florida.

Commencement at the University of West Alabama.

than 13,000 students enrolled in colleges or schools of Arts and Sciences, Business, Computer and Information Sciences, Education, Engineering, Medicine, Nursing, Allied Health Professions, Pharmacy, and Continuing Education.

THE UNIVERSITY OF WEST ALABAMA was chartered by the legislature in 1835 and opened in 1839 as Livingston Female Academy and State Normal College. The college closed during the Civil War, reopening around 1870. Although the state had provided limited assistance earlier, it took full control of the school in 1907. The school's name changed to State Teachers College in 1929. Graduate programs were added in 1957, and the college's name was changed again to Livingston State College. Ten years later, the name changed to Livingston University, and it was granted its own board of trustees. The present name was chosen in 1995. Approximately 4,000 students are enrolled at the university.

PRIVATE COLLEGES: Alabama is also home to a number of private colleges and universities. They include Birmingham-Southern College, Concordia College in Selma, Faulkner University in Montgomery, Huntingdon College in Montgomery, Judson

Above: The Administration Building at Spring Hill College, built in 1869. Below: A science class at Birmingham-Southern College.

UAB's Shelby Interdisciplinary Biomedical Research Building has more than 340,000 square feet of research space. Programs housed here include immunology and autoimmune diseases research; biomedical engineering and bone matrix research; and the Interdisciplinary Neurosciences Program. Projected research regimes include an initiative to study brain and spinal injuries, diabetes, and neurodegenerative diseases.

College in Marion, Miles College in Birmingham, Oakwood University in Huntsville, Samford University in Birmingham, Selma University, Southeastern Bible College in Birmingham, Spring Hill College in Mobile, Stillman College in Tuscaloosa, Talladega College, United States Sports Academy in Daphne, and the University of Mobile. [See page 335 for contact information.]

Research Centers

In addition to Alabama's colleges and universities, several affiliated research centers in the state are providing jobs, innovation, and opportunities for significant scientific discovery.

The University of South Alabama Mitchell Cancer Institute provides exceptional patient care through innovative treatment and both clinical and basic research. The USAMCI is the first academic cancer research institute in the upper Gulf Coast region. The institute began in 2000 and is funded through philanthropic gifts, including $22 million from the Mitchell family of Mobile; support from the State of Alabama, the City of Mobile, and Mobile County; federal appropriations; competitive contracts and grants; tobacco settlement funds; and the USA Foundation. The USAMCI is the largest research effort in the history of the University of South Alabama. By 2008, the center will represent a total investment of $125 million, including the USAMCI building, a $75 million investment in construction and equipment. In addition to improving cancer care, the institute stimulates the growth of a strong regional economy built on biomedicine and biotechnology. Together with the entire USA Health System, USAMCI focuses on discovery and development of new and more effective treatments for cancer.

Similarly, the new Richard C. and Annette N. Shelby Interdisciplinary Biomedical Research Building at the University of Alabama at Birmingham will bring together investigators from a wide variety of fields to study important health issues such as diabetes and autoimmune diseases, and to conduct bone, bioengineering, and brain research. The state-of-the-art facility is tangible evidence of the vital partnership between UAB, Birmingham, and the State of Alabama in the pursuit of better health, a stronger economy, and higher quality of life. The Shelby Building increased research space on the UAB campus by 25 percent. The 12-story facility, with 323,000 square feet of research and office space, was built at a cost of $100 million. Funding came from the federal government, the State of Alabama, Jefferson County, the City of Birmingham, and the Birmingham-based Community Foundation.

ALABAMIANS AT LEISURE

The traditional wisdom holds that all work and no play makes for dull people. Though they have a well-deserved reputation for hard work, Alabamians are anything but dull, so it must follow that they also know how to play. They do, and they always have. As we saw in the History section of this book, the first Alabamians played ball games and danced. Their pottery and clothing developed artistic embellishment. Their rituals were also social occasions. Early frontier settlers brought with them the music, stories, and pastimes of their traditional cultures, as has each new immigrant group ever since. Over the years, sports replaced combat, hunting and fishing turned into recreation, and the necessities of making clothing and furniture evolved into folk and fine arts. Today's Alabamians, like most Americans, enjoy rich leisure lives that are mostly separate from their livelihoods. There are far too many hobbies and pastimes in contemporary life to cover them all, but in this chapter we examine how Alabamians participate in sports and outdoor life, performing and fine arts, traditional arts, and enjoyment of tourist destinations and events.

Sports and Outdoor Life

Whether spectator or participatory, team or individual, amateur or pro, competitive or recreational, one can find it all in Alabama, and for all ages. Absent any major league professional teams, the leading spectator sports in the state are linked to the state's universities; auto racing and minor league baseball are the two big exceptions. Individually, hundreds of thousands hunt, fish, golf, hike, run, bowl, bicycle, birdwatch, canoe, camp, sail, water ski, skydive, rockclimb, play tennis, ride horses, and target shoot, to name just some of the avocations practiced. Amateur team sports—for adults and youth—in the state include softball, baseball, basketball, rugby, touch football, soccer, bowling, and ultimate frisbee. A select number of Alabamians also make a living as professional bass fishermen or deer hunters. The major outdoor activities include:

HUNTING AND FISHING: The 788,000-plus hunting and fishing licenses sold in Alabama in 2008 are one indicator of how avidly the state's residents and visitors pursue wild game—deer, turkey, alligator, game birds, rabbit, squirrel, wild pigs—and sport

Opposite: An afternoon at Riverwalk baseball park with the Montgomery Biscuits.

Bank fishing at Lake Eufaula, Barbour County.

fish. The fish include bass, bream, trout, catfish, mullet, mackerel, tarpon, crappie, gar, and even eels, shrimp, mussels, crayfish, and crabs.

Both the Bassmasters and Buckmasters organizations were founded in Alabama, and the Alabama Department of Conservation and Natural Resources states that hunting alone adds $840 million annually to the state's economy and supports more than 17,500 jobs. Some of these jobs are found in managed hunting preserves and camps such as Bent Creek and Water Valley lodges in Choctaw County, Piney Woods Hunting Lodge in Pike County, and Tatum Creek Hunting Camp in Dallas County, to name just a few. Other hunters simply take to the woods in bow or gun seasons and enjoy being outdoors even if they come home empty-handed.

Fishing similarly ranges from the children and adults who sit on a creek bank with a cane pole and a can of worms to the bass fishermen who have invested thousands of dollars in boats, trailers, and high-tech gear. All are welcome in Alabama, so long as they observe game and wildlife regulations. [See www.outdooralabama.com].

HIKING, CLIMBING, AND CAMPING: Alabama's varied terrain offers hiking trails for all skill and fitness levels, from leisurely walking paths leading through sand dunes

Rock climbing at Hurricane Creek Park, Cullman County.

Alabama hikers on the Pinhoti Trail.

on a Gulf Coast beach, to extended backpacking trips in the rugged Appalachian mountains.

The state's most famous trail, the Pinhoti, stretches one hundred miles from the south border of the Talladega National Forest to the Georgia state line. In the Tuskegee National Forest, the Bartram National Recreation Trail is an easy day hike or a two-day backpack trip through longleaf pine, dogwood, and oak forests to the banks and bottomlands of Choctafaula Creek. The Cherokee Ridge Alpine Trail is another day hike along the banks of beautiful Lake Martin, with its wildflowers, rock outcroppings, and history. The 33.3 mile multi-use Chief Ladiga Rail Trail begins in Anniston and is one of several rails-to-trails projects in the state. The Chief offers pastoral farmlands, wetlands, and streams, and is surrounded by mountain peaks. Those are just a few of the scores of hiking trails in Alabama. For more information and links to hiking groups, see www.800alabama.com/yooa/trails/hiking.cfm.

Alabama offers excellent rock climbing and rappelling sites. Mount Cheaha, the state's highest point, is a great place for lead and top-rope climbing, while Horse Pens 40 offers some of the best bouldering in the South. Hurricane Creek Park includes bolted sport, traditional, top rope, bouldering, and rappelling. There's also a class held each Saturday for first-time rock climbers. Palisades Park in Oneonta is a great bluff for top-rope climbing and rappelling; and Sandrock in Cherokee County offers traditional, bolted sport, top rope, rappelling, and bouldering. [See www.alabama.travel/yooa/adventure/rock.cfm.]

Whatever your idea of camping is, you can find it in Alabama. From Bear Creek Lakes in northern Alabama to Bon Secour National Wildlife Refuge along the Gulf Coast, the state's wide range of scenic camping grounds offers both cabins and campsites with amenities ranging from none to total RV luxury. There are twenty-four state parks and numerous private campgrounds. [See www.alapark.com.]

CYCLING: Bicyclists in Alabama range from casual weekend trail riders to serious road racers to weekday commuters. Excellent trail rides can be found in the state parks, national forests, and rails-to-trails routes. Several cycling clubs in the state also sponsor road rides and races of varying distances and intensity. Bicycle shops and clubs report increased interest in cycling in recent years due to energy conservation and health concerns. Links to cycling events and clubs in the state can be found at www.alabamacyclingnews.com.

Biking at Oak Mountain State Park, Pelham, Shelby County.

The Robert Trent Jones Golf Trail has become internationally known for the quality of its courses and its beauty. Top: The Shoals in Florence. Bottom: Cambrian Ridge in Greenville.

GOLF AND RACQUET SPORTS: Alabama's crown jewels of golf are the twenty-six Robert Trent Jones courses at eleven locations across the state. Developed by the Retirement Systems of Alabama, the RTJ Golf Trail offers 468 holes of championship golf in beautiful settings. The *Wall Street Journal* said the Trail "may be the biggest bargain in the country," and the *New York Times* called the Trail "some of the best public golf on Earth." For more information, see www.rtjgolf.com.

In addition, most cities in Alabama offer public and private courses; see www.al.com/golf for an overview and links to many courses. A golf variant is "frisbee golf," which has twenty-eight courses in seventeen cities around the state. See www.pdga.com to search for the locations in Alabama.

Tennis and racquetball have large followings in the state as well. The Birmingham-based Alabama Tennis Association coordinates sanctioned adult, junior, and team tournaments at locations throughout Alabama and sponsors some two dozen community tennis groups which promote the sport in their respective communities. The Westgate Tennis Center in Dothan, for example, has won three national tennis facility awards and is one of the premier tennis facilities in the southern U.S. Montgomery's annual Blue-Gray Tennis Classic hosts some of the nation's top collegiate players. Not as many people play racquetball, handball, or squash, but courts are found on college campuses and at most YMCAs and sports complexes. The Alabama Racquetball Association promotes tournaments and clinics.

Tournament play at the Dothan Westgate Tennis Center Pro Classic.

Little League Baseball at the Troy Sportsplex.

AMATEUR TEAM SPORTS: Alabamians of all ages play organized and impromptu team sports. Baseball, basketball, football, and soccer for children and youth can be found in almost every Alabama community. Softball is probably the most popular for adults, with community and church leagues enrolling thousands and thousands of players. Touch football leagues are not as common, but do exist. Adult soccer leagues have gained popularity in recent years, especially as Alabama's citizenry has become more diverse through immigration. Rugby teams can also be found in most larger cities. Contact a local recreation department for information about team sports. Bowling remains a popular individual and league sport at the state's approximately fifty bowling alleys. A sport gaining attention in Alabama is Ultimate Frisbee, which blends the constant running of soccer with the passing and catching of football. There are now three leagues with sixteen teams competing in the state, and countless more impromptu games in fields and parks.

BOATING: Alabama has more miles of navigable rivers than any other state. Our earliest inhabitants traveled these waterways in dugout canoes. We are still taking to the rivers, creeks, and lakes, but today in injection-molded kayaks, fiberglass and aluminum fishing and sailing boats, floating RVs called pontoon boats, and other pleasure craft.

Active sailing clubs sponsor recreational sailing and racing in Mobile Bay and on the state's largest man-made lakes. These include the Dixie Sailing Club on Lake Martin; the Birmingham Sailing Club on Lake Logan Martin; the Browns Creek Sailing Association on Lake Guntersville; the Buccaneer, Fairhope, and Mobile yacht clubs on Mobile Bay; and the Muscle Shoals Sailing Club on Wilson Lake and Wheeler Yacht Club on Wheeler Lake, both on the Tennessee River. The Crow's Nest Sailing Club on Lake Martin, affiliated with the commercial Lanier Sailing Academy, facilitates time-shared use of sailboats up to twenty-five feet.

Kayakers and canoeists can join paddling clubs across the state. These include Coosa River Paddling Club in Elmore County; Saddleback Canoe Club in south Alabama; Bama Backpaddlers and Birmingham Canoe Club in Birmingham; Tuscaloosa Canoe & Kayak Club, University of Alabama club, and Strokers, all in Tuscaloosa; and the Huntsville Canoe Club. These clubs stress safety and sponsor outings, whitewater rodeos, and instruction. See www.alabamawhitewater.com for more information and for links to outfitters for rentals and shuttle services.

One of Alabama's newest outdoor resources is 5 Rivers, the Delta Resource Center in the Tensaw Delta. The center features wildlife and conservation education and provides easy access to the Bartram Canoe Trail, a marked water trail (with overnight camping platforms) through beautiful cypress swamps near Mobile Bay. [See www.outdooralabama.com/outdoor-adventures/5rivers and www.outdooralabama.com/outdoor-adventures/ bartram.cfm]. Auburn University and the University of Alabama in Tuscaloosa and Huntsville compete in crew or competitive rowing, and there are rowing clubs in Huntsville, Montgomery, and Birmingham.

Kayaking on the Tombigbee River.

Recreational hot-air balloonists drifting over the Tennessee Valley near Decatur.

Sport Aviation, Skydiving, and Ballooning: Private flight instruction in small airplanes is offered at most municipal airports in Alabama. Locations in Cullman, Elberta, and Tuskegee offer skydiving instruction and supervised jumps. Balloon flights are offered by operators in Birmingham, Decatur, Gulf Shores, Huntsville, and Montgomery. Inquire at municipal airports or contact the Alabama Tourism Department for current information.

A specialized aviation hobby involves radio-controlled aircraft. The Auburn Planesman R/C Flying Club in east Alabama is a good source of information.

Running and Endurance Sports: Running clubs across Alabama have thousands of members and their sponsored events, from fun runs to marathons and triathalons, attract hundreds of thousands of participants each year. The annual Azalea Trail Run in Mobile is more than thirty years old and attracts top international athletes who finish at near world-record times. Other popular annual races are Birmingham's Vulcan Run, Montgomery's Jubilee Run, and Clanton's Peach Run. See www.runningintheusa.com or http://running.net to search for clubs or events in a particular area.

Target Shooting and Archery: Almost every county in Alabama offers safety instruction and recreational or competitive shooting venues and events in archery,

Competitors in the bike portion of the annual Florabama Mullet Man Triathlon.

Cave tours, laser light/ sound shows, kids' activities, camping, and more activities for the whole family are offered at DeSoto Caverns Park.

pistol, skeet, rifle, or sporting clays. See www.outdooralabama.com/hunting/shooting-ranges.cfm for current listings.

DIVING AND CAVING: Alabama's natural beauty is not all above ground. Its system of caves, sinkholes, and underground rivers is as extensive as anywhere in the world, thanks to the erosion over millions of years of the limestone deposits which underlie much of north Alabama. Cave exploring, however, can be dangerous to the untrained. Fortunately, the national headquarters of the National Speleological Society is located in Huntsville [see www.caves.org] and will provide information, instruction, and resources for anyone who wants to learn about or participate in caving.

You do not have to be an explorer, however, to visit Alabama caves. Russell Cave National Monument near Bridgeport and Cathedral Caverns near Grant are federal and state parks, respectively, and offer guided cave tours of the geology and history of the sites. Desoto Caverns Park near Childersburg is privately operated but has been open for public tours since the 1960s.

BIRDING AND PHOTOGRAPHY: Many Alabamians combine a love of nature and the outdoors with interests in science and photography through the hobby of birdwatching. Some 401 species have been recorded in Alabama, and the state offers a number of wildlife sanctuaries, including an Audubon bird sanctuary on Dauphin Island. The Alabama Ornithological Society [www.aosbirds.org] is the major organization in the

Birdwatching at Dauphin Island.

state for birdwatchers, but the Nature Conservancy and several local Audubon chapters also offer activities and information.

The Mobile-based Camera South is one of a number of photography groups in Alabama. The group meets monthly at the library on the University of South Alabama campus.

EQUESTRIAN AND DOG: The Alabama Horse Council [www.alabamahorsecouncil. org], the Alabama Arabian Horse Association [www.alabamaarabian.com], and the Racking Horse Breeders' Association [www.rackinghorse.com] are three of the organizations that sponsor horse-related shows, races, clinics, rides, and other activities in the state. Alabama dog fanciers are served by a number of dog, kennel, breed specialty, obedience, and specialized training clubs around the state. See www.barkbytes.com to search for local clubs and events.

SPECTATOR SPORTS: Alabama has no major league professional sports teams, but the Mobile BayBears, Birmingham Barons, Montgomery Biscuits, and Huntsville Stars

Auburn and Alabama mixing it up in the annual Iron Bowl.

are baseball teams in the AA Southern League. The Huntsville Havoc is a team in the Southern Professional Hockey League. Professional golfers, tennis players, and bass fishermen regularly compete in tournaments in Alabama, and professional athletes dominate the fields in several of the state's premier running events each year. The entertainment called professional wrestling is also eagerly followed by fans in arenas across the state. Auto racing is also a major draw and is covered separately below at "Motorsports."

But to many Alabamians, when you say *Sports*, they hear *College Football*. The University of Alabama and Auburn University have been nationally recognized football powers for a century, and their annual "Iron Bowl" showdown Thanksgiving weekend is as intense a rivalry as any in U.S. athletics.

At a slightly smaller scale, the annual "Turkey Day Classic" between Tuskegee University and Alabama State University and the "Magic City Classic" between Alabama State and Alabama A&M University are just as beloved by their fans and alumni. Collectively these teams have scores of conference and national championships, have elevated hundreds of players to the professional leagues, and have made household names of coaches and athletes like John Heisman, Paul "Bear" Bryant, Bart Starr, Joe Namath, and Bo Jackson, to mention just a few. In recent years, Troy University's football program has strengthened and gained national attention.

Football is popular at most of Alabama's other universities as well, along with basketball, baseball, soccer, swimming, gymnastics, track and field, volleyball, wrestling, tennis, golf, and other collegiate sports. But football continues to be the biggest attraction and has grown beyond just the game to include a wide variety of social activities that are set around games. Thousands of fans gather in recreational vehicles days before the kickoff. They catch up with old friends, share their special barbecue, and speculate on their teams' chances.

MOTORSPORTS: Alabamians are no different from the millions of other Americans who are fond of going fast and doing it loudly—or watching those who do. Motorsports in the state range from amateur go-cart and motocross racing for youngsters to the biggest professional thrill of them all, the flat-out, four-wide blast down the

The front-stretch dogleg in front of the grandstand at the high-banked Talladega Superspeedway.

frontstretch at Talladega Superspeedway, the "fastest, biggest motorsports facility in the world."

Talladega is part of NASCAR, a national, profitmaking organization which began in the 1940s to sanction and regulate stock car racing. Today, NASCAR racing is among the most popular spectator sports in the United States — as many as 200,000 fans pack the bleachers, skyboxes, and infield for each race around Talladega's 2.66 mile course. Over the years some of the most popular drivers cheered there by the fans have been fellow Alabamians, notably the famous "Alabama Gang," a group of drivers including Red Farmer and several members of the Allison family of Hueytown. When races are not underway, the Talladega track is used for automotive testing purposes as well as by driving schools and occasionally in film productions.

Talladega Superspeedway is big in every sense, but there are many smaller tracks around the state as well, from the paved Mobile International Speedway to short dirt tracks like the quarter-mile oval Flomaton Speedway. National Hot Rod Association-sanctioned drag races take place at strips in Phenix City, Atmore, Tuscumbia, Montgomery, Huntsville, Moulton, Woodstock, and Irvington. Motorcycle and kart racing are featured at the 1.35-mile Talladega Gran Prix Raceway. Motocross tracks are located in Gordo, Valley, Maplesville, Ozark, Tallassee, and a dozen more towns.

One of the most unusual racing facilities in the state is the Barber Motorsports Park in Leeds, near Birmingham. This 2.38-mile road track features seventeen turns and eighty feet of elevation, in an attractively landscaped natural setting. The track hosts sports car and motorcycle races that are open to the public, as well as private events organized by sports car and motorcycle clubs and driving schools that rent the track. An adjoining museum features more than nine hundred vintage and modern motorcycles as well as a collection of Lotus and other race cars.

Motorcycle racing at Birmingham's Barber Motorsports Park.

Dancers with the Alabama Ballet in Birmingham.

Performing and Fine Arts

The Alabama State Council on the Arts (ASCA), the state affiliate of the National Endowment for the Arts, is the clearinghouse for arts information, arts organizations, and arts education. ASCA's website [www.arts.state.al.us] provides listings and links to arts and artists, folklife, educational resources, grants, and other information about performing arts, literature, visual arts, folk arts and traditional culture, and local arts councils and cultural centers.

DANCE: The Alabama Dance Council in Birmingham [http://alabamadancecouncil. org] is a statewide nonprofit service organization for all dance forms and sponsors the annual Alabama Dance Festival. Alabama Ballet, Southern Danceworks, Sanspointe,

A "stomp dance" demonstration by Creek Indians and historical reenactors at Horseshoe Bend.

and Arova Contemporary Ballet, all in Birmingham, and the Montgomery Ballet are professional companies. Mobile Ballet, Birmingham Ballet, and Huntsville Ballet are semi-professional companies and are also attached to ballet schools. Pre-professional student companies include Alabama Repertory Dance Theatre at the University of Alabama, Orchesis Dance Company at the University of Montevallo, Southeast Alabama Dance Company in Dothan, Alabama Dance Theatre in Montgomery, Alabama Youth Ballet in Pelham (Stevan Grebel Center for Dance), Alabama Youth Ballet Theatre in Huntsville, Andalusia Ballet, Cullman Ballet, Downtown Dance Conservatory in Gadsden, Dunbar Dance Ensemble at Dunbar Magnet School in Mobile, Images Dance Ensemble at Grissom High School in Huntsville, and LynnTerra Ballet in Auburn.

The University of Alabama and Birmingham-Southern College offer the only dance majors in the state; the latter also has the only dance education certification program. Minors in dance are offered at Auburn, Troy, and Samford. The Alabama School of Fine Arts is the only statewide arts high school offering a concentration in dance. The Arts Council in Huntsville also hosts the only choreography competition in Alabama at the Panoply Arts Festival.

Traditional Native American dances are taught and demonstrated at Indian powwows and other ceremonial occasions; stomp dances are both a rhythmic dance form and the name for an event at which other dances may also be performed. Community-based and culturally specific dance companies include Corazon Flamenco, Devyani Dance Company (American Tribal Style Belly Dance), Jasmine Dance Troupe (traditional

Chinese Dance), M.A.D. Skillz Dance Company (Hip Hop), Nathifa Dance Company (West African Dance), Natyananda: Dance of India (classical Indian Dance), Notinée (classical-folk fusion dance of India), Sparkle Dance Company, Belly Dance Jewels (Egyptian-style belly dance), Umdabu Dance Company (South African Dance), Osumare African Drum & Dance Ensemble (West African Dance), all in Birmingham; Poza African Dance Troupe in Muscle Shoals; and Innergy, Inc., in Mobile.

Ballroom dance classes and events are sponsored by groups such as the Birmingham Ballroom Dance Association, the Ballroom Club of Montgomery, and the North Alabama Dance Club in Florence. Contra dance, a folk tradition in which couples dance in facing lines, has had a resurgence in Alabama. Dances are held regularly by the Birmingham Country Dance Society, Huntsville's North Alabama Country Dance Society, and the Tuscaloosa Contra Dancers. Clogging is another popular dance style practiced by groups such as Wetumpka's RiverBank Stompers [see www.clogdancing. com for a listing of groups and events]. Modern, hip-hop, Irish, Mexican, and belly dancing are among other forms now practiced in Alabama.

MUSIC: Alabama has rich musical traditions in forms from folk to classical. The state has produced such music giants as W. C. Handy, Hank Williams, and Nat King Cole, to name just three examples from the Alabama Music Hall of Fame in Tuscumbia [www.alamhof.org].

The Alabama Symphony Orchestra in Birmingham is the state's largest symphony,

The Huntsville Symphony Orchestra.

but Huntsville, Tuscaloosa, Montgomery, Mobile, and some smaller cities also have municipal orchestras. The Mobile Pops and the Baldwin Pops Band are among orchestras specializing in popular and show tunes. The Red Mountain Chamber Orchestra in Birmingham, the Huntsville Chamber Music Guild, Montgomery Chamber Music, and the Mobile Chamber Music Society are among groups presenting and performing compositions for string quartets or small ensembles. Mobile Opera and Opera Birmingham present professional opera productions.

Jazz and blues events are promoted and presented by the Magic City Blues Society in Birmingham, the Alabama Jazz and Blues Federation in Montgomery, and the Alabama Blues Project in Tuscaloosa, not to mention scores of nightclubs, bars, and juke joints. Similarly, country, bluegrass, rock, pop, and hip-hop/rap music are widely popular in Alabama and can be heard live at clubs throughout the state.

Gospel music is heard not only on Sunday morning but also at concerts in churches, school auditoriums, and civic centers across the state. The Central Alabama Southern Gospel Music Association [www.casgma.com] is one clearinghouse for information. The distinctive shape-note gospel music tradition is showcased with annual singing conventions, often uniting the black and white forms of the music; for more information, contact the Alabama Center for Traditional Culture, a division of Alabama State Council on the Arts [www.arts.state.al.us]. The ACTC also supports and documents musicians from recent immigrant groups into Alabama, such as Vietnamese, Cambodian, Korean, and Mexican.

VISUAL ARTS: Alabama supports a wide range of art museums, art and artist organizations, and art galleries featuring work in all disciplines. [See www.arts.state.al.us/arts-artists/visual-arts.html for a detailed listing.]

The Birmingham Museum of Art collection ranks among the Southeast's best, with more than 24,000 items, including a Wedgwood collection considered the finest outside England. Auburn's Jule Collins Smith Museum of Fine Art began with a fortuitous $1,072 purchase in 1948 of thirty-six paintings among a group acquired by the U.S. State Department but criticized as being the work of left-wingers; today the paintings are worth millions and the artists considered among America's finest. The Montgomery Museum of Art and the Westervelt Warner Museum of American Art in Tuscaloosa share a similar legacy of having major collections of American art assembled, respectively, by the Alabama industrialists Winton M. Blount and Jack Warner. Daphne's American Sport Art Museum and Archives is uniquely dedicated to the relationship between athletic competition and artistic expression and has perhaps the largest such collection in the world. Other art museums are located in Dothan, Gadsden, Huntsville, Mobile, and Ozark.

In recent decades, the state's folk artists have become especially well known. The

A patron enjoying one of the galleries at Dothan's Wiregrass Museum of Art.

Alabama Center for Traditional Culture documents the work of artists such as Bill Traylor, Mose Tolliver, Jimmie Lee Sudduth, Bernice Sims; potters Jerry Brown and the Miller family; quilters Betty Kimbrell, Nora Ezell, Yvonne Wells, and the members of the Freedom Quilting Bee; sculptor Charlie Lucas; basket-maker Lomia Nunn; and many others. Their work is sold in galleries, mounted in exhibitions, and featured in books and documentary films around the world.

LITERATURE: Alabama's distinguished literary tradition stretches from the French and British colonial period to the present in genres from fiction and poetry to autobiography, history, and travel and nature writing. The state's writers and their works are described in the online Encyclopedia of Alabama [www.encyclopediaofalabama.org/face/Article.jsp?id=h-2066]. Contemporary literature in the state is supported by the Alabama Writer's Forum [www.writersforum.org], the Alabama Center for the Book [www.alabamabookcenter.org], two university presses and a handful of independent book publishers, and by a half-dozen or more annual festivals (see the Tourism section below) devoted to writing, writers, and reading.

Public libraries located in every county and most communities are supported by the Alabama Public Library Service [http://statelibrary.alabama.gov], which also provides a regional library for the blind and physically handicapped. The Alabama Humanities Foundation [www.ahf.net] supports lectures and discussion programs by writers and scholars at many public libraries.

Tourism, Festivals, and Historic Sites

Tourists from out of state as well as Alabama's own citizens can choose their destinations for history, culture, adventure, sports, nature, or relaxation. They can choose settings from the mountains to the seashore, and accommodations from primitive campsites to luxurious resort hotels.

The best source of information about destinations and events is the Alabama Tourism Department. ADT maintains a comprehensive website at www.alabama. travel and can be called at 1-800-ALABAMA or emailed at info@tourism.alabama. gov. The department publishes online and printed guidebooks and newsletters about top tourist destinations, vacation and reunion planning, events and festivals, and specialty guides to topics such as the Civil War, Civil Rights, black heritage, music, dining, and lodging.

STATE PARKS: Alabama's twenty-two state parks—most offering lodging, RV and tent camping, and a wide variety of recreational opportunities—are operated by the Department of Conservation and Natural Resources and have their own web site at www.alapark.com. Information is also available from 1-800-ALAPARK. The parks include:

North Alabama: Joe Wheeler in Lauderdale County; Monte Sano in Madison County; Cathedral Caverns in Jackson County; Lake Guntersville in Marshall County; Buck's Pocket in DeKalb County; DeSoto in DeKalb County; and Rickwood Caverns in Blount County.

Central Alabama: Lake Lurleen in Tuscaloosa County; Oak Mountain in Shelby County; Cheaha in Clay and Cleburne counties; Wind Creek in Tallapoosa County; Chewacla in Lee County; Paul M. Grist in Dallas County; Chickasaw in Marengo County; Lakepoint Resort in Barbour County; and Roland Cooper in Wilcox County.

RV camping at Roland Cooper State Park in Wilcox County.

South Alabama: Bladon Springs in Choctaw County; Blue Springs in Barbour County; Frank Jackson in Covington County; Florala in Covington County; Chattahoochee in Houston County; Meaher in Mobile and Baldwin counties; and Gulf in Baldwin County.

NATIONAL PARKS IN ALABAMA: Six historic or scenic sites in Alabama are public attractions operated by the National Parks Service of the U.S. Department of the Interior. *Russell Cave National Monument* near Bridgeport is an important archaeological site for North American prehistoric peoples. *Little River Canyon National Preserve* atop Lookout Mountain features natural resources and Appalachian cultural heritage. The *Natchez Trace Parkway*, part of which runs through northwest Alabama, is a National Scenic Byway and All-American Road. *Horseshoe Bend National Military Park* near Dadeville commemorates the 1814 battle between the Upper Creek Indians and the force commanded by General Andrew Jackson. *Tuskegee Institute National Historic Site* is on the campus of Tuskegee University and includes the George Washington Carver Museum and the home of Booker T. Washington. Nearby is the *Tuskegee Airmen National Historic Site*, where the nation's first black pilots trained during World War II. In addition, two National Trails maintained by the Parks Service run through Alabama: the *Trail of Tears* commemorates the forced removal of Cherokee Indians from their homelands in the 1830s; and the *Selma to Montgomery Trail* memorializes the 1965 Voting Rights March. For more information on all these sites, see www.nps. gov/state/AL.

NATIONAL FORESTS IN ALABAMA: Four national forests in Alabama are under the jurisdiction of the USDA Forest Service and offer activities such as camping, boating, hiking, biking, shooting, and swimming. The forests are Bankhead in northwest Alabama; Talladega in northeast and central Alabama; Tuskegee in east Alabama; and Conecuh in south Alabama. See www.fs.fed.us/r8/alabama for more information.

FESTIVALS AND FAIRS:

The first *Mardi Gras* observance in North America was in Mobile in 1703, and three centuries later the tradition is still going strong. For weeks each spring the streets fill with marching bands, colorful floats with masked riders, and huge crowds of parade-watchers. Mobile's Mardi Gras is considered more family friendly than the one in New Orleans, but the secret krewes that organize the parades and host the elaborate balls employ just as much pomp and merriment.

The *Alabama Renaissance Faire* in Florence draws as many as 30,000 persons the last weekend of October to take part in and witness costumed pageantry, food, music, and activities. [See www.alarenfaire.org.]

A Mardi Gras parade in Mobile.

Alabama's rich literary tradition is showcased at several annual events. The largest include the *Alabama Book Fair* in Montgomery, the *Alabama Writers Symposium* in Monroeville, *Writing Today* in Birmingham, and *Southern Voices* in Hoover. [See www. writersforum.org for links to these events.]

City Stages in Birmingham, *Jubilee Cityfest* in Montgomery, *Bayfest* in Mobile, and *Big Spring Jam* in Huntsville are annual music festivals which attract many thousands of fans to hear top recording stars in all genres of music. Downtown streets are closed and stages are erected. These festivals usually include art exhibits, children's activities, running events, and food vendors. [See www.citystages.org; www.jubileecityfest.com; www.bayfest.com; and www.bigspringjam.org.]

Smaller carnivals/fairs are held in some counties, but the *Alabama State Fair* in Pelham and the *Alabama National Fair and Agricultural Exposition* in Montgomery are the largest midway carnival type events held in Alabama each year. The Montgomery event also functions as a statewide showcase for exhibitions of livestock, cooking and canning, photography and art, and 4-H and FFA/FHA projects. [See www.alabamastatefair.org and www.alnationalfair.org.]

Since 1958, the *Southeastern Livestock Exposition and Rodeo* held each spring in

Montgomery has featured the nation's top professional and amateur rodeo cowboys. [See www.bamabeef.org/SLE/sle-HOME.htm.]

The annual *Blessing of the Fleet* in Bayou La Batre is a colorful ritual that for sixty years has combined celebration and prayer for a bountiful harvest with a parade of decorated shrimp boats, arts and crafts exhibits, and food.

Dothan's *National Peanut Festival* each fall is appropriately the nation's largest peanut festival since about half the U.S. peanut crop is grown within a hundred-mile radius of this southeast Alabama city. The 10-day event attracts more than 160,000 visitors and includes games, rides, arts and crafts, parades, animal shows, beauty pageants, concerts, agricultural displays, and field crop exhibitions. [See www.nationalpeanut-festival.com.]

Mule Day in Winfield is held on the fourth Saturday in September and draws some 25,000 persons each year to a mule judging, a parade with mule- and horse-drawn buggies and wagons, music, arts and crafts, an antique car show, and other activities recalling Alabama's traditional past.

The *Opp Rattlesnake Rodeo*, featuring Eastern Diamondback snakes caught in the wiregrass countryside of south Alabama, has been a spring fixture in this south Alabama city for almost a half century. As many as 20,000 people attend activities including snake shows, snake races, music, buck dancing, and arts and crafts.

HISTORY AND EDUCATIONAL TOURISM: Alabama's many historic sites attract visitors from within the state and from around the world. The two most significant history

Rocketry exhibits at the Marshall Space Flight Center in Huntsville.

categories are Civil War and Civil Rights, but the state also has important sites related to Native Americans, African Americans, military and space, music, industry, literature, science, and architecture. Selected highlights include:

Native American sites include Moundville, one of the most important Mississippian ceremonial towns in North America; Russell Cave, with evidence of even earlier Indian civilization; Horseshoe Bend, where the climactic battle of the 1813–14 Creek War was fought; Fort Mims, site of an early battle which escalated the war; and Fort Toulouse, which was first a French then an American outpost in Indian territory and where defeated Creeks surrendered in 1814 to General Andrew Jackson.

Civil War sites include the Alabama Capitol, where the Confederacy was organized and Jefferson Davis was inaugurated; Fort Morgan, at the mouth of Mobile Bay; and Fort Blakeley, where the last major battle of the Civil War was fought.

Civil Rights sites include the locations in Montgomery where key events in the Montgomery Bus Boycott took place and leaders lived and preached; the places in Anniston, Birmingham, and Montgomery connected to the 1961 Freedom Rides; the building in Tuscaloosa where George Wallace stood in the schoolhouse door; the church where four girls died in Birmingham in 1963; the bridge in Selma where voting rights marchers were beaten in 1965; and many others. Major museums include the Birmingham Civil Rights Institute, the Rosa Parks Museum and the Civil Rights Memorial in Montgomery, the Voting Rights Museum in Selma, and the Tuskegee Multicultural Center for Human and Civil Rights and Tuskegee Airmen site.

The Marshall Space Flight Center in Huntsville offers exhibits, classes, and camps for all ages to explore the history of space exploration. Exhibits at Maxwell Air Force Base in Montgomery trace the history of military aviation, as well as the world's first flying school established by the Wright Brothers in 1910 (the site of the first night airplane flight). The U.S.S. *Alabama* is a decommissioned World War II battleship anchored in Mobile Bay, with adjoining displays of military aircraft and the U.S.S. *Drum*, a World War II submarine. The U.S. Army Aviation Museum in Ozark exhibits one of the world's largest collections of military helicopters.

The Sloss Furnaces in Birmingham and the Tannehill Ironworks near Bessemer offer exhibits and tours of two different periods in iron and steel production which figured prominently in Alabama industrial history.

Famous persons whose homes, workplaces, or burial sites in Alabama have been preserved include Jefferson Davis, Martin Luther King Jr., Hank Williams, Scott and Zelda Fitzgerald, Nat King Cole, and Ralph Abernathy in Montgomery; Helen Keller in Tuscumbia; Joe Louis near LaFayette; Bear Bryant in Tuscaloosa; Jesse Owens in Lawrence County; Red Eagle (William Weatherford) near Tensaw; William Rufus King in Selma; Booker T. Washington and George Washington Carver in Tuskegee; and W. C. Handy in Florence. Also in Florence, one of Frank Lloyd Wright's Usonian homes has been restored and is open to the public.

The previously mentioned Marshall Space Flight Center in Huntsville, the McWane Science Center in Birmingham, and the Gulf Coast Exploreum in Mobile are science museums with exhibits, hands-on activities, and IMAX theaters.

The Anniston Museum of Natural History offers exhibitions on weather, plate tectonics, and geology; the various landscapes in the state; and plants, animals, geology, archaeology, and the environment. [See www.annistonmuseum.org.]

The Alabama Museum of Natural History on the University of Alabama campus in Tuscaloosa was founded in 1831, making it the oldest museum in the state. Its exhibits showcase fossils, including a basilosaurus (see page 646); rocks and minerals, including the Hodges meteorite, the only extraterrestrial object known to have struck a human, Ann Elizabeth Hodges of Sylacauga; and archaeology. The majority of the archaeological artifacts are located at nearby Moundville Archaeological Park. [See amnh.ua.edu/wordpress and moundville.ua.edu/home.html.]

Several significant history museums in the state offer exhibits, artifacts, preserved or recreated historic structures, and interpretative reenactments. These include:

• The Alabama Department of Archives and History (ADAH) in Montgomery houses the state museum of Alabama history. Galleries include maps, portraits, and artifacts documenting Alabama life from 10,000 BC through the present. For children, a Hands-on Gallery offers educational activities, and "Grandma's Attic" has artifacts

The Alabama Department of Archives and History in Montgomery.

A period reenactor at Old Alabama Town in Montgomery.

or replicas of everyday items from the past. In addition, ADAH is the state repository for state government records and has an extensive collection of books, periodicals, private papers, genealogical records, and other documents which can be viewed in the reference room. [See www.archives.alabama.gov.]

• Montgomery's Old Alabama Town is a six-block collection of more than fifty 19th- and 20th-century structures which have been authentically restored. The structures showcase a wide variety of architecture, history, and lifestyles. [See www.oldalabamatown.com.]

• American Village in Montevallo is an American history and civics education center created by legislative act in 1995 and dedicated in 1999. It may have been the first civic education campus in the U.S. to provide experience-based learning for children. [See www.americanvillage.org.]

• Dothan's Landmark Park is a 100-acre park preserving the natural and cultural heritage of Alabama's Wiregrass Region. The park includes an 1890s living history farm with farmhouse, smokehouse, cane mill, syrup shed, and sheep, goats, and pigs; a one-room schoolhouse; a drugstore/doctor's office; a country store; and a church. Nature enthusiasts can enjoy the park's natural trail, interpretive center, planetarium, and wildlife exhibitions. The park hosts folklife festivals, antique car shows, traveling exhibits, concerts, and workshops. [See www.landmarkpark.com/index.html.]

In addition, a dozen historic sites with structures, exhibits, and activities are managed by the Alabama Historical Commission. [See http://www.preserveala.org]. These sites are:

• The Alabama Capitol in Montgomery includes the old House, Senate, and Supreme Court chambers; the historic and still-used offices of the governor and several other constitutional officers; the Goat Hill gift shop; and portraits of former governors.

• The Belle Mont Mansion in Tuscumbia is an outstanding example of Thomas Jefferson's influence on early American architecture, including high-quality brickwork with contrasting wood trim, a preference for hilltop building sites, and other neoclassical architectural ideas of the Italian Renaissance architect Andrea Palladio.

• Confederate Memorial Park in Chilton County is the site of Alabama's only Old Soldiers Home for Confederate Veterans. The site included cottages, a hospital, dairy barn, mess hall, an elaborate water and sewage system, and an administration building, but now is home to a museum on Alabama's Confederate veterans.

• Fendall Hall in Eufaula is one of Alabama's outstanding Italianate houses, with elaborate and rare interior decorative painting. Completed in 1860, its treasures include period furnishings, marble mantles, and a black and white marble tiled entry. The five-acre site includes gardens and archaeological features.

• Fort Mims in Baldwin County commemorates the battle of August 30, 1813, which is considered a leading cause of the Creek War of 1813–14 (see page 56).

• Fort Morgan in Gulf Shores was completed in 1834 and was active during the Civil War, the Spanish-American War, and World Wars I and II. The fort is most famous for its role in the 1864 Battle of Mobile Bay when Union admiral David Farragut "damned the torpedoes." The massive fort contains more than 40 million bricks laid by skilled masons, many of whom were slaves. The fort features an active living-history program that interprets all the military periods and holds an annual event commemorating the Battle of Mobile Bay.

• Fort Toulouse/Fort Jackson near Wetumpka, Elmore County, is an important archaeological site revealing the history of Native Americans, Spanish explorers, French soldiers, English and Scottish traders, and American settlers. Frequent living-history events showcase a recreated 1751 French fort and Creek Indian houses, and the partially restored 1814 Fort Jackson (see page 49).

• Gaineswood in Demopolis is one of America's finest Greek Revival houses, a masterpiece whose exceptional interior spaces have domed ceilings, elaborate plasterwork, and a facing pair of gilt mirrors that endlessly reflect each other. Gaineswood was built in 1843–61. The house museum contains many original family furnishings and objects. The grounds feature a gazebo, a slave house, and a small building that was most likely a detached kitchen.

• The Montgomery Greyhound Bus Station is the site of the 1961 attack by a white mob on the Freedom Riders, an act that shocked the nation and led the Kennedy administration to side with civil rights protestors for the first time. The most obvious result of the rides was a sweeping ruling by the Interstate Commerce Commission that effectively ended segregation in interstate bus, train, and air transportation.

• Magnolia Grove in Greensboro was the boyhood home of Spanish-American War hero and U.S. Congressman Richmond Pearson Hobson. Magnolia Grove, c. 1840,

Remnants of columns among the ruins of Old Cahawba.

is a Southern archetype—what many tourists expect to see in the Deep South. The mansion is filled with original family furniture, and the walls are lined with portraits of the Croom and Hobson families.

• Old Cahawba in Dallas County served as Alabama's first capital from 1819 to 1826. It was once a thriving antebellum river town. By 1900, however, most of Cahawba's buildings had burned, collapsed, or been dismantled. The picturesque ruins are an important archaeological site.

• Pond Spring is the post-Civil War home of General Joe Wheeler in Hillsboro, Lawrence County. Following the Civil War, Wheeler, a Confederate general, U.S. congressman, and Spanish-American War general, became a national symbol for reunification and reconciliation. The site includes a dogtrot log house built around 1818, a circa 1830 Federal-style house, the 1880s Wheeler house, eight farm-related outbuildings, two family cemeteries, an African American cemetery, a small Indian mound, a pond, a boxwood garden, and other garden areas.

ALABAMA
GOVERNMENT
DATA

Governor Riley fulfilling one of his gubernatorial duties, giving the annual State of the State address, shown here in the old House chamber in the Capitol.

4

THE EXECUTIVE DEPARTMENT

The 1901 Constitution of the State of Alabama, Section 42, divides the operation of government into "three distinct departments": Legislative, Executive, and Judicial. Section 43 provides for a separation of powers between the three functions.

Section 112 then specifies the following officers within the Executive Department:

> Governor
> Lieutenant Governor
> Attorney General
> State Auditor
> Secretary of State
> State Treasurer
> Superintendent of Education
> Commissioner of Agriculture and Industries
> and a sheriff for each county (see "Counties").

Section 114 provides for these officers to be elected for four-year terms. However, in 1969, Amendment 284 changed the office of Superintendent of Education from elected to appointed, and added an elected nine-member Board of Education (the governor serves as president).

Three additional statewide elected offices were created when the legislature established the Public Service Commission (its members also serve four-year terms).

The above state officials are profiled in this section, followed by the governor's cabinet and other state departments and agencies, most of which are overseen by the governor in his capacity as the state's chief executive officer.

BOB RILEY

52nd Governor of Alabama

2003–

OFFICE OF THE GOVERNOR

State Capitol
600 Dexter Avenue
Montgomery, AL 36130
(334) 242-7100
www.governor.alabama.gov

Governor's Authority, Responsibilities, and Qualifications

Section 113 of the Alabama Constitution declares, "The supreme executive power of this state shall be vested in a chief magistrate, who shall be styled 'The Governor of the State of Alabama.'" A governor must be thirty years old, a U.S. citizen for ten years, and a resident of Alabama for seven years at the time of election. The governor's responsibility is to faithfully execute the laws of Alabama, to present reports and budgets to the legislature, and to command the state militia. The governor has the authority to compel reports from other state officials, to call the legislature into special or emergency session, and to make appointments to many boards and commissions.

About Governor Bob Riley

Governor Riley was sworn into office for a second term in January 2007, following a successful first term marked by initiatives to improve education, to stimulate economic growth and industrial development, and to promote integrity in the operation of state government. Riley's performance in his first term and the vision he declared for a second term were popular with voters, and he won reelection with 58 percent of the vote over the Democratic nominee, then-Lieutenant Governor Lucy Baxley.

BACKGROUND: Riley is a native of Ashland, the county seat of Clay County, where his family has lived on ranches and farms for six generations. At age twenty, he earned a business degree from the University of Alabama, returned home, married his high school sweetheart, Patsy Adams, and started a business with his brother selling eggs door-to-door. That family-owned small business became one of the largest poultry operations in the Southeast. Over the next three decades, Riley ran a number of successful businesses including a grocery store, a trucking company, a car dealership, a real estate company, and a pharmacy. He also raises cattle on his Ashland ranch.

Bob and Patsy Riley are the parents of four children: Rob, Jenice (deceased), Minda, and Krisalyn. In their private lives, the Rileys have been active in church, school, and community affairs in the Ashland area.

CONGRESSIONAL SERVICE: In 1996, at age fifty-two, Riley decided to enter public service. Though politically unknown, he was elected to represent Alabama's third congressional district in the U.S. House of Representatives. In the House, Riley supported balanced budgets, tax cuts, and national defense, and served on the House Armed Services Committee. He won reelection to the House in 1998 and 2000, but had made a campaign promise to serve only three terms. As his congressional service was nearing an end, he announced his candidacy for governor and then went on to defeat two opponents in the Republican primary with 73 percent of the vote. In the November 2002 general election, he defeated the incumbent Democratic governor, Don Siegelman.

FIRST TERM: Governor Riley made economic development a major initiative of his first term. During this period, Alabama achieved low unemployment rates, experienced the creation of more than 100,000

BOB AND PATSY RILEY

new jobs, and attained a budget surplus. For its record of economic development, Alabama was named the State of the Year in 2002, 2003, 2004, and 2005 by *Southern Business and Development Magazine*, the first time in the magazine's history a state had won the title for four consecutive years. The award is based on job announcements in seventeen southern and border states.

Riley also strongly supported improvements in education. During his administration, a vigorous economy allowed funding for Alabama schools to be increased by $2 billion. Riley worked to invest much of these funds in classroom initiatives, especially the Alabama Reading Initiative and the Alabama Math, Science, and Technology Initiative. Both programs existed in only a few schools before Riley became governor. Under his leadership, the reading initiative was fully funded and was expanded to every kindergarten through third-grade classroom during his first term. The result was that Alabama's fourth graders led the nation in reading improvement on the National Assessment of Educational Progress, commonly called the "Nation's Report Card," in 2008. The Alabama Math, Science, and Technology Initiative was also significantly expanded from only 40 schools to almost 700 during his term. Students in AMSTI schools outperform those in non-AMSTI schools on every test given by the State Department of Education. In 2005, Riley launched a new education initiative designed to increase learning opportunities, especially for students in rural schools. This initiative, the ACCESS Distance Learning program, uses video-conferencing and the Internet to allow students to take advanced-level courses and electives that might not be available at their schools. In the fall of 2009, every high school in the state will have ACCESS and Alabama will become the first state in the nation to have this distance-learning capabilities in all its high schools.

Riley also was the chief proponent of a comprehensive tax reform plan that supporters projected would have made Alabama's tax system fairer while increasing state revenue by $1.2 billion over five years. The reform would have lowered the financial burden on two-thirds of the taxpayers in the state, especially poor people. That effort failed by a two-to-one margin in a 2003 referendum.

SECOND TERM: In 2007, Riley proposed an ambitious agenda called "Plan 2010," a blueprint for his second term. This allocated more funding for schools, including significant funding for construction projects and repairs and expansions of the state's reading, math, science, and distance-learning initiatives. Riley also succeeded in expanding Alabama's "First Class" pre-kindergarten program, which is rated the best in the nation for its quality by the National Institute for Early Education Research. He also proposed pro-growth tax incentives to help middle-class families, make health care more affordable, and create new jobs.

Alabama continued to successfully recruit international companies. In 2007, Riley announced the state had won the competition for the ThyssenKrupp steel facility. The project—valued at $4 billion—is the largest non-government economic development project in the nation's history. Alabama repeated in 2007 as State of the Year in the *Southern Business and Development Magazine* rankings for job creation. Riley has continued to support efforts to make government more transparent and accountable, including the creation of a website that discloses all state spending, contracts, grants, and leases. Throughout his two terms, Riley proposed tougher ethical standards for state officials and more government transparency, but these proposals were routinely defeated by the legislature. These proposals would require the disclosure of lobbyists' spending and financial ties of public officials, and grant subpoena power to the Alabama Ethics Commission.

The Governor's Cabinet

To assist him in administering the business of state government, Governor Riley has a twenty-five-member cabinet consisting of three key staff members and the heads of twenty-two state departments. Those department heads and their agencies are separately profiled beginning on page 271. Three cabinet members serve directly on the governor's staff: Chief of Staff Dave Stewart, Communications Director Jeff Emerson, and Legal Advisor Ken Wallis.

	PHONE	FAX
Governor's Office	(334) 242-7100	(334) 353-0004
Chief of Staff's Office	(334) 242-4738	(334) 242-2766
Scheduling Office	(334) 353-1188	(334) 242-0937
Press Office	(334) 242-7150	(334) 242-4495
Constituent Services Office	(334) 242-7100	(334) 353-0004
Finance Office	(334) 242-7160	(334) 353-3300
Appointments Office	(334) 353-7530	(334) 242-0936
Legal Office	(334) 242-7120	(334) 242-2335
Policy Office	(334) 242-7116	(334) 353-3012
Legislative Affairs Office	(334) 242-7989	(334) 242-4310
Governor's Mansion	(334) 834-3022	(334) 240-3466
Administrative Services Office	(334) 353-7510	(334) 353-1190

The historic Alabama Governor's Mansion near downtown Montgomery has been the home of Alabama's first families since 1950.

JIM FOLSOM, JR.
30th Lieutenant Governor of Alabama
2007–

OFFICE OF THE LIEUTENANT GOVERNOR
11 South Union Street, Suite 725
Montgomery, AL 36130
(334) 242-7900 • FAX (334) 242-4661
www.ltgov.alabama.gov

About the Office of Lieutenant Governor

The lieutenant governor is first in the line of succession to the governor and serves as president of the Alabama Senate. The office is filled by an election every four years and may be held for no more than two consecutive terms. Alabama's lieutenant governor, unlike those of many other states, is elected separately from the governor; the constitutional qualifications for election are the same for both offices.

As presiding officer of the Senate, the lieutenant governor is responsible for calling the body into session, for preserving order in the chamber, and for determining points of order. The lieutenant governor also plays important roles in the appointment of standing committees, the assignment of bills to those committees, and the appointment of citizens of Alabama to various boards, commissions, and authorities. In addition to serving as the Senate's presiding officer, the lieutenant governor assumes the duties of the governor in the event of the governor's death, impeachment, disability, or absence from the state for more than twenty days.

About Lieutenant Governor Folsom

Jim Folsom Jr., is unique among Alabama's lieutenant governors in that he has served in the office twice before and is also a former governor himself and the son of another governor.

BACKGROUND: Folsom was born May 14, 1949, the oldest son of Governor James E. "Big Jim" Folsom Sr. and Jamelle Folsom. He was raised in Montgomery and Cullman with his eight brothers and sisters. Folsom paid his way through Jacksonville State University by working at a local yarn mill and in the post office. He graduated from JSU in 1974 and subsequently worked for the Alabama Department of Industrial Relations and Reynolds Metals before beginning his political career. He is married to Marsha Guthrie Folsom; they are the parents of two children, Meghan and James III.

PUBLIC SERVICE: In 1978, Folsom was elected to the Public Service Commission, where he served two terms. In 1986, he was elected lieutenant governor and was reelected in 1990. Folsom has characterized his service while lieutenant governor as being a coalition builder to promote the passage of beneficial legislation.

In April 1993, Governor Guy Hunt was convicted of ethics law violations and was removed from office. Folsom then succeeded him, becoming Alabama's fiftieth governor.

As governor, Folsom promoted diversification in state government by appointing African Americans and women to positions in his cabinet and other state offices. The controversial Confederate flag atop the dome of the Capitol came down during his administration. Governor Folsom championed the recruitment of a Mercedes-Benz automobile plant to Alabama, thus beginning a surge in manufacturing investment and employment which has continued in the state through the past decade and a half.

CURRENT SERVICE: Folsom was elected in November 2006 to his present term as lieutenant governor, defeating the Republican nominee, Luther Strange.

The Lieutenant Governor's Staff

Chief of Staff	Mike Martin
Executive Assistant	Linda Adams
Legislative Director	Mike Martin
Director of External Affairs	Chip Hill
Director of Constituent Services	Roy Hightower
Director of Community Outreach	Janet Buskey
Office Administrative Assistant	Marilyn Taylor

OFFICE OF THE ATTORNEY GENERAL

500 Dexter Avenue
Montgomery, AL 36130
(334) 242-7900 • FAX (334) 242-4661
www.ago.alabama.gov

TROY KING
Attorney General of Alabama
2004–

About the Attorney General

The attorney general provides legal representation for the State of Alabama, its officers, departments, and agencies; defends the state in all lawsuits in which the state is named as a defendant; and represents the state in all court proceedings in which the constitutionality of a state statute is challenged.

The attorney general also may initiate civil or criminal court actions to protect the state's interests or to enforce state law. The attorney general represents the state in all criminal actions in the appellate courts of the State of Alabama and in habeas corpus proceedings in the federal courts. He has the authority to superintend and direct the prosecution of any state criminal case. The attorney general issues legal advice in formal or informal written opinions to authorized public officials and agencies.

About Attorney General Troy King

King began his public service in Alabama in 1995 as legal adviser to former Governor Fob James, and later served in the same capacity to Governor Bob Riley. In between, he served as an assistant attorney general. In 2004, Riley appointed King to succeed Attorney General Bill Pryor when the latter was appointed to the federal judiciary. King then won election in 2006 to a full term, defeating the Democratic nominee, John Tyson Jr.

BACKGROUND: King was born and raised in Elba and graduated from Troy State University and from the University of Alabama School of Law. He and his wife, Paige, have three children (Briggs, Colden, and Asher) and are members of Montgomery's First Baptist Church, where he teaches Sunday school. King serves on the VOCAL

(Victims Of Crime And Leniency) and Salvation Army boards of directors.

AS ATTORNEY GENERAL: King's Family Protection Unit is a clearinghouse for information on child abuse and exploitation, elder abuse and exploitation, consumer protection, and welfare fraud. He has supported passage of the Alabama Open Meetings Law, laws to suppress methamphetamine usage, and the Community Notification Act for stricter punishments and monitoring of sex offenders. He has prosecuted illegal gambling, corrupt public officials, and murderers. He has personally appeared at parole hearings to speak on behalf of crime victims and their families.

The Attorney General's staff

The office was classified under the judicial branch until 1868, when the attorney general was made an executive officer of the state. In 1939, the Alabama Merit System Act was passed and employees of the attorney general's office became subject to the rules and regulations of the State Personnel Board.

As of 2008, the attorney general's staff includes more than 150 employees with diversified skills and training in law, public administration, investigation, consumer affairs, utility regulation, secretarial science, and other disciplines.

Consumer Affairs Division 1-800-392-5658
Office of Victim Assistance.. 1-800-626-7676
Family Protection Unit.. 1-800-230-9485
Workers Compensation Fraud.. 1-800-923-2533
Administrative Hearings Division... (334) 242-7433
Capital Litigation Division... (334) 242-7408
Constitutional Defense, General Civil & Administrative Law .... (334) 242-7300
Criminal Appeals Division .... (334) 242-7386
Environmental Division .... (334) 242-4260
Investigations .... (334) 242-7345
Legislative Affairs .... (334) 242-7351
Medicaid Fraud Division.. (334) 353-8793
Opinions Division.. (334) 242-7403
Public Corruption & White Collar Crime...................................... (334) 353-8494
Public Information... (334) 242-7300
Violent Crimes Division... (334) 242-7407

OFFICE OF THE STATE AUDITOR

State Capitol, Room S-101
Montgomery, AL 36130
(334) 242-7010 • FAX (334) 242-7650
www.auditor.alabama.gov

SAMANTHA SHAW
State Auditor
2007–

About the State Auditor

The Alabama Constitution requires the state auditor to make a complete report to the governor each year of receipts and disbursements by the state, claims audited and paid out, and all taxes and revenues collected and paid into the Treasury, and the source thereof.

The Code of Alabama provides authority for the state auditor to perform post-audits of the accounts and records of the state treasurer and the accounts and records of the Department of Finance. In these post-audits, every voucher for which a warrant is issued by the comptroller is subject to the scrutiny of the auditor.

In addition, the state auditor serves as a member or ex officio member on the State Board of Adjustment; State Board of Appointments for Boards of Registrars; State Board of Compromise; Alabama Education Authority; and Penny Trust Fund.

The state auditor is responsible and accountable for all state personal property through a central control and by ensuring that each department has appointed a property manager who is responsible for that department's non-consumable personal property. The office audits the equipment in each state agency every two years.

About State Auditor Samantha Shaw

Shaw has spent most of her professional life as an accountant. She entered politics by working in the campaigns of her husband, Alabama Supreme Court Justice Greg Shaw, and U.S. Senator Jeff Sessions. Her 2006 election as state auditor was her first try for public office. She defeated the Democratic nominee, Janie Baker Clarke.

BACKGROUND: Shaw was born and raised in Homewood. She is the daughter of William M. "Bill" and June Daly Slimp. She earned degrees in family and child development from Auburn University and in business administration from Auburn

University Montgomery. She and her husband, Greg, have two sons, Gregory and Christopher. The Shaws are members of Frazer Memorial United Methodist Church. She is a former chairman of the Montgomery County Republican Executive Committee and is a member of the Capital City Republican Women, the Alabama Federation of Republican Women, and the Camellia Club.

Contacts in the State Auditor's Office

Samantha "Sam" Shaw .... sam.shaw@auditor.alabama.gov

Kathie Lynch, Chief of Staff .... kathie.lynch@auditor.alabama.gov

Karen Barron, Executive Assistant .... karen.barron@auditor.alabama.gov

Demea Mercer, Executive Secretary .... demea.mercer@auditor.alabama.gov

Patty Toney, IT Systems Specialist .... patty.toney@auditor.alabama.gov

Trent Wilkins, State Auditor Inventory Officer... trent.wilkins@auditor.alabama.gov

Robert Davis, State Auditor Inventory Officer...... robert.davis@auditor.alabama.gov

Ken Baker, State Auditor Inventory Officer .... ken.baker@auditor.alabama.gov

Mark Lashley, State Auditor Inventory Officer ....mark.lashley@auditor.alabama.gov

Kevinetta Marshall, Prop. Div. Account Clerk....kevi.marshall@auditor.alabama.gov

Chris McCracken, Senior Accountant .... chris.mccracken@auditor.alabama.gov

OFFICE OF THE SECRETARY OF STATE

State Capitol, Suite S-105
Montgomery, AL 36130
(334) 242-7200 • FAX (334) 242-4993
www.sos.state.al.us

BETH CHAPMAN
Secretary of State
2007–

About the Secretary of State

The secretary of state has more than one thousand duties, most of which involve processing and filing public records. The secretary of state serves as the governor's personal notary public, using the Great Seal of Alabama to attest the governor's signature on writs of arrest, contracts, deeds, leases, information on municipal incorporations, and the certificates of all notaries public registered in Alabama, as well as other executive records.

The secretary of state is Alabama's "Chief Elections Official." The office maintains elections records, which include vote totals and certified ballots, and campaign finance records, which disclose the financial transactions of candidates and political action committees. The secretary of state is also responsible for certifying certain elections results and must certify statewide amendments. Copies of certificates of election, commissions, and oaths of office are also maintained by the office. Various divisions of the office retain business records including Lands and Trademarks, Corporations, and Uniform Commercial Code (UCC). The Lands and Trademarks Records Division preserves the original state land records dating back to Alabama's statehood and records of all trademarks registered in Alabama. The state has some 200,000 corporate filings, and the Corporations Division receives some 300 requests each day for information in those files. In addition, the UCC Division maintains more than 220,000 financing statements that are filed by attorneys and banking institutions.

About Secretary of State Beth Chapman

Prior to her election in 2006, Chapman had served as appointments secretary for Governor Fob James, press secretary for Lieutenant Governor Steve Windom, and state auditor from 2002 to 2006. In addition, she has owned and operated a successful business.

BACKGROUND: Chapman grew up in Greenville and received her BS from the University of Montevallo and her MA from the University of Alabama at Birmingham. She is also a graduate of Princeton University's Executives in State Government Management Institute. She and her husband, James, have two sons, Taylor and Thatcher. Chapman has worked with the Developing Alabama Youth Program, Family Connections, and the Shelby County Child Advocacy Center, and has served on the boards of the Shelby County Family Resource Center, the Children's Policy Council, the Crisis Center, the Court Appointed Special Advocates, Lifeline Ministries, and Turning Point Foundation. She is also a motivational speaker and Christian comedian.

CURRENT SERVICE: Secretary Chapman has served as a member of the Governor's Committee on Accountability and is an active member in the National Association of Secretaries of State and the United States Election Assistance Commission. She was elected to Alabama's Electoral College in 2004. She has written two books, including *The Power of Patriotism*, which was awarded the George Washington Honor Medal.

Contacts in the Secretary of State's Office

Beth Chapman .... beth.chapman@sos.alabama.gov
Emily Thompson, Chief of Staff .... emily.thompson@sos.alabama.gov
Virginia Bunn, Executive Secretary .... virginia.bunn@sos.alabama.gov
Tamara Cofield, Public Information Secretary .... tamara.cofield@sos.alabama.gov
Adam Thompson, State HAVA Director .... adam.thompson@sos.alabama.gov
Jean Brown, Chief Legal Advisor .... jean.brown@sos.alabama.gov
Jeannie Price, Finance Division Director .... jeannie.price@sos.alabama.gov
Linda Holmes, Personnel Division Director .... linda.holmes@sos.alabama.gov
Janice McDonald, Elections Division Director .... janice.mcdonald@sos.alabama.gov
Mickey Moore, Information Systems Director .... mickey.moore@sos.alabama.gov
Jamyla Genous, Lands and Trademarks Div. Dir. ..... jamyla.genous@sos.alabama.gov
Judy Bradshaw, ACTS/Athlete Agents/Codes/Research.. judy.bradshaw@sos.alabama.gov
Sharon Staton, Corporations Division Director .... sharon.staton@sos.alabama.gov
Rebecca Morris, Business Services Director .... rebecca.morris@sos.alabama.gov
Brenda Young, UCC Division Director .... brenda.young@sos.alabama.gov

OFFICE OF THE STATE TREASURER

State Capitol, Suite S-106
Montgomery, AL 36130
(334) 242-7500 • FAX (334) 242-7592
www.treasury.alabama.gov

KAY IVEY
State Treasurer
2003–

About the State Treasurer

The state treasurer's office serves as the state's bank. Its primary goal is to promote public confidence in the Treasury through prudent investment policies. The office administers many programs designed to improve the quality of life for Alabamians. The Alabama Prepaid Affordable College Tuition (PACT) program and the Alabama Higher Education 529 Fund offer savings and investment opportunities for families planning for future college expenses. The unclaimed property program reunites rightful owners with lost or abandoned property. The Cash Management Office receives, deposits, and invests all state funds.

The state treasurer serves on the Bond Commission and performs various functions in regard to bonds issued by the state or the various state agencies having authority to issue bonds. The treasurer's specific duties depend on the provisions set out in the official statement of the bond issue. The treasurer's office maintains records of all bonds that are general obligations of the state or guaranteed by a revenue source of the state.

About State Treasurer Kay Ivey

Ivey is serving her second term as the state's chief financial official. In 2002, she defeated the Democratic nominee, Stephen Foster Black, and in 2006 she was favored by the voters over Democratic rival Steve Segrest.

BACKGROUND: A Camden native and a 1967 graduate of Auburn University, Ivey was a high school teacher before becoming an officer with Merchants National Bank in Mobile. She has also served as a hospital administrator; assistant director of the Alabama Development Office; director of Government Affairs and Communications for the Alabama Commission on Higher Education; and reading clerk for the Alabama House of Representatives. Ivey is a member of the First Baptist Church of

Montgomery, the Montgomery Rotary Club, and the board of the Montgomery YMCA. She is the first Alabama Girls State alumnus (1962) elected to an Alabama constitutional office.

CURRENT TERM: Ivey has worked on a bipartisan basis with legislators to improve Alabama's unclaimed property program and its two state-sponsored college savings programs. She has served as president of the southern region of the National Association of State Treasurers and currently serves on the executive board of the College Savings Plans Network.

Contacts in the State Treasurer's Office

Kay Ivey ....alatreas@treasury.alabama.gov
Daria Story, Assistant State Treasurer................... Daria.Story@treasury.alabama.gov
Anthony Leigh, Deputy State Treasurer.......... Anthony.Leigh@treasury.alabama.gov
Edward Dicks, Fiscal and Internal Operations..Edward.Dicks@treasury.alabama.gov
Mary Frank Crew, Executive Assistant......... Maryfrank.Crew@treasury.alabama.gov
Rita Pope, Administrative Assistant .... Rita.Pope@treasury.alabama.gov
Tom Ray, Information Systems Manager................. Tom.Ray@treasury.alabama.gov
J. Michael Manasco, General Counsel............ Mike.Manasco@treasury.alabama.gov
Linda Hopper, Personnel Manager .... Linda.Hopper@treasury.alabama.gov
Dianne Reynolds, Bonds Division Manager . Diane.Reynolds@treasury.alabama.gov
Mickey Daughtry, SAFE Director .... Mickey.Daughtry@treasury.alabama.gov
Tanya Cooley, Cash Management Director ...... Tanya.Cooley@treasury.alabama.gov
Roman McLeod, Cash Mgmt. Asst. Dir. .... Roman.Mcleod@treasury.alabama.gov
Ken Hoyle, Cash Management Asst. Director ...... Ken.Hoyle@treasury.alabama.gov
Helen Mitchell, Alabama Trust Fund ....Helen.Mitchell@treasury.alabama.gov
Ralph Ainsworth, Unclaimed Property Dir..Ralph.Ainsworth@treasury.alabama.gov
Chad Wright, Unclaimed Property Asst. Dir. ....Chad.Wright@treasury.alabama.gov
Lisa Williams, Claims Manager .... Lisa.Williams@treasury.alabama.gov
Lavonda Hairston, Business Reporting...... Lavonda.Hairston@treasury.alabama.gov
Brenda Emfinger, College Savings Program. Brenda.Emfinger@treasury.alabama.gov
Pam Stevenson, College Savings Asst. Dir.......Pam.Stevenson@treasury.alabama.gov

Department of Agriculture and Industries

1445 Federal Drive
Montgomery, AL 36107
(334) 240-7100 • FAX (334) 240-7190
www.agi.alabama.gov

About the Commissioner of Agriculture and Industries

Ron Sparks
Commissioner
2003–

The commissioner of agriculture and industries investigates, ascertains, and develops the industrial opportunities of the state, collects statistics regarding the state's industrial development, regulates measurements and weights, and fosters and develops the agricultural and industrial interests of the state. The commissioner also executes the agricultural and industrial policies of the State Board of Agriculture and Industries.

About Commissioner Ron Sparks

Ron Sparks is serving his second term as Alabama's commissioner of agriculture and industries. He had been appointed assistant commissioner in 1999.

BACKGROUND: Sparks was born and raised in Fort Payne, where he worked in the local sock mills during high school. He served as a member of the U.S. Coast Guard Honor Guard and the Coast Guard Search and Rescue Squad Division, winning the Coast Guard Commendation Medal for Meritorious Service in the Performance of Duty. After serving in the Coast Guard, Sparks graduated from Northeast State Community College and was elected a DeKalb County commissioner. He has also served as director of DeKalb County's 911 system and as state president of Alabama 911. He has owned two businesses in Fort Payne and has worked in the television industry. For more than twenty years, Sparks has coached youth athletics. He is the father of Misty, Sparky, and Luke, and the grandfather of Jake and Atticus.

AS COMMISSIONER: Sparks has promoted family farms in Alabama and markets for the state's agricultural products. He has gained notice for meeting with national and international leaders including—Cuban President Fidel Castro and the secretaries of agriculture of Benin, Puerto Rico, Ukraine, Argentina, and Brazil—to expand markets. His initiatives include the Farm to School program, country of origin label-ing, and increased consumer protection. He has also been an advocate of children's nutrition programs.

In the past two years, the department has constructed three new diagnostic labo-ratories for animal disease research and prevention. The new Auburn laboratory is the central reference laboratory in a four-lab system and replaced outdated and crowded facilities. New branch laboratories were also added in Elba and Boaz. A fourth labora-tory, in Hanceville, was opened in 1995. These labs have provided more than 900,000 laboratory test results to help ensure animal health in Alabama.

Sparks has developed the department's Emergency Preparedness and Investigations divisions to prevent agriculture-related crimes, a priority in the post-9/11 era. The department has also advanced technologically with new and improved phone systems and equipment, up-to-date computers and software, teleconferencing abilities, and a generator that will provide uninterrupted power during emergency circumstances. Sparks has served as president of the Southern Association of State Departments of Agriculture, and he is president of the National Association of State Departments of Agriculture in 2009.

Contacts in the Office of the Commissioner of Agriculture and Industries

Ron Sparks, Commissioner .... (334) 240-7100
Glen Zorn, Assistant Commissioner .... (334) 240-6594
Sharon Fulmer, Deputy Commissioner .... (334) 240-7106
Teresa Smiley, Deputy Commissioner .... (334) 240-7285
Jerome Gray, Deputy Commissioner .... (334) 240-7101
Scott Absher, Assistant Chief of Staff .... (334) 240-7105
Dr. Brad Fields, Director of Emergency Programs .... (334) 240-7278
John Key, International Trade .... (334) 240-7311
Karen Wurtz, Petroleum Commodities .... (334) 240-7127
Dr. Tony Frazier, State Veterinarian .... (334) 240-7253
Lance Hester, Food Safety .... (334) 240-7202
Dr. Terry Slaten, Meat Inspection .... (334) 240-7210
Tony Cofer, Pesticide Management .... (334) 240-7239
Dennis Barclift, Plant Protection .... (334) 240-7225
Randy Fulmer, Weights and Measures .... (334) 240-7133
Hassey Brooks, Executive Assistant .... (334) 240-3877

Public Service Commission

100 North Union Street
RSA Union, Suite 850
Montgomery, AL 36130
(334) 242-5218 • fax (334) 242-2041
www.psc.alabama.gov

About the Public Service Commission

The Public Service Commission ensures a regulatory balance between regulated companies and consumers in order to provide consumers with safe, adequate, and reliable services at rates that are equitable and economical. In 1915, the commission evolved from the Railroad Commission, which was created in 1881 to regulate railroads. Between 1881 and 1915, the Railroad Commission's jurisdiction expanded to include express companies, sleeping car companies, railroad depots, telephone and telegraph companies, and transportation companies operating as common carriers over water, toll bridges, toll ferries, and toll roads. The Public Service Commission was charged with the regulation of utilities providing electricity, gas, water, and steam; companies operating street or inter-urban railways; and rail and communication companies previously regulated by the Railroad Commission. Over the years, the commission's authority has broadened to include regulation of utility rates, motor transportation companies, natural gas transmission and distribution systems, and railroad tracks and equipment. The commission is composed of three statewide elected officials: a president and two associate commissioners.

Lucy Baxley
President
2008–

About President Lucy Baxley

Baxley was elected PSC president in 2008. As a former lieutenant governor and two-term state treasurer, she is one of Alabama's most experienced office holders. She was the first woman elected lieutenant governor in Alabama, and her election as PSC president marked the first time women had simultaneously held all three PSC seats. A native of Houston County, she has also worked in municipal

JAN COOK
Commissioner, Place 1
1992–

SUSAN PARKER
Commissioner, Place 2
2006–

and county government and at the state level in the attorney general's office and the transportation department. She then had a successful career in real estate in Birmingham before deciding to re-enter public life in 1994 with her first run for elective office. She won the state treasurer's office that year and was reelected in 1998.

As state treasurer, Baxley overhauled the unclaimed property program and expanded the Prepaid Affordable College Tuition program. She then served a term as lieutenant governor before running unsuccessfully for governor in 2006.

Baxley has two children and two grandchildren and is married to Jim Smith. They live in Montgomery and are active members of Frazer Memorial United Methodist Church.

Commissioner Jan Cook

Cook is serving her fourth term as Public Service Commissioner, Place 1. She has a BA from Auburn University. Prior to election to the PSC, Cook served on the Dozier City Council and was state auditor 1983–1991. She is a life member of the Alabama League of Aging Citizens and holds honorary memberships in the Future Homemakers of America and Delta Kappa Gamma. Cook has an honorary State Farmer's degree and has been selected as Beta Sigma Phi's Woman of the Year. She is a member of Dozier Methodist Church.

Commissioner Susan D. Parker

Parker was elected to Place 2 in 2006. She holds four college degrees, including a PhD from the University of Alabama. Prior to becoming involved in politics, Parker worked in public education for twenty-five years. Before her election to the PSC, Parker served as state auditor (1999–2003) and was the Democratic nominee for the U.S. Senate in 2002. She has served as president of numerous non-profit organizations including Boys and Girls Clubs, Heart Association, Cancer Society, Leukemia Society, Big Brothers/Big Sisters, and United Way. She has also chaired leadership programs for the chambers of commerce in Athens and Decatur. Parker has provided training programs throughout the country for non-profits on board development, communication, and fund-raising. Parker and husband Paul are members of Cumberland Presbyterian Church.

Contacts in the Public Service Commission's Office

LUCY BAXLEY'S OFFICE

Lucy Baxley, President .... lucy.baxley@psc.alabama.gov

Lisa M. Parrish, Executive Assistant .... lisa.parrish@psc.alabama.gov

JAN COOK'S OFFICE

Jan Cook, Commissioner, Place 1 .... jan.cook@psc.alabama.gov

Kelly Mulero, Executive Secretary .... kelly.mulero@psc.alabama.gov

Karen Rogers, Administrative Support Assistant ..... karen.rogers@psc.alabama.gov

SUSAN D. PARKER'S OFFICE

Susan D. Parker, Commissioner, Place 2 .... susan.parker@psc.alabama.gov

David Rountree, Chief of Staff .... david.rountree@psc.alabama.gov

Brad Williams, Executive Assistant. .... brad.williams@psc.alabama.gov

Angier Johnson, Director of Media Relations ..... angier.johnson@psc.alabama.gov

Denise Harris, Executive Secretary .... denise.harris@psc.alabama.gov

STATE BOARD OF EDUCATION

Until 1969, Alabama's superintendent of education was a constitutional officer, elected every four years. However, Amendment 284 changed the office of superintendent from elected to appointed and added a board of education with eight members elected from districts (for a map of the districts, see page 270). The members serve staggered four-year terms, and the governor serves as president by virtue of his elected office. The board sets all policy and budgets for Alabama schools in grades K-12 and also appoints the superintendent, who then serves as the chief executive officer of the Department of Education (see page 318). The board meets for K-12 matters in the Gordon Persons Building in Montgomery on the second Thursday of each month. Work sessions for K-12 are held in the same building on the fourth Thursday of each month. The board also oversees Alabama's two-year colleges and appoints the chancellor of the Department of Postsecondary Education (see page 322). The board meets in a work session for Postsecondary matters on the second Thursday of each month in the Alabama Center for Commerce in Montgomery and holds its formal Postsecondary meetings in the Gordon Persons Building on the fourth Thursday of each month. For more information, go to www.alsde.edu/html/boe.asp.

DISTRICT 01
Randy McKinney, Vice President (R)
P.O. Box 2999
Gulf Shores, AL 36547
(251) 967-2166; Fax: (251) 968-4340

DISTRICT 02
Betty Peters (R)
3507 Huntington Place
Dothan, AL 36303
(334) 794-8024; Fax: (334) 793-6303

DISTRICT 03
Stephanie W. Bell (R)
3218 Lancaster Lane
Montgomery, AL 36106
(334) 272-2777; Fax: (334) 260-0100

DISTRICT 04
Ethel H. Hall, Vice Pres. Emerita (D)
7125 Westmoreland Drive
Fairfield, AL 35064
(205) 923-6093; Fax: (205) 929-6104

DISTRICT 05
Ella B. Bell (D)
2634 Airwood Drive
Montgomery, AL 36108
(334) 229-6866; Fax: (334) 229-5050

DISTRICT 06
David F. Byers Jr. (R)
2 Metroplex Drive, Suite 111
Birmingham, AL 35209
(205) 263-2400; Fax: (205) 263-2300

DISTRICT 07
Gary Warren (R)
P.O. Box 704
Haleyville, AL 35565
(205) 486-9696

DISTRICT 08
Mary Jane Caylor, Pres. Pro Tem (D)
P.O. Box 18903
Huntsville, AL 35804
(256) 489-0541; Fax: (256) 489-0552

MEMBERS OF THE STATE BOARD OF EDUCATION, 2009

PRESIDENT
GOVERNOR BOB RILEY

DISTRICT 1
RANDY MCKINNEY

DISTRICT 2
BETTY PETERS

DISTRICT 3
STEPHANIE BELL

DISTRICT 4
ETHEL H. HALL

DISTRICT 5
ELLA B. BELL

DISTRICT 6
DAVID BYERS JR.

DISTRICT 7
GARY WARREN

DISTRICT 8
MARY JANE CAYLOR

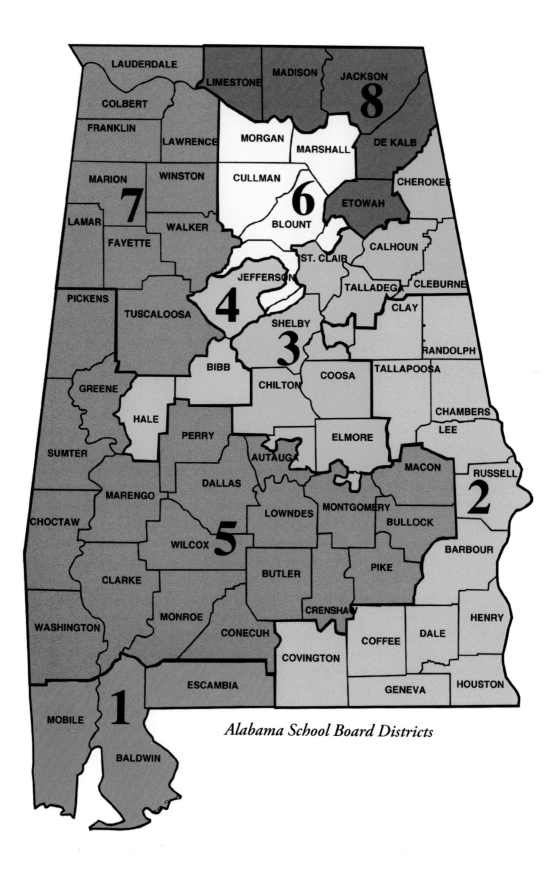

Alabama School Board Districts

CABINET LEVEL AGENCIES

Alabama's state government is a major enterprise, involving more than 35,000 state employees in several hundred departments, agencies, boards, commissions, and subagencies, and with an annual budget now exceeding $22 billion. The governor is the chief executive, but he relies on the heads of the various departments to implement policy and handle the details. The directors of twenty-two agencies under the direct control of the governor and three of his key staff members serve in the cabinet.

Under Governor Bob Riley, the cabinet officers and their agencies are charged with implementing a statewide strategic plan called "SMART Governing." State agencies set goals and benchmarks based on the governor's priorities, which gives the governor, his staff, and cabinet the ability to better manage the state and make more informed decisions in the budgeting process.

In addition to prioritizing the state's needs, the cabinet officers support the governor's mission and philosophy, monitor revenues and expenditures, manage capital assets, and work to improve efficiency in state government services.

For 2009, Governor Riley identified as his strategic priorities the creation of a "world-class" education system, the reform of state government, the expansion of economic growth, the protection of Alabamians' lives and property from crime, and the securing of quality of life through improved health care and preservation of resources.

As of June 2009, serving as cabinet members to accomplish those goals were:
- Chief of Staff   Dave Stewart
- Communications Director   Jeff Emerson
- Legal Advisor   Ken Wallis
- Director of Finance   Bill Newton
- Superintendent of Banking   John Harrison
- Director of Industrial Relations Tom Surtees

• Commissioner of Insurance	Jim Ridling
• Commissioner of Labor	Jim Bennett
• Commissioner of Mental Health	John Houston
• Commissioner of Revenue	Tim Russell
• Commissioner of Senior Services	Irene Collins
• Director of Tourism	Lee Sentell
• Director of Transportation	Joe McInnes
• Director of Public Safety	Colonel Christopher Murphy
• Director of Development Office	Neal Wade
• Director of Emergency Management	Brock Long
• Adjutant General of Military	Adjutant General A. C. Blalock
• Director of Homeland Security	Jim Walker
• Commissioner of Medicaid	Carol Herrmann-Steckel
• Commissioner of Human Resources	Nancy Buckner
• Administrator of Alcoholic Beverage Control	Emory Folmar
• Commissioner of Children's Affairs	Dr. Marquita Davis
• Director of Economic and Community Affairs	Bill Johnson
• Commissioner of Corrections	Richard Allen
• Commissioner of Conservation and Natural Resources	Barnett Lawley

ALCOHOLIC BEVERAGE CONTROL

Alcoholic Beverage Control Board
2715 Gunter Park Drive West
Montgomery, AL 36109
(334) 271-3840
www.abcboard.alabama.gov

ADMINISTRATOR
EMORY FOLMAR

The Alcoholic Beverage Control Board controls alcoholic beverages through distribution, licensing, enforcement, and education. The board enforces state and federal laws on youth access to tobacco, and it provides retailers and the general public with information relative to the laws and their consequences. The board also operates retail stores that sell the majority of liquor purchased by consumers in Alabama. In addition, the board conducts audits, collects taxes, disburses revenue obtained from those taxes, and disburses revenues from the ABC stores. In fiscal year 2006-2007 over $188 million in net revenue was generated for the State of Alabama. Recipients of these funds included the Department of Mental Health, the Education Trust Fund, the Department of Human Resources, and the General Fund.

Divisions

The ABC Board has three branches: Regulation, Enforcement, and Education; Product Management and Stores Operations; and Administrative Services and Support.

• THE ENFORCEMENT DIVISION enforces Alabama laws related to alcoholic beverages, tobacco products, and illegal drugs. The division maintains a Statewide Drug Task Force specializing in undercover investigations, which is funded by federal grants. As a part of their daily work, enforcement personnel concentrate on minors' access to alcoholic beverages and tobacco products. The division is also responsible for granting alcoholic beverage licenses.

The division's Responsible Vendor Program requires the training of all employees involved in the management, sale, or service of alcoholic beverages. Training areas include Alabama alcoholic beverage laws, legal age determination, civil and criminal penalties, and risk-reducing techniques. Licensees who voluntarily join the program are required to have policies ensuring legal and responsible sales and to train employees in these policies. ABC Board specialists monitor statewide the compliance with program requirements.

• THE PRODUCT MANAGEMENT DIVISION/STORES OPERATIONS is a system of sites for controlled sale of distilled spirits and fortified wine. It oversees all functions necessary for wholesale and retail sales of alcoholic beverages by the Alabama ABC Board. The division is responsible for the pricing, purchasing, warehousing, transporting, distributing, and merchandising of alcoholic beverages. All products for the ABC stores, private package stores, bars, and restaurants are received and shipped from the ABC warehouse.

• THE ADMINISTRATIVE area of the board consists primarily of Accounting, Information Technology, Personnel, and Administrative Support Divisions. Also located within this area are the budgeting, financial planning, and public information functions.

Administrator Emory Folmar

Governor Bob Riley appointed Emory Folmar as administrator of the Alabama Alcoholic Beverage Control Board on June 11, 2003. An Alabama political veteran, Folmar was mayor of Montgomery for twenty-two years and was the Republican nominee for governor in 1982, losing to George Wallace's unprecedented bid for a fourth term.

Folmar also had a distinguished military career and is one of the most highly decorated U.S. veterans of the Korean War. He graduated from the University of Alabama in 1951, then entered the U.S. Army, serving with the 30th Infantry Regiment, in combat as a company commander with the 2nd Infantry Division in Korea, and with the 11th ABN Division at Ft. Campbell, Kentucky. He was awarded the Silver Star, Bronze Star, Purple Heart, Combat Infantry Badge, Parachutist's Badge, Korean Campaign with Three Stars, and the Croix de Guerre with Bronze Palm.

Before being elected mayor of Montgomery, Folmar served as city council president and had a successful career as a shopping center builder and developer. He also served as chairman of the Alabama Republican Party.

He and his wife, Anita, have two children and two grandchildren.

BANKING

Banking Department
401 Adams Avenue, Suite 680
Montgomery, AL 36104
(334) 242-3452

The Banking Department, created in 1911, charters, licenses, and regulates Alabama banks and other financial service providers to foster stability, instill and protect public confidence, and promote economic development in a competitive environment.

SUPERINTENDENT
JOHN HARRISON

Divisions

• THE BUREAU OF BANKING charters and regulates banks, trust companies, and savings and loan associations. Currently, the Bureau of Banking regulates 127 banks and three trust companies with over $258 billion in assets. This makes the Bureau of Banking one of the largest in the country by assets under its control. Banks under the department's supervision have operations in twenty states. The Bureau of Banking is responsible for examining the institutions that it regulates for safety and soundness.

• THE BUREAU OF LOANS administers and enforces the Alabama Small Loan Act, the Alabama Consumer Credit Act, the Alabama Pawn Shop Act, the Alabama Mortgage Brokers Licensing Act, and the Alabama Deferred Presentment Services Act. The Bureau of Loans has more than 4,000 licensees under its jurisdiction. The bureau examines these licensees to ensure their compliance with the laws and to protect consumers.

Superintendent John Harrison

Before being appointed superintendent by Governor Riley in 2005, Harrison was the director of the Alabama Department of Economic and Community Affairs, a four-term mayor of Luverne, a banker, and a businessman.

He served as president, CEO, and board member of First Citizens Bank in Luverne; president, secretary-treasurer, and board member of the Community Bankers Association of Alabama; partner and vice-president of C&H Trucking Co, Inc; owner and president of Crenshaw Land and Timber Company; and board member of the Alabama Forestry Association Forest Fund.

Harrison graduated from Troy State University in 1967 with a double major in business administration and marketing and serves on the school's board of trustees. In 1992, he was honored as the TSU Alumnus of the Year.

CHILDREN'S AFFAIRS

Department of Children's Affairs
Business Center of Alabama Building
2 North Jackson Street, Suite 602
Montgomery, AL 36104
(334) 223-0502; FAX 240-3054
www.children.alabama.gov

The Department of Children's Affairs (DCA) provides state leadership to identify, analyze, streamline, and coordinate services and programs for children and families throughout Alabama.

**COMMISSIONER
MARQUITA DAVIS**

Divisions

• THE CHILDREN FIRST TRUST FUND was initiated in the mid-1990s by advocates and legislators who wanted to improve the lives of children in Alabama, with a strategy of funding programs and services by a proposed increase in cigarette taxes. The funding legislation never passed, but in 1998, the legislature linked Children First to the landmark agreement between the states and tobacco companies; CFTF receives funds from that settlement.

• THE CHILDREN'S POLICY COUNCIL oversees the county-level children's policy councils, chaired by local juvenile judges, which coordinate the activities of all state and local agencies and organizations dealing with children's affairs to prevent duplication and missed opportunities. The DCA commissioner serves as chairman of the Alabama Children's Policy Council.

• THE ALABAMA HEAD START STATE COLLABORATION OFFICE is a federal program that promotes collaboration between Head Start, state government initiatives and agencies, and others concerned with early care and education in Alabama. The project helps build a cohesive system of care and education for all of Alabama's children and low-income families, focusing on national, regional, and state priorities that include education, childcare, health, services to homeless families, family literacy, disability services, welfare, and community service.

• THE OFFICE OF SCHOOL READINESS works to provide Alabama's pre-kindergarten children with effective, high-quality early childhood experiences that prepare them for school. OSR funds programs that provide quality preschool experiences to four-year-olds in Alabama; provides training to pre-kindergarten teachers and administrators; and increases local and state-wide collaboration among early care and education providers, advocates, and parents.

Two new divisions will be added to DCA. The Alabama Parent Network and the Zero to Five Initiative for young children will further enhance the agency's role in providing state leadership.

Commissioner Marquita Davis

Governor Bob Riley appointed Dr. Marquita Furness Davis as commissioner of the Department of Children's Affairs on September 2, 2008. Davis succeeded Commissioner Richard H. Dorrough, who died in December 2007. Dorrough had served as commissioner since 2005.

Davis received a BS from Northern Illinois University, an MS from Alabama A&M University, and a PhD from the University of Alabama at Birmingham in Early Childhood Education and Development.

Prior to her appointment, Davis was appointed by Governor Riley to serve as the director of the Office of School Readiness. Before that, Davis was the deputy director of Child Development Services at JCCEO (Jefferson County Committee for Economic Opportunity). In that position, she directed a staff of 380 and had a budget of $16 million. The JCCEO Head Start Program is a federally funded program that provides comprehensive quality services for low-income pregnant women, infants, toddlers, and preschool children in Jefferson County.

Davis serves and has served on numerous boards and community organizations, including the American Village, Girls Inc., Junior League of Birmingham, National Conference for Community and Justice, YWCA of Central Alabama, Junior League of Birmingham Leadership Institute, Leadership Birmingham, Leadership Alabama, Leadership UAB, Momentum Women's Leadership, Youth Serve, Pathways, and the University of Montevallo's Stephens College of Business Advisory Board.

CONSERVATION AND NATURAL RESOURCES

Department of Conservation and Natural Resources
64 North Union Street
Montgomery, AL 36130
(334) 242-3151, (800) 262-3151
www.outdooralabama.com

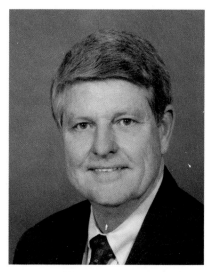

**COMMISSIONER
BARNETT LAWLEY**

The Department of Conservation and Natural Resources (ADCNR) advises the governor and the legislature on the management of freshwater fish, wildlife, marine resources, waterway safety, state lands, state parks, and other natural resources. The department also administers, manages, and maintains twenty-two state parks, twenty-three public fishing lakes, three freshwater fish hatcheries, thirty-five wildlife management areas, two waterfowl refuges, two wildlife sanctuaries, a mariculture center with forty-five ponds, and 645,000 acres of trust land managed for the benefit of several state agencies, the General Fund, and the Alabama Trust Fund. Other department functions include maintenance of a State Land Resource Information Center and administration of the Forever Wild land acquisition program.

ADCNR receives no General Fund support. Funding is generated through special revenues, which include federal monies, cigarette taxes, user and license fees, and interest from endowments and federal regulations.

The Alabama Conservation Advisory Board is a ten-member advisory board appointed by the governor to assist the department in formulating policies, examining rules and regulations, recommending changes or amendments, and publicizing programs and activities. Members include: Dan Moultrie, chair; Barnett Lawley, secretary; Louis Coles; Dr. A. Wayne May; Raymond Jones Jr.; Bill Hatley; Ross Self; Johnny Johnson; W. Grant Lynch; Dr. Warren Strickland; George Harbin; and, as ex officio members, the governor, the director of the Alabama Cooperative Extension Service, and the commissioner of the Department of Agriculture and Industries.

Divisions

• THE MARINE POLICE DIVISION enhances safety and promotes responsible use of resources on the state's waterways through enforcement, education, and community activities.

• THE MARINE RESOURCES DIVISION manages Alabama's marine fisheries resources through research and enforcement programs.

• THE STATE LANDS DIVISION manages undeveloped, state-owned trust lands in accord with their terms of acquisition. The Forever Wild land acquisition program is one of the many programs managed by this division.

• THE STATE PARKS DIVISION operates and maintains twenty-two state parks encompassing approximately 48,000 acres of land and water in Alabama.

• THE WILDLIFE AND FRESHWATER FISHERIES DIVISION manages, protects, conserves, and enhances fish and wildlife resources through enforcement, management, research, development, and educational programs.

Commissioner M. Barnett Lawley

A successful businessman before being appointed commissioner by Governor Bob Riley in 2003, Lawley has long been active in wildlife conservation and management in Alabama. He served six years on the board of directors of Alabama Wildlife Federation, was the group's vice president and legislative chairman for two terms, and is the recipient of its Member Service Award.

He is a co-founder of the St. Clair County chapters of Ducks Unlimited and the National Turkey Federation. Lawley also co-founded St. Clair County Sportsmen for the Environment and serves as its current president. He was instrumental in helping Pell City High School establish a wildlife management course in its curriculum.

In association with ADCNR, Lawley created the St. Clair County Wildlife Management Area and received Treasure Forest designation for management of the W. B. Lawley estate property.

The Pell City native recently retired after thirty years as president and owner of M. B. Lawley, Inc., a petroleum company. He served as president of the Alabama Oilmen's Association and as the group's legislative chairman. He was Oilman of the Year three times.

Lawley is a business administration graduate of Auburn University.

CORRECTIONS

Department of Corrections
301 South Ripley Street
Montgomery, AL 36130
(334) 353-3883
www.doc.alabama.gov

**COMMISSIONER
RICHARD ALLEN**

The Department of Corrections is Alabama's largest law enforcement agency, tracing its roots to 1839. Today, the department employs more than 2,700 security and 1,000 support personnel. ADOC is considered a medium-sized state correctional system, with an annual operating budget exceeding $400 million and a population of more than 25,000 inmates.

The department manages fifteen facilities with medium and higher security levels, eleven work release/community work centers, and the State Cattle Ranch, Red Eagle Honor Farm, and the Hamilton Aged and Infirmed facilities.

Divisions

• THE OPERATIONS DIVISION is responsible for ensuring the effective daily operations of prison facilities, including supervision of the Classification Review Board and the Training, Transfer, and Institutional Coordinators.

• THE ADMINISTRATIVE SERVICES DIVISION is responsible for all administrative services within the department, including personnel, finance, procurement, information systems, communications, food service, and Correctional Industries.

• THE DIVISION OF PLANS AND PROGRAMS is responsible for central records, supervised reentry, religious programs, research and planning, educational and vocational programs, and victim constituent services.

• THE DIVISION OF HEALTH SERVICES is responsible for the administration of medical and mental health services.

• THE DIVISION OF MAINTENANCE AND CONSTRUCTION is responsible for all recommended repairs and renovations as prioritized based on the most urgent needs of the department, to include implementation of a preventative maintenance program.

Commissioner Richard Allen

Richard Allen became commissioner of the Department of Corrections on February 15, 2006. Prior to his appointment, the Decatur native was a member of the Capell

& Howard law firm of Montgomery. On December 31, 2004, Commissioner Allen retired from the Alabama Attorney General's Office, where he served as chief deputy attorney general under Alabama Attorneys General Jeff Sessions, Bill Pryor, and Troy King. Commissioner Allen has also served as a law clerk to former Alabama Supreme Court Chief Justice Howell Heflin and later served as chief legislative assistant to Heflin after he was elected to the U.S. Senate.

Allen received his BA from the University of North Alabama in 1963 and his JD from the University of Alabama in 1973. He also attended the U.S. Army War College in 1983. Allen, a Vietnam veteran, retired in 1993 from the Army Reserve as a brigadier general.

DEVELOPMENT OFFICE

Alabama Development Office
401 Adams Avenue, 6th Floor
Montgomery, AL 36130
(334) 242-0400
www.ado.alabama.gov

**DIRECTOR
NEAL WADE**

Most commonly known as the state agency for economic development, the Alabama Development Office (ADO) has one mission—to create jobs in Alabama. During the Riley administration, ADO has twice been named the top state economic development agency in the United States, and Alabama's economy has been named the best in the Southeast for five straight years.

According to Director Neal Wade, "We work very hard to build relationships with site consultants and keep them up-to-date on information about our state because they are vital in supplying companies. We also work with economic development professionals across the state—some are specific to economic development organizations, some work with chambers, and some are with companies. They are our partners and our allies."

Divisions

• RECRUITMENT — To broaden Alabama's industrial base, ADO's project managers identify companies that could have an expansion project in the Southeast over the next three to five years. This division also fields calls from site consultants. The major objectives of the division are to attract industry to Alabama, to encourage and promote foreign manufacturing investment in the state, and to support expansion and retention of existing businesses. The division works cooperatively with economic development allies throughout the state. Targeted marketing efforts use direct contacts, pavilion events at selected trade shows, and business-prospecting trips. ADO considers retention and expansion of the state's existing industries to be an integral part of recruitment strategies.

• THE INFORMATION SERVICES DIVISION provides technical support and data to site selection consultants, businesses seeking to locate or expand in Alabama, and other ADO divisions, as well as to outside agencies and organizations.

• THE INTERNATIONAL TRADE DIVISION helps Alabama companies establish working relationships with export and other professionals, building knowledge that results in international business. Tools used include activities that complement the trade promotion programs of other state and federal agencies, including trade missions, trade shows, and catalog missions. Foreign buyers are encouraged to include Alabama in U.S. itineraries, and the state's exporters and importers receive mass mailings and special publications such as the *Alabama International Trade Directory*. The division co-sponsors export development activities for other Alabama organizations.

• THE SMALL BUSINESS OFFICE OF ADVOCACY provides information to meet the needs and concerns of small-business owners. Working closely with the Small Business Development Consortium, the agency coordinates with the consortium's eleven Small Business Development Centers at universities throughout the state and jointly publishes *Alabama's Answers*, a guide to doing business in Alabama. The division also works jointly with the Department of Economic and Community Affairs's Office of Minority Business Enterprise.

Director Neal Wade

Neal Wade is a veteran industrial recruiter who was appointed by Gov. Bob Riley in 2003. Wade was actively involved in many of the state's most significant recent economic development efforts, including ThyssenKrupp at Mt. Vernon, National Railcar in the Shoals area, and most recently, the Air Force tanker refueling project of Northrop Grumman Corporation/EADS in Mobile. Wade previously served as vice president for economic development of the Florida-based St. Joe Company, a real estate operating company and that state's largest private landowner. In Alabama, Wade served for nine years as president and CEO of the Economic Development Partnership of Alabama, a private economic development consortium of some of the state's leading companies. Wade graduated from Samford University, and he and his wife, Mary Ann, have three children and six grandchildren.

ECONOMIC AND COMMUNITY AFFAIRS

Alabama Department of Economic
and Community Affairs
401 Adams Avenue, 5th Floor
Montgomery, AL 36104
(334) 242-5100
www.adeca.alabama.gov

**DIRECTOR
BILL JOHNSON**

The Alabama Department of Economic and Community Affairs was created in 1983 to consolidate a number of state and federal grant programs under a single agency. ADECA's purpose is to improve and strengthen communities and the quality of life in Alabama through diverse and comprehensive programs involving economic development, infrastructure improvement, law enforcement, energy conservation, and responsible management of water resources.

Divisions

• THE DIRECTOR'S OFFICE oversees Community Development Block Grants, one of the best-known federal programs for assisting local governments with infrastructure and economic development. The director works with the Appalachian Regional Commission, the Delta Regional Authority, and special commissions to assist designated regions and rural communities. Also within the director's office, ADECA's recreational programs help communities develop trails, parks, ball fields, and other leisure opportunities. Legal, financial, audit, and other support staff help the director ensure the efficient and appropriate use of the department's resources.

• THE WORKFORCE DEVELOPMENT DIVISION focuses on jobs, education, career development, and job-training programs as it encourages economic development, prepares workers for stable and high-paying jobs, and partners with employers. The division's programs help the unemployed and welfare recipients find work, assist students preparing for future careers, serve people with disabilities, and aid workers when plants and businesses close or announce layoffs. WDD coordinates federal job-training programs that help companies identify skilled workers and that give Alabamians the tools they need to further their careers.

• THE ENERGY DIVISION develops and manages programs to conserve energy, promote biofuels and other alternative energy sources, and help low-income families with heating and cooling costs. The division fosters technology to strengthen the

Alabama economy and helps implement interactive distance learning, video medical consultations, and video arraignment.

• THE LAW ENFORCEMENT AND TRAFFIC SAFETY DIVISION administers federal funding for victims' services, law enforcement, juvenile justice, and traffic safety programs. It provides support for drug task forces, domestic violence units, child advocacy centers, and after-school programs to help children avoid drugs and violence. The division combats impaired driving by funding increased patrols and public awareness campaigns.

• THE OFFICE OF WATER RESOURCES administers programs for river-basin management, river assessment, water-supply assistance, water conservation, and water-resources development. The division also administers floodplain management in Alabama, overseeing the federal flood insurance program and updating flood insurance maps. OWR provides technical advice and analysis in support of any litigation relating to water interests shared with other states. The office also provides broad geographic information expertise to assist ADECA divisions with mapping needs.

• THE SURPLUS PROPERTY DIVISION, with warehouses at Eva and at Montgomery, sells all surplus property from state agencies that participate in the state property program. It also sells federal surplus property allocated to the state from military bases and federal agencies. State, county, and local governments and many non-profit organizations are afforded first opportunity to purchase the surplus property, often with significant savings to their budgets.

• THE COMMUNICATIONS AND INFORMATION DIVISION handles the department's public information and public relations needs, serving as the contact for citizens and the news media. CID prepares and distributes media releases about grants and other departmental activities and handles publications and graphic arts projects. The division monitors state legislation for potential impact on ADECA's programs and is the state's liaison to the Census Bureau.

Director Bill Johnson

In 2003, Governor Bob Riley appointed Johnson assistant director for ADECA, and in December 2005, named him director, succeeding John Harrison. Johnson manages a 230-member staff and is responsible for more than $200 million in federal grants. He serves as the governor's representative on the Appalachian Regional Commission, the Delta Regional Authority, and the Southern Growth Policies Board.

The son of a career soldier who retired to Birmingham in 1973, Johnson attended John Carroll High School and was awarded a full academic scholarship to Mobile's Spring Hill College. After graduating with a chemistry degree in 1981, Johnson started a commercial contracting company. In 1997, he was elected to the Birmingham City Council.

EMERGENCY MANAGEMENT

Alabama Emergency Management
Agency
5898 County Road 41
Clanton, AL 36546
(205) 280-2201
www.ema.alabama.gov

**DIRECTOR
BROCK LONG**

The Alabama Emergency Management Agency is responsible for emergency management within the state. It works with city and county governments to create and operate local emergency management organizations and to plan and coordinate statewide disaster mitigation, preparedness, and response/recovery actions for natural and man-made hazards.

Divisions

• THE EXECUTIVE BRANCH is made up of the Support Branch and Field Services Branch. The Field Services Branch consists of field service coordinators who serve as liaisons between AEMA and local emergency programs. The Support Branch facilitates external affairs and legal counsel for the agency. This division coordinates with FEMA and local EMAs before, during, and after a disaster.

• THE OPERATIONS DIVISION consists of the Response and Logistics Branch. It is tasked with coordination of the statewide mutual aid system, activation and maintenance of the State Emergency Operations Center, and coordination of volunteer organizations active in disaster and the 24-hour Warning Point Communications Room.

• THE PREPAREDNESS DIVISION consists of the Planning Branch and the NIMS, Exercise, and Training Branch. The Planning Branch oversees the Chemical Stockpile Emergency Preparedness Program, mitigation, infrastructure assistance, terrorism, radiological, natural hazards, and technical hazards. The NIMS, Exercise, and Training Branch offers training for all levels of government, private industry, and volunteer organizations.

• THE ADMINISTRATION AND RESOURCE SUPPORT DIVISION consists of the Personnel and Financial Services Branch, which includes logistics and general services, procurement, and property management.

• THE INFORMATION TECHNOLOGY DIVISION includes the Telecommunications, Database/GIS Branch, and Network/PC Support Branches. This division coordinates technology services within the agency and disaster communication statewide.

• THE RECOVERY DIVISION includes the Public Assistance Program and the Individual Assistance Program. Public Assistance involves debris removal and infrastructure issues for state and local governments, Indian tribes, and private non-profits impacted during a disaster. Individual Assistance works with FEMA to help individual citizens who need extra recovery assistance following a federally declared disaster.

Director Brock Long

Brock Long was appointed director of the Alabama Emergency Management Agency by Governor Bob Riley in January of 2008. He serves as the coordinating officer for all declared disaster events in the state of Alabama.

Within months of beginning his tenure as director, he managed three state-level disaster declarations as a result of tornadoes. In his first year he also oversaw federal disaster declarations in the aftermath of Hurricanes Gustav and Ike. He directed state resources as Alabama served as host state to 13,000 evacuees relocated during Hurricane Gustav.

One of Long's top priorities as director has been to build capability at the local level. To this end he has worked to improve funding available to county emergency managers and their agencies.

Long currently serves as the Hurricane Sub-Committee chairman and a Preparedness Committee member for the National Emergency Management Association. He represents Alabama as a member of the Board of Directors of the Central United States Earthquake Consortium. He has also served on the FEMA National Advisory Council to review possible revisions to the Stafford Act. This act outlines federal response during events of national significance.

Before coming to the Alabama Emergency Management Agency, Long worked in emergency management at the state and federal levels specializing in hurricane planning and response. He also worked in the private sector in emergency planning, disaster training, and post-event recovery.

He received a master's in public administration from Appalachian State University in 1999 and a degree in criminal justice, also from Appalachian State University, in 1997.

FINANCE

Department of Finance
600 Dexter Avenue, Room N-105
Montgomery, AL 36130
(334) 242-7160
www.finance.alabama.gov

The Finance Department provides leadership and service in financial management and operational support to all areas of state government. The finance director serves as the CFO for the State of Alabama and as a policy advisor to Governor Bob Riley.

**ACTING DIRECTOR
BILL NEWTON**

Divisions

• THE EXECUTIVE BUDGET OFFICE prepares the governor's budget proposals, administers and supervises the execution of appropriations, estimates revenues for budget preparation and administration, and helps draft budget appropriation bills.

• THE STATE COMPTROLLER provides accounting and managerial consulting services to state agencies in accordance with standards prescribed by state law and the Governmental Accounting Standards Board.

• DEBT MANAGEMENT maintains the official records of authorities for which the finance director is secretary. Additionally, the division maintains the accounts for eight authorities that borrow money for capital expenses incurred under state law.

• FINANCE ACCOUNTING AND ADMINISTRATION provides accounting services to each division of the Finance Department, prepares and processes financial transactions as required by each division in accordance with state fiscal policy and procedures, and maintains financial records for audit purposes.

• INFORMATION SERVICES is an "enabling partner" providing state agencies effective and efficient enterprise computing and voice solutions for their operations.

• LEGAL provides counsel and representation for the director and the department. It assists the legal staff of other agencies and departments when appropriate.

• THE EXECUTIVE PLANNING OFFICE develops statewide and agency-level planning for the budgeting process and for tracking the progress of state agencies in carrying out their missions.

• PURCHASING, according to state procurement laws and procedures, purchases all personal property, goods, and nonprofessional services necessary for state agencies.

• RISK MANAGEMENT is responsible for the State Insurance Fund (SIF), General Liability Trust Fund (GLTF), State Employee Injury Compensation Trust Fund (SEICTF), Employee Assistance Program (EAP), Equipment Maintenance Program (EMP), and Policy Management for all state agencies.

• THE SERVICE DIVISION maintains state-owned buildings within the Capitol complex, provides mail services to state agencies, and provides transportation and office space to state employees.

Acting Director Bill Newton

Governor Riley designated Newton as acting director of finance following the appointment of James Allen Main to the Alabama Court of Criminal Appeals in May 2009. He has served as assistant finance director since 1994 and previously served as acting finance director during transitions in the office. Newton was one of the first staff members of the Alabama Legislative Fiscal Office and then served as director of the office from 1979 to 1987, when he became finance director for the City of Huntsville.

Newton is president of the National Association of State Budget Officers. A native of Greenville, he earned undergraduate and MBA degrees from the University of Alabama and a JD from Jones School of Law.

HOMELAND SECURITY

Department of Homeland Security
P.O. Box 304115
Montgomery, AL 36130-4115
(334) 353-3050
www.dhs.alabama.gov

**DIRECTOR
JIM WALKER**

The Department of Homeland Security works with federal, state, and local partners to prevent and respond to terrorism in Alabama. The department works closely with the public and private sectors in law enforcement, emergency management, emergency medical services, fire services, public works, agriculture, public health, public safety, communications, environmental management, military, transportation, and more.

Divisions

• THE INFRASTRUCTURE PROTECTION DIVISION is responsible for the designation and protection of critical infrastructure sites throughout the state; for oversight of intelligence programs that analyze information lawfully collected by federal, state, and local law enforcement agencies with respect to threats of terrorist acts against the U.S. and Alabama; and for coordination of security matters pertaining to borders, transportation, and ports within the state.

• The SCIENCE AND TECHNOLOGY DIVISION includes the department's research and development arm and is responsible for organizing the scientific and technological resources of the state to prevent terrorism, and for unifying efforts to develop and implement scientific and technological countermeasures, including channeling the intellectual energy and capacity of Alabama's scientific institutions, such as state laboratories and universities.

• THE EMERGENCY PREPAREDNESS AND RESPONSE DIVISION coordinates emergency preparedness and response activities relating to terrorist events. In accordance with the 2003 homeland security legislation, the director of the Alabama Emergency Management Agency also serves as the deputy director for Emergency Preparedness and Response for the Alabama Department of Homeland Security.

• THE MANAGEMENT DIVISION is responsible for the oversight, management, and day-to-day administration of the department. This work includes the responsibility for homeland security strategic planning, grant management, personnel management, accounting, budgeting, information systems, and office administration.

Director Jim Walker

Walker served in the U.S. Army, 1981–2002, retiring as a lieutenant colonel. An infantry officer and Airborne Ranger, he served in both the 25th Infantry Division and the 101st Airborne Division. He has seven years' experience as an Army congressional liaison and government affairs officer. Other military assignments included service as aide-de-camp to the chairman of the Joint Chiefs of Staff, operations briefer to General Colin Powell during Operation Desert Shield, aide to President Ronald Reagan, and congressional fellow and legislative assistant to Congressman John Tanner (D-Tennessee), who was a senior member of the House Armed Services Committee.

Walker attended Austin Peay State University in Tennessee on an ROTC scholarship, graduating with a bachelor's degree in business administration. He received a master's degree in public administration from the University of Oklahoma and studied congressional and foreign affairs at the Johns Hopkins School of Advanced International Studies in Washington, D.C.

HUMAN RESOURCES

Alabama Department of
Human Resources
50 Ripley Street, Suite 2118
Montgomery, AL 36130
(334) 242-1160
www.dhr.alabama.gov

The Department of Human Resources provides for the protection, well-being, and self-sufficiency of children and adults in Alabama. The department has 4,300 employees and an annual budget of approximately $1.3 billion.

COMMISSIONER
NANCY BUCKNER

Divisions

• THE CHILD SUPPORT ENFORCEMENT DIVISION is a joint federal/state effort to help families establish paternity, obtain orders for payment of child support, and secure compliance with child support court orders.

• THE FAMILY SERVICES DIVISION, which includes the Office of Child Safety and the Office of Permanency (foster care and adoptions), maintains the Central Registry on Child Abuse and Neglect and administers the Interstate Compact on the Placement of Children. With oversight by the central administrative office in Montgomery, all services are delivered through county DHR offices.

• THE ADULT PROTECTIVE SERVICES DIVISION supports and assists county departments in protecting elderly and disabled adults from abuse, neglect, and exploitation.

• FAMILIES 4 ALABAMA'S KIDS is Alabama's recruitment and retention program that recruits adoptive and foster parents.

• THE CHILD CARE SERVICES DIVISION is the state's Child Care and Development Fund administrator and is responsible for the child care subsidy program and quality initiatives. In addition, the division licenses child care centers and monitors them for compliance with minimum standards.

• THE FAMILY ASSISTANCE DIVISION includes benefit and service programs to encourage the care of children in their own homes or in the homes of relatives. Services and benefits to eligible families include temporary cash payments, work and job training services, and child care assistance for parents engaged in work and training activities.

• THE FOOD ASSISTANCE DIVISION administers the federal food stamp program in the state. The program's purpose is to alleviate hunger and improve nutrition by providing monthly benefits to eligible low-income households to help them buy the food they need for good health. The program earned national recognition for its response to the Hurricane Ivan disaster declaration of 2004.

Commissioner Nancy Buckner

Governor Riley named Nancy T. Buckner commissioner of the Department of Human Resources on September 15, 2008 to succeed Page Walley. Commissioner Buckner was born and raised in Sylacauga, Alabama. She is a 1973 graduate of the University of Alabama in Birmingham. Buckner is devoted to her job and has worked with the Department of Human Resources for more than 35 years, most of which has been at the Talladega County Department of Human Resources. She also worked on "special assignments" from State DHR, including the child support interest project, six years as the department's legislative liaison, child welfare administrator for St. Clair County for three and one-half years, and Calhoun County DHR interim director with particular emphasis on revamping the child welfare program.

As a strong advocate for children and families, she has been affiliated with several children's advocacy organizations, including the Talladega County Easter Seals, the Alabama Child Support Association, and VOICES for Alabama's Children. She was a member of the founding committees that established Palmer Place, a child advocacy center; two family resource centers; and the Tri-Systems alternative school. Additionally, Buckner has presented training on child support issues and several child welfare issues, including special presentations on Munchausen syndrome.

Since joining Governor Riley's Cabinet, she has been appointed to the State Workforce Investment Board and is chairman of the Alabama Sheltering and Mass Care Taskforce.

INDUSTRIAL RELATIONS

Department of Industrial Relations
649 Monroe Street
Montgomery, AL 36130
(334) 242-8990
dir.alabama.gov

**DIRECTOR
TOM SURTEES**

The Alabama Department of Industrial Relations provides state and federally mandated workforce protection programs, promotes a positive economic environment for Alabama employers and workers, and disseminates information on the state's economy.

Divisions

• THE EMPLOYMENT SERVICE (ES) DIVISION delivers services through the Alabama Career Center System and through the web-based Alabama JobLink at joblink.alabama.gov, a 24/7 customer-friendly system providing job seekers and employers with self-service employment and training services. The Alabama Career Center System, located in One-Stop Career Centers throughout the state, has staff to assist job seekers and employers. All centers have resource rooms equipped with computers with high-speed Internet access for self-service job seekers.

• THE LABOR MARKET INFORMATION (LMI) DIVISION collects, analyzes, and disseminates data for evaluating the Alabama economy. What is the latest unemployment rate? What wages can be expected from a certain occupation? Which industries employ the most people? What occupations are in high demand? These are just a few examples of questions answered by LMI. Public and professional users can access the LMI data at http://dir.alabama.gov/lmi.

• THE MINING AND RECLAMATION DIVISION's Abandoned Mine Land Reclamation Program restores land and water resources adversely affected by coal mining and for which there is no continuing reclamation responsibility under state or federal law. The division's Mine Safety and Inspection Program inspects mines to ensure compliance with state laws, and, in the event of a mine disaster, coordinates rescue efforts and investigates the causes. Mine Safety and Inspection also makes certain that lands surface-mined for non-fuel minerals are reclaimed as requested by state law.

• THE UNEMPLOYMENT COMPENSATION (UC) DIVISION operates on the principle that workers who lose their jobs through no fault of their own deserve financial assistance. Providing monetary benefits to qualified unemployed workers not only assists them in meeting basic needs, but also helps employers keep their workforces together during short-term layoffs. In a recession, benefits paid to unemployed workers also help stabilize the state's economy. Qualified claimants may file for unemployment insurance by phone through UC Call Centers, or on the Internet.

An appointed volunteer Industrial Relations Advisory Council aids the director of the Department of Industrial Relations in identifying problems and formulating policies relating to the administration of the unemployment compensation program.

• THE WORKERS' COMPENSATION DIVISION administers the Alabama Workers' Compensation Law, ensuring proper payment of compensation benefits, along with necessary medical attention to employees injured on the job, or their dependents in case of death. Information and services are also provided to claimants, employers, insurance companies, attorneys, judges, legislators, labor and management groups, government agencies, and other parties.

Director Tom Surtees

Surtees was appointed director of the Department of Industrial Relations in 2007 after having served as commissioner of revenue for three years and succeeded Phyllis Kennedy. Before joining the Riley administration in 2004, Surtees was vice president for human resources with Birmingham-based Citation Corp. Before that, he was an employee-relations manager at Stockham Valves and Fittings and a personnel manager for Lamson and Sessions Co.

He has served in volunteer leadership positions with the American Cancer Society, PTA, Boys and Girls Club of Central Alabama, and the Friends of Rickwood. He has been active in the Business Council of Alabama, American Foundry Society, and the Alabama Cast Metals Association. Surtees also served on the Pleasant Grove City Council and the Jefferson County Board of Education, including four years as the latter's president.

He has bachelor's and master's degrees from the University of Alabama at Birmingham. He has served in the Alabama Army National Guard and the Army Reserves, retiring in 1997 as a lieutenant colonel.

INSURANCE

Department of Insurance
201 Monroe Street, Suite 1700
P.O. Box 303351
Montgomery, AL 36130-3351
(334) 269-3550
www.insurance.alabama.gov

**COMMISSIONER
JIM RIDLING**

The Department of Insurance regulates the insurance and pre-need industries, provides consumer protections, promotes market stability, enforces fire prevention standards, and conducts investigations.

Divisions

• THE CONSUMER SERVICES DIVISION receives, researches, investigates, and resolves individual consumer complaints against insurance companies, agents, and brokers. Completed investigations are referred to the Legal Division. The CSD provides educational materials and assistance for consumers regarding insurance questions and coverage provisions. When disasters strike, the division responds and deploys staff members to the affected areas to assist in expediting victims' insurance claims.

• THE FINANCIAL EXAMINERS DIVISION regulates the solvency of insurance companies subject to Alabama insurance laws and regulations through surveillance, monitoring, analysis, and examination. It provides technical assistance and factual information as a basis for determining regulatory action, thus serving as the first line of defense between Alabama's citizens and potentially troubled insurance companies.

• THE FIRE MARSHAL'S OFFICE investigates suspicious fires and explosions, inspects buildings for fire code compliance, and conducts fire education conferences and training seminars.

• THE LEGAL DIVISION holds hearings on agents, brokers, and companies charged with violations. Staff members review and act on charges stemming from investigations carried out by the Consumer Services Division.

• THE PRODUCER LICENSING DIVISION administers the applicable statutes and regulations governing the initial and continued licensure of all resident and non-resident producers, adjusters, service representatives, motor club representatives, surplus lines brokers, reinsurance intermediaries, managing general agents, and business entities. The division administers statutes and regulations governing the education of licensed individuals. By maintaining standards for initial and continuing education of insurance representatives, the division ensures that only qualified individuals are licensed to practice in Alabama. The division initiates regulatory action for the cancellation or suspension of the licenses of producers and service representatives who fail to comply with the annual continuing education and license renewal requirements.

• THE RATES AND FORMS DIVISION enforces Alabama insurance statutes, regulations, and bulletins pertaining to insurance companies, producers, adjusters, and other licensed entities. Its aim is to protect consumers, increase market choice, and treat all concerned fairly. To ensure companies are in compliance with statutes and regulations, the division reviews rate and form filings, assists consumers with regard to their rating and underwriter complaints, responds and deploys staff members to disaster sites, and participates in consumer outreach programs.

Commissioner Jim Ridling

Ridling was named Alabama's chief insurance regulator in 2008, succeeding Walter Bell. Ridling was born and raised in Arkansas, but has spent the last two decades in his adopted home of Alabama.

A long-time insurance executive, he served as an executive vice president of Fireman's Fund, and later as president, chairman, and CEO of Southern Guaranty Insurance until his retirement in 2003. In retirement, he helped create River Bank and Trust, where he serves as vice chairman today. He has also been involved in many civic and charitable activities.

Ridling serves as board chairman of Jackson Hospital and as a director of the Montgomery Airport Authority, Montgomery Area Chamber of Commerce, and Central Alabama Community Foundation. He is a former chairman of the River Region United Way.

He is married to the former Cathy Turner and has two daughters.

LABOR

Department of Labor
RSA Union, 6th Floor
P.O. Box 303500
Montgomery, AL 36130-3500
(334) 242-3460
www.alalabor.alabama.gov

**COMMISSIONER
JIM BENNETT**

Established in 1935, the Department of Labor promotes peaceful settlement of labor disputes and enforces state labor laws. It provides mediation services; conducts union representation elections; files annual reports on unions with more than twenty-five members; and publishes job-related illness, injury, and fatality reports through its federal surveys. Other major programs include enforcement of child labor statutes and safety inspections for boilers, pressure vessels, elevators, and escalators. Further, the Labor Department actively promotes labor/management cooperation between companies and their unions through the Governor's Annual Labor/Management Conference. The department works closely with federal agencies, including the U.S. Department of Labor.

Divisions

• THE STATISTICAL DIVISION collects information regarding job-related injuries, illnesses, and fatalities using three surveys: the Annual Survey of Occupational Injuries and Illnesses, the Census of Fatal Occupational Injuries, and the OSHA Log Data Collection Survey.

• THE SAFETY INSPECTION DIVISION is comprised of two bureaus, one covering boilers and pressure vessels, the other elevators and escalators. The Boiler and Pressure Valve Bureau oversees the estimated twelve thousand boilers and pressure vessels in use throughout the state. Operating certificates must be maintained on equipment regulated by the Act 2000-315. Permits must be obtained to install boilers and pressure valves, but installers, operators, and maintenance/service companies do not have to be certified. The main goal of the Boiler Division is to protect people from injury and death from boiler explosions. The Elevator Bureau was established when Alabama adopted an elevator code, which mandates that all elevators other than those located in industrial facilities not accessed by the general public be inspected annually and that inspections be made on elevators under construction to make sure they are properly installed and maintained. In addition, the bureau keeps accident reports and licenses persons who are engaged in construction, repair, and dismantling of elevators. The Elevator Bureau's main objective is to prevent injury and death caused by the state's estimated eleven thousand elevators.

• THE ALABAMA CHILD LABOR LAW DIVISION protects working minors. The law, which dates to 1886, prohibits youths from working in occupations or places of employment which could be harmful to their health or safety. By regulating the hours during which youths are allowed to work, the division ensures that minors also have sufficient time to take advantage of their educational opportunities.

• THE ALABAMA GOVERNOR'S LABOR/MANAGEMENT CONFERENCE provides a regular forum in which labor and management come together in a friendly setting away from the bargaining table. Topics discussed include drug testing, workplace security, and health-care costs.

Commissioner Jim Bennett

An author, former secretary of state, veteran legislator, journalist, and labor council executive, Bennett brings a wealth of state government experience to his position as labor commissioner.

He represented Homewood in the Alabama House, 1978–83, and Jefferson County in the Alabama Senate, 1983–93. He was appointed secretary of state in 1993 to fill a vacancy and won election in his own right in 1994 and 1998. From 1999 to 2000, he served as president of the National Association of Secretaries of State. No stranger to labor policy, Bennett served 1971–76 as public affairs director for the Alabama Labor Council. In the 1960s, he was an award-winning capitol reporter for the *Birmingham Post-Herald*.

He has a bachelor's degree from Jacksonville State University and a master's degree from the University of Alabama. He is chairman of the board of trustees of Jacksonville State University.

MEDICAID

Alabama Medicaid Agency
501 Dexter Avenue
Montgomery, AL 36104
(334) 242-5000
www.medicaid.alabama.gov

Medicaid is a state/federal program that pays for medical and long-term care services for eligible low-income pregnant women, children, certain people on Medicare, disabled individuals, and nursing home residents. Approximately one in five Alabama citizens is eligible for Medicaid.

COMMISSIONER
CAROL H. STECKEL

Divisions

• ADMINISTRATIVE SERVICES includes the Information Systems, Program Integrity, Fiscal Agent Liaison, and Administrative Services divisions.

• BENEFICIARY SERVICES certifies eligible individuals for Medicaid coverage through the Family Certification or the Elderly and Disabled Certification divisions. The Certification Support Division provides administrative and technical support.

• CLINICAL STANDARDS AND QUALITY operates under one of the agency's two medical directors. Statistical Support and the Quality Improvement and Standards divisions support the agency's quality improvement initiatives and overall quality assurance efforts.

• HEALTH POLICY is the responsibility of the agency's second medical director. This function determines the level and quality of medical care provided to recipients through the development and modification of health care policies and procedures.

• FINANCIAL MANAGEMENT oversees an annual budget of more than $4 billion as well as the operation of the agency's finance director's office and the Third Party and Provider Audit/Reimbursement divisions.

• PROGRAM ADMINISTRATION encompasses all program service divisions including Medical Services, Long Term Care, and Pharmacy Services.

Covered Services

Thousands of providers give health care to eligible Medicaid recipients each year. A number of services are limited to children under age twenty-one, to pregnancy-related services, or to family planning services only. Some services, such as hospital stays or doctor visits, are limited as well.

Covered services include ambulance and non-emergency transportation; dental services for children; well-child and preventive care; family planning; and home and community-based waiver programs that provide care at home instead of in a nursing home; as well as long-term care services such as home health services, durable medical equipment, hospice care, private duty nursing, and targeted case management and care in nursing and other long-term care facilities.

Other covered services available are maternity care and medical services, including doctor visits, eye care, inpatient and outpatient hospital care, lab and X-ray services, renal dialysis, transplants, mental health services, preventive health services, and pharmacy services.

Commissioner Carol H. Steckel

Steckel was appointed commissioner by Governor Bob Riley in 2003. She previously served as director of the Survey Companies, LLC, Birmingham, and as CEO of Survey Associates, LLC, Birmingham. Her prior experience includes: senior vice president of Northport Health Services; program chief of staff, March of Dimes Birth Defects Foundation, White Plains, New York; consultant, Independent Health Care; commissioner, Alabama Medicaid Agency; deputy director, Office of Prepaid Health Care, Health Care Financing Administration, Washington, D.C.; consultant and director of data and policy development, Alabama Hospital Association, Montgomery; and assistant to the special assistant to the president for health policy, the White House, Washington, D.C.

Steckel has a master's degree in public health from the University of Alabama at Birmingham and a bachelor's in sociology from Birmingham-Southern College.

MENTAL HEALTH

Department of Mental Health
100 North Union Street
Montgomery, AL 36130-1410
www.mh.alabama.gov

**COMMISSIONER
JOHN HOUSTON**

The Department of Mental Health serves Alabama citizens who have mental illness, intellectual disability, and/or substance abuse addiction. Valuing respect, inclusion, excellence, and wellness and with a vision of "a life in the community for everyone," the department fulfills its charge through the operation of psychiatric hospitals, a developmental center for individuals with intellectual disabilities, and contractual relationships with community programs throughout the state. Services offered are individualized, based in scientific research, focused on individual recovery, and outcome oriented.

Divisions

• MENTAL ILLNESS SERVICES: Mental illness is a disease of the brain that can affect the way a person feels, thinks, and relates. Affecting people of all ages, races, cultures, and socioeconomic classes, mental illness is more common than cancer, diabetes, heart disease, or arthritis. The Division of Mental Illness Services provides a comprehensive array of treatment services through state-operated psychiatric hospitals and contracted community mental health programs across the state.

• INTELLECTUAL DISABILITY SERVICES: Intellectual disability refers to a level of functioning originating in childhood that is characterized by limitations in intellectual functioning and by limitations in the daily life skills needed to live independently in the community. The Division of Intellectual Disability Services provides a broad system of services and supports through a state-operated developmental center and contracted community programs across the state.

• SUBSTANCE ABUSE SERVICES: Substance abuse refers to a diagnosis of either being dependent upon or a significant abuser of alcohol or drugs, to the extent that the ability to function appropriately is compromised. The Substance Abuse Services Division provides treatment services through contractual agreements with public and private community programs across the state. The division also contracts for prevention services intended to keep people from beginning substance abuse.

Commissioner John Houston

Houston was appointed by Governor Bob Riley in May 2005, succeeding Kathy Sawyer. A life-long resident of Alabama, Houston has been working in the human services field for more than thirty years, including more than twenty years in the Department of Mental Health central office. He was appointed executive assistant to the commissioner in 1995 with responsibilities including multi-systems planning and liaison activities with other state agencies, much of this focusing on children's services. He participated in planning, development of legislation, and program implementation of early intervention services for infants and toddlers with developmental disabilities and for multiple needs children. He has also served on several state-level policy making or planning bodies including the Governor's Interagency Council for Early Intervention Services, the Department of Youth Services Board, the Child Abuse and Neglect Prevention Board, the State Children's Services Facilitation Team, and the State Children's Policy Council.

MILITARY

State Military Department
1720 Cong. W. L. Dickinson Drive
Montgomery, AL 36109
(334) 271-7200
www.alguard.alabama.gov

ADJUTANT GENERAL
MAJOR GENERAL A. C. BLALOCK

The Alabama National Guard consists of Army and Air Guard components. The National Guard may be called into action by the president or Congress, with the president serving as commander-in-chief. The governor may call individuals or units of the Alabama National Guard to state duty during emergencies, or to assist in special situations.

Divisions

• THE JOINT FORCE HEADQUARTERS ALABAMA NATIONAL GUARD in Montgomery has subordinate units across the state. Major commands of the Alabama Army National Guard are the 62nd Troop Command (Montgomery), 167th Theater Support Command (Birmingham), 142nd Signal Brigade (Decatur), 31st Chemical Brigade (Northport), and 20th Special Forces Group (Birmingham). Alabama Air Guard Major Commands are the 117th Air Refueling Wing (Birmingham), 187th Fighter Wing (Montgomery), and the 226th Combat Communication Group (Montgomery).

• HEADQUARTERS, AIR NATIONAL GUARD is part of the Alabama National Guard Joint Force Headquarters in Montgomery and provides command and control to all Air Guard units in the state.

• THE UNITED STATES PROPERTY AND FISCAL OFFICE (USPFO) is responsible for the receipt, storage, and distribution or dispersal of all federal funds and equipment allocated to the Alabama National Guard.

• THE FAMILY READINESS PROGRAM facilitates communications, involvement, support, and recognition between families and the Alabama National Guard.

• THE 22ND RECRUITING AND RETENTION BATTALION is responsible for the recruitment of Alabama Army Guard soldiers and the retention of soldiers already in the Guard.

• THE PLANS, OPERATIONS, AND TRAINING OFFICE (POTO) handles all Army Guard special schools, annual training, ammunition, and deployment programs. One branch is in charge of mobilization readiness and new equipment, and another (Directorate of Military Support) handles military support to civilian authorities (state active duty).

- THE COUNTERDRUG PROGRAM works with law enforcement agencies and local communities to reduce the demand for drugs and drug-related violence.
- THE DIRECTORATE OF LOGISTICS (DOL) coordinates logistical support of supplies and equipment for all units in the state. A branch of the office oversees and directs the surface maintenance activities of assigned equipment in the state.
- THE INSPECTOR GENERAL (IG) is the confidential advisor to the adjutant general and an impartial fact-finder on matters relating to morale, readiness, ethics, and conduct.
- THE SENIOR ARMY ADVISOR serves on the adjutant general's staff as primary advisor on Active Army matters and as the liaison with Active Army commanders.
- THE FACILITIES MANAGEMENT OFFICE manages and directs the construction program of National Guard facilities in the state, including procurement of property, architect and engineer design, and construction.
- THE STAFF JUDGE ADVOCATE (SJA) serves as the chief legal advisor to the adjutant general and Alabama Guard members across the state.
- THE STAFF CHAPLAIN provides counseling and spiritual guidance to Guard members and serves as a member of the State Casualty Notification Team.

Adjutant General Major General Abner C. Blalock

Governor Riley appointed MG Blalock as adjutant general in August 2007, succeeding MG Mark Bowen. Prior to his appointment, General Blalock had been serving as commander of the 167th Theater Sustainment Command, a theater-level headquarters in Birmingham.

Blalock completed ROTC at Virginia Military Institute and Auburn University. He has served as a commander at six levels in the Alabama National Guard including an infantry company, a heavy support battalion, an area support group, and a chemical brigade.

Blalock's military awards include the Defense Meritorious Service Medal, Meritorious Service Medal, Army Commendation Medal, Army Achievement Medal, National Defense Service Medal, and the Humanitarian Service Medal.

He graduated from Auburn University in 1971, earned an MBA in 1981 from the University of Alabama at Birmingham, and graduated from the Army War College in 1997.

PUBLIC SAFETY

Department of Public Safety
301 South Ripley Street
Montgomery, AL 36104
(334) 242-4371
www.dps.alabama.gov

DIRECTOR
COL. J. CHRISTOPHER MURPHY

Founded in 1935, the department has evolved into a multi-faceted, comprehensive, statewide law enforcement agency. Its mission is to enhance the enjoyment of life and property in the state of Alabama and to ensure a safe environment by providing courteous service to the public, investigating criminal activities, facilitating the safe movement of traffic, and issuing driver licenses, while respecting the rights and dignity of all persons.

Divisions

• THE ADMINISTRATIVE DIVISION implements policies and procedures and facilitates the smooth operation of the department. Its sections include the Alabama Criminal Justice Training Center, Financial Services, Inspections, Legal, Personnel, Public Information, and Recruiting.

• THE ALABAMA BUREAU OF INVESTIGATION conducts criminal and drug investigations, often in support of city, county, state, federal, and foreign law enforcement agencies. ABI provides assistance in crime scene processing, searches, latent print examinations, polygraph examinations, bomb squad services, technical surveillance, hostage negotiation, marijuana eradication, and cybercrimes, including Internet crimes against children. The Criminal Information Center is responsible for the maintenance, storage, analysis, and dissemination of criminal activity information. The CIC also operates the Alabama Center for Missing and Exploited Children and the Sex Offender Registry Unit.

• THE DRIVER LICENSE DIVISION is responsible for testing and keeping records on Alabama's licensed drivers. These records include crash reports, traffic arrest forms, driver license applications, and traffic violation convictions. In addition to administering the written and road skills driver license examinations to commercial and noncommercial drivers, the division is responsible for the application of penalties that may result in the revocation or suspension of a driver license.

• THE HIGHWAY PATROL DIVISION comprises nine troops made up of seventeen posts and communications centers. The largest of Public Safety's six divisions, Highway Patrol accounts for approximately 65 percent of the total arresting officers within the department. Troopers patrol approximately 69,465 miles of rural roadways in Alabama. The division includes Motor Carrier Safety, Communications, Traffic Homicide Investigations, Felony Apprehension Patrol, the K-9 Unit, the Motorcycle Unit, Tactical Teams and Special Operations Units, Training and Career Development, Grants Administration, and Weapons of Mass Destruction.

• THE PROTECTIVE SERVICES DIVISION is responsible for providing general law enforcement/police services for all state facilities, buildings, and other designated properties within the Capitol complex and for providing protection for certain state officers and visitors to the state. Related duties include homeland security initiatives, threat assessments and related operational/response planning, intelligence gathering and analysis, and investigation of persons of interest and/or those who have made threats against public officials/facilities. The division includes Dignitary Protection, Mansion Security, and Capitol Police.

• THE SERVICE DIVISION provides supplies, equipment, assistance, and other special services necessary to the effective operation of the Department of Public Safety. The division includes State Trooper Aviation, Communications Engineering, Inventory Services, Photographic Services, Supply, and Fleet Maintenance.

Director Colonel J. Christopher Murphy

Murphy was appointed by Governor Bob Riley in December 2006, suceeding Co. W. M. Coppage. A thirty-year law enforcement veteran, Murphy began his career in 1978 with the Auburn Police Department, serving as patrol officer, corporal, and detective. He then served as a special agent with the Tennessee Bureau of Investigation, investigating major felonies in east Tennessee, before joining the U.S. Secret Service. He protected former presidents, presidential candidates, and a host of foreign heads-of-state visiting the United States, and conducted criminal investigations, including financial and computer crimes. From 2002 until his retirement from the Secret Service in 2006, he was special agent in charge of the Birmingham district office, managing the seven Secret Service offices in Alabama and Mississippi.

A native of Birmingham, Murphy earned an undergraduate degree in criminal justice at Auburn University and a master's degree in administration of criminal justice at Troy State University.

REVENUE

Department of Revenue
50 North Ripley Street
Montgomery, AL 36132
(334) 242-1170
www.revenue.alabama.gov

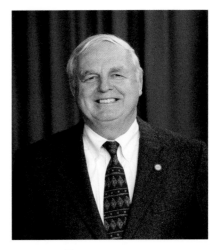

**COMMISSIONER
TIM RUSSELL**

The department administers the revenue laws and funds government services for the citizens of Alabama.

Divisions

• ADMINISTRATIVE LAW conducts impartial hearings involving contested assessments, refunds, licensing issues, and other matters administered by the department. The final decision of the administrative law judge may be appealed to circuit court by either the taxpayer or the department.

• COLLECTION SERVICES is responsible for the collection of final assessments for all tax divisions; collection of delinquent sales and withholding taxes, and bad checks; administration of the 100 percent penalty statutes; and initiation of civil legal actions against taxpayers as a result of noncompliance with Alabama's tax laws.

• HUMAN RESOURCES ensures that qualified individuals are recruited, selected, and trained for positions of responsibility within the department.

• INDIVIDUAL AND CORPORATE TAX administers, collects, and enforces the individual income, corporate income, financial institutions' excise, and business privilege taxes.

• INFORMATION TECHNOLOGY develops, programs, implements, and maintains computer systems for the department.

• INVESTIGATION investigates and enforces revenue laws regarding licensing and registration of motor vehicles, gasoline tax, motor fuels tax and substitutes, and tobacco tax. The division is also responsible for the anti-theft inspection of rebuilt motor vehicles and for the investigation and prosecution of tax evasion and other tax crimes.

• LEGAL serves as the legal advisor to the commissioner and the department, represents the department in tax litigation in state and federal courts and in hearings before the Administrative Law Division, files and processes claims in bankruptcy court for payment of delinquent taxes, issues deed and mortgage tax orders, and prosecutes violators of criminal tax statutes.

• MOTOR VEHICLE issues motor vehicle titles, maintains vehicle registration information, and enforces the Mandatory Liability Insurance Act. In addition, the division administers the International Registration Plan (IRP) and International Fuel Tax Agreement (IFTA).

• PROCESSING is responsible for the up-front processing of most tax returns received by mail, for depositing payments, and for managing the department's mailroom facilities, records retention center, and related vendor contracts.

• PROPERTY TAX oversees the reappraisal of all property in the state; sets schedules, standards, and procedures for equalization of all property values in all counties; and ensures all property is taxed uniformly throughout the state. In addition, the division assesses railroad and public utility property and collects the freight-line equipment company tax.

• SALES, USE, AND BUSINESS TAX administers, collects, and enforces state sales, use, lodgings, utility gross receipts, gasoline, motor fuels, and a number of other business-related state taxes. The division also administers local sales, use, rental, lodgings, tobacco, fuel, and solid minerals taxes for various cities and counties.

• TAX POLICY AND RESEARCH serves as the department's primary source for the determination and coordination of major tax policy issues and legislative initiatives. The division also processes and maintains rules under the Alabama Administrative Procedures Act program, directs the department's voluntary disclosure and nexus discovery program, and conducts audits related to tax avoidance schemes.

Commissioner Tim Russell

Russell was appointed by Governor Bob Riley in March 2008, succeeding Tom Surtees, who became the director of Industrial Relations in September 2007. Russell had worked in the insurance industry for more than thirty-five years, and had been president of Baldwin Mutual Insurance Company since 1998. A captain in the U.S. Army, he was awarded the U.S. Army Commendation Medal for his service during the Vietnam War.

A life-long resident of Baldwin County, Russell served three terms as mayor of Foley, 1996–2006. His community activities include volunteer leadership positions with the South Baldwin United Way, the Foley Rotary Club, the Foley Library Board, and the South Baldwin Chamber of Commerce.

He earned a BS degree in accounting from the University of Alabama and a master's in business administration from the University of South Alabama. He is also a chartered property casualty underwriter, CPCU.

Russell and his wife, the former Sandy Schultz of Foley, have three children and two grandchildren.

SENIOR SERVICES

Department of Senior Services
Suite 470 RSA Plaza
770 Washington Avenue
Montgomery, AL 36104
(334) 242-5743
www.alabamaageline.gov

COMMISSIONER
IRENE COLLINS

The Department of Senior Services promotes the independence and dignity of Alabama's aging population through a comprehensive and coordinated system of quality services. The vision of the department is to help society and state government prepare for the changing aging demographics through effective leadership, education, advocacy and stewardship. The department has received many awards, including the 2007 Rosalynn Carter Leadership in Caregiving Award.

Divisions

• ELDER RIGHTS: (1) The Elder Abuse Information and Prevention Program works with the Long-term Care Ombudsman and the departments of Human Resources and Public Health to prevent elder abuse. (2) The State Health Insurance Assistance Program (SHIP) and the Senior Medicare Patrol use certified volunteers to provide free counseling and education to Medicare/Medicaid beneficiaries on claims questions and disputes, including healthcare, waste, fraud, and abuse. (3) The Legal Assistance Program assists older adults with advice and counseling, legal representation, legal research, preparation of legal documents, negotiation, legal education, and community outreach.

• LONG-TERM CARE SERVICES: (1) The Medicaid Waiver for the Elderly and Disabled Program provides services to seniors and people with disabilities whose needs would otherwise require them to live in a nursing home. Case managers develop individualized care plans including case management, personal care, homemaker, respite, adult day care, companion services, and home-delivered frozen meals. (2) The Personal Choices Program gives older adults and those with disabilities who receive Medicaid in Alabama the opportunity to direct their own personal care services.

• Other Aging PROGRAMS: (1) Alabama Cares provides education, training, assistance, and resources to grandparents raising grandchildren and to family caregivers to help them take care of their aging loved ones and themselves. (2) Disaster Recovery responds to the needs of older victims of disasters. (3) The Long-term Care Ombudsman protects the health, safety, welfare, and rights of Alabama's senior citizens in nursing facilities, assisted living facilities, specialty care facilities, and boarding homes. Ombudsmen are advocates for residents, or their friends and families; provide administrative and technical assistance; work with legislation affecting residents of long-term care facilities; provide technical support to resident and family councils; promote the development of citizens' organizations related to long-term care facilities; and maintain accurate reporting. (4) Nutrition offers: (a) meals in a group or home setting; (b) nutrition and fitness counseling and education; and (c) fresh fruits and vegetables from farmers' markets, roadside stands, and community-supported agriculture programs. (5) The Senior Community Service Employment Program serves low-income people who are fifty-five or older and have poor employment prospects, providing community services, training, and job placement. (6) SenioRx/Wellness helps Alabama senior citizens receive free prescription drugs from pharmaceutical manufacturers, and teaches seniors about healthy eating habits, proper exercise, and chronic illness management. (7) AlabamaConnect is a fast, comprehensive service directory of links to federal, state, and other aging and disability websites; an easy-to-use medical library; an information source on health care products; a political advocacy tool; a community message board; and more. It is accessible via www.AlabamaConnect.gov or by calling 1-800-AGELINE.

Commissioner Irene Collins

Irene Collins was appointed commissioner by Governor Bob Riley in 2003. She serves on the Governor's Workforce Development Council and the FEMA National Advisory Council, is the Alabama chairman of the United We Ride initiative, and serves on the National Governors Association Policy Academy for Civic Engagement. Collins also serves as first vice president on the Executive Board of the National Association of State Units on Aging (NASUA), as well as on the Board of Directors of the National Association of Nutrition and Aging Services Programs (NANASP). She is on the National Advisory Board of the Hurricane Fund for the Elderly/Grantmakers in Aging. Collins served as the Alabama Delegation Chairperson for the 2005 White House Conference on Aging, a national event that takes place every ten years. Prior to her cabinet appointment, Collins worked as executive director for seven years at the Jefferson County Council on Aging. She is married to Richard H. (Hank) Collins, and they have five children and seven grandchildren.

TOURISM

Tourism Department
401 Adams Avenue, Suite 126
Montgomery, AL 36130
(334) 242-4169
www.alabama.travel

The department serves residents and visitors with comprehensive information about things to do and places to see in Alabama. It enhances the growth of travel and tourism as an industry through promotions and publicity and by working with travel professionals.

DIRECTOR
LEE SENTELL

Divisions

• ADMINISTRATIVE: The division supports the director with office activities, meeting planning, vendor relations, travel arrangements, and coordination of the annual Governor's Conference and Legislative Bash with a committee of tourism professionals. Administrative is responsible for scheduling and serves as a liaison between Tourism and the Governor's office as well as the Governor's Mansion.

• PUBLICATIONS: This division researches and produces materials and publications to attract visitors to the state. Publications include the *Alabama Vacation Guide* and the *Alabama Calendar of Events*; special project brochures to enhance the annual tourism theme, such as brochures on "100 Dishes to Eat in Alabama Before You Die," the "Year of Alabama Sports," and "Small Towns and Downtowns."

• PUBLIC RELATIONS: This division maintains relationships with the media and the travel industry to showcase Alabama as a travel destination. This work involves responding to media requests, originating story ideas and press trips, and writing and distributing press releases.

• GROUP TRAVEL/MARKETING/INTERNATIONAL: This division promotes Alabama's tourism destinations, attractions, events, and accommodations to domestic and international tour and travel companies at tourism trade and consumer shows.

• MAIL: This division processes the department's heavy volume of incoming and outgoing mail; keeps an inventory of departmental materials and publications; prepares a monthly report analyzing the source and type of travel and tourism inquiries to the bureau; and orders, processes, inventories, ships, and delivers all brochures for use by Alabama's eight welcome centers.

• COMMUNICATIONS: Tourist promotion representatives answer questions from callers and potential tourists who contact the department; promote the state's events, attractions, historical sites, lodging, and other areas of interest to travelers; and in times of crisis, such as hurricanes, serve as a vital source of information for travelers seeking evacuation routes, emergency shelters, hospitals, housing for animals, and other information beyond the realm of routine tourist information.

• WELCOME CENTERS: Eight of these facilities are located where major highways enter the state. They provide tourism information and make hotel reservations throughout the state. The centers are co-located with Department of Transportation rest areas.

• THE ALABAMA FILM OFFICE promotes the state to the film and video industry as a production location for feature films, television programs, music videos, industrial and corporate training films, and commercials. In addition to scouting locations for specific projects, the office keeps more than 20,000 photographs of potential sites. The office also publishes the *Alabama Production Directory*, a resource guide to locations and more than sixty categories of technicians, production staff, and support services that are used by the film and video production industry.

Director Lee Sentell

Sentell was appointed by Governor Bob Riley in 2003. He previously served as tourism director for the Huntsville Convention and Visitors Bureau and marketing director for the U.S. Space and Rocket Center.

An Auburn University graduate from Ashland, Sentell is a member of the Alabama Tourism Hall of Fame and is past president of the Alabama Travel Council and past chairman of the Alabama Bureau of Tourism and Travel Advisory Board.

He serves on the Alabama Historical Commission, the Alabama State Council on the Arts, and the Alabama Scenic Byways Commission.

Under Sentell's direction, the Tourism Department created a series of annual theme campaigns that generated attention for various segments of the state. The programs were on gardens, food, outdoors, arts, sports, and history. A brochure on "100 Dishes to Eat Before You Die" won a national award during the "food" year. The arts campaign received three major national tourism marketing awards. The final year of the Riley administration will be celebrated as "The Year of Small Towns and Downtowns."

TRANSPORTATION

Department of Transportation
1409 Coliseum Boulevard
Montgomery, AL 36110
(334) 242-6358
www.dot.state.al.us

The department seeks to provide a safe, efficient, and environmentally sound transportation system for all users, especially the taxpayers of Alabama. The department facilitates economic and social development and prosperity through the efficient movement of people and goods.

DIRECTOR
JOE McINNES

Divisions and Bureaus

As one of the largest state agencies, the department has nine divisions covering the entire state, with each division subdivided into districts to better serve the public. At a central level, the department's work is coordinated by the following bureaus:

• THE AERONAUTICS BUREAU assures that aviation fuel taxes are spent on projects and research that preserve and enhance Alabama's air transportation system.

• THE AIR TRANSPORTATION BUREAU oversees aircraft owned, operated, leased, or rented by the state, and performs maintenance on state-owned aircraft.

• THE BRIDGE BUREAU is responsible for all structural design and analysis within the department.

• THE CONSTRUCTION BUREAU provides technical advice and general supervision of all contract construction work.

• THE BUREAU OF COUNTY TRANSPORTATION serves as the liaison between the ALDOT and the state's sixty-seven counties, assisting the counties in the design, construction, and maintenance of county roads and bridges.

• THE DESIGN BUREAU consists of: (a) the Consultant Management Section, which prepares consultant agreements, negotiates fees and executes contracts, and manages and reviews roadway plans; (b) the Traffic Center Design Section, which reviews project plans, provides cost estimates, composes specifications for traffic signal installations, reviews electrical materials, manages the traffic signal design services contracts, and coordinates statewide standardization; (c) the Environmental Technical Section, which obtains environmental clearances and permits for transportation projects; (d) the Location Section, which operates survey crews, manages aerial photography, and operates the Global Positioning System (GPS) to establish ground control in remote areas; (e) the Quality Control Section, which reviews roadway plans, conducts inspections, performs quality checks, and reviews traffic control patterns; (f) the Roadway Design Section, which prepares and reviews roadway plans; and (g) the Utilities Design Section, which issues permits for utilities on rights of way and relocates utilities in conflict with highway construction.

• THE BUREAU OF EQUIPMENT, PROCUREMENT, AND SERVICES purchases, salvages, and disposes of equipment and tracks the assignment and location of equipment.

• THE BUREAU OF TRANSPORTATION PLANNING AND MODAL PROGRAMS maintains rapport with railroad companies in rail/highway safety projects; manages and oversees safety programs to reduce vehicle crashes; administers rural and urban public transportation; and administers the Transportation Enhancement, Bicycle and Pedestrian, and Transportation Community and System Preservation Pilot programs.

• THE BUREAU OF OFFICE ENGINEER advises the Transportation director, Chief Engineer's Office, bureau chiefs, and division engineers. The bureau coordinates all federal disaster relief funds and emergency relief funds with the Federal Emergency Management Agency and the Federal Highway Administration.

• THE MAINTENANCE BUREAU keeps up state highways, interstates, and roads at state institutions of higher learning, state hospitals, and some state parks.

• THE BUREAU OF MATERIALS AND TESTS selects and controls materials used by the department in road and bridge construction.

• THE BUREAU OF RESEARCH AND DEVELOPMENT incorporates new technologies and implements research findings into the department's operations.

• THE RIGHT OF WAY BUREAU obtains and clears properties needed for transportation purposes.

Director Joe McInnes

McInnes was appointed by Governor Bob Riley in 2003. Before retiring in 1999, McInnes was executive vice president and chief administration officer with Blount International, Inc. He also serves as chairman, CEO, and director of the Blount Cultural Park and as president of the Blount Foundation.

A Wetumpka native, McInnes has served as president of the Montgomery Area United Way, president of the Tukabatchee Area Council Boy Scouts of America, director of the Montgomery Area Chamber of Commerce, director of the Alabama Humanities Foundation, and trustee of the Montgomery Museum of Fine Arts.

He is a graduate of the University of Alabama and has served on its National Advisory Board and the President's Cabinet. He also received a law degree from Jones School of Law.

STATE EDUCATION AGENCIES

Educating its citizens is one of the State of Alabama's largest, most comprehensive, and most expensive responsibilities. The functions of education in the state are divided among several agencies: the Department of Education for grades K-12; the Department of Postsecondary Education for junior colleges, vocational schools, and community colleges; and the Alabama Commission on Higher Education for public colleges and universities. These agencies are all profiled in this chapter. In addition, brief listings are provided for public and private colleges and universities within Alabama, and for two special high schools that serve students from across the entire state. For specific entries, see:

Opposite: A student at Bryant High School in Tuscaloosa works in a lab at the University of Alabama in the Nanoscience Internship program.

EDUCATION

Alabama Department of Education
50 North Ripley Street
Montgomery, AL 36104
(334) 242-9700 • FAX (334) 242-9708
www.alsde.edu

**SUPERINTENDENT
JOSEPH B. MORTON**

The department oversees the implementation of educational policies for Alabama's public schools as authorized by law and determined by the State Board of Education. The department is administered by the state superintendent of education, who is appointed by the elected members of the State Board of Education (see page 268).

Divisions/Services

• ACCOUNTABILITY ROUNDTABLE AND LEA (LOCAL EDUCATION AGENCIES) SUPPORT ROUNDTABLE provide support in curriculum, instruction, fiscal responsibility, management, and leadership.

• ALABAMA READING INITIATIVE provides training for the teaching of reading with the statewide goal of 100 percent literacy among public school students.

• CAREER AND TECHNICAL EDUCATION SECTION facilitates career and technical education programming in all local education agencies and in selected institutionalized environments. The staff assists in the delivery of state-of-the-art articulated career, technical, and academic education.

• CHILD NUTRITION PROGRAM is responsible for the oversight of federal funding provided for child feeding programs. The services include the school lunch/school breakfast programs, child care center feeding programs, special milk programs, food banks, and emergency feeding programs. The program provides approximately 750,000 meals per day.

• CURRICULUM AND INSTRUCTION SECTION develops, implements, and assesses the minimum curriculum content and course design for K–12 students in the public schools. It is also responsible for instructional support, including courses of study, instructional materials and research, curriculum alignment materials, recognition and scholarship programs, the textbook adoption program (see page 320), "State Textbook Committee"), high/middle school initiatives, and counseling and guidance services.

• COMMUNICATION SECTION is responsible for defining, developing, and maintaining proactive communications with a variety of publics, including key stakeholders, internal/external audiences, and members of the media. The Alabama Learning Resources Center provides audio and video resources to education staff, teachers, and school administrators.

• COMPLIANCE ASSISTANCE PROGRAM monitors public school systems for compliance with appropriate laws and regulations.

• DISABILITY DETERMINATION SERVICES processes Social Security Disability Insurance (SSDI) and Supplemental Security Income (SSI) disability applications under the Social Security Act and in accordance with applicable federal statutes, regulations, and standards. A large portion of these claims involve applications for children's SSI benefits.

• FEDERAL PROGRAMS SECTION administers all federally funded education programs and provides technical assistance to local education agencies and schools.

• INFORMATION SYSTEMS SECTION serves as the primary supplier of teacher and student information for K–12 education and is the basis for the distribution of state funds and for the State Superintendent's Report Card.

• LEA FINANCIAL ASSISTANCE SECTION reviews and approves local school system budgets, program applications, amendments, financial statements, and various state and federal program expenditure reports, and disburses state and federal funds.

• LEA FUNDING AND ACCOUNTABILITY determines state appropriations for public school systems and ensures accountability requirements for school systems.

• LEGISLATIVE SERVICES coordinates all legislative relations in order to effectively communicate the Department of Education's position on all legislative issues to members of the legislative and executive branches of government, as well as the general public.

• TECHNOLOGY INITIATIVES assists educators and stakeholders to effectively plan, implement, and use technology in schools by providing resources, professional development, guidance in obtaining funding, and technical assistance. The section provides leadership for statewide initiatives such as ACCESS Distance Learning, Alabama Learning Exchange (ALEX), and Technology in Motion (TiM).

• PREVENTION AND SUPPORT SERVICES provides technical assistance to school and school system personnel in the areas of school safety, discipline, attendance, state at-risk programs, safe and drug-free schools and communities, Children First grants and applications, special training opportunities, and building-based student support team — a school-based, problem solving approach to meet the needs of at-risk students in regular education classroom settings.

• EDUCATOR EVALUATIONS—PROFESSIONAL EDUCATION PERSONNEL EVALUATION PROGRAM assists educators through the process of performance evaluation and professional growth to deliver quality education services and increase student achievement.

• PUPIL TRANSPORTATION SECTION manages the statewide student transportation system. Activities include school bus inspection; fleet renewal assistance; driver education programs; training and certification of school bus drivers, transportation supervisors, and other transportation personnel; technical assistance; and monitoring and evaluating state and local operations.

  • SCHOOL ARCHITECT SECTION reviews and approves schematic, preliminary, and final plans and specifications for projects involving alterations, additions, and new construction of schools as well as architectural agreements, construction contracts, and change orders; advises local boards of education with designs, cost estimates, and construction methods; advises project architects and engineers with respect to design, bidding, and construction of schools; prepares deeds and leases for property sold or exchanged by county systems; inspects and approves all new sites for school construction; and generates and maintains an inventory of all school facilities.

  • SPECIAL EDUCATION SERVICES SECTION provides technical assistance to agencies serving Alabama's gifted and disabled children, ensures compliance with federal and state laws and regulations, and processes complaints and requests for due process hearings and mediation regarding special education issues.

  • ASSESSMENT AND ACCOUNTABILITY PROGRAM manages testing and accountability.

  • TEACHER EDUCATION AND CERTIFICATION SECTION ensures that colleges and universities meet the teacher education program approval standards of the State Board of Education. The section staff assists persons who are considering education as a career, students enrolled in teacher education programs, local education agencies in need of personnel, and individuals seeking employment.

State Textbook Committee

The Textbook Adoption Program within the Curriculum and Instruction Section also administers the state textbook law and works with the annual state textbook committees. Those committees consist of twenty-three members, fourteen nominated by the superintendent of education and appointed by the Board of Education, and nine appointed by the governor, subject to confirmation by the Alabama Senate. Of the BOE's appointees, twelve must be teachers or school administrators and two must work in state higher education institutions. One member must be chosen from each of the state's seven congressional districts; the others are at-large members. Of the governor's appointees, one must be chosen from each congressional district, and the other two are at-large appointments but must be local school board members. The governor's nine appointees "shall have general knowledge of the subject area to be considered for textbook adoption and shall have a demonstrated ability to read and write at a post high school level and shall not be employed in education." The law requires that committee membership "shall be inclusive and shall reflect the racial, gender, geographic, urban/rural, and economic diversity of the state." All committee members serve for one year, focusing on one area of the curriculum. Members receive per diem expenses but no other compensation.

The Textbook Adoption Program provides assistance to local school systems in complying with the provisions of the textbook law. For information about the Alabama State Textbook program such as state-adopted lists, rejected textbooks, local adoption forms, adoption schedules, new adoptions, publisher lists, local textbook supervisors, and other information, contact Karen Benefield at karenb@alsde.edu.

About Superintendent Joseph Morton

Morton was appointed in 2004, succeeding Ed Richardson. Morton had previously served as both deputy and interim state superintendent and before that was superintendent of education of Sylacauga City Schools and of Sumter County Schools. Morton has a BS degree from Auburn University and MS and PhD degrees from the University of Alabama.

His accomplishments include being named the outstanding superintendent of education in Alabama by three different organizations, being selected by *Executive Educator* as one of the top one hundred school executives in North America, founding the Sylacauga City Schools Foundation, and being a member of the first class of Leadership Sylacauga and Leadership Alabama.

Contacts in the office of the State Superintendent of Education

Dr. Joseph B. Morton, State Superintendent .... (334) 242-9700
Dr. Eddie R. Johnson, Deputy State Supt.—Professional Services ... (334) 242-9960
Dr. Tommy Bice, Deputy State Supt.—Instructional Services .... (334) 242-8154
Feagin Johnson Jr., Asst. State Supt. .... (334) 242-9716
Craig Pouncey, Asst. State Supt.—Admin. and Financial Services.... (334) 242-9755
Sherrill Parris, Asst. State Supt.—Alabama Reading Initiative .... (334) 353-1389

POSTSECONDARY EDUCATION

Alabama Community College System
Alabama Dept. of Postsecondary Education
401 Adams Avenue*
P.O. Box 302130
Montgomery, AL 36130
(334) 242-2900
www.accs.cc

*The Department of Postsecondary Education will be relocating in fall 2009 to the following address:

135 South Union Street
Montgomery, AL 36104

**INTERIM CHANCELLOR
JOAN Y. DAVIS**

Legislative Authority

The Department of Postsecondary Education was established as a separate state agency in May of 1982 by the passage of Act No. 82-486 by the Alabama Legislature. This act authorized the State Board of Education to appoint a chancellor for the purpose of: (1) assisting the State Board in carrying out its authority with respect to the management and operation of the community, junior, and technical colleges, and Athens State University; and (2) administering the Office of the Chancellor, including the appointment of personnel as needed to carry out the tasks and responsibilities of the department.

Mission

The Alabama Department of Postsecondary Education provides a unified system of institutions for delivering academic education, adult education, and workforce development. The department's goals are to develop an educated, prosperous population by providing an affordable community college system to help citizens of any walk or stage of life succeed through quality education and training. The department has direct responsibility to the State Board of Education for the direction and supervision of educational programs and services provided by the Alabama Community College System. The department provides leadership, service, and regulatory functions for the member institutions of the Alabama Community College System to ensure educational accessibility, excellence, and equity for all citizens of Alabama.

The Alabama Community College System includes twenty-one community colleges, four technical colleges, Marion Military Institute, Athens State University, the Alabama Industrial Development Training Institute, and the Alabama Technology

Network. With a total budget of nearly $1 billion, the system serves more than 300,000 people a year.

Divisions/Services

• THE COMMUNICATIONS DIVISION provides internal and external communication services to enhance the visibility of the Alabama Community College System and the Department of Postsecondary Education and to accurately project key messages and images through electronic and online venues, news and feature releases, publications, the web site, coordinated outreach activities, advertising, and responses to media queries.

• THE EXECUTIVE DIVISION supports the chancellor's leadership of the department and the postsecondary institutions and agencies; develops proposed legislation, policies, regulations, and guidelines; develops and executes strategies for long-range planning, technical assistance, oversight, and State Board of Education relations; and provides liaison to constituencies that impact institution and agency roles.

• THE FACILITIES DIVISION, as the liaison between the department and the system's colleges, oversees new construction, renovation, and other facility needs; advises colleges in the maintenance and upkeep of their facilities; advises colleges in selection of architects, engineers, and contractors; advises in programming and planning stages of construction; verifies construction schedules and estimates; resolves periodic physical plant issues and problems; ensures that the Alabama State Bid Law and other applicable building codes are followed; gives oversight, support, and assistance to colleges for the capital expenditures for construction projects; approves all contracts with architects, engineers, and general contractors; submits drawings, specifications, and designs related to building codes, life safety, state energy code, and fire code to the Alabama Building Commission; and assists colleges in the submission of construction projects through the chancellor to the State Board of Education for approval.

• THE FISCAL SERVICES DIVISION provides leadership and guidance to the Alabama Community College System and the Department of Postsecondary Education for the effective and efficient use of available resources to accomplish the academic learning, adult education, and workforce training needs of the state. The division is responsible for fiscal research, resource analysis, fiscal planning, budgeting, monitoring, and financial management for the institutions of the Alabama Community College System and the Department of Postsecondary Education. The division develops, manages, and directs the financial reporting system for postsecondary education institutions and the department and provides technical assistance to postsecondary education institutions and the department.

• THE GOVERNMENT RELATIONS DIVISION serves the Alabama Community College System by advancing the strategic interests of the system among state, city, and federal elected officials and government agencies, as well as with civic and business leaders. In pursuit of this mission, the division strives to conduct itself in a highly transparent and ethical manner.

• THE INSTRUCTIONAL AND STUDENT SERVICES DIVISION provides technical assistance to the postsecondary education institutions in the areas of program development, staff development, and student support services; determines and maintains the standards of measurement for course and program approval and maintains the official System academic inventory; and provides liaison for the department with external agencies for academic services, occupational and economic development training, and student activities. As part of the Instructional and Student Services Division, the Adult Education and General Educational Development Testing Section assists Alabamians in achieving the basic skills and the credentials they need to be productive workers, family members, and citizens.

• THE INTERNAL AUDIT DIVISION provides all segments of the Alabama Community College System, State Board of Education, chancellor, member institutions, and personnel with independent assessments of the quality of the System's internal controls and administrative processes, and provides recommendations and suggestions for continuous improvements.

• THE LEGAL AND HUMAN RESOURCES DIVISION provides legal advice and representation to the chancellor, the Department of Postsecondary Education, the State Board of Education, and the postsecondary education institutions and agencies under the direction of the State Board of Education. The division provides technical assistance in the development of policy and the interpretation of statutes and regulations; and provides advice and assistance regarding the recruitment, selection, evaluation, management, and training of college and departmental personnel. The vice chancellor for legal and human resources also serves as general counsel and reports to the chancellor.

• THE INFORMATION TECHNOLOGY SERVICES DIVISION develops, directs, manages, and provides information to assist decision making and accountability and to support and improve computer operations; provides technical assistance and data reporting and conducts analysis to support and enhance planning, management, and resource allocation; and provides information to other entities. The Information Technology Services Division is dedicated to increasing the effectiveness and efficiency of all Department of Postsecondary Education divisions and personnel by providing the highest levels of technological and infrastructure support.

• THE WORKFORCE DEVELOPMENT DIVISION assists colleges and communities in meeting current and future workforce needs. The division manages workforce development funds and projects, provides technical assistance, and conducts state-level strategic planning and evaluation. The director of the Workforce Development Division for the two-year college system also serves as the director for the Governor's

Office of Workforce Development. The role of the Governor's Office of Workforce Development is broader than that of the division in that it includes all functions of a state-level, comprehensive workforce development system.

Interim Chancellor Joan Davis

Joan Y. Davis was appointed as interim chancellor by the Alabama State Board of Education in May 2009, following the resignation of Chancellor Bradley Byrne. As interim chancellor she serves as the chief executive officer of Alabama's two-year college system, a position she will hold until a permanent chancellor is appointed. In her permanent position, she is general counsel and vice chancellor for legal and human resources with the Alabama Department of Postsecondary Education in Montgomery. Prior to this, she engaged in private practice as well as governmental and higher education law.

Born in Macon, Georgia, Ms. Davis grew up in Tuscaloosa and is a product of Tuscaloosa City Schools. She holds BA and JD degrees from Bennett College, Greensboro, North Carolina, and The University of Alabama School of Law, respectively. In addition to serving on Alabama Bar Association committees, she serves on the Alabama Legislative Educational Advisory Committee.

Contacts in the Department of Postsecondary Education

* These phone numbers are subject to change when the department moves to its new location in fall 2009.

Joan Y. Davis, Interim Chancellor .... (334) 242-2927

Joan Y. Davis, Gen. Counsel/Vice Chancellor Legal/HR .... (334) 242-2982

Don Edwards, Vice Chancellor for Operations and Planning .... (334) 242-2925

Susan Price, Vice Chancellor for Instructional and Student Services (334) 242-2956

Martha Simmons, Director for Communications .... (334) 353-5892

Anita Archie, Director for Government Relations.......................... (334) 353-2939

Matthew Hughes, Dir., Gov.'s Office of Workforce Development ... (334) 353-1686

Steve Glover, Director for Information Technology Services .... (334) 242-2949

Alvena Williams, Director for Internal Audit................................. (334) 353-2997

HIGHER EDUCATION

Alabama Commission on Higher Education
100 North Union Street
Montgomery, AL 36104-3758
(334) 242-1998
Fax: (334) 242-0268
www.ache.alabama.gov

The twelve-member commission (ACHE) analyzes and evaluates present and future needs for instruction, research, and public service in postsecondary education in the state and assesses present and future capabilities.

**EXECUTIVE DIRECTOR
GREGORY G. FITCH**

Legislative Authority and History

State commissions in 1958 and 1968 recommended creation of an agency to coordinate higher education in Alabama. In 1969, Governor Albert Brewer proposed education reforms including a commission on higher education which would advise the legislature on "all aspects of higher learning from the junior college to the graduate level." The legislature passed Act 69-14, which created the Alabama Commission on Higher Education as an advisory agency. Throughout the 1970s, the question of how much authority ACHE should have continued to be an issue. In 1976, ACHE gained new responsibilities when Governor George Wallace transferred college student assistance functions from the State Department of Education to ACHE. Between 1976 and 1998, nine other student assistance programs were housed at the commission.

In 1979, Act 461 gave the commission approval authority over new programs of instruction, regulatory authority over nonresident institutions operating in Alabama, and approval authority over off-campus instruction. The act also strengthened ACHE's role in planning, and it mandated that overrides of the commission must be by separate bill. Act 1994-202 created the Articulation and General Studies Committee requiring ACHE to: 1) develop a general studies curriculum to be taken by all freshmen and sophomores at Alabama's public colleges and universities; 2) develop a statewide agreement for the transfer of freshman and sophomore credits among all Alabama public colleges and universities; 3) examine the need for a uniform course numbering system, course titles, and course descriptions; and 4) resolve problems in administering the foregoing. In 1995, changes in the Federal Family Educational Loan Program reduced the commission's role in the student aid arena.

In 1996, Governor Fob James called for significant reforms in education. Acts 509, 539, 557, and 771 gave ACHE responsibility for student and faculty record databases and overseeing the collection of facility master plans from each institution. The reform also included review of and mandated standards for all existing academic programs, a process which led to the consolidation or termination of more than one thousand programs in Alabama higher education.

Activities

ACHE seeks to provide reasonable access to quality higher education for Alabama citizens. The commission facilitates informed decision making and policy formulation regarding wise stewardship of resources in response to the needs of students and the goals of institutions. The agency also provides a state-level framework for institutions to respond cooperatively and individually to the needs of the citizens of the state. Specifically, the commission approves new units of instruction, including new institutions, mergers, branch campuses, colleges, schools, division and departments; approves new academic programs; approves off-campus instruction; facilitates planning for higher education, including developing a statewide plan; reviews and makes recommendations concerning existing programs; prepares a Unified Budget Recommendation to the governor and the legislature; collects and compiles information concerning higher education in Alabama; administers student assistance programs; conducts studies on higher education issues and makes recommendations to the institutions, the legislature, and the governor concerning its findings; provides a state-level framework for institutions to respond cooperatively and individually to the needs of the citizens of the state; reviews institutional facilities master plans and reports to trustees and the legislature; maintains an electronic student unit record system to provide accountability on student progress; and provides oversight for the programmatic review of private educational institutions operating as foreign corporations in Alabama in accord with the regulatory authority assigned to the commission by statute.

Commission Members

Members are appointed by the governor, lieutenant governor, and speaker of the house and confirmed by the Senate. As of November 2008, the members were:

Thomas P. Davis, Chairman (7th Congressional District)
6 Rosemont, Tuscaloosa, AL 35401; (205) 349-2624

Stephen Shaw, Vice Chairman, Commissioner at large
505 20th Street N, Suite 940, Birmingham, AL 35203; (205) 322-0457

Ralph Buffkin, 1st Congressional District
308 Gaines Avenue, Mobile, AL 36609; (251) 344-4422

William E. Powell III, 2nd Congressional District
P.O. Box 2499, Montgomery, AL 36102; (334) 265-1867

Larry Hughes, 3rd Congressional District
   72 Shoreline Court, Dadeville, AL 36853; (334) 396-6930

Roberta O. Watts, 4th Congressional District
   P.O. Box 894, Gadsden, AL 35902-0894; (256) 546-1861

Missy Ming Smith, 5th Congressional District
   100 Northside Square, Huntsville, AL 35801; (256) 532-3438

Andrew Linn Jr., 6th Congressional District
   P.O. Box 578, Birmingham, AL 35201; (205) 942-6226

Charles Ball, Commissioner at large
   1731 1st Avenue N, Suite 200, Birmingham, AL 35203; (205) 264-8401

Jeff Coleman, Commissioner at large
   102 Juniper Court, Dothan, AL 36305; (334) 983-6500

Ronald Wise, Commissioner at large
   2000 Interstate Park Dr., Suite 105, Montgomery, AL 36109; (334) 260-0003

J. R. Brooks, Commissioner at large
   P.O. Box 2087, Huntsville, AL 35804; (256) 535-1100

Executive Director Gregory G. Fitch

Fitch was named executive director in July 2006, having previously served as a state higher education executive officer (SHEEO) in Missouri and Idaho. Fitch has also served in chancellor and president roles in three community college systems and as the founding president of the Utah College of Applied Technology. He holds a PhD in administration, curriculum, and instruction from the University of Nebraska-Lincoln, an MA from Emporia State University, and a BA from Washburn University in Topeka. The Missouri native is a Vietnam War veteran and former police officer. He began his education career as a high school teacher and later entered education administration.

Commission Staff and Contact Information

Dr. Gregory G. Fitch, Executive Director.....................................(334) 242-2123

Deborah Nettles, Administrative Assistant ....(334) 242-2139

Margaret Gunter, Director, Communications and
   Governmental Relations..(334) 242-2204

Dr. Pamela Arrington, Director, Instruction, Planning &
   Special Services ....(334) 242-2207

Tim Vick, Director, Operations & Fiscal Services ....(334) 353-9153

Walter Hutcheson, Director, Technology Services ....(334) 242-2743

Diane Sherman, Director, Research Services ....(334) 242-2742

HIGH SCHOOL OF MATH AND SCIENCE

Alabama School of Mathematics and Science
1255 Dauphin Street, Mobile, AL 36604
(800) 897-2767 • www.asms.net

Established in 1989 by Act No. 89-880, ASMS is a residential, public high school for students in grades 10-12 pursuing advanced studies in mathematics, science, and technology. Tuition and room and board are free. With an advanced sequence of study in the sciences, mathematics, humanities, and liberal arts, the educational environment is enhanced by the availability of computers, modern laboratory facilities, independent research, field trips, and opportunities for special projects. The operating budget for the school is supplied by the state, while the campus is owned and maintained by the ASMS Foundation, a non-profit organization that over the years has raised nearly $14 million, much of which has been spent on capital improvement projects. Although ASMS receives state funding, the school does not fall under the jurisdiction of the state school board. The ASMS School Board governs the school and hires a president (Dr. Jane Ellis, since 2002) for administration. The governor appoints nine of the board's 21 members, including one each from the seven congressional districts and two from the Mobile-Baldwin area.

SCHOOL OF FINE ARTS

Alabama School of Fine Arts
1800 8th Avenue North, Birmingham, AL 35203
(205) 252-9241 • www.asfa.k12.al.us

Established as an after-school program in 1968, the school gradually expanded and was reauthorized in 1992 by Act 92-531 as a partially residential public school authorized and funded by the Alabama Legislature to provide tuition-free instruction to talented and impassioned students in grades 7–12. The school provides focused specialty instruction in creative writing, dance, mathematics and science, music, theatre arts, and visual arts, plus core academic courses necessary to earn an Alabama high school diploma. The school operates under its own policies and procedures, guided by a state-appointed board of trustees, which employs an executive director (John Northrop, since 1997) to supervise a staff of more than 100 administrators, teachers, and support workers. Alabama students pay a small semester matriculation fee, but no tuition. Students from outside Alabama pay tuition, which the school sets annually. Residential students pay room and board costs, set annually. Since 1976, the non-profit Alabama School of Fine Arts Foundation has raised funds for school needs and campus expansion. The school's trustees appoint members to the foundation's board of directors, which approves foundation policy and employs an executive director (Bryding Adams), who directs foundation operations.

PUBLIC COLLEGES AND UNIVERSITIES

ALABAMA A&M UNIVERSITY
4700 Meridian Street
Normal, AL 35762
(256) 372-5230 • www.aamu.edu
PRESIDENT: Dr. Beverly Edmond
FOUNDED: 1875
ENROLLMENT: 5,124

ALABAMA STATE UNIVERSITY
915 South Jackson Street
Montgomery, AL 36104
(334) 229-4100 • www.alasu.edu
PRESIDENT: Dr. Andrew Hugine Jr.
FOUNDED: 1867
ENROLLMENT: 5,608

ATHENS STATE UNIVERSITY
300 North Beaty Street
Athens, AL 35611
(256) 233-8100 • www.athens.edu
PRESIDENT: Dr. Robert Glenn
FOUNDED: 1822
ENROLLMENT: 3,348

AUBURN UNIVERSITY

AUBURN UNIVERSITY
107 Samford Hall
Auburn, AL 36849
(334) 844-4650 • www.auburn.edu
PRESIDENT: Dr. Jay Gouge
FOUNDED: 1856
ENROLLMENT: 24,137

AUBURN UNIVERSITY MONTGOMERY
P.O. Box 244023
Montgomery, AL 36124
(334) 244-3602 • www.aum.edu
CHANCELLOR: Dr. John Veres III
FOUNDED: 1969
ENROLLMENT: 5,138

JACKSONVILLE STATE UNIVERSITY
700 Pelham Road N
Jacksonville, AL 36265
(256) 782-5781 • www.jsu.edu
PRESIDENT: Dr. William Meehan
FOUNDED: 1883
ENROLLMENT: 9,077

TROY UNIVERSITY

TROY UNIVERSITY
University Avenue
Troy, AL 36082
(334) 670-3000 • www.troy.edu
CHANCELLOR: Dr. Jack Hawkins Jr.
FOUNDED: 1887
ENROLLMENT: 29,580
*Total of all four campuses

TROY UNIVERSITY DOTHAN CAMPUS
500 University Dr.
Dothan, AL 36303
(334) 983-6556 • dothan.troy.edu
VICE CHANCELLOR: Dr. Don Jeffrey

TROY UNIVERSITY MONTGOMERY CAMPUS
231 Montgomery Street
P.O. Drawer 4419
Montgomery, AL 36103
(334) 241-9591 • montgomery.troy.edu
VICE CHANCELLOR: Ray White

TROY UNIVERSITY PHENIX CITY CAMPUS
One University Place
Phenix City AL 36869
(334) 448-5106 • phenix.troy.edu
VICE CHANCELLOR: Dr. Curtis Pitts

UNIVERSITY OF ALABAMA SYSTEM
401 Queen City Avenue
Tuscaloosa, AL 35401-1551
Phone: 205-348-5861
Fax: 205-348-9788
CHANCELLOR: Dr. Malcolm Portera

UNIVERSITY OF ALABAMA
Office of Undergraduate Admissions
Box 870132
Tuscaloosa, AL 35487
(205) 348-5666 • www.ua.edu
PRESIDENT: Dr. Robert Witt
FOUNDED: 1831
ENROLLMENT: 25,544

UNIVERSITY OF ALABAMA AT BIRMINGHAM
701 20th Street South, AB 420
Birmingham, AL 35294
(205) 934-2384 • www.uab.edu
PRESIDENT: Dr. Carol Garrison
FOUNDED: 1969
ENROLLMENT: 16,246

UNIVERSITY OF ALABAMA IN HUNTSVILLE
301 Sparkman Dr.
Huntsville, AL 35899
(256) 824-1000 • www.uah.edu
PRESIDENT: Dr. David Williams
FOUNDED: 1950
ENROLLMENT: 7,264

UNIVERSITY OF MONTEVALLO
Office of Admissions Station 6030
Montevallo, AL 35115
(205) 665-6000 • www.montevallo.edu
PRESIDENT: Dr. Phillip Williams
FOUNDED: 1896
ENROLLMENT: 2,949

UNIVERSITY OF NORTH ALABAMA
122 Bibb Graves Hall
Florence, AL 35632
(256) 765-4100 • www.una.edu
PRESIDENT: Dr. William G. Cale Jr.
FOUNDED: 1830
ENROLLMENT: 7,097

UNIVERSITY OF SOUTH ALABAMA
307 University Boulevard
Mobile, AL 36688
(251) 460-6984 • www.usouthal.edu
PRESIDENT: V. Gordon Moulton
FOUNDED: 1963
ENROLLMENT: 13,779

UNIVERSITY OF WEST ALABAMA
Undergraduate Admissions Station 4
Livingston, AL 35470
(205) 652-3400 • www.uwa.edu
PRESIDENT: Dr. Richard Holland
FOUNDED: 1835
ENROLLMENT: 4,011

PUBLIC COMMUNITY COLLEGES

ALABAMA SOUTHERN COMMUNITY COLLEGE

2800 South Alabama Avenue
Monroeville, AL 36460
(251) 575-3156 • www.ascc.edu
PRESIDENT: Dr. John A. Johnson
FOUNDED: 1965
ENROLLMENT: 1,321
BRANCH: Thomasville

BEVILL STATE COMMUNITY COLLEGE

101 State Street
Sumiton, AL 35148
(205) 648-3271 • www.bscc.edu
PRESIDENT: Dr. Anne McNutt
FOUNDED: 1963
ENROLLMENT: 4,151
BRANCHES: Fayette, Hamilton, Jasper

BISHOP STATE COMMUNITY COLLEGE

351 North Broad Street
Mobile, AL 36603
(251) 405-7000 • www.bishop.edu
PRESIDENT: Dr. James Lowe
FOUNDED: 1927
ENROLLMENT: 3,224
BRANCHES: Carver, Central, Southwest

CENTRAL ALABAMA COMMUNITY COLLEGE

1675 Cherokee Road
Alexander City, AL 35010
(256)234-6346 • www.cacc.edu
PRESIDENT: Dr. Stephen Franks
FOUNDED: 1963
ENROLLMENT: 2,249
BRANCHES: Childersburg

CHATTAHOOCHEE VALLEY COMMUNITY COLLEGE

2602 College Drive
Phenix City, AL 36869
(334) 291-4900 • www.cv.edu
PRESIDENT: Dr. Laurel Blackwell
FOUNDED: 1973
ENROLLMENT: 2,005

ENTERPRISE-OZARK COMMUNITY COLLEGE

600 Plaza Dr.
Enterprise, AL 36330
(334) 347-2623 • www.eocc.edu
PRESIDENT: Dr. Nancy Chandler
FOUNDED: 1965
ENROLLMENT: 2,350
BRANCH: Aviation Campus

GADSDEN STATE COMMUNITY COLLEGE

1001 George Wallace Dr.
Gadsden, AL 35903
(256) 549-8200 • www.gadsdenstate.edu
PRESIDENT: Dr. Darryl Harrison
FOUNDED: 1925
ENROLLMENT: 5,803
BRANCHES: Ayers, East Broad Street, Valley Street

GEORGE CORLEY WALLACE COMMUNITY COLLEGE

3000 Earl Goodwin Pkwy.
Selma, AL 36702
(334) 876-9227 • www.wccs.edu
PRESIDENT: Dr. James Mitchell
FOUNDED: 1963
ENROLLMENT: 1,896

H. COUNCILL TRENHOLM STATE TECHNICAL COLLEGE

1225 Air Base Boulevard
Montgomery, AL 36108
(334) 420-4300 • www.trenholmtech.
cc.al.us
PRESIDENT: Sam Munnerlyn
FOUNDED: 1961
ENROLLMENT: 1,368
BRANCHES: Patterson

J.F. DRAKE STATE TECHNICAL COLLEGE

3421 Meridian Street North
Huntsville, AL 35811
(256) 539-8161 • www.drakestate.edu
PRESIDENT: Dr. Helen McAlpine
FOUNDED: 1961
ENROLLMENT: 825
BRANCH: Atmore

J.F. INGRAM STATE TECHNICAL COLLEGE

5375 Ingram Road
Deatsville, AL 36022
(334) 285-5177 • www.ingram.cc.al.us
PRESIDENT: Dr. J. Douglas Chambers
FOUNDED: 1965
ENROLLMENT: 537

JAMES H. FAULKNER STATE COMMUNITY COLLEGE

1900 U.S. Highway 31 South
Bay Minette, AL 36507
(251) 580-2100 • www.faulknerstate.
edu
PRESIDENT: Dr. Gary Branch
FOUNDED: 1965
ENROLLMENT: 3,664
BRANCHES: Fairhope, Gulf Shores

JEFFERSON DAVIS COMMUNITY COLLEGE

P.O. Box 958
Brewton, AL 36427
(251) 867-4832 • www.jdcc.edu
PRESIDENT: Dr. Susan McBride
FOUNDED: 1963
ENROLLMENT: 1,242
BRANCH: Atmore

JEFFERSON STATE COMMUNITY COLLEGE

2601 Carson Road
Birmingham, AL 35215
(205) 853-1200 • www.jeffstateonline.
com
PRESIDENT: Dr. Judy Merritt
FOUNDED: 1963
ENROLLMENT: 8,284
BRANCH: Shelby

JOHN C. CALHOUN COMMUNITY COLLEGE

Highway 31 North
Decatur, AL 35601
(256) 306-2500 • www.calhoun.edu
PRESIDENT: Dr. Marilyn Beck
FOUNDED: 1947
ENROLLMENT: 9,713
BRANCH: Huntsville

LURLEEN B. WALLACE COMMUNITY COLLEGE

1000 Dannelly Boulevard
Andalusia, AL 36420
(224) 881-2212 • www.lbwcc.edu
PRESIDENT: Dr. Herbert Riedel
FOUNDED: 1963
ENROLLMENT: 1,700
BRANCHES: Greenville, MacArthur
(Opp), Luverne

MARION MILITARY INSTITUTE

1101 Washington Street
Marion, AL 36756
(334) 683-2302 • www.marionmilitary.
edu
PRESIDENT: Col. James Benson, USMC
(Ret.)
FOUNDED: 1887
ENROLLMENT: 461

NORTHEAST ALABAMA COMMUNITY COLLEGE

138 Ala Highway 35
Rainsville, AL 35986
(256) 638-4418 • www.nacc.edu
PRESIDENT: Dr. David Campbell
FOUNDED: 1963
ENROLLMENT: 2,798

NORTHWEST-SHOALS COMMUNITY COLLEGE

800 George Wallace Boulevard
Muscle Shoals, AL 35661
(256) 331-5200 • www.nwscc.edu
PRESIDENT: Dr. Humphrey Lee
FOUNDED: 1963
ENROLLMENT: 4,052
BRANCH: Phil Campbell

REID STATE TECHNICAL COLLEGE

P.O. Box 588
Evergreen, AL 36401
(251) 578-5355 • www.rstc.edu
PRESIDENT: Dr. Douglas Littles
FOUNDED: 1963
ENROLLMENT: 610
BRANCH: Atmore

SHELTON STATE COMMUNITY COLLEGE

9500 Old Greensboro Road
Tuscaloosa, AL 35405
(205) 391-2211 • www.sheltonstate.
edu
PRESIDENT: Dr. Mark Heinrich
FOUNDED: 1951
ENROLLMENT: 5,161
BRANCH: C.A. Fredd

SNEAD STATE COMMUNITY COLLEGE

220 North Walnut Street
Boaz, AL 35957
(256) 593-5120 • www.snead.edu
PRESIDENT: Dr. Robert Exley
FOUNDED: 1935
ENROLLMENT: 2,251
BRANCHES: Arab, Oneonta

SOUTHERN UNION STATE COMMUNITY COLLEGE

750 Roberts Street
Wadley, AL 36276
(256) 395-2211 • www.suscc.edu
PRESIDENT: Dr. Amelia Pearson
FOUNDED: 1922
ENROLLMENT: 4,997
BRANCHES: Opelika, Valley, Wadley

T.A. LAWSON STATE COMMUNITY COLLEGE

3060 Wilson Road SW
Birmingham, AL 35221
(205) 925-2515 • www.lawsonstate.edu
PRESIDENT: Dr. Perry W. Ward
FOUNDED: 1949
ENROLLMENT: 3,614
BRANCH: Bessemer

WALLACE STATE COMMUNITY COLLEGE (HANCEVILLE)

801 Main Street NW
Hanceville, AL 35077
(256) 352-8000 • www.wallacestate.
edu
PRESIDENT: Dr. Vicki Hawsey
FOUNDED: 1963
ENROLLMENT: 5,557

PRIVATE COLLEGES AND UNIVERSITIES

AMRIDGE UNIVERSITY
1200 Taylor Road
Montgomery, AL 36117
(800) 351-4040 • www.amridgeuniversity.edu
PRESIDENT: Dr. Michael Clark Turner
FOUNDED: 1967
ENROLLMENT: 343

BIRMINGHAM-SOUTHERN COLLEGE
900 Arkadelphia Road
Birmingham, AL 35254
(205) 226-4620 • www.bsc.edu
PRESIDENT: Dr. David Pollick
FOUNDED: 1856
ENROLLMENT: 1,389

CONCORDIA COLLEGE
1804 Green Street
Selma, AL 36701
(334) 874-5700 • www.concordiaselma.edu
PRESIDENT: Dr. Julius Jenkins
FOUNDED: 1922
ENROLLMENT: 555

FAULKNER UNIVERSITY
5345 Atlanta Highway
Mongtomery, AL 36109
(334) 272-5820 • www.faulkner.edu
PRESIDENT: Dr. Billy Hilyer
FOUNDED: 1942
ENROLLMENT: 2,918

HUNTINGDON COLLEGE
1500 East Fairview Avenue
Montgomery, AL 36106
(334) 833-4222 • www.huntingdon.edu
PRESIDENT: J. Cameron West
FOUNDED: 1854
ENROLLMENT: 954

JUDSON COLLEGE
302 Bibb Street
Marion, AL 36756
(334) 683-5147 • www.judson.edu
PRESIDENT: Dr. David Potts
FOUNDED: 1838
ENROLLMENT: 311

MILES COLLEGE
P.O. Box 3800
Birmingham, AL 35208
(205) 929-1000 • www.miles.edu
PRESIDENT: Dr. George French Jr.
FOUNDED: 1896
ENROLLMENT: 1,210

OAKWOOD UNIVERSITY
Oakwood Road
Huntsville, AL 35896
(256) 726-7334 • www.oakwood.edu
PRESIDENT: Dr. Delbert Baker
FOUNDED: 1896
ENROLLMENT: 1,824

SAMFORD UNIVERSITY
800 Lakeshore Drive
Birmingham, AL 35229
(205) 870-2011 • www.samford.edu
PRESIDENT: Dr. Andrew Westmoreland
FOUNDED: 1858
ENROLLMENT: 4,469

SELMA UNIVERSITY
1501 Lapsley Street
Selma, AL 36701
(334) 872-7746 • selmauniversity.org
PRESIDENT: Dr. Alvin Cleveland Sr.
FOUNDED: 1878
ENROLLMENT: 287

SOUTH UNIVERSITY
5355 Vaughn Road
Montgomery, AL 36116
(800) 688-0932 • www.southuniversity.
edu/montgomery/Default.aspx
FOUNDED: 1997
ENROLLMENT: 463

SOUTHEASTERN BIBLE COLLEGE
2545 Valleydale Road
Birmingham, AL 35244
(800) 749-8878 • www.sebc.edu
PRESIDENT: Dr. Don Hawkins
FOUNDED: 1935
ENROLLMENT: 220

SPRING HILL COLLEGE
4000 Dauphin Street
Mobile, AL 36608
(251) 380-2262 • www.shc.edu
PRESIDENT: Rev. Richard P. Salami
FOUNDED: 1830
ENROLLMENT: 1,538

STILLMAN COLLEGE
3600 Stillman Boulevard
Tuscaloosa, AL 35403
(205) 349-4240 • www.stillman.edu
PRESIDENT: Dr. Earnest McNealey
FOUNDED: 1876
ENROLLMENT: 915

TALLADEGA COLLEGE
627 West Battle Street
Talladega, AL 35160
(205) 362-0206 • www.talladega.edu
PRESIDENT: Dr. Henry Ponder
FOUNDED: 1867
ENROLLMENT: 350

TUSKEGEE UNIVERSITY
Admissions Office
Tuskegee , AL 36088
(334) 727-8501 • www.tuskegee.edu
PRESIDENT: Dr. Benjamin Payton
FOUNDED: 1880
ENROLLMENT: 2,936

UNITED STATES SPORTS ACADEMY
One Academy Drive
Daphne, AL 36526
(334) 626-3303 • www.ussa.edu
PRESIDENT: Dr. Thomas Rosandich
FOUNDED: 1972
ENROLLMENT: 522

UNIVERSITY OF MOBILE
P.O. Box 13220
Mobile, AL 36663
(251) 675-5990 • www.umobile.edu
PRESIDENT: Dr. Mark Foley
FOUNDED: 1961
ENROLLMENT: 1,541

TUITION AND SCHOLARSHIPS

Alabama has a number of state-level agencies and services that help its citizens afford college or vocational education, including the Alabama Prepaid Affordable College Tuition Program (PACT) and the Alabama Education 529 Fund.

PACT, administered through the state treasurer's office (see page 261), allows purchase of a contract to prepay 135 semester hours of college tuition and eight semesters of qualified fee payments at any Alabama public college or university. PACT may also be used at private or out-of-state institutions. Flexible plans are available to pay for a contract which is priced according to the age of the child at the time of purchase. In essence, college tuition can be purchased at today's prices for tomorrow's use.

The Alabama Higher Education 529 Fund allows investment in a program selected from a number of professionally crafted investment strategies. The beneficiary of the account may be a child, adult, or the purchaser. Withdrawals from the account can be used to pay for tuition, fees, books, and room and board at any accredited college, trade, or graduate school.

Other programs for higher education financial assistance include:
- Alabama Student Assistance Program
- Alabama Education Grant Program
- Alabama National Guard Educational Assistance Program
- Police Officer's and Firefighter's Survivor's Educational Assistance Program
- Technology Scholarship Program for Alabama Teachers
- Alabama G.I. Dependents' Educational Benefit Program
- Alabama Nursing Scholarship Program
- Alabama Scholarships for Dependents of Blind Parents
- American Legion Auxiliary Scholarship Program
- American Legion Scholarship Program
- Junior and Community College Athletic Scholarship Program
- Junior and Community College Performing Arts Scholarship Program
- Senior Adult Scholarship Program
- Two-Year College Academic Scholarship Program

Links to the above programs can be found at www.ache.alabama.gov/Students&Parents/PayingforCollege.htm.

OTHER STATE AGENCIES

In addition to the constitutional and cabinet offices, the Executive Department includes a large number of other departments, agencies, boards, and commissions. Some have hundreds of employees and multiple offices and control many millions of dollars in the state budget. Some of the larger and better-known agencies are:

ARCHIVES AND HISTORY

Alabama Department of Archives and
History
624 Washington Avenue
P.O. Box 300100
Montgomery, AL 36130-0100
(334) 242-4435
www.archives.alabama.gov

DIRECTOR

EDWIN C. BRIDGES

The Alabama Department of Archives and
History preserves the state's historical records and
artifacts and promotes a better understanding of
Alabama history.

Founded in 1901, the Alabama Archives
is the oldest state historical department in the
United States. In addition to collecting, preserving, and making available records
of Alabama and her people, the Archives houses the state history museum, provides
records management services to state and local governments, promotes the study and
appreciation of Alabama history, and conducts a wide variety of educational programs
about Alabama.

Divisions

• ADMINISTRATIVE SERVICES includes security, building operations, budgeting,
financial management, development, and publications.

• GOVERNMENT RECORDS serves as the contact for government officials seeking
assistance with policies, standards, and procedures related to government records. It
also manages governmental collections within the Archives and coordinates development of the department's web site and digital resources.

• PUBLIC SERVICES provides research assistance and educational services to students, teachers, and the general public and operates the Museum of Alabama. Staff
in the Research Room provide assistance with genealogical, scholarly, legal, and other
research. The educational staff offers a wide variety of programs and learning materials for students and teachers, as well as programs for the general adult public. The
division also manages the department's artifact and private records collections and the
department's volunteer program.

COUNCIL ON THE ARTS

Alabama State Council on the Arts
& the Alabama Artists Gallery
201 Monroe Street
Montgomery, AL 36130-1800
(334) 242-4076
www.arts.alabama.gov

EXECUTIVE DIRECTOR
AL HEAD

The Alabama State Council on the Arts began with a 1966 executive order by Governor George C. Wallace and was formally established by legislative act the following year. The primary purpose of the council is to "enhance the quality of life in Alabama culturally, economically, and educationally by supporting the state's diverse and rich artistic resources." In addition, the council receives and disburses federal funds from the National Endowment for the Arts (NEA) as part of a federal-state partnership to support not-for-profit arts and arts-programming organizations, schools, and artists.

As an independent state agency, ASCA is governed by state administrative policies but is also overseen by a fifteen-member council appointed by the governor. The council assigns grant funds and approves programs; adopts long-range plans that establish agency goals and objectives; hires the executive director; and writes bylaws that guide the full-time staff of seventeen. Grant programs and services include the performing, visual, and literary arts and encompass arts education, folk arts, and community arts development, as well as assistance to underserved audiences, cultural facilities, and individual artists. Since 1967, ASCA has awarded more than 13,000 grants totaling $68.6 million. The Alabama Center for Traditional Culture, a division within the Alabama State Council on the Arts, was created in 1990 to further the agency's mission to research, document, and preserve the state's folk culture.

ASCA partners with statewide arts-service organizations with mutual goals, including the Alabama Writers Forum, the Alabama Alliance for Arts Education, Design Alabama, the Alabama Dance Council, the Alabama Folklife Association, and the Alabama Crafts Council. Such partnerships expand the agency's ability to address needs and accomplish major objectives without overburdening its resources and staff. Programs sponsored by the partnerships include the Alabama Dance Summit, Open Door (a writer-in-residence initiative), the Alabama Community Scholars Institute, the Mayor's Design Institute, the Imaginative Learning Workshops for teachers, and the Alabama Red Clay Conference for craftsmen.

CRIMINAL JUSTICE INFORMATION CENTER

Alabama Criminal Justice Information Center
201 South Union Street, Ste. 200
Montgomery, AL 36104
(334) 517-2400
www.acjic.alabama.gov

DIRECTOR

MAURY MITCHELL

Established in 1975, the Alabama Criminal Justice Information Center (ACJIC) is responsible for gathering and providing critical information for law enforcement and the criminal justice community. ACJIC connects Alabama's local, state, and federal law enforcement agencies to the National Crime Information Center (NCIC), administered by the Federal Bureau of Investigation's Criminal Justice Information System (FBI CJIS), and to law enforcement agencies in all fifty states and internationally via Nlets, the International Justice and Public Safety Network.

ACJIC operates its Command Center 24 hours a day, 7 days a week to provide and assist criminal justice agencies with authorized access to its information systems. ACJIC also operates state-specific information systems such as AlaCOP, Alabama's secure web portal for authorized law enforcement and criminal justice officers, and the Alabama Law Enforcement Tactical System (LETS). LETS is ACJIC's secure, Internet-based information system sharing vital information maintained by Alabama state agencies (such as Alabama driver license, boat registration, corrections, and automobile tag registrations) with authorized criminal justice agencies.

ACJIC also is responsible for establishing the policy governing and administering the management of an information technology security program for criminal justice agencies authorized to access NCIC. The agency also houses Statistical Analysis Center (SAC), which is responsible for collecting Uniform Crime Reports (UCR) and reporting Alabama crime information statistics to the FBI.

ACJIC is governed by the ACJIC Commission, a supervisory board responsible for establishing the policies and rules governing the operation of the agency. Responsibility for the day-to-day operations of the agency is vested in the ACJIC director, who works under the supervision of the ACJIC Commission.

DOCKS/PORT AUTHORITY

Alabama State Port Authority
P.O. Box 1588
Mobile, AL 36633
(251) 441-7200
www.asdd.com

DIRECTOR/CEO
JAMES K. LYONS

The State Port Authority owns and operates Alabama's deepwater port and inland dock facilities. The authority's container, general cargo, and bulk facilities have immediate access to two interstate systems, five Class I railroads, a rail ferry service every four days to and from Mexico, and nearly fifteen thousand miles of inland waterway connections.

The authority has an annual gross revenue budget of $125 million and manages four million square feet of warehouses and freight yards and nearly four thousand acres of real estate in Alabama. In 2008, over twenty-eight million tons of cargo passed through ASPA facilities.

The authority is overseen by an eight-member board of directors appointed by the governor, and a ninth ex officio member is represented in alternate years by either the mayor of Mobile or the president of the Mobile County Commission. As of January 2009, the members were: Tim Parker, chairman; Steve Thorton; C. Michael Fields; David Cooper; Barry Morton; Sonny Callahan; Maj. Gen. Gary Cooper; William Bru; and Mayor Sam Jones. Members serve five-year staggered terms.

Divisions

Executive: James K. Lyons, Director/CEO .... (251) 441-7200

Financial Services: Larry R. Downs, CFO, Secretary/Treasurer.... (251) 441-7050

Linda Paaymans, Vice President .... (251) 441-7036

Marketing: Judith Adams, Vice President .... (251) 441-7003

Trade and Development: Mark Sheppard, Vice President............ (251) 441-7201

Operations: Smitty Thorne, Executive Vice President/COO ...... (251) 441-7238

Brad Ojard, Vice President....................................... (251) 441-8133

Technical Services: Joseph Threadcraft, PE, Vice President .... (251) 441-7220

Information Technology: William (Stan) Hurston, Manager .... (251) 441-7017

Port Police: Jimmie Flanagan, Interim Police Chief .... (251) 441-7172

Terminal Railway: Bill Otter, Interim General Manager .... (251) 441-7305

ENVIRONMENTAL MANAGEMENT

Alabama Department of
Environmental Management
1400 Coliseum Boulevard
Montgomery, AL 36110
(334) 271-7700
www.adem.alabama.gov

DIRECTOR
OTIS "TREY" GLENN III

The Alabama Department of Environmental Management (ADEM) administers all major federal environmental laws, including the Clean Air, Clean Water, and Safe Drinking Water acts and federal solid and hazardous waste laws. ADEM was created by legislative act in 1982.

Divisions

• PERMITS AND SERVICES coordinates all permit applications. An environmental permit is the mechanism used to regulate emissions to the air and water, as well as to assure quality drinking water and the proper management of solid and hazardous waste. The division also contains the Pollution Prevention Unit, which provides assistance on recycling/pollution prevention, and the Ombudsman Office, which assists small businesses in complying with environmental regulations.

• AIR implements procedures designed to ensure that national ambient air quality standards, established by the Environmental Protection Agency to protect human health and the environment, are met.

• WATER evaluates and classifies all waters of the state based on existing and expected uses. The division sees that the Clean Water Act's standards are met. Water quality management follows directions and priorities set by the Clean Water Action Plan, the Nonpoint Source Management Plan, the Coastal Area Management Plan, and the Mobile Bay Natural Estuary Program. The Public Water Supply Program regulates public water systems to ensure Alabamians have safe drinking water.

• LAND seeks to ensure the proper management of solid and hazardous wastes currently being generated, remedies sites where waste has been improperly managed, and plans for future waste disposal.

• FIELD OPERATIONS is the primary source of scientific and technical support for the department.

• OFFICE OF ENVIRONMENTAL JUSTICE ensures that all Alabama citizens can participate in the development, implementation, and enforcement of environmental laws, regulations, and policies.

ETHICS COMMISSION

Alabama Ethics Commission
100 North Union Street, Ste. 104
Montgomery, AL 36104
(334) 242-2997
www.ethics.alabama.gov

DIRECTOR
JAMES L. SUMNER JR.

The Ethics Commission implements the Alabama Ethics Law, *Code of Ethics for Public Officials, Employees* etc., Section 36-25-1 through 36-25-30, *Code of Alabama, 1975*, as amended. The law seeks to ensure that public officials are independent and impartial; that decisions and policies are made in the proper governmental channels; that public office is not used for private gain; and, most importantly, that there is public confidence in the integrity of government. The law requires a five-member commission, "each of whom shall be a fair, equitable citizen of this state and of high moral character and ability." Members serve five-year terms and are appointed by the governor, lieutenant governor, and speaker of the Alabama House of Representatives, with confirmation by the Alabama Senate.

Commissioners

Cameron McDonald Vowell, Chair, Birmingham
Michael K. K. Choy, Vice-Chair, Birmingham
Linda Green, Huntsville
Braxton L. Kittrell Jr., Mobile
Josephine M. Venable, Tallassee

Staff Contacts

Director: James L. Sumner Jr. .... (334) 242.2806

Legal Division: Hugh R. Evans III, General Counsel .... (334) 242.2873

Administrative Division: Marie P. Malinowski, Chief................. (334) 242.2883

Investigative Division: Charles A. Aldridge, Chief...................... (334) 242.2804

Advisory Opinions: Theresa A. Davis, Legal Research Assistant... (334) 242.3747

Lobbyist/Principal Information: .... (334) 242.2997

Fiscal Officer/Personnel Manager: Barbi Lee .... (334) 242.2857

FORENSIC SCIENCES

Alabama Department of Forensic Sciences
991 Wire Road
Auburn, AL 36830
(334) 821-6255
www.adfs.alabama.gov

DIRECTOR

MICHAEL SPARKS

The Alabama Department of Forensic Sciences (ADFS) provides scientific assistance to both law enforcement agencies (local, state, and federal) and defense entities that are investigating criminal cases within the boundaries of the state. It also cooperates with district attorneys and coroners in the investigation of deaths as a result of unnatural causes. Investigations that cross state lines may also require the services of the department.

The department was established in 1935 with a mandate to conduct impartial analyses of evidence and unbiased medico-legal death investigations. The placement of ADFS as a separate entity within the Executive Department was to ensure fairness for suspects by removing political pressures and prosecution/defense bias from the agency.

Divisions

• Forensic science services are provided from ten laboratories located in Huntsville, Florence, Birmingham/Hoover, Jacksonville, Tuscaloosa, Mobile, Montgomery, Auburn, Dothan, and Calera.

• The Huntsville, Birmingham/Hoover, Mobile, and Montgomery laboratories are full-service or regional laboratories.

• Five satellite laboratories in Florence, Tuscaloosa, Jacksonville, Auburn, and Dothan provide primarily drug chemistry and crime scene investigation services.

• Death investigation services are performed in Huntsville, Montgomery, and Mobile medical examiner facilities.

• Implied consent (breath alcohol) services are centralized in Calera.

• Executive and department-wide administrative activities are performed at ADFS headquarters in Auburn, as required by law.

FORESTRY COMMISSION

Alabama Forestry Commission
513 Madison Avenue
Montgomery, AL 36104
(334) 240-9300
www.forestry.alabama.gov

**STATE FORESTER
LINDA CASEY**

Alabama is blessed with an abundance of healthy, diverse, and productive forests. These forests provide many benefits including recreational opportunities, wildlife habitat, clean water, and clean air, and they support one of the largest manufacturing industries in the state — the forest products industry.

The Alabama Forestry Commission (AFC) understands the value of forests to the state's economy and environment. As the state agency with the responsibility of protecting and promoting this vast resource, the AFC provides leadership and guidance to ensure that Alabama's forest resources are properly managed and protected, not only for today's needs but also for future generations.

The mission of the Alabama Forestry Commission is three-fold — Protect, Sustain, and Educate:

• Protect the forests from wildfire, insects, and disease.

• Help landowners responsibly manage their forests using professional technical assistance to benefit themselves, their land, and society.

• Educate the public about the importance and value of Alabama's forests to a healthy economy and environment.

Established as a state agency in 1924, the Alabama Forestry Commission is governed by a seven-member board appointed by the Governor. As of 2009, the commissioners are: Melisa Love, chair, Opelika; Don Heath, vice chair, Hoover; Jett Freeman, Spanish Fort; Randall Gilmore, McCalla; Johnny McReynolds, Russellville; Kenneth Real, Detroit; and Jerry M. Smith, Vernon.

GEOLOGICAL SURVEY/OIL AND GAS

Geological Survey of Alabama
State Oil and Gas Board
420 Hackberry Lane
Tuscaloosa, AL 35486
(205) 349-2852
www.gsa.alabama.gov
www.ogb.alabama.gov

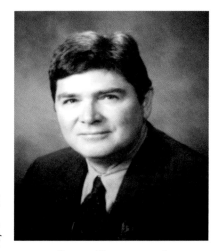

**STATE GEOLOGIST/
OIL AND GAS SUPERVISOR
BERRY H. "NICK" TEW JR.**

The Geological Survey of Alabama, established in 1848, explores and evaluates the mineral, water, energy, biological, and other natural resources of the State of Alabama and conducts basic and applied research in these fields. Its resources and information are provided to Alabama citizens, other state agencies, and educational institutions.

The State Oil and Gas Board is a regulatory agency charged with preventing waste and promoting the conservation of oil and gas while protecting the environment and the rights of owners. The Board has the authority to make and enforce regulations concerning Alabama's petroleum resources. The State Geologist/Oil and Gas Supervisor and the OGB staff implement the policies of the Board.

Divisions and Services

GEOLOGICAL SURVEY

• Geologic Investigations Program—coastal resources section, geologic mapping, geological hazards, and resources information.

• Water Investigations Program—hydrogeology, biological systems, geochemical laboratory, and water information section.

• Energy Investigations Program—coal systems and technology, petroleum systems and technology, and carbon sequestration.

OIL AND GAS BOARD

• Compliance and Hearings Division—north Alabama compliance operations, south Alabama compliance operations, and hearings.

• Technical Operations and Ground Water Protection Division—permitting, technical evaluations, engineering evaluations, geologic evaluations, ground water protection, Underground Injection Control Program, and gas storage.

• Information Technology and Records Management Division—Geographic Information Systems, maps, webpage, system administration, well records, log records, production records, and document imaging.

HISTORICAL COMMISSION

Alabama Historical Commission
468 South Perry Street
P.O. Box 300900
Montgomery, AL 36130-0900
(334) 230-2690
www.preserveala.org

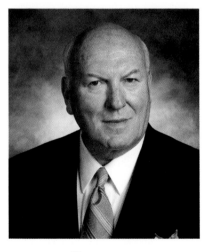

DIRECTOR

FRANK WHITE

The Alabama Historical Commission is charged with safeguarding Alabama's historic buildings and sites. Created by an act of the state legislature in 1966, the commission consists of 21 appointed members. Chair, James P. "Ike" Adams; Vice Chair, Daniel D. Bennett; Secretary, Ann Bedsole. Members: Governor Bob Riley, Janice Hawkins, Jeff Jakeman, Edwin C. Bridges, J. Danny Cooper, Ralph Draughon Jr., Lieutenant Governor Jim Folsom Jr., John Franklin Grant, Seth Hammett, Barnett Lawley, Stephen Martin, William F. Denson III, Lee Sentell, Craig Sheldon, Guy Spencer, Katherine Lynn, Gregory A. Waselkov, and Becky Fendley.

Divisions

Executive Director and
   State Historic Preservation Officer: Frank White .... (334) 230-2690
Executive Assistant: Stacey Little .... (334) 230-2690
Historic Preservation: Elizabeth Ann Brown, Director .... (334) 230-2667
State Archaeologist: Stacye Hathorn .... (334) 230-2649
Review and Compliance: Amanda Hill, Program Head .... (334) 230-2692
Survey and Registration: Lee Anne Wofford, Cemetery Programs (334) 230-2659
National Register Coordinator: Susan Enzweiler .... (334) 230-2644
Outreach: Ellen Mertins, Director .... (334) 230-2657
Communications Coordinator: John Greene .... (334) 230-2680
Community Services: Mary Shell, Preservation Planner .... (334) 230-2691
Senior Architectural Historian: Robert Gamble .... (334) 230-2670
Historic Sites: Mark Driscoll, Director .... (334) 230-2676
Alabama State Capitol: Christy Carl .... (334) 242-3188
Finance: Lisa D. Jones .... (334) 230-2663
Grants: John R. Powell .... (334) 230-2654
Personnel: Clara Nobles .... (334) 230-2675

INDUSTRIAL DEVELOPMENT TRAINING

Alabama Industrial Development Training
One Technology Court
Montgomery, AL 36116
(334) 242-4158
www.aidt.edu

DIRECTOR

ED CASTILE

AIDT was created in 1971 as part of the Alabama Community College System (see page 322). Consistently recognized for excellence, AIDT ranks as one of the top U.S. state workforce training programs. AIDT was the first state workforce training entity to earn international ISO 9001:2000 certification for its quality management system.

AIDT provides comprehensive workforce recruiting and training for employers who commit to create new jobs in Alabama through startup or expansion. AIDT has been a powerful incentive program involved in virtually all the new job opportunities offered to Alabama citizens over the last several years. AIDT services result in better employees and higher profits, while improving the quality of life and providing better jobs for Alabama citizens.

From automotive to aerospace and warehousing to biomedical, AIDT researches and identifies the needs of each company served and uses that information to develop a full range of technical pre-employment selection programs customized to each company. Whatever an employer needs, AIDT provides assistance for successful start-up or expansion in Alabama.

AIDT services, provided at no cost to trainees or employers, include: identification of employee work skills and knowledge, training curricula, and behavioral and performance criteria needed to meet company expectations; recruitment of qualified candidates for employment; and program development, instructors, equipment, consumable supplies, and training materials. AIDT also provides leadership development; industrial maintenance assessment; industrial safety assessment; process improvement assessment, an independent third-party review of a company's business processes as it relates to lean manufacturing; and AIDT+Extra. AIDT+Extra is a new service tailored toward businesses that do not qualify for standard AIDT services. It provides assistance, accessories, and advice to help businesses recruit, assess, train, and enhance the workforce needed for today's changing market.

PARDONS AND PAROLES

Alabama Board of Pardons and Paroles
301 South Ripley Street, Bldg. G
Montgomery, AL 36130
(334) 353-7771
www.paroles.alabama.gov

EXECUTIVE DIRECTOR
CYNTHIA S. DILLARD

The Board of Pardons and Paroles determines which parole-eligible inmates should be paroled and under what conditions, determines whether to grant partial or full pardons, and remits fines and bond forfeitures. Probation and parole officers (sworn police officers) are based in sixty-one local offices throughout the state to provide investigation, parole, and probation services to the courts and board. The board also operates two transitional facilities for inmates leaving prison or in lieu of going to prison.

Historically, Alabama governors could issue pardons. An 1897 law allowed the governor to parole as well as pardon. Additional changes in 1901, 1919, 1935, and 1939 moved the state closer to the present system and removed pardons and paroles from the governor's hands. The present statutory authority is Title 15, *Code of Alabama 1975*, as amended.

The Board

Three members of the board are appointed by the governor and confirmed by the Senate to serve six-year terms. The present members are: William W. Wynne Jr., chairman; VeLinda A. J. Weatherly; and Robert P. Longshore.

Individual board members are prohibited by law from discussing specific cases which may be before them or which may come before them in the future except during open public meetings when there is a quorum present and to which notices have been sent to all parties required by law. However, staff personnel may speak with citizens about specific cases and will receive any written correspondence directed to them by postal mail or by e-mail. Comments to the board may be sent by e-mail to questions4pardonsandparoles@alabpp.gov.

PERSONNEL

State Personnel Department
300 Folsom Administration Building
64 North Union Street
Montgomery, AL 36130
(334) 242-3389
www.personnel.alabama.gov

DIRECTOR
JACKIE B. GRAHAM

The Personnel Department's mission is to increase efficiency in state departments and agencies by improving personnel administration. The department is responsible for attracting persons of demonstrated capacity, ability, and training for state service and affording such persons an equal opportunity to compete for state employment.

Divisions

• CLASSIFICATION AND PAY ensures that the pay plan is competitive and the classification plan is equitable. These concerns are critical to the attraction and retention of the best available applicants to fill state job vacancies.

• RECRUITMENT AND EXAMINATIONS tests and ranks eligible applicants to fill state job vacancies from those who apply.

• CERTIFICATION is the central point for the enforcement of merit system rules and regulations by ensuring registers are processed and applicants appointed in accordance with the rules of the State Personnel Board.

• PAYROLL AND PERSONNEL AUDIT certifies the "lawfulness" of state payrolls and reviews personnel actions affecting payrolls and an employee's personnel record. Personnel Audit along with Payroll Audit assures the employee is properly identified in the automated personnel payroll system.

• TRAINING is responsible for a centralized training effort that reaches the needs of state agencies and all state employees regarding personnel policies and procedures. In addition, areas of management and leadership training are provided.

• HEARING OFFICER hears termination appeals on behalf of the State Personnel Board. Then, the hearing officers make a recommendation to the Board as to what action the Board should take in these matters.

• SPECIAL PROJECTS produces most department reports including the department's annual report as well as the state's personnel procedures manual. The division also manages the state's donated leave, workforce planning, and workplace mediation programs and receives appointments requests above the minimum salary of a classification.

PUBLIC HEALTH

Department of Public Health
RSA Tower, 201 Monroe Street
Montgomery, AL 36104
(334) 206-5300 or (800) 252-1818
www.adph.org

**STATE HEALTH OFFICER
DONALD WILLIAMSON, M.D.**

The Alabama Department of Public Health provides professional services for the improvement and protection of the public's health through disease prevention and the assurance of public health services to resident and transient populations of the state regardless of social circumstances or the ability to pay.

The divisions and services of the department include:

• CHILDREN'S HEALTH INSURANCE PROGRAM (ALL Kids): provides free or affordable medical and dental insurance to children who otherwise might not have access to health care.

• HEALTH CARE: cancer detection; child health; dental care, health education, and community fluoridation programs; diabetes; emergency medical services and trauma systems; family planning; HIV/AIDS; home care; immunization; infection control; laboratory; maternity; nursing; nutrition and WIC; sexually transmitted diseases; social work; tuberculosis.

• ENVIRONMENTAL PROTECTION: food services and lodging inspections and permitting; indoor lead, asbestos, air pollution; and insect and animal nuisances that can transmit disease to humans; on-site sewage disposal systems; solid waste; water supply in individual residential wells.

• HEALTH STANDARDS PROTECTION: health care facilities inspections and licensing including nursing homes and residential care; radiological health including x-ray inspections and nuclear power plant monitoring.

• HEALTH INFORMATION, EDUCATION, AND PROMOTION: chronic disease including diabetes, cardiovascular disease, and tobacco use prevention; disease surveillance and outbreak investigations; emergency preparedness and response; health statistics including birth and death certificates; and injury prevention.

• HEALTH CARE ACCESS: Breast and Cervical Cancer Early Detection Program; cancer registry; minority health and special populations; primary care; and Rural Health.

PUBLIC LIBRARY SERVICE

Alabama Public Library Service
6030 Monticello Drive
Montgomery, Alabama 36130
(334) 213-3900
www.statelibrary.alabama.gov

**DIRECTOR
REBECCA MITCHELL**

The Alabama Public Library Service is the state library agency. APLS is responsible for the administration and distribution of state aid to all public libraries in the state, as well as a competitive grant program under the Library Services and Technology Act.

APLS also serves as a resource for citizens, public libraries, and state employees to promote and support equitable access to library and information resources and services, and to enable all Alabamians to satisfy their educational, working, cultural, and leisure-time interests. These resources and services are provided through APLS's statewide programs and through direct grants and assistance to libraries.

Services and Programs

• ALABAMA VIRTUAL LIBRARY: Online databases providing citizens free access to materials either at their public library or through use of an AVL remote registration card.

• HOMEWORK ALABAMA: A free, online tutoring service for students from kindergarten to adults. Students are connected live with qualified tutors who offer one-on-one assistance with a number of subjects.

• REGIONAL LIBRARY FOR THE BLIND AND PHYSICALLY HANDICAPPED: in the Montgomery area dial (334) 213-3906; elsewhere, dial (800) 392-5671

• REFERENCE/INFORMATION SERVICES: APLS has computers and a reference collection available for state employees and public libraries.

• CHILDREN'S AND YOUTH SERVICES: APLS coordinates a number of children's and youth programs, including Alabama public libraries' participation in the annual Collaborative Summer Library Program, a consortium of states working to provide high-quality summer programs to children.

• INTERLIBRARY LOAN: Libraries across the state share their collections and other resources with one another.

• TECHNICAL SERVICES: APLS acquires, catalogs, and processes materials for APLS collections and assists public libraries with their collections.

PUBLIC TELEVISION (EDUCATIONAL TELEVISION COMMISSION)

Alabama Public Television
2112 11th Ave South, Suite 400
Birmingham, AL 35205
(205) 328-8756 or (800) 239-5233
News Hotline (800) 239-5239
www.aptv.org

**EXECUTIVE DIRECTOR
ALLAN PIZZATO**

The Alabama Educational Television Commission, licensee for the nine APT stations and WLRH-FM in Huntsville, was established by the Alabama Legislature in 1953. In January 1955, WCIQ on Mount Cheaha began operation as the nation's ninth non-commercial television station. Four months later, Birmingham's WBIQ made Alabama the first state with an educational television network. Today, APT operates nine digital transmitters, each broadcasting four separate channels, providing three distinct programming choices.

APT is a PBS affiliate, and its broadcast services are just one medium through which APT fulfills its educational mission. It also provides online educational services through APTPLUS, a resource for parents, students, and teachers; e-Learning for Educators; GED and workplace training; and TV 411, which provides strategies to manage health care and finances as well as prepare for securing a job. Through APT's website, visitors can access streamed videos of APT-produced programs and access a film archive that holds more than 20,000 hours of Alabama footage. APT also provides live seminars for schools and other educational groups in Alabama with educational content that addresses students' academic achievement needs.

The Alabama Educational Television Commission

The commission consists of seven members, each representing a congressional district, appointed by the governor to ten-year terms. As of 2008, the members were: Charles F. Boman, chair, Gadsden (4th District); Dannetta K. Thornton Owens, vice chair, Birmingham (6th District); Bebe Williams, secretary, Huntsville (5th District); Les Barnett, Mobile (1st District); John H. Mosley, Ozark (2nd District); Jan Dempsey, Auburn (3rd District); and Thomas E. Jackson, Birmingham (7th District).

Commission members also serve on the Alabama Educational Television Foundation, along with Chairman Joseph B. Mays Jr., Mark Morrison, and Robert E. Nesbitt, all of Birmingham.

REHABILITATION SERVICES

Department of Rehabilitation Services
602 South Lawrence Street
Montgomery, AL 36104
(334) 293-7500
www.rehab.alabama.gov

COMMISSIONER
STEVE SHIVERS

The department provides services to eligible children and adults with disabilities, under the oversight of a board consisting of one member from each of the seven congressional districts. Of these, three members must have a disability; one must be the parent of a child with a disability; and three must be from business and industry. As of 2008, the board members were: Stephen G. Kayes, Mobile (1st District); Jimmie Varnado, Montgomery (2nd District); Patricia Floyd, Opelika (3rd District); David Brock, Boaz (4th District); James Brown Jr., Huntsville (5th District); Roger McCullough, Birmingham (6th District); and William Strickland, Tuscaloosa (7th District).

Services

• ALABAMA'S EARLY INTERVENTION SYSTEM coordinates services for infants and toddlers with disabilities and developmental delays, preparing them and their families for the transition to the state preschool program for three-to-five-year-olds or other community programs. AEIS also provides financial and technical support to community programs that provide early intervention services and expertise to eligible families.

• CHILDREN'S REHABILITATION SERVICE provides services to children, birth to age twenty-one, with special health-care needs, and provides expertise and technology to local school systems, assisting teachers and school nurses in the education of children with special health-care needs. CRS administers the statewide Hemophilia Program, which serves children and adults who have this life-threatening blood disorder.

• VOCATIONAL REHABILITATION SERVICE provides rehabilitation, education, and employment-related services to some 47,000 adolescents and adults with disabilities through long-standing partnerships with local school systems, colleges and universities, junior colleges, vocational-technical schools, and community rehabilitation programs. VRS also provides more than 6,800 disability-management and employee-placement services to Alabama businesses each year.

• STATE OF ALABAMA INDEPENDENT LIVING/HOMEBOUND SERVICE provides services to Alabamians who have disabilities resulting from spinal cord or head injuries.

RETIREMENT SYSTEMS

Retirement Systems of Alabama
201 South Union Street
Montgomery, AL 36104
(334) 517-7100
www.rsa-al.gov

CHIEF EXECUTIVE OFFICER
DAVID G. BRONNER

The Retirement Systems of Alabama (RSA) consists of the Teachers' Retirement System (TRS), Employees' Retirement System (ERS), Judicial Retirement Fund (JRF), and the Public Education Employees' Health Insurance Plan (PEEHIP). Each system is overseen by a Board of Control. The TRS was established in 1939 to provide retirement benefits to qualified persons employed by state-supported educational institutions. The ERS was established in 1945 to provide retirement benefits to state employees, state police, and on an elective basis to qualified persons of cities, towns, and quasi-public organizations. Qualified judges and justices are provided retirement benefits under the JRF, which was established in 1973. PEEHIP, established in 1983, provides health insurance benefits for active and retired education employees. The RSA has approximately 327,000 members – 226,000 active and 101,000 retired.

The RSA currently manages 22 funds with aggregate assets of approximately $30 billion. The RSA has a diverse portfolio with many real estate holdings in Alabama. These include the Robert Trent Jones Golf Trail with its 468 holes of golf at 11 separate sites as well as several four-diamond resorts, hotels, and spas in the Shoals, Hoover, Point Clear, Mobile, and Montgomery. In addition, Alabama's tallest building is the new RSA Battle House Tower in Mobile. The RSA also owns hotels in Opelika and Prattville.

The RSA owns seven office buildings, seven parking decks, a park, a children's learning center, and an activity center in Montgomery. Its largest holding is 55 Water Street in New York City, which is the largest privately owned office building in New York and the second largest in the nation. Other holdings include Raycom Media, which owns and manages forty-three TV stations, and Community Newspaper Holdings, Inc., which owns 160 daily and weekly newspapers. The RSA invests in numerous industries to help create jobs in Alabama and improve the state's economy and image.

SECURITIES

Alabama Securities Commission
770 Washington Avenue, Suite 570
Mail: Post Office Box 304700
Montgomery, AL 36130
(334) 242-2984
www.asc.alabama.gov

DIRECTOR

JOSEPH P. BORG

The ASC regulates the securities industry in Alabama, protects investors against securities fraud, and enforces the Alabama Securities Act and other state and federal laws. The Alabama Securities Act provides for the licensing and regulation of securities broker-dealers, agents, investment advisers and investment adviser representatives, and financial planners. ASC regulates the individual securities through registration. All of the above entities must be registered with the ASC to conduct business in Alabama unless subject to a statutory exemption from registration. ASC promotes financial literacy by providing presentations, materials for financial literacy education, and free information relating to the disciplinary history (crime, complaints, civil law suits, etc.), educational background, and work experience of a firm or representative selling securities.

Divisions and Contacts

Joseph Borg, Director .... (334) 242-2984

Randal J. McNeill, Deputy Director .... (334) 242-2984

Chris Rhodes, Executive Assistant to the Director .... (334) 242-2984

Legal: Edwin L. Reed, General Counsel .... (334) 242-2984

Enforcement: Senior Investigator .... (334) 242-2984

Registration: Lisa Tolar, Manager (Licensing & Registration) ..... (334) 242-2379

Rena Davis, Manager (Audits & Examinations) .... (334) 242-2380

Education and Public Affairs: Daniel G. Lord, Manager .... (334) 353-4858

Administration: Renee Sanders, Manager .... (334) 242-2378

Data Processing: David Gilmore, Manager .... (334) 242-2395

SOIL AND WATER CONSERVATION

Alabama Soil and Water Conservation
Committee
100 North Union Street, Suite 334
Montgomery, AL 36104
(334) 242-2620
www.swcc.alabama.gov

EXECUTIVE DIRECTOR
STEPHEN M. CAUTHEN

Local soil and water conservation districts (SWCDs), entities of state government, work in conjunction with the Natural Resources Conservation Service (NRCS), a federal agency. In 1937 Congress established the forerunner of the NRCS to combat erosion on farms and ranches throughout the nation. The NRCS is a branch of the U.S. Department of Agriculture and has a headquarters in each state (in Alabama, based at Auburn). In 1939, the Alabama Legislature created the Alabama State Soil and Water Conservation District program. Today, the SWCC provides service, leadership, and assistance to all citizens for the wise use, conservation, and development of Alabama's natural resources.

State Committee Members

(Area 1) Charles W. Butler, New Hope
(2) Vice-Chairman George Robertson Jr., Waverly
(3) Josh Besh, Livingston
(4) Charles A. Holmes, Marion
(5) T. Louis Register, Slocomb
(6) Chairman Frank M. Nalty Jr., Brewton
(Ex officio) Richard Guthrie, Alabama Agricultural Experiment Station
(Ex officio) Micky Humphries, Education Administrator, Agriscience
(Ex officio) Gaines Smith, Cooperative Extension System

Staff Contacts

Stephen Cauthen, Executive Director .... (334) 242-2681

Heather Wilson, Executive Assistant .... (334) 242-2622

J. O. Norris, Water Quality Coordinator .... (334) 242-2662

Phyllis McGuire, Education/Outreach .... (334) 353-1969

VETERANS AFFAIRS

Alabama Department of Veterans Affairs
RSA Plaza, Suite 530
770 Washington Avenue
Montgomery, AL 36130
(334) 242-5077
www.va.alabama.gov

**COMMISSIONER
W. CLYDE MARSH**

At the end of World War II, Alabama established the Department of Veterans Affairs to aid former service personnel. Today the Alabama Department of Veterans Affairs assists eligible veterans, their families, and survivors in obtaining benefits under state and federal laws.

Divisions, Programs, and Services

• EDUCATION SERVICES manages the G.I. Dependents' Scholarship Program that serves the children, stepchildren, spouses, and unmarried widows/widowers of qualified veterans. Dependent spouses and children are entitled to two and four standard academic years, respectively, or part-time equivalent, at any Alabama state-supported institution of higher learning, or a prescribed course of study at any state-supported technical school without payment of any tuition, required textbooks, and instructional fees.

• FINANCE oversees the Alabama Veterans Trust Fund from public and private donations to ensure resources for the state's continuing commitment to provide quality health care for Alabama's veterans.

• VA CLAIMS provides county veterans service officers to assist veterans and their dependents with claims for federal pension, compensation, education, vocational training, health, financial assistance, and other related VA benefits.

• ALABAMA STATE VETERANS HOMES meets the long-term care needs of aging and chronically disabled veterans.

Youth Services

Alabama Department of Youth Services
1000 Industrial School Road
Montgomery, AL 36117
(334) 215-3800
www.dys.alabama.gov

The Department of Youth Services enhances public safety by holding juvenile offenders accountable through the use of institutional, educational, and community services that balance the rights and needs of victims, communities, courts, and offenders. In 2008, DYS handled 2,592 children in its programs.

**EXECUTIVE DIRECTOR
J. WALTER WOOD JR.**

Divisions

• The FACILITIES DIVISION operates the Autauga, Chalkville (girls), Mt. Meigs, Thomasville, and Vacca campuses and the Mobile Group Home. Youthful offenders are also housed under DYS supervision at a dozen contract facilities around the state. These include: Alabama Youth Homes, Inc.; Big Brothers Home Away from Home; Laurel Oaks; Lee County Youth Development Center; Montgomery Group Home (Troy University); North Alabama Group Home (University of North Alabama); Teen University (New Life Center For Change); Troy Group Home (Troy University); The Bridge Inc.; and Three Springs Inc.

• The SCHOOL DISTRICT DIVISION provides juvenile offenders with a comprehensive educational program to meet students' individual needs while preparing them to function and make positive contributions in today's rapidly changing society.

• The EMPLOYMENT DIVISION operates through the State Personnel Department and under the state merit system to screen and hire the approximately 700 DYS employees who work statewide in classifications ranging from laborer to senior psychologist.

Other Boards, Commissions, Committees, and Sub-Agencies

Alabama's government contains numerous boards, committees, commissions, and sub-agencies that serve either independently or in conjunction with the state's larger agencies. These organizations oversee special areas within the state government, such as the licensing of various professions, the protection of public assets, the recognition of outstanding Alabamians, and the provision of specialized services. Size, method of appointment, geographical focus, and term length vary according to the statutory authority for the various entities.

COMPENSATION
Board of Adjustment
Board of Commissioners of Alabama
  Peace Officers Annuity
Crime Victims Compensation
  Commission

CONSUMER AFFAIRS
Housing Finance Authority

CULTURAL-PRESERVATION
Agricultural Museum Board
Cahawba Advisory Committee
Citizenship Trust at the American
  Village
Historic Blakeley Authority
Historic Chattahoochee Commission
Historic Ironworks Commission
Historical Records Advisory Board
Indian Affairs Commission
Space Science Exhibit Commission
St. Stephens Historical Commission
USS Alabama Battleship Commission

ECONOMIC-COMMUNITY
Bear Creek Development Authority
Black Belt Action Commission
Coosa Valley Development Authority
Elk River Development Agency
Tombigbee Valley Development
  Authority

ELECTORAL
Board of Appointment of Registrars of
  Elections
Help America Vote Act Committee

ENVIRONMENTAL-CONSERVATION
Choctawhatchee, Pea, and Yellow Rivers
  Watershed Management Authority
Drycleaning Environmental Response
  Trust Fund Advisory Board
Surface Mining Commission
Water Resource Commission
Water Resource Research Institute

HEALTH-HUMAN SERVICES

Family Practice Rural Health Board
Family Trust Board of Trustees
Governor's Office of Faith Based and
Community Initiatives
Governor's Office on Disability
Safety Coordinating Committee
Sickle Cell Oversight and Regulatory
Commission
Statewide Health Coordinating Council
Women's Commission

HONORS-HALLS OF FAME

Academy of Honor
Aviation Hall of Fame Board
Chiropractors Hall of Fame Board
Men's Hall of Fame
Military Hall of Honor
Motorsports Hall of Fame Commission
Music Hall of Fame Board
Peace Officers' Hall of Fame Board
Senior Citizens Hall of Fame
Sports Hall of Fame Board
Turkey Hunters Hall of Fame Board
Women's Hall of Fame Board

PROFESSIONAL LICENSING AND CERTIFYING

Alabama State Bar
Athlete Agents Commission
Board for Registration of Architects
Board of Athletic Trainers
Board of Chiropractic Examiners
Board of Cosmetology
Board of Dental Examiners
Board of Electrical Contractors
Board of Examiners for Dietetics/
Nutrition Practice
Board of Examiners in Counseling
Board of Examiners in Marriage and
Family Therapy
Board of Examiners in Psychology
Board of Examiners of Assisted Living
Administrators
Board of Examiners of Landscape
Architects

Board of Examiners of Mine Personnel
Board of Examiners of Nursing Home
Administrators
Board of Examiners Speech-Language
Pathology and Audiology
Board of Funeral Service
Board of Hearing Instrument Dealers
Board of Heating and Air Conditioning
Contractors
Board of Licensure for Professional
Geologists
Board of Massage Therapy
Board of Medical Examiners
Board of Nursing
Board of Optometry
Board of Physical Therapy
Board of Podiatry
Board of Public Accountancy
Board of Registration for Foresters
Board of Registration for Professional
Engineers and Land Surveyors
Board of Social Work Examiners
Electronic Security Board of Licensure
Fire College and Personnel Standards
Commission
Home Builders Licensure Board
Licensing Board for General
Contractors
Medical Licensure Commission
Onsite Wastewater Board
Peace Officers Standards and Training
Commission
Plumbers and Gas Fitters Examining
Board
Real Estate Appraisers Board
Real Estate Commission
State Board of Auctioneers
State Board of Occupational Therapy
State Board of Pharmacy
State Board of Registration for Interior
Designers
State Board of Registration for
Professional Soil Classifiers
State Board of Veterinary Medical
Examiners Board

State Pilotage Commission
State Polygraph Examiners Board

REGULATORY

Building Commission
Credit Union Administration Board
Elevator Safety Review Board
Liquefied Petroleum Gas Board
Local Government Records
  Commission
Manufactured Housing Commission
State Records Commission

SCHOLARSHIPS

Board of Dental Scholarship Awards
Board of Medical Scholarship Awards
Board of Optometric Scholarship
  Awards
Board of Trustees of the Alabama
  Stonewall Jackson Memorial Fund

AGENCIES BY NAME

ACADEMY OF HONOR

624 Washington Avenue
Montgomery, AL 36130
(334) 242-4441
www.archives.alabama.gov/famous/academy/
  ahome.html

The Academy of Honor recognizes and honors living Alabamians for their outstanding accomplishments and service.

AGRICULTURAL MUSEUM BOARD

P.O. Box 6362
Dothan, AL 36302
(334) 794-3452
www.landmarkpark.com

The Agricultural Museum Board recognizes the important contribution of agriculture to Alabama and preserves, exhibits, displays, and interprets artifacts and other materials associated with agriculture in the state.

ALABAMA STATE BAR

P.O. Box 671
Montgomery, AL 36101
(334) 269-1515
www.alabar.org

The Alabama State Bar is the licensing and regulatory agency for attorneys in the state of Alabama, subject to the rules of the Alabama Supreme Court.

ATHLETE AGENTS COMMISSION

11 South Union Street, Suite 208
Montgomery, AL 36130
(334) 242-7220

The Athlete Agents Commission licenses athlete agents and makes recommendations concerning laws regulating agents' activities.

AVIATION HALL OF FAME BOARD

4343 73rd Street North
Birmingham, AL 35206
(205) 646-3276
www.southernmuseumofflight.org/AAHOF.
  html

The Aviation Hall of Fame Board promotes

the growth and public support of aviation in Alabama by providing recognition and honor to individuals who by extraordinary achievement and service have made substantial contributions to aviation.

BEAR CREEK DEVELOPMENT AUTHORITY

P.O. Box 670
Russellville, AL 35653
(205) 332-4392

Bear Creek Development Authority was created to develop a unified program for Bear Creek and its tributaries and watershed for the purposes of navigation; water conservation and supply; flood control; irrigation; industrial development; public recreation; and related purposes.

BLACK BELT ACTION COMMISSION

401 Adams Avenue, Suite 480
Montgomery, AL 36104
(334) 353-5185
http://blackbeltaction.alabama.gov

The Black Belt Action Commission's function is to improve the quality of life in Alabama's Black Belt region by actively working with all citizens of Alabama and other supportive parties.

BOARD FOR REGISTRATION OF ARCHITECTS

770 Washington Avenue, Suite 150
Montgomery, AL 36130
(334) 242-4179
www.boa.alabama.gov

The Board for Registration of Architects licenses and regulates architects to ensure the health, safety, and welfare of the public.

BOARD OF ADJUSTMENT

600 Dexter Avenue, 3rd Floor
Montgomery, AL 36130
(334) 242-7175
www.bdadj.alabama.gov

The Board of Adjustment hears and considers claims for damages to persons or property made against the state and its agencies, commissions, boards, institutions, or departments.

BOARD OF APPOINTMENT OF REGISTRARS OF ELECTIONS

11 South Union Street
Montgomery, AL 36130
(334) 242-4227

The Board of Appointment of Registrars of Elections appoints members of county boards of registration and fills vacancies on the boards with the exception of Jefferson County. In practice, each board member appoints one member in each county, and the governor names each county chairman. The board also appoints nine members of the Voter Registration Advisory Board.

BOARD OF ATHLETIC TRAINERS

P.O. Box 11477
Montgomery, AL 36111
(334) 264-1929
www.alata.org/licensure.htm

The Board of Athletic Trainers provides licensing and regulation of athletic trainers for the protection of the public as well as ensuring the integrity of the profession.

BOARD OF CHIROPRACTIC EXAMINERS

102 Chilton Place
Clanton, AL 35045
(205) 755-8000
www.chiro.alabama.gov

The Board of Chiropractic Examiners exists to protect the public by providing information on licensure, issuing and renewing licenses, investigating and acting on complaints, and approving seminars for continuing education.

BOARD OF COMMISSIONERS OF ALABAMA PEACE OFFICERS ANNUITY AND BENEFIT FUND

P.O. Box 2186
Montgomery, AL 36102
(888) 350-4079
www.apoabf.alabama.gov

The Board of Commissioners of Alabama Peace Officers Annuity and Benefit Fund oversees a supplement program for full-time peace officers with the powers of arrest throughout Alabama, providing retirement, disability, and death benefits.

BOARD OF COSMETOLOGY

100 North Union Street, Suite 320
Montgomery, AL 36130
(334) 242-1918
www.aboc.alabama.gov

The Board of Cosmetology examines and licenses cosmetologists and supervises the profession and practice of cosmetology.

BOARD OF DENTAL EXAMINERS

2327-B Pansy Street
Huntsville, AL 35801
(256) 533-4638
www.dentalboard.org

The Board of dental examiners licenses applicants who seek to practice dentistry and dental hygiene in Alabama.

BOARD OF DENTAL SCHOLARSHIP AWARDS

Volker Hall P115
Birmingham, AL 35294
(205) 934-4384

The Board of Dental Scholarship Awards provides loans and scholarships to dental students at the School of Dentistry and the University of Alabama - Birmingham.

BOARD OF ELECTRICAL CONTRACTORS

610 South McDonough Street
Montgomery, AL 36104
(334) 269-9990
www.aecb.alabama.gov

The Board of Electrical Contractors examines and licenses electrical contractors.

BOARD OF EXAMINERS FOR DIETETICS/ NUTRITION PRACTICE

400 South Union Street, Suite 445
Montgomery, AL 36104
(334) 242-4505
www.boed.alabama.gov

The Board of Examiners for Dietetics/ Nutrition Practice protects the health, safety, and welfare of the public by providing dietetic licensure and regulations of licensed dietitians/ nutritionists.

BOARD OF EXAMINERS IN COUNSELING

950 22nd Street North, Suite 765
Birmingham, AL 35203
(205) 458-8716
www.abec.alabama.gov

The Board of Examiners in Counseling protects the welfare of the public receiving mental health counseling services through oversight of statutes regulating licensed counselors. It also investigates and resolves consumer complaints.

BOARD OF EXAMINERS IN MARRIAGE AND FAMILY THERAPY

P.O. Box 240066
Montgomery, AL 36124
(334) 215-7233
www.mft.alabama.gov

The Board of Examiners in Marriage and Family Therapy is a regulatory agency which oversees and licenses marriage and family therapists in the state.

BOARD OF EXAMINERS IN PSYCHOLOGY

660 Adams Avenue, Suite 360
Montgomery, AL 36104
(334) 242-4127
www.psychology.alabama.gov

The Board of Examiners in Psychology licenses psychologists and psychological technicians and protects consumers through the regulatory process.

BOARD OF EXAMINERS OF ASSISTED LIVING ADMINISTRATORS

5912 Carmichael Road
Montgomery, AL 36117
(334) 262-6719
www.boeala.alabama.gov

The Board of Examiners of Assisted Living Administrators licenses and regulates assisted living administrators in Alabama.

BOARD OF EXAMINERS OF LANDSCAPE ARCHITECTS

908 South Hull Street
Montgomery, AL 36104
(334) 262-1351
www.abela.alabama.gov

The Board of Examiners of Landscape Architects regulates the practice of landscape architecture.

BOARD OF EXAMINERS OF MINE PERSONNEL

11 West Oxmoor Road S-201
Birmingham, AL 35209
(205) 944-1075

The Board of Examiners of Mine Personnel gives certificates of competency to persons who pass the required examinations to act as mine foremen or fire bosses in underground coal mines in Alabama.

BOARD OF EXAMINERS OF NURSING HOME ADMINISTRATORS

4156 Carmichael Road
Montgomery, AL 36106
(334) 271-2342
www.alboenha.state.al.us

The Board of Examiners of Nursing Home Administrators ensures that all nursing homes are administered by a licensed administrator; enforces standards that are prerequisite to licensure; administers examinations; issues licenses; investigates and takes appropriate action to all complaints against licensed administrators; conducts disciplinary proceedings; conducts continuing studies and investigations of nursing homes to improve standards; and approves various educational programs for continuing education credits.

BOARD OF EXAMINERS FOR SPEECH-LANGUAGE PATHOLOGY AND AUDIOLOGY

400 South Union Street, Suite 397
Montgomery, AL 36130
(334) 269-1434
http://abespa.org

The Board of Examiners for Speech-Language Pathology and Audiology regulates the practice of speech-language pathology and audiology, including granting of licenses to qualified registrants, registering individuals in clinical fellowships, providing continuing education programs to licensed speech-language pathologists and audiologists, and investigating complaints regarding speech-language pathologists and audiologists.

BOARD OF FUNERAL SERVICE

P.O. Box 309522
Montgomery, AL 36130
(334) 242-4049

The Board of Funeral Service examines, licenses, and supervises funeral directors, embalmers, and funeral establishments.

BOARD OF HEARING INSTRUMENT DEALERS

400 South Union Street, Suite 445
Montgomery, AL 36130
(334) 242-1925

The Board of Hearing Instrument Dealers protects the health, safety, and welfare of the public by providing hearing instrument licensure and regulating licensed hearing instrument dispensers, fitters, and apprentices.

BOARD OF HEATING AND AIR CONDITIONING CONTRACTORS

100 North Union Street, Suite 630
Montgomery, AL 36130
(334) 242-5550
www.hvac.alabama.gov

The Board of Heating and Air Conditioning Contractors identifies and certifies qualified contractors who have the knowledge and ability to install or service and repair heating and air conditioning systems.

BOARD OF LICENSURE FOR PROFESSIONAL GEOLOGISTS

610 South McDonough Street
Montgomery, AL 36104
(334) 269-9990
www.algeobd.alabama.gov

The Board of Licensure for Professional Geologists regulates the public practice of geology.

BOARD OF MASSAGE THERAPY

610 South McDonough Street
Montgomery, AL 36104
(334) 269-9990
www.almtbd.alabama.gov

The Board of Massage Therapy protects the health, safety, and welfare of the public by ensuring that licensed massage therapists, massage therapy schools, and massage therapy instructors meet prescribed standards of education, competency, and practice.

BOARD OF MEDICAL EXAMINERS

P.O. Box 946
Montgomery, AL 36101
(334) 242-4116
www.albme.org

The Board of Medical Examiners certifies that applicants meet the requirements for licensure; investigates complaints and initiates formal administrative actions against physicians licensed in Alabama; and issues and regulates Alabama Controlled Substance Certificates.

BOARD OF MEDICAL SCHOLARSHIP AWARDS

Volkner Hall, P115
Birmingham, AL 35294
(205) 934-4384

The Board of Medical Scholarship Awards establishes and administers scholarships for the study of medicine.

BOARD OF NURSING

770 Washington Avenue, Suite 250
Montgomery, AL 36104
(334) 242-4060
www.abn.alabama.gov

The Board of Nursing regulates nursing practice and education including the approval of nursing education programs, licensure of qualified applicants, removal of unsafe practitioners, and discipline of licensees.

BOARD OF OPTOMETRIC SCHOLARSHIP AWARDS

1530 3rd Avenue South
Volker Hall, P-115
Birmingham, AL 35294
(205) 934-4384

The Board of Optometric Scholarship Awards provides loans and scholarships to optometry students at the School of Optometry at the University of Alabama at Birmingham.

BOARD OF OPTOMETRY

1431 Second Avenue North
Bessemer, AL 35020

(205) 481-9993
www.optometry.alabama.gov

The Board of Optometry regulates and licenses the practice of optometry in Alabama.

BOARD OF PHYSICAL THERAPY

100 North Union Street, Suite 724
Montgomery, AL 36130
(334) 242-4064
www.pt.alabama.gov

The Board of Physical Therapy ensures public protection from the incompetent practice of physical therapy through licensure and regulation.

BOARD OF PODIATRY

610 South McDonough Street
Montgomery, AL 36104
(334) 269-9990
www.podiatryboard.alabama.gov

The Board of Podiatry regulates the practice of podiatry.

BOARD OF PUBLIC ACCOUNTANCY

770 Washington Avenue, Suite 226
Montgomery, AL 36104
(334) 242-5700
www.asbpa.alabama.gov

The State Board of Public Accountancy functions as the licensure and regulatory board for Certified Public Accountants, Public Accountants, non-licensee owners, and CPA and PA firms.

BOARD OF REGISTRATION FOR FORESTERS

513 Madison Avenue
Montgomery, AL 36130
(334) 353-3640
www.asbrf.alabama.gov

The Board of Registration of Foresters administers a licensing and regulatory program for the practice of forestry in order to benefit and protect the citizens of Alabama.

BOARD OF REGISTRATION FOR PROFESSIONAL ENGINEERS AND LAND SURVEYORS

100 North Union Street, Ste. 382
Montgomery, AL 36104

(334) 242-5568

www.bels.alabama.gov

The Board of Registration for Professional Engineers and Land Surveyors protects the public by helping to safeguard life, health, and property, and promotes the public welfare by providing for the licensing and regulation of persons engaged in engineering and land surveying.

BOARD OF SOCIAL WORK EXAMINERS

100 North Union Street, Suite 736

Montgomery, AL 36130

(334) 242-5860

www.socialwork.alabama.gov

The Board of Social Work Examiners protects the public from incompetent, unethical, and unlawful social work practice; licenses properly qualified social workers; and establishes requirements and standards for continuing education.

BOARD OF TRUSTEES OF THE ALABAMA STONEWALL JACKSON MEMORIAL FUND

624 Washington Avenue

Montgomery, AL 36130

(334) 242-4441

The Board of Trustees of the Alabama Stonewall Jackson Memorial Fund is responsible for memorializing General Stonewall Jackson through a program of education. Stonewall Jackson Memorial Funds are used to pay for scholarship loans, which are awarded annually to winners of a statewide essay contest.

BUILDING COMMISSION

770 Washington Avenue, Suite 444

Montgomery, AL 36130

(334) 242-4082

www.bc.alabama.gov

The Building Commission's primary function involves promulgating and enforcing the State Building Code through plan reviews, inspections, and serving as the state's contract administrator for state-funded construction.

CAHAWBA ADVISORY COMMITTEE

P.O. Box 2318; 1004 Water Avenue

Selma, AL 36702

www.cahawba.com

The Cahawba Advisory Committee advises the Alabama Historical Commission on development, fund raising, education, and publicity of the Old Cahawba State Park.

CHIROPRACTORS HALL OF FAME BOARD

3 South Jackson Street

Montgomery, AL 36104

(334) 262-2228

The Chiropractors Hall of Fame Board exists to honor those who have, by achievement or service, made outstanding and lasting contributions to the profession and exhibited outstanding civic service in Alabama.

CHOCTAWHATCHEE, PEA, AND YELLOW RIVERS WATERSHED MANAGEMENT AUTHORITY

400 Pell Avenue; Collegeview Bldg.

Troy, AL 36082

(334) 670-3780

www.cpyrwma.alabama.gov

The Choctawhatchee, Pea, and Yellow Rivers Watershed Management Authority protects and manages the Choctawhatchee, Pea, and Yellow rivers watersheds and develops and executes programs relating to water resource management to ensure water resources are wisely developed and properly used.

CITIZENSHIP TRUST AT THE AMERICAN VILLAGE

3727 Highway 119

Montevallo, AL 35115

(205) 665-3535

www.americanvillage.org

On a unique campus in Montevallo, the Citizenship Trust seeks to strengthen and renew the foundations of American liberty and self-government through citizenship education.

COOSA VALLEY DEVELOPMENT AUTHORITY

100 North Union Street, Room 224

Montgomery, AL 36130

(334) 353-3328

The Coosa Valley Development Authority's purpose is to develop a navigable waterway between Montgomery and Gadsden and to the Alabama-Georgia boundary.

CREDIT UNION ADMINISTRATION BOARD

1789 Congressman William L. Dickinson Drive
Montgomery, AL 36130
(334) 271-2381
www.acua.alabama.gov

The Credit Union Administration Board administers the laws of the state which regulate and otherwise relate to the operations of credit unions in Alabama.

CRIME VICTIMS COMPENSATION COMMISSION

P.O. Box 1548
Montgomery, AL 36102
(334) 290-4420
www.acvcc.alabama.gov

The Crime Victims Compensation Commission provides financial assistance to qualified, innocent victims of violent crime.

DRYCLEANING ENVIRONMENTAL RESPONSE TRUST FUND ADVISORY BOARD

610 South McDonough Street
Montgomery, AL 36104
(334) 269-9990
www.drycleaningtrustfund.alabama.gov

The Drycleaning Environmental Response Trust Fund Advisory Board approves reimbursement requests for drycleaning sites that require environmental cleanup.

ELECTRONIC SECURITY BOARD OF LICENSURE

7956 Vaughn Road, PMB 392
Montgomery, AL 36116
(334) 264-9388
www.aesbl.com

The Electronic Security Board of Licensure exists to require licensing of any person, sole proprietorship, company, or corporation that installs or services locks and/or burglar alarms for residential or commercial use.

ELEVATOR SAFETY REVIEW BOARD

100 North Union Street
Montgomery, AL 36130
(334) 242-3460
www.alalabor.alabama.gov/boards.htm

The Elevator Safety Review Board consults with engineers and organizations for the development of rules and regulations governing the operation, maintenance, servicing, construction, alteration, and inspection of elevators and like conveyances.

ELK RIVER DEVELOPMENT AGENCY

P.O. Box 127, Highway 127
Elkmont, AL 35620
(256) 732-4500

The Elk River Development Agency is a state agency that administers area development projects in Lauderdale and Limestone counties and oversees Elkmont Rural Village.

FAMILY PRACTICE RURAL HEALTH BOARD

19 South Jackson Street
Montgomery, AL 36104
(334) 242-5922

The Family Practice Rural Health Board was established to promote a greater supply of family physicians in Alabama, especially in the underserved rural areas.

FAMILY TRUST BOARD OF TRUSTEES

100 North Union Street, Suite 580
Montgomery, AL 36130
(800) 711-1303

The Family Trust Board of Trustees assists families in planning for the future care of their loved ones with disabilities. The trust is an allowable mechanism designed to protect vital government entitlements, while ensuring the availability of funding to provide optimum care.

FIRE COLLEGE AND PERSONNEL STANDARDS COMMISSION

501 Phoenix Drive
Tuscaloosa, AL 35405
(205) 391-3779
www.alabamafirecollege.org

The Fire College and Personnel Standards Commission provides residential and field-based training and certification for the state's career and volunteer fire services and all other emergency service personnel.

Governor's Office of Faith Based and Community Initiatives

P.O. Box 309534
Montgomery, AL 36130
(334) 954-7440
www.servealabama.gov

The Governor's Office of Faith Based and Community Initiatives provides oversight and authorizes funding for State AmeriCorps grants and serves in an advisory capacity for other programs, including the Governor's Statewide Interagency Council on Homelessness, and initiatives housed within the Governor's Office of Faith-Based and Community Initiatives.

Governor's Office on Disability

2129 East South Boulevard
Montgomery, AL 36111-0586
(334) 353-4663
www.good.alabama.gov

The Governor's Office on Disability monitors, evaluates, advocates, and facilitates the active participation of consumers with disabilities. The office coordinates with the Governor's Office the input from and output to consumers and consumer-driven organizations regarding disability policies and services across the state. The office seeks inclusion and participation of people with disabilities in all aspects of community life.

Help America Vote Act Committee

600 Dexter Avenue, Suite S-105
Montgomery, AL 36130
(334) 242-7200

The Alabama Vote Act Committee assists the Secretary of State with the state Help America Vote Act implementation plan.

Historic Blakeley Authority

P.O. Box 7279
Spanish Fort, AL 36577
(334) 580-0005
www.blakeleypark.org

The purpose of the Historic Blakeley Authority is to establish, preserve, and maintain as a state historic park lands in Baldwin County listed on the National Register of Historic Places as the Blakeley site, along with reconstructed buildings and other present and future improvements. A second purpose is to protect the natural plant and animal life and its environmental habitat.

Historic Chattahoochee Commission

P.O. Box 33
Eufaula, AL 36072
(334) 687-9755
www.hcc-al-ga.org

The Historic Chattahoochee Commission promotes tourism and historic preservation throughout the lower Chattahoochee Valley of Alabama and Georgia.

Historic Ironworks Commission

12632 Confederate Parkway
McCalla, AL 35111
(205) 477-5711
www.alaironworks.com

The Historic Ironworks Commission preserves historical resources of the Alabama iron and steel industry and interprets those resources through heritage education programs and unique outdoor education opportunities in a historical setting.

Historical Records Advisory Board

624 Washington Avenue
Montgomery, AL 36104
(334) 242-4452
www.archives.alabama.gov/hrb/hrbmain-page.htm

The Historical Records Advisory Board, created in 2006, is responsible for providing leadership and guidance in identifying, preserving, and providing access to Alabama's historical records.

Home Builders Licensure Board

445 Herron Street
Montgomery, AL 36130
(334) 242-2230
www.hblb.state.al.us

The Home Builders Licensure Board provides for the licensure of residential home-builders and remodelers that perform work in excess of $10,000; enforces the licensure law; investigates consumer complaints; and maintains a homeowners' recovery fund.

HOUSING FINANCE AUTHORITY

P.O. Box 230909
Montgomery, AL 36123
(334) 244-9200
www.ahfa.com

The Housing Finance Authority serves the housing needs of low and moderate income citizens for safe and sanitary single- and multi-family dwelling units through affordable financing.

INDIAN AFFAIRS COMMISSION

771 South Lawrence Street, Suite 106
Montgomery, AL 36104
(334) 242-2831
www.aiac.alabama.gov

The Indian Affairs Commission brings local, state, and federal resources into focus for provision of meaningful programs for Indian citizens of Alabama, including assistance in economic and social development, promotion of rights to cultural and religious traditions, and provisions for legal recognition of future Indian organizations.

LICENSING BOARD FOR GENERAL CONTRACTORS

2525 Fairlane Drive
Montgomery, AL 36116
(334) 272-5030
www.genconbd.alabama.gov

The Licensing Board for General Contractors licenses and regulates commercial and industrial contractors in the major and specialty classifications that constitute the industry.

LIQUEFIED PETROLEUM GAS BOARD

818 South Perry Street
Montgomery, AL 36102
(334) 242-5649
www.lpgb.alabama.gov

The Liquefied Petroleum Gas Board promotes the safety, health, and general welfare of the people of Alabama through the enforcement of state and federal statutes related to transportation, storage, residential, commercial, industrial installations and suitability of equipment used in the LP-Gas industry.

LOCAL GOVERNMENT RECORDS COMMISSION

624 Washington Avenue
Montgomery, AL 36130
(334) 242-4452
www.archives.alabama.gov/officials/local.
 html

The Local Government Records Commission establishes retention requirements for county and municipal government records.

MANUFACTURED HOUSING COMMISSION

350 South Decatur Street
Montgomery, AL 36104
(334) 242-4036
www.amhc.alabama.gov

The Manufactured Housing Commission regulates the manufactured housing industry in Alabama with emphasis on compliance and consumer protection.

MEDICAL LICENSURE COMMISSION

P.O. Box 887
Montgomery, AL 36101
(334) 242-4153
www.albme.org

The Medical Licensure Commission issues licenses for physicians to practice medicine or osteopathy in Alabama and annually renews licenses. The commission adjudicates formal charges brought by the Board of Medical Examiners against physicians and determines appropriate disciplinary resolution.

MEN'S HALL OF FAME

P.O. Box 2307, Samford University
Birmingham, AL 35229
(205) 870-2362
www.samford.edu/groups/amhf

The Men's Hall of Fame recognizes those men native to or identified most closely with Alabama who have made significant contributions to the state or nation.

MILITARY HALL OF HONOR

1101 Washington Street
Marion, AL 36756
(334) 683-2346
www.marionmilitary.edu/about-mmi/about-
 mmi-honor-hall.da

The Military Hall of Honor identifies and recognizes outstanding Alabamians who have distinguished themselves in the Armed Forces of the United States through extraordinary patriotism and heroism.

MOTORSPORTS HALL OF FAME COMMISSION

3198 Speedway Boulevard
Talladega, AL 35161
(256) 362-5002
www.motorsportshalloffame.com

The Motorsports Hall of Fame Commission manages an exhibit hall which houses and displays exhibits relating to the automobile racing industry and automobile industry.

MUSIC HALL OF FAME BOARD

P.O. Box 740405
Tuscumbia, AL 35674
(800) 239-2643
www.alamhof.org

The Music Hall of Fame Board honors notable music achievers from Alabama and the state's music heritage, in all styles and fields of music.

ONSITE WASTEWATER BOARD

450 South Union Street, Second Floor
Montgomery, AL 36104
(334) 269-6800
www.aowb.alabama.gov

The Onsite Wastewater Board examines, licenses, and regulates persons engaged in the manufacture, installation, or servicing of onsite wastewater systems in Alabama.

PEACE OFFICERS STANDARDS AND TRAINING COMMISSION

P.O. Box 300075
Montgomery, AL 36130
(334) 242-4045
www.apostc.alabama.gov

The primary purpose of the Peace Officers Standards and Training Commission is to prescribe standards for recruitment, appointment, and training of law enforcement officers and correctional officers.

PEACE OFFICERS' HALL OF FAME BOARD

940 Pelham Street
Montgomery, AL 36104
(334) 353-1470

The Peace Officers' Hall of Fame Board honors those living or dead who by achievement or service have made outstanding contributions to law enforcement in Alabama.

PLUMBERS AND GAS FITTERS EXAMINING BOARD

11 West Oxmoor Road, Ste. 104
Birmingham, AL 35209
(205) 945-4857
www.pgfb.alabama.gov

The purpose of the Plumbers and Gas Fitters Examining Board is the promotion of the public safety, health, and general welfare of the people statewide by requiring persons to establish their competency as plumbers and/or gas fitters before performing or supervising plumbing and/or gas fittings.

REAL ESTATE APPRAISERS BOARD

P.O. Box 304355
Montgomery, AL 36130
(334) 242-8747
www.reab.alabama.gov

The mission of Real Estate Appraisers Board is to protect the public interest by assuring that all consumers of real estate appraisal services receive such services from appraisers who are fully qualified in accordance with both federal and state law.

REAL ESTATE COMMISSION

1201 Carmichael Way
Montgomery, AL 36106
(334) 242-5544
www.arec.alabama.gov

The Real Estate Commission protects consumers and regulates the real estate business through the licensing and education of real estate salespersons and brokers and enforcement of the Alabama Real Estate License Law.

SAFETY COORDINATING COMMITTEE

400 South Union Street, Ste. 325
Montgomery, AL 36104
(334) 242-3288

www.safehomealabama.gov/committees.
asp#state

The mission of the Safety Coordinating Committee is to formulate, coordinate, and apply whatever committee resources are available to reduce automobile crash frequency and severity (including remedial first responder services) so that there is a maximum reduction in fatalities, severe injuries, fatal and injury crashes, and property damage crashes.

SENIOR CITIZENS HALL OF FAME

770 Washington Avenue, Ste. 470
Montgomery, AL 36130
(334) 242-5743

The Senior Citizens Hall of Fame bestows honor and recognition upon deserving citizens for their outstanding accomplishments, service, and contributions to the lives of older American citizens.

SICKLE CELL OVERSIGHT AND REGULATORY COMMISSION

1453 Springfield Avenue
Mobile, AL 36604
(251) 432-0301

The Sickle Cell Oversight and Regulatory Commission ensures the delivery of sickle cell services in Alabama. Services can include education, counseling, support, medical referral, and testing.

SPACE SCIENCE EXHIBIT COMMISSION

One Tranquility Base
Huntsville, AL 35805
(800) 637-7223
www.spacecamp.com

The Space Science Exhibit Commission has oversight responsibility for the U.S. Space and Rocket Center.

SPORTS HALL OF FAME BOARD

2150 Civic Center Boulevard
Birmingham, AL 35202
(205) 323-6665
www.ashof.org

The Sports Hall of Fame Board establishes procedures for determining membership in the Hall of Fame and maintains suitable rooms, halls, or displays within the Birmingham-Jefferson Civic Center Complex for the purpose of displaying exhibits relating to sports, athletics, and athletes.

ST. STEPHENS HISTORICAL COMMISSION

P.O. Box 78
St. Stephens, AL 36569
(251) 246-6790
www.oldststephens.com

The St. Stephens Historical Commission acquires, maintains, protects, and promotes properties of historical interest at St. Stephens in Washington County, in the vicinity of the first territorial capital of Alabama.

STATE BOARD OF AUCTIONEERS

610 South McDonough Street
Montgomery, AL 36104
(334) 269-9990
www.auctioneer.alabama.gov

The Board of Auctioneers regulates auctioneers and apprentice auctioneers.

STATE BOARD OF OCCUPATIONAL THERAPY

64 North Union Street, Suite 734
Montgomery, AL 36130
(334) 353-4466
www.ot.alabama.gov

The State Board of Occupational Therapy assures the availability and safe delivery of high-quality occupational therapy services.

STATE BOARD OF PHARMACY

10 Inverness Center, Suite 110
Birmingham, AL 35242
(205) 981-2280
www.albop.com

The Board of Pharmacy creates the rules and regulations for pharmaceutical practice in the state and establishes the standards and requirements for licensure.

STATE BOARD OF REGISTRATION FOR INTERIOR DESIGNERS

P.O. Box 11026
Birmingham, AL 35202
(205) 879-4232
www.idboard.alabama.gov

The Board of Registration for Interior

Designers regulates the practice of interior design and provides the registration of qualified persons as interior designers.

STATE BOARD OF REGISTRATION FOR PROFESSIONAL SOIL CLASSIFIERS

100 North Union Street, Suite 334
Montgomery, AL 36104
(334) 242-2620
www.swcc.alabama.gov

The Board of Registration for Professional Soil Classifiers regulates the soil classifiers profession, examines applicants, registers professional soil classifiers, and renews the registrations of professional soil classifiers.

STATE BOARD OF VETERINARY MEDICAL EXAMINERS

P.O. Box 1968
Decatur, AL 35602
(256) 353-3544
www.asbvme.us

The Veterinary Medical Examiners Board protects the interest of the public and aids practicing veterinarians by its efforts toward maintaining a high standard of integrity and skill in the practice of veterinary medicine and by ensuring that veterinary facilities meet all standards set forth in the Veterinary Practice Act and the Administrative Code.

STATE PILOTAGE COMMISSION

P.O. Box 273
Mobile, AL 36601
(334) 479-9247

The State Pilotage Commission makes all rules and regulations governing the piloting of ships and watercraft into and out of any harbor in the State of Alabama.

STATE POLYGRAPH EXAMINERS BOARD

P.O. Box 1511
Montgomery, AL 36104
(334) 353-1881
www.polygraph.alabama.gov

The Polygraph Examiners Board protects the citizens of Alabama by licensing polygraph examiners and enforcing the *Code of Alabama* as it pertains to polygraphs.

STATE RECORDS COMMISSION

624 Washington Avenue
Montgomery, AL 36130
(334) 242-4435
www.archives.alabama.gov/officials/state1.html

The State Records Commission establishes retention requirements for government records created by all state agencies, including publicly funded colleges and universities.

STATEWIDE HEALTH COORDINATING COUNCIL

P.O. Box 303025
Montgomery, AL 36130
(334) 242-4103
www.shpda.alabama.gov

The Statewide Health Coordinating Council prepares the State Health Plan, advises the State Health Planning and Development Agency on matters relating to health planning and resource development, and performs other functions as may be delegated to it to include an annual review of the State Health Plan.

SURFACE MINING COMMISSION

1811 2nd Avenue
Jasper, AL 35502
(205) 221-4130
www.surface-mining.alabama.gov

The Surface Mining Commission is the primary regulatory authority for surface coal mining operations for the State of Alabama under the federal Surface Mining Control and Reclamation Act of 1977.

TOMBIGBEE VALLEY DEVELOPMENT AUTHORITY

100 North Union Street, Room 224
Montgomery, AL 36130
(334) 353-3328

The Tombigbee Valley Development Authority facilitates construction of the Tennessee-Tombigbee Waterway and develops water resources of the Tombigbee River and watershed.

TURKEY HUNTERS HALL OF FAME BOARD

408 Croy Lane
Linden, AL 36748

(334) 295-8209

The Turkey Hunters Hall of Fame Board honors noteworthy and exceptionally skilled turkey hunters.

USS ALABAMA BATTLESHIP COMMISSION

P.O. Box 65
Mobile, AL 36601
(251) 433-2703
www.ussalabama.com

The U.S.S Alabama Battleship Commission operates a memorial park in Mobile to honor all Alabama veterans of all branches of the U.S. armed services and educates the public on veterans' contributions and sacrifices.

WATER RESOURCE RESEARCH INSTITUTE

101 Comer Hall, Auburn University
Auburn, AL 36849
(334) 844-4132
www.awrri.auburn.edu

The purpose of the Water Resource Research Institute is to assure that the state has an abundance of water necessary to meet the requirements of an expanding population and industrial community and to stimulate, sponsor, and provide for research, investigations, and experiments in the field of water resources.

WOMEN'S COMMISSION

One Commerce Street, Suite 620
Montgomery, AL 36104
(334) 202-6553
www.alabamawomenscommission.com

The Women's Commission is a continuing vehicle for the determination of effective policy and legislation in areas affecting Alabama's women.

WOMEN'S HALL OF FAME BOARD

302 Bibb Street
Marion, AL 36756
(334) 683-5167
www.awhf.org

The Women's Hall of Fame Board exists to recognize women native to or identified with Alabama who have made significant contributions on a state, national, or international scale.

Aerial view of Howell Heflin Lock and Dam on the Tombigbee River, near Gainesville, Greene County. The Tennessee-Tombigbee Waterway, of which the lock and dam is a part, was constructed by the U.S. Army Corps of Engineers for barge navigation from the Tennessee River to the Gulf of Mexico.

REGIONAL ORGANIZATIONS

APPALACHIAN REGIONAL COMMISSION
1666 Connecticut Avenue NW, Suite 700
Washington, DC 20009
(202) 884-7700
www.arc.gov

The Appalachian Regional Commission is a partnership of the thirteen Appalachian states and the federal government that works with the people of Appalachia to create opportunities for self-sustaining economic development and improved quality of life.

GULF STATES MARINE FISHERIES COMMISSION
P.O. Box 726
Ocean Springs, MS 39566
(228) 875-5912
www.gsmfc.org

The Gulf States Marine Fisheries Commission coordinates marine fisheries laws, policy, research, and federal funding for the Gulf of Mexico and state jurisdictions. All five states of the Gulf of Mexico are members: Texas, Louisiana, Mississippi, Alabama, and Florida.

SOUTHEAST INTERSTATE LOW-LEVEL RADIOACTIVE WASTE COMPACT COMMISSION
21 Glenwood Avenue, Suite 207
Raleigh, NC 27603
(919) 821-0500
www.secompact.org

The Southeast Compact is an agreement among six member states—Alabama, Florida, Georgia, Mississippi, Tennessee and Virginia—to share responsibility for management of and policy making regarding the region's commercial low-level radioactive waste (LLRW). The Southeast Compact Commission is required to meet twice annually.

SOUTHERN GROWTH POLICIES BOARD
P.O. Box 12293
Research Triangle Park, NC 27709
(919) 941-5145

www.southern.org

Develops and advances visionary economic development policies by providing dialog among the region's leaders. Four advisory councils guide policy work and research. The trustees meet at least once a year in conjunction with the Board's annual conference, and each of the councils meets several times per year.

SOUTHERN RAPID RAIL TRANSIT COMPACT
1340 Poydras Street, Suite 2100
New Orleans, LA 70112
(504) 568-6611

The Southern Rapid Rail Transit Compact exists to study the feasibility of rapid rail transit services between the states of Louisiana, Mississippi, and Alabama and to establish a joint interstate commission to assist in this effort.

TENNESSEE-TOMBIGBEE WATERWAY DEVELOPMENT AUTHORITY
P.O. Drawer 671
Columbus, MS 39703
(662) 325-3286
www.tenntom.org

The Authority promotes the development of the Tennessee-Tombigbee Waterway and its economic and commercial potential to the impacted region, including Alabama.

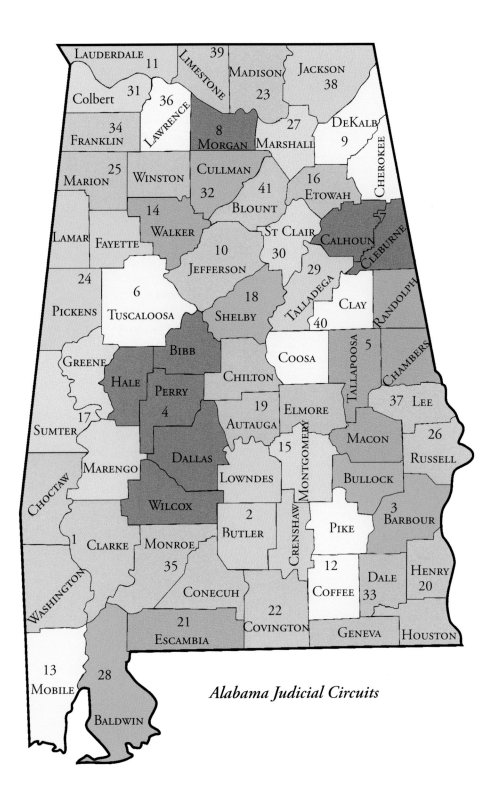

Alabama Judicial Circuits

Alabama's District Attorneys

Judicial circuit numbers refer to the map on the facing page; see alphabetical listing beginning on page 381 for office information.

District attorneys are the chief prosecutors within the state's legal system. Like all lawyers practicing in the state's courts, they are considered "officers of the court" and are governed by rules of ethics and procedure. But district attorneys are part of the executive branch of state government, not the judicial branch. District attorneys are assisted in their duties by resources provided by the State of Alabama Office of Prosecution Services and by the Alabama District Attorney's Association, both located at 515 S. Perry Street, Montgomery, AL 36104; (334) 242-4191; www. adaa-ops.org.

District attorneys are elected for six-year terms by the voters within one of Alabama's 41 judicial circuits. Several circuits include more than one county, but no county is split among more than one circuit (although Jefferson has two divisions).

District attorneys must be attorneys in good standing with the state bar. Vacancies in the office are filled by appointment of the governor.

By Judicial Circuit

01	Spencer Walker	14	Charles Baker
02	John Andrews	15	Ellen Brooks
03	Ben Reeves Jr.	16	Jimmie Harp Jr.
04	Michael Jackson	17	Greg Griggers
05	E. Paul Jones	18	Robert Owens Jr.
06	Tommy Smith	19	Randall Houston
07	Joseph "Joe" Hubbard	20	Douglas "Doug" Valeska
08	Robert "Bob" Burrell	21	Stephen Billy
09	Mike O'Dell	22	Gregory Gambril
10	M. David Barber	23	Tim Morgan
10	Arthur Green Jr.	24	J. Christopher "Chris" McCool
11	Christopher Connolly	25	John "Jack" Bostick
12	Gary McAliley	26	Kenneth "Ken" Davis
13	John Tyson Jr.	27	Steve Marshall
		28	Judy Newcomb

29   Steve Giddens
30   Richard Minor
31   Bryce Graham Jr.
32   C. Wilson Blaylock
33   Kirke Adams
34   Joseph Rushing III
35   Tommy Chapman
36   Jim Osborn
37   Nick Abbett
38   Charles Rhodes
39   Kristi Valls
40   Fred Thompson
41   Tommy Rountree

BY COUNTY

Autauga – Randall Houston
Baldwin – Judy Newcomb
Barbour – Ben Reeves Jr.
Bibb – Michael Jackson
Blount – Tommy Rountree
Bullock – Ben Reeves Jr.
Butler – John Andrews
Calhoun – Joseph "Joe" Hubbard
Chambers – E. Paul Jones
Cherokee – Mike O'Dell
Chilton – Randall Houston
Choctaw – Spencer Walker
Clarke – Spencer Walker
Clay – Fred Thompson
Cleburne – Joseph "Joe" Hubbard
Coffee – Gary McAliley
Colbert – Bryce Graham Jr.
Conecuh – Tommy Chapman
Coosa – Fred Thompson
Covington – Gregory Gambril
Crenshaw – John Andrews
Cullman – C. Wilson Blaylock
Dale – Kirke Adams
Dallas – Michael Jackson
DeKalb – Mike O'Dell
Elmore – Randall Houston
Escambia – Stephen Billy

Etowah – Jimmie Harp Jr.
Fayette – J. Christopher "Chris" McCool
Franklin – Joseph Rushing III
Geneva – Kirke Adams
Greene – Greg Griggers
Hale – Michael Jackson
Henry – Douglas "Doug" Valeska
Houston – Douglas "Doug" Valeska
Jackson – Charles Rhodes
Jefferson – M. David Barber
Jefferson (Bessemer) – Arthur Green Jr.
Lamar – J. Christopher "Chris" McCool
Lauderdale – Christopher Connolly
Lawrence – Jim Osborn
Lee – Nick Abbett
Limestone – Kristi Valls
Lowndes – John Andrews
Macon – E. Paul Jones
Madison – Tim Morgan
Marengo – Greg Griggers
Marion – John "Jack" Bostick
Marshall – Steve Marshall
Mobile – John Tyson Jr.
Monroe – Tommy Chapman
Montgomery – Ellen Brooks
Morgan – Robert "Bob" Burrell
Perry – Michael Jackson
Pickens – J. Christopher "Chris" McCool
Pike – Gary McAliley
Randolph – E. Paul Jones
Russell – Kenneth "Ken" Davis
Shelby – Robert Owens Jr.
St. Clair – Richard Minor
Sumter – Greg Griggers
Talladega – Steve Giddens
Tallapoosa – E. Paul Jones
Tuscaloosa – Tommy Smith
Walker – Charles Baker
Washington – Spencer Walker
Wilcox – Michael Jackson
Winston – John "Jack" Bostick

ALABAMA'S DISTRICT ATTORNEYS

Circuit numbers refer to the map on page 378. (R) or (D) refers to party affiliation.

NICK ABBETT (R)
Circuit: 37; Counties: Lee
  Lee County Justice Center; 2311 Gateway
  Drive, Suite 111
  Opelika, AL 36801-6858
  (334) 749-7148

KIRKE ADAMS (R)
Circuit: 33; Counties: Dale and Geneva
  P.O. Box 1688
  Ozark, AL 36361-1688
  (334) 774-9500

JOHN ANDREWS (D)
Circuit: 02; Counties: Butler, Crenshaw,
and Lowndes
  700 Court Square
  Greenville, AL 36037-2393
  (334) 282-7444

CHARLES BAKER (D)
Circuit: 14; Counties: Walker
  P.O. Box 2227
  Jasper, AL 35501-2227
  (205) 384-7272

M. DAVID BARBER (R)
Circuit: 10; Counties: Jefferson
  801 Richard Arrington Jr. Boulevard
  North; Mel Bailey Criminal Justice
  Center
  Birmingham, AL 35263-0121
  (205) 325-5252

STEPHEN BILLY (D)
Circuit: 21; Counties: Escambia
  P.O. Box 993
  Brewton, AL 36427-0993
  (251) 236-0239

C. WILSON BLAYLOCK (R)
Circuit: 32; Counties: Cullman
  Cullman County Courthouse; 500 2nd
  Avenue SW, Room 207

  Cullman, AL 35055-4155
  (256) 736-2800

JOHN "JACK" BOSTICK (D)
Circuit: 25; Counties: Marion and
Winston
  P.O. Box 1596
  Hamilton, AL 35570-1596
  (205) 921-7403

ELLEN BROOKS (D)
Circuit: 15; Counties: Montgomery
  P.O. Box 1667
  Montgomery, AL 36102-1667
  (334) 832-2550

ROBERT "BOB" BURRELL (R)
Circuit: 08; Counties: Morgan
  P.O. Box 1727
  Decatur, AL 35602-4607
  (256) 351-4610

TOMMY CHAPMAN (D)
Circuit: 35; Counties: Conecuh and
Monroe
  P.O. Drawer 860
  Evergreen, AL 36401-0860
  (251) 578-4977

CHRISTOPHER CONNOLLY (D)
Circuit: 11; Counties: Lauderdale
  P.O. Box 914; 20th South Court Street
  Florence, AL 35631-0914
  (256) 764-6351

KENNETH "KEN" DAVIS (D)
Circuit: 26; Counties: Russell
  P.O. Box 939
  Phenix City, AL 36868-0939
  (334) 298-6028

GREGORY GAMBRIL (D)
Circuit: 22; Counties: Covington
  Covington County Courthouse; 100

North Court Square
Andalusia, AL 36420-3996
(334) 222-2513

STEVE GIDDENS (D)
Circuit: 29; Counties: Talladega
P.O. Box 572
Talladega, AL 35160-0572
(256) 362-2036

BRYCE GRAHAM JR. (D)
Circuit: 31; Counties: Colbert
P.O. Box 534
Tuscumbia, AL 35674-0534
(256) 386-8520

ARTHUR GREEN JR. (D)
Circuit: 10; Counties: Jefferson
(Bessemer)
701 Courthouse Annex; 1801 3rd Avenue
North
Bessemer, AL 35020-4973
(205) 481-4145

GREG GRIGGERS (D)
Circuit: 17; Counties: Greene, Marengo,
and Sumter
P.O. Box 1054
Demopolis, AL 36732
(334) 289-2149

JIMMIE HARP JR. (D)
Circuit: 16; Counties: Etowah
P.O. Box 8248
Gadsden, AL 35902-8248
(256) 549-5363

RANDALL HOUSTON (R)
Circuit: 19; Counties: Autauga, Chilton,
and Elmore
P.O. Box 700
Wetumpka, AL 36092-0700
(334) 567-2237

JOSEPH "JOE" HUBBARD (D)
Circuit: 07; Counties: Calhoun and
Cleburne
Calhoun County Courthouse; 25 West
11th Street, Suite 400

Anniston, AL 36201-0910
(256) 231-1770

MICHAEL JACKSON (D)
Circuit: 04; Counties: Bibb, Dallas,
Hale, Perry, and Wilcox
P.O. Box 987
Selma, AL 36701-0987
(334) 874-2540

E. PAUL JONES (D)
Circuit: 05; Counties: Chambers,
Macon, Randolph, and Tallapoosa
P.O. Box 997
Alexander City, AL 35011-0997
(256) 234-3741

STEVE MARSHALL (D)
Circuit: 27; Counties: Marshall
P.O. Box 458
Guntersville, AL 35976-0458
(256) 582-8113

GARY McALILEY (D)
Circuit: 12; Counties: Coffee and Pike
P.O. Box 311102
Enterprise, AL 36331-1102
(334) 347-1142

J. CHRISTOPHER "CHRIS" McCOOL (D)
Circuit: 24; Counties: Fayette, Lamar,
and Pickens
P.O. Box 520
Carrollton, AL 35447
(205) 367-9915

RICHARD MINOR (R)
Circuit: 30; Counties: St. Clair
1815 Cogswell Avenue, Suite 221
Pell City, AL 35125
(205) 338-9429

TIM MORGAN (D)
Circuit: 23; Counties: Madison
100 Northside Square
Huntsville, AL 35801-4820
(256) 532-3460

JUDY NEWCOMB (R)
 Circuit: 28; Counties: Baldwin
   P.O. Box 1269
   Bay Minette, AL 36507
   (251) 937-0274

MIKE O'DELL (D)
 Circuit: 09; Counties: Cherokee and
 DeKalb
   505 County Courthouse; 300 Grand
    Avenue South, Suite 505
   Ft. Payne, AL 35967
   (256) 845-8550

JIM OSBORN (D)
 Circuit: 36; Counties: Lawrence
   P.O. Box 625
   Moulton, AL 35650-0625
   (256) 974-2446

ROBERT OWENS JR. (R)
 Circuit: 18; Counties: Shelby
   P.O. Box 706
   Columbiana, AL 35051-0706
   (205) 669-3750

BEN REEVES JR. (D)
 Circuit: 03; Counties: Barbour and
 Bullock
   P.O. Box 61
   Eufaula, AL 36072-0061
   (334) 687-7638

CHARLES RHODES (D)
 Circuit: 38; Counties: Jackson
   P.O. Box 923
   Scottsboro, AL 35768-0923
   (256) 574-9240

TOMMY ROUNTREE (R)
 Circuit: 41; Counties: Blount
   220 2nd Avenue East, Room 210
   Oneonta, AL 35121
   (205) 625-4171

JOSEPH RUSHING III (D)
 Circuit: 34; Counties: Franklin
   P.O. Box 119
   Russellville, AL 35653-0119

   (256) 332-8870

TOMMY SMITH (D)
 Circuit: 06; Counties: Tuscaloosa
   410 County Courthouse; 714 Greens-
    boro Avenue
   Tuscaloosa, AL 35401-1894
   (205) 349-1252

FRED THOMPSON (D)
 Circuit: 40; Counties: Clay and Coosa
   P.O. Box 688
   Ashland, AL 36251-0688
   (256) 354-3578

JOHN TYSON JR. (D)
 Circuit: 13; Counties: Mobile
   P.O. Box 2841
   Mobile, AL 36652-2841
   (251) 574-8400

DOUGLAS "DOUG" VALESKA (D)
 Circuit: 20; Counties: Henry and
 Houston
   P.O. Box 1632
   Dothan, AL 36302-1632
   (334) 677-4894

KRISTI VALLS (D)
 Circuit: 39; Counties: Limestone
   P.O. Box 415
   Athens, AL 35611-0415
   (256) 233-6416

SPENCER WALKER (D)
 Circuit: 01; Counties: Choctaw, Clarke,
 and Washington
   P.O. Box 850
   Grove Hill, AL 36451-0850
   (251) 275-3144

The Heflin-Torbert Judicial Building in Montgomery houses the Supreme Court, the Courts of Civil and Criminal Appeals, the State Law Library, and the Administrative Office of Courts.

5

THE JUDICIAL DEPARTMENT

Alabama has a three-tiered judicial system. At the local level, there are probate, municipal, district, and circuit courts. Verdicts may be appealed to the courts of civil or criminal appeals, and from there to the state supreme court.

Supreme Court

Under the 1819 state constitution, the general assembly elected the Supreme Court justices, who also served as circuit court judges. Originally, the state had five judicial circuits, thus the first Supreme Court consisted of five justices, with future governor Clement Comer Clay serving as chief justice. The court first met on May 8, 1820, at Cahaba, the state capital. From 1819 to 1832, the judges continued to serve on both the Supreme Court and their respective circuit courts.

In 1832, the Supreme Court became a separate entity and the circuit court judges no longer served as Supreme Court justices. The number of justices was reduced from seven—the number of circuit courts in 1832—to three who served six-year terms.

In 1889, the number of justices was increased from three to four. Two years later, another judge was added, and in 1903, two additional judges brought the total to seven. The last increase occurred in 1969, when Act 602 set the total members at nine, including the chief justice and eight associate justices.

The Supreme Court has authority to review decisions by other state courts, to determine certain legal matters over which no other court has jurisdiction, to issue such orders necessary to carry out its general superintendence over the courts in Alabama, and to make rules governing administration, practice, and procedures in all courts. The Supreme Court has exclusive jurisdiction over appeals from the Alabama Public Service Commission and over all appeals where the amount in controversy exceeds $50,000. The chief justice is the administrative head of the state's judicial system.

Appellate Courts

In 1911, to ease the Supreme Court's case load, the legislature established a three-member Court of Appeals. That appellate court existed until 1969, when the legislature established the Court of Criminal Appeals and the Court of Civil Appeals.

The Court of Civil Appeals consists of five judges, with the most senior judge presiding. The court has jurisdiction in all civil appeals where the amount in controversy does not exceed $50,000 and all appeals from administrative agencies in which a judgment was rendered in a circuit court. The Court of Civil Appeals also exercises jurisdiction over appeals in workmen's compensation cases and domestic relations cases, including annulment, divorce, alimony, child support, adoption, and child custody cases.

The Court of Criminal Appeals is also composed of five judges, who choose the presiding judge. The court hears all appeals of felony and misdemeanor cases, including violations of city ordinances, and all post-conviction writs in criminal cases.

Circuit and District Courts

Established in 1819, the circuit courts operate as general trial courts with appellate jurisdiction over inferior courts within the circuit. The circuit courts hear both criminal and civil cases, including all civil matters exceeding $5,000, and all felony offenses.

Circuit judges are elected by voters in their circuits. Judges must be licensed to practice law in Alabama, must have resided within the circuit for one year, and must continue to reside in the circuit while serving as a circuit judge. Circuit judges serve for six-year terms. There are currently forty-one circuits, encompassing one or more counties. No county is divided between circuits. The number of judges varies between circuits, with some having only one, while Circuit 10, Jefferson County, has twenty-two.

Created in 1975, district courts serve as trial courts with limited civil and criminal jurisdiction. Each district court is a court of record. District judges try all cases in a district court without a jury. The requirements for district judges are the same as for circuit judges. Each county has its own district court and the number of judges depends on the population of the county.

Municipal Courts

Municipal courts hear misdemeanor criminal and traffic cases which involve offenses committed within their municipality's police jurisdiction. There are 257 municipal courts in Alabama.

Unlike all other judges in Alabama, municipal judges are not elected; they are appointed by the governing body of the municipality. Full-time municipal court judges are appointed for four-year terms, while part-time municipal judges are appointed for two-year terms.

Probate Courts

Probate courts have original and general jurisdiction over the probate of wills; the granting of letters of testamentary and of administration and the repeal or revocation of the same; all controversies over the right of executorship or of administrations; the settlement of accounts of executors and administrators; the sale and disposition of the property belonging to and the distribution of intestate estates; the appointment and removal of guardians for minors and persons of unsound mind; all controversies as to the right of guardianship; the allotment in dower in land in the cases provided by law; the partition of land by law; and name changes.

Probate judges are elected to six-year terms by the voters of each county. Current probate judges are listed with other county officials in the county section of this book beginning on page 503.

Judicial Administrative Agencies

• **ADMINISTRATIVE OFFICE OF COURTS** supports the operation of the state's court system; develops procedures and systems to enhance the operational capacity of the courts, including training, education, and development of the employees of the Unified Judicial System; and collects and disseminates information necessary for efficient court operations. These tasks are implemented in part by and through the Alabama Judicial College, along with the support of statewide technological expertise and implementation of the Court Services and Information Technology Division. The AOC also houses basic support departments such as Human Resources and Finance, and more specialized departments such as the Family Court Division, the Legal Division, the Judicial Study Commission, and the Public Information Office. The chief justice of the Alabama Supreme Court is the chief administrative officer of the state's court system and appoints the administrative director of courts; the current director is Callie T. Dietz. The AOC is located in the Alabama Judicial Building, 300 Dexter Avenue, Montgomery, AL 36104; (334) 954-5000; www.alacourt.gov.

• **CENTER FOR DISPUTE RESOLUTION** is the administrative arm of the Alabama Supreme Court Commission on Dispute Resolution. The Center develops and implements mediation programs in the courts, neighborhoods, educational facilities, and government agencies within Alabama. Judith Keegan, JD, executive director; P.O. Box 671, Montgomery, AL 36101; (334) 269-0409; www.alabamaadr.org.

• **JUDICIAL COMPENSATION COMMISSION** recommends to the legislature the salary and expense allowances for all judges of the state except municipal and probate judges. The five members are appointed by the governor, president of the senate, speaker of the house, and the Alabama State Bar. The commission may be contacted through the Administrative Office of Courts (see above).

• **JUDICIAL INQUIRY COMMISSION** consists of nine members appointed by the governor, Supreme Court, Circuit Court Judges Association, and State Bar to hear, investigate, and prosecute before the Court of the Judiciary any complaints of ethical misconduct or disability concerning any state judge. Jenny Garrett, executive director; 800 South McDonough Street, Suite 201; Montgomery, AL 36104; (334) 242-4089; www.alalinc.net/jic.

• **SUPREME COURT LAW LIBRARY** maintains one of the largest collections of legal materials in the state, including all of the reported decisions of the state and federal appellate courts in the United States; the statutes of all fifty states and the District of Columbia; the Acts of Congress, the United States Code and the regulations of the various agencies of the U.S. government; and other legal periodicals and treatises, as well as the computer-assisted legal research databases, WESTLAW and LEXIS. It is a public law library, open 8 a.m. to 6 p.m., Monday through Friday, on the main floor of the Judicial Building, 300 Dexter Avenue; 334-242-4347 or 1-800-236-4069; reference@alalinc.net. Tim Lewis is the state law librarian.

ALABAMA UNIFIED JUDICIAL SYSTEM STRUCTURE

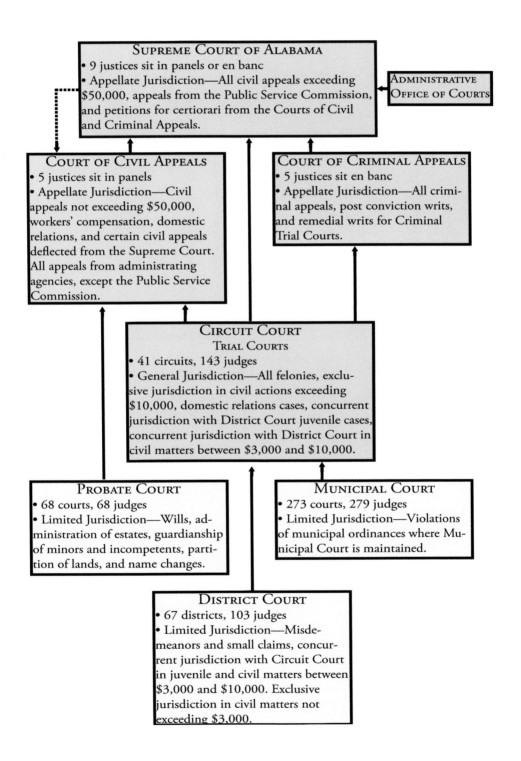

SUPREME COURT OF ALABAMA
- 9 justices sit in panels or en banc
- Appellate Jurisdiction—All civil appeals exceeding $50,000, appeals from the Public Service Commission, and petitions for certiorari from the Courts of Civil and Criminal Appeals.

ADMINISTRATIVE OFFICE OF COURTS

COURT OF CIVIL APPEALS
- 5 justices sit in panels
- Appellate Jurisdiction—Civil appeals not exceeding $50,000, workers' compensation, domestic relations, and certain civil appeals deflected from the Supreme Court. All appeals from administrating agencies, except the Public Service Commission.

COURT OF CRIMINAL APPEALS
- 5 justices sit en banc
- Appellate Jurisdiction—All criminal appeals, post conviction writs, and remedial writs for Criminal Trial Courts.

CIRCUIT COURT
TRIAL COURTS
- 41 circuits, 143 judges
- General Jurisdiction—All felonies, exclusive jurisdiction in civil actions exceeding $10,000, domestic relations cases, concurrent jurisdiction with District Court juvenile cases, concurrent jurisdiction with District Court in civil matters between $3,000 and $10,000.

PROBATE COURT
- 68 courts, 68 judges
- Limited Jurisdiction—Wills, administration of estates, guardianship of minors and incompetents, partition of lands, and name changes.

MUNICIPAL COURT
- 273 courts, 279 judges
- Limited Jurisdiction—Violations of municipal ordinances where Municipal Court is maintained.

DISTRICT COURT
- 67 districts, 103 judges
- Limited Jurisdiction—Misdemeanors and small claims, concurrent jurisdiction with Circuit Court in juvenile and civil matters between $3,000 and $10,000. Exclusive jurisdiction in civil matters not exceeding $3,000.

The Supreme Court Courtroom occupies the central point under the dome of the Heflin-Torbert Judicial Building, directly over the rotunda. The room is patterned after the Rotunda Library designed by Thomas Jefferson at the University of Virginia. Around the perimeter of the room are twelve pairs of classical columns replicating the limestone columns on the building front.

The Alabama Supreme Court

300 Dexter Avenue

Montgomery, AL 36104

(334) 229-0700

www.judicial.state.al.us/supreme.cfm

Chief Justice Sue Bell Cobb

Democrat; Elected 2006

Justice Cobb, formerly a resident of Evergreen, is the first female chief justice of the Alabama Supreme Court. She became one of the state's youngest judges when appointed a Conecuh County district judge in 1981, and while a district judge was known for accepting trial court assignments in some forty counties. She subsequently served two terms on the Alabama Court of Criminal Appeals. Her biography includes:

B. 1956, Louisville, Kentucky. BA, history (Phi Alpha Theta Scholarship key), University of Alabama, 1978; JD, University of Alabama School of Law (Bench and Bar Honor Society, Farrah Law Society, and Moot Court Board), 1981. Conecuh County district judge, 1981–94; Alabama Court of Criminal Appeals in 1994–2006; alternate chief judge, Alabama Court of the Judiciary, 1997. Faculty, Alabama Judicial College. Former president, Alabama Council of Juvenile and Family Court Judges; chair, Children First Foundation; graduate, Leadership Alabama; Stennis Center Pacesetter; member, Farrah Law Society board, Montgomery Kiwanis Club, and First United Methodist Church (pianist for children's choir). She is married to William J. Cobb. They have three children, Bill, Andy, and Caitlin, and two grandchildren.

JUSTICE CHAMP LYONS JR.
Republican; Elected 2000

B. 1940, Boston, Mass. BA, American Government, 1962, Harvard University; LLB, 1965, University of Alabama School of Law; editor-in-chief of the *Alabama Law Review* and elected to Omicron Delta Kappa. Clerked for federal court at Mobile, then practiced law 9 years in Montgomery with Capell, Howard, Knabe & Cobbs and 21 years in Mobile with Helmsing, Lyons, Sims & Leach. Appointed March 1998, by Governor Fob James Jr., as associate justice; elected November 2000; reelected November 2006. From 1971–98, served as reporter and later as chair of Supreme Court Standing Committee on Rules of Civil Procedure and as chair of Supreme Court's Advisory Committee on Civil Rules of Practice and Procedure for District Courts. Authored treatise on civil procedure, *Alabama Practice*, now in 4th edition. Member, Alabama Law Institute and American Law Institute; fellow, American Bar Foundation; former president, Harvard Alumni Association, Mobile Bar Association, Mobile Bar Foundation. Justice Lyons married the former Emilee Oswalt in 1967; they have two children and four grandchildren. The Lyonses live in Point Clear and attend Christ Anglican Church in Mobile.

JUSTICE THOMAS A. WOODALL
Republican; Elected 2000

B. 1950, Meridian, Miss. Meridian Senior High School, National Merit Semifinalist. BA, history, Millsaps College, 1972, magna cum laude, Omicron Delta Kappa, Eta Sigma, Phi Alpha Theta, Who's Who in American Colleges and Universities. JD, University of Virginia School of Law, 1975. While in law school, he was an editor at the Michie Company where he was involved in revising or updating legal publications. From 1975–91, Woodall was employed by the Birmingham firm of Rives and Peterson. He served on that firm's first executive committee and as its managing partner. He was recognized in 1989 by the *Birmingham Business Journal* as one of its "Top 40 Under 40." From 1991–96, Justice Woodall practiced civil litigation in state and federal courts with the Birmingham firm of Woodall and Maddox, PC. He served on the executive committee of the Birmingham Bar Association and chaired the association's Grievance, Civil Courts Procedures, Membership and Lawyer Referral Service committees. He served on the Alabama Pattern Jury Instructions Civil Committee from 1985–2001.

Justice Michael Bolin
Republican; Elected 2004

Justice Tom Parker
Republican; Elected 2004

B. 1948, Birmingham. Shades Valley High School, 1966 (National Honor Society). BS, business administration, Samford University, 1970. J. D., Cumberland School of Law, 1973, cum laude, associate editor of the *Cumberland-Samford Law Review*, Curia Honors. Practiced in Birmingham with Hanes, Hanes, and Bolin 1973–80, and with Frey, Rogers, and Bolin 1980–88. Probate judge of Jefferson County, 1988–2004. Served as president, vice president, and treasurer, Alabama Probate Judges Association. He authored Alabama's putative father registry law, designed to protect the rights of all parties in adoption proceedings. Received national "Angel of Adoptions" award for service to adoptive families. Member of Alabama Child Abuse and Neglect Prevention—Children's Trust Fund Committee. Board member of Glenwood, the nonprofit autism and behavioral health center. Bolin is a long-time member of the Vestavia-Hoover Kiwanis Club. Bolin and his wife, Rosemary, have one daughter, Leigh Anne, and they live in Vestavia Hills, where they are active members of St. Peter the Apostle Church.

B. 1951, Montgomery. Dartmouth College, cum laude; JD, Vanderbilt University School of Law. He won a Rotary International Fellowship to study law at the University of Sao Paulo, Brazil, where he was the first foreign student in Brazil's most prestigious law school. He was a partner in the Montgomery law firm of Parker & Kotouc, PC, before becoming an Alabama assistant attorney general. Later he was special projects manager for the Foundation for Moral Law. In January 2001, Parker was appointed by then Alabama Chief Justice Roy Moore deputy administrative director of courts, where he served as general counsel for the Alabama court system, and as director of the Alabama Judicial College. He also served as legal adviser to Moore. He was founding executive director of the Alabama Family Alliance (now the Alabama Policy Institute) and founding executive director for Alabama Family Advocates. Parker is married to the former Dottie James of Auburn, who was supervisor of the Alabama Governor's Mansion during the Fob James administration. They are members of Frazer Memorial United Methodist Church.

JUSTICE PATRICIA SMITH
Republican; Elected 2004

JUSTICE GLENN MURDOCK
Republican; Elected 2006

B. 1951. Montgomery Catholic High School, 1970; Troy University, 1973, Outstanding Female Graduate. She attended Jones Law School while working full-time for the Veteran's Administration. She practiced law with Bell, Johnson and Medaris until hired as the first female assistant district attorney for the 18th Judicial Circuit in 1977. She served as presiding district court judge in Shelby County, 1980–2003. In Shelby County, she helped establish the Developing Youth Foundation and the Court-Appointed Special Advocate program. She has served on the Governor's Commission on Crime; Commission of the Future of the Juvenile Justice System; Interagency Conference on Youth (chair); Governor's Child Welfare Data Review Commission; State Department of Human Resources' Quality Assurance Committee. She married Jerry Smith in 1975. They have two children: Shelly Marck and Jarrett Smith.

B. 1956, Enterprise. Enterprise High School. BA, political science and economics, University of Alabama, 1978, SGA vice president, Phi Beta Kappa, and summa cum laude; JD, University of Virginia Law School, 1981, national moot court team. Clerked for U.S. Dist. Judge Clarence W. Allgood, Northern District of Alabama. Since that time, he has engaged in private practice, served as in-house counsel to a national corporation, and served as a state administrative law judge. In 1992, Judge Murdock joined the Birmingham/Montgomery firm of Wallace, Jordan, Ratliff & Brandt. In 1994-95, he represented Perry O. Hooper Sr., in the successful year-long federal court litigation to establish the winner of the 1994 Alabama chief justice election. A member of the Birmingham and Alabama Bar Associations, he has practiced before the state and federal courts in Alabama, as well as the Eleventh Circuit Court of Appeals. Murdock is married to the former Margaret Gilchrist of Hartselle. They have three children, Emily, Bailey, and John Taylor, and they are active members of Covenant Presbyterian Church of Birmingham.

JUSTICE LYN STUART
Republican; Elected 2006

B. 1955, Atmore, Alabama. BA with high honors, sociology and education, Auburn University, 1977; JD, University of Alabama School of Law, 1980, secretary of the Student Bar Association and member of the John A. Campbell Moot Court Board. Stuart has worked as an Alabama assistant attorney general, executive assistant to the commissioner and special assistant attorney general for the Alabama Department of Corrections, and assistant district attorney for Baldwin County. She was elected district judge in 1988, and reelected in 1994. Governor Fob James Jr., appointed Stuart a circuit judge in January 1997. She was elected, without opposition, to a six-year term in 1998. Stuart is a past president of the Alabama Council of Juvenile and Family Court Judges and a former speaker for the National Council of Juvenile and Family Court Judges. She served as president of the Blue Ridge Institute for Juvenile and Family Court Judges in 2002. Stuart and her husband, George, have two sons, Tucker and Shepard, and a daughter, Kelly.

JUSTICE GREG SHAW
Republican; Elected 2008

B. 1957, Birmingham. BS, chemistry, Auburn University, 1979; JD, Cumberland School of Law, 1982; LLM, judicial process, University of Virginia School of Law, 2004. General law practice, St. Clair County and Birmingham, 1982–84; staff attorney to Supreme Court Associate Justice Janie L. Shores, 1984; senior staff attorney to Supreme Court Associate Justice James Gorman Houston Jr., 1985–2000; Alabama Court of Criminal Appeals, 2000–08; Chief judge of the Alabama Court of the Judiciary, 2007–. He is an honorary Master of the Bench of the Hugh Maddox Inn of Court, and serves on the Chief Justice's Commission on Professionalism and the Alabama State Bar's committees on Archives and History and Judicial Liaison. Shaw is a Kiwanian and is married to Samantha "Sam" Shaw, who was elected Alabama's state auditor in 2006. They have two sons, Gregory and C. J., and are members of Montgomery's Frazer Memorial United Methodist Church.

CLERKS OF THE ALABAMA APPELLATE COURTS

SUPREME COURT
ROBERT ESDALE SR.

CIVIL APPEALS
JOHN H. WILKERSON JR.

CRIMINAL APPEALS
LANE MANN

B. 1927, Birmingham. Gulf Coast Military Academy, 1945; BS, University of Alabama, 1953; LLB, 1954. U.S. Army, 1950-52; private practice, Birmingham, 1954–74; vice-president and general counsel, Moore-Handley, Inc., 1974–83; municipal judge, Pelham, 1975–83; Clerk of the Alabama Supreme Court, 1983–. Served on the Alabama State Bar Committee on the revision of the Criminal Code. Esdale is a member of Saint Mary's on the Highlands. He is married to the former Susanne Sageser Flack, and they have six children: Graham, James, Phillip, Mary Masoner, Wesley Lister, and Hunter Flack.

B. 1943, Mobile. University Military School, Mobile, 1961; A.B., University of Alabama, 1966; JD, University of Alabama Law School, 1972. Law clerk for Chief Justice Howell Heflin, 1972; research analyst for Alabama Supreme Court, 1972–75; law professor, Jones Law School, 1974– ; Clerk of the Court of Civil Appeals, 1975–. Past president, National Conference of Appellate Court Clerks. Married the former Janice Elaine Blackledge of Huntsville, 1968. Three children: Wendy, John III, and Lee. Deacon, First Baptist Church, Montgomery; member, Kiwanis Club of Montgomery.

B. 1950, Alexander City. Lanett High School, 1968; BS, Auburn University, 1971; JD, Jones Law Institute, 1977. Assistant attorney general, Alabama Attorney General's office, 1972–73; U.S. Postal Inspector, Philadelphia, Pa., 1973-74; special investigator and special assistant attorney general, Alabama Attorney General's office, 1974–79; legal director, Administrative Office of Courts, 1979–90; director, Alabama Judicial System Study Commission, 1987; Clerk of the Court of Criminal Appeals, 1990–. He is married to the former Lana R. Bush of Montgomery. They have three daughters: Julie, Katie, and Lucy.

THE COURT OF CIVIL APPEALS

300 Dexter Avenue
Montgomery, AL 36104
(334) 242-4095
http://www.judicial.state.al.us/civil.cfm

The Court of Civil Appeals is located on the second floor of the west wing of the Heflin-Torbet Judicial Department. The courtroom, above, is small compared with a trial court and the Supreme Court. Usually, only the lawyers appear to argue each side of the case before the panel of judges. There is no need for a jury, witnesses, or a large area for spectators.

PRESIDING JUDGE WILLIAM THOMPSON
Republican; Elected 1996

JUDGE CRAIG SORRELL PITTMAN
Republican; Elected 2000

B. 1962, Jacksonville, FL. BA, University of Alabama, 1984; JD, Cumberland School of Law, 1988. General law practice in Birmingham and Montgomery, including the firm of former Chief Justice Perry Hooper; assistant legal adviser to Governor Guy Hunt. Elected to Court of Civil Appeals, 1996; reelected, 2002; presiding judge, 2007–. Thompson is a member of the Alabama Juvenile Code Revision Committee, the Alabama Court Improvement Project Advisory Committee, and the Chief Justice's Commission on Professionalism. He is also a member of the Appellate Rules Committee, the Legislative Coordinating Council, and the Judicial System Study Commission. He is a former chief judge of the Court of the Judiciary and a former advisory board member of the Service Guild of Birmingham's Early Intervention Program. He grew up in Autauga and Elmore counties. He is married to the former Melinda Rainey of Greenville, and they have three children. The family attends St. Stephen's Episcopal Church.

B. 1956, Enterprise. Indian Springs School, Birmingham; BA, political science, Middlebury College, 1978, with honors; JD, Cumberland School of Law, 1981. Admitted to practice in Alabama and Florida. Clerk for U.S. District Judge T. Virgil Pittman, Mobile, 1981–83. General law practice: Hamilton, Butler, Riddick, Tarlton, and Sullivan, 1983–86; Pittman, Pittman, Carwie and Fuquay, 1986–2000. Deputy attorney general and general counsel for Alabama State Docks, 1995–98. Member of the Mobile, Alabama, and Florida bar associations, Maritime Law Association, and Southeastern Admiralty Law Institute. Pittman is married to the former Janet Rich of Mobile. They have two children, Craig Jr., and Jennifer Leigh. The Pittmans are members of All Saints Episcopal Church in Mobile.

JUDGE TOMMY BRYAN
Republican; Elected 2004

JUDGE TERRY MOORE
Republican; Elected 2006

B. 1956, Opp. Brantley High School, 1974; BS, education, 1978, and MS, education, 1979, Troy State University; JD, Jones School of Law, 1983. Staff attorney, Alabama Court of Criminal Appeals, 1984–1986; assistant attorney general, associate general counsel, Alabama Department of Environmental Management, 1987–2004. Elected to the Court of Civil Appeals, 2004. Member, Montgomery and Alabama bar associations, past chair of state bar Environmental Law Section and member of Appellate Practice Section and co-chair Quality of Life Committee as well as the Supreme Court's Rules of Judicial Administration Committee, Appellate Rules Committee, and Commission on Dispute Resolution. Admitted to practice before the U.S. Supreme Court, U.S. Court of Appeals for the Eleventh Circuit, and the District of Columbia. Bryan is married to the former Pamela Mizzell of Tuscaloosa, and they have two children, a daughter, Thomason, and a son, Tucker. The family attends Montgomery's First Baptist Church.

B. 1965, Mobile. Macon Junior College; BA, political science, University of South Alabama, 1990; JD, University of Alabama, 1993, magna cum laude. General law practice, especially defense of workers' compensation cases: Adams & Reese, 1993–98; Vickers, Riis, Murray & Curran, 1998–2004; Austill, Lewis, Simms, Pipkin & Moore, 2004–2006. Elected to Court of Civil Appeals, 2006. Moore wrote the often-cited *Alabama Workers' Compensation* (West Publishing, 1998). His published articles include "Does the Supreme Court Have the Power to Make Rules of Evidence?" 25 *Cumberland Law Review* 331 (1994-95). Moore grew up in Mobile County. He is married to the former Ashlee Stewart of Mobile, and they have two children, Alex and Pierce. The family attends Christ United Methodist Church in Mobile.

JUDGE TERRI WILLINGHAM THOMAS
Republican; Elected 2006

B. 1964, Cullman. AA, Wallace State Community College; BA, business, Athens State University; JD, Cumberland School of Law, 1993. General law practice in Cullman, 1993–96; Cullman County district and juvenile judge, 1996–2006. Elected to the Court of Civil Appeals, 2006. President of the Alabama Juvenile and Family Courts Judges Association, 2004–05. Faculty of the Alabama Judicial College. She has also served as a member of Alabama's Juvenile Code Revision Committee, the Judicial System Legislative Coordinating Council, and the Standing Committee on Juvenile Procedure of the Juvenile Justice Committee. She is a founder and board member of Traditions Bank in Cullman and has served on the Children's First board and the Children's Policy Council. Thomas and her husband, Dave, have four girls: Tara, Miranda, Ella, and Eliza. She is an active member of Cullman Church of Christ.

THE COURT OF CRIMINAL APPEALS

300 Dexter Avenue

Montgomery, AL 36104

(334) 242-4590

http://www.judicial.state.al.us/criminal.cfm

The Court of Criminal Appeals is located on the second floor of the east wing of the Heflin-Torbet Judicial Building. The courtroom, above, is small compared with a trial court and the Supreme Court. Usually, only the lawyers appear to argue each side of the case before the panel of judges. The space is relatively small since there are no juries or witnesses and usually only a few spectators.

PRESIDING JUDGE ALISA KELLI WISE
Republican; Elected 2000

JUDGE SAMUEL HENRY WELCH
Republican; Elected 2006

B. 1962, Geneva. Prattville High School, 1980; BS, biology, Auburn University, 1985; JD, Jones School of Law, 1994; MPA, Auburn University Montgomery, 2000. Internship, criminal appeals division, Alabama Attorney General's office; staff, Governor's legislative office; legal counsel, ProStaff HRM, Inc.; general law practice with John Taber & Associates and Pittman, Pittman, Carwie & Fuquay; staff attorney to Justice Jean Brown on Alabama Supreme Court and Court of Criminal Appeals. Elected to Court of Criminal Appeals, 2000; Presiding Judge, 2008– . Member, Alabama and Montgomery bar associations, Envision 2020 Riverfront Development Task Force, Family Sunshine Center board, Montgomery Junior League, Camellia Garden Club, Max Federal Credit Union board, Federalist Society, State Bar Criminal Law Section Task Force, Leadership Council of the Stennis Center for Public Service, and advisory board of AUM's School of Public Administration. Past president of the Capital City Republican Women. National Young Republican of the Year, 1999. American Council of Young Political Leaders bilateral exchange with Indonesia, 2002. Wise and her husband, Arthur Ray, are members of St. James United Methodist Church, where they teach kindergarten Sunday School. They have one child, Hanah-Mathis.

B. 1950, Carrollton, GA., grew up in Monroeville. AA, Patrick Henry Junior College, 1970; BA, Birmingham-Southern College, 1972, cum laude, Omicron Delta Kappa; JD, University of Alabama School of Law, 1976; editor of *Law & Psychology Review*, Bench and Bar Legal Honor Society, American Jurisprudence Prize for Constitutional Law. Practiced law in Birmingham, Demopolis, and Monroeville, 1976–83. Municipal judge, 1981–83; district judge, 1983–89; circuit judge, 1989–2006. Welch is also a colonel and staff judge advocate in the U.S. Army Reserve. He has served in the Alabama Air National Guard and Army Reserve since 1972 and is a veteran of the Gulf War 1990–91 in Saudi Arabia, Kuwait, and Iraq. He is a member of the American Legion and Veterans of Foreign Wars. He has served as a Boy Scout troop leader, Little League coach, board of Monroeville Community Concerts, and with the Kiwanis Club. He helped found and was president of Parents Awareness in Monroe County. Welch is a lifelong member of First Baptist Church of Monroeville, where he has taught Sunday school and served as a counselor. He is married to the former Sandra Carol Phillips of Frisco City. They have two children, Bryon and Allison, and one grandson.

JUDGE MARY BECKER WINDOM
Republican; Elected 2008

JUDGE J. ELIZABETH KELLUM
Republican; Elected 2008

B. 1959, Mobile. BS, business administration, University of South Alabama, 1982; JD, Jones School of Law, magna cum laude, 1999. Executive secretary, Bay Minette Area Chamber of Commerce, 1984; executive director, Bay Minette Area Chamber of Commerce, 1985–86; coordinator, Economic Development Dept. of Mobile Area Chamber of Commerce, 1987–89; director of member relations, Mobile Area Chamber of Commerce, 1990–92; sole practitioner, 2000–03; assistant U.S. attorney, Southern District of Alabama, 2003–04 ; deputy attorney general, 2004–. Christ Church; Bay Minette Chamber of Commerce; Mobile Chamber of Commerce; Board of Directors: Junior Achievement of Mobile and Montgomery Humane Society; National Board of America's Junior Miss. She is married to Steve, former lieutenant governor of Alabama. They have two children, Robert and Thomas.

B. 1959, Tuscaloosa. BA, cum laude, political science, University of Alabama, 1981; JD, University of Alabama, 1984. Assistant attorney general, 1985–1987; staff attorney, Judge Sam Taylor, Alabama Court of Criminal Appeals, 1987–1990; attorney, Robison & Belser, PA, 1990–1996; senior staff attorney, Judge Jean Brown, 1997–1999; senior staff attorney, Justice Jean Brown, Alabama Supreme Court, 1999–2001; senior staff attorney, Judge Kelli Wise, 2001–2008. Alabama State Bar; American Bar Association; Federalist Society; Farrah Law Alumni Society; First Baptist Church of Montgomery; Montgomery Museum of Fine Arts; Landmarks Foundation of Montgomery; Capital City Republican Women.

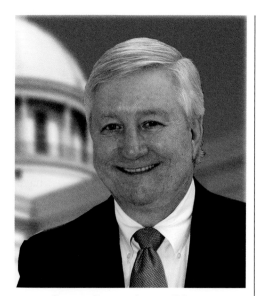

JUDGE JAMES ALLEN MAIN
Republican; Appointed 2009

B. 1945, Union Springs. BS, pharmacy, Auburn University, 1968; JD, University of Alabama, 1972. Lawyer, Main and Smith Law, 1972–89 and Beasley Allen Law Firm, 1989–1997; legal advisor and chief of staff, Governor Fob James, 1997–99; senior counselor, Governor Bob Riley, 2003–04; director, Department of Finance, 2004–09. Member, American, Alabama and Montgomery bar associations and Montgomery County Inn of Court; past president, American Pharmacists Association; past chairman, Dean's Council for the Auburn School of Pharmacy; and founding fellow, Alabama Law Foundation. Main and his wife, Gale, have three children: Jay, Saxon, and Ashley. Governor Riley appointed Main in May 2009 to the seat vacated when Judge Greg Shaw won election to the Alabama Supreme Court in 2008.

CIRCUIT AND DISTRICT JUDGES

The 143 circuit judges in Alabama's forty-one judicial circuits preside over trial courts of general jurisdiction. Elections are by circuit, for six-year terms. Cases before these judges can include any felony or civil matter. Circuit courts have exclusive jurisdiction over civil cases in which the amount at issue exceeds $10,000. Circuit courts have concurrent jurisdiction with district courts in civil matters between $3,000 and $10,000, and concurrent jurisdiction with district courts over juvenile cases. Appeals from circuit court are to the Court of Criminal Appeals, the Court of Civil Appeals, or directly to the Supreme Court, depending on the type of case and the amount of money at issue.

Alabama's 103 district judges in the sixty-seven counties (districts) preside over courts of limited jurisdiction. Elections are by judicial circuit and county, for six-year terms. Cases heard include misdemeanors, small claims, juvenile matters, and civil matters up to $10,000, with exclusive jurisdiction over civil matters up to $3,000. Appeals from district court are to circuit court.

NOTE: Municipal judges also preside over courts of limited jurisdiction. These judges handle violations of municipal ordinances—traffic laws, nuisance ordinances, building codes, etc.—in towns and cities having municipal judges; otherwise, such cases are heard in district court. Unlike other Alabama judges, municipal judges are appointed rather than elected. They serve four-year terms if full-time, or two years if part-time. Appeals from municipal courts are to the respective circuit courts. As of 2009, Alabama had 279 municipal judges in 273 courts. These judges are not listed by name in this book.

Alabama Judicial Circuits, 2009

ALABAMA'S CIRCUIT JUDGES, BY CIRCUIT

Numbers refer to the map on the facing page; see alphabetical listing beginning on page 409 for office information.

01	Baxter, James Thomas		10	Horn III, Allwin
01	DuBose, Stuart		10	Huff, James
02	McFerrin, H. Edward		10	Jones, Clyde
03	Smithart, Burt		10	King III, Dan
04	Jones, Thomas		10	King Jr., Tom
04	Meigs, Jack		10	Lee, Helen Shores
04	Wiggins, Marvin		10	Nail, C. Tommy
05	Martin, Ray		10	Noble, G. William
05	Perryman, Steven		10	Parsons, Douglas Mac
05	Young Jr., Tom		10	Pate, Gary
06	Almond, Michael Brad		10	Petelos, Teresa
06	Donaldson, Scott		10	Petro, Laura
06	England Jr., John		10	Privett, Caryl
06	Hamner Jr., Herschel		10	Pulliam, Teresa
06	Lisenby, Philip		10	Ramsey, Edward
06	Malone, Charles		10	Vance Jr., Robert
07	Bankson Jr., Mannon		10	Verin, Eugene
07	Howell, Brian		10	Vinson, Virginia
07	Laird Jr., R. Joel		10	Vowell, J. Scott
07	Street Jr., Malcolm		11	Jones, Michael
07	Thomason, John		11	Sandlin, James
08	Haddock, Steven		11	Suttle, Ned Michael
08	Paler, Sherrie		12	Barr, Robert
08	Thompson, Glenn		12	Head III, Thomas
09	Cole, Randall		12	Kelley, Jeffery
09	Grimes, J. Kevin		13	Banks, Julian
09	Rains, David		13	Chambers, Rosemary
10	Bahakel, Gloria		13	Graddick, Charles
10	Bahakel, Alfred		13	Johnston, Joseph
10	Boohaker, Joseph		13	Lockett, John
10	Brown, Houston		13	Namen, Edmond
10	Childers, Suzanne		13	Smith, Robert
10	Cole, William "Bill"		13	Stewart, Sarah
10	Ferguson, Sonny		13	Stout, Roderick
10	Graffeo, Michael		13	Wood, James

13 Youngpeter, Michael	26 Greene, George
14 Elliott, Jr., Hoyt	26 Johnson, Albert
14 Farris Jr., James	27 Hawk, Howard
14 Selman, Jerry	27 Jolley, Allen
15 Capell III, John	28 Bosch, Carmen
15 Hardwick, Johnny	28 Floyd, J. Langford
15 Hobbs Jr., Truman	28 Partin, Charles
15 Kelly, Anita	28 Reid, James
15 McCooey, Tracy	28 Wilters, Robert
15 Price, Charles	29 Hollingsworth III, Willliam
15 Reese, Eugene	29 King, Julian
15 Shashy, William	30 Hill Jr., James
15 Warner, Patricia	30 Robinson, Charles
16 Hall, Anthony Clark	31 Hatcher, Jacqueline
16 Kimberley, David	31 Hughston Jr., Harold
16 Millican, William	32 Brunner Jr., Harry
16 Rhea III, William	32 Hardeman, Don
17 Hardaway Jr., Eddie	33 McLauchlin Jr., P. B.
18 Conwill, H. L.	33 Quattlebaum, Kenneth
18 Harrington, Hub	34 Dempsey, Terry
18 Joiner, J. Micahel	35 Hare, Dawn
18 Reeves, G. Daniel	36 Reich, II, A. Philip
19 Bush, John	37 Denson, John
19 Fuller, Benjamin	37 Lane, Richard
19 Reynolds, Sibley	37 Walker III, Jacob
20 Anderson, Larry	38 Graham, John
20 Binford, Henry	38 Holt, Jennifer
20 Jackson, Edward	39 Baker, Robert
20 Little, Charles	39 Woodroof Jr., James
21 Byrne, Bradley	40 Rochester, John
21 Rice, Bert	41 King, Steven
22 McKathan, M. Ashley	
22 Short, Charles	
23 Bell, William	
23 Hall, Karen	
23 Hamilton, Laura	
23 Little Jr., Loyd	
23 Smith, James	
23 Williams, Bruce	
24 Moore Jr., James	
25 Bentley, John	
25 Carter, Talmage Lee	

Alabama's Circuit Judges, by Name

See page 407 for a list organized by circuit. (P = presiding)

Judge Michael Brad Almond (R)
Circuit: 06
205 County Courthouse; 714 Greensboro Avenue
Tuscaloosa, AL 35401
(205) 349-3870

Judge Larry Anderson (R)
Circuit: 20
113 North Oates Street; P.O. Drawer 6406
Dothan, AL 36302
(334) 671-8761

Judge Gloria Bahakel (R)
Circuit: 10
Courtroom 405, CJC; 801 Richard Arrington Jr. Boulevard
Birmingham, AL 35203
(205) 325-5323

Judge Alfred Bahakel (R)
Circuit: 10
Courtroom 606, CJC; 801 Richard Arrington Jr. Boulevard
Birmingham, AL 35203
(205) 325-5648

Judge Robert Baker (D)
Circuit: 39
Courthouse Square; P.O. Box 895
Athens, AL 35611
(256) 233-8083

Judge Julian Banks (R)
Circuit: 13
205 Government Street; Courtroom 2500
Mobile, AL 36644
(251) 574-8488

Judge Mannon Bankson Jr. (R)
Circuit: 07
County Courthouse; 25 West 11th
Street, Suite 210
Anniston, AL 36201
(256) 231-1735

Judge Robert Barr (D)
Circuit: 12
503 County Courthouse; 120 West Church Street
Troy, AL 36081
(334) 566-1307

Judge James Thomas Baxter (D) P
Circuit: 01
P.O. Box 1418
Chatom, AL 36518
(251) 847-2304

Judge William Bell (D) P
Circuit: 23
Madison County Courthouse; 100 North Side Square
Huntsville, AL 35801
(256) 532-3636

Judge John Bentley (D) P
Circuit: 25
P.O. Box 297
Hamilton, AL 35570
(205) 921-2200

Judge Henry Binford (R)
Circuit: 20
114 North Oates Street; P.O. Drawer 6406
Dothan, AL 36302
(334) 677-4848

Judge Joseph Boohaker (D)
Circuit: 10
Courtroom 360, CJC; 716 Richard Arrington Jr. Boulevard North
Birmingham, AL 35203
(205) 325-5753

JUDGE CARMEN BOSCH (R)
Circuit: 28
312 Courthouse Square, Suite 23
Bay Minette, AL 36507
(251) 937-0235

JUDGE HOUSTON BROWN (D)
Circuit: 10
Courtroom 640, CJC; 716 Richard Arrington Jr. Boulevard North
Birmingham, AL 35203
(205) 325-5367

JUDGE HARRY BRUNNER JR. (D) P
Circuit: 32
500 2nd Avenue SW, Room 313
Cullman, AL 35055
(256) 775-4653

JUDGE JOHN BUSH (R)
Circuit: 19
County Courthouse, Room 232; 8935
Highway 231, North
Wetumpka, AL 36092
(334) 567-1148

JUDGE BRADLEY BYRNE (D) P
Circuit: 21
318 Bellville Avenue; P.O. Box 1211
Brewton, AL 36426
(251) 867-0281

JUDGE JOHN CAPELL III (R)
Circuit: 15
County Admin. Bldg. & Courthouse
Annex; 100 South Lawrence Street
Montgomery, AL 36104
(334) 832-7761

JUDGE TALMAGE LEE CARTER (R)
Circuit: 25
P.O. Drawer C
Hayleyville, AL 35565
(205) 921-2400

JUDGE ROSEMARY CHAMBERS (R)
Circuit: 13
205 Government Street; Courtroom
2600
Mobile, AL 36644

(251) 574-8463

JUDGE SUZANNE CHILDERS (D)
Circuit: 10
Courtroom 210, DRCH; 2124 7th
Avenue North
Birmingham, AL 35203
(205) 325-5406

JUDGE RANDALL COLE (D) P
Circuit: 09
County Courthouse, Suite 403; 300
Grand Avenue South
Ft. Payne, AL 35967
(256) 845-8540

JUDGE WILLIAM "BILL" COLE (R)
Circuit: 10
Courtroom 605, CJC; 801 Richard Arrington Jr. Blvd.
Birmingham, AL 35203
(205) 325-5290

JUDGE H. L. CONWILL (R)
Circuit: 18
County Courthouse; 112 North Main
Street; P.O. Box 1136
Columbiana, AL 35051
(205) 669-3800

JUDGE TERRY DEMPSEY (D) P
Circuit: 34
410 North Jackson Street; P.O. Box 148
Russellville, AL 35653
(256) 332-8893

JUDGE JOHN DENSON (R)
Circuit: 37
2311 Gateway Drive; Lee County Justice
Center
Opelika, AL 36801
(334) 737-3411

JUDGE SCOTT DONALDSON (R)
Circuit: 06
County Courthouse; 714 Greensboro
Avenue
Tuscaloosa, AL 35401
(205) 349-3870

JUDGE STUART DUBOSE (D)
Circuit: 01
P.O. Box 914; 117 Court Street
Grove Hill, AL 36451
(251) 275-8667

JUDGE HOYT ELLIOTT JR. (D)
Circuit: 14
19th Street/2nd Avenue; P.O. Box 4
Jasper, AL 35502
(205) 384-7263

JUDGE JOHN ENGLAND JR. (D) P
Circuit: 06
County Courthouse, 2nd Floor; 714
Greensboro Avenue
Tuscaloosa, AL 35401
(205) 349-3870

JUDGE JAMES FARRIS JR. (D)
Circuit: 14
18th Street/2nd Avenue; P.O. Box 1030
Jasper, AL 35502
(205) 384-7234

JUDGE SONNY FERGUSON (R)
Circuit: 10
Courtroom 240 DRCH; 2124 7th Avenue North
Birmingham, AL 35203
(205) 325-5562

JUDGE J. LANGFORD FLOYD (R)
Circuit: 28
312 Courthouse Square, Suite 21
Bay Minette, AL 36507
(251) 937-0237

JUDGE BENJAMIN FULLER (R)
Circuit: 19
134 North Court Street, Suite 206
Prattville, AL 3606
(334) 361-3766

JUDGE CHARLES GRADDICK (D) P
Circuit: 13
205 Government Street; Courtroom 6200
Mobile, AL 36644
(251) 574-5369

JUDGE MICHAEL GRAFFEO (D)
Circuit: 10
Courtroom 310, CJC; 716 Richard Arrington Jr. Blvd. North
Birmingham, AL 35203
(205) 325-5644

JUDGE JOHN GRAHAM (D)
Circuit: 38
302 County Courthouse; 102 East Laurel Street, Suite 302
Scottsboro, AL 35768
(256) 574-9345

JUDGE GEORGE GREENE (D) P
Circuit: 26
County Courthouse; 501 14th Street;
P.O. Box 1188
Phenix City, AL 36867
(334) 297-4567

JUDGE J. KEVIN GRIMES (D)
Circuit: 09
County Courthouse Annex, Suite 300;
102 Main Street
Centre, AL 35960
(256) 927-0500

JUDGE STEVEN HADDOCK (D) P
Circuit: 08
P.O. Box 668; 302 Lee Street
Decatur, AL 35602
(256) 351-4750

JUDGE ANTHONY CLARK HALL (D)
Circuit: 16
Judicial Building, Suite 307; 801 Forrest Avenue
Gadsden, AL 35901
(256) 549-5368

JUDGE KAREN HALL (R)
Circuit: 23
Madison County Courthouse; 100 North Side Square
Huntsville, AL 35801
(256) 532-3455

JUDGE LAURA HAMILTON (D)
Circuit: 23
Madison County Courthouse; 100
North Side Square
Huntsville, AL 35801
(256) 532-3631

JUDGE HERSCHEL HAMNER JR. (D)
Circuit: 06
County Courthouse, 5th Floor; 714
Greensboro Avenue
Tuscaloosa, AL 35401
(205) 349-3870

JUDGE EDDIE HARDAWAY JR. (D) P
Circuit: 17
P.O. Drawer 290; Franklin Street
Livingston, AL 35470
(205) 652-6169

JUDGE DON HARDEMAN (D)
Circuit: 32
500 2nd Avenue SW
Cullman, AL 35055
(256) 775-4765

JUDGE JOHNNY HARDWICK (D)
Circuit: 15
County Courthouse; 251 South Law-
rence Street
Montgomery, AL 36104
(334) 832-5381

JUDGE DAWN HARE (D) P
Circuit: 35
Courthouse Square; P.O. Box 601
Monroeville, AL 36461
(251) 743-3649

JUDGE HUB HARRINGTON (D)
Circuit: 18
County Courthouse; 112 North Main
Street; P.O. Box 1374
Columbiana, AL 35051
(205) 669-3810

JUDGE JACQUELINE HATCHER (D)
Circuit: 31
County Courthouse; 201 North Main
Street

Tuscumbia, AL 35674
(256) 386-8528

JUDGE HOWARD HAWK (D)
Circuit: 27
424 Blount Avenue
Guntersville, AL 35976
(256) 571-7776

JUDGE THOMAS HEAD III (R)
Circuit: 12
1501 Forest Lake Drive
Elba, AL 36323
(334) 897-5525

JUDGE JAMES HILL JR. (R)
Circuit: 30
County Courthouse, Suite 307; 1815
Cogswell Avenue
Pell City, AL 35125
(205) 338-9491

JUDGE TRUMAN HOBBS JR. (D)
Circuit: 15
County Courthouse; One Church Street
Montgomery, AL 36104
(334) 832-4950

**JUDGE WILLIAM HOLLINGSWORTH III
(D)**
Circuit: 29
148 East Street North; P.O. Box 541
Talladega, AL 35160
(256) 761-2108

JUDGE JENNIFER HOLT (D) P
Circuit: 38
Room 337, Jackson County Courthouse;
Market Street
Scottsboro, AL 35768
(256) 574-9350

JUDGE ALLWIN HORN III (R)
Circuit: 10
Suite 350, CJC; 716 Richard Arrington
Jr. Boulevard North
Birmingham, AL 35203
(205) 325-5365

JUDGE BRIAN HOWELL (D)
Circuit: 07
County Courthouse; 25 West 11th
Street, Suite 240
Anniston, AL 36201
(256) 231-1821

JUDGE JAMES HUFF (R)
Circuit: 10
120 Second Court North
Birmingham, AL 35204
(205) 325-5538

JUDGE HAROLD HUGHSTON JR. (D) P
Circuit: 31
County Courthouse; 201 North Main
Street
Tuscumbia, AL 35674
(256) 386-8526

JUDGE EDWARD JACKSON (R)
Circuit: 20
114 North Oates Street; P.O. Drawer
6406
Dothan, AL 36302
(334) 677-4854

JUDGE ALBERT JOHNSON (D)
Circuit: 26
501 14th Street
Phenix City, AL 36868
(334) 297-1366

JUDGE JOSEPH JOHNSTON (R)
Circuit: 13
205 Government Street; Courtroom
6600
Mobile, AL 36644
(251) 574-8685

JUDGE J. MICAHEL JOINER (D) P
Circuit: 18
County Courthouse; 112 North Main
Street; P.O. Box 975
Columbiana, AL 35051
(205) 669-3861

JUDGE ALLEN JOLLEY (D)
Circuit: 27
133 South Emmett Street; P.O. Box 546

Albertville, AL 35950
(256) 878-8597

JUDGE THOMAS JONES (D) P
Circuit: 04
Courthouse Annex; 102 Church Street;
P.O. Box 1225
Selma, AL 36702
(334) 624-4334

JUDGE CLYDE JONES (D)
Circuit: 10
Courtroom 710, CJC; 801 Richard Ar-
rington Jr. Boulevard
Birmingham, AL 35203
(205) 325-5395

JUDGE MICHAEL JONES (D)
Circuit: 11
503 County Courthouse; 200 South
Court Street
Florence, AL 35630
(256) 760-5831

JUDGE JEFFERY KELLEY (R) P
Circuit: 12
County Courthouse; 104 North Edwards
Street; P.O. Box 311446
Elba, AL 36331
(334) 347-4785

JUDGE ANITA KELLY (D)
Circuit: 15
County Admin. Bldge. & Courthouse
Annex; 100 South Lawrence Street
Montgomery, AL 36104
(334) 832-1375

JUDGE DAVID KIMBERLEY (D)
Circuit: 16
Judicial Building, Suite 300; 801 Forrest
Avenue
Gadsden, AL 35901
(256) 549-5372

JUDGE JULIAN KING (D) P
Circuit: 29
148 East Street North; P.O. Box 697
Talladega, AL 35160
(256) 761-2106

JUDGE STEVEN KING (R) P
Circuit: 41
220 2nd Avenue East, Room 207
Oneonta, AL 35121
(205) 625-4145

JUDGE DAN KING III (R)
Circuit: 10
615 Courthouse Annex; 1801 3rd Avenue North
Bessemer, AL 35020
(205) 481-4175

JUDGE TOM KING JR. (D)
Circuit: 10
Courtroom 340; 716 Richard Arrington Jr. Boulevard North
Birmingham, AL 35203
(205) 325-5025

JUDGE R. JOEL LAIRD JR. (D)
Circuit: 07
County Courthouse; 25 West 11th Street, Suite 320
Anniston, AL 36201
(256) 231-1822

JUDGE RICHARD LANE (R)
Circuit: 37
2311 Gateway Drive, Suite 115; Lee County Justice Center
Opelika, AL 36801
(334) 749-7141

JUDGE HELEN SHORES LEE (D)
Circuit: 10
Courtroom 650, CJC; 716 Richard Arrington Jr. Boulevard North
Birmingham, AL 35203
(205) 325-5635

JUDGE PHILIP LISENBY (R)
Circuit: 06
County Courthouse, 5th Floor; 714 Greensboro Avenue
Tuscaloosa, AL 35401
(205) 349-3870

JUDGE CHARLES LITTLE (D) P
Circuit: 20
114 North Oates Street; P.O. Drawer 6406
Dothan, AL 36302
(334) 677-4889

JUDGE LOYD LITTLE JR. (D)
Circuit: 23
Madison County Courthouse; 100 Northside Square
Huntsville, AL 35801
(256) 532-3440

JUDGE JOHN LOCKETT (D)
Circuit: 13
205 Government Street; Courtroom 6500
Mobile, AL 36644
(251) 574-8477

JUDGE CHARLES MALONE (R)
Circuit: 06
County Courthouse, 2nd Floor; 714 Greensboro Avenue
Tuscaloosa, AL 35401
(205) 349-3870

JUDGE RAY MARTIN (D) P
Circuit: 05
County Courthouse, Room 204; 125 North Broadnax Street
Dadeville, AL 36853
(256) 357-2066

JUDGE TRACY McCOOEY (D)
Circuit: 15
County Courthouse; 251 South Lawrence Street
Montgomery, AL 36104
(334) 832-4950

JUDGE H. EDWARD McFERRIN (D) P
Circuit: 02
700 Court Square; P.O. Box 515
Greenville, AL 36037
(334) 382-3621

JUDGE M. ASHLEY McKATHAN (I) P
Circuit: 22
County Courthouse; Court Square
Andalusia, AL 36420
(334) 428-2585

JUDGE P. B. McLAUCHLIN JR. (D) P
Circuit: 33
Court Square; P.O. Box 1305
Ozark, AL 36361
(334) 774-8011

JUDGE JACK MEIGS (D) P
Circuit: 04
P.O. Box 475
Centreville, AL 35042
(205) 926-3120

JUDGE WILLIAM MILLICAN (D) P
Circuit: 16
Judicial Building, Suite 303; 801 Forrest
Avenue
Gadsden, AL 35901
(256) 549-5364

JUDGE JAMES MOORE JR. (D) P
Circuit: 24
103 North Temple Avenue; P.O. Box 788
Fayette, AL 35555
(205) 932-3169

JUDGE C. TOMMY NAIL (D)
Circuit: 10
Courtroom 505, CJC; 801 Richard Ar-
rington Jr. Boulevard
Birmingham, AL 35203
(205) 327-8205

JUDGE EDMOND NAMEN (R)
Circuit: 13
Strickland Youth Center; 2315 Costar-
ides Street
Mobile , AL 36617
(251) 574-8470

JUDGE G. WILLIAM NOBLE (R)
Circuit: 10
Courtroom 610, CJC; 716 Richard Ar-
rington Jr. Boulevard North
Birmingham, AL 35203

(205) 325-5020

JUDGE SHERRIE PALER (D)
Circuit: 08
P.O. Box 668; 302 Lee Street
Decatur, AL 35602
(256) 351-4700

JUDGE DOUGLAS MAC PARSONS (D)
Circuit: 10
613 Courthouse Annex; 1801 Third
Avenue North
Bessemer, AL 35020
(205) 481-4170

JUDGE CHARLES PARTIN (R)
Circuit: 28
Courthouse Square; P.O. Box 358
Bay Minette, AL 36507
(251) 937-0273

JUDGE GARY PATE (R)
Circuit: 10
Courtroom 230, DRCH; 2124 7th
Avenue North
Birmingham, AL 35203
(205) 325-5022

JUDGE STEVEN PERRYMAN (D)
Circuit: 05
#2 LaFayette Street
LaFayette, AL 36862
(334) 864-4328

JUDGE TERESA PETELOS (R)
Circuit: 10
607 Courthouse Annex; 1801 Third
Avenue North
Bessemer, AL 35020
(205) 325-4181

JUDGE LAURA PETRO (D)
Circuit: 10
Courtroom 506, CJC; 801 Richard Ar-
rington Jr. Boulevard
Birmingham, AL 35203
(205) 325-5646

JUDGE CHARLES PRICE (D) P
Circuit: 15

County Courthouse; 251 South Lawrence Street
Montgomery, AL 36104
(334) 832-1331

JUDGE CARYL PRIVETT (D)
Circuit: 10
Courtroom 550, CJC; 716 Richard Arrington Jr. Boulevard North
Birmingham, AL 35203
(205) 325-5388

JUDGE TERESA PULLIAM (R)
Circuit: 10
Courtroom 406, CJC; 801 Richard Arrington Jr. Boulevard
Birmingham, AL 35203
(205) 325-5349

JUDGE KENNETH QUATTLEBAUM (R)
Circuit: 33
Court Square; P.O. Box 908
Ozark, AL 36361
(334) 774-3726

JUDGE DAVID RAINS (D)
Circuit: 09
County Courthouse, Suite 406; 300 Grand Avenue South
Ft. Payne, AL 35967
(256) 845-8545

JUDGE EDWARD RAMSEY (R)
Circuit: 10
Courtroom 670, CJC; 716 Richard Arrington Jr. Boulevard North
Birmingham, AL 35203
(205) 325-5280

JUDGE EUGENE REESE (D)
Circuit: 15
County Courthouse; 251 South Lawrence Street
Montgomery, AL 36104
(334) 832-1360

JUDGE G. DANIEL REEVES (D)
Circuit: 18
County Courthouse; 112 North Main Street; P.O. Box 1209

Columbiana, AL 35051
(205) 669-8588

JUDGE A. PHILIP REICH, II (D)
Circuit: 36
14330 Court Street; P.O. Box 395
Moulton, AL 35650
(256) 974-2444

JUDGE JAMES REID (R) P
Circuit: 28
312 Courthouse Square, Suite 22
Bay Minette, AL 36507
(251) 937-0290

JUDGE SIBLEY REYNOLDS (R) P
Circuit: 19
500 2nd Avenue North; P.O. Box 70
Clanton, AL 35045
(334) 361-3766

JUDGE WILLIAM RHEA III (D)
Circuit: 16
Judicial Building, Suite 305; 801 Forrest Avenue
Gadsden, AL 35901
(256) 549-5317

JUDGE BERT RICE (D)
Circuit: 21
P.O. Box 795; 318 Bellville Avenue
Brewton, AL 36426
(251) 867-0253

JUDGE CHARLES ROBINSON (D) P
Circuit: 30
County Courthouse, Suite 217; 1815 Cogswell Avenue
Pell City, AL 35125
(205) 594-2187

JUDGE JOHN ROCHESTER (D) P
Circuit: 40
County Courthouse, Court Square; P.O. Box 40
Ashland, AL 36251
(256) 354-2242

JUDGE JAMES SANDLIN (D)
Circuit: 11

317 County Courthouse; 200 South
Court Street
Florence, AL 35630
(256) 760-5825

JUDGE JERRY SELMAN (D) P
Circuit: 14
1801 Third Avenue, Room 224; P.O.
Box 2388
Jasper, AL 35502
(205) 384-7237

JUDGE WILLIAM SHASHY (R)
Circuit: 15
County Courthouse; 251 South Law-
rence Street
Montgomery, AL 36104
(334) 832-1370

JUDGE CHARLES SHORT (D)
Circuit: 22
County Courthouse; Court Square
Andalusia, AL 36420
(334) 428-2580

JUDGE ROBERT SMITH (R)
Circuit: 13
205 Government Street; Courtroom
6100
Mobile , AL 36644
(251) 574-8485

JUDGE JAMES SMITH (D)
Circuit: 23
Madison County Courthouse; 100
North Side Square
Huntsville, AL 35801
(256) 532-3394

JUDGE BURT SMITHART (D) P
Circuit: 03
P.O. Box 230; 217 North Praire Street
Eufaula, AL 36089
(334) 738-3286

JUDGE SARAH STEWART (R)
Circuit: 13
205 Government Street; Courtroom
8600
Mobile, AL 36644

(251) 574-8457

JUDGE RODERICK STOUT (D)
Circuit: 13
205 Government Street; Courtroom
8100
Mobile, AL 36644
(251) 574-8481

JUDGE MALCOLM STREET JR. (D) P
Circuit: 07
County Courthouse; 25 West 11th
Street, Box 1
Anniston, AL 36201
(256) 231-1820

JUDGE NED MICHAEL SUTTLE (D) P
Circuit: 11
County Courthouse, 4th Floor; 200
South Court Street
Florence, AL 35630
(256) 760-5820

JUDGE JOHN THOMASON (R)
Circuit: 07
County Courthouse; 25 West 11th
Street, Suite 326
Anniston, AL 36201
(256) 231-1830

JUDGE GLENN THOMPSON (D)
Circuit: 08
P.O. Box 668; 302 Lee Street
Decatur, AL 35602
(256) 351-4785

JUDGE ROBERT VANCE JR. (D)
Circuit: 10
Courtroom 330, CJC; 716 Richard Ar-
rington Jr. Boulevard North
Birmingham, AL 35203
(205) 325-5035

JUDGE EUGENE VERIN (D)
Circuit: 10
708 Courthouse Annex; 1801 3rd Avenue North
Bessemer, AL 35020
(205) 481-4198

JUDGE VIRGINIA VINSON (R)
Circuit: 10
Courtroom 705, CJC; 801 Richard Arrington Jr. Boulevard
Birmingham, AL 35203
(205) 325-8683

JUDGE J. SCOTT VOWELL (D) P
Circuit: 10
Courtroom 406, CJC; 801 Richard Arrington Jr. Boulevard North
Birmingham, AL 35203
(205) 325-5200

JUDGE JACOB WALKER III (R) P
Circuit: 37
2311 Gateway Drive; Lee County Justice Center
Opelika, AL 36801
(334) 749-7156

JUDGE PATRICIA WARNER (D)
Circuit: 15
County Admin. Bldg. & Courthouse Annex; 100 South Lawrence Street
Montgomery, AL 36104
(334) 832-2556

JUDGE MARVIN WIGGINS (D)
Circuit: 04
County Courthouse; 1001 Main Street, Room 52
Greensboro, AL 36744
(334) 624-5620

JUDGE BRUCE WILLIAMS (R)
Circuit: 23
Madison County Courthouse; 100 North Side Square
Huntsville, AL 35801
(256) 532-3754

JUDGE ROBERT WILTERS (R)
Circuit: 28
Courthouse Square; P.O. Box 835
Bay Minette, AL 36507
(251) 580-2570

JUDGE JAMES WOOD (D)
Circuit: 13
205 Government Street, Courtroom 8200
Mobile, AL 36644
(251) 574-8475

JUDGE JAMES WOODROOF JR. (D) P
Circuit: 39
Courthouse Square; P.O. Box 486
Athens, AL 35612
(256) 233-6410

JUDGE TOM YOUNG JR. (D)
Circuit: 05
395 Lee Street
Alexander City, AL 35010
(256) 234-7901

JUDGE MICHAEL YOUNGPETER (R)
Circuit: 13
205 Government Street; Courtroom 8200
Mobile, AL 36644
(251) 574-8799

Autauga: Wood, Phillip
Baldwin: Bishop, Jody
Baldwin: Hart, Michelle
Barbour: Hart III, Charles
Bibb: Owings, William Donovan
Blount: Dobson, John
Bullock: Daniel, Theresa
Butler: Russell Jr., James
Calhoun: Colvin Jr., Gus
Calhoun: Phillips, Laura
Calhoun: Warren, Larry
Chambers: Milford Jr., Myron
Cherokee: Carver, Sheri
Chilton: Hardesty, Rhonda
Choctaw: Thompson, Joe
Clarke: Kimbrough, William
Clay: Simpson, George
Cleburne: Sarrell Jr. , Warren
Coffee: Sherling, Braxton
Colbert: Carpenter, George
Conecuh: Brock, Jeffery
Coosa: Teel, Carlton
Covington: McGuire III, Frank
Crenshaw: Sport, Thomas
Cullman: Chaney, Kim
Cullman: Nicholas, Greg
Dale: Garner Jr., William Stanley
Dale: Steagall, Fred
Dallas: Armstrong III, Robert
DeKalb: Whitmire, II, Steven
Elmore: Culberson, Mary Elizabeth
Elmore: Goggans, James Glenn
Escambia: Jordan, J. David
Etowah: Owen, Charles
Etowah: Russell Jr., William

Fayette: Clary, Jerry
Franklin: McDowell, Paula
Geneva: Fleming Jr., Charles
Greene: Jones-Osborne, Lillie
Hale: Ryan, William
Henry: Peterson, James
Houston: Mendheim, Brady
Houston: Steensland Jr., M. John
Jackson: Grider, Ralph
Jefferson: Barclay, Elise
Jefferson: Bynon Jr., Robert
Jefferson: Coleman Jr., Ralph
Jefferson: Fancher, Eric
Jefferson: Ganus, Jill
Jefferson: Lawley, David
Jefferson: Lichtenstein , David
Jefferson: Lowther, John
Jefferson: Ross, Katrina
Jefferson: Summers Jr., W. Alan
Jefferson: Watkins, Sheldon
Jefferson: Winston Jr., Norman
Lamar: Lambert, Donald
Lauderdale: Medley, Carole
Lawrence: Mullican, Randall
Lee: Bush, Russell
Lee: Nix, Michael
Limestone: Anderson, Jeanne
Limestone: Batts, Jerry
Lowndes: Bozeman-Lovell, Terri
Macon: Ford Jr., Aubrey
Madison: Hall, Ruth Ann
Madison: O'Dell, Dennis
Madison: Richardson, Schuyler
Madison: Sherrod, Martha
Marengo: Drinkard, W. Wade

Marion: Cashion, James
Marshall: Burke, Liles
Marshall: Riley, F. Timothy
Mobile: Brown, George
Mobile: Hardesty Jr., George
Mobile: McKnight, Charles
Mobile: McMaken, Michael
Mobile: Sherling Jr., Barber
Monroe: Elbrecht, George
Montgomery: Ray, II, Arthur
Montgomery: Robinson-Higgins, Pamela
Montgomery: Yates, Sharon
Morgan: Langham, Charles
Morgan: Waters, Shelly
Perry: McMillan, Donald
Pickens: Kirk Jr., William
Pike: Hightower, William

Randolph: Whaley, W. Patrick
Russell: Bellmay, Michael
Russell: Funderburk, Eric
Shelby: Jackson, Ronald
Shelby: Kramer, James
St. Clair: Seay, Phil
Sumter: Montgomery, Tammy
Talladega: Dobson, Tommy
Talladega: Sims, George
Tallapoosa: Taylor, Clayton
Tuscaloosa: Chandler, Joel
Tuscaloosa: Guin III, James
Walker: Lapkovitch, Larry
Walker: Wells, Jimmy
Washington: Turner, Jerry
Wilcox: Pettway, Jo Celeste
Winston: Newell, Michael

JEANNE ANDERSON (D)
Limestone County
P.O. Box 1102; Courthouse Square
Athens, AL 35611
(256) 233-6419

ROBERT ARMSTRONG III (D)
Dallas County
County Courthouse, 102 Church Street;
P.O. Box 23
Selma, AL 36702
(334) 874-2529

ELISE BARCLAY (R)
Jefferson County
120 North 2nd Court
Birmingham, AL 35204
(205) 325-5489

JERRY BATTS (D)
Limestone County
200 West Washington Street; P.O. Box 338
Athens, AL 35612
(256) 233-6440

MICHAEL BELLMAY (D)
Russell County
501 14th Street; P.O. Box 1770
Phenix City, AL 36868
(334) 298-0931

JODY BISHOP (R)
Baldwin County
312 Courthouse Square Suite 24
Bay Minette, AL 36507
(251) 580-1647

TERRI BOZEMAN-LOVELL (D)
Lowndes County
P.O. Box 455
Hayneville, AL 36040
(334) 548-2591

JEFFERY BROCK (D)
Conecuh County
P.O. Box 227; Courthouse Square
Evergreen, AL 36401
(251) 578-2421

GEORGE BROWN (R)
Mobile County
Strickland Youth Center; 2315 Costarides Street
Mobile, AL 36617
(251) 574-5245

LILES BURKE (D)
Marshall County
424 Blount Avenue
Guntersville, AL 35976
(256) 571-7779

RUSSELL BUSH (R)
Lee County
2311 Gateway Drive, Suite 106; Lee County Judicial Center
Opelika, AL 36801
(334) 737-3378

ROBERT BYNON JR. (D)
Jefferson County
Courtroom 510 CJC; 716 Richard Arrington Jr. Boulevard North
Birmingham, AL 35203
(205) 325-5328

GEORGE CARPENTER (D)
Colbert County
County Courthouse; 201 North Main Street
Tuscumbia, AL 35674
(256) 386-8524

SHERI CARVER (D)
Cherokee County
County Courthouse; 100 Main Street
Centre, AL 35960
(256) 927-3682

JAMES CASHION (D)
Marion County
132 South Military; P.O. Box 1476
Hamilton, AL 35570
(205) 921-3181

JOEL CHANDLER (D)
Tuscaloosa County
County Courthouse, 6th Floor; 714
Greensboro Avenue
Tuscaloosa, AL 35401
(205) 349-3870

KIM CHANEY (D)
Cullman County
Room 213, County Courthouse; 500
Second Avenue, SW
Cullman, AL 35055
(205) 775-4766

JERRY CLARY (D)
Fayette County
Courthouse, 103 North Temple Avenue;
P.O. Box 616
Fayette, AL 35555
(205) 932-4613

RALPH COLEMAN JR. (R)
Jefferson County
517 Courthouse Annex; 1801 3rd Avenue North
Bessemer, AL 35020
(205) 481-4195

GUS COLVIN JR. (D)
Calhoun County
County Courthouse; 25 West 11th Street
Anniston, AL 36201
(256) 231-1870

MARY ELIZABETH CULBERSON (R)
Elmore County
8935 Highway 231 North; P.O. Box 924
Wetumpka, AL 36092
(334) 567-1153

THERESA DANIEL ()
Bullock County
P.O. Box 8; 217 North Prairie
Union Springs, AL 36089

(334) 738-2730

JOHN DOBSON (R)
Blount County
County Courthouse, Room 209; 220
2nd Avenue East
Oneonta, AL 35121
(205) 625-4147

TOMMY DOBSON (D)
Talladega County
400 North Norton; P.O. Box 1326
Sylacauga, AL 35150
(256) 249-1005

W. WADE DRINKARD (D)
Marengo County
101 East Coats Avenue; P.O. Box
480445
Linden, AL 36748
(334) 295-8774

GEORGE ELBRECHT (D)
Monroe County
County Courthouse; Courthouse Square
Monroeville, AL 36461
(251) 743-4381

ERIC FANCHER (R)
Jefferson County
505 Courthouse Annex; 1801 3rd Avenue North
Bessemer, AL 35020
(205) 481-4190

CHARLES FLEMING JR. (D)
Geneva County
200 North Commerce Street; P.O. Box
758
Geneva, AL 36340
(334) 684-5630

AUBREY FORD JR. (D)
Macon County
101 East Northside Street; P.O. Box
830703
Tuskegee , AL 36083
(334) 727-6110

ERIC FUNDERBURK (D)
Russell County
501 14th Street; P.O. Box 2488
Phenix City, AL 36868
(334) 297-1347

JILL GANUS (R)
Jefferson County
511 Courthouse Annex; 1801 3rd Avenue North
Bessemer, AL 35020
(205) 744-3555

WILLIAM STANLEY GARNER JR. (R)
Dale County
County Courthouse; Court Square
Ozark, AL 36361
(334) 774-4431

JAMES GLENN GOGGANS (R)
Elmore County
P.O. Box 1196
Wetumpka, AL 36092
(334) 512-0828

RALPH GRIDER (D)
Jackson County
County Courthouse; 102 East Laurel Street
Scottsboro, AL 35768
(256) 574-9355

JAMES GUIN III (D)
Tuscaloosa County
County Courthouse, 6th Floor; 714 Greensboro Avenue
Tuscaloosa, AL 35401
(205) 349-3870

RUTH ANN HALL (R)
Madison County
Madison County Courthouse; 100 North Side Square
Huntsville, AL 35801
(256) 532-3618

RHONDA HARDESTY (R)
Chilton County
County Courthouse, 500 2nd Avenue North; P.O. Box 1187

Clanton, AL 35045
(205) 755-1558

GEORGE HARDESTY JR. (R)
Mobile County
205 Government Street; Courtroom 4300
Mobile, AL 36644
(251) 574-6615

MICHELLE HART (R)
Baldwin County
Foley Satellite Courthouse; 201 East Section Avenue
Foley, AL 36535
(251) 972-8573

CHARLES HART III (D)
Barbour County
303 East Broad Street Rm. 201
Eufaula, AL 36027
(334) 687-1510

WILLIAM HIGHTOWER (I)
Pike County
County Courthouse; 120 West Church Street
Troy, AL 36081
(334) 566-5222

RONALD JACKSON (R)
Shelby County
P.O. Box 1398; 112 North Main Street
Columbiana, AL 35051
(205) 669-3787

LILLIE JONES-OSBORNE (D)
Greene County
400 Morrow Avenue; P.O. Box 310
Eutaw, AL 35462
(205) 372-3143

J. DAVID JORDAN (D)
Escambia County
P.O. Box 982
Brewton, AL 36427
(251) 867-0252

WILLIAM KIMBROUGH (D)
Clarke County
114 Court Street; P.O. Box 931
Grove Hill, AL 36451
(251) 275-8296

WILLIAM KIRK JR. (R)
Pickens County
P.O. Box 426; 1 Courthouse Square
Carrollton, AL 35447
(205) 367-2076

JAMES KRAMER (R)
Shelby County
112 North Main Street; P.O. Box 1115
Columbiana, AL 35051
(205) 669-3730

DONALD LAMBERT (R)
Lamar County
330 1st Street NE; P.O. Box 643
Vernon, AL 35592
(205) 695-9427

CHARLES LANGHAM (R)
Morgan County
P.O. Box 668; 302 Lee Street
Decatur, AL 35602
(256) 351-4760

LARRY LAPKOVITCH (D)
Walker County
P.O. Box 150; County Courthouse, 19th
Street
Jasper, AL 35501
(205) 384-7240

DAVID LAWLEY (R)
Jefferson County
Courtroom 205 CJC; 801 Richard Ar-
rington Jr. Boulevard North
Birmingham, AL 35203
(205) 325-5013

DAVID LICHTENSTEIN (D)
Jefferson County
Courtroom 806 CJC; 716 Richard Ar-
rington Jr. Boulevard North
Birmingham, AL 35203
(205) 325-5339

JOHN LOWTHER (D)
Jefferson County
Courtroom 560 CJC; 716 Richard Ar-
rington Jr. Boulevard North
Birmingham, AL 35203
(205) 325-5593

PAULA McDOWELL (D)
Franklin County
410 North Jackson
Russellville, AL 35653
(256) 332-8886

FRANK McGUIRE III (D)
Covington County
County Courthouse; Court Square
Andalusia, AL 36420
(334) 428-2570

CHARLES McKNIGHT (R)
Mobile County
205 Government Street; Courtroom
4400
Mobile, AL 36644
(251) 574-8439

MICHAEL McMAKEN (R)
Mobile County
205 Government Street; Courtroom
4100
Mobile, AL 36644
(251) 574-8681

DONALD McMILLAN (D)
Perry County
P.O. Box 146; Washington Street
Marion, AL 36756
(334) 683-2215

CAROLE MEDLEY (D)
Lauderdale County
County Courthouse; 200 South Court
Street
Florence, AL 35630
(256) 760-5815

BRADY MENDHEIM (R)
Houston County
114 North Oates Street; P.O. Drawer 6406
Dothan, AL 36302
(334) 677-4881

MYRON MILFORD JR. (D)
Chambers County
2 LaFayette Street
LaFayette, AL 36862
(334) 864-4320

TAMMY MONTGOMERY (D)
Sumter County
P.O. Box 9; Franklin Street, Courthouse Square
Livingston, AL 35470
(205) 652-7364

RANDALL MULLICAN (D)
Lawrence County
14330 Court Street, Suite 307
Moulton, AL 35650
(256) 974-2450

MICHAEL NEWELL (R)
Winston County
2539 6th Avenue; P.O. Box 613
Haleyville, AL 35565
(205) 486-9554

GREG NICHOLAS (R)
Cullman County
County Courthouse; 500 Second Avenue SW
Cullman, AL 35055
(256) 775-4767

MICHAEL NIX (R)
Lee County
2311 Gateway Drive, Suite 118; Lee County Justice Center
Opelika, AL 36801
(334) 737-3484

DENNIS O'DELL (D)
Madison County
Madison County Courthouse; 100 North Side Square

Huntsville, AL 35801
(256) 532-3432

CHARLES OWEN (D)
Etowah County
Judicial Building, Suite 201; 801 Forrest Avenue
Gadsden, AL 35091
(256) 549-5321

WILLIAM DONOVAN OWINGS (R)
Bibb County
Bibb County Courthouse; 35 Court Street East
Centreville, AL 35042
(205) 926-3106

JAMES PETERSON (D)
Henry County
P.O. Box 338; RTR Square, Suite H
Abbeville, AL 36310
(334) 585-5712

JO CELESTE PETTWAY (D)
Wilcox County
P.O. Box 549; 12 Waters Avenue
Camden, AL 36726
(334) 682-4619

LAURA PHILLIPS (R)
Calhoun County
County Courthouse; 25 West 11th Street
Anniston, AL 36201
(256) 231-1733

ARTHUR RAY, II (D)
Montgomery County
County Courthouse; 251 South Lawrence Street
Montgomery, AL 36104
(334) 832-2559

SCHUYLER RICHARDSON (R)
Madison County
Madison County Courthouse; 100 Northside Square
Huntsville, AL 35801
(256) 532-1633

F. TIMOTHY RILEY (R)
Marshall County
200 West Main Street; P.O. Box 388
Abbeville, AL 35950
(256) 878-2007

PAMELA ROBINSON-HIGGINS (D)
Montgomery County
County Courthouse; 251 South Law-
rence Street
Montgomery, AL 36104
(334) 832-1359

KATRINA ROSS (D)
Jefferson County
Courtroom 205 CJC; 801 Richard Ar-
rington Jr. Boulevard North
Birmingham, AL 35203
(205) 325-5296

JAMES RUSSELL JR. (D)
Butler County
700 Court Square
Greenville, AL 36037
(334) 382-6125

WILLIAM RUSSELL JR. (D)
Etowah County
Judicial Building, Suite 200; 801 Forrest
Avenue
Gadsden, AL 35901
(256) 549-5319

WILLIAM RYAN (D)
Hale County
1001 Main Street; P.O. Box 27
Greensboro, AL 36744
(334) 624-8561

WARREN SARRELL JR. (D)
Cleburne County
120 Vickery Street, Room 202; P.O. Box
266
Heflin, AL 36264
(256) 463-5955

PHIL SEAY (R)
St. Clair County
County Courthouse; 1815 Cogswell
Avenue, Suite 308

Pell City, AL 35128
(205) 338-3869

BRAXTON SHERLING (R)
Coffee County
104 North Edwards Street; P.O. Box
311244
Enterprise, AL 36331
(334) 393-2949

BARBER SHERLING JR. (R)
Mobile County
205 Government Street; Courtroom
4600
Mobile, AL 36644
(251) 574-8722

MARTHA SHERROD (D)
Madison County
Madison County Courthouse; 100
North Side Square
Huntsville, AL 35801
(256) 532-6990

GEORGE SIMPSON (D)
Clay County
County Courthouse, Court Square; P.O.
Box 880
Ashland, AL 36251
(256) 354-7633

GEORGE SIMS (D)
Talladega County
P.O. Box 764
Talladega, AL 35160
(256) 761-2113

THOMAS SPORT (D)
Crenshaw County
County Courthouse; P.O. Box 66
Luverne, AL 36049
(334) 335-6568

FRED STEAGALL (D)
Dale County
P.O. Box 1346; Court Square
Ozark, AL 36361
(334) 774-7008

M. JOHN STEENSLAND JR. (R)
Houston County
114 North Oates Street; P.O. Drawer 6406
Dothan, AL 36302
(334) 677-4857

W. ALAN SUMMERS JR. (D)
Jefferson County
120 Second Court North
Birmingham, AL 35204
(205) 214-8688

CLAYTON TAYLOR (D)
Tallapoosa County
County Courthouse; 125 North Broadnax Street, Room 212
Dadeville, AL 36826
(256) 825-1086

CARLTON TEEL (D)
Coosa County
P.O. Box 115; Main Street
Rockford, AL 35136
(256) 377-4957

JOE THOMPSON (D)
Choctaw County
117 South Mulberry Street
Butler, AL 36904
(205) 459-3828

JERRY TURNER (D)
Washington County
County Courthouse, Court Street; P.O. Box 1025
Chatom, AL 36518
(251) 847-2164

LARRY WARREN (D)
Calhoun County
County Courthouse; 25 West 11th Street
Anniston, AL 36201
(256) 231-1866

SHELLY WATERS (R)
Morgan County
P.O. Box 668; 302 Lee Street
Decatur, AL 35602
(256) 351-4765

SHELDON WATKINS (R)
Jefferson County
Room 206 CJC; 801 Richard Arrington Jr. Boulevard North
Birmingham, AL 35203
(205) 325-5018

JIMMY WELLS (D)
Walker County
Courthouse Annex, 18th & 3rd Avenue; P.O. Box 3165
Jasper, AL 35502
(205) 384-7260

W. PATRICK WHALEY (D)
Randolph County
P.O. Box 267; Highway 431
Wedowee, AL 36278
(256) 357-4921

STEVEN WHITMIRE, II (D)
DeKalb County
300 Grand Avenue South
Ft. Payne, AL 35967
(256) 845-8574

NORMAN WINSTON JR. (R)
Jefferson County
570 JCCH; 716 Richard Arrington Jr. Boulevard North
Birmingham, AL 35203
(205) 325-5336

PHILLIP WOOD (R)
Autauga County
134 North Court Street
Prattville, AL 36067
(334) 361-3733

SHARON YATES (D)
Montgomery County
County Courthouse; 251 South Lawrence Street
Montgomery, AL 36104
(334) 832-1391

Old Senate Chamber, in Capitol, c. 1940. Following the Capitol's renovation in the late 1980s, the Senate Chamber was returned to its appearance as of February 1861, when the Confederacy was formed in that space. The Alabama Senate now meets in a chamber on the seventh floor of the State House.

6

THE LEGISLATIVE DEPARTMENT

Article IV of the 1901 Alabama Constitution defines the role and responsibilities of the two houses of the legislative department of state government, the House of Representatives and the Senate. Article IX, sections 197 and 198, establishes membership in the Senate at not less than one-fourth nor more than one-third of the total membership of the House, and allows for additional representation in the event new counties are created. The House can have no more than 105 members—its present size—unless new counties are created. Thus, the thirty-five-member Senate is precisely one-third the size of the House. Based on the estimated 2006 Alabama population of 4.6 million, each senator currently represents a district of approximately 130,000 Alabamians while each House district includes about 44,000 persons. The legislature redraws district lines every ten years based on state's population as determined by the U.S. Census.

Article IV, Section 47, requires that senators be at least twenty-five years old and House members at least twenty-one at the time of election, and that they be U.S. citizens who have lived in Alabama for at least three years and in their district for at least one year prior to election. Members of both bodies are elected for four-year terms and assume office at midnight of the day of their election. There are no term limits. Amendment 97 provides that the governor is required to call a special election should a vacancy occur in either house of the legislature. While the House has exclusive power to originate revenue bills, such legislation can be amended and/or substituted by the Senate. Because the Senate is considered to be the "deliberative body," rules concerning length of debate are more liberal than those of the House.

In both houses, a quorum (or majority of members) must be present to transact business. Passage of a bill requires an affirmative vote of a majority of each house. Exceptions to this rule include votes on constitutional amendments, which need a three-fifths vote of the elected members of each house, and appropriations to nongovernmental organizations, which require two-thirds of the total members.

Votes are recorded differently in the two houses. In the Senate, while many procedural matters can be decided with a simple "voice vote," the roll is formally called for all votes on bills and amendments and the votes are written in a journal as the senators call out "yea," "nay," or "abstain." In the House, with three times as many members, roll call votes would take much longer, so electronic voting has been used since 1945.

Though not elected officials, the secretary of the Senate and the clerk of the House serve as the administrative officers to handle the business of their respective bodies. Both officers are elected by the members of their respective legislative bodies. They also serve as parliamentarian for their respective bodies.

At the beginning of each quadrennium, each house adopts a set of rules that will regulate its operations. These rules address a wide variety of issues, from who is permitted on the floor of a chamber when the body is in session to an outline of the regular order of business for each meeting day. The House and Senate together adopt "Joint Rules of the Alabama Legislature," which cover such issues as communications between the two houses and the establishment of conference committees to reconcile conflicting versions of a bill.

In addition, most states, including Alabama, have a Legislative Council. In Alabama, this is a permanent committee composed of, from the Senate: the lieutenant governor and president pro-tempore, the chairs of the Finance and Taxation, Rules, Judiciary, and Governmental Affairs committees, and six senators elected by the Senate; and, from the House: the speaker and speaker pro-tempore, the chairs of the Ways and Means, Rules, Judiciary, and Local Government committees, and six representatives elected by the House. Also serving are the majority and minority leaders of each house. The Legislative Council meets quarterly to consider problems for which legislation may be needed and to make recommendations for the next legislative session. The Legislative Council also supervises the operations of the Legislative Reference Service, and, sitting as the Joint Committee on Administrative Regulation Review, reviews administrative rules.

The Senate

Like the United States Senate, the Alabama Senate has sole power of confirmation of certain appointees designated by the Constitution and by statute. The legislative antecedent of this role is a similar power vested in the Roman Senate during the period of the Republic.

The lieutenant governor of Alabama is ex officio president of the Senate, as provided under Article V, Section 117 (see page 253). The lieutenant governor can vote on Senate matters only to break a tie. The Senate may grant other powers to the lieutenant governor, in his capacity as president of the Senate. The office of lieutenant governor was first created by the Constitution of 1868, then revived in the Constitution of 1901. The prior constitutions of 1819, 1861, 1865, and 1875 had provided that the Senate elect its own president, as the speaker of the House of Representatives is elected. The Senate president pro tempore (Latin, "for a time") is elected during each organizational session from the ranks of the senators to serve in the event of absence of the president, as outlined in Article IV, Section 51. During the organizational session, members are assigned to Senate committees. The secretary of the Senate is responsible for the daily calendaring of bills, photocopying bills, and carrying communications from the Senate to the House. Members of the Alabama Senate, by rule, select a majority leader and a minority leader.

The House

The leader of the House of Representatives is the speaker of the House. The speaker is elected during the organizational session held during the January following each four-year election. The speaker keeps order and decorum in the House and recognizes members to speak. During the organizational session, the speaker assigns members to House committees. If the speaker is absent, the speaker pro tempore assumes the position. The clerk of the House is responsible for the daily calendaring of bills, photocopying bills, and carrying communications from the House to the Senate. As in the U.S. House of Representatives, members of the Alabama House select a majority leader and a minority leader.

Agencies of the Legislature

Several nonpartisan state agencies provide support to the legislature and the public. They assist in the drafting, research, and analysis of bills and budgets, and the evaluation of the financial operations of state agencies, county governments, and other entities receiving or disbursing state funds. For fiscal year 2007, the budgets of the legislative service agencies were: Examiners of Public Accounts, $12.4 million; Alabama Law Institute, $540,000; Legislative Council, $760,000; Legislative Fiscal Office, $1.86 million; and Legislative Reference Service, $2.7 million. The agencies are:

ALABAMA LAW INSTITUTE

P.O. Box 861425, Tuscaloosa, AL 35486-0013 • (205) 348-7411

www.ali.state.al.us • Robert McCurley, director

Created by act of the legislature in 1967, the ALI is located at the University of Alabama School of Law so it can have access to the research resources and faculty of the law school. The purpose of the Institute is to clarify and simplify the laws of Alabama, to revise laws that are out of date, and to develop proposals for new legislation in areas of need. The Institute works closely with the Legislative Reference Service in the yearly placing of acts passed by the legislature within the *Code of Alabama* for proper placement and codification. Major code revision work, such as revision of an entire section of law (Alabama's business corporation law, for example), is handled by the ALI. The Institute receives its projects from members of the legislature, state government, and the State Bar Association, or it may initiate studies itself when revisions are needed.

LEGISLATIVE REFERENCE SERVICE

11 South Union Street, Suite 613, Montgomery, AL 36130 • (334) 242-7560

www.lrs.state.al.us • Jerry L. Bassett, director

LRS, created in 1945 by Act 1945-152, drafts bills as requested by members of the legislature and conducts legal research for the legislature. The LRS director is appointed by the Legislative Council. LRS responds to questions concerning the organization and administration of state government or the operation of constitutional or statutory law; studies and reports on problems of state and local government; analyzes federal, state, and local government operations in Alabama and makes recommendations to the Legislative Council as appropriate; compiles and publishes the statutes of Alabama; acts as code commissioner in determining the content of the *Code of Alabama* and prepares an annual codification bill to adopt changes enacted by the legislature; and publishes the *Alabama Administrative Monthly* and the *Alabama Administrative Code.*

LEGISLATIVE FISCAL OFFICE

11 South Union Street, Room 620, Montgomery, AL 36130-3525 • (334) 242-7950
www.lfo.alabama.gov • Joyce Bigbee, Legislative Fiscal Officer (director)

LFO was established by Act 1975-108 to provide independent, accurate, and objective fiscal information—including fiscal notes on bills, budget analysis, drafting of legislative budget documents, and revenue estimating—to members of the Alabama House and Senate. The LFO is supervised by the ten-member Joint Fiscal Committee, and chaired by the chair of the Senate Finance and Taxation Committee. The Joint Fiscal Committee selects and appoints the LFO director, who coordinates with the Senate Fiscal Officer (Norris Green) and House Fiscal Officer (Frank Gitschier).

EXAMINERS OF PUBLIC ACCOUNTS

50 North Ripley Street, Room 3201, Montgomery, AL 36104-3833 • (334) 242-9200
www.examiners.state.al.us • Ronald L. Jones, Chief Examiner

The Department of Examiners of Public Accounts was created in 1947 (*Code of Alabama 1975*, Sections 41-5-1 through 41-5-24), although the title Examiner of Public Accounts originated in 1883, when the Alabama General Assembly, the forerunner of today's legislature, authorized the governor to appoint an examiner of public accounts. The department operates under the direction of the Legislative Committee on Public Accounts. The Examiners of Public Accounts is empowered to audit the books, accounts, and records of all state and county offices, officers, bureaus, boards, commissions, corporations, departments, and agencies, and all entities receiving or disbursing public funds, and to report on expenditures, contracts, or other audit findings found to be in violation of law. The department has the authority to assist other governmental officers such as the attorney general, district attorneys, and federal agencies. The chief examiner can issue subpoenas to compel the attendance of witnesses and the production of records in connection with audits. Each state and county officer must keep books, records, and accounts, and make reports as prescribed by the chief examiner.

THE ALABAMA STATE SENATE

Alabama State House, 11 South Union Street
Montgomery, AL 36130
(334) 242-7800
www.legislature.state.al.us/senate/senate.html

OFFICERS OF THE SENATE

LT. GOV. JIM FOLSOM JR.
President

RODGER MELL SMITHERMAN
President Pro Tempore

CHARLES McDOWELL LEE
Secretary of the Senate

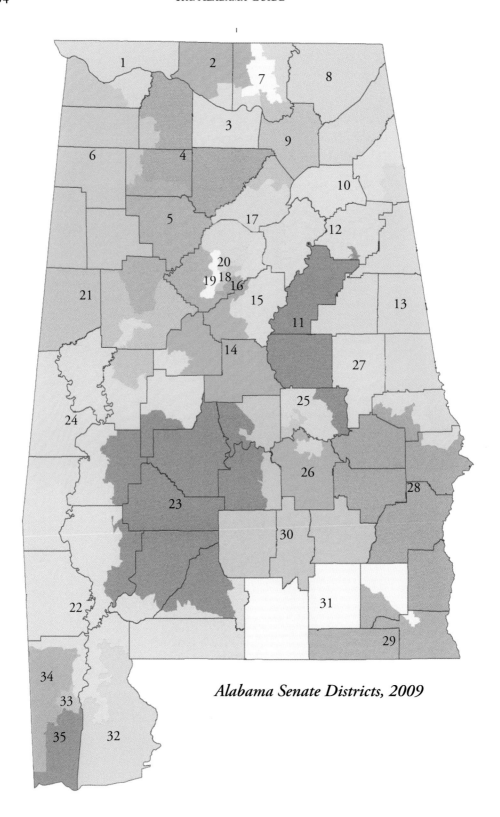

Alabama Senate Districts, 2009

Members of the Alabama State Senate
As of June 10, 2009

District	Senator
1	Bobby Denton
2	Tom Butler
3	Arthur Orr
4	Zeb Little
5	Charles Bishop
6	Roger Bedford
7	Paul Sanford
8	Lowell Barron
9	Hinton Mitchem
10	Larry Means
11	Jim Preuitt
12	Del Marsh
13	Kim Benefield
14	Henry "Hank" Erwin Jr.
15	Steve French
16	J. T. "Jabo" Waggoner
17	Scott Beason
18	Rodger Mell Smitherman
19	Vacant*
20	Linda Coleman
21	Victor "Phil" Poole
22	Marc Keahey
23	Henry "Hank" Sanders
24	Bobby Singleton
25	Larry Dixon
26	Quinton Ross Jr.
27	T. D. "Ted" Little
28	Myron Penn
29	Harri Anne Smith
30	Wendell Mitchell
31	Jimmy Holley
32	Lee "Trip" Pittman
33	Vivian Davis Figures
34	Rusty Glover
35	Ben Brooks

*Vacant following the depature of E. B. McClain. Special election pending at time of publication.

LOWELL BARRON (D)

District 8: DeKalb, Jackson, and Madison

Committees: Rules (chair); Banking and Insurance; Commerce, Transportation, and Utilities; Constitution, Campaign Finance, Ethics, and Elections; Economic Expansion and Trade; Finance and Taxation, General Fund; Local Legislation No. 1; Tourism and Marketing

Room 729-B; 11 South Union Street
Montgomery, AL 36130
(334) 242-7858

P.O. Box 65
Fyffe, AL 35971
(256) 623-2298

B. 1942, Jackson County. BS, pharmacy, Auburn University, 1965. Owner: Sand Mountain Drug Store, 1966–79, Fyffe Construction, 1970–, All Temp Windows, 1975–, Barron Land Company, 1976–. Fyffe City Council, 1969; mayor, Town of Fyffe, 1969–82; Alabama Senate, 1983–; president pro tem, 1999–2006; in 1983, the only successful write-in candidate in the history of the Senate. Baptist; former member, Auburn University board of trustees. Children: Shala, Lowell, Lauren, and Collier.

SCOTT BEASON (R)

District 17: Blount, Jefferson, and St. Clair

Committees: Banking and Insurance; Children, Youth Affairs, and Human Resources; Finance and Taxation, General Fund; Fiscal Responsibility and Accountability; Governmental Affairs; Local Legislation No. 2; Small Business and Economic Development

Room 737-B; 11 South Union Street
Montgomery, AL 36130
senatorsbeason@gmail.com
(334) 242-7794

P.O. Box 31
Gardendale, AL 35071
(205) 325-5308

B. 1969, Hartselle. BS, geology, 1991, University of Alabama. Environmental consultant, RUST Environment and Infrastructure and Bondurant Environmental, 1992–97; owner: Beason Construction and Renovation, 1997–2003, UFindEm.com (Internet start-up), 2000–01, Old South Construction, 2003–05, Planet Smoothie franchisee, 2002–05, Custom Renovators, 2005–08, Leonidas Group LLC, 2008–. Alabama House, 1998–2006; Alabama Senate, 2006–. Jefferson County and Alabama Republican executive committees; Rotary Club (honorary); Civitans; Gideons; Gardendale First Baptist Church. Spouse: Lori. Children: Keller, Merritt, and McCalan.

ROGER BEDFORD (D)

District 6: Colbert, Fayette, Franklin, Lamar, Lawrence, Marion, and Winston

Committees: Finance and Taxation, General Fund (chair); Agriculture, Conservation, and Forestry; Banking and Insurance; Commerce, Transportation, and Utilities; Confirmations; Constitution, Campaign Finance, Ethics, and Elections; Energy and Natural Resources; Finance and Taxation, Education; Health; Judiciary; Local Legislation No. 1; Rules

Room 730-B; 11 South Union Street
Montgomery, AL 36130
senbedford@aol.com
(334) 242-7862

P.O. Box 370
Russellville, AL 35653
(256) 332-2880

B. 1956, Richmond, VA. BS, political science, University of Alabama, 1976; JD, Cumberland School of Law, 1981. Attorney: Bedford, Bedford, Rogers, 1983–90, Bedford, Rogers, Bowling, P.C., 1990–. Alabama Senate, 1983–. Baptist Church; Rotary Club; Alabama Bar Association; Cattlemen's Association; NRA; Ducks Unlimited; American Cancer Society; board member: Boy Scouts of America, Tennessee Valley Council. Spouse: Maudie Darby. Child: Roger III.

KIM BENEFIELD (D)

District 13: Chambers, Cherokee, Clay, Cleburne, Lee, and Randolph

Committees: Agriculture, Conservation, and Forestry (chair); Banking and Insurance; Education; Energy and Natural Resources; Finance and Taxation, General Fund; Fiscal Responsibility and Accountability; Governmental Affairs; Industrial Development and Recruitment; Judiciary

Room 729-C; 11 South Union Street
Montgomery, AL 36130
kbenefield@acs-isp.com
(334) 242-7874

P.O. Box 123
Woodland, AL 36280

B. 1956, Anniston. BS, accounting, Jacksonville State University, 1985. Randolph County Circuit Clerk, 1988–2006; Alabama Senate, 2006–. Pianist and Sunday School teacher, Zion Baptist Church. Spouse: Dennis. Child: Kelly.

CHARLES BISHOP (R)

District 5: Jefferson, Tuscaloosa, Walker, and Winston

Committees: Business and Labor; Commerce, Transportation, and Utilities; Local Legislation No. 2; Rules; Tourism and Marketing

Room 737; 11 South Union Street
Montgomery, AL 36130
(334) 242-7894

P.O. Box 1585
Jasper, AL 35502
(205) 221-4950

B. 1937, Moro, AR. Dexter High School, Dexter, MO. President and CEO, B&D Industrial Mining Services, Inc., 1975–. Senate, 1983–90, 2006–; Alabama Commissioner of Agriculture and Industry, 1999–2003. Church of Christ; Chamber of Commerce. Spouse: Cynthia. Children: Todd, Charlene, Charles Dean Jr., Brandy, and Jessica.

BEN BROOKS (R)

District 35: Mobile

Committees: Banking and Insurance; Constitution, Campaign Finance, Ethics, and Elections; Fiscal Responsibility and Accountability; Local Legislation No. 3; Judiciary; Veterans and Military Affairs

Room 735; 11 South Union Street
Montgomery, AL 36130
benbrooksiii@aol.com
(334) 242-7882

1495 University Boulevard
Mobile, AL 36619
(251) 344-7744

B. 1958, Mobile. BA, political science, University of South Alabama, 1980; JD, University of Alabama, 1983. Attorney, Wright, Green, PC, 1983–93, 2004–; special judge of the Mobile County District Court, 1993–. Mobile City councilman, 2001–06; chairman of the council finance committee, 2001–06; Alabama Senate, 2006–. Council of the Alabama Law Institute, Alabama Judicial System Study Commission. Spouse: Kathy. Children: Megan, Benjamin, IV, and Elizabeth.

TOM BUTLER (D)

District 2: Limestone and Madison

Committees: Children, Youth Affairs, and
Human Resources (chair); Agriculture, Con-
servation and Forestry; Commerce, Transpor-
tation, and Utilities; Finance and Taxation,
Education; Finance and Taxation, General
Fund; Health; Industrial Development and
Recruitment; Local Legislation No. 1; Rules

Room 733; 11 South Union Street
Montgomery, AL 36130
senbutler@aol.com
(334) 242-7854

136 Hartington Drive
Madison, AL 35758
(256) 837-8374

B. 1944, Huntsville. BS, chemistry, University of
Alabama, 1966; BS, pharmacy, Auburn University,
1970. Pharmacist. Alabama House of Representatives, 1982–94; Alabama Senate, 1994–. Baptist;
Optimist Club; Alabama Pharmaceutical Association; North Alabama Health Underwriters Association. Spouse: Karen. Children: Robin and Jill.

LINDA COLEMAN (D)

District 20: Jefferson

Committees: Health (chair); Commerce,
Transportation, and Utilities; Confirmations;
Finance and Taxation, Education; Fiscal
Responsibility and Accountability; Govern-
mental Affairs; Local Legislation No. 2; Small
Business and Economic Development

Room 732; 11 South Union Street
Montgomery, AL 36130
lindacoleman60@bellsouth.net
(334) 242-7864

926 Chinchona Drive
Birmingham, AL 35214
(205) 254-2079

B. 1950, Birmingham. BS, education, Alabama
A&M University, 1971; MA, education, special-
ization in special-needs children, University of
Alabama at Birmingham, 1976. Teacher, Birmingham Public School System, 1972–82; marketing,
Birmingham-Jefferson County Transit Authority, 1999–; compliance officer, Americans With
Disabilities, 2005–. Birmingham City Council,
1985–97; Alabama House of Representatives,
2002–06; Alabama Senate, 2006–. American
Red Cross; Positive Maturity Board in Jefferson
County; National Foundation for Women Legislators; Saint Mary's Catholic Church.

BOBBY DENTON (D)

District 1: Colbert and Lauderdale

Committees: Banking and Insurance (chair); Business and Labor; Education; Finance and Taxation, Education; Governmental Affairs; Industrial Development and Recruitment; Rules

Room 719; 11 South Union Street
Montgomery, AL 36130
bobby@bobbydenton.com
(334) 242-7888

2206 Lisa Avenue
Muscle Shoals, AL 35661
(256) 383-1317

B. 1938, Colbert County. BA, human relations, cum laude, University of Alabama, 1996. Director of development, Northwest Shoals Community College, Muscle Shoals, 1985–2004; singer, 1956–60, 1997–. Alabama Senate, 1978–; dean of Senate, 2002–. Church of Christ. Spouse: Barbara. Children: Three.

LARRY DIXON (R)

District 25: Elmore and Montgomery

Committees: Confirmations; Finance and Taxation, Education; Governmental Affairs; Health; Veterans and Military Affairs

Room 737-D; 11 South Union Street
Montgomery, AL 36130
ldixon@albme.org
(334) 242-7895

P.O. Box 946
Montgomery, AL 36101
(334) 242-4116

B. 1942, Nowata, OK. BS, history, 1968, and MA, history, Washington State University, 1970. Sergeant E-5, United States Army Infantry, 1961–64; director of continuing medical education, State Medical Association, 1972–78; director, Jackson Hospital Foundation, 1978–81; executive director, Alabama Board of Medical Examiners, 1981–. Montgomery City Council, 1975–78; Alabama House of Representatives, 1978–82; Alabama Senate, 1982–. Methodist; Montgomery Lions Club; National Administrators in Medicine. Spouse: Gaynell. Children: Katherine and Elizabeth.

HENRY "HANK" ERWIN JR. (R)

District 14: Bibb, Chilton, Jefferson, and Shelby

Committees: Agriculture, Conservation, and Forestry; Education; Industrial Development and Recruitment; Local Legislation No. 2; Veterans and Military Affairs

Room 738-A; 11 South Union Street
Montgomery, AL 36130
senatorerwin@aol.com
(334) 242-7873

106-B South First Street
Alabaster, AL 35007
(205) 621-6681

B. 1949, Birmingham. BS, Troy University, 1972; BA, Southwestern Bible College, 1974; MA, Dallas Seminary, 1981. Talk show host: American Weekend, 1994–95, WDJC Radio, 1996–99, WYDE Radio, 1999–2001; president and CEO, Save America Foundation, 1993–. Alabama Senate, 2002–. Birmingham's Lakeside Baptist Church; board member: Alabama Citizens Action Program, Freedoms Foundation. Spouse: Sheila. Children: Andrew and Jonathan.

VIVIAN DAVIS FIGURES (D)

District 33: Mobile

Committees: Education (chair); Local Legislation No. 3 (chair); Children, Youth Affairs, and Human Resources; Confirmations; Finance and Taxation, Education; Governmental Affairs; Judiciary; Rules; Small Business and Economic Development

Room 736-A; 11 South Union Street
Montgomery, AL 36130
vdfigures@comcast.net
(334) 242-7871

104 South Lawrence Street
Mobile, AL 36602
(251) 208-5480

B. 1957, Mobile. BS, management science, University of New Haven, 1980; attended Jones School of Law. Summer lunch program manager and director of foster grandparents program, Mobile Community Action, Inc., 1980–82; co-owner and vice president, *The New Times*, 1982–96; majority owner and president, PerfectPrint, Inc., 1986–96; president and CEO, Figures Legacy Education Foundation, 1998–. Mobile City Council, 1993–97; Alabama Senate, 1997–. Baptist; board member, Mobile Area Education Foundation. Spouse: Michael (deceased). Children: Akil, Shomari, and Jelani.

STEVE FRENCH (R)

District 15: Jefferson and Shelby

Committees: Finance and Taxation, General Fund; Health; Industrial Development and Recruitment; Local Legislation No. 2; Rules

Room 733-A; 11 South Union Street
Montgomery, AL 36130
steve.french@alsenate.gov
(334) 242-7851

P.O. Box 131428
Birmingham, AL 35213
(205) 325-5308

B. 1962, Lynchburg, VA. BS, personnel and industrial relations, Auburn University, 1985. Founder/operator, Political Consulting Company, 1992–98; investment and insurance specialist, Turner Insurance and Bonding, 2005–. Alabama Senate, 1998–. EPSCOR Panel of the University of Alabama; Alabama Commission on Infrastructure; SMART Governing Legislative Task Force. Spouse: Elizabeth. Children: Alex, Sally, Lizzie, and Virginia.

RUSTY GLOVER (R)

District 34: Mobile

Committees: Agriculture, Conservation, and Forestry; Commerce, Transportation, and Utilities; Education; Energy and Natural Resources; Finance and Taxation, General Fund; Local Legislation No. 3; Small Business and Economic Development

Room 735-B; 11 South Union Street
Montgomery, AL 36130
(334) 242-7886

P.O. Box 2175
Semmes, AL 36575
(251) 208-5480

B. 1966, Mobile. BS, secondary education, University of South Alabama, 1989; MEd, secondary education, University of South Alabama, 1997; MA, history, University of South Alabama, 1999. History teacher, Mary G. Montgomery High School, 1989–. Alabama House of Representatives, 2002–06; Alabama Senate, 2006–. Southern Baptist. Spouse: Connie. Children: Katie and Kellie.

JIMMY HOLLEY (R)

District 31: Coffee, Covington, Dale, and Houston

Committees: Commerce, Transportation, and Utilities; Finance and Taxation, Education; Veterans and Military Affairs

Room 731-C; 11 South Union Street
Montgomery , AL 36130
(334) 242-7845

4212 County Road 364
Elba, AL 36323
(334) 897-5181

B. 1944, Coffee County. BS, political science, East Tennessee State University, 1967; MA, school administration, East Tennessee State University, 1973. Alabama National Guard, 1967–73; educator, Troy University, 1984–2007; Southeast Pharmaceuticals, 2008–. Alabama House of Representatives, 1974–94; Alabama Senate, 1998–. College Avenue Church of Christ in Enterprise. Spouse: Mary. Children: John and Jason.

MARC KEAHEY (D)

District 22: Baldwin, Choctaw, Clarke, Conecuh, Escambia, Mobile, Monroe, and Washington

Committees: To be assigned.

11 S. Union St.
Montgomery, AL 36130
(334) 242-7700

128 Main St.
P.O. Box 297
Grove Hill, AL 36451
(251) 275-3127

B. 1980, Mobile. Lurleen B. Wallace Community College; BS, business management, University of Alabama, 2002; JD, Cumberland School of Law, 2008. Staff, State Representative Seth Hammett; Clarke County Public Defender; attorney, Keahey Law Office. Alabama House of Representatives, 2006–09; Alabama Senate, 2009–, elected in a special election on June 2, 2009 to fill the vacancy caused by the death of Sen. Pat Lindsey on January 11, 2009. Grove Hill Baptist Church. Spouse: Lara. Child: Marc.

T. D. "TED" LITTLE (D)

District 27: Lee, Russell, and Tallapoosa

Committees: Fiscal Responsibility and Accountability (chair); Children, Youth Affairs, and Human Resources; Confirmations; Economic Expansion and Trade; Finance and Taxation, Education; Judiciary; Rules; Small Business and Economic Development

Room 740; 11 South Union Street
Montgomery, AL 36130
tedlittle@mindspring.com
(334) 242-7865

P.O. Box 2366
Auburn, AL 36831
(334) 887-3472

B. 1942, Andalusia. BS, industrial management, University of Alabama, 1964; JD, University of Alabama School of Law, 1967. Faculty, Auburn University School of Business, 1968–85; guest lecturer, Lyman-Ward Military Academy, 1988–; attorney, 1975–. Senate, 1975–86, 1991–. Baptist; member of several boards and councils, including Dean's Advisory Council of Auburn University's College of Human Sciences, Chattahoochee Valley Community College Foundation. Widower. Children: Mollie and Terre.

ZEB LITTLE (D)

District 4: Cullman, Lawrence, and Winston

Committees: Local Legislation No. 1 (chair). Pursuant to Senate Rule 47 (c), the Senate majority leader serves on all Senate standing committees, with the exception of local legislation committees.

Room 721; 11 South Union Street
Montgomery, AL 36130
zeb@zeblittlelawfirm.com
(334) 242-7855

P.O. Box 2278
Cullman, AL 35056
(256) 775-7707

B. 1968, Cullman. BA, history, University of Alabama at Birmingham, 1991; JD, Cumberland School of Law, 1994. Attorney, Zeb Little Law Firm, LLC, 1994–. Senate, 1998–, Senate floor leader and majority leader, 2002–. St. John's Evangelical Protestant Church; Alabama and Cullman County bar associations; admitted to the bars of the U.S. District Court for the Northern and Middle districts of Alabama. Spouse: Deanna. Children: Zeb and Emily.

DEL MARSH (R)

District 12: Calhoun and St. Clair

Committees: Confirmations; Finance and Taxation, Education; Judiciary; Tourism and Marketing

Room 735-D; 11 South Union Street
Montgomery, AL 36130
del.marsh@alsenate.gov
(334) 242-7877

P.O. Drawer 2365
Anniston, AL 36202
(256) 237-8647

B. 1956, Wheeling, WV. BS, industrial management, Auburn University, 1980. Owner: Aerospace Coatings International, 1988–, Industrial Plating Company, 1988–, Marsh Properties, 1994–. Alabama Senate, 1998–. Episcopalian; organizing director, Southern States Bank; finance director, Alabama Republican Party. Spouse: Ginger. Children: Justin and Christine.

LARRY MEANS (D)

District 10: Cherokee and Etowah

Committees: Industrial Development and Recruitment (chair); Agriculture, Conservation, and Forestry; Business and Labor; Commerce, Transportation, and Utilities; Confirmations; Energy and Natural Resources; Finance and Taxation, Education; Governmental Affairs; Health

Room 731-A; 11 South Union Street
Montgomery, AL 36130
larry.means@alsenate.org
(334) 242- 7857

1106 6th Street
Attalla, AL 35954
(256) 538-2014

B. 1947, Attalla. BBA, business administration, Jacksonville State University, 1970. Supervisor, Gulf States Steel Corporation; McCartney Construction Company. Attalla City Council, 1976–80, 1984–88; mayor, City of Attalla, 1992–98; Alabama Senate, 1998–. Attalla First Baptist Church; Attalla Lions Club; Chamber of Commerce board; former chair, Metropolitan Planning Organization. Spouse: Karen. Children: Tanya and Brent.

WENDELL MITCHELL (D)

District 30: Autauga, Butler, Crenshaw, Elmore, Lowndes, and Pike

Committees: Pursuant to Senate Rule 47(e),
the deputy president pro tempore serves on all
Senate standing committees, with the exception of the local legislation committees.

Room 726-B; 11 South Union Street
Montgomery, AL 36130
wmitchell@faulkner.edu
(334) 242-7883

P.O. Box 225
Luverne, AL 36049
(334) 335-3449

B. 1940, Montgomery. BS, history and political
science, Auburn University, 1962; JD, University
of Alabama, 1965. Dean emeritus, Jones School
of Law, 2003–. Alabama Senate, 1982–, president
pro tempore, 2007–09, deputy president pro tempore, 2009–. Church of Christ; Luverne Rotary
Club; American Bar Association; Alabama Bar
Association. Spouse: Rosalind. Children: Maury,
Shelly, and Wendy.

HINTON MITCHEM (D)

District 9: Blount, Madison, and Marshall

Committees: Confirmations (chair); Agriculture, Conservation, and Forestry; Commerce,
Transportation, and Utilities; Finance and
Taxation, General Fund; Health; Rules; Veterans and Military Affairs

Room 726-A; 11 South Union Street
Montgomery, AL 36130
legislator@mclo.org
(334) 242-7876

412-A Gunter Avenue
Guntersville, AL 35976
(256) 582-0619

B. 1938, Oconee County, GA. BS, education,
University of Georgia, 1960. Owner, Hinton
Mitchem Tractor Co., Inc, 1965–2005; retired.
Alabama House of Representatives, 1974–78;
Alabama Senate, 1978– , president pro tempore,
2007–09. Rotary Club. Spouse: Judy. Children:
Todd, Tonya, and Derrick.

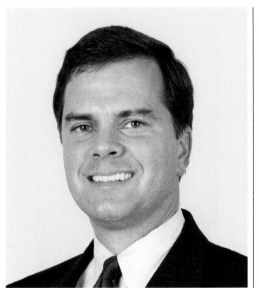

ARTHUR ORR (R)

District 3: Limestone, Madison, and Morgan

Committees: Confirmations; Constitution, Campaign Finance, Ethics, and Elections; Economic Expansion and Trade; Finance and Taxation, General Fund; Judiciary; Local Legislation No. 1

Room 737-A; 11 South Union Street
Montgomery, AL 36130
(334) 242-7891

P.O. Box 305
Decatur, AL 35602
(256) 345-3861

B. 1964, Decatur. BA, English, Wake Forest University, 1986; JD, University of Alabama, 1989. Peace Corps volunteer, Nepal, 1989–91; partner/attorney, Harris, Caddell, and Shanks PC, 1992–97; new country developer/staff attorney, Habitat for Humanity International, Asia/Pacific, 1997–2001; general counsel, Cook's Pest Control, Inc., 2001–. Alabama Senate, 2006–. First Bible Church. Spouse: Amy. Child: Jack.

MYRON PENN (D)

District 28: Barbour, Bullock, Henry, Lee, Macon, and Russell

Committees: Judiciary (chair); Agriculture, Conservation, and Forestry; Confirmations; Constitution, Campaign Finance, Ethics, and Elections; Economic Expansion and Trade; Education; Energy and Natural Resources; Finance and Taxation, General Fund; Fiscal Responsibility and Accountability; Governmental Affairs; Health; Tourism and Marketing

Room 734-B; 11 South Union Street
Montgomery, AL 36130
myronpenn28@hotmail.com
(334) 242- 7868

P.O. Box 688; 5 Court Square
Clayton, AL 36016
(334) 738-4486

B. 1972, Tuskegee. BA, history, University of Alabama at Birmingham, 1996; JD, Cumberland School of Law, 1998. Director of constituent affairs, Governor Jim Folsom, 1993–95; attorney: Gorham and Waldrep, PC, 1999–2000, Penn and Seaborn, LLC, Union Springs and Clanton, 2002–. Bullock County Commission, chair, 2000–02; Alabama Senate, 2002–. Methodist; Alabama Bar Association; Bullock County Partners in Education; Bullock County YMCA board; Union Springs Chamber of Commerce. Spouse: Holley.

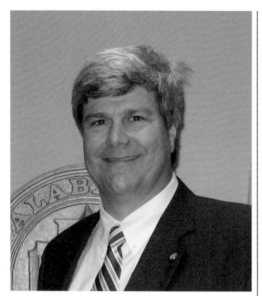

LEE "TRIP" PITTMAN (R)

District 32: Baldwin

Committees: Constitution, Campaign Finance, Ethics, and Elections; Economic Expansion and Trade; Education; Energy and Natural Resources; Finance and Taxation, General Fund; Judiciary

Room 738-B; 11 South Union Street
Montgomery, AL 36130
trip.pittman@alsenate.gov
(334) 242-7897

P.O. Box 1812
Daphne, AL 36526
(251) 621-3555

B. 1960, Birmingham. BS, commerce and business administration, University of Alabama, 1982. Businessman; owner, Pittman Tractor Co., Inc., 1988–. Alabama Senate, 2007–, elected in a special election on October 16, 2007 to fill the vacancy due to the resignation of Sen. Bradley Byrne. Fairhope United Methodist Church. Spouse: Lynn. Children: Reynolds, Virginia, and Lee.

VICTOR "PHIL" POOLE (D)

District 21: Hale, Pickens, and Tuscaloosa

Committees: Veterans and Military Affairs (chair); Children, Youth Affairs, and Human Resources; Finance and Taxation, Education

Room 736-B; 11 South Union Street
Montgomery, AL 36130
poole@mound.net
(334) 242-7889

P.O. Box 609
Moundville, AL 35474
(205) 371-6337

B. 1959, Tuscaloosa. BS, business, University of Alabama, 1980; JD, University of Alabama School of Law, 1982. First lieutenant, Alabama National Guard, 1982–88; captain, Army Reserve, 1989–96; attorney: Phil Poole LLC, 1984–, Cross, Poole, Goldasich, and Fischer, 2000–. Alabama House of Representatives, 1982–94; Alabama Senate 1994–. Methodist; Alabama State Bar; Moundville Masonic Lodge; Tuscaloosa Jaycees; Tuscaloosa County Bar Association; West Alabama Chamber of Commerce. Spouse: Leigh Ann.

JIM PREUITT (D)

District 11: Calhoun, Coosa, Elmore, and Talladega

Committees: Small Business and Economic Development (chair); Banking and Insurance; Commerce, Transportation, and Utilities; Finance and Taxation, General Fund; Governmental Affairs

Room 733-B; 11 South Union Street
Montgomery, AL 36130
(334) 242-7898

723 East Battle Street
Talladega, AL 35160
(256) 362-6900

B. 1935, Moulton. Attended school in Lawrence and Morgan counties. Automobile dealer, Ford Mercury, General Motors, and Chrysler dealerships, 1999–; farmer. Alabama House of Representatives, 1982–86; Alabama Senate, 1986–92, 1998–. Church of Christ; Kiwanis Club; Chamber of Commerce; Alabama Automobile Dealers Association; National Automobile Dealers Association. Spouse: Rona. Children: Lynne and Leigh.

QUINTON ROSS JR. (D)

District 26: Montgomery

Committees: Commerce, Transportation, and Utilities (chair); Constitution, Campaign Finance, Ethics, and Elections (chair); Education; Energy and Natural Resources; Finance and Taxation, Education; Governmental Affairs; Health; Rules; Tourism and Marketing; Veterans and Military Affairs

Room 734-A; 11 South Union Street
Montgomery, AL 36130
quinton.ross@alsenate.gov
(334) 242-7880

P.O. Box 6183
Montgomery, AL 36106
(334) 242-7880

B. 1968, Mobile. BS, political science, Alabama State University, 1992; MA, education, Alabama State University, 1995; pursuing PhD, educational leadership, policy, and law. English teacher, McIntyre Junior High School, 1995–96; administrative assistant, Goodwyn Junior High School, 1997–98; principal, Booker T. Washington Magnet High School, 1998–2003; director of Adult Education Consortium, Trenholm State Technical College, 2003–. Alabama Senate, 2002–. Hutchinson Missionary Baptist Church; Omega Psi Phi fraternity. Spouse: Kelley. Children: Quinmari and Quinton III.

HENRY "HANK" SANDERS (D)

District 23: Autauga, Clarke, Conecuh, Dallas, Lowndes, Marengo, Monroe, Perry, and Wilcox

Committees: Finance and Taxation, Education (chair); Commerce, Transportation, and Utilities; Confirmations; Constitution, Campaign Finance, Ethics, and Elections; Economic Expansion and Trade; Education; Energy and Natural Resources; Finance and Taxation, General Fund; Judiciary; Local Legislation No. 1

Room 730-A; 11 South Union Street
Montgomery, AL 36130
(334) 242-7860

P.O. Box 1305; 1405 Jeff Davis Avenue
Selma, AL 36702
(334) 875-9264

B. 1942, Baldwin County. BA, history, Talladega College, 1967; JD, Harvard Law School, 1970. Attorney, Chestnut, Sanders, Sanders, and Pettaway, 1971–. Alabama Senate, 1982–. Baptist; C.A.R.E.; Alabama New South Coalition; National Conference of Black Lawyers; National and American bar associations; Alabama Lawyers Association. Spouse: Faya Rose. Children: Malkia, Kindaka, Ainka, Charles, Maurice, Rosie, and Jennifer.

PAUL SANFORD (R)

District 7: Madison

Committees: To be assigned.

11 South Union Street
Montgomery, AL 36130
(334) 242-7700

B. 1967, Huntsville. AOS, culinary arts, Culinary Institute of America, 1991. Ruth's Chris Steakhouse (Nashville), 1997–98; assistant general manager, Legend's Club of Tennessee, 1998–2000; Gibson's Barbeque, executive chef, 2000–02; co-owner, Little Paul's Barbecue, 2002–. Alabama Senate, 2009–, elected in special election on June 9, 2009 to fill the vacancy caused by the resignation of Sen. Parker Griffith on November 24, 2008. Volunteer coach: Randolph School, Upward Basketball Program, American Youth Soccer Organization, and Kicks Soccer Club; volunteer, Habitat for Humanity. Spouse: Danielle. Children: Chase and Ryan.

BOBBY SINGLETON (D)

District 24: Bibb, Choctaw, Greene, Hale, Marengo, Perry, Sumter, and Tuscaloosa

Committees: Tourism and Marketing (chair); Agriculture, Conservation, and Forestry; Banking and Insurance; Confirmations; Economic Expansion and Trade; Finance and Taxation, General Fund; Fiscal Responsibility and Accountability; Industrial Development and Recruitment; Judiciary

Room 732-B; 11 South Union Street
Montgomery, AL 36130
bsingle164@yahoo.com
(334) 242-7935

P.O. Box 548
Greensboro, AL 36744

B. Greensboro. BS, criminal justice, Alabama State University, 1984; JD, Miles Law School. Alabama House of Representatives, 2002–2005; Alabama Senate, 2005–. Greenleaf Missionary Baptist Church.

HARRI ANNE SMITH (R)

District 29: Dale, Geneva, and Houston

Committees: Agriculture, Conservation, and Forestry; Banking and Insurance; Commerce, Transportation, and Utilities; Confirmations; Finance and Taxation, Education; Governmental Affairs; Health; Local Legislation No. 1; Rules

Room 735-C; 11 South Union Street
Montgomery, AL 36130
harriannesmith@graceba.net
(334) 242-7879

P.O. Box 483
Slocomb, AL 36375
(334) 886-3208

B. 1962, Houston County. BBA, business administration, Troy State University, 1985. Board of directors, executive vice president, and operations officer, Slocomb National Bank (now Friend Bank), 1984–. Council member, City of Slocomb, 1989–96; mayor, City of Slocomb, 1996; Alabama Senate, 1998–. Baptist; Southeast Alabama Regional Planning and Development Revolving Loan Fund; Alabama Federation of Republican Women. Spouse: Charlie.

RODGER MELL SMITHERMAN (D)

District 18: Jefferson

President Pro Tempore of the Senate

Committees: Local Legislation No. 2 (chair); Banking and Insurance; Business and Labor; Confirmations; Constitution, Campaign Finance, Ethics, and Elections; Finance and Taxation, Education; Industrial Development and Recruitment; Judiciary; Rules; Tourism and Marketing

Room 722; 11 South Union Street
Montgomery, AL 36130
rodger99@bellsouth.net
(334) 242-7870

2029 2nd Avenue North
Birmingham, AL 35203
(205) 322-0012

B. 1953, Montgomery. BBA, University of Montevallo, 1976; JD, with honors, Miles Law School, 1986. Consultant law professor, Miles Law School, seventeen years; attorney, Smitherman and Smitherman, twenty years; junior varsity girls' basketball coach and assistant varsity girls' basketball coach, Ramsey High School, eleven years. Alabama Senate, 1994–, president pro tempore, 2009–. Birmingham Chamber of Commerce; Alabama Trial Lawyers Association; Birmingham Bar Association; Presbyterian Church, elder. Spouse: Carole. Children: Rodger, Tonya, Mary, and Crystal.

J. T. "JABO" WAGGONER (R)

District 16: Jefferson and Shelby

Committees: Pursuant to Senate Rule 47 (i and j), the Senate minority leader serves on all Senate standing committees, with the exception of the local legislation committees; Local Legislation No. 2.

Room 737-C; 11 South Union Street
Montgomery, AL 36130
jabo.waggoner@alsenate.gov
(334) 242-7892

P.O. Box 660609
Vestavia Hills, AL 35266
(205) 978-7405

B. 1937, Birmingham. BA, business administration, Birmingham-Southern College, 1960; JD, Birmingham School of Law, 1964. Vice president of community and public affairs, Health-South Corporation, 1990–2003; president, Birmingham Business Consultants Limited Liability Company, 2003–. Alabama House of Representatives, 1966–83; Alabama Senate, 1990–, minority leader, 2002–. Homewood Church of Christ; board member: Metropolitan Development Board, Better Business Bureau, Greater Birmingham Convention and Visitors Bureau, Alabama Sports Hall of Fame, Pinnacle Bank. Spouse: Marilyn. Children: Scott (deceased), Mark, Lyn, and Jay.

The State House in Montgomery has housed the Alabama Legislature since 1985, when the two houses moved from their original chambers in the Capitol. From 1963 to 1985, the building housed the Alabama Highway Department.

The Old House Chamber in the Capitol. Today, the House and Senate meet in the State House across Union Street from the Capitol, and the historic Old House Chamber is used on ceremonial occasions such as the annual delivery of the governor's "State of the State" address to the assembled legislature and judiciary.

The Alabama State House of Representatives

Alabama State House, 11 South Union Street
Montgomery, AL 36130
(334) 242-7600
www.legislature.state.al.us/house/house.html

Officers of the House

SETH HAMMETT
Speaker of the House

DEMETRIUS NEWTON
Speaker Pro Tempore of the House

GREG PAPPAS
Clerk of the House

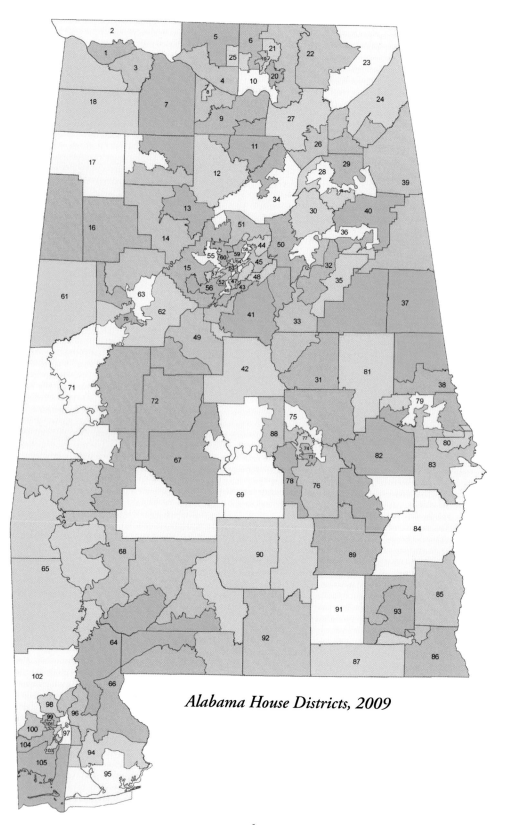

Alabama House Districts, 2009

MEMBERS OF THE ALABAMA HOUSE OF REPRESENTATIVES
As of June 10, 2009

Dist.	Representative
1	Tammy Irons
2	Mike Curtis
3	Marcel Black
4	Micky Hammon
5	Henry White
6	Vacant*
7	John "Jody" Letson
8	Bill Dukes
9	Ronald Grantland
10	Mike Ball
11	Jeremy Oden
12	James Fields Jr.
13	Tommy Sherer
14	Ken Guin
15	Pat Moore
16	William Thigpen Sr.
17	Michael Millican
18	Johnny Mack Morrow
19	Laura Hall
20	Howard Sanderford
21	Randy Hinshaw
22	Butch Taylor
23	John Robinson
24	Todd Greeson
25	Mac McCutcheon
26	W. Frank McDaniel
27	Jeffrey McLaughlin
28	Craig Ford
29	John "Jack" Page III
30	Blaine Galliher
31	Barry Mask
32	Barbara Boyd
33	Ronald Johnson
34	Elwyn Thomas
35	Steve Hurst
36	Randy Wood
37	Richard Laird
38	Duwayne Bridges
39	Richard Lindsey
40	Lea Fite
41	Mike Hill
42	James "Jimmy" Martin
43	Mary Sue McClurkin
44	Arthur Payne
45	Owen Drake
46	Paul DeMarco
47	Jack Williams
48	Greg Canfield
49	Cam Ward
50	Jim McClendon
51	Benjamin "Allen" Treadaway
52	John Rogers Jr.
53	Demetrius Newton
54	Patricia Todd
55	Rod Scott
56	Priscilla Dunn
57	Merika Coleman
58	Oliver Robinson
59	Mary Moore
60	Earl Hilliard Jr.
61	Alan Harper
62	Gerald Allen
63	Robert Bentley
64	Harry Shiver
65	Vacant†
66	Alan Baker
67	Yusuf Salaam
68	Thomas Jackson
69	James Thomas
70	Chris England
71	Artis "A. J." McCampbell
72	Ralph Howard
73	David Grimes
74	Jay Love
75	Greg Wren
76	Thad McClammy
77	John Knight Jr.
78	Alvin Holmes
79	Mike Hubbard
80	Lesley Vance
81	Betty Carol Graham
82	Pebblin Warren
83	George Bandy
84	Billy Beasley
85	Locy "Sonny" Baker
86	Benjamin Lewis
87	Warren Beck
88	H. Mac Gipson Jr.
89	Alan Boothe
90	Charles Newton
91	Terry Spicer
92	Seth Hammett
93	Steve Clouse
94	Joe Faust
95	Stephen McMillan
96	Randy Davis
97	Yvonne Kennedy
98	James Gordon
99	James Buskey
100	Victor Gaston
101	Jamie Ison
102	Chad Fincher
103	Joseph Mitchell
104	Jim Barton
105	Spencer Collier

*Seat vacated by Rep. Sue Schmitz on February 26, 2009. Special election pending at time of publication.
† Seat vacated by Marc Keahey following his election to the Alabama Senate on June 2, 2009.

GERALD ALLEN (R)

District 62: Tuscaloosa

Committees: Commerce;
Government Appropriations;
Tuscaloosa County Legisla-
tion

Rm. 531; 11 S. Union St.
Montgomery, AL 36130
gerald.allen@alhouse.org
(334) 242-7758

P.O. Box 71001
Tuscaloosa, AL 35407
(205) 556-5310

B. 1950, Tuscaloosa. BS, educa-
tion, University of Alabama,
1973. Coach, Tuscaloosa County
Board of Education, 1973–76;
athletic director, Tuscaloosa
County Parks and Recreation,
1976–78; sales, CASHCO,
1978–80; owner, CASHCO
Marketing, 1980–. Alabama
House of Representatives, 1994–.
Deacon, Gilgal Baptist Church;
University of Alabama Alumni
Association; West Alabama
Chamber of Commerce; Civitan
Club; Holt High School boost-
ers; Cottondale Elementary and
Holt High School PTAs. Spouse:
Sheila. Children: Wes, Kellie,
and Jill.

ALAN BAKER (R)

District 66: Baldwin and
Escambia

Committees: Baldwin County
Legislation; Education
Policy; Public Safety

Rm. 538-A; 11 S. Union St.
Montgomery, AL 36130
staterep@co.escambia.al.us
(334) 242-7720

P.O. Box 975
Brewton, AL 36427
(251) 867-0244

B. 1956, Brewton. BS, history,
Auburn University, 1978. His-
tory teacher and coach, South
Girard School, 1978–80; Earnest
Ward School, 1980–84; teacher
and football and track coach, T.
R. Miller High School, 1984–
2005; director, Mortgage and
Refinance Business, 2005–06;
retired. Alabama House of
Representatives, 2006-. Board
member: Escambia County
American Red Cross, Brewton
Area YMCA, Habitat for Hu-
manity; First Baptist Church of
Brewton. Spouse: Kaki.

LOCY "SONNY" BAKER (D)

District 85: Henry and
Houston

Committees: Government
Appropriations; Health

Rm. 522-D; 11 S. Union St.
Montgomery, AL 36130
LocyBaker@al.house.org
(334) 242-7693

115 Bryant St.
Abbeville, AL 36310
(334) 726-1144

B. 1945, Abbeville. AA, BS, and
MA, Alabama State University.
Army, 1968–71; Daniel Con-
struction Company, 1976–77;
National Guard, 1973–2004;
director of student support
services, George C. Wallace Col-
lege, Dothan. Barbour County
Board of Education, 1973–76;
Dothan City Board of Educa-
tion, 1977–80; Henry County
Commissioner, 1991; Alabama
House of Representatives, 1994-.
Deacon, Mary Magdalene Bap-
tist Church; Alabama Education
Association; Free and Accepted
Masonry; Kappa Alpha Psi;
Kiwanis Club. Spouse: Idena.
Children: Paul, Brandon, and
Corey.

MIKE BALL (R)

District 10: Madison

Committees: Education Policy; Internal Affairs; Madison County Legislation; Public Safety

Rm. 526-D; 11 S. Union St. Montgomery, AL 36130

mikeball@knology.net

(334) 242-7683

P.O. Box 6302

Huntsville, AL 35824

(256) 539-5441

B. 1954, Stockton, CA. AS, criminal justice, Jefferson State Junior College, 1982; BS, political science, Athens State University, 2004. Sergeant, Marine Corps, 1973–77; state trooper, Alabama Highway Patrol, 1978–86; agent-supervisor/hostage negotiator, Alabama Bureau of Investigation, Major Crimes Unit, 1986–2003; co-owner, Ball Roofing, 2003–. Alabama House of Representatives, 2002–. Singer and mandolin player, Madison Mountaintop Band. Spouse: Debbie. Children: Chris, Cara, and Mandy.

GEORGE BANDY (D)

District 83: Lee and Russell

Committees: Constitution and Elections; Lee County Legislation; Local Legislation

Rm. 529; 11 S. Union St. Montgomery, AL 36130

george.bandy@alhouse.org

(334) 242-7721

1307-A Glenn Cir.

Opelika, AL 36801

(334) 749-0051

B. 1945, Opelika. BA, Morehouse College. Pastor, Saint James Missionary Baptist Church, 1985–2009. Opelika City Council 1986–90, president pro tem, 1986–90; Lee County Commission, 1990-94; Alabama House of Representatives, 1994-. Chair, Alabama Democratic Conference; president, Lee County Alliance; Lee County Concerned Citizens; Lee County Voters League; NAACP. Children: George and Jennifer.

JIM BARTON JR. (R)

District 104: Mobile

Committees: Banking and Insurance; Health; Mobile County Legislation

Rm. 540-D; 11 S. Union St. Montgomery, AL 36130

jbarton@msg-inc.com

(334) 242-7754

3824 St. Andrews Dr.

Mobile, AL 36693

(251) 208-5480

B. 1968, Mobile. BA, political science, University of South Alabama. Sales, Accelerated Technology, Inc., 1993–2001; owner: Bay Area Resources, Inc., 1995–; Old South Construction, 2000–. Alabama House of Representatives, 2001–. Saint Ignatius Catholic Church; Alabama Chapter of National Multiple Sclerosis Society. Spouse: Kim. Children: Ward and Georgianne.

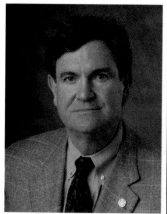  

BILLY BEASLEY (D)

District 84: Barbour, Bullock, and Russell

Committees: Government Appropriations; Health

Rm. 625-A; 11 S. Union St. Montgomery, AL 36130 billy.beasley@alhouse.org (334) 242-7686

P.O. Box 220 Clayton, AL 36016 (334) 775-3291

B. 1940, Clayton. BS, pharmacy, Auburn University, 1962. Captain, U.S. Army, Medical Services Corps, 1964–66; operator, Louisville Drug Store, 1982–2005; president, Pratts Station, LLC, 1993–; operator, Clayton Drug Company, 1996–; operator, Clio Drug Companies, 1997–. Alabama House of Representatives, 1998–. Clayton United Methodist Church; Eufaula/ Barbour County Chamber of Commerce; Barbour County Hospital; Auburn Alumni Association. Spouse: Rebecca. Children: Martin, Brad, Margaret, Tom, and Rebecca.

WARREN BECK (R)

District 87: Geneva and Houston

Committees: Commerce; Tourism and Travel

Rm. 630-C; 11 S. Union St. Montgomery, AL 36130 warren.beck@alhouse.org (334) 242-7774

1410 Center Plaza Geneva, AL 36340 (334) 684-9549

B. 1944, Geneva. BS, marketing, Troy University, 1966; MS, education, Troy University, 1974. Operator, Center Insurance Agency, 1983–. Mayor, City of Geneva, 2001–02; Alabama House of Representatives, 2002–. Rotary Club. Spouse: Carolyn (deceased). Children: Two.

ROBERT BENTLEY (R)

District 63: Tuscaloosa

Committees: Agriculture and Forestry; Education Appropriations; Internal Affairs; Tuscaloosa County Legislation

Rm. 537-D; 11 S. Union St. Montgomery, AL 36130 robert.bentley@alhouse.org (334) 242-7691

11 Ridgeland Tuscaloosa, AL 35406 (205) 349-3675

B. 1943, Columbiana. BS, chemistry, University of Alabama, 1964; MD, dermatology, University of Alabama School of Medicine, 1968; residency, University of Alabama School of Medicine. Captain, Air Force Medical Corp, 1969–71; founding partner/president, Alabama Dermatological Associates, 1974–. Alabama House of Representatives, 2002–. American Academy of Dermatology; Medical Association of Alabama; Vietnam Veterans of America; American Legion; First Baptist Church; Youth for Christ Advisory Board. Spouse: Dianne. Children: John, Paul, Luke, and Matthew.

MARCEL BLACK (D)

District 3: Colbert

Committees: Judiciary (chair); Boards and Commissions

Rm. 516-F; 11 S. Union St. Montgomery, AL 36130 marcel.black@alhouse.org (334) 242-7667

210 North Main St. Tuscumbia, AL 35674 (256) 383-2435

B. 1951, Colbert County. BA, political science, University of Alabama, 1972; JD, University of Alabama, 1975. Attorney: Richard Shelby and Associates, 1975–76; independent practice, 1976–81, 1994–99; Hewitt and Black, 1981–94; Black and Hughston, PC, 2000–. Alabama House of Representatives, 1990–. First Presbyterian Church of Tuscumbia. Spouse: Martha. Children: Edgar and Virginia Fern.

ALAN BOOTHE (D)

District 89: Dale and Pike

Committees: Boards and Commissions; Education Appropriations; Internal Affairs

Rm. 627-A; 11 S. Union St. Montgomery, AL 36130 alan.boothe@alhouse.org (334) 242-7710

P.O. Box 561 Troy, AL 36081 (334) 566-5742

B. 1945, Opp. BS, social science, 1973, MS, administration of criminal justice, Troy University, 1975. Air Force, 1966–70, Alabama National Guard, 1975–95; Pike County Coroner, 1975–85; director of governmental relations and chief of police, Troy University, 1993–. Troy City Councilman, 1985–96; Alabama House of Representatives, 1998–. International Association of Chiefs of Police; Rotary Club; First Baptist Church of Troy. Spouse: Anne. Children: Melissa and Jason.

BARBARA BOYD (D)

District 32: Calhoun and Talladega

Committees: Education Policy; Government Operations; Rules

Rm. 530; 11 S. Union St. Montgomery, AL 36130 bboyd@calhouncounty.org (334) 242-7692

2222 McDaniel Ave. Anniston, AL 36202 (256) 236-3521 Ext. 39

B. 1937, Anniston. BA, French and English, Miles College, 1960; MA, supervision and curriculum development, 1976; EdD, University of Alabama, 1976. Instructor: J. W. Darden High School, 1960–62; Calhoun County Training School, 1962–70; Weaver Junior High and High schools, 1970–85. Alabama House of Representatives, 1994–. NAACP; Alabama Democratic Conference; Southern Christian Leadership Conference; NEA-retired; Alpha Kappa Alpha; Phi Delta Kappa; trustee board of Christian Education, Murray Temple Christian Methodist Episcopal Church. Children: Frank and Reginald.

Duwayne Bridges (R)

District 38: Chambers and
Lee

Committees: Banking and
Insurance; Commerce; Lee
County Legislation

Rm. 528-C; 11 S. Union St.
Montgomery, AL 36130
duwayne.bridges@alhouse.org
(334) 242-7708

P.O. Box 729
Valley, AL 36854
(334) 756-6373

B. 1946, Shawnee, OK. AA,
business marketing, Albany
Junior College, 1990; BA, business administration, Faulkner
University, 1998; MA, human
resources management, Troy
University, 1992. Sergeant, Marine Corps, Vietnam, 1964–68;
owner, Bridges Western Wear
and Antiques, 1978–; owner/
president, Bridges/Perlis Travel
Plaza, 1978–. Alabama House
of Representatives, 2000–. Hike/
Bike/Run Event for Valley
Haven School for the Mentally
Retarded; Chattahoochee Valley Hospital, 1991 Outstanding
ARC Volunteer. Spouse: Pat.
Children: Duwayne and Karen.

James Buskey (D)

District 99: Mobile

Committees: Banking and
Insurance; Education Ap-
propriations; Mobile County
Legislation; Rules

Rm. 540-C; 11 S. Union St.
Montgomery, AL 36130
james.buskey@alhouse.org
(334) 242-7757

104 S. Lawrence St.
Mobile, AL 36602
(251) 208-5480

B. 1937, Greenville. BS, secondary education, Alabama State
University, 1959; MA, teach-
ing mathematics, University of
North Carolina at Chapel Hill,
1964; EdS, University of Colo-
rado, 1974. Assistant principal:
LeFlore High School, 1966–76;
Williamson High School, 1976–
87; principal, E. S. Chastang
Middle School, 1987–1992.
Alabama House of Representa-
tives, 1976-. Aimwell Baptist
Church; Omega Psi Phi; Ala-
bama Democratic Conference;
executive board, Alabama Demo-
cratic Party; board of directors,
Franklin Primary Health Center;
Commonwealth National Bank.
Spouse: Virginia.

Greg Canfield (R)

District 48: Jefferson and
Shelby

Committees: Constitution
and Elections; Government
Appropriations; Jefferson
County Legislation; Shelby
County Legislation

Rm. 625-D; 11 S. Union St.
Montgomery, AL 36130
gcanfield@bellsouth.net
(334) 242-7663

804 Park View Cir.
Vestavia Hills, AL 35242
(205) 453-0883

B. 1960, Birmingham. BS,
finance, University of Alabama
at Birmingham, 1983. Account
executive, general manager, and
regional sales manager, Purolator,
1983–89; national account executive, Transus Freight Systems,
1989–91; president and agent,
Canfield Insurance & Financial
Services, 1993–2008; agent, J.
H. Berry Insurance, 1993–2008.
Vestavia Hills City Council,
2000–06; Alabama House of
Representatives, 2006–. Leadership Vestavia Hills; Leadership
Birmingham; Our Lady of Sor-
rows Catholic Church. Spouse:
Denise. Children: Rachel and
John.

STEVE CLOUSE (R)

District 93: Dale and Houston

Committees: Banking and Insurance; Health

Rm. 526-A; 11 S. Union St. Montgomery, AL 36130 steve.clouse@alhouse.org (334) 242-7717

P.O. Box 818 Ozark, AL 36361 (334) 774-9122

B. 1956, Dale County. BA, political science, University of Alabama, 1978. Vice president, Clouse Marketing Company, 1979–. Alabama House of Representatives, 1994–. First United Methodist Church; past president, Ozark Rotary Club; board member, Ozark Boys and Girls Club; American Cancer Society; Regional Revolving Loan Committee; former chair, Dale County United Way. Spouse: Diane. Children: Anne Myrre and Todd.

MERIKA COLEMAN (D)

District 57: Jefferson

Committees: Boards and Commissions (chair); Government Operations; Jefferson County Legislation

Rm. 208; 11 S. Union St. Montgomery, AL 36130 merika.coleman@alhouse.org (334) 242-7755

P.O. Box 28888 Birmingham, AL 35228 (205) 325-5308

B. 1973, Lakenheath AFB, England. BA, mass communication, 1995, MPA, 1997, University of Alabama at Birmingham. Instructor of social and behavioral sciences, Miles College, 1997–99, 2008–; Greater Birmingham Ministries, 1999–; director, community and economic development and adjunct instructor of government, Lawson State Community College, 2000–04; economic and community development director, City of Bessemer, 2004–06. Alabama House of Representatives, 2002–. Saint Mary's Catholic School; Midfield Neighborhood Association; Midfield Voter's League. Spouse: Edward. Children: Elexia and Xaviar.

SPENCER COLLIER (R)

District 105: Mobile

Committees: Agriculture and Forestry; Judiciary; Mobile County Legislation

Rm. 540-D; 11 S. Union St. Montgomery, AL 36130 jsc@cunninghambounds.com (334) 242-7719

P.O. Box 550 Irvington, AL 36544 (251) 208-5480

B. 1973, Mobile. BS, criminal justice, Troy University, 1995. Supervisor, state troopers, 1996–2006; legal advisor, Cunningham Bounds, 2006–. Alabama House of Representatives, 2002–. Mobile Christian Center. Spouse: Melissa. Children: Christopher, Connor, Colby, and Caroline.

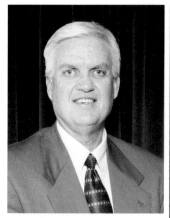

MIKE CURTIS (D)

District 2: Lauderdale

Committees: County and Municipal Government; Public Safety

Rm. 522-E; 11 S. Union St.
Montgomery, AL 36130
mike.curtis@alhouse.gov
(334) 242-7725

115 E. Mobile St.
Florence, AL 35634
(256) 760-5707

B. 1955, Russellville. BS, sociology and history, University of North Alabama, 1977; County Commission College, 1998. Associate agent, Nationwide Insurance, 1996–. Lauderdale County Commission, 1996–2006; Alabama House of Representatives, 2006–. Alabama Special Olympics; Shoals Special Olympics; Harlon Hill Trophy; Division II Hall of Fame; Shoals National Championship Committee; board of directors, 911; Association of County Commissions of Alabama; Retired Senior Volunteer Program; Atlas Church of Christ; Lauderdale County Career Technical Advisory Committee. Spouse: Janice. Children: Britney, Mellany, and Bryce.

RANDY DAVIS (R)

District 96: Baldwin and Mobile

Committees: Agriculture and Forestry; Constitution and Elections; Baldwin County Legislation; Local Legislation; Mobile County Legislation

Rm. 538-B; 11 S. Union St.
Montgomery, AL 36130
rmdavis14@aol.com
(334) 242-7724

6590 Thompson Ln.
Daphne, AL 36526
(251) 990-4615

B. 1952, Mobile. BMEd, 1974, and MMEd, 1976, University of Southern Mississippi; EdS, Alabama State University, 1998. Teacher, 1973–87, supervisor, 1989–2000, Mobile County School System; salesperson, Princeton Industries Corporation, 1987–89; public relations coordinator, Baldwin County School System, 2000–04; assistant professor of music, University of Mobile, 2004–. Alabama House of Representatives, 2002–. Mobile Opera; Mobile Symphony; Baldwin Pops; Baldwin County Pops Band. Spouse: Martha. Child: Judson.

PAUL DeMARCO (R)

District 46: Jefferson

Committees: Boards and Commissions; Jefferson County Legislation; Judiciary

Rm. 537-F; 11 S. Union St.
Montgomery, AL 36130
paul@pljpc.com
(334) 242-7740

111 Edgewood Blvd.
Homewood, AL 35209
(205) 802-7285

B. 1967, Birmingham. BA, Journalism, Auburn University, 1990; JD, University of Alabama, 1993. Editor-in-chief, *Alabama Law Review*, 1993; partner, Parsons, Lee, and Juliano P.C., 1993–. Alabama House of Representatives, 2005–. Past president, Birmingham Bar Foundation; Homewood, Hoover, Mountain Brook, and Vestavia Hills chambers of commerce. Spouse: Jacqueline.

OWEN DRAKE (R)

District 45: Jefferson and St. Clair

Committees: County and Municipal Government; Jefferson County Legislation; Public Safety

Rm. 528-B; 11 S. Union St. Montgomery, AL 36130 odrake208@charter.net (334) 242-7727

P.O. Box 865 Leeds, AL 35094 (205) 699-6655

B. 1936, Anniston. AS, management, Jefferson State Community College, 1972; University of Maryland overseas extension classes. Air Force, 1955–59, 1962–88; police detective, City of Fairfield, 1959–61; director of communications, Jefferson County Commission, 1989–2002. Leeds City Council, 2002–06; Alabama House of Representatives, 2006–. Leeds Chamber of Commerce; Leeds High School Technical Education Advisory Committee; Lions Club; First Baptist Church of Leeds; Leeds City Schools 5-year Planning Commission; Rotary Club. Spouse: Kathye. Children: Six.

BILL DUKES (D)

District 8: Morgan

Committees: County and Municipal Government (chair); Commerce

Rm. 523-A; 11 S. Union St. Montgomery, AL 36130 bill.dukes@alhouse.org (334) 242-7689

2209 Parkplace St. SE Decatur, AL 35601 (256) 353-1725

B. 1927, Tarma, KY. BA, education, Bowling Green College of Commerce, 1952. Army, 1945–47; business manager, Northwest Mississippi Junior College, 1952–54; State of Kentucky, State Tuberculosis Commission, 1954–57; Chemstrand Corp., 1957–71; administrative assistant to mayor of Decatur, 1971–76. Decatur City Council, 1968–70; mayor, City of Decatur, 1976–94; Alabama House of Representatives, 1994–. Alabama Congress of Parents and Teachers; American Legion; Decatur Boys Club; Jaycees; Salvation Army. Spouse: Juanita. Children: Ronnie, Jeffrey, Sandra, and Pamela.

PRISCILLA DUNN (D)

District 56: Jefferson

Committees: Education Policy; Internal Affairs; Jefferson County Legislation; Judiciary; Local Legislation

Rm. 540-B; 11 S. Union St. Montgomery, AL 36130 priscilla.dunn@alhouse.org (334) 242-7689

460 Carriage Hills Dr. Bessemer, AL 35022 (205) 426-3795

B. 1943, St. Clair County. BS, elementary education, Alabama State University, 1966; MA, physical education, University of Montevallo, 1971. Homeless education coordinator, Bessemer City Schools, 1994–. Alabama House of Representatives, 1998–. Trustee and Sunday school teacher, Shady Grove Baptist Church; Jefferson/Shelby Counties American Cancer Society Advisory Board; State Democratic Executive Committee; Humanistic Challengers Federated Club; Concerned Citizens of Bessemer Cut-Off; Girls, Inc. of Central Alabama; Jefferson County Congress of Christian Education. Spouse: Grover. Child: Karen.

CHRIS ENGLAND (D)

District 70: Tuscaloosa

Committees: County and
 Municipal Government;
 Judiciary; Tuscaloosa County
 Legislation

Rm. 539-B; 11 S. Union St.
Montgomery, AL 36130
cengland@hotmail.com
(334) 242-7703

P.O. Box 2089
Tuscaloosa, AL 35403-2089
(205) 349-0101

B. 1976, Tuscaloosa. BA, English
and political science, Howard
University, 1999; JD, University of Alabama, 2002. Assistant
attorney, City of Tuscaloosa,
2004–. Alabama House of Representatives, 2006–. Spouse: Shea.
Children: Kennedy, Autumn,
and Christopher Jr.

JOE FAUST (R)

District 94: Baldwin

Committee: Baldwin County
 Legislation; Tourism and
 Travel

Rm. 524-C; 11 S. Union St.
Montgomery, AL 36130
jfaust@co.baldwin.al.us
(334) 242-7699

20452 Bishop Rd.
Fairhope, AL 36532
(251) 990-4615

B. 1940, Birmingham. Marietta
Johnson School of Organic Edu-
cation, 1959; attended Faulkner
Community College. National
Guard, 1958–66; retail sales
manager, Woodhaven Dairy,
1962–68; owner, Commercial
Insulation Company, 1963–81;
salesman: Independent Insur-
ance, 1968–, Woodman of the
World Life Insurance, 1981–93.
Baldwin County Commission,
1996–2002; Alabama House of
Representatives, 2002–. Marietta
Johnson School of Organic Edu-
cation; Eastern Shore Chamber
of Commerce; Mason; First
Baptist Church. Spouse: Sharon.
Children: Teddy, Christopher,
Andrea, and Mallory.

JAMES FIELDS JR. (D)

District 12: Cullman

Committees: Commerce;
 Government Operations
11 S. Union St.
Montgomery, AL 36130
james.fields@alhouse.org
(334) 242-7600

P.O. Box 635
Hanceville, AL 35077
(256) 287-0007

B. 1954, Colony. BS, sociology and law enforcement,
Jacksonville State University,
1977. Unemployment fraud
investigator and assistant director, Alabama Department of Industrial Relations, 1978–2007.
Alabama House of Representatives, 2008–, elected in a
special election on January 29,
2008 to fill the vacancy due to
the resignation of Neal Morrison. Hanceville Civitan Club;
Colony Lions Club; Victim Services; North Alabama Council
of Governments; Community
Action Partnership of North
Alabama; Alabama Wildlife
Federation. Spouse: Yvette.
Children: Seven.

CHAD FINCHER (R)

District 102: Mobile

Committees: Agriculture and Forestry; Constitution and Elections; Mobile County Legislation

Rm. 528-A; 11 S. Union St.
Montgomery, AL 36130
chad.fincher@alhouse.org
(334) 242-7778

P.O. Box 981
Semmes, AL 36575
(251) 649-2372

B. 1974, Mobile. BS, forestry operations, Auburn University, 1996. Registered forester, State of Alabama, 1996–2002; realtor and owner, Fincher & Associates Realty Services, 2002–. Alabama House of Representatives, 2006–. Mobile County Republican Executive Committee; Mobile County GOP; Mobile Area Association of Realtors; Friends of Semmes; Semmes Historical Society; Citronelle Historical Society; Mobile County Landowners Association; Alabama Farmers Federation; Alabama Treasure Forest Association; Alabama Forestry Association; vice president, Tanner Williams Civic and Historical Society. Spouse: Caresse. Child: Anna.

LEA FITE (D)

District 40: Calhoun

Committees: Education Policy; Government Operations; Tourism and Travel

Rm. 534-A; 11 S. Union St.
Montgomery, AL 36130
lea.fite@alhouse.org
(334) 242-7681

2413 Alabama Hwy. 202
Anniston, AL 36201
(256) 236-0533

B. 1955, Anniston. Attended Jacksonville State University. Owner, Food Outlet, 1985–. Alabama House of Representatives, 2002–. Kiwanis Club of Jacksonville; Exchange Club of Jacksonville. Spouse: Judy. Children: Laurie, Wes, Trae, and Jerrod.

CRAIG FORD (D)

District 28: Etowah

Committees: Banking and Insurance; Public Safety; Rules; Tourism and Travel

Rm. 517-F; 11 S. Union St.
Montgomery, AL 36130
craig.ford@alhouse.org
(334) 242-7690

P.O. Box 8208
Gadsden, AL 35902
(256) 413-7611

B. 1968, Gadsden. BS, marketing, Auburn University, 1991. Claims, State Farm Insurance, 1992–2000; captain, Army Reserves, 1989–; owner, Hodges Ford Insurance Agency, 2000–; co-owner, *The Messenger*, 2003–. Alabama House of Representatives, 2000–. Breakaway Ministries; First Baptist Church of Gadsden; Little League Baseball coach; YMCA; Church Royal Ambassadors Basketball League; National Conference of State Legislators; Financial Service Committee; National Conference of Legislators from Gaming States; Alabama Retired Teachers Association. Spouse: Gwen. Children: Jon and Wells Elizabeth.

BLAINE GALLIHER (R)

District 30: Etowah and St. Clair

Committees: Banking and Insurance; Health; Rules

Rm. 628-C; 11 S. Union St. Montgomery, AL 36130 blaine2@mindspring.com (334) 242-7760

P.O. Box 4353 Gadsden, AL 35904 (256) 832-1201

B. 1949, Abingdon, VA. BS, technology, Jacksonville State University, 2001. Army, 1968–71; general foreman and purchasing agent, Gulf State Steel Transportation Department, 1978–2000; director of business and industry training for Calhoun County, Gadsden State Community College, 2002–. Alabama House of Representatives, 1994–. Crosspoint Baptist Church; board of directors: Clark Smeltzer Adult Education Center, Sarrell Dental Clinic, Talladega Motor Sports Hall of Fame; Gadsden Etowah Chamber of Commerce; Rainbow City Lions Club; advisory board member, C.I.T.Y. Program of Etowah County. Children: Terry and Charlie.

VICTOR GASTON (R)

District 100: Mobile

Committees: Government Appropriations; Government Operations; Mobile County Legislation

Rm. 526-C; 11 S. Union St. Montgomery, AL 36130 victor.gaston@alhouse.org (334) 242-7675

1136 Hillcrest Crossing W Mobile, AL 36695 (251) 639-2555

B. 1943, Mobile. BS, history, University of Southern Mississippi, 1965; MA, secondary education, University of South Alabama, 1974; EdD, Auburn University, 1980. Marine Reserves, 1969–79; Alabama Army National Guard, 1989–99; timber farmer; teacher and administrator, Mobile County Public School System, 1969–97; retired. Alabama House of Representatives, 1982–. Home of Grace for Women; Volunteers of America; Mobile ARC; 3-10 Board; 4-H Club Foundation; Penelope House; Mobile Museum of Art; Assistance League. Spouse: Jean. Children: Hank and George.

H. MAC GIPSON JR. (R)

District 88: Autauga and Elmore

Committees: Education Appropriations; Tourism and Travel

Rm. 522-E; 11 S. Union St. Montgomery, AL 36130 macgipson@knology.net (334) 242-7695

507 Cook Rd. Prattville, AL 36067 (334) 365-9529

B. 1935, Camden. Starke Military School, 1952; attended Troy University. Wholesale division manager, Jones Tire Company, 1968–77; sergeant, Army, 1954–58; sales manager, Goodyear Tire and Rubber Company, 1958–77; manager, Kelly-Springfield Tire Company, 1977–81; president/owner, Gipson's Auto Tire, Inc., 1981–2005. Alabama House of Representatives, 1994–. First United Methodist Church; American Legion; Autauga Cattlemen's Association; Alabama Tire Dealers Association; Children First Board. Spouse: Mary Lee. Children: Mary, H. M. "Hoot," Robert, and Jo Ella.

James Gordon (D)

District 98: Mobile

Committees: Boards and Commissions; Constitution and Elections; Health; Mobile County Legislation

Rm. 522-C; 11 S. Union St. Montgomery, AL 36130
james@jamesogordon.com
(334) 242-7772

607 South Wilson Ave. #B
Mobile, AL 36617
(251) 476-7246

B. 1964, Rome, GA. PhD, chiropractic, Life University, 1995. Navy, 1982–85; scrub nurse, Floyd Medical Center; Chiropractor, 1995–. Alabama House of Representatives, 2006–. Mobile ARC; NAACP; Pleasant Valley Optimist Club; Utopia Club; Veterans of Foreign Wars; president, Prichard Boys and Girls Club Advisory Board. Spouse: Annie. Children: Adelle and Dominique.

Betty Carol Graham (D)

District 81: Lee and Tallapoosa

Committees: Banking and Insurance; Education Appropriations; Lee County Legislation

Rm. 531; 11 S. Union St. Montgomery, AL 36130
bcgraham@cacc.cc.al.us
(334) 242-7741

3485 Cowpens Rd.
Alexander City, AL 35010
(256) 234-7068

B. 1943, Tallapoosa County. AA, education, Auburn University; BS, English, Jacksonville State University, 1971; MA, English, University of Montevallo, 1975. Teacher, Tallapoosa County Board of Education, 1972–89; dean of students, Central Alabama Community College, 1998–2008. Alabama House of Representatives, 1994–. National Energy Council; Cattlemen's and Cattlewomen's Association; Elks; Civitans; Chamber of Commerce; Rocky Creek Baptist Church. Spouse: Joel. Child: Jeffery.

Ronald Grantland (D)

District 9: Cullman and Morgan

Committees: Government Appropriations; Health; Local Legislation

Rm. 524-A; 11 S. Union St. Montgomery, AL 36130
ronald.grantland@alhouse.org
(334) 242-7736

P.O. Box 1085
Hartselle, AL 35640
(256) 773-6796

B. 1947, Hartselle. BA, history, Athens State University, 1971; MPH, University of Alabama at Birmingham, 1982; CPM, Auburn University Montgomery, 1991. Health representative, Alabama Department of Public Health, 1972–88; administrator: Madison County Health Department, 1981–87, Cullman and Winston County Health Department, 1987–. Hartselle City Council, 1992–96; Alabama House of Representatives, 1998–. Habitat for Humanity; Hartselle Planning Commission; Alabama Public Health Association; Southern Health Association; East Highland Baptist Church. Spouse: Joan. Children: Landon and Loren.

TODD GREESON (R)

District 24: DeKalb

Committees: Education Appropriations; Rules; Tourism and Travel

Rm. 528-A; 11 S. Union St. Montgomery, AL 36130 todd.greeson@alhouse.org (334) 242-7743

P.O. Box 159 Ider, AL 35981 (256) 632-3963

B. 1971, Ft. Payne. AS, business, Northeast State Junior College, 1994; BS, political science, 1997, BBA, management, Athens State College, 1997; MA, public administration, Troy University, 2007. Coordinator of business and industry, Northeast State Junior College, 2004–. Alabama House of Representatives, 1998–. Past chair, DeKalb County Young Republicans; Mountain View Baptist Church; Alabama Cattlemen's Association. Spouse: Dana. Children: Garrett and Daniel.

DAVID GRIMES (R)

District 73: Montgomery

Committees: Banking and Insurance; Commerce; Internal Affairs; Montgomery County Legislation

Rm. 537-A; 11 S. Union St. Montgomery, AL 36130 grimesdg@birch.net (334) 242-7707

P.O. Box 6176 Montgomery, AL 36106 (334) 834-3989

B. 1953, Detroit, MI. BS, business, Troy University, 1974. Barb's on Mulberry, 1978–; life insurance broker, thirty years; Mediation Services, 2004–. Alabama House of Representatives, 2002–. Coach, Little League Baseball; deacon, Trinity Presbyterian Church; board member: Lifeline Children's Services, Inc., YMCA Camp Chandler; president: Garden District Homeowners Association, Cloverdale Homeowners Association; Montgomery Rotary Club; Montgomery Lions Club. Spouse: Barbara. Children: John-David and Tyler.

KEN GUIN (D)

District 14: Tuscaloosa, Walker, and Winston

Committees: Rules (chair); Constitution and Elections; Tuscaloosa County Legislation

Rm. 517-E; 11 S. Union St. Montgomery, AL 36130 ken@kenguin.com (334) 242-7674

P.O. Box 470 Carbon Hill, AL 35549 (205) 924-0061

B. 1962, Birmingham. BA, English, Auburn, 1984; JD, Cumberland School of Law, 1987. Attorney: Laird and Wiley, 1987–88; Hardin, Taber, and Tucker, 1988–90; Ken Guin Attorney at Law, PC, 1991–. Alabama House of Representatives, 1994–, House majority leader, 1997–. Lay leader and young adult Sunday school teacher, First United Methodist Church of Carbon Hill; chair of trustees, Jasper District of the United Methodist Church; State Legislative Leader Foundation; Walker Baptist Medical Center; Walker County Extension Service. Spouse: Tanya. Children: J. K. and Emma.

LAURA HALL (D)

District 19: Madison

Committees: Government Appropriations; Judiciary; Madison County Legislation.

Rm. 518; 11 S. Union St. Montgomery, AL 36130 laura.hall2@att.net (334) 242-7688

P.O. Box 3367 Huntsville, AL 35810 (256) 539-5441

B. 1943, Sandy Springs, SC. BA, biology, Morris College, 1965; MA, science education, Ohio State University, 1973; certification in K–12 administration. High school teacher, Huntsville City Schools, 1965–98; administrator, Calhoun Community College, 1998–2008; retired. Alabama House of Representatives, 1993–. Madison County Women's Political Caucus; Madison County Democratic Women; advisory board of directors: AIDS Action Coalition, Central North Alabama Health Center. Spouse: John. Child: Janeka.

SETH HAMMETT (D)

District 92: Covington and Escambia

Speaker of the House

Rm. 519-A; 11 S. Union St. Montgomery, AL 36130 seth.hammett@alhouse.org (334) 242-7668

P.O. Box 1776 Andalusia, AL 36420 (334) 222-4469

B. 1946, Andalusia. BS, business administration, Auburn University, 1968; MBA, Auburn University, 1970. Air Force, 1968–69; founder and president, First National Bank of Andalusia, 1984–91; president emeritus, Lurleen B. Wallace Community College, 2002–; director of economic development, Power-South, 2004–. Alabama House of Representatives, 1978–, speaker pro tempore, 1995–2000, speaker of the House, 2001–. First United Methodist Church of Andalusia; Council of State Governments; National Conference of State Legislatures; National Speakers Conference; Southern Legislative Conference; State Legislative Leaders Foundation. Spouse: Nancy. Children: Merrill and Catherine.

MICKY HAMMON (R)

District 4: Limestone and Morgan

Committees: Constitution and Elections; Tourism and Travel

Rm. 523-C; 11 S. Union St. Montgomery, AL 36130 micky.hammon@alhouse.org (334) 242-7709

1344 East Upper River Rd. Decatur, AL 35603 (205) 350-0375

B. 1957, Morgan County. AS, electrical, Calhoun County Community College, 1977. Electrical contractor, 1987–2005. Alabama House of Representatives, 2002–. Business Council of Alabama; Morgan County Economic Development Association; Decatur Chamber of Commerce; U.S. Chamber of Commerce; National Federation of Independent Businesses; Associated Builders and Contractors; Tennessee Valley Training Center. Spouse: Pam. Children: Jake, Colter, and Davis-Anne.

ALAN HARPER (D)

District 61: Pickens and Tuscaloosa

Committees: Agriculture and Forestry; Boards and Commissions; Commerce; Tuscaloosa County Legislation

Rm. 538-C; 11 S. Union St. Montgomery, AL 36130 saharper@nctv.com (334) 242-7732

P.O. Box 403 Aliceville, AL 35442 (205) 373-2433

B. 1957, Northport. BA, public relations, University of Alabama, 1986. Project manager, Tuscaloosa County Industrial Development Authority, 1993–2003; director of economic development, City of Aliceville, 2005–. Alabama House of Representatives, 2006–. Economic Development Association of Alabama; Tennessee-Tombigbee Waterway Development Council; Rotary Club; DCH Regional Medical Center Institutional Review Commission; Aliceville Area, Gordon Area, and Reform Chambers of Commerce; Cattlemen's Association. Spouse: Jean. Children: Brant and Sam.

MIKE HILL (R)

District 41: Shelby

Committees: Banking and Insurance; Government Operations

Rm. 628-D; 11 S. Union St. Montgomery, AL 36130 mhillcolum@aol.com (334) 242-7715

114 Arlington Ave. Columbiana, AL 35051 (205) 669-6264

B. 1949, Birmingham. BS, quantitative methods, Auburn University, 1972; attended School of Banking of the South, Louisiana State University, and Oklahoma State University. Army, 1972; senior vice president, First National Bank of Columbiana, 1973–86; title insurance agent, Cahaba Title, Inc., 1986–2000; community business banker and assistant vice president, Regions Bank, 2008–. Alabama House of Representatives, 1986–. First Baptist Church of Columbiana; Birmingham Occupational Rehabilitation Center; Kiwanis Club. Spouse: Carol. Children: Hayden and Hunter.

EARL HILLIARD JR. (D)

District 60: Jefferson

Committees: Agriculture and Forestry; Commerce; County and Municipal Government; Jefferson County Legislation; Tourism and Travel

Rm. 539-A; 11 S. Union St. Montgomery, AL 36130 earl.hilliard@alhouse.org (334) 242-7684

B. 1969, Montgomery. BA, marketing, Morehouse College, 1991; Howard University School of Law, 1996. Civic affairs specialist in corporate external affairs, 1996–97; director of government relations, Morehouse College, 1997–98; Hilliard, Smith, and Hunt, 2000–; president and filmmaker, Magic City Films, 2000–. Alabama House of Representatives, 2006–. Mt. Moriah Missionary Baptist Church of North Pratt; Alpha Phi Alpha; Screen Actors Guild; Greater Birmingham Foster and Adoptive Parent Association; Alabama Jazz Hall of Fame; Birmingham/Jefferson County Film Advisory Board; Sidewalk Moving Picture Festival. Spouse: Janine. Children: Earl and Nya.

Randy Hinshaw (D)

District 21: Madison

Committees: Madison
County Legislation; Rules;
Tourism and Travel

Rm. 535; 11 S. Union St.
Montgomery, AL 36130
randy.hinshaw@alhouse.org
(334) 242-7733

100 St. Clair Ave., Suite A
Huntsville, AL 35801
(256) 539-5441

B. 1960, Huntington Park, CA.
AS, John C. Calhoun Com-
munity College, 1990; attended
Athens State University. Program
coordinator, Southern Union
State Community College.
Alabama House of Representa-
tives, 1994–98, 2002–. Alabama
Education Association; Alabama
New South Coalition; Alabama
Democratic Conference; past
member, Madison County
Mental Health Board; past vice
president, Northeast Huntsville
Civic Association. Spouse: Leslie.
Children: Anna, Alan-Michael,
Jeremy, Whitney, and Morgan.

Alvin Holmes (D)

District 78: Montgomery

Committee: Montgomery
County Legislation

Rm. 525-A; 11 S. Union St.
Montgomery, AL 36130
alvin.holmes@alhouse.org
(334) 242-7706

P.O. Box 6064
Montgomery, AL 36106
(334) 264-7807

B. 1939. Attended: Atlanta
University, Rochester Business
Institute, and University of
Alabama; BS, MA, and MEd,
Alabama State University; OIC,
University of Pennsylvania; LLD,
Jones School of Law. Military
service, 1963–65; real estate
broker, Alvin Holmes Realty
Co., 1975–; college educator,
Alabama State University. Ala-
bama House of Representatives,
1974–. Hutchinson Missionary
Baptist Church; State Democrat-
ic Executive Committee; Kappa
Alpha Psi; Southern Christian
Leadership Conference; Mont-
gomery Improvement Associa-
tion; NAACP. Child: Veronica.

Ralph Howard (D)

District 72: Bibb, Hale,
Marengo, and Perry

Committees: Agriculture and
Industries; Government
Operations

Rm. 527-D; 11 S. Union St.
Montgomery, AL 36130
ralph.howard@alhouse.org
(334) 242-7759

700 M. W. Rollins Ln.
Greensboro, AL 36744
(334) 624-1887

B. 1969, Montgomery. Uni-
versity of Maryland's branch in
Okinawa; BA, criminal justice,
University of Alabama, 1998.
Marine Corps, 1988–97; adult
education instructor, Shelton
State Community College,
2005–06. Alabama House of
Representatives, 2005–. Pleasant Grove Missionary Baptist
Church; Friendship Lodge 228;
Alabama Democratic Conference; Disabled American Veterans; vice chair, Alabama House
of Representatives Black Caucus;
board member: American Village
in Montevallo, Alabama Military
Hall of Honor. Spouse: Yolande.
Children: Makaila, Keonna,
and Trey.

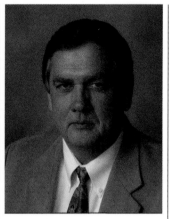

MIKE HUBBARD (R)

District 79: Lee

Committees: Agriculture
and Forestry; Government
Operations; Lee County
Legislation

Rm. 536-A; 11 S. Union St.
Montgomery, AL 36130
hubbard@mikehubbard.com
(334) 242-7739

P.O. Box 950
Auburn, AL 36831
(334) 826-9946

B. 1962, Hartwell, GA. ABJ,
broadcasting, University of
Georgia, 1983. Associate sports
information director, Auburn
University, 1984–90; general
manager, Host Communica-
tions, 1990–94; founder/presi-
dent, Auburn Network, 1994–
2003; president, International
Sports Properties, 2003–. Alabama House of Representatives,
1998–, minority leader, 2007–,
Governor's House floor leader,
2003–. Chair, Governor Riley's
Inauguration 2003 and 2007;
Business Council of Alabama;
Alabama Broadcasters Association; Auburn United Methodist
Church. Spouse: Susan. Children: Clayte and Riley.

STEVE HURST (D)

District 35: Calhoun and
Talladega

Committees: Agriculture and
Forestry; Public Safety

Rm. 630-A; 11 S. Union St.
Montgomery, AL 36130
steve.hurst@alhouse.org
(334) 353-9215

155 Quail Run Rd.
Munford, AL 36268
(256) 761-1935

B. 1948, Walker County. Tal-
ladega High School, 1967.
Electrician, Georgia Pacific Cor-
poration, 1975–2005; retired.
Talladega County commissioner,
1985-93; Alabama House of
Representatives, 1998–. Calhoun
County Chamber of Commerce;
Talladega County Chamber
of Commerce. Spouse: Linda.
Children: Michael, Kenneth,
and Vance.

TAMMY IRONS (D)

District 1: Lauderdale

Committees: Boards and
Commissions; Judiciary

Rm. 526-B; 11 S. Union St.
Montgomery, AL 36130
tammy@ironslawfirm.com
(334) 353-9032

219 N. Court St.
Florence, AL 35630
(256) 766-9201

B. 1963, Florence. BS, account-
ing, University of North Ala-
bama, 1986; JD, University of
Memphis, 1989. Law clerk, Hon.
Hewitt Tomlin, presiding judge,
Western Section of Tennessee
Court of Appeals, 1989–90;
owner/attorney, Irons Law Firm,
1999–. Alabama House of
Representatives, 2006–. Shoals
Entrepreneurial Center; Shoals
Economic Development Author-
ity; SafePlace, Inc.; Boys and
Girls Clubs; president, Lauder-
dale County Bar Association;
President's Cabinet, University of
North Alabama; Sherrod Avenue
Church of Christ. Single.

JAMIE ISON (R)

District 101: Mobile

Committees: Agriculture and Forestry; Judiciary; Mobile County Legislation

Rm. 527-B; 11 S. Union St. Montgomery , AL 36130 isonfor101@comcast.net (334) 242- 7711

104 S. Lawrence St. Mobile, AL 36602 (251) 208-5480

B. 1953, New Albany, MS. BA, speech pathology, University of Mississippi, 1974; MA, communicative disorders, University of Mississippi, 1975. Regional director, Alabama Institute for Deaf and Blind, 1985–2003; retired. Alabama House of Representatives, 2002–. Board member: Leadership Mobile, Habitat for Humanity; past-president, Mobile Sunrise Rotary Club; co-chair, Mobile Advisory Commission for the Disabled; All Saints Episcopal Church. Spouse: M. Harland. Children: Philip and Wyatt.

THOMAS JACKSON (D)

District 68: Choctaw, Clarke, Conecuh, Marengo, and Monroe

Committees: Agriculture and Forestry (chair); Health

Rm. 522-C; 11 S. Union St. Montgomery, AL 36130 thomas.jackson@alhouse.org (334) 242-7738

P.O. Box 656 Thomasville, AL 36784 (334) 246-3597

B. 1950, Thomasville. AA, education, Selma University, 1970; BS, psychology, Knoxville College, 1972; MA, education and counseling, Alabama State University, 1972. Director, Upward Bound Program for Alabama Southern College, 1997–2000. Alabama House of Representatives, 1994–. Church of God in Christ; Kappa Alpha Psi; National Black Caucus for State Legislators; Alabama and National Education Associations; Kiwanis Club; coordinator, Thomasville Precinct-ADC; board member, Southwest Alabama Boys and Girls Club. Spouse: Dorothy. Children: Kimberly, Terence, Thomas, and Trumaine.

RONALD JOHNSON (R)

District 33: Coosa and Talladega

Committees: Health; Rules

Rm. 627-D; 11 S. Union St. Montgomery, AL 36130 ronald.johnson@alhouse.org (334) 242-7777

3770 Sylacauga-Fayette Hwy. Sylacauga, AL 35151 (256) 249-9489

B. 1943, Bonifay, FL. BS, biology and chemistry, Florida State University, 1965; Pharmacy degree, Auburn University, 1968. Partner/pharmacist, Medical Care Equipment, Inc., 1980–2000. Alabama House of Representatives, 1978–. Executive Board of the South; Talladega and Auburn Kiwanis Clubs; American, Alabama, Maryland, and South Talladega County Pharmaceutical Associations; Sylacauga Chamber of Commerce; Sylacauga Retail Merchants Association; National Federation of Independent Business. Spouse: Susan. Child: Stephanie.

YVONNE KENNEDY (D)

District 97: Mobile

Committees: Education Policy (chair); Education Appropriations; Mobile County Legislation

Rm. 537-C; 11 S. Union St. Montgomery, AL 36130 yvonne.kennedy@alhouse.org (334) 242-7737

1205 Glennon Ave. Mobile, AL 36603 (251) 690-6416

B. 1945, Mobile. BS, English and social science, Alabama State University, 1966; MA, English, Morgan State University, 1968; PhD, higher education administration, University of Alabama, 1979. English instructor, co-chair for SACS accreditation, Higher Education Achievement Program coordinator, 1968–74, president, 1981–2007, S.D. Bishop State Junior College. Alabama House of Representatives, 1982–. American Association for Higher Education; America's Junior Miss Scholarship Foundation, Inc.; Delta Sigma Theta; Mobile County United Negro College Fund Campaign; Board of Christian Education, Southeast Alabama Conference.

JOHN KNIGHT JR. (D)

District 77: Montgomery

Committees: Government Appropriations (chair); Montgomery County Legislation; Public Safety

Rm. 516-A; 11 S. Union St. Montgomery, AL 36130 john.knight@alhouse.gov (334) 242-7660

P.O. Box 6300 Montgomery, AL 36106 (334) 229-4286

B. Montgomery. BS, with honors, business administration, Alabama State University. Alabama State University, assistant vice president for institutional advancement, special assistant to the president, and executive vice president. Alabama House of Representatives, 1993–. Kershaw YMCA; Montgomery Housing Authority; Montgomery Improvement Association; Southern Development Council, Inc.; Montgomery County Democratic Executive Committee; Montgomery County Democratic Conference, chair. Children: Tamara and Tehrik.

RICHARD LAIRD (D)

District 37: Chambers, Clay, and Randolph

Committees: County and Municipal Government; Health; Rules

Rm. 528-D; 11 S. Union St. Montgomery, AL 36130 rjlsrdo@teleclipse.net (334) 242-7744

341 Bonner Dr. Roanoke, AL 36274 (334) 863-7938

B. 1939, Rome, GA. Attended University of Alabama. Multiple positions, ended as manager, V. J. Elmore Company, 1956–66; owner, Laird's 5 and 10, 1966–84; president, Ranco Inc., Real Estate and Development, 1979–. Roanoke City Council, 1972–76; Alabama House of Representatives, 1978–. Handley Avenue Church of God; Randolph County Camp of Gideons International; Alabama Farmers Federation; Alabama and Randolph County Cattlemen's Association and Farm Bureau. Spouse: Peggy. Child: Richard "Joel."

JOHN "JODY" LETSON (D)

District 7: Lawrence and Winston

Committees: Government Appropriations; Government Operations

Rm. 541-A; 11 S. Union St. Montgomery, AL 36130 legislativeoffice@aol.com (334) 242-7767

12001 Alabama Hwy. 157 Moulton, AL 35650 (256) 974-5175

B. 1949, Lawrence County. Courtland High School, 1967; attended Calhoun Community College. Cotton and corn farming, Letson Brothers Farm, 1975–; jobsetter, General Motors, 1977–2006; Letson's Grocery, 1980–. Lawrence County commissioner, 1976–80; Alabama House of Representatives, 1996–. Lawrence County Chamber of Commerce; Hillsboro Baptist Church. Spouse: Diane. Child: Kim.

BENJAMIN LEWIS (R)

District 86: Houston

Committees: Agriculture and Forestry; Public Safety

Rm. 540-A; 11 S. Union St. Montgomery, AL 36130 benjamin.lewis@alhouse.org (334) 242-7756

2209 Eddins Rd. Dothan, AL 36301 (334) 793-5555

B. 1975, Dothan. BS, magna cum laude, history, Troy University, 2000; JD, Jones School of Law, 2005; graduate-level agricultural law studies, Arkansas School of Law. Dairy farmer; lawyer. Alabama House of Representatives, 2006–. Alabama Law Institute; Boy Scouts of America; Alabama State Bar Association; Houston County Bar Association; Florida Bar Association; American Agricultural Law Association; Alabama Farmers Federation; Alabama Cattlemen's Association; Dothan Area Chamber of Commerce; Church of Jesus Christ of Latter-day Saints; National Rifle Association; Eagle Scout. Spouse: Becky. Children: Marshall, Carson, Weston, and John "Brooks."

RICHARD LINDSEY (D)

District 39: Cherokee, Cleburne, and DeKalb

Committees: Education Appropriations (chair)

Rm. 514; 11 S. Union St. Montgomery, AL 36130 richard.lindsey@alhouse.org (334) 242-7713

14160 County Rd. 22 Centre, AL 35960 (256) 475-3400

B. 1956, Floyd County, GA. BS, business administration - management, Jacksonville State University, 1978. Manager, Lindsey Brothers, Inc., 1978–. Alabama House of Representatives, 1983–. Ebenezer United Methodist Church; Cherokee County Chamber of Commerce; Farmers and Merchants Bank; board member: Cherokee County ALFA Organization, Coosa-Alabama River Improvement Association; president, Howells Cemetery Association; secretary, Southeastern Cotton Ginners Association. Spouse: Johna. Children: Rich and Anna.

JAY LOVE (R)

District 74: Montgomery

Committees: Constitution and Elections; Government Appropriations; Montgomery County Legislation

Rm. 527-A; 11 S. Union St. Montgomery, AL 36130 jlove32376@aol.com (334) 242-7716

P.O. Box 3221 Montgomery, AL 36109 (334) 224-0822

B. 1968, Montgomery. BA, business administration, Auburn University Montgomery, 1990. Owner, Subway Sandwich Shops, 1992–2006; SE Subway Development. Alabama House of Representatives, 2002–. First Baptist Church of Montgomery. Spouse: Cheri. Children: Rachel, Addison, Rebecca, and Caroline.

JAMES "JIMMY" MARTIN (D)

District 42: Chilton and Shelby

Committees: Banking and Insurance; Constitution and Elections; Shelby County Legislation

Rm. 530-D; 11 S. Union St. Montgomery, AL 36130 jamesmmartin@bellsouth.net (334) 242-7714

P.O. Box 1214 Clanton, AL 35046 (205) 755-3550

B. 1938, Montgomery County. BS, mortuary science, John A. Grupton College, 1962. Co-owner, Martin Funeral Home, Inc., 1959–. Chilton County coroner, 1963–98; Alabama House of Representatives, 1998–. Board member, Chilton County Chamber of Commerce; Alabama Funeral Directors' Association; First Baptist Church. Spouse: Norma. Children: Jim and Kim.

BARRY MASK (R)

District 31: Coosa and Elmore

Committees: Constitution and Elections; Local Legislation; Tourism and Travel

Rm. 527-C; 11 S. Union St. Montgomery, AL 36130 barry.mask@alhouse.org (334) 242-7732

41 Brookland Ct. Wetumpka, AL 36093 (334) 328-9231

B. 1959, Alexander City. BS, public administration, Auburn University, 1983. Governmental affairs: Alabama State Employees Association, 1984–89, Alabama Association of Realtors, 1990–94, Business Council of Alabama, 1994–96, Alabama Industry and Manufactures Association, 1996–99; project manager, Riverfront Master Plan, 2000–01. Alabama House of Representatives, 2006–. Life member, Auburn Alumni Association; co-founder: Elmore County Economic Development Authority, Joe Sewell Memorial Award; Wetumpka Lions Club. Spouse: Jill.

ARTIS "A. J." McCAMPBELL (D)

District 71: Greene, Marengo, Sumter, and Tuscaloosa

Committees: Agriculture and Forestry; Commerce; Public Safety; Tourism and Travel; Tuscaloosa County Legislation

Rm. 539-C; 11 S. Union St. Montgomery, AL 35130
artis.mccampbell@alhouse.org
(334) 242-7747

P.O. Box 487
Demopolis, AL 36732
(334) 652-6531

B. 1953, Greene County. BA, political science, University of Alabama, 1976. Patrolman and investigator, City of Tuscaloosa, 1975–79; juvenile probation officer, Greene County, 1979–85; investigator, District Attorney's Office, 17th Judicial Circuit, 1985–90; insurance agent, State Farm, 1990–. Alabama House of Representatives, 2006–. Leadership Marengo County; Rotary International; MOPASS, Inc.; Marengo County Hospital Board; Demopolis Chamber of Commerce; Christian Chapel Baptist Church. Spouse: Diana. Children: Erica and Calida.

THAD McCLAMMY (D)

District 76: Montgomery

Committees: Public Safety (chair); Banking and Insurance; Montgomery County Legislation; Tourism and Travel

Rm. 525-D; 11 S. Union St. Montgomery, AL 36130
thad.mcclammy@alhouse.org
(334) 242-7780

858 West South Blvd.
Montgomery, AL 36105
(334) 284-1769

B. 1942, Beatrice. BA, business administration, Alabama State University, 1966; MS, vocational and adult education, Auburn University Montgomery, 1975; honorary JD, Selma University. Real estate broker, City of Montgomery, 1968–74; dean and president, Trenholm State Technical College, 1974–85. Alabama House of Representatives, 1994–. Alabama and Montgomery Democratic Conferences; Lion's Club; Alabama and National Education Associations; Southern Placement Council; Omega Psi Phi; Iota Lambda Sigma; Tots and Teens, Inc. Spouse: Patricia. Children: Patrice and Christopher.

JIM McCLENDON (R)

District 50: St. Clair and Shelby

Committees: County and Municipal Government; Health; Shelby County Legislation

Rm. 527-C; 11 S. Union St. Montgomery, AL 36130
jim.mcclendon@alhouse.org
(334) 242-7749

361 Jones Rd.
Springville, AL 35146
(205) 467-2656

B. 1943, Mobile. BS, pre-med, Birmingham-Southern College, 1965; OD, University of Houston, 1967. Navy Medical Service Corps, Vietnam, 1969–71; instructor of clinical optometry, University of Alabama at Birmingham, 1971–76; optometrist, Leeds and Moody, 1977–2000. Alabama House of Representatives, 2002–. Past president, Alabama Optometric Association; former board member, St. Anne's Home; Jefferson County Health Planning Commission; board member, Davis Lake Fire Department; finance committee, First Methodist Church of Springville. Spouse: El. Children: Molly and Lara.

MARY SUE McCLURKIN (R)

District 43: Jefferson and Shelby

Committees: Boards and Commissions; Education Appropriations; Jefferson County Legislation; Shelby County Legislation

Rm. 517-D; 11 S. Union St. Montgomery, AL 36130 mary.mcclurkin@alhouse.org (334) 242-7682

1134 County Services Dr. Pelham, AL 35124 (205) 620-6610

B. 1947, Abbeville. BS, home economics, Huntington College, 1969; MA, education, Auburn University, 1971. Executive director, Pelham Chamber of Commerce, 1981–83; account executive, Riverchase Business Brokers, 1983–85; owner: Alabama Butane Company, Inc., 1985–2001, McClurkin Enterprises, 2001–. Alabama House of Representatives, 1998–. Briarwood Presbyterian Church; Alabama Republican Party; Shelby County Republican Executive Committee; board member, Business Council of Alabama. Spouse: Van. Children: Burt, Ben, and Daniel.

MAC McCUTCHEON (R)

District 25: Limestone and Madison

Committees: Education Policy; Madison County Legislation; Public Safety

Rm. 524-B; 11 S. Union St. Montgomery, AL 36130 macmccutcheon@knology.net (334) 242-7705

100 St. Clair St. Huntsville, AL 35801 (256) 539-5441

B. 1952, Ft. Benning, GA. AS, criminal justice, Calhoun Community College, 2002; BS, criminal justice administration, Trinity University, 2002. Farmer; major crimes investigator, Huntsville Police Department, 1974–2002; College Park Church of God, associate pastor, 2000–07; probation officer, City of Huntsville Municipal Court System, 2002–06; City of Huntsville Planning Department, 2006–. Alabama House of Representatives, 2006–. American Legion; Fraternal Order of Police; Alabama Peace Officers; North Alabama Emmaus Community. Spouse: Debbie. Children: Christopher and April Nicole.

W. FRANK McDANIEL (D)

District 26: DeKalb and Marshall

Committees: Commerce (chair); County and Municipal Government

Rm. 522-B; 11 S. Union St. Montgomery, AL 36130 legislator@mclo.org (334) 242-7697

412-A Gunter Ave. Guntersville, AL 35976 (256) 582-0619

B. 1937, Union Springs. BS, business administration, Auburn University, 1959. Airman, Alabama Air National Guard, 1959–67; Air Force, 1961–62; salesman/sales manager, Burroughs Corporation, 1959–73; president, McDaniel Tom's Sales, 1973–2000. Alabama House of Representatives, 1990–. Deacon, First Baptist Church of Albertville; Marshall County Corrections Program; Snead College Advisory Board; Joint State Park Committee; Southern Legislative Conference's Committee on Commerce and Economic Development; Alabama Regional Councils' Revolving Loan Policy Committee. Spouse: Pat. Children: David and Don.

JEFFREY McLAUGHLIN (D)

District 27: Marshall

Committees: County and Municipal Government; Education Appropriations

Rm. 526-D; 11 S. Union St. Montgomery, AL 36130

jeff@mcedlaw.com

(334) 242-7600

412-A Gunter Ave. Guntersville, AL 35976

(256) 582-0619

B. 1960, Decatur. BA, history, Birmingham-Southern College, 1982; JD, Harvard Law School, 1990. History, government, and biology teacher, John Carroll High School, 1982–87; law clerk: U.S. district judge Seybourn Lynn, 1990–95, Maynard Cooper and Gale, 1990–95; attorney, McLaughlin and Edmondson, LLC, 1995–. Alabama House of Representatives, 2001–. St. Williams Church; Lake City Civitans; Lake Guntersville Chamber of Commerce. Spouse: Stacy. Children: Frank, William, and Mary.

STEPHEN McMILLAN (R)

District 95: Baldwin

Committees: Baldwin County Legislation; County and Municipal Government; Judiciary

Rm. 532; 11 S. Union St. Montgomery, AL 36130

bcld07@gmail.com

(334) 242-7723

P.O. Box 337 Bay Minette, AL 36507

(251) 943-5061 Ext. 2240

B. 1941, Mobile. BA, psychology, Auburn University, 1964. Owner/broker, McMillan and Associates, 1972–. Alabama House of Representatives, 1982–. Rotary Club; Board and Foundation of Alabama School of Mathematics and Science; former president, Alabama Association of Realtors. Spouse: Gayle. Children: Adrienne, Scott, and Jason.

MICHAEL MILLICAN (D)

District 17: Marion and Winston

Committee: Health (chair)

Rm. 628-F; 11 S. Union St. Montgomery, AL 36130

mike.millican@alhouse.gov

(334) 242-7768

995 Country Estates Dr. Hamilton, AL 35570

(205) 921-3214

B. 1950, Sulligent. Barbering degree, Northwest Technical College, 1970; BS, education, Athens State University, 1980. Instructor and director of business and industry, Northwest Community College (Bevill State Community College), 1974–2008. Alabama House of Representatives, 1990–. First Baptist Church of Hamilton; Marion County Cattleman's Association; Masonic Lodge; Adult Education Advisory Council; Winston-Marion Community Action Association; Advisory Board of the Marion County Extension Service. Spouse: Debbie. Child: Jennifer (deceased).

JOSEPH MITCHELL (D)

District 103: Mobile

Committees: Constitution
and Elections; Education
Policy; Internal Affairs; Mobile County Legislation

Rm. 517-A; 11 S. Union St.
Montgomery, AL 36130
house3@alhouse.org
(334) 242-7735

465 Dexter Ave.
Mobile, AL 36604
(334) 473-5020

B. 1948, Mobile. BA, health,
Morehouse College, 1969; MA,
secondary education, University
of South Alabama, 1974; CASE,
University of Alabama-Birming-
ham, 1979; PhD, engineering
and educational psychology,
Texas A&M University, 1983.
Independent consultant, King-
dom of Saudi Arabia, 1984–;
owner, Bantu Family Association, 1988–; engineering consultant, 1988–; award winning jazz
musician and educator. Mobile
County School Board, 1990-94;
Alabama House of Representatives, 1994–. Metropolitan
African Methodist Episcopal
Church; American Federation
of Musicians; American Research
Association. Spouse: Janetta.

MARY MOORE (D)

District 59: Jefferson

Committees: Boards and
Commissions; Constitu-
tion and Elections; Jefferson
County Legislation

Rm. 539-D; 11 S. Union St.
Montgomery, AL 36130
mamoor48@bellsouth.net
(334) 242-7608

1622 36th Ave. N.
Birmingham, AL 35207
(205) 322-0254

B. 1948, Birmingham. BS, biol-
ogy, Tuskegee University, 1970;
Certificate of Medical Technol-
ogy, University of Alabama
at Birmingham, 1971; MBA,
human resource development,
Alabama A&M University,
1983. Medical technologist,
Department of Veterans Affairs
Hospital, 1971–2000. Member,
Birmingham City School Board,
1998–2002; Alabama House of
Representatives, 2002–. Delta
Sigma Theta; Evergreen Mis-
sionary Baptist Church. Child:
Michael.

PAT MOORE (R)

District 15: Jefferson

Committees: Boards and
Commissions; Govern-
ment Operations; Jefferson
County Legislation

Rm. 523-C; 11 S. Union St.
Montgomery, AL 36130
patmoore15d@aol.com
(334) 242-7775

49 7th St., Suite A
Pleasant Grove, AL 35127
(205) 744-1593

B. 1945, Chattanooga, TN. BS,
industrial food management
and history, Auburn University,
1966; MA, secondary math-
ematics education, University of
Alabama at Birmingham, 1990.
Co-owner: Moore Home Builders and Rentals, 1968–; timber
farm, 1995–. Alabama House
of Representatives, 2006–. Alabama Republican State Executive
Committee; Jefferson County
Executive Committee; Greater
Birmingham Republican Wom-
en; Western Area Republican
Club; Hueytown Chamber of
Commerce. Spouse: Dan. Children: Danlyn and Kit.

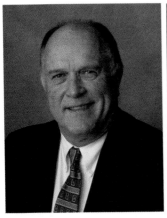

JOHNNY MACK MORROW (D)

District 18: Colbert and Franklin

Committees: Tourism and Travel (chair); Government Operations

Rm. 628-B; 11 S. Union St. Montgomery, AL 36130

johnny.morrow@alhouse.org

(334) 242-7698

1895 Hwy. 28
Red Bay, AL 35582

B. 1942, Vina. BS, agricultural economics, Mississippi State University, 1965; MBA, business administration, Samford University, 1970. Business and economics instructor, Northwest Junior College, 1970-98; retired. Alabama House of Representatives, 1990–. First Baptist Church of Red Bay; Cahaba Shrine Temple; Alabama Education Association; Franklin County Cattlemen's Association. Children: Three.

CHARLES NEWTON (D)

District 90: Butler, Conecuh, and Crenshaw

Committees: Government Appropriations; Judiciary

Rm. 541-E; 11 S. Union St. Montgomery, AL 36130

charles.newton@alhouse.org

(334) 242-4460

1216 South Conecuh St. Greenville, AL 36037

(334) 382-3370

B. 1947, Greenville. BS, political science, University of Alabama, 1968; MA, history, 1970, University of Alabama. Newton Oil Company, 1975– (currently serving as president). Greenville City Councilman, 1984–89; Alabama House of Representatives, 1989–. First Baptist Church of Greenville; Alabama Cattleman's Association; Greenville Rotary Club; Greenville Chamber of Commerce; Alabama Historical Association. Spouse: Jan. Children: Ollie, Seth, and Lila.

DEMETRIUS NEWTON (D)

District 53: Jefferson

Speaker Pro Tempore

Committees: Jefferson County Legislation; Public Safety

Rm. 516-D; 11 S. Union St. Montgomery, AL 36130

demetrius.newton@alhouse. org

(334) 242-7663

P.O. Box 2525
Birmingham, AL 35202

(205) 252-9203

B. 1928, Fairfield. BA, economics and political science, Wilberforce University, 1949; JD, Boston University, 1952. Army, 82nd Airborne Division, 1952–54; city judge, City of Brownville, 1972–78; city attorney, City of Birmingham, 1991–; attorney, Demetrius C. Newton, Attorney, 2000–. Alabama House of Representatives, 1986–, speaker pro tem, 1998–. Mt. Olive Baptist Church; Alabama, National, and American Bar Associations; American Judicature Society; NAACP; 101 Black Men; Vulcan Golf Club; past president and C.E.O, Birmingham Urban League. Children: Deirdre and Demetrius Jr.

JEREMY ODEN (R)

District 11: Blount, Cullman, and Morgan

Committees: County and Municipal Government; Education Appropriations

Rm. 527-D; 11 S. Union St.
Montgomery, AL 36130
jeremy.oden@alhouse.org
(334) 242-7722

P.O. Box 9
Eva, AL 35621
(256) 734-3188

B. 1968, Birmingham. BA, Bible and Christian administration, Asbury College, 1991; two years post-graduate work, Asbury Theological Seminary. Delta Discount Corporation; president and CEO, O and O Construction Incorporated, 1992–; VP/M&PR/Lender, Eva-Bank, 2005–. Alabama House of Representatives, 1998–. Eva United Methodist Church; Eva Lion's Club; Arrites Oden Masonic Lodge; Huntsville Scottish Rite; Decatur York Rite; Huntsville Shrine Association. Spouse: Samantha. Child: Anika

JOHN "JACK" PAGE III (D)

District 29: DeKalb and Etowah

Committees: Constitution and Elections; Government Appropriations; Rules

Rm. 628-E; 11 S. Union St.
Montgomery, AL 36130
reppage@bellsouth.net
(334) 242-7742

P.O. Box 227
Gadsden, AL 35902
(256) 546-5365

B. 1950, Kokura, Kyushu, Japan. AS, history, cum laude, Gadsden State Community College, 1975; BS, secondary education, history and sociology, Jacksonville State University, 1976. U.S. Marine Corps, Vietnam; community liaison, Gadsden State Community College, 2002–. Gadsden City Council, 1990–93; Alabama House of Representatives, 1993–. Mason; Veterans of Foreign Wars; National Rifle Association; Vietnam Veterans Association; Alabama Gun Collectors Association; Independent Order of Odd Fellows; Gadsden-Etowah Chamber of Commerce. Spouse: Rebecca. Children: Courtney, John, and Gill.

ARTHUR PAYNE (R)

District 44: Jefferson

Committees: Boards and Commissions; Government Operations; Jefferson County Legislation; Rules

Rm. 627-B; 11 S. Union St.
Montgomery, AL 36130
arthur.payne@alhouse.org
(334) 242-7753

7763 Peppertree Highlands Cir.
Trussville, AL 35173
(205) 655-5845

B. 1946, Trussville. BS, business administration, Auburn University, 1968; MBA, University of Alabama in Birmingham, 1974; MA, education administration, University of Alabama, 1975. Army, 1969–70; owner, Arthur Payne Sporting Goods, 1981–2006; retired. Alabama House of Representatives, 1978–. First Baptist Church of Trussville; past president, Center Point Civitan Club. Spouse: Deborah. Children: Mark and Marty.

JOHN ROBINSON (D)

District 23: Jackson

Committees: Education
Policy; Judiciary; Rules

Rm. 534-D; 11 S. Union St.
Montgomery, AL 36130
john.robinson@alhouse.org
(334) 242-7728

100 East Peachtree St.
Scottsboro, AL 35768
(256) 218-3090

B. 1950, Albertville. Attended Jacksonville State University; JD, Birmingham School of Law, 1984. Trial coordinator, Jackson County District Attorney's Office, 1975–99. Alabama House of Representatives, 1994–, majority whip. St. Luke's Episcopal Church; Jackson County Historical Association. Child: Lawson.

OLIVER ROBINSON (D)

District 58: Jefferson

Committees: Government
Operations (chair); Bank-
ing and Insurance; Jefferson
County Legislation

Rm. 534-B; 11 S. Union St.
Montgomery, AL 36130
oliver.robinson@alhouse.org
(334) 242-7769

9640 Eastpoint Cir.
Birmingham, AL 35217
(205) 849-6765

B. 1960, Birmingham. BS, urban affairs, University of Alabama at Birmingham, 1987. Basketball player, San Antonio Spurs, 1982–83; vice president of community affairs, AmSouth Bank, 1987–99; co-founder: Robinson & Robinson Communications, 1994–, ABI Capital Management, 1999–. Alabama House of Representatives, 1998–. Bethel Baptist Church in West End; Phi Beta Sigma; Birmingham Public Park and Recreation Board; 1991 class of Leadership Birmingham; treasurer, Keep Birmingham Beautiful Commission. Spouse: Sakina. Children: Amanda, Adriana, and Oliver III.

JOHN ROGERS JR. (D)

District 52: Jefferson

Committees: Boards and
Commissions; Education
Appropriations; Jefferson
County Legislation

Rm. 541-D; 11 S. Union St.
Montgomery, AL 36130
yke@cec.conteduc.uab.edu
(334) 242-7761

1424 18th St. SW
Birmingham, AL 35211
(205) 934-0364

B. 1940, Birmingham. BS, biology and chemistry, Tennessee State University, 1962; MS, vocational guidance counseling, University of Alabama. Air Force, 1962–80; director of minority affairs, University of Alabama at Birmingham, 1982–; president, Rogers and Rogers, Inc., 1989–; CEO, Wilson and Associates, 2001–. Alabama House of Representatives, 1982–. St. Mary's Catholic Church; Alpha Phi Alpha; Mt. Meigs Advisory Council; Alabama Council on Crime and Delinquency; Birmingham Convention and Visitors Bureau; St. Andrews Foundation; Sickle Cell Foundation. Spouse: Gennie. Children: Jerena, Tammy, and John III.

YUSUF SALAAM (D)

District 67: Dallas

Committees: Government
Appropriations; Judiciary

Rm. 539-E; 11 S. Union St.
Montgomery, AL 36130
yusuf.salaam@alhouse.org
(334) 242-7746

230 Franklin St.
Selma, AL 36703
(334) 872-7571

B. 1947, Ft. Benning, GA. AB,
history, University of Georgia,
1971; JD, University of Miami,
1975; LLM, University of Wis-
consin, 1977. Attorney, Yusuf
Salaam Attorney PC, 1993–. Alabama House of Representatives,
2002–. Alabama Trial Lawyers;
Alabama Bar Association; Alabama Democratic Committee;
Dallas County Bar; Coalition
for Good Government. Spouse:
Khayriyyah. Children: Fatima,
Rastreeda, Gaaiyya, Safiyyah,
and Yusuflibril.

HOWARD SANDERFORD (R)

District 20: Madison

Committees: Boards and
Commissions; Judiciary;
Madison County Legislation

Rm. 528-B; 11 S. Union St.
Montgomery, AL 36130
hs1989@aol.com
(334) 242-4368

908 Tannehill Dr. SE
Huntsville, AL 35802
(256) 533-1989

B. 1935, Meridian, MS. AS,
Meridian Junior College, 1955;
BS, accounting, Mississippi State
University, 1957. Marine Corps,
1957–61; general systems division manager–Huntsville, IBM
World Trade and manager of new
systems, IBM, 1961–87; president, Computer Leasing Company, Inc., 1985. Alabama House
of Representatives, 1989–. First
Baptist Church; Alabama Commission on Aerospace Sciences;
Alabama Management Improvement Program; Alabama Board
of Medical Scholarship Awards.
Spouse: Dot. Children: Mary
Ann, Peggy, and Betty.

ROD SCOTT (D)

District 55: Jefferson

Committees: Commerce;
County and Municipal Gov-
ernment; Jefferson County
Legislation; Rules

Rm. 525-C; 11 S. Union St.
Montgomery, AL 36130
scotthrod@yahoo.com
(334) 242-7752

Miles College; 5500 Myron
Massy Blvd.
Birmingham, AL 35208
(205) 929-1534

B. 1958, Fairfield. BA, econom-
ics, Yale University, 1980; MBA,
Amos Tuck School of Business
Administration at Dartmouth
College, 1983. Economics pro-
fessor, Miles College, 2002–. Ala-
bama House of Representatives,
2006–. National Conference
of State Legislatures; National
Black Caucus of State Legislators;
Southern Legislative Conference;
Legislative Leadership Founda-
tion; Southern Region Education
Board. Children: Sara-Valena,
Jordan, and Bradlea-roi.

TOMMY SHERER (D)

District 13: Walker

Committees: Constitution and Elections; Education Policy; Government Appropriations; Local Legislation

Rm. 522-A; 11 S. Union St. Montgomery, AL 36130

tommysherer@yahoo.com

(334) 242-7694

P.O. Box 1384

Jasper, AL 35502

(205) 522-2348

B. 1948, Walker County. BS, music education, Jacksonville State University, MEd music, Samford University, 1970; EdS, administration, University of Alabama at Birmingham, 1991. Teacher, 1971–85; principal/assistant principal, Walker County School System, 1985–1988; public relations director, Jasper City Schools, 1988–90; principal, Jasper City Schools, 1990–2002. Alabama House of Representatives, 2002–. Kiwanis Club; Cattlemen's Association; Children's Policy Council; Sons of the American Legion; First Baptist Church of Jasper. Spouse: Jeanette. Children: Christopher and Sondra.

HARRY SHIVER (R)

District 64: Baldwin, Conecuh, Escambia, and Monroe

Committees: Baldwin County Legislation; Education Policy; Government Operations

Rm. 526-D; 11 S. Union St. Montgomery, AL 36130

harryshiver@aol.com

(334) 242-7745

46007 Sunset Dr.

Bay Minette, AL 36507

(251) 937-0240

B. 1946, Bay Minette. BS, social science and physical education, Livingston University, 1968; MS, secondary education, Troy University, 1982; EdS, Troy University, 1984. Teacher, Stockton Junior High School, 1968–74; Bay Minette Middle School, 1974–2004. Alabama House of Representatives, 2006–. First United Methodist Church of Bay Minette; North Baldwin and Monroe County Chambers of Commerce; Alabama Retired Teachers Association; Baldwin County Retired Teachers Association; officiates high school football and basketball and college softball. Spouse: Jean. Child: Julie.

TERRY SPICER (D)

District 91: Coffee

Committees: Education Appropriations; Education Policy

Rm. 630-B; 11 S. Union St. Montgomery, AL 36130

terry.spicer@alhouse.org

(334) 242-7773

2665 Taylor Mill Rd.

Elba, AL 36323

(334) 347-2623 ext.2246

B. 1965, Opp. AA, air conditioning and refrigeration, Douglas McArthur State Technical College, 1985; BS, technical education, Athens State College, 1991; MPA, Auburn University Montgomery, 1998; honorary doctorate, University of West Alabama. Manager/owner, Spicer Heating and Cooling, 1983–97; dean of workforce development, Lurleen B. Wallace Community College, 1997–2004; assistant to the president for economic and community development, Enterprise-Ozark Community College, 2004–. Alabama House of Representatives, 1998–. First Baptist Church of Elba; Coffee County Cattlemen's Association. Spouse: Ceina. Children: Hayes and J. Cole.

BUTCH TAYLOR (D)

District 22: Jackson and Madison

Committees: County and Municipal Government; Government Operations

Rm. 524-C; 11 S. Union St. Montgomery, AL 35130 butch.taylor@alhouse.org (334) 242-7219

224 Taylor Ave. New Hope, AL 35760 (256) 723-8436

B. 1950, New Hope. BS, biology, University of North Alabama, 1972. Teacher and coach, Madison County Board of Education, 1972–2002; retired. New Hope City Council, 2000–02; Madison County Board of Education, 2002–06, president, 2005–06; Alabama House of Representatives, 2007–, elected in a special election held March 6, 2007 to fill the vacancy due to the death of Albert Hall on November 12, 2006. Methodist; Alabama High School Athletics Association. Spouse: Ann. Children: Jake, Shellie, and Sherrie.

WILLIAM THIGPEN SR. (D)

District 16: Fayette, Lamar, and Tuscaloosa

Committees: Banking and Insurance; Health; Tuscaloosa County Legislation

Rm. 538-D; 11 S. Union St. Montgomery, AL 36130 william.thigpen@alhouse.org (334) 242-7766

103 1st Ave. NW Fayette, AL 35555 (205) 270-0749

B. 1940, Greenville. BS, secondary education, Troy University, 1964. Alabama Army National Guard, 1958–86; plant superintendent, Boss Manufacturing Company Industrial Work Gloves, 1965–69; plant manager, Fayette Manufacturing Company Children's Outer Wear, 1969–72; owner, Fayette Sportswear-Men's Sports Coats, 1972–85; insurance agent, 1986–90; owner and dealer principal, Thigpen Doric Vaults, 1990–93; Thigpen Ford Mercury, 1994–2000. Alabama House of Representatives, 1998–. Secretary, adult Sunday School class, Fayette First Baptist Church; Fayette Chamber of Commerce. Spouse: Betty. Children: Three.

ELWYN THOMAS (R)

District 34: Blount and Jefferson

Committees: Government Appropriations; Jefferson County Legislation; Public Safety

Rm. 541-B; 11 S. Union St. Montgomery, AL 36130 elwyn.thomas@alhouse.org (334) 242-7762

124 Cliff Springs Rd. Oneonta, AL 35121 (205) 237-4672

B. 1943, Oneonta. Attended Lincoln Graduate Center at Snead State Community College and Alabama Bankers' Seminars. Real estate evaluator, Nashville Savings, 1990–. Alabama House of Representatives, 1998–. First Baptist Church of Oneonta; Blount County Chamber of Commerce; Alabama Realtors' Association; St. Clair County Board of Realtors; Gideons. Spouse: Linda. Child: Teresa.

James Thomas (D)

District 69: Autauga, Dallas, Lowndes, and Wilcox

Committees: Banking and Insurance; Education Appropriations; Tourism and Travel

Rm. 525-B; 11 S. Union St.
Montgomery, AL 36130
james.thomas@alhouse.org
(334) 242-7701

P.O. Box 1089
Camden, AL 36726
(334) 682-9590

B. 1943, Lowndes County. BS, 1965, Alabama State University. Principal, Wilcox Central High School, 1989–. Alabama House of Representatives, 1982–. First Missionary Baptist Church in White Hall; Alabama and National Education Associations; Administrators Association; president, National Black Caucus of State Legislatures. Spouse: Evelyn. Child: Angela.

Patricia Todd (D)

District 54: Jefferson

Committees: Boards and Commissions; Constitution and Elections; Jefferson County Legislation

Rm. 541-C; 11 S. Union St.
Montgomery, AL 36130
patricia.todd@alhouse.org
(334) 242-7718

P.O. Box 130201
Birmingham, AL 35222
(205) 324-9822

B. 1955, Richmond, KY. BS, political science, University of Kentucky, 1980; MPA, University of Alabama at Birmingham, 1994. Staff member, Bill Baxley for Governor, 1986; owner, One on One Computer Training, 1999–2001; program director, Central Alabama Women's Business Center, 2001–04; associate director, AIDS Alabama, 2004–. Alabama House of Representatives, 2006–. Past secretary: Crestwood Neighborhood Association, Episcopal Church Women at Grace Episcopal Woodlawn; board member, Equality Alabama; NAACP; League of Women Voters. Partner: Jennifer. Child: Samantha.

Benjamin "Allen" Treadaway (R)

District 51: Jefferson

Committees: Education Policy; Health; Jefferson County Legislation; Local Legislation

Rm. 536-D; 11 S. Union St.
Montgomery, AL 36130
bsketa@aol.com
(334) 242-7685

P.O. Box 126
Morris, AL 35116
(205) 566-6835

B. 1961, Birmingham. Peace Officers Standards and Training Commission, Birmingham Police Academy, 1989. Sergeant, Birmingham Police Department, 1989–. Alabama House of Representatives, 2006–. Past president, Birmingham Fraternal Order of Police; City of Birmingham Officer of the Year, 1992; Alabama State Fraternal Order of Police, Most Outstanding Member, 2004–05; board member, Birmingham Retirement and Relief System. Spouse: Susan. Children: Kelsey, Erin, Tyler, Ally, and Cody.

LESLEY VANCE (D)

District 80: Lee and Russell

Committees: Banking and Insurance (chair); Commerce; Lee County Legislation

Rm. 630-E; 11 S. Union St. Montgomery, AL 36130 lesley.vance@alhouse.org (334) 242-7687

3738 U.S. 431 N. Phenix City, AL 36868 (334) 298-0668

B. 1939, Troy. Advanced business courses, Mortuary College. Owner, Vance Memorial Chapel, 1972–; co-owner, Vance-Brooks Funeral Home, 2002–. Russell County coroner, 1963–90; Russell County commissioner, 1992–94; Alabama House of Representatives, 1994–. First Baptist Church. Spouse: Patricia. Children: Leslie, Carmen, and Chris.

CAM WARD (R)

District 49: Bibb and Shelby

Committees: Education Policy; Judiciary; Rules; Shelby County Legislation

Rm. 625-C; 11 S. Union St. Montgomery, AL 36130 camjulward@aol.com (334) 242-7750

1134 County Services Dr. Pelham, AL 35124 (205) 664-6848

B. 1971, Milton, FL. BS, international relations and political science, Troy University, 1993; JD, Cumberland School of Law, 1996. Deputy attorney general, Alabama State Auditor's Office, 1996–98; deputy secretary of state, 1998; district director, Congressman Spencer Bacchus, 1998–2001; executive director, Industrial Development Board of Alabaster, 2001–. Alabama House of Representatives, 2002–. Leadership Shelby County; Alabaster/Pelham Rotary Club; Greater Education Foundation of Shelby County; American Bar Association; Alabama Republican Party State Executive Committee; Hunter Street Baptist Church in Hoover. Spouse: Julie. Child: Riley.

PEBBLIN WARREN (D)

District 82: Bullock, Lee, and Macon

Committees: Commerce; County and Municipal Government; Health; Lee County Legislation; Rules

Rm. 517-C; 11 S. Union St. Montgomery, AL 36130 pebblin.warren@alhouse.gov (334) 242-7734

P.O. Box 1328 Tuskegee Institute, AL 36087 (334) 280-4469

B. 1952, Keysville, GA. BS, business administration, 1972, and MEd, personal administration, 1986, Tuskegee University. Director of student services, Department of Postsecondary Education, 1989–2005; community resource specialist, Alabama Industrial Development Training, 2006–. Alabama House of Representatives, 2005–. Elder, Tuskegee Westminster Presbyterian Church; board, Aid to Inmate Mothers; Delta Sigma Theta; vice president, Democrats of the 82nd District. Spouse: David. Children: Sharon and Pebblin.

HENRY WHITE (D)

District 5: Limestone

Committees: Agriculture and Forestry; Education Policy; Public Safety

Rm. 528-C; 11 S. Union St. Montgomery, AL 36130 henrywhite@pclnet.net (334) 242-7712

P.O. Box 1085 Athens, AL 35612 (256) 278-8033

B. 1948, Limestone County. AA, school administration, 1987, and BS, physical education, University of North Alabama, 1971; MEd, University of Montevallo, 1975. Principal, Reed Elementary School, 1986–89, 1993–2006; superintendent, Limestone County School District, 1989–93. Athens City Council, 2000–06; Alabama House of Representatives, 2006–. Baptist Church. Spouse: Marsha. Children: Cory and Lindsey.

JACK WILLIAMS (R)

District 47: Jefferson

Committees: Commerce; County and Municipal Government; Jefferson County Legislation

Rm. 536-D; 11 S. Union St. Montgomery, AL 36130 jack@jackwilliams.org (334) 242-7779

3273 Brashford Rd. Birmingham, AL 35216 (205) 414-7539

B. 1957, Jasper. BA, Bible, Southeastern Bible College. Real estate consultant, Jefferson Group, 2005–. Alabama House of Representatives, 2004–; Alabama Department of Human Resources, Quality Assurance Committee, 2000–02 . Fullness Christian Fellowship; board chair, Greater Birmingham Habitat for Humanity; past chair, Greater Birmingham Young Republicans. Spouse: Glenda. Children: Regan and Jordan.

RANDY WOOD (R)

District 36: Calhoun and St. Clair

Committees: County and Municipal Government; Public Safety

Rm. 524-E; 11 S. Union St. Montgomery, AL 36130 randy.wood@alhouse.org (334) 242-7700

P.O. Box 4432 Anniston, AL 36204 (256) 237-8114

B. 1947, Tift County, GA. AA, business, Southern Union College, 1967. Alabama National Guard, 1967–73; owner, Wood's Auto Body Shop, 1982–; Calhoun County Commission, 1999–2002; Alabama House of Representatives, 2002–. Saks Civitan Club; Weaver Lions Club; Fraternal Order of Police, Lodge #4. Spouse: Linda. Child: Allison.

GREG WREN (R)

District 75: Elmore and
Montgomery

Committees: Boards and
Commissions; Commerce;
Montgomery County Leg-
islation

Rm. 517-B; 11 S. Union St.
Montgomery, AL 36104
repgregwren@aol.com
(334) 242-7764

4213 Carmichael Rd.
Montgomery, AL 36106
(334) 395-0123

B. 1955, Ithaca, NY. BA, public
administration, University of
Alabama, 1977. Director of gov-
ernmental affairs, Alabama As-
sociation of Realtors, 1977–81;
chartered financial consultant,
Northwestern Mutual, 1981–;
owner, Wren and Associates,
2002–. Alabama House of Rep-
resentatives, 1994–2002; 2006–.
YMCA; Envision 2020; Alabama
Asthma and Allergy Foundation;
Alabama Mental Illness Planning
Council; First Baptist Church
Disaster Relief and Resource
Center Team. Spouse: Susan.
Children: Rachael, Christa, and
Catherine.

7

Federal Offices in Alabama

Alabama is represented in Congress by two members of the United States Senate and seven members of the United States House of Representatives. The senators are elected statewide and serve six-year terms. The representatives serve two-year terms and are elected by districts. The number of senators is fixed by the U.S. Constitution at two per state, but the number of representatives apportioned to each state varies according to the changing U.S. population. There are 435 House districts nationally, and after each U.S. Census, the districts are adjusted, if necessary, so that each state's population has an equal voice.

In addition, Alabama has three United States judicial districts, with U.S. attorneys, district and magistrate judges, and marshals assigned to each. Alabama is a part of the U.S. Eleventh Circuit Court of Appeals, and several of the circuit judges live in Alabama and have their chambers at one of the federal courthouses in the state. All these officials are appointed rather than elected. U.S. circuit and district judges are nominated by the president and confirmed by the Senate for life terms. U.S. magistrate judges are nominated by a committee of lawyers and approved by a majority of the sitting judges in their respective districts for eight-year terms. U.S. attorneys and marshals are appointed by the president and typically serve until there is a change of administration.

U.S. SENATOR
RICHARD SHELBY

Alabama's senior U.S. senator was born May 6, 1934, in Birmingham, and lives now in Tuscaloosa with his wife, Annette (Nevin). They have two sons: Richard Jr. and Claude Nevin.

Shelby earned his BA and LLB degrees from the University of Alabama, then practiced law and served as Tuscaloosa city prosecutor, U.S. magistrate judge, special assistant to the Alabama attorney general, and state senator before being elected to Congress in 1978. He served four terms in the House and was first elected to the U.S. Senate in 1986 as a Democrat. He switched to the Republican Party in 1994.

Shelby is the ranking member on the Banking, Housing, and Urban Affairs Committee and the Commerce, Justice, and Science Appropriations Subcommittee. In addition, he is a senior member of the full Appropriations Committee and the Special Committee on Aging. From 1995 to 2003 he served on the Senate Select Committee on Intelligence, which he chaired from 1997 to 2001.

WASHINGTON OFFICE: 304 Russell Senate Office Building, Washington, DC 20510 www.shelby.senate.gov; senator@shelby.senate.gov; Tel: (202) 224-5744, Fax: (202) 224-3416

BIRMINGHAM OFFICE: 1800 5th Avenue North, 321 Federal Building, Birmingham, AL 35203; Tel: (205) 731-1384, Fax: (205) 731-1386

HUNTSVILLE OFFICE: 1000 Glenn Hearn Boulevard #20127, Huntsville, AL 35824; Tel: (256) 772-0460, Fax: (256) 772-8387

MOBILE OFFICE: 113 St. Joseph Street, 445 U.S. Federal Courthouse, Mobile, AL 36602; Tel: (251) 694-4164, Fax: (251) 694-4166

MONTGOMERY OFFICE: 15 Lee Street, B-28 Federal Courthouse, Suite 208, Montgomery, AL 36104 ; Tel: (334) 223-7303, Fax: (334) 223-7317

TUSCALOOSA OFFICE: 1118 Greensboro Avenue, Room 240, Tuscaloosa, AL 35401; Tel: (205) 759-5047, Fax: (205) 759-5067

U.S. SENATOR
JEFF SESSIONS

Alabama's junior U.S. senator was born in Selma, on December 24, 1946, and lives now in Mobile with his wife, Mary (Blackshear). They have three children: Mary Abigail Reinhardt, Ruth Walk, and Sam.

Sessions earned his BA from Huntington College and his JD from the University of Alabama. He practiced law in Russellville and Mobile, and served as an assistant U.S. attorney, U.S. attorney for the Southern District of Alabama, and attorney general of Alabama before being elected to the U.S. Senate in 1996 as a Republican.

Sessions serves on the Senate Armed Services Committee, the Senate Judiciary Committee, the Senate Energy and Natural Resources Committee, the Senate Budget Committee, the International Narcotics Control Caucus, and the Committee Meetings/Hearings Schedule Committee.

WASHINGTON OFFICE: 335 Russell Senate Office Building, Washington, DC 20510; www.sessions.senate.gov; Tel: (202) 224-4124, Fax: (202) 224-3149

BIRMINGHAM OFFICE: 341 Vance Federal Building, 1800 Fifth Avenue North, Birmingham, AL 35203, Tel: (205) 731-1500, Fax (205) 731-0221

HUNTSVILLE OFFICE: AmSouth Center, Suite 802, 200 Clinton Avenue NW, Huntsville, AL 35801, Tel: (256) 533-0979, Fax: (256) 533-0745

MOBILE OFFICE: 41 West I-65 Service Road North, Suite 2300-A, Mobile, AL 36608, Tel: (251) 414-3083, Fax (251) 414-5845

MONTGOMERY OFFICE: 7550 Halcyon Summit Drive, Suite 150, Montgomery, AL 36117; Tel: (334) 244-7017, Fax: (334) 244-7091

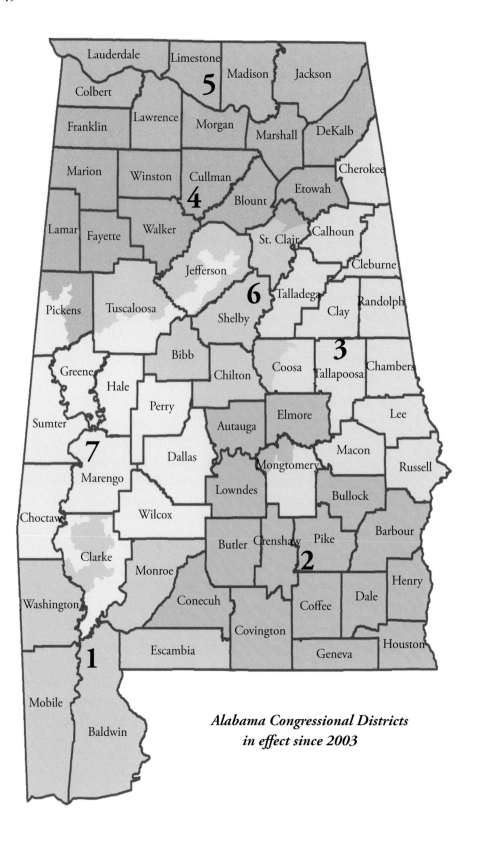

Alabama Congressional Districts
in effect since 2003

U.S. REPRESENTATIVE DIST. 1
JO BONNER

Bonner, R-Mobile, served as press secretary and chief of staff to former 1st District Congressman Sonny Callahan from 1984 to 1999, then won Callahan's seat when Callahan retired in 2000. Bonner serves on the House Appropriations, Budget, and Ethics committees. A Selma native, he is a graduate of the University of Alabama. He and his wife, Janée, have a daughter, Lee, and son, Robins.

WASHINGTON OFFICE: 422 Cannon House Office Building, Washington, DC 20515; http://bonner.house.gov; Tel: (202) 225-4931, Fax: (202) 225-0562

BALDWIN COUNTY OFFICE: 1302 North McKenzie Street, Foley, AL 36535; Tel: (251) 943-2073, Fax: (251) 943-2093

MOBILE OFFICE: 1141 Montlimar Drive, Suite 3010, Mobile, AL 36609; Tel: (251) 690-2811 or 1-800-288-8721, Fax: (251) 342-0404

U.S. REPRESENTATIVE DIST. 2
BOBBY BRIGHT

Bright, D-Montgomery, is in his first term. A former three-term mayor of Montgomery, he is a native of Dale County. He has degrees from Auburn University and Jones Law School and is a former practicing attorney. Bright serves on the Agriculture, Armed Service, and Small Business committees. He is married to the former Lynn Clardy and has three children, Neal, Lisa, and Katie.

WASHINGTON OFFICE: 1205 Longworth House Office Building, Washington, DC 20515; www.bright.house.gov; Tel: (202) 225-2901, Fax: (202) 225-8913

MONTGOMERY OFFICE: 3500 Eastern Boulevard, #250, Montgomery, AL 36116; Tel: (334) 277-9113, Fax: (334) 277-8534

U.S. REPRESENTATIVE DIST. 3
MIKE ROGERS

Rogers, R-Anniston, previously served on the Calhoun County Commission and in the Alabama Legislature. A lawyer, he was elected to Congress in 2002. He is the ranking minority member of the Homeland Security Subcommittee on Management, Integration, and Oversight, and serves on the Armed Services and Agriculture committees. He and his wife, Beth, have three children and live near Anniston.

WASHINGTON OFFICE: 324 Cannon House Office Building, Washington, DC 20515; www.house.gov/mikerogers; Tel: (202) 225-3261, Fax: (202) 225-8485

ANNISTON OFFICE: 1129 Noble Street, 104 Federal Building, Anniston, AL 36201; Tel: (256) 236-5655, Fax: (256) 237-9203

MONTGOMERY OFFICE: 7550 Halcyon Summit Drive, Montgomery, AL 36117; Tel: (334) 377-4210; Fax: (334) 277-4257

OPELIKA OFFICE: 1819 Pepperell Parkway, Suite 203, Opelika, AL 36801; Tel: (334) 745-6221, Fax: (334) 742-0109

U.S. REPRESENTATIVE DIST. 4
ROBERT ADERHOLT

Aderholt, R-Jasper, is serving his sixth term. He previously was legal assistant to Governor Fob James and a municipal judge in Haleyville. He serves on the Appropriations and Budget committees. He and his wife, Caroline, have two children.

WASHINGTON OFFICE: 1433 Longworth House Office Building, Washington, DC 20515; www.aderholt.house.gov; Tel: (202) 225-4876, Fax: (202) 225-5587

CULLMAN OFFICE: 205 Fourth Avenue NE, Suite 104, Cullman, AL 35055, Tel: (256) 734-6043; Fax: (256) 737-0885

DECATUR OFFICE: Morgan County Courthouse, P.O. Box 668, Decatur, AL 35602, Tel: (256) 350-4093; Fax (256) 350-5056

GADSDEN OFFICE: 107 Federal Building, 600 Broad Street, Gadsden, AL 35901, Phone: (256) 546-0201, Fax: (256) 546-8778

JASPER OFFICE: 247 Carl Elliott Building, 1710 Alabama Avenue, Jasper, AL 35501; Tel: (205) 221-2310; Fax: (205) 221-9035

U.S. REPRESENTATIVE DIST. 5
PARKER GRIFFITH

Griffith, D-Huntsville, is serving his first term. A retired oncologist and businessman, he previously served in the Alabama Senate. He received his MD from Louisiana State University Medical School in New Orleans and served his residency at the University of Texas. Prior to attending medical school, he taught 7th grade math in New Orleans. He serves on the Science and Technology, Small Business, and Transportation and Infrastructure committees. He and his wife have five children and ten grandchildren.

WASHINGTON OFFICE: 417 Cannon House Office Building, Washington, DC 20515; www.griffith.house.gov; Tel: (202) 225-4801, Fax: (202) 225-4392

HUNTSVILLE OFFICE: 200 Pratt Avenue NE, Suite A, Huntsville, AL 35801; Tel: (256) 551-0190, Fax: (256) 551-0194

U.S. REPRESENTATIVE DIST. 6
SPENCER BACHUS

Bachus, R-Birmingham, is serving his eighth term. He is the ranking minority member on the Financial Services Committee. A lawyer, he previously served in both the Alabama House and Senate, where he drafted Alabama's domestic abuse statutes and authored the state's first law penalizing repeat DUI offenders. In Congress, he has authored several laws, including laws to provide Medicare coverage for prostate cancer screenings and to establish the Cahaba River National Wildlife Refuge. He and his wife, Linda, live in Vestavia Hills and are the parents of five children.

WASHINGTON OFFICE: 2246 Rayburn Building, Washington, DC 20515; www.bachus.house.gov; Tel: (202) 225-4921, Fax: (202) 225-2082

BIRMINGHAM OFFICE: 1900 International Park Drive, Birmingham, AL 35243, Tel: (205) 969-2296; Fax: (205) 969-3958

CLANTON OFFICE: 703 2nd Avenue North, P.O. Box 502, Clanton, AL 35046, Tel: (205) 280-0704; Fax (205) 280-3060

U.S. REPRESENTATIVE DIST. 7
ARTUR DAVIS

Davis, D-Birmingham, was elected in 2004. He serves on the Ways and Means and Judiciary committees. He previously served as an assistant U.S. attorney and had a general legal practice. He is a native of Montgomery and is a magna cum laude graduate of Harvard University and Harvard Law School.

WASHINGTON OFFICE: 208 Cannon House Office Building, Washington, DC 20515; www.arturdavis.house.gov; Tel: (202) 225-2665, Fax: (202) 225-9567

BIRMINGHAM OFFICE: 2 20th Street North, Suite #1130, Birmingham, AL 35203, Tel: (205) 254-1960; Fax: (205) 254-1974

DEMOPOLIS OFFICE: 102 E. Washington Street, Suite F, Demopolis, AL 36732, Tel: (334) 287-0860; Fax (334) 287-0870

LIVINGSTON OFFICE: 205 North Washington Street, Webb Hall 236–237, Livingston, AL 35470; Tel: (205) 652-5834; Fax: (205) 652-5935

SELMA OFFICE: 908 Alabama Avenue, Suite 112, Selma, AL 36701; Tel: (334) 877-4414; Fax: (334) 877-4489

VISITING ALABAMA CONGRESSIONAL MEMBERS IN WASHINGTON

Meeting with a member of Congress or congressional staff is an effective way to express interest in policy or legislative issues.

Plan your visit by calling ahead to determine in advance which member or committee staff you need to meet.

Then contact the Appointment Secretary/Scheduler. Explain your purpose and whom you represent.

When it is time to meet with a member, be punctual and be patient. Members have crowded schedules. If interruptions do occur, be flexible.

When possible, bring supporting information and materials. It is helpful to share information and examples that demonstrate clearly the impact or benefits associated with a particular issue or piece of legislation.

Be political (which does not mean partisan). Members of Congress want to represent the best interests of their districts and state. Wherever possible, demonstrate the connection between what you are requesting and the interests of the member's constituency. Where it is appropriate, feel free to ask for a commitment.

Be prepared to answer questions or provide additional information. Follow up the meeting with a thank you letter that outlines the different points covered during the meeting, and send along any additional information and materials requested.

(Adapted from CongressLink)

ALABAMA'S FEDERAL JUDGES, ATTORNEYS, AND MARSHALS

MIDDLE DISTRICT OF ALABAMA

Frank M. Johnson Jr., U.S. Courthouse
One Church Street
Montgomery, AL 36104
(334) 954-3600

Chief District Judge Mark Fuller
District Judge Myron Thompson
District Judge W. Keith Watkins
Senior District Judge W. Harold
  Albritton
Senior District Judge Ira DeMent
Senior District Judge Truman Hobbs
Chief Magistrate Judge Susan Russ
  Walker
Magistrate Judge Wallace Capel Jr.
Magistrate Judge Charles S. Coody
Magistrate Judge Terry F. Moorer
U.S. Attorney Leura Canary
U.S. Marshal Jesse Seroyer
Clerk of Court Debra Hackett

NORTHERN DISTRICT OF ALABAMA

Hugo L. Black U.S. Courthouse
1729 Fifth Avenue North
Birmingham, AL 35203
(205) 278-1700

Chief District Judge Sharon Blackburn
District Judge Karon Bowdre
District Judge U. W. Clemon
District Judge L. Scott Coogler
District Judge Virginia Emerson
  Hopkins
District Judge Inge Johnson
District Judge R. David Proctor
District Judge C. Lynwood Smith Jr.
Senior District Judge William Acker Jr.
Senior District Judge J. Foy Guin Jr.
Senior District Judge James Hancock
Senior District Judge Robert Propst
Chief Magistrate Judge Paul Greene

Magistrate Judge Robert Armstrong Jr.
Magistrate Judge Harwell Davis III
Magistrate Judge John Ott
Magistrate Judge T. Michael Putnam
U.S. Attorney Alice Martin
U.S. Marshal Chester Martin Keely
Clerk of Court Sharon Harris

SOUTHERN DISTRICT OF ALABAMA

U.S. Courthouse
113 St. Joseph Street
Mobile, AL 36602
(251) 690-2371

Chief District Judge Callie Granade
District Judge Kristi DuBose
District Judge William Steele
Senior District Judge Charles Butler Jr.
Magistrate Judge Sonja Bivins
Magistrate Judge William Cassady
Magistrate Judge Bert Milling Jr.
U.S. Attorney Deborah Rhodes
U.S. Marshal William Taylor
Clerk of Court Charles Diard Jr.

ELEVENTH CIRCUIT COURT OF APPEALS

56 Forsyth St. N.W.
Atlanta, GA 30303
(404) 335-6100.

Circuit Judge Ed Carnes*
Circuit Judge Joel Dubina*
Circuit Judge William Pryor†
Senior Circuit Judge Emmett R. Cox‡
Senior Circuit Judge John Godbold*

*chambers in Montgomery courthouse
†chambers in Birmingham courthouse
‡chambers in Mobile courthouse

8

COUNTIES

Alabama has sixty-seven counties, twenty-two of which are older than the state itself, having been created before 1819 under the authority of either the Mississippi or Alabama territorial governments. Washington, established in 1800, is the oldest. In the decade after statehood, the legislature created fourteen more counties. Then, in 1832, cessions of land from the Creek, Cherokee, and Choctaw Indians made way for the creation of thirteen more counties. Two more were established in the 1840s, fourteen more during Reconstruction, and the last—Houston—in 1903.

Counties are corporate bodies with legislative and administrative functions. They can sue or be sued. They collect taxes, maintain official records, and administer schools, public safety, and health. They also build and maintain roads and bridges. The authority of the counties is established by statutes passed by the legislature.

The political forces that led to creation of the 1901 Constitution were heavily dominated by agricultural interests, but the influence of old county political organizations diminished during the subsequent decades as people left the farms and moved to cities. Also, court decisions requiring one-man, one-vote apportionment for electoral districts diluted both rural and county influences.

Toward the close of the twentieth century, however, population trends reversed, and many rural areas gained residents. This trend created new demand for municipal-type services such as zoning; nuisance abatement; building standards; and provisions for water, sewage, and public safety. County governments in recent years have scrambled to keep up with these demands.

The Shelby County Courthouse, Columbiana.

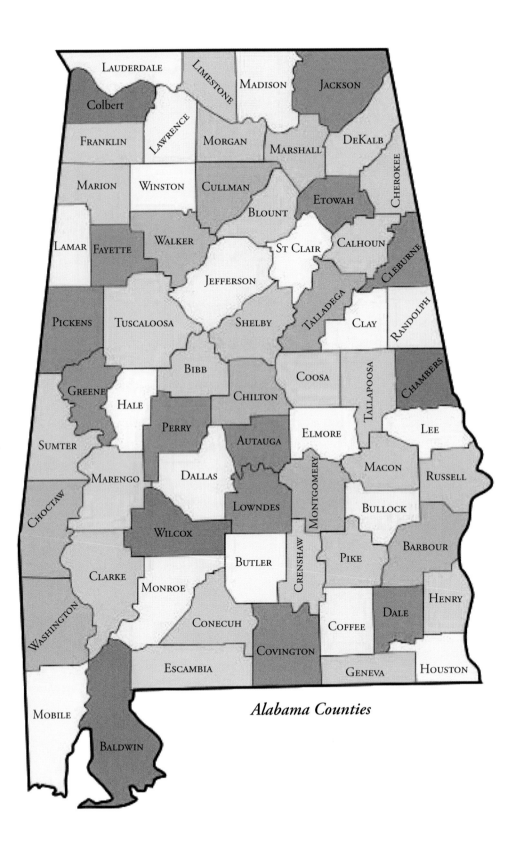

Alabama Counties

AUTAUGA

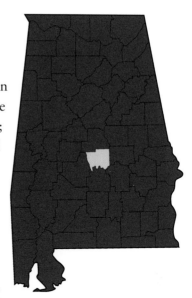

Autauga County was created by the legislature on November 21, 1818. On December 13, 1820, the boundaries in the north and northwest were enlarged; on January 12, 1827, the line between Autauga and Shelby counties was more definitely fixed. In 1866 part of its territory was taken to establish the new county of Elmore. In 1868 another portion of the county was taken to establish Baker, later known as Chilton, County. Autauga County is located in the central part of the state. It is bounded by Chilton, Lowndes, Elmore, Montgomery, and Dallas counties. It comprises 604 square miles. The county was named for Autauga Creek, which runs through it. The word "Autauga," meaning "pure water," comes from the Indian village Atagi, located on the Alabama River at the mouth of Autauga Creek. The first county seat was established at Washington, on the site of the Indian village of Atagi, in 1819. In 1830 the county seat was moved to Kingston. In 1868 the legislature relocated the county seat to Prattville, which was named after cotton gin manufacturer Daniel Pratt.

COURTHOUSE: 176 West 5th Street, Prattville, AL 36067-3041; (334) 361-3725

PROBATE JUDGE: Alfred Booth (R)

SHERIFF: Herbie Johnson (R)

CIRCUIT CLERK: William "Whit" Moncrief (R)

DISTRICT ATTORNEY: Randall Houston

REVENUE COMMISSIONER: T. T. "Tommy" Ray

COUNTY COMMISSIONERS: Clyde Chambliss; Danny Chavers; A. G. Carter; Michael Morgan; Carl Johnson

POPULATION: 49,730

MUNICIPALITIES WITHIN: Autaugaville; Billingsley; Prattville

FOR MORE INFORMATION: www.autaugaco.org

BALDWIN

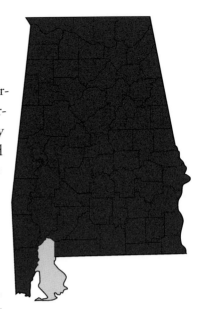

Baldwin County was created by the Mississippi Territorial Legislature on December 21, 1809, from territory taken from Washington County. The county was named for Abraham Baldwin, a distinguished citizen of Georgia. Its size was altered several times before 1868, when it received its present dimensions. Baldwin County lies in the southwestern part of the state. It is bordered by Washington, Mobile, Clarke, Monroe, and Escambia counties and Florida, Mobile Bay, and the Gulf of Mexico. Baldwin County encompasses 1,590 square miles, making it the largest county in Alabama and larger than the state of Rhode Island. MacIntosh Bluff, Blakeley, and Daphne each served for a time as county seat before 1901, when Bay Minette was so designated.

COURTHOUSE: 220 Courthouse Square, Bay Minette, AL 36507; (251) 580-2596

PROBATE JUDGE: Adrian Johns (R)

SHERIFF: Huey Hoss Mack Jr. (R)

CIRCUIT CLERK: Jody Wise Campbell (R)

DISTRICT ATTORNEY: Judy Newcomb

REVENUE COMMISSIONER: James "Phil" Nix Jr.

COUNTY COMMISSIONERS: Frank Burt Jr.; David Ed Bishop; Wayne Gruenloh; Charles "Skip" Gruber

POPULATION: 140,415

MUNICIPALITIES WITHIN: Bay Minette; Daphne; Elberta; Fairhope; Foley; Gulf Shores; Loxley; Magnolia Springs; Orange Beach; Robertsdale; Silverhill; Spanish Fort; Summerdale

FOR MORE INFORMATION: www.co.baldwin.al.us

Barbour

Barbour County was created on December 18, 1832, from former Creek Indian territory and a portion of Pike County. Its boundaries were altered in 1866 and 1868. Barbour County is located in the southeastern section of the state, bounded on the east by the Chattahoochee River and Georgia. The county encompasses 884 square miles. The county was named for Virginia governor James Barbour. The county seat was established in Louisville in 1833 and moved to Clayton in 1834. Today Barbour County maintains two courthouses—one in Clayton and one in Eufaula.

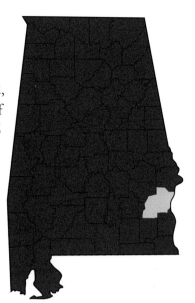

Courthouse: 303 East Broad Street, Eufaula, AL 36027; (334) 775-3203. In Clayton: Court Square, Clayton, AL 36016; (334) 775-8371

Probate Judge: Nancy Robertson (D)

Sheriff: Leroy Upshaw (D)

Circuit Clerk: David Nix (D)

District Attorney: Ben Reeves Jr.

Revenue Commissioner: Orvie Locklar

County Commissioners: Henry Franklin; Frank Straughn; Grover Forte; Kenneth Earl Gilmore; Fred Cooper; Patricia Ivey; Trip Horne

Population: 28,171

Municipalities within: Baker Hill; Blue Springs; Clayton; Clio; Eufaula; Louisville

BIBB

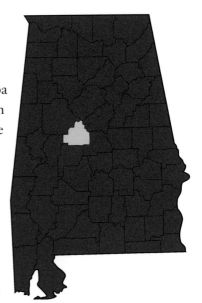

Bibb County was originally created as Cahawba County by the Alabama Territorial Legislature on February 7, 1818. Alterations were made to the boundaries in 1818, 1819, 1820, 1821, and 1868. The county name was changed to Bibb on December 4, 1820, in honor of Alabama's first governor, William Wyatt Bibb. The county is located near the center of the state and is drained by the Cahaba River. The terrain is hilly, and there are significant mineral deposits in the northern part of the county. Bibb County encompasses 625 square miles. The county seat is located at Centreville, the site of the falls in the Cahaba River.

COURTHOUSE: 8 Court Square West, Suite A, Centreville, AL 35042; (205) 926-3108

PROBATE JUDGE: Jerry Pow (R)

SHERIFF: Keith Hannah (D)

CIRCUIT CLERK: Gayle Bearden (R)

DISTRICT ATTORNEY: Michael Jackson

TAX ASSESSOR/COLLECTOR: Angie Langston

COUNTY COMMISSIONERS: Charles Beasley; Ricky Hubbard; Al Green; James Kelley; Jerome Chism

POPULATION: 21,482

MUNICIPALITIES WITHIN: Brent; Centreville; West Blocton; Woodstock

FOR MORE INFORMATION: www.bibbal.com

Blount

Blount County was created by the Alabama Territorial Legislature on February 6, 1818, from land ceded to the federal government by the Creek Nation on August 9, 1814. The county was named for Governor Willie G. Blount of Tennessee, who provided assistance to settlers in Alabama during the Creek War of 1813–14. It lies in the northeastern section of the state generally known as the mineral region. Blount County is bordered by Cullman, Marshall, Etowah, Jefferson, and Walker counties. The county is drained by the Locust and Mulberry forks of the Black Warrior River. Blount County contains 651 square miles. Beginning in 1818, Blountsville, originally known as Bear Meat Cabin, served as the county seat. An election in 1889 resulted in its transfer to Oneonta.

Courthouse: 220 2nd Avenue East, Room 101, Oneonta, AL 35121; (205) 625-4191

Probate Judge: David Standridge (R)

Sheriff: Lloyd Arrington (R)

Circuit Clerk: Michael Criswell (R)

District Attorney: Tommy Rountree

Revenue Commissioner: Donny B. Ray

County Commissioners: David Cochran; Robert Bullard; Tom Ryan; Waymon Pitts

Population: 56,436

Municipalities within: Allgood; Blountsville; Cleveland; Hayden; Highland Lake; Locust Fork; Nectar; Oneonta; Rosa; Snead; Susan Moore

For more information: www.co.blount.al.us

BULLOCK

Bullock County was created on December 5, 1866, though its boundaries were changed in February 1867. The county was named to honor Confederate colonel Edward C. Bullock of Barbour County. The county is in the southeastern section of the state, in the prairie region. Bullock County encompasses 625 square miles. The Chunnennuggee Ridge runs through the center of the county. The county seat is Union Springs.

COURTHOUSE: 217 North Prairie Street, Union Springs, AL 36089; (334) 738-2250

PROBATE JUDGE: Johnny Williamson (D)

SHERIFF: Raymond "Buck" Rodgers (D)

CIRCUIT CLERK: Wilbert Jernigan (D)

DISTRICT ATTORNEY: Ben Reeves Jr.

REVENUE COMMISSIONER: Neara S. Reed

COUNTY COMMISSIONERS: James Perry; John Adams; Dock McGowan; Alonza Ellis; Ronald Smith

POPULATION: 11,714

MUNICIPALITIES WITHIN: Midway; Union Springs

BUTLER

Butler County was created by the first session of the Alabama Legislature on December 13, 1819, from parts of Monroe and Conecuh counties. Butler County occupies 778 square miles in the south-central part of the state, and it borders Lowndes, Crenshaw, Covington, Conecuh, Monroe, and Wilcox counties. The county was named for Captain William Butler, a soldier of the Creek War of 1813–14. The county seat is Greenville.

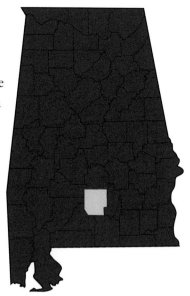

COURTHOUSE: 700 Court Square, Greenville, AL 36037; (334) 382-3612

PROBATE JUDGE: Steve Norman (D)

SHERIFF: Kenny Harden (D)

CIRCUIT CLERK: Allen Stephenson (D)

DISTRICT ATTORNEY: John Andrews

REVENUE COMMISSIONER: Belle Peavy until October 2009, then Deborah Crews

COUNTY COMMISSIONERS: Jerry Hartin; Jesse McWilliams; Frank Hickman; Daniel Robinson; Glenn King

POPULATION: 21,399

MUNICIPALITIES WITHIN: Georgiana; Greenville; McKenzie

CALHOUN

Calhoun County was created on December 18, 1832, from ceded Creek Indian territory. It was originally named Benton County in honor of Thomas Hart Benton. The county seat was established in Jacksonville in 1833. On January 29, 1858, the name was changed to Calhoun County in honor of John C. Calhoun of South Carolina. The county seat was moved to Anniston in 1899. Calhoun County is located in the northeastern section of the state, at the southern end of the Appalachian Mountain chain. It encompasses 611 square miles. The Coosa River flows along the western boundary of the county.

COURTHOUSE: 1702 Noble Street, Suite 102, Anniston, AL 36201; (256) 241-2825

PROBATE JUDGE: Alice Martin (D)

SHERIFF: Larry Amerson (D)

CIRCUIT CLERK: Ted Hooks (D)

DISTRICT ATTORNEY: Joseph "Joe" Hubbard

REVENUE COMMISSIONER: Karen Roper

COUNTY COMMISSIONERS: James "Pappy" Dunn; Robert Downing; Eli Henderson; J. D. Hess; Rudy Abbott

POPULATION: 112,903

MUNICIPALITIES WITHIN: Anniston; Hobson City; Jacksonville; Ohatchee; Oxford; Piedmont; Weaver

FOR MORE INFORMATION: www.calhouncounty.org

Chambers

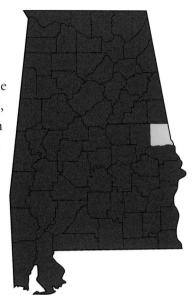

Chambers County was created by an act of the Alabama General Assembly on December 18, 1832, from former Creek Indian territory. It is located in the east-central portion of the state and is bounded on the east by the Chattahoochee River. Chambers County encompasses 603 square miles. The county is named for Henry Chambers, a U.S. senator from Alabama. The location of the county seat was selected in 1833, and the town of LaFayette was built specifically for that purpose.

COURTHOUSE: #2 LaFayette Street, LaFayette, AL 36862; (334) 864-4384

PROBATE JUDGE: John Crowder (D)

SHERIFF: Sid Lockhart (D)

CIRCUIT CLERK: Charles Story (D)

DISTRICT ATTORNEY: E. Paul Jones

REVENUE COMMISSIONER: Wendy Williams

COUNTY COMMISSIONERS: Rosa Dunn; Wayne White; Danny Kendrick; Charles Hardage; Jack Bunn; Debbie Wood

POPULATION: 35,176

MUNICIPALITIES WITHIN: Five Points; LaFayette; Lanett; Valley

FOR MORE INFORMATION: www.chamberscounty.com

Cherokee

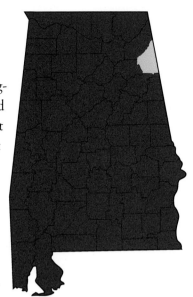

Cherokee County was created by the Alabama Legislature on January 9, 1836. The county was named
for the Cherokee Indians, who ceded the land that
now comprises the county to the federal government
by the Treaty of New Echota, December 29, 1835.
Cherokee County is located in the northeastern portion of the state, in the Appalachian Mountains, and
it encompasses 600 square miles. It is bordered by
DeKalb, Etowah, Calhoun, and Cleburne counties
and Georgia. For Cherokee County's first ten years,
its residents quarreled over the location of a county
seat. In 1837 the Alabama Legislature authorized
the seat of county government to be established at Cedar Bluff. In 1844 an election
was held, and the county seat was moved to the town of Centre.

Courthouse: 100 Main Street, Centre, AL 35960; (256) 927-3363
Probate Judge: Melvyn Salter (D)
Sheriff: Jeff Shaver (D)
Circuit Clerk: Dwayne Amos (D)
District Attorney: Mike O'Dell
Revenue Commissioner: Johnny A. Roberts
County Commissioners: Melvyn Salter; Wade Sprouse; Kimball Parker; Elbert
    St. Clair; Carlton Teague
Population: 23,998
Municipalities within: Cedar Bluff; Centre; Gaylesville; Leesburg; Sand Rock

CHILTON

Chilton County is located in the central part of the state. It was created as Baker County by the Alabama Legislature on December 30, 1868, from lands taken from Autauga, Bibb, Perry, and Shelby counties. It was named for Alfred Baker, a prominent citizen, former Confederate soldier, and postmaster in Grantville, the county seat from 1868 to 1870. Baker was responsible for enlarging Goosepond, later renamed Clanton, after Bridgadier General James Holt Clanton, as the new county seat and served as its first mayor. The county was renamed Chilton County on December 17, 1874, in honor of William Parish Chilton, chief justice of the Alabama Supreme Court and a member of the provisional and regular congresses of the Confederate States of America. The county encompasses 695 square miles. The Coosa River forms the eastern boundary of the county. The county is famous for its peach crop.

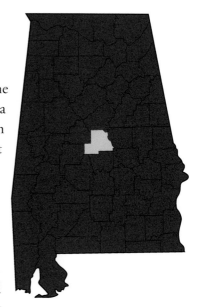

COURTHOUSE: P.O. Box 270, Clanton, AL 35046; (205) 755-1555

PROBATE JUDGE: Robert Martin (D)

SHERIFF: Kevin Davis (D)

CIRCUIT CLERK: Glenn McGriff (R)

DISTRICT ATTORNEY: Randall Houston

TAX ASSESSOR: Tom Powers

COUNTY COMMISSIONERS: Bobby Agee; Charles Bryant; Lamar Hayes; Joe Headley; Carl Allen Wyatt; Tim Mims; Allen Caton

POPULATION: 41,953

MUNICIPALITIES WITHIN: Clanton; Jemison; Maplesville; Thorsby

FOR MORE INFORMATION: www.chiltoncounty.org

CHOCTAW

Choctaw County was created by the Alabama Legislature on December 29, 1847. The county is located in the southwestern part of the state and is bordered by Sumter, Marengo, Clarke, and Washington counties and Mississippi. It encompasses 909 square miles. The county was named for the Choctaw Indians, who were original inhabitants of that part of the state and one of the major Indian tribal groups in Alabama. Choctaw County is the site of Alabama's first producing oil well, which was drilled near Gilbertown in 1944. The county's population reached its peak in the 1920s due to jobs created by the E. E. Jackson and Choctaw lumber companies. The county seat is Butler.

COURTHOUSE: 117 South Mulberry Street, Suite 9, Butler, AL 36904; (205) 459-2100

PROBATE JUDGE: D'Wayne May (D)

SHERIFF: James Lovette (D)

CIRCUIT CLERK: Donna Murphy (D)

DISTRICT ATTORNEY: Spencer Walker

REVENUE COMMISSIONER: David H. Sparrow

COUNTY COMMISSIONERS: Dandy Brown; C. D. Ruffin; Clyde Dixon; Henry Lovette

POPULATION: 15,922

MUNICIPALITIES WITHIN: Butler; Gilbertown; Lisman; Needham; Pennington; Silas; Toxey

Clarke

The Mississippi Territorial Legislature created Clarke County on December 10, 1812. The county seat was not established until 1820, when it was located at Clarksville. In 1831 the seat of government was moved to Grove Hill, previously known as Magoffin's Store, Smithville, and Macon. Clarke County is located in the southwestern portion of the state at the juncture of the Alabama and Tombigbee rivers. It encompasses 1,230 square miles and is the third largest county in the state. The county was named for General John Clarke of Georgia.

Courthouse: 114 Court Street, Grove Hill, AL 36451; (251) 275-3251

Probate Judge: Becky Presnall (D)

Sheriff: Bobby Moore (D)

Circuit Clerk: Jay Duke (D)

District Attorney: Spencer Walker

Revenue Commissioner: Chris Beverly

County Commissioners: Elma Averett; Paul Bradford; Patrica DuBose; Joe Hunt; Rhondel Rhone

Population: 27,248

Municipalities within: Coffeeville; Fulton; Grove Hill; Jackson; Thomasville

For more information: www.clarkecountyal.com

Clay

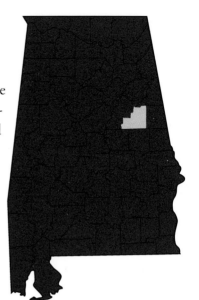

Clay County was created by the Alabama Legislature on December 7, 1866, from land taken from Randolph and Talladega counties. The county is located in the east-central part of the state, in the foothills of the Appalachian Mountains. It encompasses 606 square miles. The county was named for U.S. senator Henry Clay of Kentucky. The Talladega National Forest is located in the western part of the county. Clay County is the home of former Supreme Court Justice Hugo Black and Alabama's fifty-second governor, Bob Riley. The county seat is Ashland.

Courthouse: Courthouse Square, Ashland, AL 36251; (256) 354-7888

Probate Judge: George Ingram (D)

Sheriff: Jean "Dot" Alexander (D)

Circuit Clerk: Jeffery Colburn (D)

District Attorney: Fred Thompson

Revenue Commissioner: Ronald Robertson

County Commissioners: Wayne Watts; J. D. Davidson; Jimmy Patterson; Kevin Kiser; Ricky Burney

Population: 14,254

Municipalities within: Ashland; Lineville

CLEBURNE

Cleburne County is located in the northeastern part of Alabama. It was created by an act of the Alabama Legislature on December 6, 1866, from territory formerly contained in Calhoun, Randolph, and Talladega counties. The county currently comprises 561 square miles. The county was named for Patrick Ronayne Cleburne, a Confederate major general. The county seat was established at Edwardsville in 1867 and moved to Heflin in 1906. A large area in the western portion of the county is part of the Talladega National Forest.

COURTHOUSE: 120 Vickery Street, Heflin, AL 36264; (256) 463-2951

PROBATE JUDGE: Ryan Robertson (R)

SHERIFF: Joseph Jacks (D)

CIRCUIT CLERK: Jerry Paul Owen (D)

DISTRICT ATTORNEY: Joseph "Joe" Hubbard

REVENUE COMMISSIONER: Nikki Smallwood

COUNTY COMMISSIONERS: Joel Robinson; Tracy Lambert; Dwight Williamson; Bobby Brooks

POPULATION: 14,123

MUNICIPALITIES WITHIN: Edwardsville; Fruithurst; Heflin; Ranburne

COFFEE

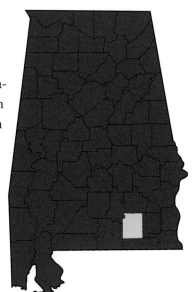

Coffee County was created by the Alabama Legislature on December 29, 1841, from what had been part of Dale County. Coffee County is located in the southeastern part of the state and is bordered by Pike, Dale, Geneva, Covington, and Crenshaw counties. It encompasses 680 square miles. The county was named for General John Coffee, a hero of the Creek War of 1813-14. The first county seat was at Wellborn. The county courthouse was destroyed by fire in 1851, and the following year the legislature authorized an election to select another site. The town of Elba, then called Bentonville, was chosen. Today the county also maintains a courthouse in Enterprise and administrative offices in New Brockton.

COURTHOUSE: 230 Court Street, Elba, AL 36323; (334) 894-5556
PROBATE JUDGE: William Gammill (R)
SHERIFF: Dave Sutton (R)
CIRCUIT CLERK: Mickey Counts (R)
DISTRICT ATTORNEY: Gary McAliley
REVENUE COMMISSIONER: Ronald L. Burns
COUNTY COMMISSIONERS: Linda Westbrook; J. L. Weeks; Robert Stephens; Doug Dalrymple; Bernest Brooks; Jim Thompson; Tom Grimsley
POPULATION: 46,027
MUNICIPALITIES WITHIN: Elba; Enterprise; Kinston; New Brockton

COLBERT

Originally settled as early as 1810 and part of Franklin County, Colbert County was created by the Alabama Legislature on February 6, 1867. It was abolished by the constitutional convention on November 29, 1867, and re-established by the legislature on February 24, 1870. Colbert County is located in the northwestern part of the state. It encompasses 589 square miles. The county was named after George and Levi Colbert, noted Chickasaw chiefs who resided in the county. It is bordered by Lauderdale, Lawrence, and Franklin counties, Mississippi, and the Tennessee River. An election in 1870 established the county seat at Tuscumbia. Colbert County was the birthplace of Helen Keller.

COURTHOUSE: 201 North Main Street, Tuscumbia, AL 35674; (256) 386-8542

PROBATE JUDGE: W. Thomas Crosslin (D)

SHERIFF: Ronnie May (D)

CIRCUIT CLERK: Nancy Lewis Hearn (D)

DISTRICT ATTORNEY: Bryce Graham Jr.

REVENUE COMMISSIONER: Bill Thompson

COUNTY COMMISSIONERS: Phillip "Rex" Burleson; Troy Woodis; Tim Leigh; Emmitt Jimmar; James Bingham; Howard Keeton

POPULATION: 54,824

MUNICIPALITIES WITHIN: Cherokee; Leighton; Littleville; Muscle Shoals; Sheffield; Tuscumbia

FOR MORE INFORMATION: www.colbertcounty.org

CONECUH

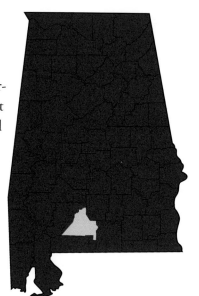

Conecuh County was created by the Alabama Territorial Legislature on February 13, 1818, from part of Monroe County. The county's size was altered several times before 1868, when it received its present dimensions. It currently comprises 853 square miles. The county's name comes from the Muscogee language and has been interpreted to mean "land of cane." Conecuh County lies in the southern portion of the state and is bordered by Monroe, Butler, Covington, and Escambia counties. The county seat was at Sparta from 1818 until 1868, when it was moved to Evergreen.

COURTHOUSE: Jackson Street, Courthouse Square, Evergreen, AL 36401; (251) 578-7034

PROBATE JUDGE: Rogene Booker (D)

SHERIFF: Edwin Booker (D)

CIRCUIT CLERK: David Jackson (D)

DISTRICT ATTORNEY: Tommy Chapman

REVENUE COMMISSIONER: Terry Sullivan

COUNTY COMMISSIONERS: Hugh Barrow; Jerold Dean; D. K. Bodiford; Wendell Byrd; Leonard Millender

POPULATION: 14,089

MUNICIPALITIES WITHIN: Castleberry; Evergreen; Repton

COOSA

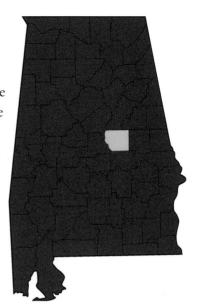

Coosa County was created by the Alabama Legislature on December 18, 1832, from lands included in the Creek Indian Treaty of Cusseta, March 24, 1832. Coosa County lies in the east-central part of the state. It is bordered by Shelby, Talladega, Clay, Tallapoosa, Elmore, and Chilton counties. It currently comprises 666 square miles. The county was named for the Coosa River, which forms its western boundary. The word "Coosa" is believed to mean "cane-brake" in the Alibama-Kossati Indian dialect. A site on Albert Crumpler's plantation on Hatchemalega Creek was chosen as the county seat and given the name Lexington. In 1835 the name was changed to Rockford.

COURTHOUSE: Main Street, Rockford, AL 35136; (256) 377-2420

PROBATE JUDGE: Terry Mitchell (D)

SHERIFF: Terry Wilson (R)

CIRCUIT CLERK: Jeff Wood (D)

DISTRICT ATTORNEY: Fred Thompson

REVENUE COMMISSIONER: Charles Luker (D)

COUNTY COMMISSIONERS: Randall Dunham; Corey Thomas; Unzell Kelley; Anthony Thornton; Todd Adams

POPULATION: 11,044

MUNICIPALITIES WITHIN: Goodwater; Kellyton; Rockford

COVINGTON

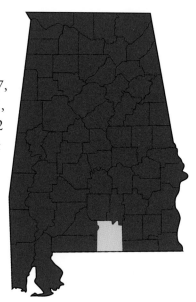

Covington County was created on December 17, 1821. Its boundaries were rearranged in 1824, 1841, and 1868. It was named in honor of War of 1812 hero General Leonard Wailes Covington. In August 1868 the name was changed to Jones County, but the original name was restored in October 1868. The county occupies 1,038 square miles in the south-central part of the state, bordering Florida. The county seat was first established at Montezuma, later named Covington, but flooding and a yellow fever epidemic in 1841 forced the settlers to move the county seat to the highest ground in the vicinity, the present city square of Andalusia. The town was called "New Site" until 1846, when a post office was established and the name was changed to Andalusia. The southwestern portion of the county contains the Conecuh National Forest.

COURTHOUSE: 1 Court Square, Andalusia, AL 36420; (334) 428-2513

PROBATE JUDGE: Benjamin M. Bowden (R)

SHERIFF: Dennis Meeks (D)

CIRCUIT CLERK: Roger Powell (D)

DISTRICT ATTORNEY: Gregory Gambril

REVENUE COMMISSIONER: Janice Hart

COUNTY COMMISSIONERS: Kent Colquett; Bragg Carter; Harold Elmore; Carl Turman; Greg White

POPULATION: 37,234

MUNICIPALITIES WITHIN: Andalusia; Babbie; Carolina; Florala; Gantt; Heath; Horn Hill; Libertyville; Lockhart; Onycha; Opp; Red Level; River Falls; Sanford

FOR MORE INFORMATION: www.covingtoncountyal.org

CRENSHAW

Crenshaw County was created by an act of the Alabama General Assembly on November 30, 1866. It was formed from parts of Butler, Coffee, Covington, Pike, and Lowndes counties. It is located in the south-central section of the state, in the coastal plain area. Crenshaw County encompasses 611 square miles. The county was named for Anderson Crenshaw, an early settler of Butler County. The county seat was established in Rutledge in 1867 and was moved to Luverne in 1893.

COURTHOUSE: 29 South Glenwood Avenue, Luverne, AL 36049; (334) 335-6568

PROBATE JUDGE: James Purdue (D)

SHERIFF: Charles West (D)

CIRCUIT CLERK: Jeannie Gibson (D)

DISTRICT ATTORNEY: John Andrews

REVENUE COMMISSIONER: Sherry McSwean

COUNTY COMMISSIONERS: Ricky McElwain; Ronnie Blackmon; Ed Beasley; Ronnie Hudson; Charlie Sankey

POPULATION: 13,665

MUNICIPALITIES WITHIN: Brantley; Dozier; Glenwood; Luverne; Petrey; Rutledge

CULLMAN

Cullman County was created by the Alabama Legislature on January 24, 1877, from portions of Blount, Morgan, and Winston counties. Cullman County lies in the north-central part of the state and is bordered by Morgan, Marshall, Blount, Walker, and Winston counties. It encompasses 755 square miles. The county was named after John G. Cullmann, a native of Germany who encouraged the immigration of Germans to northern Alabama. The county seat is Cullman.

COURTHOUSE: 500 2nd Avenue SW, Cullman, AL 35055; (256) 775-4665

PROBATE JUDGE: Leah Patterson-Lust (D)

SHERIFF: J. Tyler Roden (D)

CIRCUIT CLERK: Robert Bates (D)

DISTRICT ATTORNEY: C. Wilson Blaylock

REVENUE COMMISSIONER: Kay D. Williams-Smith

COUNTY COMMISSIONERS: Doug Williams; Wayne Willingham; Wiley Kitchens

POPULATION: 77,483

MUNICIPALITIES WITHIN: Baileyton; Colony; Cullman; Dodge City; Fairview; Garden City; Good Hope; Hanceville; Holly Pond; South Vinemont; West Point

FOR MORE INFORMATION: www.co.cullman.al.us

DALE

Dale County was created by the Alabama Legislature on December 22, 1824, from land ceded by the Creek Nation in the Treaty of Fort Jackson of 1814. Dale County is located in the southeastern part of the state, wholly within the coastal plain. It is bordered by Pike, Barbour, Henry, Houston, Geneva, and Coffee counties. It encompasses 563 square miles. The county was named for General Sam Dale, pioneer and Indian fighter. Originally, the county seat was located at Dale Court House, which later became Daleville. An election in 1870 resulted in the removal of the county seat to Ozark. Fort Rucker, located in Dale County, is the primary flight training base for U.S. Army Aviation.

COURTHOUSE: 1702 Highway 123 South, Suite C, Ozark, AL 36360; (334) 774-6262

PROBATE JUDGE: Eunice Hagler (D)

SHERIFF: Wally Olson (R)

CIRCUIT CLERK: Mary Bludsworth (D)

DISTRICT ATTORNEY: Kirke Adams

REVENUE COMMISSIONER: Tommy Lavender

COUNTY COMMISSIONERS: Doug Williamson; Glenn Grantham; Gerald Harden; Kurt McDaniel

POPULATION: 49,129

MUNICIPALITIES WITHIN: Ariton; Clayhatchee; Daleville; Grimes; Level Plains; Midland City; Napier Field; Newton; Ozark; Pinckard

DALLAS

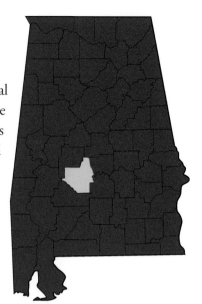

Dallas County was created by the Alabama Territorial Legislature on February 9, 1818, from portions of the Creek cession of August 9, 1814. Dallas County is located in the Black Belt region of the west-central portion of the state, and is traversed by the Alabama River. Dallas is bordered by Perry, Chilton, Autauga, Lowndes, Wilcox, and Marengo counties. It encompasses 993 square miles. The county was named for Alexander J. Dallas of Pennsylvania, U.S. Treasury Secretary. Originally, the county seat was at Cahaba, which also served as the state capital for a brief period. In 1865 the county seat was transferred to Selma.

COURTHOUSE: 105 Lauderdale Street, Selma, AL 36702; (334) 876-4830

PROBATE JUDGE: Kim Ballard (D)

SHERIFF: Harris Huffman Jr. (D)

CIRCUIT CLERK: Cheryl Curtis-Strong (D)

DISTRICT ATTORNEY: Michael Jackson

TAX ASSESSOR: Frances Hughes

COUNTY COMMISSIONERS: Connell Towns; Roy Moore; Curtis Williams; Clifford Hunter

POPULATION: 43,945

MUNICIPALITIES WITHIN: Orrville; Selma; Valley Grande

DeKalb

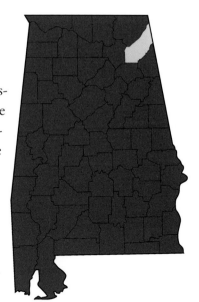

DeKalb County was created by the Alabama Legislature on January 9, 1836, from land ceded to the federal government by the Cherokee Nation. Willstown, later Fort Payne, was, for a time, the home of Sequoyah, who invented the Cherokee syllabary. The county is located in the northeast corner of the state and is bordered by Jackson, Marshall, Etowah, and Cherokee counties and Georgia. It encompasses 778 square miles. The county was named for Major General Johann, Baron de Kalb, a hero of the American Revolution. Its county seat is Fort Payne,

COURTHOUSE: 300 Grand Avenue SW, Ft. Payne, AL 35967; (256) 845-8510

PROBATE JUDGE: Ronnie Osborn (R)

SHERIFF: Jimmy Harris (D)

CIRCUIT CLERK: Pam Bailey Simpson (D)

DISTRICT ATTORNEY: Mike O'Dell

REVENUE COMMISSIONER: Martha Crye Ogle

COUNTY COMMISSIONERS: Ricky Harcrow; Ed Nix; Brant Craig; Dewitt Jackson; Sid Holcomb

POPULATION: 64,452

MUNICIPALITIES WITHIN: Crossville; Fort Payne; Fyffe; Geraldine; Hammondville; Henagar; Ider; Lakeview; Mentone; Pine Ridge; Powell; Rainsville; Shiloh; Sylvania; Valley Head

FOR MORE INFORMATION: www.dekalbcountyal.us

ELMORE

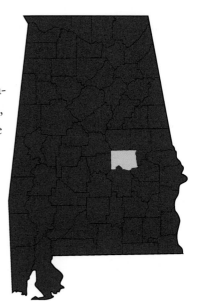

Elmore County was created by the Alabama Legislature on Feb. 15, 1866, from parts of Autauga, Coosa, Montgomery, and Tallapoosa counties. It lies in the east-central part of the state and is drained by the Coosa and Tallapoosa rivers, which merge to form the Alabama River a few miles south of Wetumpka, the county seat. It encompasses 622 square miles. The county is named for General John Archer Elmore, a veteran of the American Revolution and early settler of Alabama. The French established Fort Toulouse at the confluence of the Coosa and Tallapoosa in 1717, upon which General Andrew Jackson erected Fort Jackson in 1814, following the Battle of Horseshoe Bend.

COURTHOUSE: 100 East Commerce Street, Wetumpka, AL 36092; (334) 567-1144

PROBATE JUDGE: Jimmy Stubbs (D)

SHERIFF: Bill Franklin (R)

CIRCUIT CLERK: Larry Dozier (R)

DISTRICT ATTORNEY: Randall Houston

REVENUE COMMISSIONER: William M. Harper

COUNTY COMMISSIONERS: T. J. Eason; Mickey Shaw; Don Whorton; Joe Faulk; Earl Reeves

POPULATION: 75,688

MUNICIPALITIES WITHIN: Coosada; Deatsville; Eclectic; Elmore; Millbrook; Wetumpka

FOR MORE INFORMATION: www.elmoreco.org

ESCAMBIA

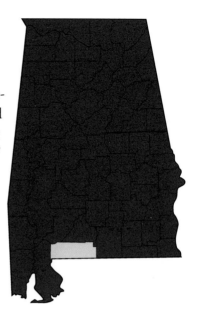

Escambia County was created by the Alabama Legislature on Dec. 10, 1868, from parts of Baldwin and Conecuh counties. It is located in the southern part of the state and lies on the northern boundary of Florida. It is also bordered by Monroe, Conecuh, Covington, and Baldwin counties and encompasses 953 square miles. The county name is derived from the Escambia River, which runs through it. The Creek Indians called the river "Shambia," meaning clearwater. The county seat was originally located at Pollard; in 1880 it was transferred to Brewton, originally named Newport. Brewton was named in honor of Edmund Troupe Brewton, a great-nephew of the first settler of the area and station agent of the town's railroad depot.

COURTHOUSE: 314 Belleville Avenue, Brewton, AL 36427; (251) 867-0297

PROBATE JUDGE: Emille Mims (R)

SHERIFF: Grover Smith (D)

CIRCUIT CLERK: James Kenneth Taylor (D)

DISTRICT ATTORNEY: Stephen Billy

TAX ASSESSOR: Jim Hildreth

COUNTY COMMISSIONERS: David Stokes; Todd Williamson; Larry White; William H. Brown; Wiley Tait

POPULATION: 37,849

MUNICIPALITIES WITHIN: Atmore; Brewton; East Brewton; Flomaton; Pollard; Riverview

FOR MORE INFORMATION: www.co.escambia.al.us

ETOWAH

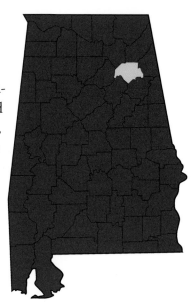

Etowah County was created by the Alabama Legislature on December 7, 1866, and was originally named Baine County in honor of General David W. Baine, a Confederate soldier from Lowndes County. The county was abolished on December 1, 1868, by the constitutional convention, and re-established on the same day, under the name of Etowah—a Cherokee Indian name. Etowah County is located in the northeastern section of the state, in the southern Appalachians. It is bordered by Marshall, DeKalb, Cherokee, Calhoun, St. Clair, and Blount counties. It encompasses 542 square miles. Sand Mountain and part of Lookout Mountain are located in Etowah County. Gadsden is the county seat, named after Colonel James Gadsden, distinguished soldier, diplomat, and railroad president.

COURTHOUSE: 800 Forrest Avenue, Gadsden, AL 35901; (256) 549-5342

PROBATE JUDGE: Bobby Junkins (D)

SHERIFF: Todd Entrekin (D)

CIRCUIT CLERK: Billy Yates (D)

DISTRICT ATTORNEY: Jimmie Harp Jr.

REVENUE COMMISSIONER: Judy Pitts

COUNTY COMMISSIONERS: Jimmy McKee; Perry Gwin; Larry Payne; Jeff Overstreet; Willie Brown; Tim Choate

POPULATION: 103,362

MUNICIPALITIES WITHIN: Altoona; Attalla; Gadsden; Glencoe; Hokes Bluff; Mountainboro; Rainbow City; Reece City; Ridgeville; Sardis City; Southside; Walnut Grove

FOR MORE INFORMATION: www.etowahcounty.org

FAYETTE

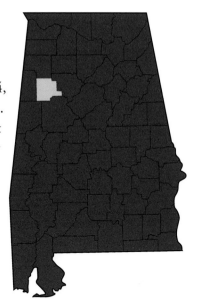

Fayette County was created on December 20, 1824, from portions of Tuscaloosa and Marion counties. It encompasses 629 square miles in the northwest central section of the state. The county was named for Gilbert du Motier, Marquis de la Fayette, the French general and hero of the American Revolution, who was touring the nation at the time of the county's formation. The county seat is also named Fayette.

COURTHOUSE: 103 1st Avenue NE, Fayette, AL 35555; (205) 932-4510

PROBATE JUDGE: William Oswalt (D)

SHERIFF: Rodney Ingel (D)

CIRCUIT CLERK: J. Eddy Smith (D)

DISTRICT ATTORNEY: J. Christopher "Chris" McCool

REVENUE COMMISSIONER: Ruby Porter

COUNTY COMMISSIONERS: Charlie Jones; Mark Atkinson; Gorman "Nicky" Whitehead; RoDolphus "Sonny" Cotton; Mark Duckworth; John Underwood

POPULATION: 18,005

MUNICIPALITIES WITHIN: Belk; Berry; Fayette

FRANKLIN

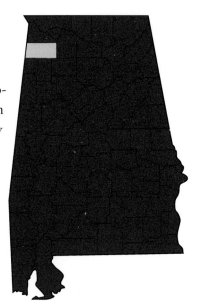

Franklin County was created by the Alabama Territorial Legislature on February 6, 1818. It is situated in the northwestern part of the state and is bordered by Colbert, Lawrence, Winston, and Marion counties and Mississippi. It encompasses 643 square miles. The county was named in honor of Benjamin Franklin. The county seat was originally located at Russellville, named after William Russell, an early settler and chief scout for General Andrew Jackson during the Creek Indian War of 1813–14. In 1849 the county seat was transferred to Frankfort, where it remained until 1879 when it was moved to Belgreen. A courthouse fire in 1890 probably accounted for the return of the county seat to Russellville in 1891.

COURTHOUSE: 410 North Jefferson Avenue, Russellville, AL 35653; (256) 332-8801

PROBATE JUDGE: Barry Moore (R)

SHERIFF: Larry Plott (D)

CIRCUIT CLERK: Anita Morgan Scott (D)

DISTRICT ATTORNEY: Joseph Rushing III

REVENUE COMMISSIONER: Don Garrard

COUNTY COMMISSIONERS: Jackie Bradford; Gene Graham; Rayburn Massey; Norris Lewey

POPULATION: 30,847

MUNICIPALITIES WITHIN: Hodges; Phil Campbell; Red Bay; Russellville; Vina

Geneva

Geneva County was created by the Alabama Legislature on December 26, 1868. Geneva County is located in southeastern Alabama and is drained by the Choctawhatchee River. It is bordered by Coffee, Covington, Dale, and Houston counties and Florida. It encompasses 579 square miles. The county was named for Geneva, its principal town and county seat. The town of Geneva was named for Geneva, Switzerland, by Henry Yonge, a native of Switzerland who served as an early postmaster in the town.

Courthouse: 200 North Commerce Street, Geneva, AL 36340; (334) 684-2276

Probate Judge: Fred Hamic (R)

Sheriff: Greg Ward (D)

Circuit Clerk: Gale Laye (R)

District Attorney: Kirke Adams

Revenue Commissioner: Dean Shields

County Commissioners: Larry Everett; Gary Shields; Ray Minshew; Dennis Finch

Population: 25,868

Municipalities within: Black; Coffee Springs; Geneva; Hartford; Malvern; Samson; Slocomb

For more information: www.genevacounty.net

GREENE

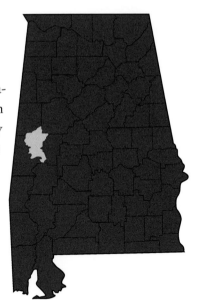

Greene County was created by the Alabama Legislature in its first session on December 13, 1819, from part of the land ceded to the federal government by the Choctaw Cession of October 24, 1816. Greene County is located in the west-central portion of the state, between the Tombigbee and Black Warrior rivers. It is bordered by Pickens, Tuscaloosa, Hale, Marengo, and Sumter counties. It encompasses 631 square miles. The county was named in honor of General Nathanael Greene, a hero of the American Revolution. The first county seat was located at Erie, now in Hale County. In 1838 the county seat was transferred to Eutaw.

COURTHOUSE: 400 Morrow Avenue, Eutaw, AL 35462; (205) 372-3340

PROBATE JUDGE: Earlean Isaac (D)

SHERIFF: Ison Thomas (D)

CIRCUIT CLERK: Etta Edwards (D)

DISTRICT ATTORNEY: Greg Griggers

REVENUE COMMISSIONER: Brenda J. Goree

COUNTY COMMISSIONERS: Nick Underwood; Tennyson Smith; Donald Means; William Johnson; Marvin Childs

POPULATION: 9,574

MUNICIPALITIES WITHIN: Boligee; Eutaw; Forkland; Union

HALE

Hale County was created by the Alabama Legislature on January 30, 1867. Hale County is located in the west-central section of the state and is drained by the Black Warrior River. Hale County is bordered by Tuscaloosa, Bibb, Perry, Marengo, and Greene counties. It encompasses 656 square miles. The county was named for Lieutenant Colonel Stephen Fowler Hale, a Confederate officer killed at Gaines' Mill, Virginia. An important site of the Mississippian Indian culture, Moundville, is located in Hale County. The county seat is Greensboro.

COURTHOUSE: 1001 Main Street, Greensboro, AL 36744; (334) 624-8740

PROBATE JUDGE: Leland Avery (D)

SHERIFF: Kenneth Ellis (D)

CIRCUIT CLERK: Catrinna Long Perry (D)

DISTRICT ATTORNEY: Michael Jackson

TAX ASSESSOR: Juliaette Tubbs

COUNTY COMMISSIONERS: Fred McNeill; Elijah Knox; Joe Lee Hamilton; Joe Kyser

POPULATION: 17,185

MUNICIPALITIES WITHIN: Akron; Greensboro; Newbern

HENRY

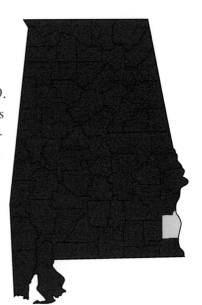

Henry County was created on December 13, 1819. Known as "The Mother County" of the Wiregrass region, Henry County was vast in size until its boundaries were reduced by the establishment of Pike and Covington counties in 1821, Dale County in 1824, Barbour County in 1832, and Houston County in 1903. Henry County is located in the southeastern corner of the state, bounded to the east by Georgia and the Chattahoochee River. It encompasses 557 square miles. The county was named for Revolutionary War patriot Patrick Henry. The county seat is Abbeville.

COURTHOUSE: 101 Court Square, Abbeville, AL 36310; (334) 585-3257

PROBATE JUDGE: Jo Anne Smith (D)

SHERIFF: Will Maddox (D)

CIRCUIT CLERK: Shirlene Vickers (D)

DISTRICT ATTORNEY: Douglas Valeska

REVENUE COMMISSIONER: Kristie Allums

COUNTY COMMISSIONERS: Franklin Swann; Billy Barnes; Kip Platt; Roger Scott; Tommy Jones

POPULATION: 16,706

MUNICIPALITIES WITHIN: Abbeville; Haleburg; Headland; Newville

HOUSTON

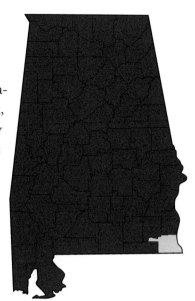

Houston County was created by the Alabama Legislature on February 9, 1903, from parts of Dale, Geneva, and Henry counties. It is Alabama's youngest county and encompasses 578 square miles. The county was named in honor of Alabama Governor George Smith Houston. Houston County lies in the extreme southeastern corner of the state, in the Wiregrass region, and borders Georgia on the east and Florida to the south. The county seat is Dothan, which was known as Poplar Head prior to 1871. Houston County is home to the National Peanut Festival.

COURTHOUSE: 462 North Oates Street, Dothan, AL 36302; (334) 677-4729

PROBATE JUDGE: Luke Cooley (R)

SHERIFF: Andy Hughes (R)

CIRCUIT CLERK: Carla Woodall (R)

DISTRICT ATTORNEY: Douglas "Doug" Valeska

REVENUE COMMISSIONER: Starla M. Matthews

COUNTY COMMISSIONERS: Curtis Harvey; Bobby Snellgrove; Frances Cook; Phillip Forrester; Mark Culver

POPULATION: 97,171

MUNICIPALITIES WITHIN: Ashford; Avon; Columbia; Cottonwood; Cowarts; Dothan; Gordon; Kinsey; Madrid; Rehobeth; Taylor; Webb

FOR MORE INFORMATION: www.houstoncounty.org

JACKSON

Jackson County was created by the Alabama Legislature on December 13, 1819, from land acquired from the Cherokee Indians. Jackson County is located in the northeastern corner of the state. It is bordered by DeKalb, Marshall, and Madison counties and Tennessee and Georgia. It encompasses 1,127 square miles. Jackson County is home to Russell Cave, which was continually used by Indians from the Archaic into the Mississippian periods. The county was named in honor of General Andrew Jackson. Most of the county is drained by the Tennessee River. The act establishing Jackson County designated Sauta Cave as a temporary seat of justice. Bellefonte was the county seat from 1821 until 1859, at which time it was transferred to Scottsboro, which was named for Robert T. Scott, an early settler from North Carolina.

COURTHOUSE: 102 East Laurel Street, Scottsboro, AL 35768; (256) 574-9290

PROBATE JUDGE: Floyd Hambrick Jr. (D)

SHERIFF: Dennis Miller (D)

CIRCUIT CLERK: Ken Ferrell (D)

DISTRICT ATTORNEY: Charles Rhodes

REVENUE COMMISSIONER: Ron Crawford

COUNTY COMMISSIONERS: Jack Allen; Carl Marona; James Darren Blizard; Glenda Hodges; James Tidmore

POPULATION: 53,926

MUNICIPALITIES WITHIN: Bridgeport; Dutton; Hollywood; Hytop; Langston; Paint Rock; Pisgah; Pleasant Groves; Scottsboro; Section; Skyline; Stevenson; Woodville

FOR MORE INFORMATION: www.jacksoncountyal.com

Jefferson

Jefferson County was created by the Alabama Legislature on December 13, 1819. The county is located in the north-central portion of the state, on the southern extension of the Appalachians, in the center of the iron, coal, and limestone belt of the South. Jefferson County is bordered by Blount, Bibb, St. Clair, Shelby, Tuscaloosa, and Walker counties. It encompasses 1,119 square miles. The county was named in honor of Thomas Jefferson. The county seat was at Carrollsville in 1819-21, Elyton in 1821-73, and since 1873 has been at Birmingham, which was named for England's iron and steel center. There are two courthouses, one in Birmingham and one in Bessemer.

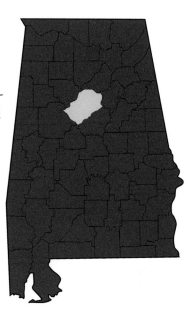

Courthouse: 716 Richard Arrington Jr. Boulevard North, Birmingham, AL 35263; (205) 325-5203; Bessemer Annex Courthouse; 1801 3rd Avenue North, Room 101, Bessemer, AL 35020; (205) 481-4100

Probate Judge: Alan King (D) (in Birmingham, Place 1); Sherri Friday (in Birmingham, Place 2); Deputy Probate Judge: Cynthia Vines Butler (D) (in Bessemer)

Sheriff: Michael Hale (R)

Circuit Clerk: Anne-Marie Adams (D); Earl Carter Jr. (D) (in Bessemer)

District Attorney: Brandon Falls; M. David Barber (in Bessemer)

Tax Assessor: Gaynell Hendricks (in Birmingham); Assistant Tax Assessor: Andrew Bennett (in Bessermer)

County Commissioners: William Bell Sr.; Shelia Smoot; Bobby Humphryes; Bettye Fine Collins; Jim Carns

Population: 662,047

Municipalities within: Adamsville; Argo; Bessemer; Brighton; Brookside; Cardiff; Center Point; Clay; Fairfield; Fultondale; Gardendale; Graysville; Homewood; Hueytown; Irondale; Kimberly; Lipscomb; Maytown; Morris; Mountain Brook; Mulga; North Johns; Pinson; Pleasant Grove; Sylvan Springs; Tarrant; Trafford; Warrior; West Jefferson

For more information: www.jeffcointouch.com

LAMAR

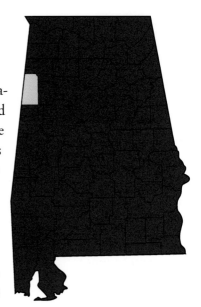

Lamar County was created by the Alabama Legislature on February 4, 1867, and was originally named Jones County after E. P. Jones, a resident of Fayette County. On November 13, 1867, the county was abolished. On October 8, 1868, the county was re-created under the name of Sanford County, honoring H. C. Sanford of Cherokee County. On February 8, 1877, the name was changed to Lamar in honor of Senator L. Q. C. Lamar of Mississippi. Lamar County is bordered by Marion, Fayette, and Pickens counties and Mississippi. It encompasses 605 square miles. The county is drained by the Tombigbee River. In 1866 the community known as Swayne Courthouse, named for General Wager Swayne, military governor of the state, was designated as the county seat. In 1868 the name was changed to Vernon, after Edmund Vernon, an immigrant from Vernon, England.

COURTHOUSE: 44690 Highway 17, Vernon, AL 35592; (205) 695-7333
PROBATE JUDGE: Johnny Rogers (D)
SHERIFF: Terry Perkins (D)
CIRCUIT CLERK: Mary Ann Jones (D)
DISTRICT ATTORNEY: J. Christopher "Chris" McCool
REVENUE COMMISSIONER: Donna Holsonback
COUNTY COMMISSIONERS: Greg Norton; Dewey Carruth; Terry Roberts; Gary Beard
POPULATION: 15,904
MUNICIPALITIES WITHIN: Beaverton; Detroit; Millport; Sulligent; Vernon

Lauderdale

Lauderdale County was created by the Alabama Territorial Legislature on February 6, 1818. It is located in the northwestern corner of the state. The Tennessee River forms the county's southern boundary. It encompasses 661 square miles. The county was named for Colonel James Lauderdale, a Tennessean killed at the Battle of New Orleans. Since Lauderdale County's creation, the county seat has been at Florence, named by the city's architect and engineer, Ferdinand Sannoner, for his home, Florence, Italy.

Courthouse: 200 South Court Street, Florence, AL 35631; (256) 760-5804

Probate Judge: Dewey Mitchell (D)

Sheriff: Ronnie Willis (D)

Circuit Clerk: Missy Horman Hibbett (D)

District Attorney: Christopher Connolly

Revenue Commissioner: Danny Hendrix

County Commissioners: William Smith; D. C. Thornton; Larry Irons; Ronnie Brown

Population: 87,891

Municipalities within: Anderson; Florence; Killen; Lexington; Rogersville; Saint Florian; Waterloo

For more information: lauderdalecountyonline.com

LAWRENCE

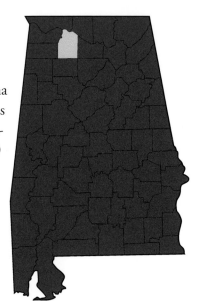

Lawrence County was created by an act of the Alabama Territorial Legislature on February 6, 1818. It was formed from former Cherokee Indian land. It encompasses 718 square miles, of which more than 100,000 acres is included in the Bankhead National Forest. The county is named for Captain James Lawrence, a naval hero of the War of 1812. It is located in the northwestern part of the state and is bounded on the north by the Tennessee River. The county seat is Moulton, named for Lt. Michael Moulton, a hero of the Creek War of 1813–14.

COURTHOUSE: 14330 Court Street, Moulton, AL 35650; (256) 974-0063

PROBATE JUDGE: Mike Praytor (D)

SHERIFF: Gene Mitchell (D)

CIRCUIT CLERK: Harce Hill (D)

DISTRICT ATTORNEY: Jim Osborn

REVENUE COMMISSIONER: Tommy Praytor

COUNTY COMMISSIONERS: Mose Jones Jr.; John Terry; Bradley Cross; Harold LouAllen; Alma Whitlow

POPULATION: 34,321

MUNICIPALITIES WITHIN: Courtland; Hillsboro; Moulton; North Courtland; Town Creek

LEE

Lee County was created by the Alabama Legislature on December 5, 1866. It is bordered by Chambers, Tallapoosa, Macon, and Russell counties, and on the east by the Chattahoochee River and Georgia. It encompasses 609 square miles. The county was named for Confederate general Robert E. Lee. The county seat is located at Opelika, which means "big swamp" in the Creek Indian language. Auburn University is located in nearby Auburn, the county's largest city.

COURTHOUSE: 215 South 9th Street, Opelika, AL 36803; (334) 745-9761

PROBATE JUDGE: Bill English (R)

SHERIFF: Jay Jones (R)

CIRCUIT CLERK: Corrine Hurst (R)

DISTRICT ATTORNEY: Nick Abbett

REVENUE COMMISSIONER: Oline W. Price

COUNTY COMMISSIONERS: Mathan Holt; Johnny Lawrence; Harry Ennis; Annell Smith; John Andrew Harris

POPULATION: 125,781

MUNICIPALITIES WITHIN: Auburn; Loachapoka; Opelika; Smiths Station

FOR MORE INFORMATION: www.leeco.us

LIMESTONE

Limestone County was created by an act of the Alabama Territorial Legislature on February 6, 1818. The county was formed from land comprising Elk County, which was created on May 24, 1817, and is no longer extant. Limestone County received additional land from Lauderdale County in 1821. Limestone County is bordered by Lauderdale, Lawrence, Morgan, and Madison counties and Tennessee. It encompasses 559 square miles. The name of the county comes from a stream which flows through it in a creek bed of hard limestone. Athens, named for the Greek city, is the county seat.

COURTHOUSE: 310 Washington Street, Athens, AL 35611; (256) 233-6427

PROBATE JUDGE: Michael Davis (D)

SHERIFF: Mike Blakely (D)

CIRCUIT CLERK: Charles Page Jr. (D)

DISTRICT ATTORNEY: Kristi Valls

REVENUE COMMISSIONER: G. Brian Patterson

COUNTY COMMISSIONERS: Gary Daly; Gerald Barksdale; Bill Latimer; Bill Daws; David Seibert

POPULATION: 72,446

MUNICIPALITIES WITHIN: Ardmore; Athens; Elkmont; Lester; Mooresville

FOR MORE INFORMATION: www.limestonecounty.net

LOWNDES

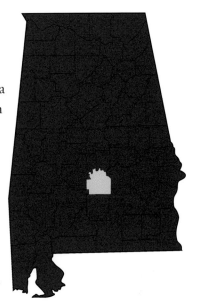

Lowndes County was created by an act of the Alabama Legislature on January 20, 1830. It was formed from parts of Montgomery, Dallas, and Butler counties. Lowndes County is located in the south-central portion of the state, in the Black Belt. It encompasses 714 square miles. The county is named for South Carolina statesman William Lowndes. Hayneville, named for South Carolina Senator Robert Hayne, is the county seat. The county is home to the National Parks Service's Lowndes County Interpretive Center in Hayneville, which is dedicated to the memory of the protesters of the Selma to Montgomery March in March 1965.

COURTHOUSE: Tuskeena Street, Hayneville, AL 36040; (334) 548-2331

PROBATE JUDGE: John Hulett (D)

SHERIFF: Chip Williams (D)

CIRCUIT CLERK: Ruby Jones (D)

DISTRICT ATTORNEY: John Andrews

TAX ASSESSOR: Willie Ruth Myrick

COUNTY COMMISSIONERS: Robert Harris; Charlie King; Marzett Thomas; Joey Barganier; W. Dickson Farrior

POPULATION: 13,473

MUNICIPALITIES WITHIN: Benton; Fort Deposit; Gordonville; Hayneville; Lowndesboro; Mosses; White Hall

MACON

Macon County was created by the Alabama Legislature on December 18, 1832, from territory acquired
from the last cession of the Creek Indians, March
24, 1832. Its present boundaries were fixed in 1866.
It is located in the east-central portion of the state
and is bordered by Elmore, Tallapoosa, Lee, Russell,
Bullock, and Montgomery counties. It encompasses
614 square miles. Macon County was named for
Nathaniel Macon, a distinguished soldier and statesman from North Carolina. The county seat is located
at Tuskegee, which means "warrior" in the
Muscogeen dialect of the Creek Indian language.
Tuskegee is also the site of Tuskegee University. The Tuskegee National Forest is located in Macon County.

COURTHOUSE: 101 East Northside Street, Tuskegee, AL 36083; (334) 727-5120

PROBATE JUDGE: Alfonza Menefee (D)

SHERIFF: David Warren (D)

CIRCUIT CLERK: David Love (D)

DISTRICT ATTORNEY: E. Paul Jones

REVENUE COMMISSIONER: Ed Corbitt

COUNTY COMMISSIONERS: Miles Robinson; Albert Daniels; Andrew Thompson;
    Tommy King; Jesse Upshaw

POPULATION: 22,594

MUNICIPALITIES WITHIN: Franklin; Shorter; Tuskegee

MADISON

Madison County was created by Mississippi Territory governor Robert Williams on December 13, 1808. Additional land was added until the county achieved its current boundaries in 1824. The county is located in the north-central part of the state, bounded to the north by Tennessee and to the south by the Tennessee River. It encompasses 806 square miles. Madison County was named for President James Madison. The first white settlers entered the area in 1804. The area was previously inhabited by Cherokee and Chickasaw Indians. Huntsville, the county seat, is named for its first settler, John Hunt. The county is the home of the Marshall Space Flight Center.

COURTHOUSE: 100 North Side Square, Huntsville, AL 35801; (256) 532-3330

PROBATE JUDGE: Tommy Ragland (D)

SHERIFF: Blake Dorning (R)

CIRCUIT CLERK: Jane Chandler Smith (D)

DISTRICT ATTORNEY: Tim Morgan

TAX ASSESSOR: Fran Hamilton

COUNTY COMMISSIONERS: Roger Jones; Faye Dyer; Jerry Craig; Dale Strong; Morris Brooks; Bob Harrison; Mike Gillespie

POPULATION: 304,307

MUNICIPALITIES WITHIN: Gurley; Huntsville; Madison; New Hope; Owens Cross Roads; Triana

FOR MORE INFORMATION: www.co.madison.al.us

MARENGO

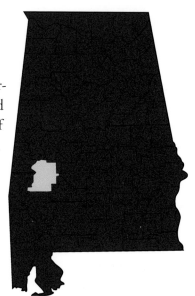

Marengo County was created by the Alabama Territorial Legislature on February 6, 1818, from land acquired from the Choctaw Indians by the treaty of October 24, 1816. It is situated in the west-central part of the state. It is bordered by Hale, Greene, Perry, Dallas, Wilcox, Clarke, Choctaw, and Sumter counties. It encompasses 982 square miles. The name of the county was suggested by Judge Abner Lipscomb, and was given as a compliment to the first white settlers, expatriated French soldiers who founded the Vine and Olive Colony. The name commemorates Napoleon's great victory at Marengo over the Austrian armies on June 14, 1800. The county seat was originally known as "Town of Marengo." In 1823 the name was changed to Linden, a shortened version of "Hohenlinden," site of a French victory in Bavaria in 1800. Demopolis, "city of the people," is the county's largest municipality.

COURTHOUSE: 101 East Coats Avenue, Linden, AL 36748-0715; (334) 295-2200
PROBATE JUDGE: Cindy Neilson (D)
SHERIFF: Jesse Langley (D)
CIRCUIT CLERK: Robert "Rusty" Nichols (D)
DISTRICT ATTORNEY: Greg Griggers
REVENUE COMMISSIONER: W. J. "Bo" McAlpine
COUNTY COMMISSIONERS: Freddie Armstead; Ken Tucker; John Crawford; Calvin Martin; Jerry Loftin
POPULATION: 21,842
MUNICIPALITIES WITHIN: Dayton; Demopolis; Faunsdale; Linden; Myrtlewood; Providence; Sweet Water; Thomaston

MARION

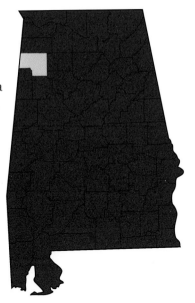

Marion County was created by an act of the Alabama Territorial Legislature on February 13, 1818. It is located in the northwestern part of the state, bounded on the west by Mississippi. It encompasses 744 square miles. Marion County was named for General Francis Marion of South Carolina. The county seat was established in 1820 and is named for Albert J. Hamilton, an early settler.

COURTHOUSE: 152 Military Street South, Hamilton, AL 35570; (205) 921-2471

PROBATE JUDGE: Judy Miller (D)

SHERIFF: Kevin Williams (D)

CIRCUIT CLERK: Sheila Silas Bozman (D)

DISTRICT ATTORNEY: John "Jack" Bostick

REVENUE COMMISSIONER: Janetta Garner

COUNTY COMMISSIONERS: Kenny Jackson; Eddie Byrd; Don Barnwell; Michael Davis; Bobby Burleson

POPULATION: 31,214

MUNICIPALITIES WITHIN: Bear Creek; Brilliant; Guin; Gu-Win; Hackleburg; Hamilton; Twin

FOR MORE INFORMATION: www.sonet.net/marioncounty

MARSHALL

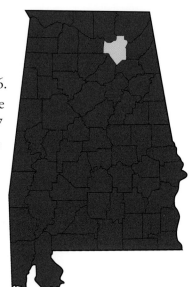

Marshall County was created on January 9, 1836. The county is located in the northeastern part of the state on the Appalachian ridge. It encompasses 567 square miles. The Tennessee River cuts through the northern part of the county, creating Guntersville Lake. Marshall County was named to honor Chief Justice John Marshall. The county seat was established in 1836 at Claysville, moved to Marshall in 1838, to Warrenton in 1841, and was finally located at Guntersville in 1848.

COURTHOUSE: 425 Gunter Avenue, Guntersville, AL 35976; (256) 571-7764

PROBATE JUDGE: Tim Mitchell (D)

SHERIFF: Scott Walls (D)

CIRCUIT CLERK: Cheryl Pierce (R)

DISTRICT ATTORNEY: Steve Marshall

REVENUE COMMISSIONER: Joey Masters

COUNTY COMMISSIONERS: Bill Stricklend; R.E. Martin; C. W. "Buddy" Allen; Tim Bollinger; Doug Fleming

POPULATION: 87,185

MUNICIPALITIES WITHIN: Albertville; Arab; Douglas; Grant; Guntersville; Union Grove

FOR MORE INFORMATION: www.marshallco.org

Mobile

Mobile County was created by proclamation of Governor David Holmes of the Mississippi Territory on December 18, 1812. The area was occupied by the French in 1702–63, the British in 1763–80, and the Spanish in 1780–1812. Mobile County is located in the southwestern corner of the state and is bordered by Mississippi, Washington, and Baldwin counties, Mobile Bay, and the Gulf of Mexico. It encompasses 1,238 square miles. Mobile County derives its name from a tribe of Indians the French encountered living in the area around Mobile Bay in 1702.

COURTHOUSE: 205 Government Street, Mobile, AL 36633; (251) 574-8540

PROBATE JUDGE: Don Davis (R)

SHERIFF: Sam Cochran (R)

CIRCUIT CLERK: JoJo Schwarzauer (R)

DISTRICT ATTORNEY: John Tyson Jr.

REVENUE COMMISSIONER: Marilyn E. Wood

COUNTY COMMISSIONERS: Merceria Ludgood; Stephen Nodine; Mike Dean

POPULATION: 404,157

MUNICIPALITIES WITHIN: Bayou La Batre; Chickasaw; Citronelle; Creola; Mobile; Mount Vernon; Prichard; Saraland; Satsuma

FOR MORE INFORMATION: www.mobilecountyal.gov

MONROE

Monroe County was created by the Mississippi territorial governor David Holmes on June 29, 1815. It was comprised of Creek Indian lands ceded by the Treaty of Fort Jackson. It was reduced in size by the creation of Montgomery, Conecuh, and Wilcox counties. Monroe County is located in the southwestern area of the state, in the Piney Woods region. It encompasses 1,019 square miles. Monroe County was named for U.S. President James Monroe. The first county seat was established at Fort Clairborne; it was moved to Monroeville in 1832. Monroeville is the home of Harper Lee, author of *To Kill a Mockingbird*.

COURTHOUSE: Courthouse Square, Monroeville, AL 36461; (251) 743-4107

PROBATE JUDGE: Greg Norris (D)

SHERIFF: Thomas Tate (D)

CIRCUIT CLERK: John Sawyer (D)

DISTRICT ATTORNEY: Tommy Chapman

REVENUE COMMISSIONER: Fonde Melton

COUNTY COMMISSIONERS: Jeral Jordan; Tim McKenzie; Billy Ghee; Charlie McCorvey Jr.

POPULATION: 24,342

MUNICIPALITIES WITHIN: Beatrice; Excel; Frisco City; Monroeville

FOR MORE INFORMATION: www.monroecountyal.com

MONTGOMERY

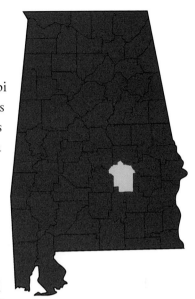

Montgomery County was created by the Mississippi Territorial Legislature on December 6, 1816. It is located in the south-central part of the state and is bounded on the north by the Alabama and Tallapoosa rivers. It encompasses 793 square miles. Montgomery County was named in honor of Major Lemuel Putnam Montgomery of Tennessee, who was killed in the Battle of Horseshoe Bend, 1814. The county seat, also named Montgomery, is the state capital and was briefly the capital of the Confederacy in 1861. The city of Montgomery was named after General Richard Montgomery, who died in the Battle of Quebec during the American Revolution.

COURTHOUSE: 100 South Lawrence Street, Montgomery, AL 36101-0223; (334) 832-1240

PROBATE JUDGE: Reese McKinney Jr. (R)

SHERIFF: D. T. Marshall (D)

CIRCUIT CLERK: Melissa Rittenour (D)

DISTRICT ATTORNEY: Ellen Brooks

REVENUE COMMISSIONER: Sarah G. Spear

COUNTY COMMISSIONERS: Vacant; Elton Dean Sr.; Dimitri Polizos; Jiles Williams Jr.; Reed Ingram

POPULATION: 223,571

MUNICIPALITIES WITHIN: Montgomery; Pike Road

FOR MORE INFORMATION: www.mc-ala.org

MORGAN

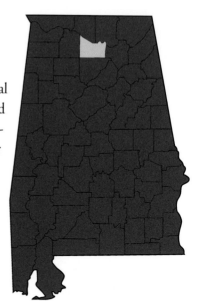

Morgan County was created by the Alabama Territorial Legislature on February 8, 1818, from land acquired from the Cherokee Indians by the Treaty of Turkeytown. The county was originally named Cotaco for a creek that flows through it. On June 14, 1821, the name was changed to Morgan, in honor of General Daniel Morgan of Virginia, a hero of the American Revolution. Morgan County lies in the northern section of the state, on the Tennessee River. It is bordered by Limestone, Madison, Marshall, Cullman, Winston, and Lawrence counties. Morgan County encompasses 575 square miles. The county seat was at Somerville from 1818 until 1891. Then it was transferred to Decatur, named after Stephen E. Decatur, hero of the 1804 war with Tripoli.

COURTHOUSE: 302 Lee Street NE, Decatur, AL 35602; (256) 351-4675

PROBATE JUDGE: Greg Cain (R)

SHERIFF: Greg Bartlett (R)

CIRCUIT CLERK: John Pat Orr (D)

DISTRICT ATTORNEY: Robert "Bob" Burrell

REVENUE COMMISSIONER: Amanda Scott

COUNTY COMMISSIONERS: Jeff Clark; Ken Livingston; Kevin Murphy; Stacy Lee George; John Glasscock

POPULATION: 115,237

MUNICIPALITIES WITHIN: Decatur; Eva; Falkville; Hartselle; Priceville; Somerville; Trinity

FOR MORE INFORMATION: www.co.morgan.al.us

Perry

Perry County was created by the Alabama Legislature on December 13, 1819. It was named for Commodore Oliver Hazard Perry of Rhode Island, hero of the War of 1812. In 1822 the courthouse was established at Muckle's Ridge, now known as Marion. The county is located in the west-central part of the state, in the Black Belt region. It encompasses 724 square miles. Coretta Scott King was born near Marion.

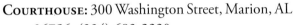

Courthouse: 300 Washington Street, Marion, AL 36756; (334) 683-2220

Probate Judge: Eldara Anderson (D)

Sheriff: James Hood (D)

Circuit Clerk: Mary Cosby Moore (D)

District Attorney: Michael Jackson

Revenue Commissioner: Christine Jackson

County Commissioners: Albert Turner; Timothy Sanderson; Brett Harrison; Fairest Cureton; Clarence Black

Population: 11,186

Municipalities within: Marion; Uniontown

PICKENS

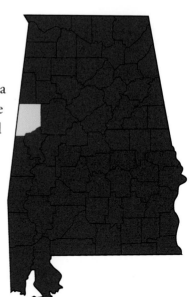

Pickens County was created by an act of the Alabama Legislature on December 19, 1820. It is located in the western part of the state. Its boundaries were changed several times between 1820 and 1866, when its present boundaries were fixed. The county is bounded by Fayette, Greene, Lamar, Sumter, and Tuscaloosa counties and Mississippi. It encompasses 890 square miles. Pickens County was named for Revolutionary War general Andrew Pickens of South Carolina. The first county seat was established at Pickens Courthouse, later called Pickens, then Pickensville, and moved to Carrollton in 1830.

COURTHOUSE: 50 Courthouse Square, Carrollton, AL 35447; (205) 367-2010
PROBATE JUDGE: John Paluzzi (D)
SHERIFF: David Abston (D)
CIRCUIT CLERK: Bobby Cowart (D)
DISTRICT ATTORNEY: J. Christopher "Chris" McCool
REVENUE COMMISSIONER: John A. "Jack" Somerville, IV
COUNTY COMMISSIONERS: William Latham; Earnest Summerville; Sentell Harper; Willie Colvin; Ted Ezelle Jr.
POPULATION: 20,949
MUNICIPALITIES WITHIN: Aliceville; Carrollton; Ethelsville; Gordo; McMullen; Memphis; Pickensville; Reform

PIKE

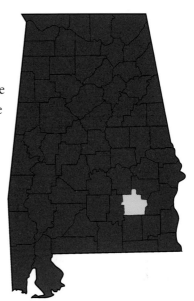

Pike County was created on December 17, 1821. The county is located in the southeastern section of the state, in the Wiregrass area. The county boundaries changed several times before being set at their current locations in 1866. The first county seat was established at Louisville, later moved to Monticello, and finally located in Troy in 1839. Pike County encompasses 672 square miles. It was named for General Zebulon Pike of New Jersey, an explorer and a soldier in the War of 1812. A teachers' training college, Troy Normal School, was established in Troy in 1887. Today it exists as Troy University.

COURTHOUSE: 120 West Church Street, Troy, AL 36081; (334) 566-1246

PROBATE JUDGE: William "Bill" Stone (D)

SHERIFF: Russell Thomas (D)

CIRCUIT CLERK: Brenda Meadows Peacock (R)

DISTRICT ATTORNEY: Gary McAliley

REVENUE COMMISSIONER: Curtis Blair

COUNTY COMMISSIONERS: Adam Drinkwater; Homer Wright; Robin Sullivan; Jimmy Barron; Ray Goodson; Charlie Harris

POPULATION: 29,620

MUNICIPALITIES WITHIN: Banks; Brundidge; Goshen; Troy

RANDOLPH

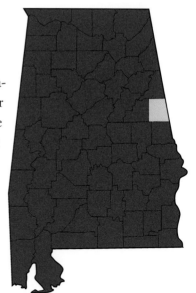

Randolph County was created by an act of the Alabama Legislature on December 18, 1832, from former Creek Indian territory. It borders Georgia in the central part of the state, in the Piedmont plateau. It encompasses 585 square miles. Randolph County is named for John Randolph, a prominent U.S. senator from Virginia. Wedowee became the county seat in 1835, although Roanoke is the largest city.

COURTHOUSE: 1 Main Street, Wedowee, AL 36278; (256) 357-4933

PROBATE JUDGE: George "Mack" Diamond (D)

SHERIFF: Jeffrey Fuller (D)

CIRCUIT CLERK: Chris May (D)

DISTRICT ATTORNEY: E. Paul Jones

REVENUE COMMISSIONER: Josh Burns

COUNTY COMMISSIONERS: Larry Raughton; Edward Creed Sr.; Kevin Spears; T. J. "June" Waldrep; Lathonia Wright

POPULATION: 22,673

MUNICIPALITIES WITHIN: Roanoke; Wadley; Wedowee; Woodland

FOR MORE INFORMATION: www.ircusa.com/randolph/county.htm

Russell

Russell County was created by an act of the Alabama Legislature on December 18, 1832, from former Creek Indian territory. It is located in the south-central part of the state and is bounded on the east by the Chattahoochee River and Georgia. Russell County encompasses 647 square miles. It is named for Colonel Gilbert C. Russell of Mobile, a U.S. military officer who fought in the Creek Wars. The first county seat was established at Girard and was moved to Seale in 1868. In 1935, it moved to Phenix City which had merged with Girard.

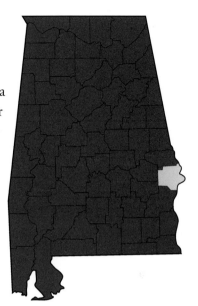

COURTHOUSE: 501 14th Street, Phenix City, AL 36868-0700; (334) 298-7979

PROBATE JUDGE: Alfred Harden (D)

SHERIFF: Thomas Boswell (D)

CIRCUIT CLERK: Kathy Coulter (D)

DISTRICT ATTORNEY: Kenneth "Ken" Davis

REVENUE COMMISSIONER: Naomi Elliott

COUNTY COMMISSIONERS: Gentry Lee; Gordon Cox; Peggy Martin; Johnnie Robinson; J. D. Upshaw; Cattie Epps; Mervin Dudley

POPULATION: 50,085

MUNICIPALITIES WITHIN: Hurtsboro; Phenix City

SHELBY

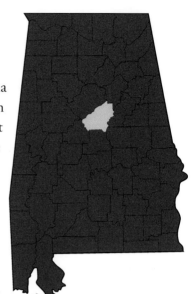

Shelby County was created by an act of the Alabama Territorial Legislature on February 7, 1818, from Creek Indian territory ceded in the Treaty of Fort Jackson on August 9, 1814. It is located in the north-central part of the state and is bounded by Bibb, Chilton, Jefferson, St. Clair, and Talladega counties. About one-half of the county is in the mineral belt. Shelby County encompasses 800 square miles and is named for Isaac Shelby, first governor of Kentucky. The location of the first county seat was Shelbyville. In 1826 the town of Columbia changed its name to Columbiana and became the permanent county seat.

COURTHOUSE: 112 North Main Street, Columbiana, AL 35051; (205) 669-3713

PROBATE JUDGE: James W. Fuhrmeister (R)

SHERIFF: Chris Curry (R)

CIRCUIT CLERK: Mary H. Harris (D)

DISTRICT ATTORNEY: Robert Owens Jr.

PROPERTY TAX Commissioner: Don Armstrong

COUNTY COMMISSIONERS: Corley Ellis; Earl Cunningham; Jon Parker; Dan Acker; Joel Bearden; Larry Dillard; Lindsey Allison; Ted Crockett; Robbie Hayes

POPULATION: 171,465

MUNICIPALITIES WITHIN: Alabaster; Calera; Chelsea; Columbiana; Harpersville; Helena; Indian Springs; Montevallo; Pelham; Vincent; Westover; Wilsonville; Wilton

FOR MORE INFORMATION: www.shelbycountyalabama.com

St. Clair

St. Clair County was created by the Alabama Territorial Legislature on November 20, 1818. It is located in the north-central part of the state and is bordered by Blount, Calhoun, Talladega, Shelby, and Jefferson counties. It encompasses 646 square miles. St. Clair County was named for General Arthur St. Clair of Pennsylvania, a hero of the American Revolution and the only governor of the Northwest Territory. St. Clair has two county seats, Pell City and Ashville. Ashville, originally called St. Clairsville, was named for John Ash, a senator in the state's first general assembly. Pell City, founded in 1890, is named after John Pell of the Pell City Iron and Land Company.

Courthouse: 129 Fifth Avenue, Ashville, AL 35953; (205) 594-2120

Probate Judge: Micheal Bowling (R)

Sheriff: Terry Surles (R)

Circuit Clerk: Annette Hall (R)

District Attorney: Richard Minor

Revenue Commissioner: Elizabeth Mealer

County Commissioners: Jeff Brown; Michael Bowling; Paul Manning; Jimmy Roberts; Stan Batemon

Population: 75,232

Municipalities within: Ashville; Margaret; Moody; Odenville; Pell City; Ragland; Riverside; Springville; Steele

For more information: www.stclairco.com

SUMTER

Sumter County was created on December 18, 1832, from former Choctaw Indian territory ceded in 1830 by the Treaty of Dancing Rabbit Creek. The county is located in the west-central part of the state, bordering Mississippi to the west and the Tombigbee River to the east. Sumter County encompasses 913 square miles. It was named for General Thomas Sumter of South Carolina, who served during the American Revolution and later represented South Carolina in the U.S. House of Representatives and Senate. The county seat was established at Livingston in 1833. The Livingston State Normal School, now the University of West Alabama, was established in 1883.

COURTHOUSE: Washington Street, Livingston, AL 35470; (205) 652-2731

PROBATE JUDGE: Willie Pearl Watkins-Rice (D)

SHERIFF: Johnny Lee Hatter (D)

CIRCUIT CLERK: Edmund Bell (D)

DISTRICT ATTORNEY: Greg Griggers

TAX ASSESSOR: Joyce Paige

COUNTY COMMISSIONERS: Marie D. Carter; Drucilla Russ-Jackson; Grodie Hall; Ben Walker; Ronnie Beard; Aubrey Ellis

POPULATION: 14,798

MUNICIPALITIES WITHIN: Cuba; Emelle; Epes; Gainesville; Geiger; Livingston; York

TALLADEGA

Talladega County was created by an act of the Alabama Legislature on December 18, 1832, from land ceded by the Creek Indians. The county's courthouse, built in 1836, is the oldest in the state. Talladega County is located near the geographic center of the state, in the Coosa River Valley. It encompasses 760 square miles. Talladega County is named for a Creek Indian village. Talladega, the county seat, is home of the Talladega Superspeedway.

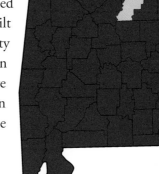

COURTHOUSE: Courthouse Square, Talladega, AL 35161-0737; (256) 362-4175

PROBATE JUDGE: Billy Atkinson (D)

SHERIFF: Jerry Studdard (D)

CIRCUIT CLERK: Clarence Haynes (D)

DISTRICT ATTORNEY: Steve Giddons

REVENUE COMMISSIONER: Harvey Bowlin

COUNTY COMMISSIONERS: Edward Lackey; Tony Haynes; Kelvin Cunningham; Jimmy Roberson; John Carter

POPULATION: 80,271

MUNICIPALITIES WITHIN: Bon Air; Childersburg; Lincoln; Munford; Oak Grove; Sylacauga; Talladega; Talladega Springs; Waldo

FOR MORE INFORMATION: www.talladegacountyal.org

TALLAPOOSA

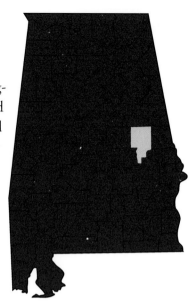

Tallapoosa County was created by the Alabama Legislature on December 18, 1832, from land acquired from the Creek Cession of March 24, 1832. It received its present dimensions in 1866. Tallapoosa County is located in the east-central part of the state and is bordered by Clay, Randolph, Chambers, Lee, Macon, Elmore, and Coosa counties. The county lies almost entirely in the Piedmont plateau, immediately south of the Appalachian plateau province. It encompasses 766 square miles. The county derives its name from the Tallapoosa River. From 1832 to 1838, the county seat was at Okfuskee. Since 1838, it has been at Dadeville, although the county government also has an office in Alexander City. Dadeville was named for Major Francis Langhorne Dade, who died in the Seminole War. Horseshoe Bend National Military Park is located in Tallapoosa County.

COURTHOUSE: 125 North Broadnax Street, Dadeville, AL 36853; (256) 825-4266

PROBATE JUDGE: Gloria Sinclair (D)

SHERIFF: Jimmy Abbett (D)

CIRCUIT CLERK: Frank Lucas (D)

DISTRICT ATTORNEY: E. Paul Jones

REVENUE COMMISSIONER: Linda Harris

COUNTY COMMISSIONERS: T. C. Coley; Charles Shaw; Frank Tapley; Emma Jean Thweatt; Johnny Allen

POPULATION: 41,475

MUNICIPALITIES WITHIN: Alexander City; Camp Hill; Dadeville; Daviston; Goldville; Jacksons' Gap; New Site

FOR MORE INFORMATION: www.tallaco.com

TUSCALOOSA

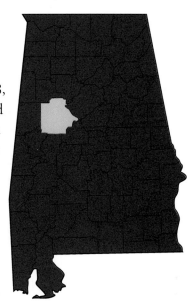

Tuscaloosa County was created on February 6, 1818, though its present boundaries were not established until 1820. The county is located in the Appalachian foothills and the coastal plain. The county was inhabited by both Creek and Choctaw Indians. It encompasses 1,351 square miles. Tuscaloosa County received its name from the Choctaw Indian word for the Black Warrior River, which flows through the area. The county seat was first established in the town of Tuscaloosa in 1819, moved to Newton in 1822, and then went back to Tuscaloosa shortly thereafter. Tuscaloosa was designated the state capital from 1826 to 1845. The University of Alabama was established in Tuscaloosa in 1831.

COURTHOUSE: 714 Greensboro Avenue, Tuscaloosa, AL 35402; (205) 349-3870

PROBATE JUDGE: W. Hardy McCollum (D)

SHERIFF: Ron Abernathy (acting)

CIRCUIT CLERK: Magaria Hamner Bobo (R)

DISTRICT ATTORNEY: Tommy Smith

TAX ASSESSOR: Doster McMullen

COUNTY COMMISSIONERS: Don Wallace; Gary Youngblood; Bobby Miller; Reginald Murray; Hardy McCollum

POPULATION: 171,159

MUNICIPALITIES WITHIN: Brookwood; Coaling; Lake View; Northport; Tuscaloosa; Vance

FOR MORE INFORMATION: www.tuscco.com

WALKER

Walker County was created by the Alabama Legislature on December 26, 1823. The county is located in the northwestern part of the state and is bordered by Winston, Cullman, Blount, Jefferson, Tuscaloosa, Fayette, and Marion counties. It encompasses 803 square miles. Walker County was once a world leader in coal production. The county is drained by the Black Warrior River and Mulberry and Sipsey forks. Walker County was named for Alabama's first U.S. senator, John Williams Walker. The county seat is Jasper, named for William Jasper, a hero of the American Revolution.

COURTHOUSE: 1801 Third Avenue, Jasper, AL 35502-0502; (205) 384-7284

PROBATE JUDGE: Rick Allison (D)

SHERIFF: John Tirey (D)

CIRCUIT CLERK: Susan "Suzie" Odem (D)

DISTRICT ATTORNEY: Charles Baker

REVENUE COMMISSIONER: Jerry Guthrie

COUNTY COMMISSIONERS: Dual Tubbs; Larry Farris; Ben Huggins; James Bridges; Bruce Hamrick

POPULATION: 70,034

MUNICIPALITIES WITHIN: Carbon Hill; Cordova; Dora; Eldridge; Jasper; Kansas; Nauvoo; Oakman; Parrish; Sipsey; Sumiton

FOR MORE INFORMATION: www.walkercounty.com

WASHINGTON

Washington County was created on June 4, 1800, as a county of the Mississippi Territory. Originally the county contained 26,400 square miles, and its original boundaries were the Chattahoochee River to the east, the Pearl River to the west, the 32nd parallel to the north, and the 31st parallel to the south. The area of Washington County was later divided into 16 Mississippi counties and 29 Alabama counties. Today the county encompasses 1,081 square miles and is bounded by Mississippi, the Tombigbee River, and Mobile and Choctaw counties. Washington County was named for George Washington. Early county  seats included McIntosh's Bluff, Wakefield, and St. Stephens, the first capital of the Alabama Territory. The county seat is now located at Chatom.

COURTHOUSE: 45 Court Square, Chatom, AL 36518; (251) 847-2201
PROBATE JUDGE: Charles Singleton (D)
SHERIFF: Richard Stringer (D)
CIRCUIT CLERK: Steven Grimes (D)
DISTRICT ATTORNEY: Spencer Walker
REVENUE COMMISSIONER: Laura L. Taylor
COUNTY COMMISSIONERS: Johnny Johnston; J. Allen Bailey Jr.; William Beasley; Hilton Robbins
POPULATION: 17,651
MUNICIPALITIES WITHIN: Chatom; McIntosh; Millry
FOR MORE INFORMATION: www.washingtoncountyal.com

WILCOX

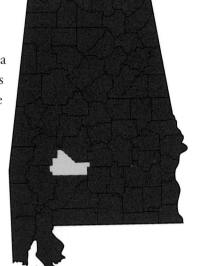

Wilcox County was created by an act of the Alabama Legislature on December 13, 1819. The county is located in the south-central part of the state, in the Black Belt region. It encompasses 907 square miles. Wilcox County was named for Lieutenant Joseph M. Wilcox, who died in the Creek War. The county was a center of Alabama antebellum plantation life. Today it is largely agricultural and rural. The county seat is Camden.

COURTHOUSE: 100 Broad Street, Camden, AL 36726; (334) 682-4883

PROBATE JUDGE: Jerry Boggan (D)

SHERIFF: Prince Arnold (D)

CIRCUIT CLERK: Ralph Ervin (D)

DISTRICT ATTORNEY: Michael Jackson

TAX ASSESSOR: Shelly D. Dale

COUNTY COMMISSIONERS: Mark Curl; David Manzie; John Matthews; Elijah Shaw III; Ricky Powell; Reginald Southall

POPULATION: 13,183

MUNICIPALITIES WITHIN: Camden; Oak Hill; Pine Apple; Pine Hill; Yellow Bluff

FOR MORE INFORMATION: www.wilcoxcountyalabama.com

Winston

Winston County was created as Hancock County on February 12, 1850, from territory formerly in Walker County. It was named for Governor John Hancock of Massachusetts. On January 22, 1858, the name was changed to Winston in honor of Alabama governor John A. Winston. The county is located in the northwestern part of the state, in the Appalachian foothills. It encompasses 632 square miles. The county seat is located in Double Springs. The county gained notoriety during the Civil War due to its threat to secede from the Confederacy as "The Free State of Winston." The county contains rich mineral deposits. A large portion of the county is part of the William B. Bankhead National Forest.

Courthouse: Main Street, Courthouse Square, Double Springs, AL 35553; (205) 489-5026

Probate Judge: Sheila Moore (R)

Sheriff: Edward Townsend (D)

Circuit Clerk: John Snoddy (R)

District Attorney: John "Jack" Bostick

Revenue Commissioner: Sandra Thorn Wright

County Commissioners: Thomas Farmer; Roger Hayes; Jerry Mobley

Population: 24,634

Municipalities within: Addison; Arley; Double Springs; Haleyville; Lynn; Natural Bridge

For more information: www.winstoncountyalabama.org

MULTICOUNTY AGENCIES IN ALABAMA

The twelve member organizations of the Alabama Association of Regional Councils are public agencies serving multi-jurisdictional regional communities whose residents have common economic, social, and geographic concerns. Each agency is founded on, sustained by, and directly tied to local governments through local and/or state government laws, agreements, or other actions. The regional councils provide communication, planning, poli-cymaking, coordination, advocacy, and technical assistance for issues and needs which cross city, town, county, and, in some instances, state boundaries.

Regional councils have different names such as regional planning and development commissions, councils of government, and economic or local development districts. Their governing bodies are primarily com-posed of local government elected officials and appointed representatives of local communities and state government.

Each region can also provide special services determined by the board of di-rectors. The emphasis and program mix depend upon local needs and priorities within the region.

Alabama's twelve regional councils were created following the passage in Congress of the Public Works and Economic Devel-opment Act of 1965 and the Appalachian Regional Development Act of 1965. In 1969, Alabama Act 1126 revamped the state's enabling legislation, authorizing the governing bodies of local governments to establish regional planning and develop-

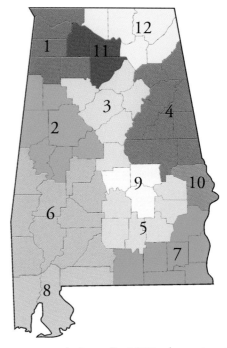

ment commissions. By 1971, the regional councils of Alabama had emerged in the form which is seen today.

—Adapted from www.alarc.org

ALABAMA ASSOCIATION OF REGIONAL COUNCILS
5900 Carmichael Place
Montgomery, AL 36117
(334) 277-2221
www.alarc.org

(1) NORTHWEST ALABAMA COUNCIL OF LOCAL GOVERNMENTS
103 Student Drive
Muscle Shoals, AL 35661
(256) 389-0500
nacolg.com
Serves Colbert, Franklin, Lauderdale, Marion, and Winston counties.

(2) WEST ALABAMA REGIONAL COMMISSION
4200 Highway 69, Suite 1

Northport, AL 35473

(205) 333-2990

www.warc.info

Serves Bibb, Fayette, Greene, Hale, Lamar, Pickens, and Tuscaloosa counties.

(3) REGIONAL PLANNING COMMISSION OF GREATER BIRMINGHAM

1731 1st Avenue North #200

Birmingham, AL 35203

(205) 251-8139

www.rpcgb.org

Serves Blount, Chilton, Jefferson, Shelby, St. Clair, and Walker counties.

(4) EAST ALABAMA REGIONAL PLANNING AND DEVELOPMENT COMMISSION

1130 Quintard Avenue

Anniston, AL 36202

(256) 237-6741

www.earpdc.org

Serves Calhoun, Chambers Cherokee, Clay, Cleburne, Coosa, Etowah, Randolph, Talladega, and Tallapoosa counties.

(5) SOUTH CENTRAL ALABAMA DEVELOPMENT COMMISSION

5900 Carmichael Place

Montgomery, AL 36117

www.scadc.alabama.gov

Serves Bullock, Butler, Crenshaw, Lowndes, Macon, Montgomery, and Pike counties.

(6) ALABAMA-TOMBIGBEE REGIONAL COMMISSION

107 Broad Street

Camden, AL 36726

(334) 682-4234

www.alarc.org/atrc/

Serves Choctaw, Clarke, Conecuh, Dallas, Marengo, Monroe, Perry, Sumter, Washington, and Wilcox counties.

(7) SOUTHEAST ALABAMA REGIONAL PLANNING & DEVELOPMENT COMMISSION

P.O. Box 1406

Dothan, AL 36302

(334) 794-4093

www.southeastalabama.com

Serves Barbour, Coffee, Covington, Dale, Geneva, Henry, Houston, and Pike counties.

(8) SOUTH ALABAMA REGIONAL PLANNING COMMISSION

110 Beauregard

Mobile, AL 36633

(251) 433-6541

www.sarpc.org

Serves Baldwin, Escambia, and Mobile counties.

(9) CENTRAL ALABAMA REGIONAL PLANNING AND DEVELOPMENT COMMISSION

430 S. Court Street

Montgomery, AL 36104

(334) 262-4300

www.carpdc.com

Serves Autauga, Elmore, and Montgomery counties.

(10) LEE-RUSSELL COUNCIL OF GOVERNMENTS

2207 Gateway Drive

Opelika, AL 36801-6834

334) 749-5264

www.lrcog.com

Serves Lee and Russell counties.

(11) NORTH CENTRAL ALABAMA REGIONAL COUNCIL OF GOVERNMENTS

216 Jackson SE

Decatur, AL 35602

(256) 355-4515

www.narcog.org

Serves Cullman, Lawrence, and Morgan counties.

(12) TOP OF ALABAMA REGIONAL COUNCIL OF GOVERNMENTS

5075 Research Drive NW

Huntsville, AL 35805

(256) 830-0818

www.tarcog.org

Serves DeKalb, Jackson, Limestone, Madison, and Marshall counties.

Downtown Gadsden, Etowah County, population 38,978.

9

MUNICIPALITIES

In Alabama, all powers of its approximately 450 municipalities flow directly from the legislature under what is known as the *Dillon* rule. This rule provides that municipalities have no powers beyond those expressively given to them by the state. The authorization must be either explicit or clearly implied from the language of a state statute, a provision of the 1901 Constitution, or an amendment.

The Extent of Municipal Power

Municipalities are established by incorporation through the procedures set out in the *Code of Alabama*. Municipalities grow through annexations. The methods of annexing property are also provided for in the code.

Municipalities are divided into cities and towns on the basis of population. If the municipality has less than two thousand citizens, it is a town. Once the population reaches two thousand, the municipality is defined as a city.

Municipalities may exercise two types of power: legislative and corporate. Legislative powers affect the public generally. In exercising these powers, the municipality acts as an arm of the state. Corporate powers are more comparable to those of a private corporation and are exercised to benefit the municipality in its proprietary capacity.

Municipalities also have authority to exercise certain powers within their police jurisdictions, a legislatively created area extending either a mile-and-a-half or three miles beyond the corporate limits, depending on the population of the municipality. This authority ensures orderly development beyond the municipal limits and allows fire and police protection within these areas. Municipalities can levy certain taxes in the police jurisdiction to pay for services provided in the area.

Appropriations

Municipal expenditures are limited by state law. Section 94 of the Alabama Constitution prohibits municipalities from giving anything of value to any private individual or group of individuals and bars donations to private, nonprofit corporations, even if these organizations benefit the public.

Section 94 does not prohibit municipalities from contracting with private companies and individuals for services nor does it ban appropriations to public organizations that serve the municipality. For instance, municipalities may contribute funds to public schools their citizens attend. However, municipalities may not make donations to band booster clubs or other private clubs organized by students or parents because these are private groups.

Municipalities must also comply with the state bid law.

The Division of Duties between Elected Officials

One of the most misunderstood aspects of municipal government is the separation of powers between the mayor and the council. Like government on the state and federal levels, municipal government is divided into three separate but equal branches: executive, legislative, and judicial. Each of these branches has distinct duties, powers, and restrictions on how far it can intrude into the affairs of the other branches.

At the municipal level the mayor serves as the head of the executive branch. As such, the mayor is responsible for overseeing the day-to-day operations of the municipality. He or she oversees municipal employees; makes sure that bills are paid on time; executes municipal contracts; and, in general, performs many of the same functions as a C.E.O. of a private corporation.

In municipalities of fewer than twelve thousand inhabitants, the mayor also presides over council meetings and serves as a member of the council. In these cities and towns, the mayor may vote on any issue before the council, introduce measures, and participate in debates to the same extent as members of the council.

In cities with populations of more than twelve thousand, the mayor is not a member of the council. However, he or she has veto power over any permanent action taken by the council. The council can override a veto by a two-thirds vote.

The council is the legislative branch. Individual council members have no greater power or authority than any other citizen of the municipality. The council can only act as a body at a legally convened meeting.

The council has authority over the finances and property of the municipality. The council establishes policies, passes ordinances, sets tax levels, determines what sorts of services the municipality will offer, and has authority over all other legislative aspects of municipal government.

A council meeting is not a public hearing. The meeting is open to the public not so much to obtain citizen input as to allow the public to observe the affairs of government and ensure appropriate and legal representation by their elected officials.

Citizens have no right to speak at a council meeting, although most councils do set aside a time for public comment. The Sunshine Law grants citizens the right to be present at public meetings, but it does not grant them an absolute right to express their views at the meeting.

Similarly, most records maintained by a municipality are open to public inspection. The municipality is entitled to establish reasonable procedures governing access to public records. Citizens who wish to view public records must follow these procedures. Also, the municipality may charge for making copies. Additionally, not all records are open to public inspection. Some records, such as on-going police investigation files, some material in personnel records, and similar records which contain information not for public consumption, are not open to the public. Further, individual council members have no greater right to inspect municipal records than do any other members of the public.

Relationships with Boards

Not all municipal services are provided by the municipality itself. Many are provided by municipal boards. Some of these boards are separately incorporated, while others are not. Municipalities have the authority to create a broad range of boards to control particular functions. Utility boards, such as water boards, provide the most common example.

Boards are usually created when the governing body takes on the duty of performing so many functions that it needs to give a particular responsibility to another entity so that it can adequately provide for the other needs of the citizens. Once a board is created, its powers are specified by the statute under which it was organized. The council may not change the duties of the board from those set out in the statute. Nor can a council create boards that are not authorized by the legislature. Although a council may create an advisory board, it cannot delegate power over any municipal function under its control unless the legislature has given it that authority. An advisory board can only make recommendations to the council.

Frequently, municipal officials are asked to remove board members or to order the board to take certain actions. However, once a board is created, it has the sole power to act, and the council has no power to make demands on the members of the board. Members of these boards are appointed for terms, and generally they cannot be removed until their terms expire. This is especially true for separately incorporated boards.

Incorporated boards usually cannot be dissolved until some event defined in the *Code of Alabama* occurs. Frequently this is the payment of the debts of the board. Therefore, members of incorporated boards are totally independent from council members. Unincorporated boards may be dissolved by a governing body, although the council may not change the duties of the board from those set out in the Code.

Conclusion

This article does not answer every conceivable question regarding municipal government, nor could it. Municipal government is multifaceted. It is difficult to even list all the functions performed by municipalities, and even harder to explain the laws which govern their operation. Multi-volume sets of books have been written which provide only a brief overview.

However, what is often overlooked is the community nature of a municipality. Although municipal governments are legally recognized entities with a certain amount of control over the affairs of their citizens, municipalities are still communities. They are organized by citizens who feel a need for the services and protection the government provides. In order to make the government effective, elected officials, and the citizens they represent, must work together in a spirit of cooperation based on an understanding of what the municipality is permitted to do under state law.

The above information was provided by the Alabama League of Municipalities, which was organized in 1935 to represent the interests and needs of the state's towns and cities and their citizens. For more information, visit www.alalm.org.

INCORPORATED MUNICIPALITIES IN ALABAMA

POPULATION 100,000 AND GREATER*

Birmingham	242,820
Montgomery	201,568
Mobile	198,915
Huntsville	158,216

POPULATION 50,000–99,999

Tuscaloosa	77,906
Hoover	62,742
Dothan	57,737
Decatur	53,929

POPULATION 25,000–49,999

Auburn	42,987
Gadsden	38,978
Florence	36,264
Vestavia Hills	30,418
Bessemer	29,672
Madison	29,329
Prichard	28,633
Phenix City	28,265
Homewood	25,043

POPULATION 10,000–24,999

Prattville	24,303
Anniston	24,276
Opelika	23,498
Alabaster	22,619
Enterprise	21,178
Mountain Brook	20,604
Selma	20,512
Northport	19,435
Athens	18,967
Albertville	17,247
Daphne	16,581
Hueytown	15,364
Center Point	15,296
Talladega	15,143
Ozark	15,119
Alexander City	15,008
Scottsboro	14,762
Oxford	14,592
Pelham	14,369
Jasper	14,052
Cullman	13,995
Troy	13,935
Eufaula	13,908
Fort Payne	12,938
Trussville	12,924
Sylacauga	12,616
Fairhope	12,480
Fairfield	12,381
Saraland	12,288
Hartselle	12,019
Muscle Shoals	11,924
Tuskegee	11,846
Gardendale	11,626
Leeds	10,455
Millbrook	10,386
Helena	10,296

*All population figures are from 2006 U.S. Census data provided by the Alabama League of Municipalities as is the data in the following list of Alabama municipalities.

All Municipalities

ABBEVILLE. Henry County. Pop. 2,987. P.O. Box 427, 36310. (334) 585-6444. www.cityofabbeville.org. Mayor Ryan Blalock. Clerk J. M. Giganti Jr.

ADAMSVILLE. Jefferson County. Pop. 4,965. P.O. Box 309, 35005. (205) 674-5671. Mayor Pam Palmer. Clerk Susan Luster-

Gilmore.

ADDISON. Winston County. Pop. 723. P.O. Box 98, 35540. (256) 747-2971. Mayor Marsha Pigg. Clerk Cindy Luker.

AKRON. Hale County. Pop. 521. P.O. Box 8, 35441. (205) 372-3148. Mayor Stanley Hollie. Clerk Jennifer Jones.

ALABASTER. Shelby County. Pop. 22,619. 201 First Street North, 35007. (205) 664-6800. www.cityofalabaster.com. Mayor David M. Frings. Clerk Marsha Massey.

ALBERTVILLE. Marshall County. Pop. 17,247. P.O. Box 1248, 35950. (256) 891-8200. www.cityofalbertville.com. Mayor Lindsey Lyons. Clerk Phyllis Webb.

ALEXANDER CITY. Tallapoosa County. Pop. 15,008. P.O. Box 552, 35011. (256) 329-6700. www.alexandercityonline.com. Mayor Barbara H. Young. Clerk Luise Hardman.

ALICEVILLE. Pickens County. Pop. 2,567. 419 Memorial Parkway NE, 35442. (205) 373-6611. www.cityofaliceville.com. Mayor W. R. McKinzey Jr. Clerk Mary Bess Paluzzi.

ALLGOOD. Blount County. Pop. 629. P.O. Box 150, 35013. (205) 274-7138. Mayor Gene Armstrong. Clerk Teresa Blackmon.

ALTOONA. Etowah County. Pop. 984. P.O. Box 279, 35952. (205) 589-2311. Mayor Richard R. Nash. Clerk Amy Simmons.

ANDALUSIA. Covington County. Pop. 8,794. P.O. Box 429, 36420. (334) 222-3313. www.cityofandalusia.com. Mayor Earl Johnson. Clerk John M. Thompson.

ANDERSON. Lauderdale County. Pop. 354.

P.O. Box 8, 35610. (256) 247-3617. Mayor B. J. Tully. Clerk Rebecca Grisham.

ANNISTON. Calhoun County. Pop. 24,276. P.O. Box 2168, 36202. (256) 236-3422. www.anniston.org. Mayor Gene Robinson. Clerk Alan B. Atkinson.

ARAB. Marshall County. Pop. 71,74. 740 North Main Street, 35016. (256) 586-3544. www.arabcity.org. Mayor Gary W. Beam. Clerk Tony Willis.

ARDMORE. Limestone County. Pop. 1,034. 26494 First Street, 35739. (256) 423-3011. Mayor Eugene Shannon. Clerk Sandra Tucker.

ARGO. Jefferson County. Pop. 1,780. 8885 Gadsden Highway, 35173. (205) 655-3379. Mayor Paul D. Jennings. Clerk Andrea Jennings.

ARITON. Dale County. Pop. 772. P.O. Box 53, 36311. (334) 762-2266. Mayor Marie Black. Clerk Jacqueline Danner.

ARLEY. Winston County. Pop. 290. P.O. Box 146, 35541. (205) 387-0103. Mayor Allan Harbison. Clerk Wanda Farmer.

ASHFORD. Houston County. Pop. 1,853. P.O. Box 428, 36312. (334) 899-3366. Mayor Norman Burgess. Clerk Gwen Hubbard.

ASHLAND. Clay County. Pop. 1,965. P.O. Box 849, 36251. (256) 354-2121. www.cityofashland.net. Mayor Larry J. Fetner. Clerk Charles E. Foster.

ASHVILLE. St. Clair County. Pop. 2,260. P.O. Drawer 70, 35953. (205) 594-4151. www.cityofashville.org. Mayor Robert L. McKay. Clerk Bertha Wilson.

ATHENS. Limestone County. Pop. 18,967. P.O. Box 1089, 35612. (256) 233-8720. www.athens.al.us. Mayor Dan Williams.

Clerk John Hamilton.

ATMORE. Escambia County. Pop. 7,676. P.O. Drawer 1297, 36504. (251) 368-2253. www.cityofatmore.com. Mayor Howard Shell. Clerk Becca Smith.

ATTALLA. Etowah County. Pop. 6,592. 612 Fourth Street NW, 35954. (256) 538-9986. Mayor Jane Phillips. Clerk Sharon Jones.

AUBURN. Lee County. Pop. 42,987. 144 Tichenor Avenue, Suite 1, 36830. (334) 501-7260. www.auburnalabama.org. Mayor Bill Ham Jr. Clerk/City Mgr. Charles M. Duggan Jr.

AUTAUGAVILLE. Autauga County. Pop. 820. P.O. Box 237, 36003. (334) 365-9563. Mayor F. B. Ward. Clerk Valerie Seabon.

AVON. Houston County. Pop. 466. P.O. Box 462, Ashford, 36312. (334) 899-3715. Mayor Timothy Prevatt. Clerk Neda Womack.

BABBIE. Covington County. Pop. 627. 24123 Bethel Road, Opp, 36467. (334) 493-3995. Mayor Chris Caldwell. Clerk Elaine Williamson.

BAILEYTON. Cullman County. Pop. 684. P.O. Box 116, 35019. (256) 796-6447. Mayor Johnny B. Dyar. Clerk Patricia Gilbert.

BAKER HILL. Barbour County. Pop. 354. 1896 Highway 131, 36027. (334) 616-6888. Mayor Aaron Grubbs. Clerk Virginia O. Wood.

BANKS. Pike County. Pop. 224. P.O. Box 6666, 36005. (334) 243-5768. Mayor Dewayne Henderson. Clerk Jennifer Smith.

BAY MINETTE. Baldwin County. Pop. 7,820. P.O. Box 1208, 36507. (251) 580-1619. Mayor Jamie Tillery. Clerk Rita Findley.

BAYOU LA BATRE. Mobile County. Pop. 2,313. 13785 South Wintzell Avenue, 36509. (251) 824-2171. Mayor Stan Wright. Clerk Donna Gainey.

BEAR CREEK. Marion County. Pop. 1,053. P.O. Box 186, 35543. (205) 486-4707. bearcreekal.com. Mayor Connie Morrison. Clerk Ava McCurley.

BEATRICE. Monroe County. Pop. 412. P.O. Box 56, 36401. (251) 789-2241. Mayor Hugh A. Bishop. Clerk Lisa Joyner.

BEAVERTON. Lamar County. Pop. 226. P.O. Box 70, 35544. (205) 698-0744. Mayor Joe L. Collier. Clerk Tracy Gann.

BELK. Fayette County. Pop. 214. P.O. Box 195, 35545. (205) 932-9292. Mayor Ronald Waldrop. Clerk Barbara Sullivan.

BENTON. Lowndes County. Pop. 47. 379 Washington Street, 36785. (334) 874-7878. Mayor John D. Cooper. Clerk Edie H. Hornsby.

BERRY. Fayette County. Pop. 1,238. 30 School Avenue, 35546. (205) 689-4562. Mayor Roy H. Dobbs. Clerk Marie McCluskey.

BESSEMER. Jefferson County. Pop. 29,672. 1800 Third Avenue North, 35020. (205) 424-4060. www.bessemeral.org. Mayor Edward E. May. Clerk Travis A. Brooks.

BILLINGSLEY. Autauga County. Pop. 116. P.O. Box 142, 36006. (205) 755-9809. Mayor Gregg Davis. Clerk Eloise Chandler.

BIRMINGHAM. Jefferson and Shelby counties. Pop. 242,820. 710 North 20th Street, 35203. (205) 254-2000. www.

informationbirmingham.com. Mayor Larry Langford. Clerk Paula R. Smith.

BLACK. Geneva County. Pop. 202. P.O. Box 301, 36314. (334) 684-1340. Mayor Tom Ed Majors. Clerk Nancy M. Hawthorne.

BLOUNTSVILLE. Blount County. Pop. 1,768. P.O. Box 186, 35031. (205) 429-2406. Mayor Randy Millwood. Clerk Alethea Bailey.

BLUE SPRINGS. Barbour County. Pop. 121. 2571 Highway 10, Clio, 36017. (334) 397-4791. Mayor Vince Moates. Clerk Amanda Merritt.

BOAZ. Etowah and Marshall counties. Pop. 7,411. P.O. Box 537, 35957. (256) 593-9537. www.cityofboaz.org. Mayor Tim Walker. Clerk Jill Bright.

BOLIGEE. Greene County. Pop. 369. P.O. Box 245, 35443. (205) 336-8531. Mayor Bonny Olayiwola. Clerk Susie Morrow.

BON AIR. Talladega County. Pop. 96. P.O. Box 117, 35032. (256) 245-4831. Mayor Pamila C. Pilkington. Clerk Allison Morris.

BRANTLEY. Crenshaw County. Pop. 920. P.O. Box 44, 36009. (334) 527-8624. townofbrantley.com. Mayor Bernie Sullivan. Clerk Philip Mosley.

BRENT. Bibb County. Pop. 4,024. P.O. Box 220, 35034. (205) 926-4643. cityofbrentalabama.com. Mayor Dennis Stripling. Clerk Rosalyn T. Adams.

BREWTON. Escambia County. Pop. 5,498. P.O. Box 368, 36427. (251) 809-1770. www.cityofbrewton.org. Mayor Ted Jennings. Clerk John F. P. Angel.

BRIDGEPORT. Jackson County. Pop. 2,728. P.O. Box 747, 35740. (256) 495-3892. Mayor David C. Hughes. Clerk Tanya M. Pace.

BRIGHTON. Jefferson County. Pop. 3,640. 3700 Main Street, 35020. (205) 428-9547. Mayor Angelo Hinkle. Clerk LaSonya Walker.

BRILLIANT. Marion County. Pop. 762. P.O. Box 407, 35548. (205) 465-2281. www.brilliantal.org. Mayor Perry Franks. Clerk Kay Stanford.

BROOKSIDE. Jefferson County. Pop. 1,393. P.O. Box 142, 35036. (205) 674-9275. www.brooksidealabama.com. Mayor Roger McCondichie. Clerk Debbie Keedy.

BROOKWOOD. Tuscaloosa County. Pop. 1,483. 15689 Hwy. 216, 35444. (205) 556-1300. brookwoodalabama.com. Mayor Alton Hyche. Clerk Linda Barger.

BRUNDIDGE. Pike County. Pop. 2,341. P.O. Box 638, 36010. (334) 735-2385. www.brundidge.org. Mayor James T. Ramage III. Clerk Britt Thomas.

BUTLER. Choctaw County. Pop. 1,952. P.O. Box 455, 36904. (205) 459-3793. Mayor Ben Smith. Clerk Lana Stafford.

CALERA. Shelby County. Pop. 3,158. 10947 Highway 25, 35040. (205) 668-3500. cityofcalera.org. Mayor George Roy. Clerk Linda Steele.

CAMDEN. Wilcox County. Pop. 2,257. 223-A Clairborne St., 36726. (334) 682-4603. Mayor Henrietta Blackmon. Clerk Oletha Miller.

CAMP HILL. Tallapoosa County. Pop. 1,273. P.O. Box 100, 36850. (256) 896-4148. Mayor Samuel Ellis. Clerk Dorothy Woodall.

CARBON HILL. Walker County. Pop. 2,071. P.O. Box 519, 35549. (205) 924-9961.

Mayor Chris Hart. Clerk Polly Haley.

CARDIFF. Jefferson County. Pop. 82. 128 Main St. Graysville, 35073. (205) 674-6638. Mayor Joseph Country. Clerk Rose Mary Nail.

CAROLINA. Covington County. Pop. 248. 13700 U.S. 29, Andalusia, 36420. (334) 222-5581. Mayor James C. Garner. Clerk Betty Wilhite.

CARROLLTON. Pickens County. Pop. 987. P.O. Box 169, 35447. (205) 367-8711. Mayor John D. Lammers. Clerk Elizabeth B. Goodson.

CASTLEBERRY. Conecuh County. Pop. 590. P.O. Box 97, 36432. (251) 966-2141. Mayor J. B. Jackson. Clerk Lola Edwards.

CEDAR BLUFF. Cherokee County. Pop. 1,467. P.O. Box 38, 35959. (256) 779-6121. www.cedarbluff-al.org. Mayor Martha Baker. Clerk DeLana Martin.

CENTER POINT. Jefferson County. Pop. 15,296. P.O. Box 9847, 35220. (205) 854-4460. thecityofcenterpoint.org. Mayor Tom Henderson. Clerk Jackie Davidson.

CENTRE. Cherokee County. Pop. 3,216. 401 E. Main St., 35960. (256) 927-5222. cityofcentre.org. Mayor Tonny Wilkie. Clerk Mary Lee Tucker.

CENTREVILLE. Bibb County. Pop. 2,466. 1270 Walnut Street, 35042. (205) 926-4995. www.cityofcentreville.com. Mayor Tom Bamberg. Clerk Stephanie Scott.

CHATOM. Washington County. Pop. 1,193. P.O. Box 817, 36518. (251) 847-2580. www.chatom.org. Mayor Harold L. Crouch. Clerk Sharron Sheffield.

CHELSEA. Shelby County. Pop. 2,949. P.O. Box 111, 35043. (205) 678-8455. www. cityofchelsea.com. Mayor Samuel Earl Niven Sr. Clerk Becky C. Landers.

CHEROKEE. Colbert County. Pop. 1,237. P.O. Box D, 35616. (256) 359-4959. Mayor Charles K. Landsdell. Clerk Melinda Malone.

CHICKASAW. Mobile County. Pop. 6,364. 224 N. Craft Hwy., 36611. (251) 452-6450. www.cityofchickasaw.org. Mayor Byron Pittman. Clerk Judi Smith.

CHILDERSBURG. Talladega County. Pop. 4,927. 201 8th Avenue, SW, 35044. (256) 378-5521. childersburg.org. Mayor B. J. Meeks. Clerk Sandra G. Donahoo.

CITRONELLE. Mobile County. Pop. 3,659. 19135 S. Main St., 36522. (251) 866-7973. www.cityofcitronelle.com. Mayor Loretta Presnell. Clerk Lori Bryan.

CLANTON. Chilton County. Pop. 7,800. P.O. Box 580, 35045. (205) 755-1105. www.clanton.al.us. Mayor Billy Joe Driver. Clerk Debra Orange.

CLAY. Jefferson County. Pop. 8,633. P.O. Box 345, 35048. (205) 680-1223. Mayor Ed McGuffie. Clerk Bobby Christmas.

CLAYHATCHEE. Dale County. Pop. 501. 1 West Main Street, Daleville, 36322. (334) 598-4321. Mayor Deloris Salter. Clerk Kim Baker.

CLAYTON. Barbour County. Pop. 1,475. P.O. Box 385, 36016. (334) 775-9176. Mayor Rebecca P. Beasley. Clerk Norean Kennedy.

CLEVELAND. Blount County. Pop. 1,241. P.O. Box 186, 35049. (205) 274-9640. Mayor Larry Longshore. Clerk Debra Millwood.

CLIO. Barbour County. Pop. 2,206. P.O. Box 219, 36017. (334) 397-2723. Mayor

David S. Grice. Clerk Vivian Hagler.

COALING. Tuscaloosa County. Pop. 1,115. P.O. Box 10, 35449. (205) 507-0200. Mayor Charley F. Foster. Clerk Sylvia Rouse.

COFFEE SPRINGS. Geneva County. Pop. 251. P.O. Box 8, 36318. (334) 684-8181. Mayor Leala E. Aycock. Clerk Barbara L. Shirah.

COFFEEVILLE. Clarke County. Pop. 360. P.O. Box 10, 36524. (251) 276-3266. Mayor Robert H. Cox. Clerk Summer Scruggs.

COKER. County. Pop. 808. P.O. Box 278, 35452. (205) 333-8181. Mayor Marla Shaw. Clerk Yvonne Phillips.

COLLINSVILLE. Cherokee and DeKalb counties. Pop. 1,644. P.O. Box 390, 35961. (256) 524-2135. www.collinsvillealabama.net. Mayor Johnny Traffanstedt. Clerk Peggy Wright.

COLONY. Cullman County. Pop. 385. 65 Byars Road, Hanceville, 35077. (256) 287-1192. www.co.cullman.al.us/colony.htm. Mayor Morris Fitts. Clerk Tyrone Turner.

COLUMBIA. Houston County. Pop. 804. P.O. Box 339, 36319. (334) 696-4417. Mayor Sandra Lovett. Clerk Patricia Kindberg.

COLUMBIANA. Shelby County. Pop. 3,316. 107 Mildred Street, 35051. (205) 669-5800. cityofcolumbiana.com. Mayor J. Allan Lowe. Clerk Gina Antolini.

COOSADA. Elmore County. Pop. 1,382. P.O. Box 96, 36020. (334) 285-3700. Mayor Frank Rives Houston. Clerk Jeannie Ward.

CORDOVA. Walker County. Pop. 2,423. 74 Main Street, 35550. (205) 483-

9266. Mayor Jack Scott. Clerk Elaine S. Stewart.

COTTONWOOD. Houston County. Pop. 1,170. P.O. Box 447, 36320. (334) 691-2671. www.townofcottonwood.org. Mayor Lomax Smith. Clerk Augusta Habron.

COUNTY LINE. Blount and Jefferson counties. Pop. 257. P.O. Box 130, 35172. (205) 590-1649. Mayor James Larry Calvert. Clerk Bill Ivey.

COURTLAND. Lawrence County. Pop. 769. P.O. Box 160, 35618. (256) 637-2707. courtlandalabama.com. Mayor Ted H. Letson. Clerk Bettie K. Hollis.

COWARTS. Houston County. Pop. 1,546. P.O. Box 69, 36321. (334) 792-8920. Mayor Randy Roland. Clerk Annette Whaley.

CREOLA. Mobile County. Pop. 2,002. P.O. Box 490, 36525. (251) 675-8142. Mayor Donald Nelson. Clerk Kim W. Pettway.

CROSSVILLE. DeKalb County. Pop. 1,431. P.O. Box 100, 35962. (256) 528-7121. www.crossvillealabama.com. Mayor James T. Johnston. Clerk Debbie Stepleton.

CUBA. Sumter County. Pop. 363. P.O. Box 385, 36907. (205) 392-7181. Mayor Carl Storey. Clerk Lamar W. Hardin.

CULLMAN. Cullman County. Pop. 13,995. P.O. Box 278, 35056. (256) 775-7109. www.cullmancity.org. Mayor Max A. Townson. Clerk Ruth W. Rose.

DADEVILLE. Tallapoosa County. Pop. 3,212. 216 S. Broadnax Street, 36853. (256) 825-9242. Mayor Mike Ingram. Clerk Sharon Harrelson.

DALEVILLE. Dale County. Pop. 4,653. P.O. Box 188, 36322. (334) 598-2345. www.

dalevilleal.com. Mayor Wess Etheredge. Clerk Angelia F. Filmore.

DAPHNE. Baldwin County. Pop. 16,581. P.O. Box 400, 36526. (251) 621-9000. www.daphneal.com. Mayor Fred Small. Clerk David Cohen.

DAUPHIN ISLAND. Mobile County. Pop. 1,371. 1011 Bienville Boulevard, 36528. (251) 861-5525. www.townofdauphin-island.org. Mayor Jeffrey Collier. Clerk Nannette Davidson.

DAVISTON. Tallapoosa County. Pop. 267. P.O. Box 26, 36256. (334) 395-2260. Mayor Tim East. Clerk Linda K. Hodnett.

DAYTON. Marengo County. Pop. 60. 27181 Highway 28, Faunsdale, 36738. (334) 289-2006. Mayor William S. Poole Jr.

DEATSVILLE. Elmore County. Pop. 340. P.O. Box 220167, 36022. (334) 285-9881. Mayor W. Clayton Edgar. Clerk Sandy Bradshaw.

DECATUR. Morgan County. Pop. 53,929. P.O. Box 488, 35602. (256) 341-4500. www.decaturalabamausa.com. Mayor Don Stanford. Clerk Betty Marshall.

DEMOPOLIS. Marengo County. Pop. 7,540. P.O. Box 580, 36732. (334) 289-0577. www.demopolisal.gov. Mayor Mike Grayson. Clerk Paula Bird.

DETROIT. Lamar County. Pop. 247. P.O. Box 114, 35552. (205) 273-4294. Mayor James G. Mullins. Clerk Donald Puckett.

DODGE CITY. Cullman County. Pop. 612. 130 Howard Circle, Hanceville, 35077. (256) 287-0364. Mayor Perry Ray. Clerk Vicki Ogletree.

DORA. Walker County. Pop. 2,413. 1485 Sharon Boulevard, 35062. (205) 648-

3211. Mayor Christopher Edwards. Clerk Tracey Glover.

DOTHAN. Houston County. Pop. 57,737. P.O. Box 2128, 36302. (334) 615-3000. www.dothan.org. Mayor Pat Thomas. Clerk Pam McCoy.

DOUBLE SPRINGS. Winston County. Pop. 1,003. P.O. Box 279, 35553. (205) 489-5447. Mayor Elmo Robinson. Clerk Kim Ownby.

DOUGLAS. Marshall County. Pop. 530. P.O. Box 45, 35964. (256) 593-9531. Mayor Paula Phillips. Clerk Debra Brown.

DOZIER. Crenshaw County. Pop. 391. P.O. Box 216, 36028. (334) 496-3742. Mayor Kaye S. Moody. Clerk Mary W. Dozier.

DUTTON. Jackson County. Pop. 310. P.O. Box 6, 35744. (256) 228-6392. Mayor Bryan Stewart. Clerk Patricia Romans.

EAST BREWTON. Escambia County. Pop. 2,496. P.O. Box 2010, 36427. (251) 867-6092. eastbrewton.net. Mayor Terry Clark. Clerk Karen Singleton.

ECLECTIC. Elmore County. Pop. 1,037. P.O. Box 240430, 36024. (334) 541-4429. townofelectic.org. Mayor Gary Wright. Clerk Dawn Webb.

EDWARDSVILLE. Cleburne County. Pop. 186. P.O. Box 8, 36261. (256) 463-8608. Mayor Billy J. Driggers Jr. Clerk Larry R. Thompson.

ELBA. Coffee County. Pop. 4,185. 200 Buford Street, 36323. (334) 897-2333. www.elbaalabama.net. Mayor James E. Grimes. Clerk N. Wayne Grantham.

ELBERTA. Baldwin County. Pop. 552. P.O. Box 277, 36530. (251) 986-5995. Mayor Marvin Williams. Clerk Sandy Germany.

ELDRIDGE. Walker County. Pop. 184. P.O. Box 99, 35554. (205) 924-4383. Mayor Bobbie Jean Dodd. Clerk Bobby L. McGowen.

ELKMONT. Limestone County. Pop. 470. P.O. Box 387, 35620. (256) 732-4211. Mayor Tracy Compton. Clerk Billie Sue Pressnell.

ELMORE. Elmore County. Pop. 199. P.O. Box 204, 36025. (334) 514-5988. www.townofelmore.com. Mayor Margaret White. Clerk Rita Raye Murchison.

EMELLE. Sumter County. Pop. 158. P.O. Box 97, 35459. (205) 652-4385. www.emellealabama.com. Mayor Roy Willingham Sr. Clerk Gloria Mayo.

ENTERPRISE. Coffee County. Pop. 21,178. P.O. Box 311000, 36331. (334) 348-2602. cityofenterprise.net. Mayor Kenneth Boswell. Clerk Steve Hicks.

EPES. Sumter County. Pop. 206. P.O. Box 127, 35460. Mayor Walter C. Porter Sr. Clerk Mary Porter.

ETHELSVILLE. Pickens County. Pop. 81. P.O. Box 85, 35461. (205) 658-2651. Mayor Linwood Hughes. Clerk Jimmie N. Jolly.

EUFAULA. Barbour County. Pop. 14,478. P.O. Box 219, 36072-0219. (334) 688-2000. www.eufaulaalabama.com. Mayor Jay Jaxon Jr. Clerk Joy White.

EUTAW. Greene County. Pop. 1,878. P.O. Box 431, 35462. (205) 372-4212. Mayor Raymond Steele. Clerk Peggy H. Stripling.

EVA. Morgan County. Pop. 491. P.O. Box 68, 35621. (256) 796-7360. Mayor Gary Livingston. Clerk Judy H. Fortenberry.

EVERGREEN. Conecuh County. Pop. 3,630. P.O. Box 229, 36401. (251) 578-1574. www.evergreenal.org. Mayor Larry Fluker. Clerk Peggy W. Howell.

EXCEL. Monroe County. Pop. 582. P.O. Box 369, 36439. (251) 765-2558. Mayor Jenny Countryman. Clerk Loretta L. Bradley.

FAIRFIELD. Jefferson County. Pop. 12,381. 4701 Gary Avenue, 35064. (205) 788-2492. www.fairfieldal.us. Mayor Kenneth Coachman. Clerk Vacant.

FAIRHOPE. Baldwin County. Pop. 12,480. P.O. Drawer 429, 36533. (251) 928-2136. www.cofairhope.com. Mayor Timothy Kant. Clerk Lisa Hanks.

FAIRVIEW. Cullman County. Pop. 522. 7525 AL. Highway 69 North, Cullman, 35058. (256) 796-5424. Mayor Randall Shedd. Clerk Debbie Shedd.

FALKVILLE. Morgan County. Pop. 1,202. P.O. Box 407, 35622. (256) 784-5922. Mayor Jimmie Walker. Clerk Belinda G. Ealey.

FAUNSDALE. Marengo County. Pop. 87. P.O. Box 211, 36738. (334) 628-4871. Mayor George Kelly. Clerk Sheila Averette.

FAYETTE. Fayette County. Pop. 4,922. 203 Temple Avenue North, 35555. (205) 932-5367. Mayor Ray Nelson. Clerk Dawn Clapp.

FIVE POINTS. Chambers County. Pop. 146. P.O. Box 147, 36855. (334) 864-0004. Mayor Geneva Bledsoe. Clerk Heather McWhorter.

FLOMATON. Escambia County. Pop. 1,588. P.O. Box 632, 36441. (251) 296-2431. Mayor Dewey J. Bondurant Jr. Clerk Diane Killam.

FLORALA. Covington County. Pop. 1,964. P.O. Box 351, 36442. (334) 858-3612.

Mayor Robert Williamson. Clerk Kathy Rathel.

FLORENCE. Lauderdale County. Pop. 36,264. P.O. Box 98, 35631. (256) 760-6678. www.florenceal.org. Mayor Bobby E. Irons. Clerk Robert M. Leyde.

FOLEY. Baldwin County. Pop. 7,590. P.O. Box 1750, 36536. (251) 943-1545. www.cityoffoley.org. Mayor John E. Koniar. Clerk /Admin. Perry Wilbourne.

FORKLAND. Greene County. Pop. 629. 13327 U.S. Highway 43 North, 36740. (334) 289-3033. Mayor Eddie J. Woods. Clerk Cynthia K. Stone.

FORT DEPOSIT. Lowndes County. Pop. 1,270. P.O. Box 260, 36032. (334) 227-4841. Mayor Fletcher Fountain Sr. Clerk Cynthia Jones.

FORT PAYNE. DeKalb County. Pop. 12,938. 100 Alabama Avenue North, 35967. (256) 845-1524. www.fortpayne.org. Mayor William H. Jordan. Clerk James C. McGee.

FRANKLIN. Macon County. Pop. 149. 1660 Alabama Highway. 49, Tuskegee, 36083. (334) 727-2111. Mayor Rufus C. Carson. Clerk Margaret Floyd.

FRISCO CITY. Monroe County. Pop. 1,460. P.O. Box 119, 36445. (251) 267-3439. Mayor Sue Starr. Clerk Charlene Harrison.

FRUITHURST. Cleburne County. Pop. 270. P.O. Box 160, 36262. (256) 434-0996. Mayor Tony Butler. Clerk Tawanna Gibson.

FULTON. Clarke County. Pop. 308. P.O. Box 67, 36446. (334) 636-9527. Mayor Michael Norris. Clerk Murphy Clarke.

FULTONDALE. Jefferson County. Pop. 6,595. P.O. Box 699, 35068. (205) 841-4481. www.cityoffultondale.com. Mayor Jim Lowery. Clerk Jane H. Hicks.

FYFFE. DeKalb County. Pop. 971. P.O. Box 8, 35971. (256) 623-7298. fyffecitylimits.com. Mayor Kathy Woodall. Clerk Brandi Clayton.

GADSDEN. Etowah County. Pop. 38,978. P.O. Box 267, 35902. (256) 549-4516. cityofgadsden.com. Mayor Sherman Guyton. Clerk Iva Nelson.

GAINESVILLE. Sumter County. Pop. 220. P.O. Box 73, 35464. (205) 652-7551. Mayor Carrie Mae Fulghum. Clerk Thelma Palmer.

GANTT. Covington County. Pop. 241. P.O. Box 8, 36038. (334) 388-4786. Mayor Melissa Grissett. Clerk Christina Cartwright.

GARDEN CITY. Cullman County. Pop. 564. P.O. Box 172, 35070. (256) 352-5408. Mayor Harden Davis. Clerk Pam Leslie.

GARDENDALE. Jefferson County. Pop. 11,626. P.O. Box 889, 35071. (205) 631-8789. www.cityofgardendale.com. Mayor Othell Phillips. Clerk Keith Mosley.

GAYLESVILLE. Cherokee County. Pop. 140. P.O. Box 156, 35973. (256) 422-3378. Mayor Elizabeth Stafford. Clerk Cindy Miller.

GEIGER. Sumter County. Pop. 161. 201 Broadway Street, 35459. (205) 455-2811. Mayor Michael Cunningham Sr. Clerk Sandra G. Yarbrough.

GENEVA. Geneva County. Pop. 4,388. P.O. Box 37, 36340. (334) 684-2485. Mayor Wynnton Melton. Clerk/Treasurer Lisa Johnson.

GEORGIANA. Butler County. Pop. 1,737.

P.O. Box 310, 36033. (334) 376-2555. Mayor Mike Middleton. Clerk Ann Browder.

GERALDINE. DeKalb County. Pop. 786. P.O. Box 183, 35974. (256) 659-2122. Mayor Billy Smothers. Clerk Kimberly Cleveland.

GILBERTOWN. Choctaw County. Pop. 187. P.O. Box 152, 36908. (251) 843-2766. Mayor Robert H. Graham. Clerk Alice Carlisle.

GLEN ALLEN. Marion and Fayette counties. Pop. 442. P.O. Box 40, 35559. (205) 487-2014. Mayor Allen J. Dunavant. Clerk Shirley Stewart.

GLENCOE. Etowah County. Pop. 5,152. 201 West Chastain Boulevard, 35905. (256) 492-1424. www.cityofglencoe. net. Mayor Charles Gilchrist. Clerk Susan Casey.

GLENWOOD. Crenshaw County. Pop. 191. P.O. Box 217, 36034. (334) 335-4463. Mayor Becky Hughes. Clerk Sandra Berry.

GOLDVILLE. Tallapoosa County. Pop. 37. 4233 Goldville Cutoff Road, Daviston, 36256. (256) 329-1786. Mayor James C. Powell. Clerk Dorothy H. Harry.

GOOD HOPE. Cullman County. Pop. 1,966. 134 Town Hall Drive, Cullman, 35057. (256) 739-3757. Mayor Corey Harbison. Clerk Joanner Jones.

GOODWATER. Coosa County. Pop. 1,633. P.O. Box 45, 35072. (256) 839-6301. Mayor Lonnie Caldwell. Clerk Ida James.

GORDO. Pickens County. Pop. 1,677. P.O. Box 348, 35466. (205) 364-7111. Mayor Daryl Craig Patterson. Clerk Kay Perkins.

GORDON. Houston County. Pop. 408. P.O. Box 46, 36343. (334) 522-3113. Mayor Charles Dismuke. Clerk Gwendolyn Howard.

GORDONVILLE. Lowndes County. Pop. 318. 404 Wall Street, 36040. (334) 563-7730. Mayor Willie C. Davis. Clerk Brenda Davis.

GOSHEN. Pike County. Pop. 300. P.O. Box 146, 36035. (334) 484-3246. Mayor Jack A. Waller. Clerk Traci Shaver.

GRANT. Marshall County. Pop. 665. P.O. Box 70, 35747. (256) 728-2007. www. grantalabama.com. Mayor Larry Walker. Clerk Carolyn May.

GRAYSVILLE. Jefferson County. Pop. 2,344. P.O. Box 130, 35073. (205) 674-5643. www.graysvillecity.com. Mayor Doug Brewer. Clerk Kathy Dumas.

GREENSBORO. Hale County. Pop. 2,731. 1101 Main Street, 36744. (334) 624-8119. Mayor Johnnie B. Washington. Clerk Lorrie Cook.

GREENVILLE. Butler County. Pop. 7,228. P.O. Box 158, 36037. (334) 382-2647. www.greenville-alabama.com. Mayor Dexter McLendon. Clerk Sue R. Arnold.

GRIMES. Dale County. Pop. 459. 1473 County Road 25, Midland City, 36350. (334) 983-3835. Mayor Frankie Adkins. Clerk Phillip Horne.

GROVE HILL. Clarke County. Pop. 1,438. P.O. Box 847, 36451. (251) 275-3153. Mayor Jerry Newton. Clerk Cheryl Hicks.

GUIN. Marion County. Pop. 2,389. P.O. Box 249, 35563. (205) 468-2242. www. guinal.org. Mayor Phil Segraves. Clerk Norma J. Nelson.

GULF SHORES. Baldwin County. Pop. 5,044. P.O. Box 299, 36547. (251) 968-2425. www.gulfshores.org. Mayor Robert S. Craft. Clerk Renee Moore.

GUNTERSVILLE. Marshall County. Pop. 7,395. 341 Gunter Avenue, 35976. (256) 571-7560. www.guntersvilleal. org. Mayor Robert L. Hembree Jr. Clerk Betty Jones.

GURLEY. Madison County. Pop. 876. P.O. Box 128, 35748. (256) 776-3313. Mayor Stan Simpson. Clerk Tawnie Bryant.

GU-WIN. Marion County. Pop. 204. P.O. Box 550, 35563. (205) 412-9750. Mayor Brandon Webster. Clerk Deborah Webster.

HACKLEBURG. Marion County. Pop. 1,527. P.O. Box 279, 35564. (205) 935-3133. Mayor Douglas Gunnin. Clerk Sandra Bishop.

HALEBURG. Henry County. Pop. 108. 1396 Main Street, Columbia, 36319. (334) 696-2277. Mayor Roger Money. Clerk C. J. Elliott.

HALEYVILLE. Winston County. Pop. 4,182. 1901 11th Avenue, 35565. (205) 486-3121. www.haleyvillechamber.org. Mayor Ken Sunseri. Clerk Debra Hood.

HAMILTON. Marion County. Pop. 6,786. P.O. Box 188, 35570. (205) 921-2121. www.cityofhamilton.org. Mayor Bobby Holliday. Clerk Jan Williams.

HAMMONDVILLE. DeKalb County. Pop. 486. 37669 U.S. Highway 11, 35989. (256) 635-6374. Mayor Larry J. Watson. Clerk Deborah Graves.

HANCEVILLE. Cullman County. Pop. 2,951. 112 Main Street SE, 35077. (256) 352-9830. Mayor Kenneth Nail. Clerk Tania Wilcox.

HARPERSVILLE. Shelby County. Pop. 1,620. P.O. Box 370, 35078. (205) 672-9961. townofharpersville.com. Mayor Theoangelo Perkins. Clerk Joyce Robertson.

HARTFORD. Geneva County. Pop. 2,369. 203 West Main Street, 36344. (334) 588-2245. Mayor Jeff Sorrells. Clerk Vicky Marsh.

HARTSELLE. Morgan County. Pop. 12,019. 200 Sparkman Street NW, 35640. (256) 773-2535. www.hartselle.org. Mayor Dwight Tankersley. Clerk Rita Lee.

HAYDEN. Blount County. Pop. 470. P.O. Box 493, 35079. (205) 647-7191. Mayor Thelma Smith. Clerk Ann Stone.

HAYNEVILLE. Lowndes County. Pop. 1,177. P.O. Box 365, 36040. (334) 548-2128. Mayor Helenor T. Bell. Clerk Susie A. Smith.

HEADLAND. Henry County. Pop. 3,523. 9 Park Street, 36345. (334) 693-3365. www.ci.headand.al.us. Mayor Ray Marler. Clerk Susan Money.

HEATH. Covington County. Pop. 249. P.O. Box 1414, Andalusia, 36420. Mayor Earl Baker. Clerk Glenda Grimes.

HEFLIN. Cleburne County. Pop. 3,002. P.O. Box 128, 36264. (256) 463-2290. www.cityofheflin.org. Mayor Anna Berry. Clerk Terri C. Daulton.

HELENA. Shelby County. Pop. 10,296. P.O. Box 262, 35080. (205) 663-2161. www.cityofhelena.org. Mayor Charles W. Penhale. Clerk Amanda C. Traywick.

HENAGAR. DeKalb County. Pop. 2,400. P.O. Box 39, 35978. (256) 657-6282. www.cityofhenagar.org. Mayor Winston Jenkins. Clerk Deborah Raines.

HIGHLAND LAKE. Blount County. Pop. 408. 612 Lakeshore Drive, 35121. (205)

625-6407. Mayor James A. Bryson. Clerk Cheryl Storey.

HILLSBORO. Lawrence County. Pop. 608. 11355 Main Street, 35643. (256) 637-2070. Mayor Charles Owens. Clerk Canary Lucious.

HOBSON CITY. Calhoun County. Pop. 878. 715 Martin L. King Jr. Drive, 36201. (256) 831-4940. Mayor Alberta C. McCrory. Clerk Nikita Allen.

HODGES. Franklin County. Pop. 261. P.O. Box 87, 35571. (205) 935-3445. Mayor Edward Crouch. Clerk Frankie Petree.

HOKES BLUFF. Etowah County. Pop. 4,149. P.O. Box 2338, 35903. (256) 492-2414. Mayor Gary W. Reeves. Clerk Sheila H. Burns.

HOLLY POND. Cullman County. Pop. 645. P.O. Box 9, 35083. (256) 796-2124. Mayor Herman Nail. Clerk Linda Pope.

HOLLYWOOD. Jackson County. Pop. 950. P.O. Box 240, 35752. (256) 259-4845. Mayor Tommy Allen. Clerk Lona Bradford.

HOMEWOOD. Jefferson County. Pop. 25,043. 2850 19th Street South, 35209. (205) 332-6100. www.homewoodal.org. Mayor Scott McBrayer. Clerk Linda J. Cook.

HOOVER. Jefferson and Shelby counties. Pop. 62,742. 100 Municipal Drive, 35216. (205) 444-7500. www.hooveral. org. Mayor Tony Petelos. Clerk Linda Crump.

HORN HILL. Covington County. Pop. 235. 19019 Horn Hill Road, Opp, AL, 36467. (334) 493-3737. Mayor Rowayne Harper. Clerk Ann Smith.

HUEYTOWN. Jefferson County. Pop. 15,364.

P.O. Box 3650, 35023. (205) 491-7010. Mayor Delor Baumann. Clerk Janice Wilhite.

HUNTSVILLE. Madison County. Pop. 158,216. P.O. Box 308, 35804. (256) 427-5000. www.hsvcity.com. Mayor Tommy Battle. Clerk Charles E. Hagood.

HURTSBORO. Russell County. Pop. 592. P.O. Box 358, 36860. (334) 667-7771. Mayor Rayford E. Tapley. Clerk Kimberly Key.

HYTOP. Jackson County. Pop. 315. 30332 Alabama Highway 79, Scottsboro, 35768. (256) 587-6094. Mayor Leslie Thackerson. Clerk Julie N. Avans.

IDER. DeKalb County. Pop. 664. P.O. Box 157, 35981. (256) 657-4184. Mayor Brad Hannah. Clerk Wilma Fletcher.

INDIAN SPRINGS. Shelby County. Pop. 2,225. 2635 Cahaba Valley Road, 35124. (205) 982-1755. www.indianspringsvillage.org. Mayor Stephen W. Zerkis. Clerk Kelly Rasco.

IRONDALE. Jefferson County. Pop. 9,813. P.O. Box 100188, 35210. (205) 956-9200. www.cityofirondale.org. Mayor Tommy Joe Alexander. Clerk/Treasurer Glenda Cox.

JACKSON. Clarke County. Pop. 5,419. P.O. Box 1096, 36545. (251) 246-2461. Mayor G. Richard Long. Clerk Betty Powell.

JACKSONS' GAP. Tallapoosa County. Pop. 761. P.O. Box 162, 36861. (256) 825-8518. Mayor J. D. Ayers. Clerk Teresa Freeman.

JACKSONVILLE. Calhoun County. Pop. 8,404. 320 Church Avenue SE, 36265. (256) 435-7611. jacksonville-al.org.

Mayor Johnny L. Smith. Clerk Dorothy Wilson.

JASPER. Walker County. Pop. 14,052. P.O. Box 1589, 35502. (205) 221-2100. Mayor V. L. "Sonny" Posey. Clerk Kathy Chambless.

JEMISON. Chilton County. Pop. 2,248. P.O. Box 609, 35085. (205) 688-4492. www.jemisonalabama.org. Mayor Eddie Reed. Clerk Mary Ellison.

KANSAS. Walker County. Pop. 260. P.O. Box 186, 35573. (205) 924-0072. Mayor Joey Bagwell. Clerk Mary Ann Parrish.

KELLYTON. Coosa County. Pop. 321. P.O. Box 75, 35089. (256) 839-9737. Mayor Jane Harris. Clerk Karen Keel.

KENNEDY. Lamar County. Pop. 541. P.O. Box 70, 35574. (205) 596-3670. Mayor Ray Holsonback. Clerk James A. Vice Jr.

KILLEN. Lauderdale County. Pop. 1,119. P.O. Box 27, 35645. (256) 757-1246. Mayor Jerry Mitchell. Clerk Wonda Simpson.

KIMBERLY. Jefferson County. Pop. 1,801. P.O. Box 206, 35091. (205) 647-5551. Mayor Ralph Lindsey. Clerk Sandra Waid.

KINSEY. Houston County. Pop. 1,796. 6947 Walden Drive, 36303. (334) 793-5409. Mayor Jason R. Reneau. Clerk Faye Douglas.

KINSTON. Coffee County. Pop. 602. P.O. Box 26, 36453. (334) 565-3188. Mayor C. Heflin Smith. Clerk Paula Katauskas.

LaFAYETTE. Chambers County. Pop. 3,234. P.O. Box 87, 36862. (334) 864-7181. Mayor Matthew K. Hurst. Clerk Diane W. Perry.

LAKE VIEW. Tuscaloosa County. Pop. 1,357. 22757 Central Park Drive, 35111. (205) 477-1999. Mayor Joe Allcorn. Clerk Luann Higginbotham.

LAKEVIEW. DeKalb County. Pop. 163. P.O. Box 85, Geraldine, 35974. (256) 659-4021. Mayor Debra Maddox. Clerk Joan Chandler.

LANETT. Chambers County. Pop. 7,897. P.O. Box 290, 36863. (334) 644-2141. www.cityoflanett.com. Mayor Oscar Crawley. Clerk Deborah Daniel.

LANGSTON. Jackson County. Pop. 254. P.O. Box 33, 35755. (256) 228-6414. Mayor Floyd Vaught. Clerk Lora Johnson.

LEEDS. Jefferson, St. Clair, and Shelby counties. Pop. 10,455. 8373 First Avenue, 35094. (205) 699-2585. www.leedsalabama.gov. Mayor Eric Patterson. Clerk /Manager Kevin Fouts.

LEESBURG. Cherokee County. Pop. 799. P.O. Box 1, 35983. (256) 526-8890. www.leesburg-al.org. Mayor Edward Mackey. Clerk Jennifer Sharpe.

LEIGHTON. Colbert County. Pop. 849. P.O. Box 308, 35646. (256) 446-8477. Mayor Lawayne Harrison. Clerk Destin Berryman.

LESTER. Limestone County. Pop. 107. P.O. Box 25, 35647. (256) 232-1191. Mayor Thomas Gatlin. Clerk Charlotte Gatlin.

LEVEL PLAINS. Dale County. Pop. 1,544. 1708 Joe Bruer Road, Daleville, 36322. (334) 347-0422. Mayor Tyrus L. Waters. Clerk Patricia Wambles.

LEXINGTON. Lauderdale County. Pop. 840. P.O. Box 457, 35648. (256) 229-5221. www.lexingtonal.org. Mayor Bobby McGuire. Clerk Jennifer Hendershot.

LIBERTYVILLE. Covington County. Pop. 106. 20,998 Alabama Highway 55, Andalusia, 36420. (334) 222-2996. Mayor Byron D. Dozier. Clerk Marilyn Walker.

LINCOLN. Talladega County. Pop. 4,577. P.O. Box 172, 35096. (205) 763-7777. Mayor Carroll L. Watson. Clerk Laura S. Carmack.

LINDEN. Marengo County. Pop. 2,424. 211 North Main St., 36748. (334) 295-5051. www.lindenalabama.net. Mayor Mitzi Gates. Administrator Cheryl Hall.

LINEVILLE. Clay County. Pop. 2,401. P.O. Box 247, 36266. (256) 396-2581. www.cityoflineville.com. Mayor Roy Adamson. Clerk Cynthia Harris.

LIPSCOMB. Jefferson County. Pop. 2,458. 5512 Avenue H, 35020. (205) 428-6374. Mayor Melanie Bouyer. Clerk Beverly Chatman.

LISMAN. Choctaw County. Pop. 653. P.O. Box 157, 36912. (205) 398-3889. Mayor Thomas E. Jackson. Clerk Donzie M. Spears.

LITTLEVILLE. Colbert County. Pop. 978. 1810 George Wallace Hwy., Russellville, 35654. (256) 332-3567. Mayor Kenneth Copeland. Clerk Alice Vandiver.

LIVINGSTON. Sumter County. Pop. 3,297. P.O. Box W, 35470. (205) 652-2505. www.ci.livingston.al.us. Mayor Thomas M. Tartt III. Clerk Tom Luke Jr.

LOACHAPOKA. Lee County. Pop. 165. P.O. Box 10, 36865. (334) 821-1921. Mayor Larry Justice. Clerk Alice Grout.

LOCKHART. Covington County. Pop. 548. P.O. Box 216, 36455. (334) 858-6744. Mayor Eugene R. Birge. Clerk Barbara Roberts.

LOCUST FORK. Blount County. Pop. 1,016. P.O. Box 67, 35097. (205) 681-4581. Mayor Joseph Hughes. Clerk Tammy Riebe.

LOUISVILLE. Barbour County. Pop. 612. P.O. Box 125, 36048. (334) 266-5210. Mayor James B. Grant. Clerk Janice Clark.

LOWNDESBORO. Lowndes County. Pop. 140. P.O. Box 130, 36752. (334) 278-3434. townoflowndesboro.org. Mayor Rick Pate. Clerk Melanie B. McPherson.

LOXLEY. Baldwin County. Pop. 1,348. P.O. Box 9, 36551. (251) 964-5162. www.townofloxley.org. Mayor Billy J. Middleton. Clerk Carol P. Middleton.

LUVERNE. Crenshaw County. Pop. 2,635. P.O. Box 249, 36049. (334) 335-3741. Mayor Joe R. Sport. Clerk Charlotte W. Flynn.

LYNN. Winston County. Pop. 597. P.O. Box 145, 35575. (205) 893-5250. www. lynnalabama.com. Mayor Ronald Haley. Clerk Marcia Manasco.

MADISON. Madison County. Pop. 29,329. 100 Hughes Road, 35758. (256) 772-5600. www.madisonal.gov. Mayor Paul Finley. Clerk Melanie Williard.

MADRID. Houston County. Pop. 303. 764 Decatur Rd., Box C-48, Cottonwood, 36320. (334) 677-5312. Mayor Elaine Williams. Clerk Luann Hill.

MAGNOLIA SPRINGS. Baldwin County. Pop. 729. P.O. Box 890, 36555. (251) 965-9888. www.townofmagnoliasprings. org. Mayor Charles Houser. Clerk Karen S. Biel.

MALVERN. Geneva County. Pop. 1,215. P.O. Box 98, 36349. (334) 793-6537. Mayor Carl R. Marsh. Clerk Frances Harrison.

MAPLESVILLE. Chilton County. Pop. 672. P.O. Box 9, 36750. (334) 366-4211. Mayor Kurt Wallace. Clerk Sheila Haigler.

MARGARET. St. Clair County. Pop. 1,169. P.O. Box 309, 35112. (205) 629-5742. www.margaretal.com. Mayor Jeffrey G. Wilson. Clerk Marelyn Johnson.

MARION. Perry County. Pop. 3,511. P.O. Drawer 959, 36756. (334) 683-6545. www.marional.gov. Mayor Anthony J. Long. Clerk Carolyn G. Thomas.

MAYTOWN. Jefferson County. Pop. 435. 4505 Town Hall Drive, 35118. (205) 786-8611. Mayor Ann H. Goolsby. Clerk Ann Higgins.

McINTOSH. Washington County. Pop. 244. P.O. Box 385, 36553. (251) 944-2428. Mayor Carrol Daugherty. Clerk Sharon Ross-Akridge.

McKENZIE. Butler County. Pop. 644. P.O. Box 151, 36456. (334) 374-2311. Mayor Melvin Shufford. Clerk Tina Brooks.

McMULLEN. Pickens County. Pop. 66. P.O. Box 469, Aliceville, 35442. (205) 373-2003. Mayor Essie B. Madison. Clerk Carolyn Cleveland.

MEMPHIS. Pickens County. Pop. 33. 128 Memphis Circle, Aliceville, 35442. (205) 373-6726. Mayor Eddie Windham. Clerk Evelyn B. Hinton.

MENTONE. DeKalb County. Pop. 451. P.O. Box 295, 35984. (256) 634-4444. www.town-of-mentone-alabama.com. Mayor Rob Hammond. Clerk Marie S. Dillenbeck.

MIDFIELD. Jefferson County. Pop. 5,626. 725 Bessemer Super Hwy., 35228. (205) 923-7578. www.cityofmidfield.com. Mayor Gary Richardson. Clerk Tameeka Ephriam.

MIDLAND CITY. Dale County. Pop. 1,703. P.O. Box 69, 36350. (334) 983-3511. Mayor Virgil Skipper. Clerk Melissa Knighton.

MIDWAY. Bullock County. Pop. 457. P.O. Box 36, 36053. (334) 529-3261. Mayor James N. Robbins Sr. Clerk Margaret Hill.

MILLBROOK. Elmore County. Pop. 10,386. P.O. Box 630, 36054. (334) 285-6428. www.cityofmillbrook.org. Mayor Al Kelley. Clerk Teresa Mercer.

MILLPORT. Lamar County. Pop. 1,160. P.O. Box 365, 35576. (205) 662-4228. Mayor Waymon Fields. Clerk Lynnette Ogden.

MILLRY. Washington County. Pop. 615. P.O. Box 563, 36558. (251) 846-2698. Mayor Roy Chapman. Clerk Kay Singley.

MOBILE. Mobile County. Pop. 198,915. P.O. Box 1827, 36633. (251) 208-7411. www.cityofmobile.org. Mayor Samuel L. Jones. Clerk Lisa C. Lambert.

MONROEVILLE. Monroe County. Pop. 6,862. P.O. Box 147, 36461. (251) 575-2081. cityofmonroeville.com. Mayor Mike Kennedy. Clerk Toni L. McKelvey.

MONTEVALLO. Shelby County. Pop. 4,825. 545 Main Street, 35115. (205) 665-2555. www.cityofmontevallo.com. Mayor Ben McCrory. Clerk Herman Lehman.

MONTGOMERY. Montgomery County. Pop. 201,568. P.O. Box 1111, 36101. (334) 241-4400. www.montgomeryal.gov. Mayor Todd Strange. Clerk Brenda G. Blalock.

MOODY. St. Clair County. Pop. 8,053. 670

Park Ave., 35004. (205) 640-5121. www. moodyalabama.gov. Mayor Joe Lee. Clerk Patsy Beard.

MOORESVILLE. Limestone County. Pop. 59. P.O. Box 42, 35,649. (256) 353-3628. mooresvillealabama.com. Mayor Susan Goldby. Clerk Margaret-Anne Crumlish.

MORRIS. Jefferson County. Pop. 1,827. P.O. Box 163, 35116. (205) 647-0596. Mayor Craig Drummonds. Clerk Rachael Turner.

MOSSES. Lowndes County. Pop. 1,101. P.O. Box 296, Hayneville, 36040. (334) 563-9141. Mayor William Scott. Clerk Libby L. Burke.

MOULTON. Lawrence County. Pop. 3,260. 720 Seminary Street, 35650. (256) 974-5191. Mayor Ray Alexander. Clerk Shirley Gilley.

MOUNDVILLE. Hale and Tuscaloosa counties. Pop. 1,809. P.O. Box 98, 35474. (205) 371-2641. Mayor Joshua Wyatt. Clerk Carol Townsend.

MOUNT VERNON. Mobile County. Pop. 844. P.O. Box 309, 36560. (251) 829-6633. www.mtvernonal.com. Mayor Jerry C. Lundy. Clerk Bonnie Byrd.

MOUNTAIN BROOK. Jefferson County. Pop. 20,604. P.O. Box 130009, 35213. (205) 870-3532. www.mtnbrook.org. Mayor Lawrence Terry Oden. Clerk Steve Boone.

MOUNTAINBORO. Etowah County. Pop. 338. 19 North Main Street, Boaz, 35956. (256) 593-0087. Mayor John Willis. Clerk Angelia D. Pullen.

MULGA. Jefferson County. Pop. 973. P.O. Box 549, 35118. (205) 781-0645. Mayor Dennis McCrary. Clerk Miranda Black.

MUNFORD. Talladega County. Pop. 1,508. P.O. Box 10, 36268. (256) 358-9050. Mayor D. Lynn Swinford. Clerk Tanya Thomas.

MUSCLE SHOALS. Colbert County. Pop. 11,924. P.O. Box 2624, 35662. (256) 386-9200. cityofmuscleshoals.com. Mayor David Bradford. Clerk Ricky Williams.

MYRTLEWOOD. Marengo County. Pop. 139. P.O. Box 70, 36763. (334) 295-4191. Mayor Fred Sakon. Clerk Betty Barkley.

NAPIER FIELD. Dale County. Pop. 404. 400 Headquarters Street, 36303. (334) 983-3548. Mayor Greg Ballard. Clerk Jackie Holloway.

NATURAL BRIDGE. Winston County. Pop. 28. P.O. Box 367, 35577. (205) 486-8449. www.geocities.com/naturalbridge 35577. Mayor A. G. Parrish. Clerk Barbara Tidwell.

NAUVOO. Walker County. Pop. 284. P.O. Box 186, 35578. (205) 697-5890. Mayor Darrell Mote. Clerk Sheila Bridgmon.

NECTAR. Blount County. Pop. 372. P.O. Box 235, Cleveland, 35049. (205) 559-7780. Mayor Rickey Box. Clerk Sue Gaither.

NEEDHAM. Choctaw County. Pop. 97. 2553 Needham Road, 36915. (205) 673-3088. Mayor Quinnie Donald. Clerk Donna Grice.

NEW BROCKTON. Coffee County. Pop. 1,250. P.O. Box 70, 36351. (334) 894-5283. Mayor Lenwood Herron. Clerk Catina Tyson.

NEW HOPE. Madison County. Pop. 2,539. P.O. Box 419, 35760. (256) 723-2616. Mayor John Howard. Clerk Sherrie

Davis.

NEW SITE. Tallapoosa County. Pop. 848. 12791 Highway. 22 East, 36256. (256) 234-2049. Mayor Curtis Mims. Clerk Deloris Riddle.

NEWBERN. Hale County. Pop. 231. P.O. Box 147, 36765. (334) 624-3633. Mayor Haywood F. Stokes III. Clerk Lynn O. Williams.

NEWTON. Dale County. Pop. 1,708. P.O. Box 10, 36352. (334) 299-3361. Mayor Ted Stanford. Clerk Nina Dickerson.

NEWVILLE. Henry County. Pop. 553. P.O. Box 119, 36353. (334) 889-2222. Mayor Kent Whiddon. Clerk Debra Gordon.

NORTH COURTLAND. Lawrence County. Pop. 799. P.O. Box 93, 35618. (256) 637-6378. Mayor Ronald Jones. Clerk Della Miller-Taylor.

NORTH JOHNS. Jefferson County. Pop. 142. P.O. Box 156, Adger, 35006. (205) 425-6524. Mayor Kenneth Lindsey. Clerk Cynthia Dunn.

NORTHPORT. Tuscaloosa County. Pop. 19,435. P.O. Box 569, 35476. (205) 339-7000. www.cityofnorthport.org. Mayor Bobby Herndon. Clerk Rosemary Nichols.

NOTASULGA. Lee and Macon counties. Pop. 916. P.O. Box 207, 36866. (334) 257-1454. Mayor Frank Tew. Clerk Wanda Ingram.

OAK GROVE. Talladega County. Pop. 457. 2364 Forest Glen Road, 35150. (256) 249-9971. Mayor Charles R. Merkel. Clerk Carolyn Zeigler.

OAK HILL. Wilcox County. Pop. 37. P.O. Box 9, 36766. (251) 746-2443. Mayor F. David Fuller. Clerk Olivia S. Dale.

OAKMAN. Walker County. Pop. 944. P.O. Box 267, 35579. (205) 622-3232. Mayor Joyce Todd. Clerk Deanna Woods.

ODENVILLE. St. Clair County. Pop. 1,956. P.O. Box 113, 35120. (205) 629-6366. Mayor Rodney Christian. Clerk Priscilla Newton.

OHATCHEE. Calhoun County. Pop. 1,215. P.O. Box 645, 36271. (256) 892-3233. Mayor Steve Baswell. Clerk Kelli Lee.

ONEONTA. Blount County. Pop. 5,576. 202 Third Avenue East, 35121. (205) 274-2150. cityofoneonta.us. Mayor Darryl Ray. Clerk Tammie Noland.

ONYCHA. Covington County. Pop. 208. 16901 U.S. Highway 331, Opp, 36467. (334) 493-4202. Mayor Jerry Smith. Clerk Annette Johns.

OPELIKA. Lee County. Pop. 23,498. P.O. Box 390, 36803. (334) 705-5150. www.opelika.org. Mayor Gary Fuller. Clerk Bob Shuman.

OPP. Covington County. Pop. 6,607. P.O. Box 610, 36467. (334) 493-4572. Mayor H. D. Edgar. Clerk Connie Smith.

ORANGE BEACH. Baldwin County. Pop. 3,784. P.O. Box 458, 36561. (251) 981-6979. www.cityoforangebeach.com. Mayor Anthony T. Kennon. Clerk Cathy Constantino.

ORRVILLE. Dallas County. Pop. 230. P.O. Box 98, 36767. (334) 996-9726. Mayor Gene McHugh. Clerk Vernon Anderson.

OWENS CROSS ROADS. Madison County. Pop. 1,124. P.O. Box 158, 35763. (256) 725-4163. Mayor Curtis J. Craig Sr. Clerk Barbara Webster.

OXFORD. Calhoun County. Pop. 14,592. P.O. Box 3383, 36203. (256) 835-6100. www.oxfordalabama.org. Mayor Leon

Smith. Clerk Shirley Henson.

OZARK. Dale County. Pop. 15,119. P.O. Box 1987, 36361. (334) 774-5393. www.ozarkalabama.us. Mayor William E. "Billy" Blackwell. Clerk Melissa Robinson.

PAINT ROCK. Jackson County. Pop. 185. P.O. Box 143, 35764. (256) 776-3393. Mayor Michael Counts. Clerk Shirley Johnson.

PARRISH. Walker County. Pop. 1,268. P.O. Box 89, 35580. (205) 686-9991. Mayor Wayne Gross. Clerk Marcy Brown.

PELHAM. Shelby County. Pop. 14,369. P.O. Box 1419, 35124. (205) 620-6400. www.pelhamonline.com. Mayor Don Murphy. Clerk Donna Treslar.

PELL CITY. St. Clair County. Pop. 9,565. 1905 First Avenue North, 35125. (205) 338-2244. www.cityofpellcity.com. Mayor Bill Hereford. Clerk Jennifer Brown.

PENNINGTON. Choctaw County. Pop. 353. P.O. Box 40, 36916. (205) 654-2688. Mayor Jack Fendley. Clerk Vanessa C. Woodard.

PETREY. Crenshaw County. Pop. 63. 44 Community House Road, Luverne, 36049. (334) 335-6700. Mayor Curtis Petrey. Clerk Sue Beasley.

PHENIX CITY. Russell County. Pop. 28,265. 601 12th Street, 36867. (334) 448-2726. www.phenixcityal.us. Mayor H. S. "Sonny" Coulter. Clerk Charlotte L. Sierra.

PHIL CAMPBELL. Franklin County. Pop. 1,091. P.O. Box 489, 35581. (205) 993-5313. Mayor Jerry Mays. Clerk Ann Bragwell.

PICKENSVILLE. Pickens County. Pop. 662. 16831 Highway. 14, 35447. (205) 373-2068. Mayor Mary L. Fuseyamore. Clerk Shirley Fields.

PIEDMONT. Calhoun County. Pop. 5,120. P.O. Box 112, 36272. (256) 447-9007. www.piedmontcity.org. Mayor Brian Young. Clerk Michelle Franklin.

PIKE ROAD. Montgomery County. Pop. 312. 4902 Pike Road, 36064. (334) 272-9883. www.pikeroad.us. Mayor Gordon Stone. Clerk Charlene Rabren.

PINCKARD. Dale County. Pop. 667. P.O. Box 202, 36371. (334) 983-3517. Mayor Fred M. McNab. Clerk Dana H. Courtney.

PINE APPLE. Wilcox County. Pop. 145. P.O. Box 8, 36768. (251) 746-2514. Mayor Chris Stone. Clerk Lynn Grimes.

PINE HILL. Wilcox County. Pop. 966. P.O. Drawer 397, 36769. (334) 963-4351. Mayor Harry A. Mason. Clerk Marjorie H. Sheffield.

PINE RIDGE. DeKalb County. Pop. 243. 58 Municipal Drive, Fort Payne, 35968. (256) 845-2200. Mayor Mary Jo Chandler. Clerk Sybil Jones.

PINSON. Jefferson County. Pop. 6,081. P.O. Box 1599, 35126. (205) 680-5556. www.thecityofpinson.com. Mayor Hoyt Sanders. Clerk Marie Turner.

PISGAH. Jackson County. Pop. 706. P.O. Box 2, 35765. (256) 451-3232. Mayor Chris Woods. Clerk Jennifer Hall.

PLEASANT GROVE. Jefferson County. Pop. 9,983. 501 Park Road, 35127. (205) 744-1720. www.cityofpg.com. Mayor Jerry W. Brasseale. Clerk Karen Duncan.

PLEASANT GROVES. Jackson County. Pop. 447. 3973 County Road 8, Woodville, 35776. (256) 587-3132. Mayor Mickey

L. West. Clerk Deveda Cain.

POLLARD. Escambia County. Pop. 120. 415 Canterbury Street, 36441-1415. (251) 296-0195. Mayor Valeria P. Osby. Clerk Sharon Pleasant.

POWELL. DeKalb County. Pop. 926. 110 Broad Street North, Fyffe, 35971. (256) 638-4283. Mayor Eugene Byrum. Clerk Cora (Susie) Wilbourn.

PRATTVILLE. Autauga County. Pop. 24,303. 101 West Main Street, 36067. (334) 361-3609. www.prattville.com. Mayor Jim Byard Jr. Clerk Gina Smith.

PRICEVILLE. Morgan County. Pop. 2,151. 242 Marco Drive, 35603. (256) 355-5476. www.townofpriceville.com. Mayor Melvin Duran. Clerk Kelly Dean.

PRICHARD. Mobile County. Pop. 28,633. P.O. Box 10427, 36610. (251) 452-7861. thecityofprichard.org. Mayor Ronald K. Davis. Clerk Darlene P. Lewis.

PROVIDENCE. Marengo County. Pop. 311. P.O. Box 581, Linden, 36748. (334) 295-8419. Mayor John Ed Crawford. Clerk Marvene C. Pickard.

RAGLAND. St. Clair County. Pop. 1,918. 220 Fredia Street, Suite 102, 35131. (205) 472-0400. Mayor Lanis White. Clerk Penny Owens.

RAINBOW CITY. Etowah County. Pop. 8,428. 3700 Rainbow Drive, 35906. (256) 442-2511. rbcalabama.com. Mayor Terry John Calhoun. Clerk Barbara T. Wester.

RAINSVILLE. DeKalb County. Pop. 4,499. P.O. Box 309, 35986. (256) 638-6331. Mayor Donnie Chandler. Clerk Judy Lewis.

RANBURNE. Cleburne County. Pop. 459. P.O. Box 219, 36273. (256) 568-3483.

Mayor Owen Lowery. Clerk Pamela W. Richardson.

RED BAY. Franklin County. Pop. 3,374. P.O. Box 2002, 35582. (256) 356-4473. www.cityofredbay.org. Mayor Bobby Forsythe. Clerk Linda B. Holcomb.

RED LEVEL. Covington County. Pop. 556. P.O. Box 236, 36474. (334) 469-5351. www.redleveltown.com. Mayor Michael Purnell. Clerk Deborah Hoffman.

REECE CITY. Etowah County. Pop. 634. 1023 Valley Drive, Attalla, 35954. (256) 538-6521. Mayor Randall Scott. Clerk Kathy Jones.

REFORM. Pickens County. Pop. 1,978. P.O. Box 489, 35481. (205) 375-6363. Mayor Frank Criswell. Clerk Annette Reed.

REHOBETH. Houston County. Pop. 993. 5449 County Road 203, 36301. (334) 671-5829. www.rehobethalabama.com. Mayor Joe P. Collins. Clerk Barbara E. Hall.

REPTON. Conecuh County. Pop. 280. P.O. Box 35, 36475. (251) 248-2370. Mayor Terri B. Carter. Clerk Lisa Bartlett.

RIDGEVILLE. Etowah County. Pop. 158. P.O. Box 423, Attalla, 35954. (256) 538-8968. Mayor Deborah Adair. Clerk Beluah Lawrence.

RIVER FALLS. Covington County. Pop. 616. P.O. Box 17, 36476. (334) 222-3510. Mayor Mary G. Hixon. Clerk Christine Morgan.

RIVERSIDE. St. Clair County. Pop. 1,564. P.O. Box 130, 35135. (205) 338-7692. www.riversidealabama.net. Mayor M. S. "Rusty" Jessup. Clerk Rhonda F. Burns.

RIVERVIEW. Escambia County. Pop. 99. P.O. Box 2368, Brewton, 36427. (251) 867-5378. Mayor Carl O. Smith. Clerk

Jeanette Moore.

ROANOKE. Randolph County. Pop. 6,563. P.O. Box 1270, 36274. (334) 863-4129. Mayor Mike Fisher. Clerk Ellen Farmer.

ROBERTSDALE. Baldwin County. Pop. 3,782. P.O. Box 429, 36567. (251) 947-8900. www.robertsdale.org. Mayor Charles H. Murphy. Clerk Shannon Ellison.

ROCKFORD. Coosa County. Pop. 428. P.O. Box 128, 35136. (256) 377-4911. Mayor Randall Lewis. Clerk Doris Culver.

ROGERSVILLE. Lauderdale County. Pop. 1,199. P.O. Box 540, 35652. (256) 247-5446. www.rogersvillealabama. org. Mayor Richard Herston. Clerk Lisa Crumbley.

ROSA. Blount County. Pop. 313. P.O. Box 1454, Oneonta, 35121. (205) 625-6088. Mayor Andy Ellis. Clerk Julia K. Whisenant.

RUSSELLVILLE. Franklin County. Pop. 8,971. P.O. Box 1000, 35653. (256) 332-6060. www.russellvillegov.com. Mayor Troy Oliver. Clerk Kimberly Wright.

RUTLEDGE. Crenshaw County. Pop. 476. P.O. Box 85, 36071. (334) 335-6624. www.rutledge-al.com. Mayor Joe Dexter Flynn. Clerk Rita Brown.

SAINT FLORIAN. Lauderdale County. Pop. 335. 4508 County Road 47, Florence, 35634. (256) 767-3690. www.stflori-analabama.com. Mayor Louis A. Stumpe. Clerk Carlene Moomaw.

SAMSON. Geneva County. Pop. 2,071. 104 East Main Street, 36477. (334) 898-7541. cityofsamson.com. Mayor Clay King. Clerk Hazel McGowan.

SAND ROCK. Cherokee County. Pop. 509. 1925 Sand Rock Avenue, 35983. (256) 523-5898. Mayor Bill Glenn Jr. Clerk Melanie Garrett.

SANFORD. Covington County. Pop. 269. P.O. Box 248, Andalusia 36420. (334) 493-3888. Mayor John P. Thomasson. Clerk Robin Bowers.

SARALAND. Mobile County. Pop. 12,288. 716 Highway 43 South, 36571. (251) 675-5103. www.saraland.org. Mayor Ken Williams. Clerk Denise Jernigan-Bush.

SARDIS CITY. Etowah County. Pop. 1,438. 1335 Sardis Drive, 35956. (256) 593-6492. www.sardiscity.com. Mayor Terry W. Stephens. Clerk Doug Gamblin.

SATSUMA. Mobile County. Pop. 5,687. P.O. Box 517, 36572. (251) 675-1440. www.cityofsatsuma.com. Mayor William Stewart III. Clerk Vicki Miller.

SCOTTSBORO. Jackson County. Pop. 14,762. 316 S. Broad Street, 35768. (256) 574-3100. cityofscottsboro.com. Mayor Melton Potter. Clerk Cathy O'Shields.

SECTION. Jackson County. Pop. 769. P.O. Box 310, 35771. (256) 228-3280. Mayor Bob Matthews. Clerk Linda Tolbert.

SELMA. Dallas County. Pop. 20,512. P.O. Box 450, 36702. (334) 874-2102. www.selma-al.gov. Mayor George P. Evans. Clerk Ivy S. Harrison.

SHEFFIELD. Colbert County. Pop. 9,652. P.O. Box 380, 35660. (256) 383-0250. Mayor Ian T. Sanford. Clerk Clayton Kelly.

SHILOH. DeKalb County. Pop. 289. P.O. Box 924, Rainsville, 35986. (205) 623-1094. Mayor Charles D. Liles. Clerk Shelia Phillips.

SHORTER. Macon County. Pop. 355. P.O. Box 117, 36075. (334) 727-9190. www.shorteralabama.com. Mayor Willie Mae

Powell. Clerk Harold Powell.

SILAS. Choctaw County. Pop. 529. P.O. Box 147, 36916. (251) 542-9716. Mayor Shirley M. Perry. Clerk Sara Jane Welford.

SILVERHILL. Baldwin County. Pop. 616. P.O. Box 309, 36576. (251) 945-5198. Mayor Timothy C. Wilson. Clerk Bonnie McNeil.

SIPSEY. Walker County. Pop. 552. P.O. Box 156, 35584. (205) 648-8154. Mayor Anita Sanders. Clerk Terry Kizziah.

SKYLINE. Jackson County. Pop. 843. 21638 Ala. Hwy. 79, Scottsboro, 35768. (256) 587-3335. Mayor Archie Rice. Clerk Angie Scarberry.

SLOCOMB. Geneva County. Pop. 2,052. P.O. Box 1147, 36375. (334) 886-2955. www.slocombcity.com. Mayor Rob Hinson. Clerk Peggy Armstrong.

SMITHS STATION. Lee County. Pop. 4,752. P.O. Box 250, 36877. (334) 297-8771. www.smithsstation.us. Mayor LaFaye Dellinger. Clerk Jerry Bentley.

SNEAD. Blount County. Pop. 748. P.O. Box 505, 35952. (205) 466-3200. Mayor Tim Kent. Clerk Rae Ware.

SOMERVILLE. Morgan County. Pop. 347. P.O. Box 153, 35670. (256) 778-8282. Mayor Ray Long. Clerk Regina Long.

SOUTH VINEMONT. Cullman County. Pop. 425. P.O. Box 130, Vinemont, 35179. (256) 737-5411. Mayor Melba Patton. Clerk Angie Chambers.

SOUTHSIDE. Etowah County. Pop. 7,036. 2255 Highway 77, 35907. (256) 442-9775. www.cityofsouthside.com. Mayor Wally Burns. Clerk Cynthia B. Osborne.

SPANISH FORT. Baldwin County. Pop. 5,423. P.O. Box 7226, 36577. (251) 626-4884. cityofspanishfort.com. Mayor Joseph C. Bonner. Clerk Mary Lynn Williams.

SPRINGVILLE. St. Clair County. Pop. 2,521. P.O. Box 919, 35146. (205) 467-6133. www.cityofspringvilleal.org. Mayor William Isley Jr. Clerk Brenda Roberts.

STEELE. St. Clair County. Pop. 1,093. P.O. Box 425, 35987. (256) 538-8145. Mayor John W. McHugh Jr. Clerk Patricia Coffee.

STEVENSON. Jackson County. Pop. 1,770. 104 Kentucky Avenue, 35772. (256) 437-3000. Mayor Rickey Steele Sr. Clerk Katye Tipton.

SULLIGENT. Lamar County. Pop. 2,151. P.O. Box 365, 35586. (205) 698-9111. Mayor J. Scott Boman. Clerk Gary Mosley.

SUMITON. Walker County. Pop. 2,665. P.O. Box 10, 35148. (205) 648-9191. thecityofsumiton.com. Mayor Harry L. Ellis. Clerk Judy M. Glover.

SUMMERDALE. Baldwin County. Pop. 655. P.O. Box 148, 36580. (251) 989-6202. summerdalealabama.com. Mayor David Wilson. Clerk Tiffany Lynn.

SUSAN MOORE. Blount County. Pop. 721. 39989 State Highway 75, Altoona, 35952. (205) 466-7400. Mayor Jamie Brothers. Clerk Beverly Mize.

SWEET WATER. Marengo County. Pop. 234. P.O. Box 33, 36782. (334) 994-4120. Mayor Wilbon R. Davis. Clerk Mary Jo Windham.

SYLACAUGA. Talladega County. Pop. 12,616. P.O. Box 390, 35150. (256) 401-2400. www.sylacauga.net. Mayor Sam Wright. Clerk Patricia G. Carden.

SYLVAN SPRINGS. Jefferson County. Pop.

1,465. 300 Town Hall Drive, 35118. (205) 491-3210. www.sylvansprings. net. Mayor Stevan H. Parsons. Clerk Peggy Shadix.

SYLVANIA. DeKalb County. Pop. 1,186. P.O. Box 150, 35988. (256) 638-2604. Mayor Mitchell Dendy. Clerk Michael P. Kling.

TALLADEGA. Talladega County. Pop. 15,143. P.O. Box 498, 35161. (256) 362-8186. www.talladega.com. Mayor Brian York. Clerk Beth Cheeks.

TALLADEGA SPRINGS. Talladega County. Pop. 124. 32 Old Cedar Creek Road, Sylacauga, 35151. (256) 245-2214. Mayor Franklin D. Mitchell. Clerk Nancy Mitchell.

TALLASSEE. Elmore and Tallapoosa counties. Pop. 4,934. 3 Freeman Avenue, 36078. (334) 283-6571. tallassee.al.us. Mayor George A. McCain. Clerk Barbara B. Garnett.

TARRANT. Jefferson County. Pop. 7,022. 1604 Pinson Valley Parkway, 35217. (205) 849-2800. Mayor Loxcil Tuck. Clerk Cheryl Green.

TAYLOR. Houston County. Pop. 1,898. 1469 South County Road 59, 36301. (334) 677-5079. Mayor Joel H. Napier. Clerk Barbara F. Benton.

THOMASTON. Marengo County. Pop. 383. P.O. Box 276, 36783. (334) 627-3434. Mayor Jeff Laduron. Clerk Carolyn H. Finley.

THOMASVILLE. Clarke County. Pop. 4,649. P.O. Box 127, 36784. (334) 636-5827. www.thomasvilleal.com. Mayor Sheldon A. Day. Clerk Deborah P. Ballard.

THORSBY. Chilton County. Pop. 1,820. P.O. Box 608, 35171. (205) 646-3575.

Mayor Richard "Dearl" Hilyer. Clerk Denise D. Gunn.

TOWN CREEK. Lawrence County. Pop. 1,216. P.O. Box 190, 35672. (256) 685-3344. Mayor Mike Parker. Clerk Christy Welborn.

TOXEY. Choctaw County. Pop. 152. P.O. Box 318, 36921. (251) 843-5222. Mayor Jeanette F. Carney. Clerk Mary Mooney.

TRAFFORD. Jefferson County. Pop. 523. 9239 East Commercial Avenue, 35172. (205) 647-3751. Mayor Robert E. Niblett. Clerk Carolyn Tyler.

TRIANA. Madison County. Pop. 458. 640 Sixth Street, Madison, 35756. (256) 772-0151. Mayor Mary Caudle. Clerk Sharron Humphrey.

TRINITY. Morgan County. Pop. 1,841. 35 Preston Drive, 35673. (256) 353-2474. Mayor Vaughn Goodwin. Clerk Barbara Jones.

TROY. Pike County. Pop. 13,935. P.O. Box 549, 36081. (334) 566-0177. www.troy-alabama.com. Mayor Jimmy E. Lunsford. Clerk Alton Starling.

TRUSSVILLE. Jefferson and St. Clair counties. Pop. 12,924. P.O. Box 159, 35173. (205) 655-7478. www.trussville.org. Mayor Eugene A. Melton. Clerk Lynn B. Porter.

TUSCALOOSA. Tuscaloosa County. Pop. 77,906. P.O. Box 2089, 35403. (205) 248-5010. www.tuscaloosa.com. Mayor Walt Maddox. Clerk Tracy Croom.

TUSCUMBIA. Colbert County. Pop. 7,856. P.O. Box 29, 35674. (256) 383-5463. cityoftuscumbia.org. Mayor Billy S. Shoemaker. Clerk Jo Ann Armstead.

TUSKEGEE. Macon County. Pop. 11,846.

P.O. Box 830687, 36083. (334) 720-0500. www.tuskegeealabama.org. Mayor Omar Neal. Clerk Alfred Davis.

TWIN. Marion County. Pop. 450. 6125 State Highway 253, Guin, 35563. (205) 384-8978. Mayor Charles R. Baccus. Clerk Johnny Walker.

UNION. Greene County. Pop. 227. 7657 County Road 191, Eutaw, 35462. (205) 372-3498. Mayor James Gaines Jr. Clerk Marilyn Sanford.

UNION GROVE. Marshall County. Pop. 94. P.O. Box 67, 35175. (256) 753-2210. Mayor David Dwayne Smith. Clerk Sarah Bunch.

UNION SPRINGS. Bullock County. Pop. 3,670. P.O. Box 549, 36089. (334) 738-2720. Mayor John McGowan. Clerk Cathy Dickerson.

UNIONTOWN. Perry County. Pop. 1,636. P.O. Box 1069, 36786. (334) 628-2011. www.uniontownalabama.org. Mayor Jamaal Hunter. Clerk Alfreda B. Washington.

VALLEY. Chambers County. Pop. 9,198. P.O. Box 186, 36854. (334) 756-5220. www.cityofvalley.com. Mayor Arnold Leak. Clerk Martha Cato.

VALLEY GRANDE. Dallas County. Pop. 1,979. 5914 Alabama Highway 22, 36703. (334) 872-0104. www.cityofvalleygrande.com. Mayor Tom Lee. Clerk Janet Frasier.

VALLEY HEAD. DeKalb County. Pop. 611. P.O. Box 144, 35989. (256) 635-6814. Mayor Kenneth Hammond. Clerk Debra Rhodes.

VANCE. Tuscaloosa County. Pop. 500. P.O. Box 107, 35490. (205) 553-8278. www.vanceusa.com. Mayor Keith Mahaffey.

Clerk Tracy Burt.

VERNON. Lamar County. Pop. 2,143. P.O. Box 357, 35592. (205) 695-7718. Mayor Dupree Pennington. Clerk Rebecca Cantrell.

VESTAVIA HILLS. Jefferson and Shelby counties. Pop. 30,418. 513 Montgomery Highway, 35216. (205) 978-0100. www.vestaviahills.net. Mayor Alberto "Butch" Zaragoza Jr. Clerk Rebecca Leavings.

VINA. Franklin County. Pop. 400. P.O. Box 6, 35593. (256) 356-4996. Mayor D. W. Franklin. Clerk Sue Raper.

VINCENT. Shelby County. Pop. 1,853. P.O. Box 49, 35178. (205) 672-2261. Mayor Ray McAllister. Clerk Joy Marler.

VREDENBURGH. Wilcox and Monroe counties. Pop. 327. P.O. Box 285, 36481. (334) 337-4587. Mayor Delois Adams. Clerk Pricilla M. Castophney.

WADLEY. Randolph County. Pop. 640. P.O. Box 9, 36276. (256) 395-2261. Mayor Jim Dabbs. Clerk Marsha Poe.

WALDO. Talladega County. Pop. 281. 39 Sorghum Lane, Talladega, 35160. (256) 362-9313. www.waldoal.com. Mayor Henry Howard. Clerk Iris Jemison.

WALNUT GROVE. Etowah County. Pop. 710. P.O. Box 100, 35990. (205) 589-2553. Mayor Autry Works. Clerk Kelly Hollingsworth.

WARRIOR. Jefferson County. Pop. 3,169. 215 Main Street, 35180. (205) 647-0520. Mayor Rena Hudson. Clerk Demetra Mixon.

WATERLOO. Lauderdale County. Pop. 208. P.O. Box 38, 35677. (256) 764-3237. Mayor Neil Scott. Clerk Kimberly Franks.

WAVERLY. Chambers and Lee counties.

Pop. 184. P.O. Box 115, 36879. (334) 887-0999. Mayor Ellen L. Hilyer. Clerk Carolyn Moreman.

WEAVER. Calhoun County. Pop. 2,619. P.O. Box 1060, 36277. (256) 820-1125. Mayor Garry D. Bearden. Clerk Teresa H. Summerlin.

WEBB. Houston County. Pop. 1,298. P.O. Box 127, 36376. (334) 792-0386. Mayor Vicky Hunter. Clerk Kim Brown.

WEDOWEE. Randolph County. Pop. 818. P.O. Box 270, 36278. (256) 357-2122. www.cityofwedowee.org. Mayor Timothy Coe. Clerk Susan Cooper.

WEST BLOCTON. Bibb County. Pop. 1,372. P.O. Box 187, 35184. (205) 938-7622. Mayor J. E. "Jabo" Reese. Clerk Pamela H. Morse.

WEST JEFFERSON. Jefferson County. Pop. 344. P.O. Box 158, Quinton, 35130. (205) 674-3219. Mayor Charles D. Nix. Clerk Angela Romano.

WEST POINT. Cullman County. Pop. 295. P.O. Box 1641, Cullman, 35056. (256) 734-0006. Mayor Kenneth Kilgo. Clerk Joyce Sapp.

WESTOVER. Shelby County. Pop. 918. P.O. Box 356, 35185. (205) 678-3375. www.westoveralabama.org. Mayor Mark McLaughlin. Clerk Wayne Jones.

WETUMPKA. Elmore County. Pop. 5,726. P.O. Box 1180, 36092. (334) 567-5147. cityofwetumpka.com. Mayor Jerry Willis. Clerk Janice G. Whorton.

WHITE HALL. Lowndes County. Pop. 1,014. 625 Freedom Road, 36040. (334) 875-5703. Mayor John Jackson. Clerk Bertha White.

WILSONVILLE. Shelby County. Pop. 1,551. P.O. Box 70, 35186. (205) 669-6180.

Mayor Rosemary C. Liveoak. Clerk Kay M. Ray.

WILTON. Shelby County. Pop. 580. P.O. Box 159, 35187. (205) 665-2021. Mayor Joe H. Fancher. Clerk April Price.

WINFIELD. Fayette and Marion counties. Pop. 4,540. P.O. Drawer 1438, 35594. (205) 487-4337. www.winfieldcity.org. Mayor Wayne Silas. Clerk Candace Reed.

WOODLAND. Randolph County. Pop. 192. P.O. Box 156, 36280. (256) 449-2222. Mayor Tim Prince. Clerk Lucy Arrington.

WOODSTOCK. Bibb County. Pop. 986. P.O. Box 250, 35188. (205) 938-9790. www.woodstockalabama.com. Mayor Rickey Kornegay. Clerk Faye Gamble.

WOODVILLE. Jackson County. Pop. 761. P.O. Box 94, 35776. (256) 776-2860. www.woodvilleonline.com. Mayor Faye Cook. Clerk Brenda Austin.

YELLOW BLUFF. Wilcox County. Pop. 181. 80 Park Avenue, 36769. (334) 963-4881. Mayor Glen McCord. Clerk Bairjail Atwood.

YORK. Sumter County. Pop. 2,854. 607 2nd Avenue, 36925. (205) 392-5231. Mayor Glenda DuBose. Clerk LaKetha Fluker.

10

STATISTICS AND DEMOGRAPHICS

DON BOGIE

Dramatic changes have characterized Alabama's population since the achievement of statehood in 1819. From a count of only 128,000 people in the state's first census in 1820 to an estimated 4.6 million people in 2007, its population has increased more than thirty-six fold. While Alabama was a predominantly rural and agricultural state from 1820 until well into the twentieth century, a majority of the population now lives in metropolitan areas and its major industries include education, health, manufacturing, and retail trade. Recent growth in the manufacturing and high-tech sectors has drawn attention, if not envy, from across the nation, with Alabama becoming one of the South's leaders in motor-vehicle manufacturing.

No longer the youthful population it was at the time of statehood, or even at the turn of the twentieth century, the median age of Alabamians is approaching forty and the elderly now account for nearly one of every seven people in the state. Likewise, education and income levels have increased exponentially, and the state is increasingly diverse. Alabamians listed more than one hundred ancestry and nationality groups in the last census, while the state's Hispanic population has quadrupled over the last twenty-five years. In addition to experiencing social and economic gains, today's Alabamians are living much longer than their predecessors. While life expectancy at birth was estimated to have been less than fifty years at the turn of the twentieth century, it is now seventy-five years for the general population. Thus, the twenty-five years of life added since 1900 totals one-third of the life expectancy Alabamians enjoy today.

Although many of the population-related changes that have taken place over the years clearly indicate progress, other trends and indicators cast a more ominous shadow over the Alabama landscape. Changes in the agricultural sector and limited economic and employment opportunities have led to heavy out-migration at various junctures in the state's history. The gaps are generally closing, but the state continues to lag behind U.S. averages relative to many social and economic benchmarks, including educational attainment, income levels, and the proportion of the population living in poverty. The settlement and accompanying growth of minority populations has not always been welcome in some Alabama communities, fostering conditions that have hindered socioeconomic advancement. Health-related issues—including higher rates of diabetes, obesity, heart disease, and stroke than in most other states—have acted as impediments to even larger gains in life expectancy.

The graphics in this chapter of *The Alabama Guide* attempt to capture some of the most noteworthy demographic changes that have marked Alabama over the decades. Thus, almost all of the tables, charts, and graphs included herein contain historical information. Several of the graphics also look forward in time. Projections of future demographic trends provide educated guesses of what may lie ahead as the Alabama population moves beyond the formative years of the twenty-first century. While two centuries of demographic events and history can hardly be captured in a few graphic snapshots, the attempt has been made to include at least some of the most essential information that can be derived from U.S. decennial census publications and other reports.

The study of population begins with the number of people, clearly the most basic demographic fact about any geographic area whether large or small. Thus, the initial graphics presented in this chapter examine population totals for the state as a whole and for other major sectors of the Alabama population (including rural and urban areas, counties, metropolitan areas, and cities).

Next, the "composition" of the Alabama population is analyzed through a series of charts and graphs that address age, gender distribution, the race and ethnic composition of the population, the foreign-born population, and some of the myriad groups to which Alabamians trace their ancestry. Most of the graphics pertain to the social and economic characteristics of the Alabama population. Family and household composition, income, poverty, educational attainment, and the occupational pursuits of Alabamians are among the topics that are addressed. The chapter concludes with an examination of changes in life expectancy for the Alabama population over the last half century.

Collectively, these graphics present a series of snapshots of the "way we were" and the direction in which the state may be headed. They indicate that major challenges still lie ahead in adequately educating our youth, providing good jobs and opportunities for economic advancement, strengthening families, and lifting people out of poverty. Many rural communities across the state have been depleted by years of out-migration and are now virtually stagnant, even as Alabama has become, at least on paper, an urban/metropolitan state. Alabama can hardly afford to ignore the rural communities where nearly half of the population still lives. As the diversity of the state continues to increase, intolerance and discrimination still create social tensions that prevent us from realizing our full potential as a people and as a state. With the "graying of Alabama," the needs of our senior citizens will become much more visible and immediate in the years ahead, with significant implications for housing, recreation, health care, and transportation. These, as well as demographic challenges yet unseen, will evolve as the state's population continues to change.

At approximately 4.6 million people, Alabama comprises only 1.5 percent of the U.S. population. Still, it is the twenty-third most populous state in the union, ranking ahead of South Carolina by approximately two hundred thousand people and behind Colorado by about the same number. Alabama is characterized by a slowly growing population, ranking thirty-second in numerical increase over the period 2000–2007.

Traditionally, Alabama has depended on many more births than deaths to fuel population growth. But the birth rate has declined and moved much closer to the death rate. Thus, migration has become a much more significant factor in the state's continued growth. Indeed, the extent to which Alabama can attract more people than it is losing in the years ahead will be critical to whether it will continue to be ranked in the upper half of the nation's most-populous states and maintain the congressional seats that it currently has in Washington.

The South has emerged as one of the nation's fastest-growing regions in recent decades, but Alabama has not shared fully in that growth. Although recent economic and demographic gains suggest that Alabama is rising, the state has often ranked in the third tier of southern states in population increase. Will Alabama continue to play only a secondary role in the South's resurgence, or will it emerge as one of the region's main players as we move deeper into the twenty-first century? Continued advancement across the entire institutional framework—education, the economy, the workplace, government and political leadership, and human relationships—will be essential to the outcome.

SOCIOLOGIST DON BOGIE retired as director of the Center for Demographic Research at Auburn University Montgomery. Dr. Bogie is the author or coauthor of more than fifty journal articles, chapters in books, monographs, and other reports and has been a frequent contributor to the op-ed pages of the state's major newspapers. He continues to be active in community and professional groups, and, as a consultant to the Mid-Alabama Coalition for the Homeless, his proposals to the U.S. Department of Housing and Urban Development have helped to generate approximately $13.5 million for local programs.

TABLE 1:

ALABAMA CENSUS TOTALS AND PERCENT CHANGE IN POPULATION, 1820–2000

Year	Census Total	Percent Change in Population from Preceding Census
1820*	127,901	-
1830	309,527	142.0
1840	590,756	90.9
1850	771,623	30.6
1860	964,201	25.0
1870	996,992	3.4
1880	1,262,505	26.6
1890	1,513,401	19.9
1900	1,828,697	20.8
1910	2,138,093	16.9
1920	2,348,174	9.8
1930	2,646,248	12.7
1940	2,832,961	7.1
1950	3,061,743	8.1
1960	3,266,740	6.7
1970	3,444,354	5.4
1980	3,894,025**	13.1
1990	4,040,578	3.8
2000	4,447,100	10.1

*First census after statehood.

**Revised census total.

Sources: U.S. Census Bureau, Decennial Censuses of the Population for 1820–2000.

TABLE 2:

PERCENT CHANGE IN THE ALABAMA
AND U.S. POPULATION, 1940–2007

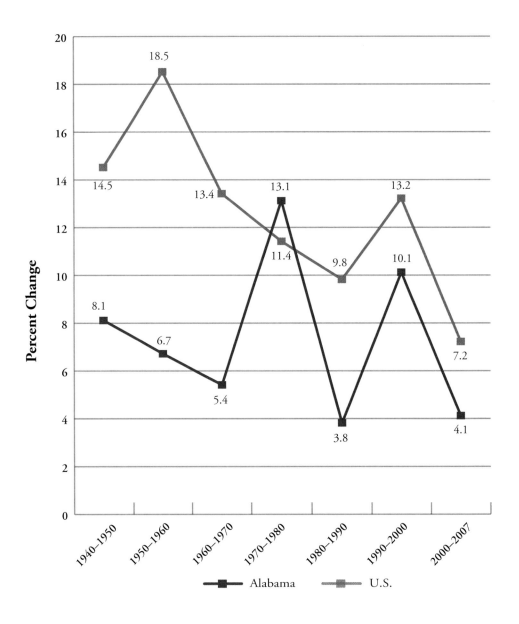

Sources: U.S. Census Bureau, Decennial Censuses of the Population for 1940–2000; Annual Estimates of the Population for the U.S., Regions, and States, 2000–2007.

Table 3:

RURAL-URBAN DISTRIBUTION
OF THE ALABAMA POPULATION, 1900–2000

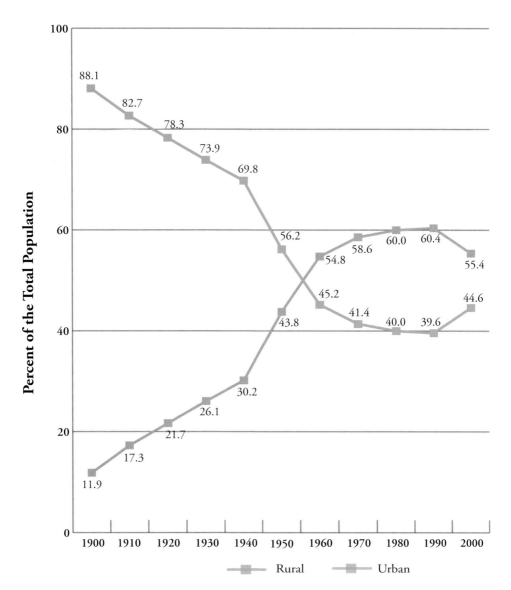

Note: Definitions of "rural" and "urban" have been revised periodically by the Census Bureau. Thus, the above data reflect the differing definitions that were used from 1900–1940, 1950–1990, and beginning in 2000. According to the latest definition of "urban," an urban area generally consists of a central place and adjacent densely settled areas that together have a total population of at least 2,500. Other technical qualifications are also included in the current definition.

Sources: U.S. Census Bureau, Decennial Censuses of the Population for 1950–2000.

TABLE 4:

PERCENTAGE OF THE POPULATION LIVING
IN METROPOLITAN AREAS, 2007

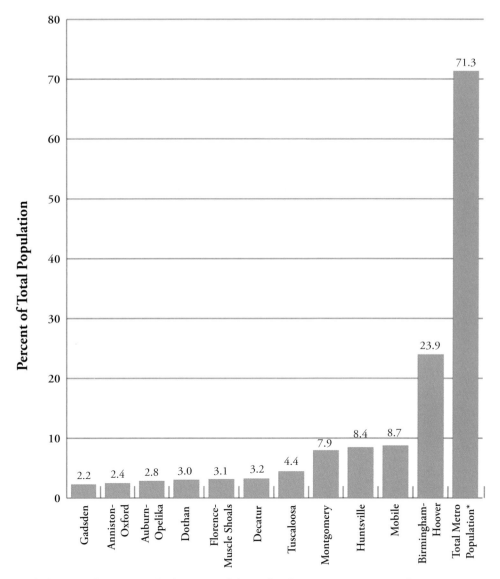

*Includes Russell County, which is part of the Columbus, Georgia, metropolitan area.

Note: A "metropolitan area" consists of a core urban area of 50,000 or more in population, the remainder of the county in which the urban core is located, and any adjacent counties that are socially and economically integrated with the urban core.

Source: U.S. Bureau of the Census, Annual Estimates of the Population of Metropolitan and Micropolitan Statistical Areas, 2000–2007.

TABLE 5:

NET MIGRATION ESTIMATES, 1950–2007

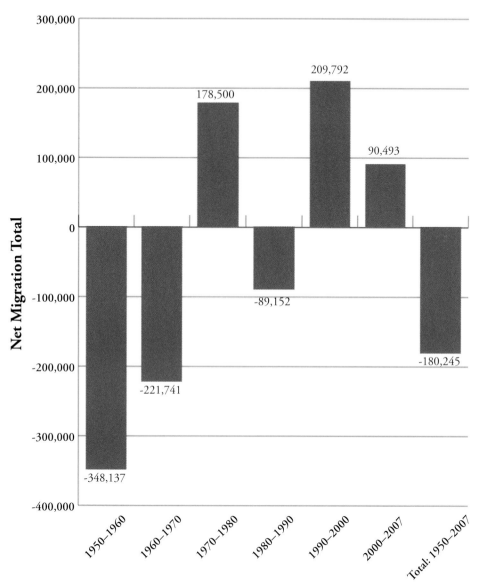

Note: "Net migration" is the number that is derived after both in-movement and out-movement
are taken into consideration. An excess of in-movement over out-movement produces a
positive number, while an excess of out-movement over in-movement yields a negative
number.

Sources: U.S. Census Bureau, Decennial Censuses of the Population for 1950–2000 (population
totals for 1950–2000); Alabama Department of Public Health, Center for Health Statistics
(birth and death data for 1950–2000); and U.S. Census Bureau, Cumulative Estimates of the
Components of Population Change for the U.S., Regions, and States, 2000–2007.

Table 6:

POPULATION TOTALS AND PERCENT CHANGE IN POPULATION FOR ALABAMA COUNTIES, 1950 AND 2007

	Census Population Total, 1950	Estimated Population, 2007	Percent Change in Population, 1950–2007
Autauga	18,186	49,960	174.7
Baldwin	40,997	171,769	319.0
Barbour	28,892	27,941	-3.3
Bibb	17,987	21,535	19.7
Blount	28,975	56,614	95.4
Bullock	16,054	10,781	-32.8
Butler	29,228	20,157	-31.0
Calhoun	79,539	113,103	42.2
Chambers	39,528	34,764	-12.1
Cherokee	17,634	24,560	39.3
Chilton	26,922	42,299	57.1
Choctaw	19,152	14,173	-26.0
Clarke	26,548	26,496	-0.2
Clay	13,929	13,788	-1.0
Cleburne	11,904	14,700	23.5
Coffee	30,720	46,793	52.3
Colbert	39,561	54,588	38.0
Conecuh	21,776	13,160	-39.6
Coosa	11,766	10,864	-7.7
Covington	40,373	37,007	-8.3
Crenshaw	18,981	13,805	-27.3
Cullman	49,046	80,554	64.2
Dale	20,828	48,150	131.2
Dallas	56,270	43,079	-23.4
DeKalb	45,048	68,016	51.0
Elmore	31,649	77,525	145.0
Escambia	31,443	37,600	19.6
Etowah	93,892	103,217	9.9
Fayette	19,388	17,648	-9.0
Franklin	25,705	30,439	18.4
Geneva	25,899	25,707	-0.7
Greene	16,482	9,201	-44.2
Hale	20,832	18,111	-13.1

TABLE 6:

Henry	18,674	16,621	-11.0
Houston	46,522	97,171	108.9
Jackson	38,998	53,030	36.0
Jefferson	558,928	658,779	17.9
Lamar	16,441	14,447	-12.1
Lauderdale	54,179	88,561	63.5
Lawrence	27,128	34,229	26.2
Lee	45,073	130,516	189.6
Limestone	35,766	73,898	106.6
Lowndes	18,018	12,686	-29.6
Macon	30,561	22,336	-26.9
Madison	72,903	312,734	329.0
Marengo	29,494	21,276	-27.9
Marion	27,264	29,580	8.5
Marshall	45,090	87,644	94.4
Mobile	231,105	404,406	75.0
Monroe	25,732	22,764	-11.5
Montgomery	138,965	225,791	62.5
Morgan	52,924	115,050	117.4
Perry	20,439	10,602	-48.1
Pickens	24,349	19,651	-19.3
Pike	30,608	29,925	-2.2
Randolph	22,513	22,425	-0.4
Russell	40,364	50,183	24.3
St. Clair	26,687	78,054	192.5
Shelby	30,362	182,113	499.8
Sumter	23,610	13,306	-43.6
Talladega	63,639	80,255	26.1
Tallapoosa	35,074	40,747	16.2
Tuscaloosa	94,092	177,906	89.1
Walker	63,769	68,816	7.9
Washington	15,612	17,226	10.3
Wilcox	23,476	12,779	-45.6
Winston	18,250	24,240	32.8
ALABAMA	**3,061,743**	**4,627,851**	**51.2**

Sources: U.S. Census Bureau, 1950 Census of the Population and Annual Estimates of the Population for Counties of Alabama, 2000–2007.

TABLE 7:

ALABAMA'S TEN LARGEST CITIES, 1900, 1950, 2000

	1900			1950			2000	
1	Mobile	38,469	1	Birmingham	320,037	1	Birmingham	242,820
2	Birmingham	38,415	2	Mobile	129,009	2	Montgomery	201,568
3	Montgomery	30,346	3	Montgomery	106,525	3	Mobile	198,915
4	Anniston	9,695	4	Gadsden	55,725	4	Huntsville	158,216
5	Selma	8,713	5	Tuscaloosa	46,396	5	Tuscaloosa	77,906
6	Huntsville	8,068	6	Anniston	31,066	6	Hoover	62,742
7	Florence	6,478	7	Bessemer	28,445	7	Dothan	57,737
8	Bessemer	6,358	8	Florence	23,870	8	Decatur	53,929
9	Tuscaloosa	5,094	9	Phenix City	23,305	9	Auburn	42,987
10	Talladega	5,056	10	Selma	22,840	10	Gadsden	38,978

Sources: U.S. Census Bureau, Decennial Censuses of the Population for 1900, 1950, and 2000.

TABLE 8:

MEDIAN AGE OF THE ALABAMA AND U.S. POPULATION, 1900–2030

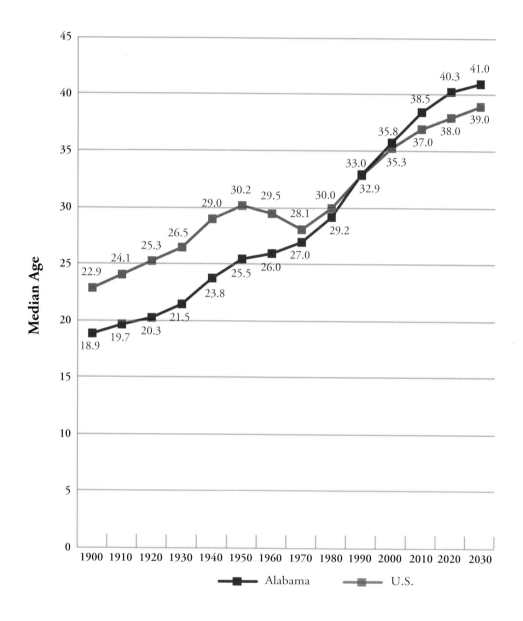

Note: "Median age" refers to the point at which half the population is above a given age and half the population is below.

Sources: U.S. Census Bureau, Decennial Censuses of the Population for 1900–2000 and Interim State Population Projections for 2000–2030.

TABLE 9:

PERCENTAGE OF THE ALABAMA POPULATION
UNDER 20 AND 65+, 1950–2030

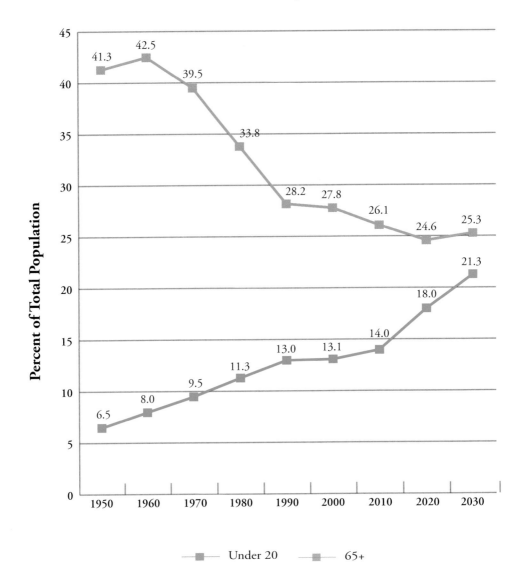

Sources: U.S. Census Bureau, Decennial Censuses of the Population for 1950–2000 and Interim State Population Projections, 2000–2030.

TABLE 10:

SEX RATIO OF THE ALABAMA POPULATION
UNDER 20 AND 65+, 1900–2030

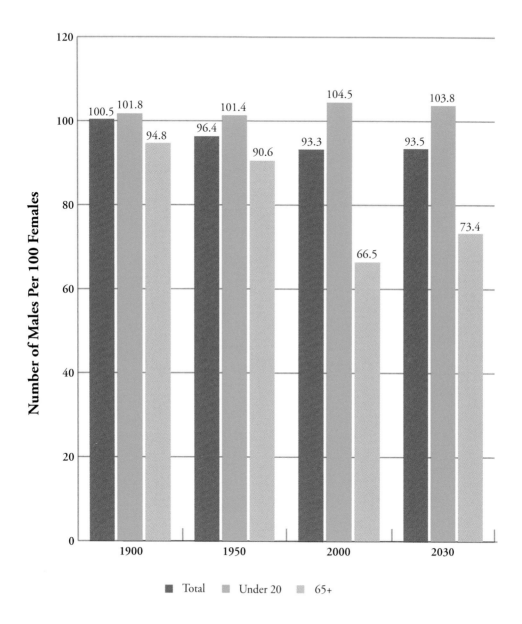

Note: The "sex ratio" is defined as the number of males per 100 females.

Sources: U.S. Census Bureau, Decennial Censuses of the Population for 1900, 1950, and 2000 and Interim State Population Projections for 2000–2030.

TABLE 11:

AGE-SEX DISTRIBUTION OF THE ALABAMA POPULATION

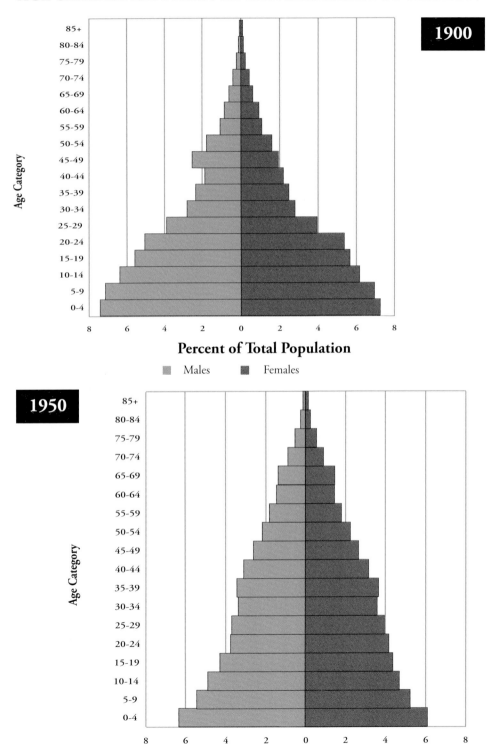

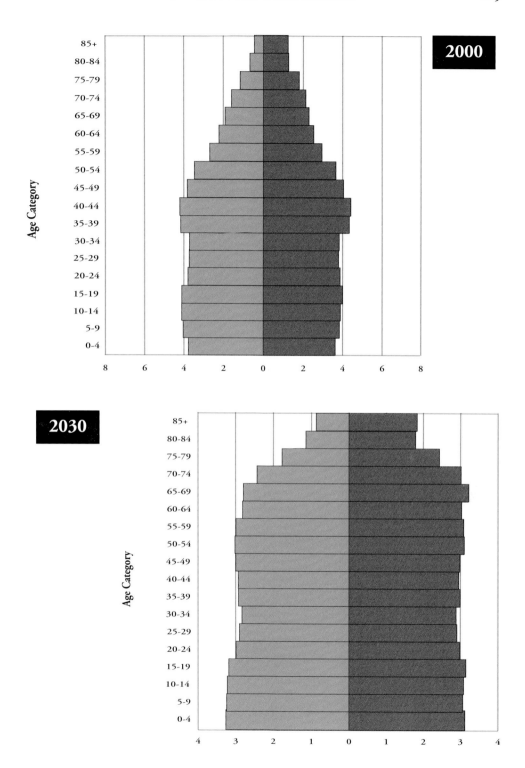

Sources: U.S. Census Bureau, Decennial Censuses of the Population for 1900, 1950, and 2000 and Interim State Projections of Population for 2030.

TABLE 12:

RACE AND ETHNIC DISTRIBUTION
OF THE ALABAMA POPULATION, 1950–2007

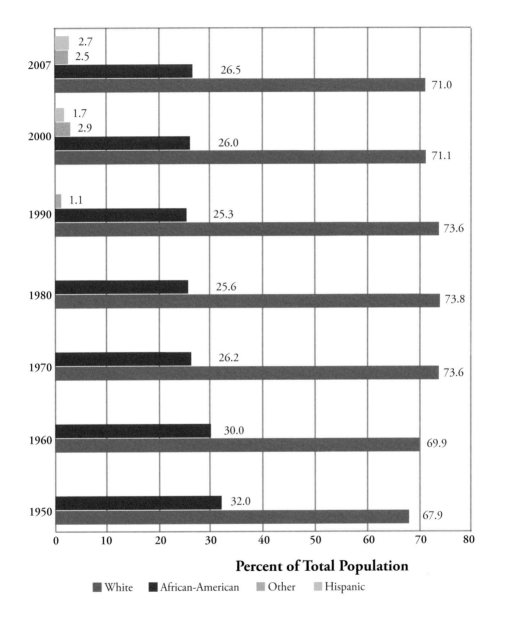

Percent of Total Population

■ White   ■ African-American   ■ Other   ■ Hispanic

Notes: Hispanics may be of any race. Values less than 1.0 percent are not reported.
Sources: U.S. Census Bureau, Decennial Censuses of the Population for 1950–2000 and Annual Estimates of the Population by Age, Sex, and Hispanic Origin for Alabama 2000–2007.

TABLE 13:

PERCENTAGE OF THE ALABAMA AND U.S. POPULATION FOREIGN BORN, 1900–2006

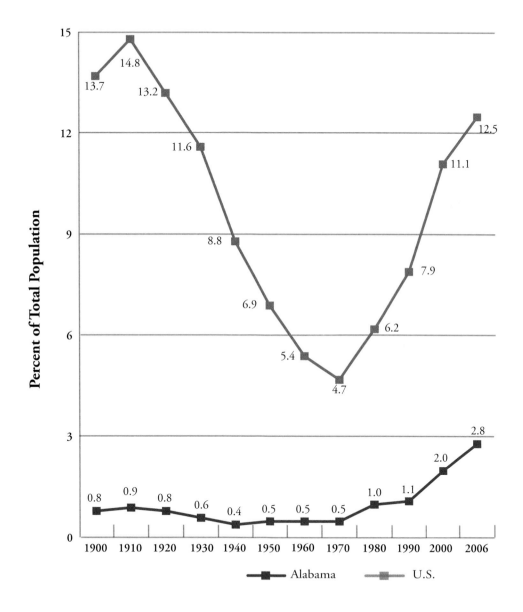

Sources: U.S. Census Bureau, Decennial Censuses of the Population for 1990–2000 and 2006 American Community Survey.

Table 14:

ALABAMA HOUSEHOLD, FAMILY, AND PER CAPITA INCOME AS A PERCENTAGE OF U.S. INCOME, 1969–2006

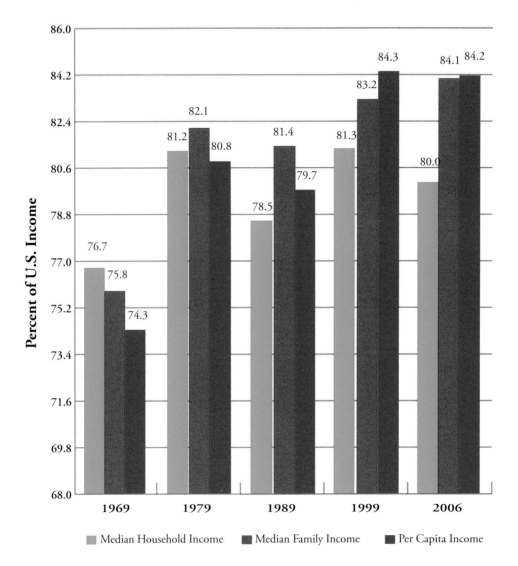

Notes: A "household" is comprised of one or more persons, while a "family" consists of two or more persons who are related. "Median" refers to the point at which half of the households are above a given income value and half are below. "Per capita income" is derived by dividing the aggregate income for all persons by the total population.

Sources: U.S. Census Bureau, Decennial Censuses of the Population for 1970–2000 and 2006 American Community Survey.

TABLE 15:

PERCENTAGE OF THE ALABAMA AND U.S. POPULATION BELOW THE POVERTY LEVEL, 1969–2006

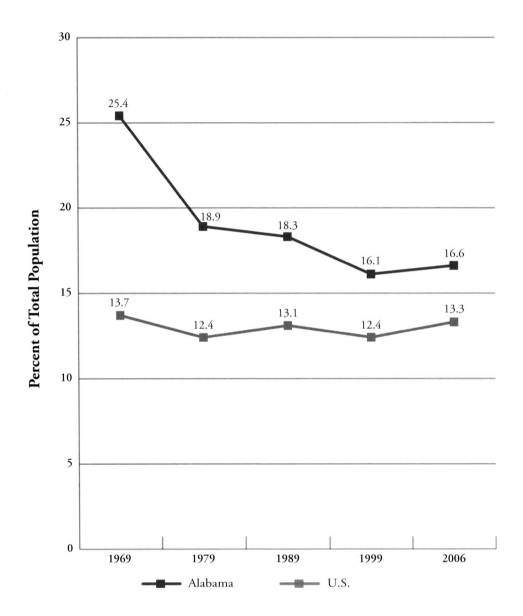

Sources: *U.S. Census Bureau, Decennial Censuses of the Population for 1970, 1980, 1990, and 2000, and 2006 American Community Survey.*

TABLE 16:

PERCENTAGE OF THE ALABAMA AND U.S. POPULATION HIGH SCHOOL GRADUATES OR HIGHER, 1950–2006

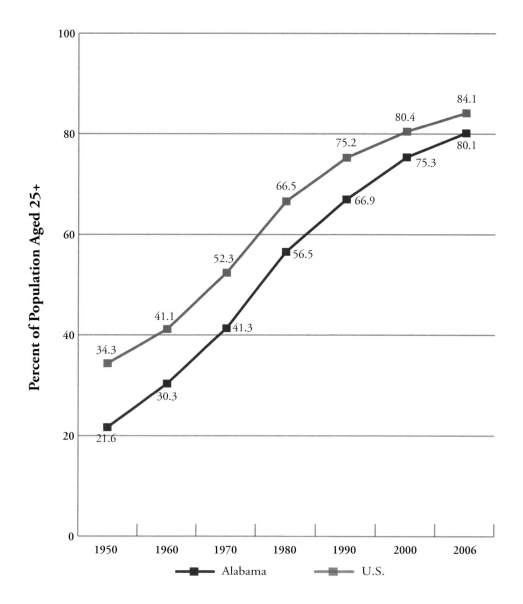

Note: Data reported are for persons aged 25+. Questions used to measure educational attainment may vary slightly depending on the census.

Sources: U.S. Census Bureau, Decennial Censuses of the Population for 1950–2000 and 2006 American Community Survey.

TABLE 17:

PERCENTAGE OF THE ALABAMA AND U.S. POPULATION COLLEGE GRADUATES OR HIGHER, 1950–2006

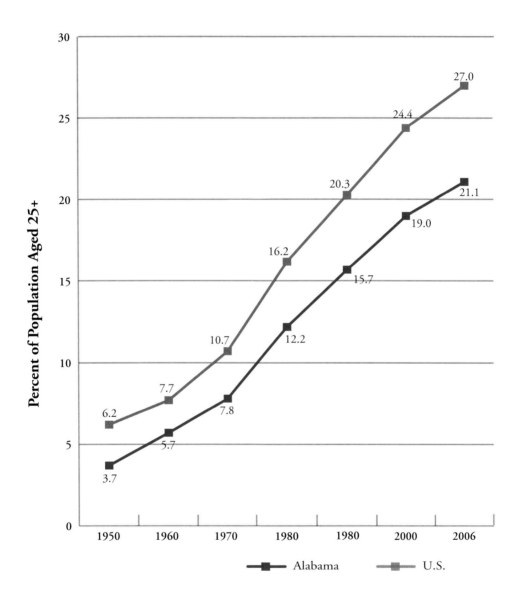

Note: Data reported are for persons aged 25+. Questions used to measure educational attainment may vary slightly depending on the census.

Sources: U.S. Census Bureau, Decennial Censuses of the Population for 1950–2000 and 2006 American Community Survey.

TABLE 18:

HOUSEHOLD AND FAMILY COMPOSITION OF THE ALABAMA POPULATION, 1980–2000

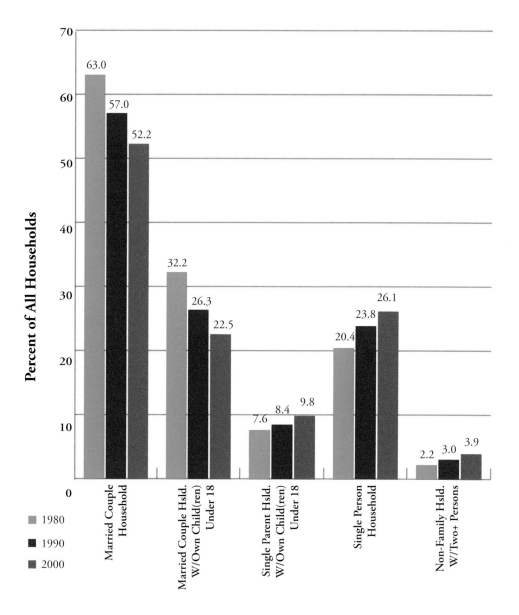

Note: Percentages will not add to 100.0 because the first two categories are overlapping. In addition, not all household categories within the population are represented. A "non-family household" consists of unrelated persons (partners, roommates, boarders, etc.) who share a single dwelling unit.

Sources: U.S. Census Bureau, Decennial Censuses of the Population for 1980, 1990, and 2000.

Table 19:

DISTRIBUTION OF THE ALABAMA AND U.S. WORKFORCE BY OCCUPATION, 2006

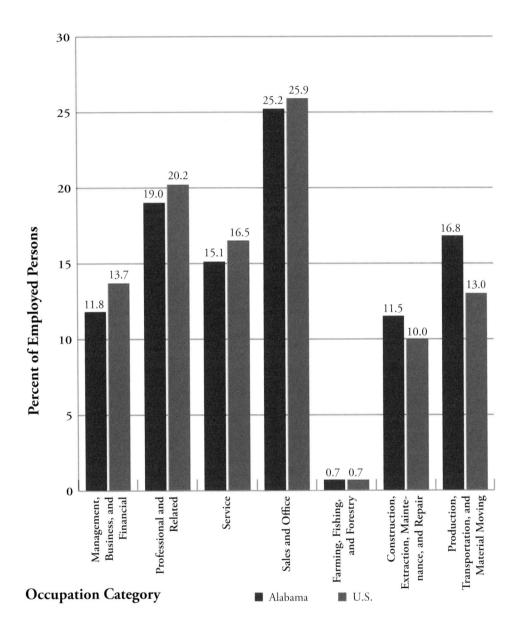

Note: Data are for civilian employees aged 16+.

Source: U.S. Census Bureau, 2006 American Community Survey.

TABLE 20:

DISTRIBUTION OF THE ALABAMA AND U.S. WORKFORCE BY INDUSTRY, 2006

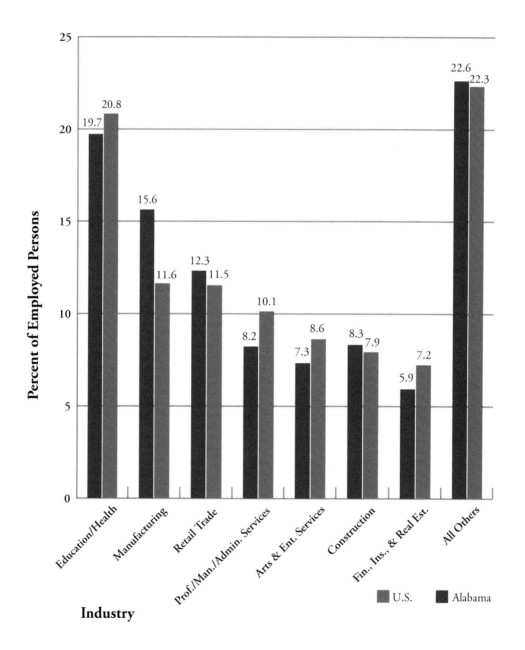

Note: Data are for civilian employees aged 16+.

Source: U.S. Census Bureau, 2006 American Community Survey.

TABLE 21:

MARKET VALUE OF AGRICULTURAL PRODUCTS SOLD BY ALABAMA FARMERS, 2002

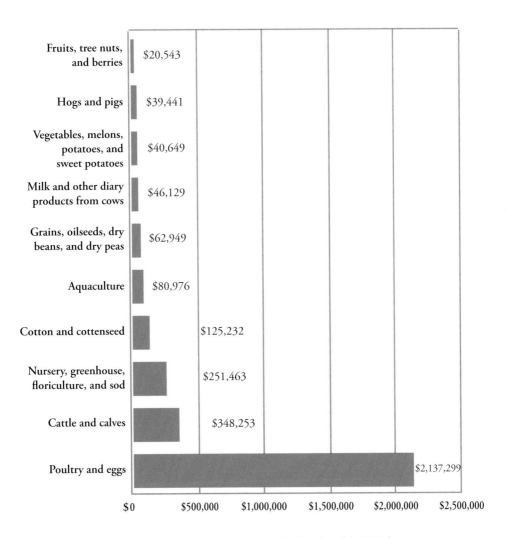

Sales (in $1,000s)

Source: U.S. Department of Agriculture, 2002 Census of Agriculture.

TABLE 22:

BIRTH AND DEATH RATES FOR THE ALABAMA POPULATION, 1950–2006

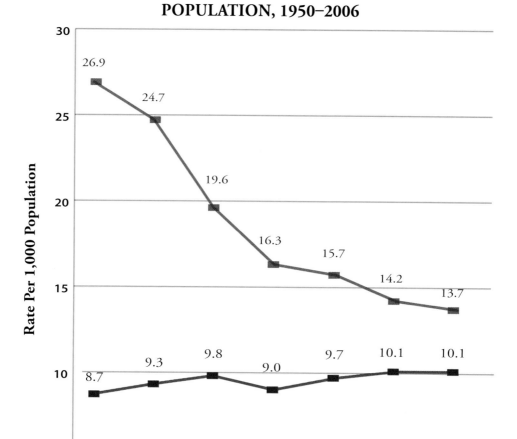

*Number of births/deaths per 1,000 persons in the total population.
Source: Alabama Department of Public Health, Center for Health Statistics, Alabama Vital Statistics: 2006.

TABLE 23:

LIFE EXPECTANCY AT BIRTH FOR THE ALABAMA
AND U.S. POPULATION, 1950–2006

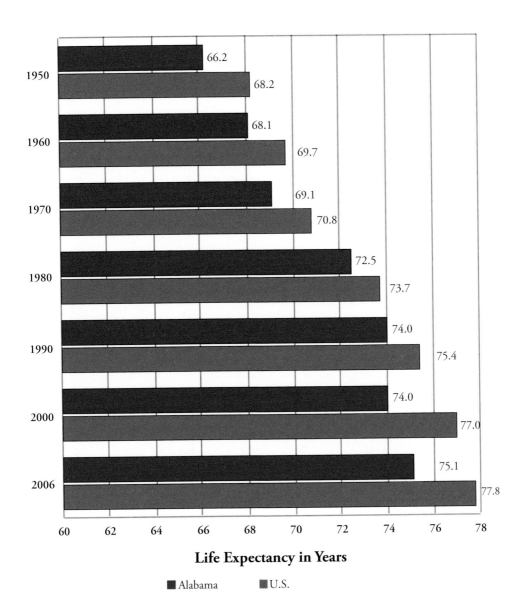

Life Expectancy in Years

■ Alabama   ■ U.S.

*Sources: Unpublished data provided by the Alabama Department of Public Health, Center
for Health Statistics, and National Center for Health Statistics, National Vital Statistics
Reports, Vol. 56, No. 10, April, 2008.*

The Alabama Theatre in Birmingham.

11

Symbols and Emblems

In the years since Alabama became the twenty-second state in 1819, several dozen items have been designated by the governor and legislature as official symbols. The list includes:

This section also includes a complete list of all the persons who have served as governor since Alabama achieved statehood in 1819.

"Alabama"

Official State Song

The words of "Alabama," the state song, were written by Julia S. Tutwiler, a distinguished educator and reformer. The inspiration for "Alabama" came to Tutwiler after she returned to her native state from Germany, where she had been studying new educational methods for girls and women. She recalled that in Germany patriotism was kept aflame by spirited songs. She thought that it would restore the spirits of her own people to give them a new patriotic song, so she wrote a fatherland song and called it "Alabama." It was first sung to an Austrian air, but in 1931 the Alabama Federation of Music Clubs promoted a version of the song with music written by Edna Gockel Gussen of Birmingham. This version was adopted as the state song by House Joint Resolution 74 on March 9, 1931, and was subsequently officially approved as Act 31-126 by Governor B. M. Miller.

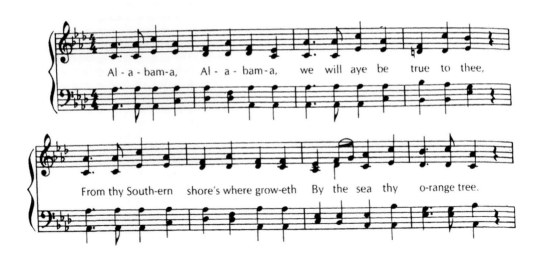

1

Alabama, Alabama,
We will aye be true to thee,
From thy Southern shore where groweth,
By the sea thine orange tree.
To thy Northern vale where floweth
Deep and blue thy Tennessee.
Alabama, Alabama
We will aye be true to thee!

2

Broad the Stream whose name thou bearest;
Grand thy Bigbee rolls along;
Fair thy Coosa-Tallapoosa
Bold thy Warrior, dark and strong.
Goodlier than the land that Moses
Climbed lone Nebo's Mount to see
Alabama, Alabama,
We will aye be true to thee!

3

From thy prairies broad and fertile,
Where thy snow-white cotton shines.
To the hills where coal and iron
Hide in thy exhaustless mines.
Strong-armed miners—sturdy farmers:
Loyal hearts what'er we be.
Alabama, Alabama,
We will aye be true to thee!

4

From the quarries where the marble
White as that of Paros gleams
Waiting till thy sculptor's chisel,
Wake to like thy poet's dream;
For not only wealth of nature,
Wealth of mind hast thou to fee.
Alabama, Alabama,
We will aye be true to thee!

5

Where the perfumed south-wind whispers,
Thy magnolia groves among,
Softer than a mother's kisses
Sweeter than a mother's song;
Where the golden jasmine trailing,
Woos the treasure-laden bee,
Alabama, Alabama,
We will aye be true to thee!

6
Brave and pure thy men and women,
Better this than corn and wine,
Make us worthy, God in Heaven,
Of this goodly land of Thine;
Hearts as open as our doorways,
Liberal hands and spirits free,
Alabama, Alabama,
We will aye be true to thee!

7
Little, little, can I give thee,
Alabama, mother mine;
But that little—hand, brain, spirit,
All I have and am are thine.
Take, O take the gift and giver.
Take and serve thyself with me,
Alabama, Alabama,
I will aye be true to thee.

ALABAMA GREAT SEAL

OFFICIAL STATE SEAL

In 1817, when he was appointed governor of the new Alabama Territory, William Wyatt Bibb recognized the need for an official seal for commissions and other state papers. Bibb believed the best seal would be a map of the territory showing its rivers. The seal also showed the bordering states and the Spanish colony of Florida. In 1819 Alabama became a state, and the first legislature designated the territorial seal as the state seal. That seal remained in use until the Reconstruction period when the legislature approved a new seal depicting an eagle perched upon the shield of the United States seal. In the beak of the eagle was a banner reading "Here We Rest." In 1939, a bill was introduced and unanimously passed by the legislature to restore the original seal. Governor Frank M. Dixon approved the new seal under Act 39-20.

ALABAMA STATE FLAG

OFFICIAL STATE FLAG

According to the 1895 Acts of Alabama, the state flag is to be a crimson St. Andrew's cross on a field of white. The bars forming the cross are not to be less than six inches broad and are to extend diagonally across the flag from side to side. By law (Acts of Alabama, 2001-472), the flag is to be displayed in this manner: "Each facility or building located in this state that is affiliated with any department or agency of the state and supported in whole or in part by public funds, shall prominently display the Alabama State Flag, in accordance with appropriate flag display protocol, on a flag pole or flag poles located near the main entrance of

each facility or building. Any facility or building that is not in public view or open to the general public, or is used only for storage or other warehouse purposes, may be exempt from the requirements of this section at the discretion of the director or chief official of the department or agency." Under an Act approved September 26, 1923, the flags of Alabama and the United States must be displayed on every school day at all schools which receive any public funds. The official salute is (per the *Code of Alabama* 1-2A-2): "Flag of Alabama, I salute thee. To thee I pledge my allegiance, my service, and my life."

YELLOWHAMMER

OFFICIAL STATE BIRD

The yellowhammer (*Colaptes auratus*) is more terrestrial than other woodpeckers. It is commonly observed feeding on lawns and is perhaps the most obvious woodpecker of the city and suburban areas. Yellowhammers begin nesting in April when the female lays six to ten white eggs in a cavity of a dead tree, fence post, or, occasionally, some other site including nest boxes, roofs of buildings, or banks and cliffs. One egg is laid each day until the clutch is completed. Incubation takes about seventeen days, and the chicks are ready to fly three weeks to a month after hatching. Both parents take part in the care and feeding of the young. Yellowhammers are reported to eat more ants than any other American bird. They also eat other insects such as grasshoppers, crickets, and caterpillars, and many plants including berries, nuts, seeds, and fruits; the berries of poison ivy appear to be a favorite food. Other names commonly given to yellowhammers include: Northern Flicker (the correct common name, according to the American Ornithologists Union), Flicker, Yellow-shafted Flicker, Southern Flicker, and Common Flicker. Act 27-542 designated the yellowhammer as Alabama's state bird in 1927.

ALABAMA COAT OF ARMS

OFFICIAL STATE COAT OF ARMS

The original design of the Alabama coat of arms was drawn in 1923 by B. J. Tieman of New York, an authority on heraldry. A few years later, Naomi Rabb Winston of Washington, D.C., painted the completed design in oil. A bill to adopt a state coat of arms was introduced in the legislature in 1939 by James Simpson of Jefferson County and passed unanimously in both houses. The Alabama coat of arms consists of a shield on which appears the emblems of the five governments that have held sovereignty over Alabama. The flags of Spain, France, Great Britain, and the Confederacy are bound by the flag and shield of the United States. This shield is supported on either side by bald eagles, symbolizing courage. The crest is a model of the *Baldine*, the ship on which Iberville and Bienville sailed from France to establish a colony near present-day Mobile. The state motto, "Audemus jura nostra defendere," appears on a sash beneath the shield. The motto has been translated as: "We Dare Maintain Our Rights" or "We Dare Defend Our Rights." The source of the motto, according to a *Birmingham News-Age Herald* article, was Marie Bankhead Owen, former director of the Alabama Department of Archives and History. She wrote in that article that she came upon the idea for the motto while searching for "a phrase that would interpret the spirit of our peoples in a terse and energetic sentence." A poem, "What Constitutes a State?" by the eighteenth-century author Sir William Jones (see Bartlett's *Familiar Quotations*) includes the stanza, "Men who their duties know. But know their rights, and knowing, dare maintain." The motto was translated into Latin by Professor W. B. Saffold of the University of Alabama. Act 39-140 designated both the coat of arms and motto as official state symbols.

ALABAMA CREED

OFFICIAL STATE CREED

"I believe in Alabama, a state dedicated to a faith in God and the enlightenment of mankind; to a democracy that safeguards the liberties of each citizen and to the conservation of her youth, her ideals, and her soil. I believe it is my duty to obey her laws, to respect her flag and to be alert to her needs and generous in my efforts to foster her advancement within the statehood of the world." The creed was written by Mrs. H. P. Thetford of Birmingham and was adopted by the Alabama Federation of Women's Clubs. In 1953, the Federation recommended the creed to the legislature, which adopted it under Act 53-244.

CAMELLIA

OFFICIAL STATE FLOWER

The camellia (*Camellia japonica L.*) replaced the goldenrod as Alabama's state flower under Act 59-124 in 1959. Camellias are evergreen shrubs or trees that bloom in the fall, winter, and early spring. Camellias are native to China, Japan, and Southeast Asia. The genus was named for George Kamel, a botanist and Jesuit missionary to Asia. Red camellias symbolize intrinsic worth, while white camellias symbolize loveliness. Whatever their color, all camellias represent longevity and faithfulness.

FIGHTING TARPON

OFFICIAL STATE SALTWATER FISH

The fighting tarpon (*Tarpon atlanticus*) is a silvery, saltwater game fish that can reach weights of one hundred pounds and ranges off the Gulf Coast of Alabama and in the Mobile estuary. The tarpon was originally designated as the state fish of Alabama by Act 55-564 in 1955. But in 1975, it became the state saltwater fish after the designation of the largemouth bass as the state freshwater fish.

SQUARE DANCE

OFFICIAL STATE FOLK DANCE

Square dancing is performed by four couples, or groups of four couples, each couple forming a side of a compact square. Traditionally accompanied by a fiddle, accordion, banjo, and guitar, the couples perform a variety of movements prompted by the patter or singing calls (instruction) of a "caller." Cooperative movement is the hallmark of well-executed square dancing. Square dancing is to be distinguished from related dances called contra or longways dance where couples stand double file in a line, and from round dances where couples stand in a circle. The origin of the square dance can be traced to England in the 1600s and to the stately French cotillion popular at the court of Louis XV. The square dance was designated the American Folk Dance of Alabama in 1981 by Act 81-48.

HEMATITE

OFFICIAL STATE MINERAL

Hematite, an oxide of iron (Fe_2O_3), is also known as "red iron ore." Hematite was mined for many years in the Valley and Ridge area of central and northeastern Alabama. The mining of hematite was once a major Alabama industry, and the occurrence of hematite with nearby deposits of coal and limestone led to Birmingham's development as an industrial center after the Civil War. Iron ore mining in the state ceased in 1975 primarily due to the availability of inexpensive higher-grade imported ores. Red iron ore has been mined in Bibb, Blount, DeKalb, Cherokee, Etowah, Jefferson, St. Clair, and Tuscaloosa counties. The Red Mountain Formation of hematite occurs along the entire length of Red Mountain, which passes through these counties. From about 1840 to 1975, approximately 375 million tons of iron ore were mined in Alabama, principally from the Birmingham red-ore district. In 1904, Birmingham iron ore was used in casting the statue of Vulcan, which stands atop Red Mountain as the largest cast-iron structure ever made. In 1967 the legislature approved Act 67-503 adopting hematite as the state mineral.

The "Head of Christ" by Giuseppe Moretti is the first known work of fine art created from Alabama marble. The sculpture was displayed at the 1904 World's Fair in St. Louis, as was Moretti's largest work, "Vulcan," which now overlooks downtown Birmingham. Moretti's widow donated the "Head of Christ" to the Alabama Department of Archives and History in 1940.

MARBLE

OFFICIAL STATE ROCK

Marble is a metamorphic rock consisting of fine- to coarse-grained recrystallized calcite (limestone) or dolomite. It may be white, pink, gray, red, or black, depending on the impurities in the original limestone or dolomite. In Alabama the major source of marble is the Sylacauga Marble Belt in Talladega County, where it occurs in a narrow outcrop from the Coosa River to southeast of Talladega. However, marble is also plentiful in Bibb, Calhoun, Clay, Coosa, Etowah, Lee, Macon, St. Clair, and Shelby counties. Alabama marble has been used in buildings all over the United States. The Sylacauga marble is known for its high-grade crystalline texture, whiteness, and beauty, and has been quarried, cut, and polished for more than 160 years for use as monument stone, building stone, and works of fine art. Since 1900, approximately thirty million tons of marble have been quarried in Sylacauga. Crushed marble is also used as an agricultural soil conditioner and in textiles, paints, electrical insulation, and plastics. Micronized marble is shipped as a slurry for use in paper pigment and coating. Marble became the state rock after the legislature passed Act 69-755 in 1969.

RACKING HORSE

OFFICIAL STATE HORSE

The racking horse (*Equus caballus*) is similar to the Tennessee walking horse. It has a smooth, natural gait and can sustain a rapid pace for long periods of time. The "rack" of the racking horse is a bi-lateral four-beat gait which is neither a pace nor a trot. It is often called a "single-foot" because only one foot strikes the ground at a time. A true racking horse comes by this gait as naturally as walking comes to other breeds. The racking horse is a good mount for beginning riders, not only for its extremely comfortable ride, but also because of its unusual friendliness to humans. The racking horse is attractive and gracefully built with a long sloping neck, full flanks, well-boned smooth legs, and finely textured hair. It is considered a "light" horse in comparison with other breeds, averaging 15.2 hands high (a "hand" is about four inches) and weighing 1,000 pounds. Colors may be black, bay, sorrel, chestnut, brown, gray, yellow, and spotted. Act 75-1153 of 1975 designated the racking horse as the state horse.

FLORENCE RENAISSANCE FAIRE

OFFICIAL STATE RENAISSANCE FAIRE

The two-day Florence Renaissance Faire takes place each fourth weekend in October. Florence is named for Florence, Italy, the founding city of the Renaissance movement in Europe during the fifteenth century. The Renaissance Faire celebrates the period from the twelfth through the sixteenth centuries. Authentic costumes, arts and crafts, and food are all a part of the Faire. Visitors can take part in medieval games and hear musicians playing authentic instruments. Artisans and merchants offer coins of the realm, hand-thrown pottery, jewelry, dried flower wreaths, and many other delights. Magicians, mirthmakers, and minstrels wander the grounds in period attire. The Florence Renaissance Faire became the official state Renaissance faire in 1988 by Act 88-43.

EASTERN WILD TURKEY

OFFICIAL STATE GAME BIRD

The wild turkey (*Meleagris gallopavo*) is one of the most common game birds in the United States. It is also one of the most difficult to hunt because of its craftiness and cautious nature. The Alabama Game and Fish Division of the Department of Conservation and Natural Resources established a wild turkey restocking program in the 1940s to compensate for a shortage caused by over-hunting. Now, Alabama has one of the largest per-acre populations of wild turkeys of any state. Act 80-734 established the eastern wild turkey as Alabama's game bird.

LARGEMOUTH BASS

OFFICIAL STATE FRESHWATER FISH

The largemouth bass (*Micropterus salmoides*) is abundant in Alabama's inland waters and is popular with sport fishermen. It can be found throughout the United States in ponds, lakes, and rivers. Largemouth bass grow to four to six inches during their first year, eight to twelve inches in two years, and to sixteen inches in three years. They are usually green with dark blotches that form a horizontal stripe along the middle of the fish on either side. The belly ranges from light green to almost white. They have a nearly divided dorsal fin with the anterior portion containing nine spines and the posterior portion containing twelve to thirteen soft rays. Their upper jaw reaches far beyond the rear margin of the eye. Hatchlings feed primarily on zooplankton and insect larvae. At about two inches in length, they become active predators. Adults feed almost exclusively on other fish and large invertebrates such as crayfish. Larger fish prey upon smaller bass. Act 75-1183 in 1975 designated the largemouth bass as the state freshwater fish.

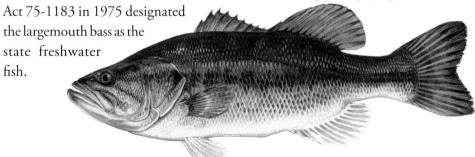

Pecan

Official State Nut

Pecans (*Carya illinoinensis*) are thin-shelled nuts found all over the U.S., but primarily in the southern states. Pecan trees are grown throughout Alabama. Pecans are good sources of vitamin B-6 and are used in many southern recipes, such as pralines and pecan pie. Act 82-17, adopted in 1982, made the pecan the Alabama state nut.

Basilosaur

Official State Fossil

In 1834 a complete skeleton of a basilosaur (*Basilosaurus cetoides*, king of the lizards) was found on a plantation in southwestern Alabama. Staff of the Philadelphia Academy of Natural Sciences studied the skeleton and said it was not a lizard, but a squid- and fish-eating member of the whale family. Because of this they renamed it the zeuglodon (however, in scientific taxonomy, a scientific name once given does not change, so the creature is still a *Basilosaurus cetoides)*. Since it was a sea animal they estimated it to be more than forty-five million years old. Zeuglodons averaged from fifty-five to seventy feet long and had tails up to forty feet long. The ancient whale fossil is most abundant in Alabama. A zeuglodon skeleton found in 1982 in Washington County is now displayed at the McWane Center in Birmingham. Another Alabama specimen was sent to the Smithsonian Institution in Washington, D.C. These are the two most comprehensive *Basilosaurus cetoides* skeletons ever found. A cast of the creature is also mounted in Smith Hall at the Alabama Museum of Natural History in Tuscaloosa. Act 84-66 made the zeuglodon the state fossil in 1984.

Star Blue Quartz

Official State Gemstone

Star blue quartz is a beautiful and plentiful gemstone. Quartz rocks are typically formed when volcanic heat melts silica, which then flows with water into crevices where it crystallizes into silicon dioxide (SiO_2), often with traces of other minerals. Quartz is both decorative and useful, and is made into glass, lenses, electrical components, abrasives, and gemstone and building stone. The star blue quartz was designated the state gemstone in 1990 by Act 90-203.

Eastern Tiger Swallowtail

Official State Mascot and Butterfly

Male eastern tiger swallowtails (*Papilio glaucus*) are yellow with dark tiger stripes. Females come in two forms: one yellow like the male and the other black with shadows of dark stripes. The hindwing of both female forms has many iridescent blue scales and an orange marginal spot. In both female forms, the row of marginal spots on the underside of the forewing merges into a continuous band. Selma is designated as the Butterfly Capital of Alabama, and the eastern tiger swallowtail is its mascot. Legislation to make the eastern tiger swallowtail the state's official mascot and butterfly was requested by the Selma City Council and was enacted in 1989 by Act 89-676.

Monarch Butterfly

Official State Insect

The monarch butterfly is a native butterfly well-known to Alabama. The monarch butterfly is known by scientists as *Danaus plexippus*, which in Greek literally means "sleepy transformation." The name reflects the species' ability to hibernate and metamorphize. Adult monarchs possess two pair of brilliant orange-reddish wings, featuring black veins and white spots along the edges. Their wingspan is about four inches, and they weigh less than half an ounce. Males, which possess distinguishing black dot (stigmata) along the veins of their wings, are slightly bigger than the females. Each adult butterfly lives only about four to five weeks. But one of the wonders of the monarchs is the annual creation of a unique "Methuselah generation," born in autumn, who live seven or eight months. This generation performs the incredible feat of flying from Canada and the United States to the center of Mexico, where it spends the winter in hibernation. After mating in the second half of February, the monarchs begin the journey north. Once they reach the United States, a kind of relay race begins: their short-lived offspring, with only four or five weeks to live, continue making the trek northward over several generations. Monarchs use the sun's orbit to guide them on their migration. On cloudy days, they are guided by an internal biological compass that functions according to the movement of the sun. In 1989 the legislature made the monarch butterfly the state insect by Act 89-935.

Open Horseman Association Horse Show

Official State Horse Show

The first Alabama Open Horseman Association Alabama State Championship Horse Show—the dream of horseman Don Witt—was held in W. O. Crawford Arena in Montgomery in September 1988 with 994 entries. By 2002, the show had grown to three days with more than 2,000 entries. It is held at Garrett Coliseum in Montgomery over Labor Day weekend and is the second largest horse show east of the Mississippi River. Act 88-656 designated the Alabama Open Horseman Association Horse Show as the official state championship horse show in May 1988.

Alabama Red-bellied Turtle

Official State Reptile

The Alabama red-bellied turtle (*Pseudemys alabamensis*) is native to Alabama and is found nowhere else in the world, although its family, Emydidae, is the largest turtle family. The red-belly and related species are often seen basking on logs in the fresh to brackish waters of the Mobile Delta. Adult male turtles are approximately one foot long. Females are slightly larger with a carapace (upper shell) length reaching thirteen inches. Carapace color may be green to dark brown or black with yellow, orange, or red vertical markings along the sides. The plastron (under shell) may be pale yellow to red with or without dark markings. Colors and markings are usually more intense in young turtles. The head, neck, and legs are marked with yellowish striping. Males have elongated foreclaws. A unique distinguishing characteristic of the Alabama red-bellied turtle is the presence of tooth-like cusps on either side of the upper jaw. Male and female Alabama red-bellied turtles reach maturity at four and six years, respectively. Nesting occurs from May through July. Females leave their aquatic environment and venture onto dry land to lay their eggs. A shallow nest is excavated in generally sandy soil where four to nine eggs are deposited. Hatchlings usually emerge during the summer. The Alabama red-bellied turtle was placed on the U.S. Fish and Wildlife Service's Endangered Species List in 1987. The turtle is also protected under Nongame Species Regulations by the Alabama Department of Conservation and Natural Resources. Act 90-82 made the Alabama red-bellied turtle the state reptile.

SOUTHERN LONGLEAF PINE

OFFICIAL STATE TREE

The southern longleaf pine (*Pinus palustris miller*) is distributed primarily in the lower two-thirds of the state. It is distinguished by the needles which occur in bundles of threes and are about a foot long. Its large cones are six to ten inches long. The longleaf pine is unique among all trees in that it develops very little above ground in the first one to five years of its life. During this time the top is a dense bunch of green needles and is often mistaken for grass. This tree is found on a variety of sites but grows best on well-drained sandy soils. Longleaf pines can grow to a height of 150 feet and a diameter of four feet. The legislature first designated the southern pine as the state tree in 1949. But because there are so many kinds of pine trees, the southern longleaf was specified as the state tree of Alabama by the legislature by Act 97-548 in 1997.

THE MIRACLE WORKER

OFFICIAL STATE OUTDOOR DRAMA

The play by William Gibson relates the story of Helen Keller's early life and her teacher, Anne Sullivan. In 1962, the first production was performed on the grounds of Ivy Green, the birthplace of Helen Keller at Tuscumbia. The play is now performed at Ivy Green each summer from the end of June through July on Friday and Saturday nights. *The Miracle Worker* was designated the state outdoor drama in 1991 by Act 91-37.

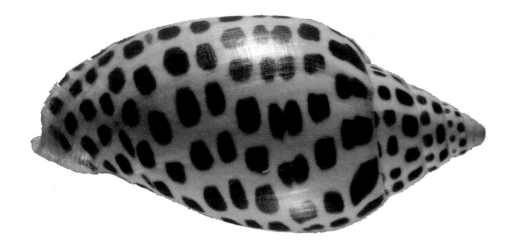

JOHNSTONE'S JUNONIA

OFFICIAL STATE SHELL

The Johnstone's junonia (*Scaphella junonia johnstoneae*) is an offshore seashell common to the Gulf Coast. The shell was described by a Harvard scientist, Dr. William J. Clench, who named it in honor of Kathleen Yerger Johnstone, an amateur conchologist from Mobile who popularized seashells through speeches and books. The *Scaphella junonia johnstoneae* was made the state shell in 1990 by Act 90-567.

THE ALABAMA THEATRE

OFFICIAL STATE HISTORIC THEATER

The Alabama Theatre opened in downtown Birmingham on December 16, 1927, and was dubbed the "Showplace of the South" by the movie producer Adolph Zuker. The ornate movie palace was once a part of the Paramount theater chain. Numerous stars of Broadway and the silver screen appeared on the Alabama's stage, including John Barrymore, Roy Rogers, and Tallulah Bankhead. By late 1981, the growth of suburbs and mall multi-screen theaters had drained away most of the Alabama's audience, and it closed its doors. In 1987, Birmingham Landmarks, Inc., purchased the theatre and turned it into a performing arts center. Today, the Alabama Theatre hosts more than 250 evenings of entertainment each year and draws some four hundred thousand patrons into downtown Birmingham for a wide variety of events: broadway shows, ballets, operas, rock & roll concerts, parties, weddings, fashion shows, beauty pageants, and the occasional classic film. The Alabama Theatre for the Performing Arts was designated the state historic theatre in 1993 by Act 93-26.

BAMA SOIL SERIES

OFFICIAL STATE SOIL

The Bama soil series is the official state soil of Alabama. Bama soils occur in twenty-six counties in Alabama on more than 360,000 acres in the state, mainly in the western and central part of the state, paralleling major river systems. Bama soils are well drained, have desirable physical properties, and are located on high positions of the landscape. These characteristics make them well suited to most agricultural and urban uses. They are well suited to cultivated crops, pasture, hay, and woodland. Cotton and corn are the principal cultivated crops grown on these soils. A soil series is a naturally occurring entity on the landscape. Therefore, a given series does not necessarily occur within the confines of only one state. Bama soil occurs in Alabama, Mississippi, Florida, and Virginia. The Professional Soil Classifiers Association of Alabama adopted a resolution at its 1996 annual meeting recommending the Bama soil series as the state soil. The Alabama Soil and Water Conservation Committee and the Alabama Association of Conservation Districts supported the recommendation, and the Bama soil series was designated as the state soil by Act 97-233 in 1997.

OAK-LEAF HYDRANGEA

OFFICIAL STATE WILDFLOWER

This medium-size (six to eight feet tall) deciduous shrub is found in every section of Alabama. In the 1770s, naturalist William Bartram was the first to describe the plant. He named it *Hydrangea quercifolia* (querci: oak, and folia: leaf). Oak-leaf hydrangea will grow in most soils but prefers well-drained, moisture-retentive soil. It will grow in full sun or shade and is easily rooted from softwood cuttings taken in July. Large spikes of white blooms in April and May rise above large green oak-shaped leaves. In summer, these blossoms turn a deep rose color and persist into the winter. The leaves turn red in the fall, and the peeling bark of the stems and branches adds to its attractive appearance. The oak-leaf hydrangea was designated the state wildflower in 1999 by Act 99-313; the law requires Auburn University to maintain specimens of the plant.

PINE BURR QUILT

OFFICIAL STATE QUILT

The resolution naming the state quilt recognizes the work of the Freedom Quilting Bee, a well-known group of African American women quilters in Wilcox County. Loretta Pettway Bennett created the state's official pine burr quilt while participating in the Alabama State Council on the Arts Folklife Apprenticeship Program. Her mother, Qunnie Pettway, a Gee's Bend quilter, taught her the pine burr quilt pattern. Act 97-111 in 1997 designated Bennett's pine burr quilt as Alabama's state quilt.

Red Hills Salamander

Official State Amphibian

The secretive and rarely seen Red Hills salamander (*Phaeognathus hubrichti*) is thought to exist only in a limited area of south Alabama in Butler, Conecuh, Crenshaw, Covington, and Monroe counties. The Red Hills salamander has a dark brown tail and body and grows to about ten inches in length. The salamander's diet consists primarily of insects and spiders. Under federal protection since 1976, the Red Hills salamander is near extinction because of its limited range, specific habitat requirements, low reproductive rates, and loss of habitat from logging and other practices. Under the Endangered Species Act, habitat for the Red Hills salamander cannot be damaged or changed without a special permit. The Red Hills salamander was designated the state amphibian in 2000 by Act 2000-232.

Dothan Landmark Park

Official State Agricultural Museum

Landmark Park is a hundred-acre facility operated by Dothan Landmarks Foundation to preserve the cultural and natural heritage of the Wiregrass region of southeast Alabama. The park features an 1890s living history farm, a one-room schoolhouse, a general store, a turn-of the-century church, elevated boardwalks, nature trails, wildlife exhibits, a planetarium, and a picnic area. Landmark Park also serves as headquarters for the Alabama Agricultural Museum Board. Special programs include Spring Farm Day in March, Antique and Collector Car Show in October, Wiregrass Heritage Festival in October, and Victorian Christmas in December. Landmark Park was designated the state agricultural museum in 1992 by Act 92-541.

BLACKBERRY

OFFICIAL STATE FRUIT

The blackberry (*Rubus occidentalis*) is an aggregate fruit composed of many smaller fruits called drupes. The fruit is dark purple with smooth, fragile skin. In the middle of the cluster is a greenish-white core that extends to almost the bottom of the berry. Blackberries can be easily confused with raspberries, but raspberries have a hollow center. Blackberries are red and hard when they are immature and turn black and shiny when they ripen. Senate Bill 163, passed as Act 2004-363 in 2004, designated the blackberry as the state fruit.

BLACK BEAR

OFFICIAL STATE MAMMAL

Black bears (*Ursus americanus pallas*) in Alabama are normally black with a brown muzzle and an occasional white blaze on the chest. Average body weights range from 150 to 350 pounds for adult males and 120 to 250 pounds for females with body

lengths from three to six feet. Black bears are classified as carnivores even though their omnivorous diet consists mainly of plant material. They are poor predators and eat vertebrate animals only when the opportunity presents itself. Female black bears typically begin having cubs at three to five years of age; however, in marginal habitats, this may increase to seven years. Mating generally occurs in the summer months, and cubs are born in winter dens in January and February. Litter size can range from one to five with twins being most common. Newborn cubs measure only eight inches in length and weigh from eight to twelve ounces. In 2006, Act 2006-245 designated the black bear as the state mammal.

PEACH

OFFICIAL STATE TREE FRUIT

The peach (*Prunus persica*) belongs to the family Rosaceae, a large family of herbs, shrubs, and trees distributed over most of the earth, and, for plants of the genus Rosa, the true roses. The peach appears to have originated in China, where it was mentioned in literature five thousand years ago. It was introduced into Persia before Christian times and was spread by the Romans throughout Europe. Several of its horticultural varieties were brought by the Spanish to North America, where it became naturalized as far north as Pennsylvania by the late seventeenth century. Thirty to forty varieties of peaches are grown commercially throughout Alabama. The harvest season begins in south Alabama in early May and is completed in north Alabama in early September. Alabama producers harvest their peaches riper than many southeastern producers who ship them long distances. Because fruits are more mature when picked, they tend to have the full flavor of the variety grown. Freshly harvested fruits are available not only in grocery stores but also at roadside outlets and pick-your-own operations. In 2006, by Act 2006-520, the legislature designated the peach as the official state tree fruit of Alabama.

CHRISTMAS ON THE RIVER COOK-OFF

OFFICIAL STATE BARBECUE CHAMPIONSHIP

The "Christmas on the River Cook-off" started in Demopolis in 1989 as part of that river town's annual holiday festivities. Today, the Cook-off involves teams from nine states, seventy-five judges, and eight thousand barbecue fanatics. Judging is conducted in three categories: ribs, shoulders, and whole hog. The winner is eligible to participate in the World Championship "Memphis in May Barbeque Cooking Contest." In addition to the barbecue contest, arts, crafts, parades, and dancing go on for a whole week. The Demopolis Cook-Off was designated the official state barbecue championship by Act 91-739.

Governors of Alabama

General Notes: In this numbering scheme, a governor serving a subsequent term does not get a new number. Thus James E. Folsom, the 42nd governor, is not ranked also as the 44th governor when he returned to office after the end of term number 43, Gordon Persons. Nor are acting governors numbered in the official sequence. ¶ Initially, the governor served a two-year term. The Constitution of 1901 set the term at four years and prohibited a governor from serving consecutive terms. Constitutional Amendment No. 282, ratified in 1968, allows the governor to serve two consecutive terms. ¶ The Constitution of 1901 designated the lieutenant governor as next in line to succeed the governor followed by the president pro tempore of the Senate. ¶ The Constitution of 1901 states that if the governor is absent from the state for more than twenty days, then the lieutenant governor shall assume the powers and duties of the governor until his return.

No.	Name	Dates of Service	Party	Home county
(D=Democrat, R=Republican, W=Whig)				
1	William Wyatt Bibb	Nov 9, 1819–Jul 25, 1820	D	Autauga
2	Thomas Bibb[1]	Jul 25, 1820–Nov 9, 1821	D	Limestone
3	Israel Pickens	Nov 9, 1821–Nov 25, 1825	D	Greene
4	John Murphy	Nov 25, 1825–Nov 25, 1829	D	Monroe
5	Gabriel Moore	Nov 25, 1829–Mar 3, 1831	D	Madison
6	Samuel B. Moore[2]	Mar 3, 1831–Nov 26, 1831	D	Jackson
7	John Gayle	Nov 26, 1831–Nov 21, 1835	D/W	Greene
8	Clement Comer Clay	Nov 21, 1835–Jul 17, 1837	D	Madison
9	Hugh McVay[3]	Jul 17, 1837–Nov 22, 1837	D	Lauderdale
10	Arthur P. Bagby	Nov, 22, 1837–Nov 22, 1841	D	Monroe
11	Benjamin Fitzpatrick	Nov 22, 1841–Dec 10, 1845	D	Autauga
12	Joshua L. Martin	Dec 10, 1845–Dec 16, 1847	D	Tuscaloosa
13	Reuben Chapman	Dec 16, 1847–Dec 17, 1849	D	Madison
14	Henry W. Collier	Dec 17, 1849–Dec 20, 1853	D	Tuscaloosa
15	John A. Winston	Dec 20, 1853–Dec 1, 1857	D	Sumter
16	Andrew B. Moore	Dec 1, 1857–Dec 2, 1861	D	Perry
17	John Shorter	Dec 2, 1861–Dec 1, 1863	D	Barbour
18	Thomas H. Watts	Dec 1, 1863–Jun 1865	D	Montgomery
19	Lewis E. Parsons[4]	Jun 1865–Dec 12/13, 1865	D	Talladega
20	Robert M. Patton[5]	Dec 12/13, 1865–Jul 1867	W	Lauderdale
	Wager Swayne[6]	Jul 1867–Jul 14, 1868	R	Montgomery
21	William H. Smith	Jul 14, 1868–Nov 26, 1870	R	Randolph

22	Robert B. Lindsay	Nov 26, 1870–Nov 17, 1872	D	Colbert
23	David P. Lewis	Nov 17, 1872–Nov 24, 1874	R	Madison
24	George S. Houston	Nov 24, 1874–Nov 28, 1878	D	Limestone
25	Rufus W. Cobb	Nov 28, 1878–Dec 1, 1882	D	Shelby
26	Edward A. O'Neal	Dec 1, 1882–Dec 1, 1886	D	Lauderdale
27	Thomas Seay	Dec 1, 1886–Dec 1, 1890	D	Hale
28	Thomas G. Jones	Dec 1, 1890–Dec 1, 1894	D	Montgomery
29	William C. Oates	Dec 1, 1894–Dec 1, 1896	D	Henry
30	Joseph F. Johnston	Dec 1, 1896–Dec 1, 1900	D	Jefferson
	William D. Jelks[7]	Dec 1, 1900–Dec 26, 1900	D	Barbour
31	William J. Samford	Dec 26, 1900–Jun 11, 1901	D	Lee
32	William D. Jelks[8]	Jun 11, 1901–Jan 14, 1907	D	Barbour
	Russell Cunningham[9]	Apr 25, 1904–Mar 5, 1905	D	Jefferson
33	Braxton B. Comer	Jan 14, 1907–Jan 17, 1911	D	Jefferson
34	Emmett O'Neal	Jan 17, 1911–Jan 18, 1915	D	Lauderdale
35	Charles Henderson	Jan 18, 1915–Jan 20, 1919	D	Pike
36	Thomas E. Kilby	Jan 20, 1919–Jan 15, 1923	D	Calhoun
37	William W. Brandon	Jan 15, 1923–Jan 17, 1927	D	Tuscaloosa
	Charles McDowell[10]	Jul 10–11, 1924	D	Barbour
38	Bibb Graves	Jan 17, 1927–Jan 19, 1931	D	Montgomery
39	Benjamin M. Miller	Jan 19, 1931–Jan 14, 1935	D	Wilcox
	Bibb Graves	Jan 14, 1935–Jan 17, 1939	D	Montgomery
40	Frank M. Dixon	Jan 17, 1939–Jan 19, 1943	D	Jefferson
41	Chauncey M. Sparks	Jan 19, 1943–Jan 20, 1947	D	Barbour
42	James E. Folsom	Jan 20, 1947–Jan 15, 1951	D	Cullman
43	Gordon Persons	Jan 15, 1951–Jan 17, 1955	D	Montgomery
	James E. Folsom	Jan 17, 1955–Jan 19, 1959	D	Cullman
44	John M. Patterson	Jan 19, 1959–Jan 14, 1963	D	Russell
45	George C. Wallace	Jan 14, 1963–Jan 16, 1967	D	Barbour
46	Lurleen B. Wallace	Jan 16, 1967–Mar 7, 1968	D	Tuscaloosa
47	Albert P. Brewer[11]	Mar 7, 1968–Jan 18, 1971	D	Morgan
	George C. Wallace	Jan 18, 1971–Jun 5, 1979	D	Barbour
	Jere Beasley[12]	Jun 5–Jul 7, 1972	D	Barbour
48	Forrest "Fob" James	Jan 15, 1979–Jan 17, 1983	D	Lee
	George C. Wallace	Jan 17, 1983–Jan 19, 1987	D	Barbour
49	Guy Hunt	Jan 19, 1987–Apr 22, 1993	R	Cullman
50	James E. Folsom, Jr.[13]	Apr 22, 1993–Jan 16, 1995	D	Cullman
	Forrest "Fob" James	Jan 16, 1995–Jan 18, 1999	R	Lee
51	Don Siegelman	Jan 18, 1999–Jan 20, 2003	D	Mobile
52	Bob Riley	Jan 20, 2003–	R	Clay

SPECIFIC NOTES:

[1] President of the Senate Thomas Bibb became governor upon the death of his brother, Governor William Wyatt Bibb.

[2] President of the Alabama Senate Samuel Moore became governor upon Governor Gabriel Moore's election to the U.S. Senate.

[3] President of the Senate Hugh McVay became governor upon Governor Clement Comer Clay's appointment to the U.S. Senate.

[4] Parsons was appointed provisional governor by President Andrew Johnson.

[5] Patton was a long-time Whig leader before the Civil War, but supported the Democratic candidate Stephen Douglas in the 1860 presidential election, after the break-up of the Whig Party.

[6] Governor Wager Swayne was appointed military governor.

[7] President of the Senate William Jelks became acting governor because Governor William Samford sought medical treatment out-of-state during the initial days of his administration which began Dec 1.

[8] President of the Senate William Jelks became governor upon the death of Governor William Samford and was elected subsequently to a four-year term as governor.

[9] Lieutenant Governor Russell Cunningham became acting governor during Governor William Jelks's illness.

[10] Lieutenant Governor Charles McDowell became acting governor when Governor William Brandon spent twenty-one days in New York City chairing the state delegation to the 1924 Democratic National Convention.

[11] Lieutenant Governor Albert Brewer became acting governor for a portion of one day as Governor Lurleen Wallace received medical treatment out-of-state for more than twenty days. He became governor upon her death.

[12] Lieutenant Governor Jere Beasley became acting governor while Governor George Wallace was in a Maryland hospital for more than twenty days recovering from an assassination attempt.

[13] Lieutenant Governor Jim Folsom, Jr., became governor upon conviction of Guy Hunt for ethics violations.

ACKNOWLEDGMENTS

This book took several years to plan, research, and produce, and many persons inside and outside of state government helped make it possible. The list that follows will inevitably be incomplete, but it is a start at acknowledging the contributors to the project.

Governor Bob Riley had the idea for this book and asked John Harrison, director of the Banking Department, to make it possible. Harrison asked the Alabama Department of Archives and History (ADAH) to produce the book, and he subsequently convened and chaired a committee of state department heads and their representatives to guide the project. The committee members include: Larry Childers, Lee Sentell, Jeff Emerson, Barnett Lawley, Gerri Miller, and Hobbie Sealy. Within ADAH, Director Ed Bridges created a publications office to produce the book, and he and Assistant Director Steve Murray supervised the process.

Bridges also notes that his essay, which makes up Chapter 2, "Historical Alabama," depends heavily on the work of many other historians. Some who graciously critiqued parts of his draft were Leah Atkins, Richard Bailey, Kathryn Braund, Michael Fitzgerald, John Hall, Craig Sheldon, Mills Thornton, and Greg Waselkov. Colleagues at the Archives also provided information and/or editorial reviews and their names are included in the listing on the next page. Martha Bridges edited the entire draft.

Special thanks are also due to Alabama geologist James Lacefield and to the editors and contributors of the *Encyclopedia of Alabama* (EOA). Lacefield's *Lost World in Alabama Rocks* and several articles in the *EOA*—especially those by Mike Neilson on the state's physiographic sections, Everett Smith on the Tensaw Delta, David T. King Jr. on the Wetumpka crater, and David C. Kopaska-Merkel on the Minkin Paleozoic Footprint Site—were adapted for Chapter 1, "The Land." Similarly, the section in Chapter 3 on "Alabamians at Work" drew heavily from information compiled by the staff of the Economic Development Partnership of Alabama; the introduction to the

Legislature in Chapter 6 was adapted from information compiled by legislative staff; and the introduction to "Municipalities" in Chapter 9 was adapted from information provided by the Alabama League of Municipalities. Any errors of interpretation, however, are those of the staff of *The Alabama Guide*, not the original authors.

Statistician and demographer Don Bogie also deserves special recognition for coming out of retirement to assemble the tables and charts in Chapter 10, "Demographics."

Other ADAH staffers who provided illustrations, checked facts, read proofs, or provided operational support for the book include Darlene Adams, Iris Bailey, Ken Barr, Tracey Berezansky, Jessamyn Boyd, Bob Bradley, Mike Breedlove, Frank Brown, Rickie Brunner, Bob Cason, Clarice Crosby, Drew Davis, Susan DuBose, Nancy Dupree, Christine Garrett, Frankie George, John Hardin, Kelly Hoomes, George Jennings, Norwood Kerr, Alan Legleiter, Cynthia Luckie, Taylor McGaughy, Meredith McLemore, Alden Monroe, Steve Murray, Mark Palmer, Debbie Pendleton, Glenda Puckett, Mary Jo Scott, Frazine Taylor, Tom Turley, Richard Wang, Debra Wilkins, Randall Williams, and Pat Wilson.

Within many state departments, key persons provided photos, biographies, and facts. These include: Jon Morgan (Alabama Senate); Judith Adams (State Docks); Norman Arnold and Katrina Timmons (Military Department); Lauree Ashcom and Yasamie Richardson (Emergency Management); John Bradford, Candice Lanier, and Barry Spear (Human Resources); Elizabeth Bressler (Banking); Elishia Ballentine (Forestry); Amy Belcher, Christy Rhodes Kirk, Cathy Johnson, and Sharon Fulmar (Agriculture); Robin Cooper, Lisa Castaldo, Mark Dixon, Jeff Emerson, Sue Dahrouge, Robin Cooper, Elaine LeFleur, and Taylor Nichols (Governor's Office); Peggy Collins, Edith Parten, Ami Simpson, Marilyn Stamps, and Tommy Cauthen (Tourism); Lynn Childs (ACJIC); Tamara Cofield, Adam Thompson, and Emily Thompson (Secretary of State's Office); E. J. Cooper (Postsecondary Education); Phyllis Wesley (Industrial Development Training); Brian Corbett (Corrections); Linda Crockett (Transportation); Donna Dodd, Windy Leavell, Kelly Mulero, David Rountree, Lisa Parrish, and Angier Johnson (Public Service Commission); Brittany DuBose (Homeland Security); Margaret Gunter (ACHE); Mary Hasselwander (Medicaid); Chip Hill (Lieutenant Governor's Office); Ed Johnson, Keith Camp, and Jason Hodges (Administrative Office of Courts); Robert Horton (Veterans' Affairs); Beverly Davis, Mary Nell Shaw, Sara Wright, Nancy Ray, Cynthia Brown, Benjamin Hicks, Karen Benefield, and Mitch Edwards (Education); Scott Hughes and John T. Pate (Environmental Management); Renae Easterly (Labor); Anne Evans (Mental Health); Ashley Farmer, Melissa Senn, and Joy Patterson (Attorney General's Office).

Also, Kaleigh Flatt and Nancy Leigh (Senior Services); Renee Ferraz (ABC Board); Tommy Giles, Doris Teague, and John Reese (Public Safety); Joey Brackner, Diana Green, and Barbara Reed (Arts Council); David Bolin and David Kopaska-Merkel (Oil and Gas Board); Jann Fomby and Heather Wilson (Soil and Water); Jackie Graham (Personnel); Ragan Ingram (Insurance); Mattie Jackson and Robin Rawls (Medicaid); Frances Kennamer and Kathy Vincent (Public Health); Kathy Johnson, Susan Jana, and Donna Newman (Finance); Ned Jenkins and Stacey Little (Alabama Historical Commission); Doug Durr, Rebecca Leigh White, Garry L. Rumph, and Hobbie Sealy (Conservation); Rod Kennette (Forensic Sciences); Jeanie Key and Kathie Lynch (State Auditor's office); Anthony Leigh (State Treasurer's Office); Lena Littlefield and Jason Swann (District Attorneys Association); Dan Lord (Securities Commission); Ron Macksoud, David White and Tonya Lee (Industrial Relations); Marie Malinowski (Ethics Commission); Kathie Martin (APTV); Carolyn Middleton (Budget Office); Gerri Miller, Linda Swann, and Adrienne Washington (ADO); Rebecca Mitchell and Crystal Bonvillian (Public Library Service); Allen Peaton, Marcia Calendar, and Walter Wood (Youth Services); Mike Pegues and Amanda Spurlin (RSA); Jim Plott and Larry Childers (ADECA); Sue Poe and Candance Williams (BOE); Clay Redden (Alabama House of Representatives); Carla Snellgrove (Revenue); Tammy Williams (Childrens' Affairs); Clark Bruner (Health Planning and Development); Kathleen McGehee (Rehabilitation Services); Cynthia Dillard (Pardons and Paroles); Irene Burgess, Dan Irvin, Sandy Ebersole, and Lewis S. Dean (Geological Survey).

Within the Alabama Judicial System, photos and information were provided by Katrena Bailey, Mike Bolin, Barbara Fischer, Nathan Bruner, Sharon Gaston, Helen Gray, Marilyn Horsley, Lynn Knight, John Lazenby, Suzie Long, Sue McCall, Lane Mann, Vickie Mims, Evelyn Moore, Amberly Page, Alma Surles, Gwyn Bruner, Beth Kellum, Sharon Gaston, Carrie Adams, Tim Lewis, Callie Dietz, Ed Johnson, Donna Newman, and Helen Gray.

Photos and helpful information were provided by staffers in Congressional offices, federal agencies or courts, universities, associations and others. These included: Jennifer Datcher and Lori Qullier (Association of County Commissioners); Edye Goertz and Laura Whatley (Alabama League of Municipalities); Jennie Gibson (U.S. Rep. Bud Cramer); Heather Johnson (U.S. Rep. Parker Griffith); Jesper Düring Jørgensen (Dutch Royal Library); Tim Pennycuff (UAB Medical School Archives); Laura Shill and Erin Tapp (UAB Public Relations); Claus Martel (Redstone); Mitch Relfe (U.S. Rep. Spencer Bachus); Jenny Selzer (U.S. Rep. Bobby Bright); Bonnie Shanholtzer (Legislative Reapportionment Office); John Varner, Dana M. Caudle, and Aaron Trehub (AU Libraries); Wendy Wallace (Economic Development Partnership of Alabama); Linda Hallmark (Birmingham-Southern); Larry Percy (Troy University); Vicky Cook (Baldwin County Public Schools); Meaghen Gordon (University of West Alabama); Brad Green (Paul W. Bryant Museum); Sam Duvall (Forestry); Randall Becker, Shelia Reed, and Shawn Williams (National Park Service); Silvano Wueschner (Maxwell AFB); Laura Shill (UA); Debra Barrentine (Northeast Alabama Community College);

Brian Seidman (NewSouth Books); Tommy Brown (Continental Eagle Archives); Charles Scribner and Nelson Brooke (Black Warrior Riverkeepers); David King, Mac W. Martin, and Luke Marzan (AU); Ron Buta (Alabama Paleontological Society); Craig Remington (UA Cartographic Research Lab); Steve Latham (JSU); Erika Day (ThyssenKrupp); Leslie Evelyn (Alabama A&M Research Institute); Brian Dowler (National Wild Turkey Foundation); Fay Garner and Julie Yates (USDA–Natural Resources Conservation Service); David Bundy and Wanda Lloyd (*Montgomery Advertiser*); Peggy Perazzo (Stone Quarries and Beyond); and Debbie Babb, Tamra Trull, Jim Bennett, Matt Arnett, Stephanie Burak, Gene Hanson, Terry Hartley, Peggy B. Perazzo, Beth Rogers, Tom Seale, Ginny Shaver, Jeffrey C. Motz, Alan Pitts, Pamela J. W. Gore, M. Lewis Kennedy, and Rosemary Johnson.

Photo Sources

All images not mentioned in the list below are from the holdings of the Alabama Department of Archives and History.

End sheets: Alabama Tourism Department (ATD)

Front Matter: Page i, ATD. ii, Cartographic Research Lab, University of Alabama (CRL, UA). iv–v, ATD. vi, ATD. viii, Robin Cooper, Governor's Office (GO). x, ATD.

Chapter 1: Page 1, ATD. 2, ATD. 4, Peggy Perazzo, Stone Quarries and Beyond. 6, CRL, UA. 7, Dr. James Lacefield. 8–9, CRL, UA. 10, Dr. James Lacefield. 11, Nelson Brooke, Black Warrior Riverkeeper. 12, Dr. Pamela Gore. 14, ATD. 15, ATD. 17, Division of Wildlife and Freshwater Fisheries, Alabama Department of Conservation and Natural Resources. 18, ATD. 20, John T. Pate, Water Quality Branch, Alabama Department of Environmental Management. 21, The Yacht Club On Lake Logan Martin. 22, Dennis Hold, courtesy of NewSouth Books (Holt, NSB). 23, Holt, NSB. 24–25, Dr. Ed Bridges. 26-27, ATD. 28, Holt, NSB. 29, Darren Swanson. 30, Dr. David King and Dr. Luke Marzen, Auburn University. 32, Alabama Paleontological Society (APS). 33, APS.

Chapter 2: Page 38, top, National Parks Service (NPS). 42–43, ATD. 47, top, The Royal Library, the Netherlands; bottom, Alabama Historical Commission, Fort Toulouse/ Jackson Park. 50, top, ATD. 58, top, NPS. 64, bottom right, Continental Eagle Archives. 70, Town of Mooresville. 76, bottom, Jim Bennett. 77, top, Jim Bennett; bottom right, *Pictorial War Record, Battles of the Late Civil War*, September 1, 1883. 85, *Harper's Weekly*. 114, bottom, The Loveliest Village Photograph Collection, Auburn University Special Collections and Archives (AU). 120, top, Alabama Power Company Archives. 121, middle, Rob Flynn, USDA/ARS (Agriculture Research Service). 132, top, U.S. Army. 133, Maxwell Air Force Base (Maxwell). 137, inset and bottom, Eugene B. Sledge Collection, AU. 140, The Loveliest Village Photograph Collection, AU. 142, bottom right, *Associated Press*. 143, bottom, Paul Robertson. 153, Paul W. Bryant Museum. 154, U.S. Army. 156, top, University of Alabama at Birmingham Archives; bottom, University of

Alabama at Birmingham Public Relations. 157, Alabama Supreme Court and State Law Library. 159, top, Alabama Oil and Gas Board; bottom, ATD. 150, top, Hyundai Press Kit 1; bottom, Hyundai Press Kit 2 (Hyundai). 161, ATD. 162, ATD. 163, Alabama State Department of Education (ASDOE). 164, ATD. 165, ATD. 166, "Quilts of Gee's Bend" exhibition. 167, ATD. 168, ATD.

CHAPTER 3: Page 170, Hyundai. 172, Economic Development Partnership of Alabama. 173, Alabama Development Office (ADO). 175, ADO. 176, NASA/courtesy of nasaimages.com (NASA). 178, Maxwell. 180, ATD. 181, Alabama Forestry Association (AFA). 182, Jim Walter Resources, Dennis Hall photographer. 183, ThyssenKrupp. 184, UAB Public Relations. 187, Retirement Services of Alabama. 189, Ciba. 190, AFA. 192, top, Foley Middle School, Baldwin County Public Schools; bottom, William L. Radney Elementary, Alexander City Schools. 193, ASDOE. 194, Sumter County High School, Sumter County Schools. 195, Alabama State Council on the Arts (COA). 196, Northeast Alabama Community College. 197, The Alabama Technology Network. 199, University Relations Photography, The University of Alabama. 200, Auburn University. 201, Tuskegee University, Media and Public Affairs. 202, U.S. Army. 203, Alabama State University. 204, Jacksonville State University, Steven Latham photographer. 205, Ralph Ford. 206, University of Montevallo. 207, University of South Alabama. 208, University of West Alabama. 209, top, Altairisfar on Wikimedia Commons; bottom, Birmingham-Southern College. 210, UAB. 212–229, ATD. 230, COA. 231–242, ATD. 233.

CHAPTER 4: Page 243, GO. 244, GO. 250, GO. 270, ASDOE. 316, URP, UA. 376, U.S. Army Corps of Engineers.

CHAPTER 5: Page 390, GO. 397, GO. 401, GO. 406, Alabama District Attorney's Association.

CHAPTER 6: Page 434, Alabama Legislative Reapportionment Office (LRO). 456, CRL, UA. 473, *Montgomery Advertiser.*

CHAPTERS 7–9: Page 496, LRO. 502, Tom Seale. 574, ATD.

CHAPTER 10: Page 632, © 1998, Lewis Kennedy, www.mlewiskennedy.com.

CHAPTER 11: Page 638, ATD. 639, Terry Hartley, Due South Photography. 640, ATD. 641, ATD. 642, Daniel Irvine, Geological Society of Alabama. 644, Racking Horse Breeders' Association of America, 2007 World Champion, "The Finalizer," owned by John L. Denny of Blountsville, ridden by Lamar Denny of Blountsville. 645, top, National Wild Turkey Federation; bottom, ATD. 646, top, Alabama Department of Agriculture and Industry (ADAI); bottom, Birmingham Paleontological Society. 647, Gene Hanson. 648, U.S. Fish and Wildlife Services, Division of Public Affairs. 650, AFA. 651, ATD. 652, top, U.S. Department of Agriculture-Natural Resources Conservation Service; bottom, Mississippi State University. 654, Emmett Blankenship, U.S. Fish and Wildlife Services. 655, top, Oregon Berry Packing, Inc.; bottom, Holt, NSB. 656, ADAI.

INDEX

NOTE ON ORGANIZATION: Because this entire book is about the State of Alabama, many index entries that might be found under *Alabama, State of* are instead under their respective letter sections. For example, for *Alabama Department of Public Safety*, see *Public Safety Department* under section *P*. For *Alabama, capitals of*, see *Capitals of Alabama* under section *C*.

Bellingrath Gardens,
Mobile County.